MISCELLANEOUS ESSAYS
RELATING TO
INDIAN SUBJECTS

MISCELLANEOUS ESSAYS
RELATING TO
INDIAN SUBJECTS

BY

BRIAN HOUGHTON HODGSON, ESQ., F.R.S.

LATE OF THE BENGAL CIVIL SERVICE;

CORRESPONDING MEMBER OF THE INSTITUTE;
CHEVALIER OF THE LEGION OF HONOUR;
HONORARY MEMBER OF THE GERMAN ORIENTAL
SOCIETY AND THE SOCIETE
ASIATIQUE; MEMBER OF THE ASIATIC SOCIETIES OF
CALCUTTA AND
LONDON; OF THE ETHNOLOGICAL AND ZOOLOGICAL
SOCIETIES
OF LONDON; AND LATE BRITISH MINISTER AT THE
COURT OF NEPAL

VOL. I

Published by

Gyan Publishing House
5, Ansari Road
Daryaganj, New Delhi-110002
Phone: 011-47034999, 9811692060
E-mail: books@gyanbooks.com

Distribution Network
gyanbooks.com
India, USA, Canada, UK, Australia, France

ISBN : 978-81-212-3781-9 (Set)
ISBN : 978-81-212-5005-4 (PB)
First Published, 1880

2nd Impression 2020

Printed at: Gyan Press, Delhi.

The book at your disposal is the edition of an old book originally published long back. The Text quality of this book may not be at par as compared to our other books but many readers approached us to reprint this important book so that it could satiate their hunger. We request all the readers of this book to help us to improve its quality by providing the necessary text of those pages which are not properly visible. Your valuable support in this case will be highly appreciated and acknowledged and our future readers will be benefitted immensely.

MISCELLANEOUS ESSAYS

RELATING TO

INDIAN SUBJECTS.

BY

BRIAN HOUGHTON HODGSON, Esq., F.R.S.

LATE OF THE BENGAL CIVIL SERVICE;

CORRESPONDING MEMBER OF THE INSTITUTE; CHEVALIER OF THE LEGION OF HONOUR; HONORARY MEMBER OF THE GERMAN ORIENTAL SOCIETY AND THE SOCIÉTÉ ASIATIQUE; MEMBER OF THE ASIATIC SOCIETIES OF CALCUTTA AND LONDON; OF THE ETHNOLOGICAL AND ZOOLOGICAL SOCIETIES OF LONDON; AND LATE BRITISH MINISTER AT THE COURT OF NEPAL.

VOL. I.

LONDON:
TRÜBNER & CO., LUDGATE HILL.
1880.

PREFACE.

IN the notice prefixed to the "Essays on the Languages, Literature, and Religion of Nepal and Tibet" (1874), reference is made to the probability of a republication of the remaining papers of Mr. Hodgson, comprising not only Articles IV., V., and XI. of the "Selections from the Records of the Government of Bengal, No. XXVII.," which would have found their fittest place in that re-issue, but also his various Papers on the Tribes and Languages of the Northern Non-Aryans adjacent to India, with other Essays of a more general character. That probability has now become a reality, Mr. Hodgson having readily granted permission to the publishers of the "Essays" to bring out in a collected form also his remaining papers on Indian languages and ethnology. And inasmuch as the previous volume has already proved of essential service to scholars by placing within their easy reach materials theretofore accessible only to the favoured few who could consult the scarce serials in which the several articles had originally appeared, the present completion of the re-issue will, it is hoped, be sure of as cordial a welcome.

To the Papers numbered I. to VIII. the same value and interest attach at the present day as were accorded to them when they were published for the first time, hardly any fresh materials having since come to light concerning the tribes and languages there treated of. This does not apply in the same degree to the various Papers comprised in the Ninth Section, which have been incorporated in the re-issue only with a view of completing Mr. Hodgson's conspectus of the general character and structural affinities of the Non-Aryan languages of India.

Lastly, the Papers, here reproduced in a more complete form, on the Pre-eminence of the Vernaculars have lost none of their significance even at the present moment, as the frequent reference made to them by the Press shews the abiding vitality of the subject.

Almost all the Papers, more especially the longer Linguistical Essays, have been reprinted from copies revised and annotated by the author himself, who has earned a fresh and lasting title to the gratitude of all students of Indian glossology and ethnology by allowing the rare and valuable Papers comprised in these volumes to be made generally available.

R. R.

CONTENTS OF VOL. I.

SECTION I.

ON THE KOCCH, BÓDÓ, AND DHIMÁL TRIBES.

["*Essay on the Kocch, Bódó, and Dhimál Tribes:*" *Calcutta*, 1847.]

SECTION II.

ON HIMÁLAYAN ETHNOLOGY.

[*Journal of the Bengal Asiatic Society*, Vol. XXII. pp. 317–427; Vol. XXVII. pp. 113–270.]

SECTION I.

ON THE KOCCH, BÓDO, AND DHIMÁL TRIBES.*

PART I.—VOCABULARY.

NOUNS.

1ST.—THINGS AND BEINGS.

	English.	Kocch.	Bodo.	Dhimál.
THINGS AND BEINGS.	The Universe,	Songsár,	...	...
	Creator,	...	...	...
	Creature,	...	...	...
	Matter, universal,	...	...	...
	Spirit, universal,	...	...	..
	Space ditto,	...	...	...
	Time ditto,	Kál,	Khál,	Khál.
	Motion, universal,	Chalan, gaman,	Thángbai,	Hánka.
	Immotion or rest,	Thirta, Rahan,	Thábai,	Hiká.
	Action, conscious motion,	Korom,	Habba,	Kámpáka.
	Inaction ditto,	...	Habbagéyá,	Kámmánthuka.
	Light, lux,	Jyoti,	Shráng,	Jolka.
	Darkness,	Andhér,	Khomshi,	Kitikitika.
	Figure or form,	Rúp,	Rúp,	Rúp.
	Formlessness,	Arúp,	Rúpgéyá,	Rúpmánthuka.
	Star,	Tárá,	Háthotki,	Phúró.
	Planet,	Graha,	...	...
	Saturn,	Súni,	...	...
	Jupiter,	Brihaspati,	...	...
	Venus,	Súkra,	...	...
	Mars,	Mongol,	...	...
	Eclipse,	Grohon,	...	...
	Heaven,	Sworg: Dévá,	Nókhoráng, visible arch,	...
	Earth,	Prithivi,	...	...
	Hades or Hell,	Pátál, Norok,	...	...
	This world,	Lók,	...	...
	The next world,	Pórlók,	...	...
	God,	Bhagaván,	Bátho (the Síj plant),	Waráng-Béráng (mas et fœm).

*The prominence and extent given to this portion of my work are explained in the Introduction, p. 2, and the principle on which the vocabulary is constructed at pp. 6 7. [Published at Calcutta, 1847.]

	English.	*Kocch.*	*Bodo.*	*Dhimál.*
THINGS AND BEINGS.	A God, any	Dév'ta,	Madai,	Dír, Grám.
	Angel or Kalodemon,	Súr, Dév'ta,	...	...
	Devil or Kakodemon,	Dait, Rák-shas, Asúr,	...	..
	The Devil,	...	...	...
	Fairy, good,	...	Madai,	...
	Ogre, Gnome, Sprite, } bad,	...	Jomon,	..
	Ghost,	Bhút,	Gathaicho,	...
	Witch (*fem.*),	Dákini,	Háshá-Hinjou, Hinjouni Daina,	Mhái Béwal Dhaina.
	Sun,	Bélá,	Shán,	Bélá.
	Moon,	Chánd,	Nókhábir,	Táli.
	Dark half of,	Badi,	Dán khomshi,	...
	Bright ditto,	Súdi,	Dáu shráng,	...
	Body, limited,	Gotor,	Modom,	Dhór.
	Shadow,	Chíá,	Sáikhlúm,	Dápká.
	Human body,	Gotor,	Modom,	Dhor.
	Human soul,	Jíú,	...	...
	Life,	Jíú,	Gótháng,*	Singlhóka.
	Death,	Moron,	Gothoi,*	Síká.
	A being, moving,	...	...	...
	A thing, motionless,	...	...	...
	A name,	Nám,	Múng,	Ming.
	An animal,	Pasú,	Gothing,	...
	A vegetal,	Trin,	...	...
	A mineral,	Dhátú,	...	...
	Human kind,	Mánushi,	Mánushi,	Dyáng.
	Quadruped,	Chárpáyá,	Athéng thónglré,	Diálong-khókoi.
	Bat kind,	Chám chilka,	Badamali,	...
	Bird kind,	Pókhi,	Dáuchen or Dau,	Jihá.
	Fish kind,	Máchá,	Gná,	Haiyú.
	Shelled fish kind,	...	...	...
	Testudines,	...	...	...
	Lacertine Reptiles,	...	...	...
	Batrachians,	...	Imbú,	...
	Serpent kind,	Sámp,	Jibo,	Púnhiá.
	Insect kind,	Póká,	Impho,	Nhámoi.
	Mind, understanding, Reason, the thinking organ,	Mon,	Gasho?	...
	Instinct, animal reason,	...	...	...
	Meditation, thought, reflection, the act,	Bhávana,	...	...
	Consciousness,	...	...	...
	Reasoning, ratiocination,	...	..	...
	Debate, argument,	Báda bádi,	Raijalaiyu,	Dopka warka.

* Rather alive and dead.

THINGS AND BEINGS.

English.	*Kocch.*	*Bodo.*	*Dhimál.*
Memory,	Phom,	Shútrúng,	Phom.
Forgetfulness,	Béphom,	Bouwa, Shút-rúnggeya,	Phommántthó.
Sensation, physical,	Dishapáu,	Dásmanno,	Dishaménku.
Perception, mental, or, Apprehension,	Phom,	Gashomanuo,	Phom.
Quantity,	...	...	...
Degree,	...	...	...
Quality,	Gún,	...	...
Number,	Ganti,	Shanno,	Ganéká.
Time, limited,	Bélá,	Bélá,	Bélá.
Place, ditto,	Thán,	Núptbi,	Chól.
Circumstance, event, external,	Británt,	...	...
Condition, state, internal,	Gati, Dasha,	...	...
Constitution, Temperament, Nature,	Swobhau,	...	...
Manner, the how,	Doul, Prakár,	...	...
Occasion, the when,	...	...	...
Object, end in view,	Bishoi,	...	...
Reason, the human, why,	Hétú, Sobob,	...	...
Cause, causa causans,	Káran,	...	...
Effect, consequence,	...	...	...
Feeling, affection, passion,	Máyá,	Wanna,	...
Parental affection,	Máyá,	Wanna,	...
Filial ditto,	Máyá,	Wanna,	...
Conjugal ditto,	Prém, Móh,	Wanna,	...
Appetite, bodily desire,	U'dhar,	Gashojáyú !	Mondhámi.
Mental desire, wish,	Iccha,	Gashojáyú,	Mondháni.
Motive, inducement,	Sobob, káron,	...	...
Intention, purpose, design, aim,	Sobob, Nimitt,	...	...
Endeavour, attempt,	Chéshta, Ánt,	...	...
Act or deed,	Kám, Kormo,	Habba,	...
Disposition, temper,	Mizág,	...	...
Behaviour, conduct, Demeanour, manners,	Chalan,	...	...
Habit, wont,	Chál,	...	...
Practice, use,	Chál,	...	...
Custom, usage,	Bhés, Dastúr,	...	...

	English.	Kocch.	Bodo.	Dhimál.
	Use, enjoyment of,	Bhóg,	...	...
	Use, mere act of,	...	...	...
	Disuse, cessation of,	...	...	...
	Abuse, wrong use,	...	...	...
	The material elements,	Panj Bhút,	...	...
2nd, EARTH.	Earth, the terrene element,	Prithivi,	...	...
	Earth, land, terra firma,	Máti, Bhúmi,	Há,	Bhanói.
	Soil, cultivable,	Sárúk máti,	Húsharhá,	Bhanói.
	Mould,	Sárúk máti,	...	...
	Marl,	Sárúk máti,	...	...
	Mud,	Kádó,	Habdú,	Kadéó.
	Dust,	Dhúlá,	Háduri,	...
	Manure,	Sár,	Hásár,	Sár.
	Stone, a fragment of rock,	Páthar,	Onthái,	U'nthúr.
	Gravel, the heap,	Kankar,	...	...
	Rock, the mass,	Páthar,	Onthai,	U'nthúr.
	Clay rock, alumina,	...	...	...
	Potter's clay,	Kúmhálermáti,	Aithálihá,	Chikthálì Bhanói.
	Limestone, rock calx,	...	...	...
	Chalk,	Khárimáti,	...	...
	Lime, prepared,	Chún,	...	...
	Quick-lime,	Alwa, Jhúri,	...	...
	Sandstone rock,	...	...	...
	Sand, loose,	Bálú,	Bálá,	Bálá.
	Flint rock, silex,	Páthar,	...	...
	Gun flint,	Páthari,	...	...
	Glass,	Kánch,	...	...
	Soda,	...	...	...
	Alkali,	...	...	...
	Acid,	...	...	...
	Rock-salt,	...	...	...
	Salt, any,	Nún,	Sankhri,	Désé.
	Saltpetre,	Jaikhar,	...	...
	Borax,	Sohága,	...	...
	Sulphur,	Gandarak,	...	...
	Antimony, or mercury,	Pársá,	...	...
	Arsenic,	...	...	...
	Talc,	Abór,	Alongbár,	Bálápát.
	Mica,	...	...	...
	Crystal,	Bilour,	...	...
	Mineral ore,	Dhátú,	...	...
	Gold,	Sóna,	Sona,	Sona.
	Silver,	Rúpá,	Rúpá,	Rúpá.
	Iron,	Lóhá,	Shúrr,	Chír,
	Copper,	Támba,	Támbo,	Támbo.
	Tin,	Ránga,	...	...
	Zinc,	Jasta,	...	...
	Lead,	Síshá,	...	...
	Pewter,	...	...	...
	Brass,	Pítal,	...	...

	English.	*Kocch.*	*Bodo.*	*Dhimál.*
EARTH.	Bell metal,	...	...	...
	A mountain or hill,	Parbot,	Hájo,	Rá.
	A plain,	Dángá,	Photár, Háyen,	Dhaidhaika.
	A hill top,	Máthi,	Khró,	Púring.
	A hill side,	Májha,	Géjér,	...
	A hill base,	Gór,	Khíbo,	Lélá.
	A wooded plain or weald,	Jhárbári,	Hágrá ?*	Sing bári.
	A naked plain or wold,	Dhaidhai dánga,	Phótár,	Dhaidhaika.
	Dry uplands,	Dángi,	Hágúng,	Tika.
	Low flooded lands,	Dóhalla,	Dohala,	...
	A valley, large,	Khál,	Hákor,	...
	A valley, small,	Khál,	Hákor,	...
	A ravine,	Dhordhora,	...	...
	A forest,	Sál bári,	Hágrá má,	Sing bári.
	A jungle,	Jhár bári,	Thúri hágrá, or Hágrá,	Dincha.
	Copse or brush-wood,	Jhári,	Joulia,	Jhápsi.
	A sandy waste or desert,	Dhúdúa dánga,	Hágúng ?	Tíkar.
	A marsh, or swampy plain,	Démdévi,	Dalbári,	...
	A quagmire, or quicksand,	Dhasna,	Hábráng,	...
3rd, WATER.	Water,	Jal,	Dói,	Chí.
	Salt water,	Nóna Jal,	...	...
	Fresh water,	Mítha Jal,	...	...
	Tide,	...	...	...
	Ocean or sea,	...	...	...
	A river,	Nodi,	Dói (water),	Chí (ditto).
	A great river,	Bada nodi,	Dói gédét,	Badka Chí.
	A rivulet,	Chota nodi,	Dóishá,	Mhoika Chí.
	Still water,	Dhí páni,	Dongo,	Dángi.
	Running water,	Bohonti páni,	...	Phoika Chí.
	Coast or bank,	Dhádani,	Dóijing,	Chéngsho.
	Bay or inlet,	Ghéná,	Míri,	Ghékana.
	A canal,	Dánṛá,	...	...
	Aqueduct, small and crude,	Shán,	Phoiri,	Ráhi.
	A torrent,	Tarang,	...	...
	A rapid,	Khúrkhúria or Bajna,	Doibájana,	...
	A waterfall,	Dhordhora,	...	...
	A lake, natural,	Jhíl,	Dhángi ?	Dhángi ?
	A pond, natural,	Kháṛi, Dobha,	Dóba,	Dóba.
	A tank, artificial,	Diggi, Choka,	...	...
	A wave,	Dhéyú,	Doi dhö,	Chíko dhéö.
	A stream or current,	Sont,	...	Rághá.
	A spring, natural,	Bhúl,	Bimú,	Bhúl.
	A well, artificial,	Chúá,	Dói khor,	...
	A fountain, do.,	Dhárá,	...	...

* Forest, and Sing bári the same.

	English.	Kocch.	Bodo.	Dhimál.
	A bridge,	Khorkhori,	Saikhóng,	...
	A ferry,	Ghát,	...	...
	A ford,	Ghát,	...	...
	Ether, the element,	Déwá,	Nokhoráng,	...
4th, Air.	Air, do.,	Batás,	Bár,	Bhirma.
	Wind, moving air,	Batás,	Bár,	Bhirma.
	Storm, tempest,	Dúnd,	Bárhúrka,	...
	Atmosphere, weather,	Samay,	Din,	Din.
	Bad weather,	Búra samay,	Hamma din,	Má elka din.
	Good weather,	Bhalo samay,	Ghám din,	Elka din.
	Cloud,	Mégh,	Jamóï,	...
	Sunshine,	Rávad,	Shandúng,	Sáné.
	Season,	Samay,	Din,	Din.
	Spring,	Basant,	...	...
	Summer,	Grish samay,	Galam Battar,	Sá kó din.
	Autumn,	...	...	...
	Winter,	Jár samay,	Gajáng battar,	Chúmko din.
	The rains,	Barsh kál,	...	...
	Rain,	Páni,	Nókhá,	Wái.
	Drop of rain,	Tóp,	...	...
	Shower of rain,	...	...	...
	Thunder,	Charak,	Kharammo,	...
	Lightning,	Deva chilak,	Mú phlámo,	Kapli gái.
	Hail,	Páthar,	Krothai,	U'nthúr.
	Snow,	Hém,	...	...
	Frost,	Púla,	...	...
	Thaw,	Galay,	...	...
	Dew,	Sít,	Níhúr,	Nihari.
	Mist or haze,	Kúhá,	...	...
	Fog,	Kúhá,	...	...
5th, Fire.	Fire (the element),	Agni,	Wát,	Méṇ.
	Temperature,	...	...	...
	Heat, caloric,	Grísh,	Gúdúng,	Bhémka.
	Cold,	Jár,	Gajáng,	Chúnka.
	Fire, any,	Agni,	Wát,	Méṇ.
	Flame,	Jálá,	Wát chalai,	Méṭika.
	Smoke,	Dhúṇa,	Wákan doï,	Dhúṇa.
	Fireplace or grate,	Ákha,	Dou dap, / Wag dap,	Méṇ dhoka. / Méṇ pondho.
	Forge,	Áphar,	Wát gadáp,	...
	Furnace,	Bhatti,	...	...
	Kiln,	Bhátta,	...	...
	Oven,	Ákhá,	Doudap,	...
	Still,	Bhatti,	Bháti,	Bháti.
	Fuel,	Khori,	Bón,	Mising.
	Wood,	Lakri,	Bón,	Khútáng.
	Charcoal,	Àngrá,	Hangár,	Ángrá.
	Cinders,	...	...	...
	Ashes,	Músh,	Hátoplá,	Chai Léö.
	Turf,	Chokri,	I'tha,	Chapra.
	Cowdung,	Chán,	Múshokhi,	Piá kolishi.
	Straw,	Lárá,	Maijigáp,	Nárá.
6th, Human Body.	The human body,	Gótór,	Modom,	Dhór.
	The head,	Múra,	Khóró,	Púrin.
	The limbs,	Ang,	...	...

	English.	*Kocch*	*Bodo.*	*Dhimál.*
HUMAN BODY.	The skin,	Chamra,	Bigúr,	Dhálé.
	The hair of body,	Rom,	Khomon,	Moishú.
	The hair of head,	Chúli,	Khanai,	Poshom.
	The neck,	Gardhan,	...	Nirga.
	The throat,	Túti,	Garáng bá,	Totoá.
	The arm, all,	Háth,	Nákhánti,	Khúrbáha.
	The true arm,	Báhún,	Yágdo,	Khúr.
	The fore arm,	Nalli,	Nakhánti,	Báhá.
	The hand,	Háth,	Akhai or Nákhai,	Khúr.
	The palm,	Tálá, Akhai or Nákhai,	Thálka,	Tálá.
	The back hand,	Háthér pith, *Nákhai or Akhai,	Bikhúng,	Gándi.
	The finger, any,	Angúl,	Náshi,	Khúrsing.
	The thumb,	Búdi angúl,	Náshimá,	Mengta khursing.
	The wrist,	Háther lúlú,	Nágódó,	...
	Finger nail,	Khól,	Náshi gúr,	Khóltá.
	Thumb nail,	Khól,	Náshi gúr,	Khóltá.
	The leg, all,	Théngá,	Gnáthéng,	Khókoï.
	The true leg, tibia,	Mókchá,	Yádoï,	Khókoï.
	The thigh, femur,	Chórú,	Phéndá,	Whálténg.
	The knee,	Hatwa,	Hánthú,	Whálteng Túrhúï.
	The ankle,	Théngér lúlú,	Yágréng,	Khóï ganti.
	The heel,	Gúdárá,	Yáphá doudoï,	Gúdni.
	The foot,	Bhóri,	Yáphá,	Khókóï.
	The toe, any,	Théngér angúl,	Náthéng nashi,	Khókoï ko khursing.
	Great toe,	Budi angúl,	Náshi má,	Amabúndi.
	Toe-nail,	Khúlká,	Náshi gúr,	...
	Sole of foot,	Tálá,	Tálkhá,	Khúrsing talà.
	A joint, any,	Lúlú,	Jóra,	Gánti.
	A bone, any,	Harwá,	Régéng,	Hár.
	Flesh, muscle,	Másang,	Bidat,	Béhá.
	Blood,	Lóhú,	Thóï,	Hitti.
	Blood-vessel,	Sir,	Sir,	Jhiré.
	Sinew or tendon,	...	Róta,	...
	The face,	Múkh,	Múkháng,	Rhúai.
	The eye,	Chakhú,	Mogon,	Mí.
	The eyebrow,	Bhúr,	Múshúgúr,	Mí pátá.
	The eyelash,	Chakhú nóá,	Moïshrám,	Mimúí.
	The nose,	Nák,	Gúnthúng,	Nhápú.
	The nostril,	Nák ka bind,	Bolong or Gúdúng,	Nhápú phonga.
	The forehead,	Kópál,	Jobom,	Kopál.
	The cheek,	Gál,	Khoulai,	Galbúng.
	The chin,	Thútúli,	Khúkháp,	Kátó.
	The ear,	Kán,	Khomá,	Náháthong.
	The beard,	Dáḍhi,	Dáḍhi,	Dáḍhi.
	The mustache,	Dádhi,	Dádhi,	Dádhi.
	The mouth,	Múkh,	Khougá,	Núï.
	The lips,	Thót,	Kúsúthï,	Dilvé.
	The teeth,	Dánt,	Háthai,	Sitong.
	The jaws,	Chouwá,	Hágmá,	Jambai.

* N is frequently a superadded and often a commuted letter.

	English.	Kocch.	Bodo.	Dhimál.
HUMAN BODY.	The tongue,	Jívha,	Chálai,	Détóng.
	The palate,	Tálú,	Jérkhóng,	Núi-ko-kilo.
	The chest, male,	Búkh,	Jarbá,	Túmtá.
	The breast, fem.,	Dúdhyá,	Jarba : Abú,	Túmtá.
	The nipple,	Thomona,	Abú bijú ; or Ahárbánthú,	Dúdú konáshi.
	The hip,	Chorú Joṛá,	Phéndá kani bégéng,	Whálténg-jora.
	The buttocks,	Tholmá,	Kithúthái,	Líshura thúmá.
	The anus,	Kóti,	Khibú,	Líshura.
	The penis,	Chént,	Chúchi,	Tau.
	The testes,	Bicha,	Ladoï,	Séshé.
	The vulva,	Máng,	Chiphá,	Lí.
	The womb,	Bacha Dhúkri,	Bishákhó,	Chánteréng.
	The back,	Píth,	Bikhúng,	Gándi.
	The belly or front,	Pét,	U'dóï,	Hémáng.
	The stomach,	Bhóti,	Bhándár,	Pátám.
	The bowels,	Lár,	Bibú,	Téréng.
	The navel,	Lébhí,	Wáthú mai,	Botereng.
	The liver,	Kúljá,	Bikha,	Túmsing.
	The lungs,	Phéphéra,	Sompholo,	Khúsló.
	The heart,	Gotma,	Moikhún,	Mókcha : khondáng.
	The gall-bladder,	Pitt,	Biklo,	Pitá.
	The spleen,	Tilli,	Nokhabír,	...
	The bladder,	Páni mútári,	Chithóp,	Páni mutári.
	The kidneys,	Gila,	Gila,	Kẹbá.
	The skeleton,	...	...	...
	The back-bone or spinal column,	Líldárú,	Chinchiri,	Líldárú.
	A rib, any,	Panjár,	Khamibár,	Panjár.
	The skull,	Khópri,	Khóró bógéng,	Púring ko hár.
	The brain,	Gidhú,	Mélém,	Pú nhúï.
	Marrow,	Magaz,	Mélém,	Dúng.
	Spittle,	Thúpá,	Júmúdoï,	Thopchi.
	Phlegm,	Ghéngór,	Hágárdoï,	Háká.
	Snot,	Singani,	Gúng grái,	Nháthí.
	Turd, human,	Gúh,	Khí,	Lishi.
	Horsedung,	Ládí,	Gorainikhí,	O'nhya-ko-lishi.
	Cowdung,	Ghán,	Múshúnikhí,	Piá ko lishi.
	Wild beast's do.,	Gúh,	Móchánikhí,	Khúna ko lishi.
	Urine, human,	Múth,	Háshú doï,	Chicho.
	Cow's urine,	Múth,	Múshúni háshú doï,	Piá ko chicho.
	Sweat,	Jhóṇs,	Galám dóï,	Bhémtí.
	Semen, animal,	Brij,	Phédá,	Tou ko chi.
	Menses,	Mátághósa,	Roti chinam,	Lí-ko-chi.
	Pus,	Pújh,	Gúmó doï,	Bití.
	Bile,	...	Biklóni doï,	Píto-ko-chi.
	Fat,	Charbi,	...	...
	Grease or Tallow,	Charbi,	...	...
	Gravy,	Másangérras,	Bidatni dóï,	Béhá ko chi.
	Slime,	...	...	...
	Spray,	Phén,	...	...
	Moult, of birds,	Kúrich,	...	...
	Casting hair, of beasts,	...	...	...
	Rust,	Múrchá,	Mámúrkhí,	...

	English.	Kocch.	Bodo.	Dhimál.
	Mildew or blight,	Sóllá,	Mairúng,	Patna.
	Mouldiness,	Sáwó,	Soyo,	Soulúng.
	Rot, putrescence,	Póchá,	Géchéö,	Pách.
	Paring, peel,	Chhál,	Bigúr,	Dhálé.
	Lees and refuse of expressed seed, &c.,	Sitti : Chimri,	Chábá,	Chónchá.
	Litter, dirt,	Kútá,	Jábór,	Jábór.
7th, Appetites, Affections, and Passions.	Cobweb,	Jálshi,	Bémádóng,	...
	Hunger,	Bhúk,	U'kidóng,	Mhitú.
	Thirst,	Piás,	Gángdóng,	Chiám.
	Nakedness,	Léngtápan,	...	...
	Cold, pain of,	Jár,	Gajáng,	Chúng.
	Sexual desire, simple,	Thánrá,	Hinjouni lúbi dong,	Mondhápka.
	Animal heat, fem.,	Rajh,	Gúnnáng,	...
	Libidinousness, vicious,	Kám,	Chúchi thengai,	...
	Gluttony,	...	...	...
	Drunkenness,	...	...	...
	Idle talk,	Kéch-kéch,	Phétphét,	...
	Foul-mouthedness or Abusiveness,	Gáli,	Rái khám, Rái chúá,	Náiká.
	Slander, backbiting,	Múkhú,	Chokhú póra kothásondong,	...
	Censure, blame,	Ninda,	Shúbúdong,	...
	Praise, approval,	Prasan,	...	...
	Continence, bodily,	Jitindratá,	...	...
	Continence, mental,	Sila,	...	...
	Incontinence, bodily or sensuality,	Indribas,	...	...
	Incontinence, mental,	Mattatá,	...	...
	Virtue,	Pún,	...	...
	Vice,	Páp,	...	...
	Error or fault,	Ghóti,	Bouá,	...
	Love, charitas, benevolence,	Moh, máyá, Chéma,	...	...
	Hate, malevolence,	Ghin,	Ninoháyá,	Chiká.
	Hope,	Bhórsá,	...	...
	Fear,	Hatás, Dór,	Giyir,	Láchi.
	Justice,	Dharam,	...	...
	Injustice,	Adharam,	...	...
	Right, just,	...	...	...
	Duty, obligation,	...	...	...
	Cunning, deceit, hypocrisy,	Chhal,	...	...
	Candour, openness,	...	...	...
	Modesty, shame,	Láj, sharam,	Lájyo,	Lódér.
	Impudence,	Nilajta,	Láji rúngá,	Lédér mántho.
	Joy,	U'lash,	...	...
	Sorrow,	Khéd,	Jingá siö,	...

	English.	*Kocch.*	*Bodo.*	*Dhimál.*
APPETITES, AFFECTIONS, AND PASSIONS.	Avarice, covetousness,	Lóbh,	...	...
	Generosity, liberality,	Dánsilta,	...	...
	Pride, vanity,	...	...	...
	Humility,	...	...	...
	Industry,	Maskat, kismat,	Habba moucho,	Kámpáka.
	Idleness,	A'las,	Búdong, Báyú,	...
	Truth,	Sacchouti,	Chaléyá,	Saccha dopka.
	Falsehood,	Jhútapan,	Chaléyo,	Micha dopka.
	Patience,	Táp,	...	...
	Impatience,	Asantáp,	...	...
	Rage, anger,	Práptong,	...	...
	Mercy, gentleness,	Doya,	Wánno,	...
	Cruelty, savageness,	Kóthú,	Wanná,	...
	Bravery,	Húp,	Gúhúdong,	Jivédhámka.
	Cowardice,	Nihúp,	Gikho,	Jivé mhoika.
	Good manners, politeness, grace,	Sishtáchár,	...	...
	Bad manners, vulgarity,	Dústáchár,	...	...
	Curiosity,	...	...	...
	Indifference,	...	...	...
	Revenge,	Bodol,	...	...
	Forgiveness,	Khéma,	...	...
	Perfidy,	Kapat,	Chímak,	...
	Fidelity,	...	...	...
	Jealousy,	...	...	...
	Sanity, mental,	...	...	...
	Madness,	Págla pan,	...	...
	Idiocy, cretanism,	...	...	...
8th, FOOD.	Food, victuals,	Khórák,	Jánai jinis,	Cháka jinis.
	Eatables,	Khábar khorák,	Jánai jinis,	Cháka jinis.
	Drinkables,	Pívar khorák,	Longnai jinis,	A'mka jinis.
	Animal food,	Máshong,	Bidot,	Béhá.
	Vegetable food,	Phalhár,	Máigong,	Sár.
	Fish meat,	Mácch máshong,	Gnábidot,	Haiyú Béha.
	Fowl meat,	Múrgh máshong,	Doubidot,	Kíya kobeha.
	Flesh meat,	Máshong,	Bidot,	Béhá.
	Grain diet,	Phalhár,	...	...
	Fruit diet,	Phalhár,	...	...
	Hot condiments,	Garam masála,	...	...
	Cold condiments,	Thanda masála,	...	...
	Water,	Jal,	Dóï,	Chí.
	Fermented liquor,	...	Jou,	Yú.
	Distilled liquor,	Madh,	Pitika,	Phatika.
	Milk,	Dúdh,	Dúdú,	Dúdhé.
	Buttermilk,	...	...	...
	Whey,	Máthá,	...	...
	Ghee,	Ghiú,	Ghiú,	Ghiú.
	Curds,	Dahi,	Dúdú,	Dahí.
	Roast or grilled flesh,	Bhájá,	Manbai,	Khinka béhá.
	Boiled flesh,	Jhól,	Bidai,	Jhól.
	Beef,	Gaiko másang,	Músho bidot,	Píá ko béhá.

	English.	*Kocch.*	*Bodo.*	*Dhimál.*
	Mutton,	Bheri ko másang,	Mónda bidot,	Mónda ko béhá.
	Goat flesh,	Bakri ko másang,	Búrma bidot,	Eócha ko béhá.
	Pork,	Súwar ko másang,	Yóma bidot,	Páyá ko béhá.
	Venison,	Mriga ko másang,	Moini bidot,	Yénga ko báha.
	Breakfast,	...	Phúnjáni jáyá,	Rhéma cháka.
	Dinner,	...	Sánjiphú moikham,	Mánjh béláchákа.
9th,	Supper,	...	Biléyomoikham,	Ditima-cháka.
DRESS.	Clothes : dress,	Kapra,	Hí,	Dhábá.
	Man's dress,	...	Hiwáni Hí,	Wáwal ko Dhába.
	Woman's dress,	...	Hinjouni Hí,	Béwal ko Bóná or bolha.
	Man's headdress,	Pa'gri,	Pháli,	Pátuka.
	Woman's ditto,	Ghúngar,	Khákiúkdong,	Béwal ko púchara.
	Man's upper vest,	Pachura,	Búchúla,	Dhábá.
	Woman's ditto,	Khári,	Dókna matta, Dokna-glou,	Bólhá.
	Man's lower vest,	Dhóti,	Gámcha,	Dhári.
	Woman's ditto,	Phóta, Patani,	Dokna matta,	Bólhá.
	Man's foot-cover,	Jota,	Jóta,	Jóta.
	Woman's ditto,	Jota,	Jóta,	Jota.
	Cotton clothes,	Súkulá kapra,	Higúphút,	Kapaiko Dhábá.
	Linen clothes,	...	...	...
	Woollen clothes,	Lúi ko kapra,	...	...
	Silk or satin clothes,	Pát ko kapra,	Injini hí,	...
10th, GAMES	A sport, game, pastime,	Khélá,	Gélénai,	Ghalló.
	Chess,	...	...	...
	Drafts,	...	...	...
	Dicing,	...	...	...
	A dice,	...	...	...
	Card-playing,	...	...	...
	A card,	...	...	...
	Kite-flying,	...	...	..
	A kite (paper),	...	...	...
	Putting the stone,	...	...	...
	Hockey,	..	...	...
	Wrestling,	..	...	...
	Fencing or single-stick,	... ..	...	...
	Ram-fights,	...	...	...
	Cock-fights,	...	...	..
	Hunting, or the chase,	Shikár,	..	...
	Visiting, society,	Sákaját,	Lago manno,	Dóhéhá.
	An assembly, soiree,	...	Gotha jádong,	Dyángjómbi.
	A feast,	Bhój,	Madáihúdúng (sacred),	Néváchápi.
11th, ORNAMENTS.	An ornament, personal, or jewel,	Gahana,	...	...
	A mirror,	Aïná,	...	Bahoti.
	A bracelet,	Matha, sakho,	Náchúng,	...
	An armlet,	Báhúng,	...	...
	An anklet,	Khárú,	...	...
	A ring,	Angúthi,	Nashithám,	...

	English.	*Kocch.*	*Bodo.*	*Dhimál.*
	An ear-ring,	Phúlkori kadama,	Onti, karan-phúl,	Onti.
	A nose-ring,	Phúl,	Nákha phúl,	Chatia.
	A necklace,	Hásúli,	...	...
	A chain of gold,	Sikal, jhinjiri,	...	...
	A chain of silver,	Sikal, jhinjiri,	...	...
	A precious stone,	...	...	...
	Diamond,	Hírá,	...	...
	Pearl,	Moti,	...	...
	Coral,	Múngá,	...	...
	Firoza,	...	...	...
12th, ANIMALS, QUADRUPEDAL.	Animal,	Rasú,	...	...
	Mankind,	Mánushi,	Mánushí,	Dyáng.
	Quadruped,	Chárpáya,	Gnáthéng thúngbré,	Diálong-khokoï.
	Bat, common,	Chámchila,	Bádá málí,	Chámchil.
	Pteropine or frugivorous Bats,	Bogdor,	Bilin,	Bogdor.
	Monkey, Macacus,	Bándor,	Mokhóra,	Nhóyá.
	Monkey, Semnopithecus,	Húlmán,	Thiá mokhora,	Húlmán.
	Cat, domestic,	Bilai,	Mouji,	Ménkou.
	Male cat,	Bilai,	Mouji jóla,	Dánkha menkou.
	Female cat,	Billi,	Mouji jo,	Mahani menkou.
	Kitten,	Bilaiér chóá,	Mouji galai,	Menkou ko chan.
	Wild cat, Viverriceps,	Happa,	Happa,	Happa.
	Chaus lynx,	...	...	...
	Tiger,	Bág,	Móchá,	Khúná.
	Leopard,	Túká bág,	Chitia mócha,	Nákshi khúna.
	Dog, domestic,	Kúkúr,	Choïmá,	Khiá.
	Male dog,	Kúkúr,	Choïmá jolá,	Dánkhá khiá.
	Bitch,	Kúkurni,	Choïmá jo,	Mahani khiá.
	Young or whelp,	Chóá kúkúr,	Choisya galai,	Khiá ko chan.
	Wild dog or Cúón,	Kúhók,	Chikú,	Dincha ko khiá.
	Hyæna,	Lékrá,	Lókra,	Lékra.
	Jackal,	Síyál,	Síyál,	Síyál.
	Wolf,	...	...	...
	Fox,	Khéki,	Khak siál,	Khéki.
	Mungoose, Herpestes,	Biji,	Nyúlai,	Nyúl.
	Civet, large, Viverra,	Mátch gai,	Múrú,	...
	Civet, small, Viverricula,	Katás,	Gandouri,	Katás.
	Paradoxurus, or screw-tail,	...	...	...
	Weasel, mustelá,	...	...	...
	Marten, martes,	...	...	...
	Otter, Lutra,	U'd,	Mathám,	U'd.
	Bear, Helarctos,	Bhoul, Bhándá,	Múphúr,	Naibhri.
	Bear, Prochilus,	Bhándi,	Khak bhálú,	...
	Ratel, Mesobema,	...	...	...
	Hedgehog,	...	...	...
	Musk shrew or sorex,	Chiká,	Chiká,	Chiká.
	Mole,	Pari nindú,	...	...

	English.	*Kocch.*	*Bodo.*	*Dhimál.*
ANIMALS, QUADRUPEDAL.	Elephant,	Háthi,	Moïdét,	Náría.
	Male elephant,	Háthi,	Moïdet jola,	Dánkha nária.
	Female elephant,	Hathni,	Moïdet jo,	Mahani nária.
	Elephant's trunk,	Súnr,	Súndi,	Súndáng.
	Elephant's tusk,	Háthi dánt,	Moïdet nipathai,	Nária ko shitong.
	Rhinoceros,	Génda,	Génda,	Láyá.
	His horn,	Khág,	Génda ni góng,	Láyá ko sing.
	Hog, tame,	Súvar,	Nong yoma,	Páyá.
	Male hog,	Pangár,	Yóma jola,	Dánkha páyá.
	Female or sow,	Páthi,	Yóma jo,	Mahani páyá.
	Wild hog,	Banwa súvár,	Hágráni yoma,	Dincha ko páyá.
	Manis,	Kéwat,	Khéötai,	Kéwata Háyá.
	Ox, tame, Bos,	Górú,	Múshó,	Piá.
	Bull,	A'ndhia,	Músho dámra,	Dánkha piá.
	Cow,	Gái,	Músho jo,	Mahani piá.
	Calf,	Báchrú,	Músho galái,	Piá ko chan.
	Bibos or Gaur,	Gouri gáó,	Báns bolod,	Dincha ko piá.
	Buffalo, tame,	Bhainsa,	Moïsho,	Diá.
	Male buffalo,	Rángá,	Moïsho jola,	Dánkha diá.
	Female buffalo,	Sáral, Dhénú,	Moïsho jo,	Mahani diá.
	Bison or Yak,	Khopoli,	Bima Khúkuli gáo,	Chouri piá.
	Wild buffalo, male,	Arná,	Hágráni Moïsho jola,	Dánkha diá dincha ko.
	Ditto, female,	Arni,	Hágráni Moïsho jo,	Mahani diá dincha ko.
	Antelope, black,	Latti,	...	...
	Ditto, four-horned,	...	...	...
	Ditto, Goral,	...	...	...
	Ditto, Thár,	...	...	...
	Goat, domestic, male,	Chágol,	Búrmá,	Eéchá.
	Ditto, female,	Bákrí,	Búrma jo,	Mahani Eéchá.
	Kid,	Pátha, páthí,	Búrma galai,	Eécha ko chan.
	Wild goat or Hermitragus,	...	Móïsh théngá,	...
	Domestic sheep,	Bhérá,	Méndá,	Méndá.
	The ram,	Bhéra,	Ménda phántá,	Dánkha ménda.
	The ewe,	Bhérí,	Ménda jo,	Mahani ménda.
	The lamb,	Báchá,	Ménda galai,	Ménda kó chan.
	Wild sheep,	...	...	...
	Stag, Elaphus,	Gónr,	...	Géná.
	Stag, Kusa,	Gáwaj,	...	...
	Cervus, all,	Harin, Mirga,	Móchó,	Yéngbá.
	Axis, chittal,	Phútka khátia,	Khátia pháglá,	Phútki.
	Stylocerus or Stilt,	Sókra,	Móchói,	Sókra.
	Musk deer,	Kastúri,	Kastúri,	Kostúri.
	Horse, male,	Ghora,	Gorai thángan,	O'nyhá.
	Mare,	Ghori,	Gorai thángani,	Thangani onyha.
	Foal,	Báchá,	Gorai galai,	Onyha ko chan.
	Ass,	Gadha,	Gadha,	Gadha.
	Mule,	Khachar,	Khachar,	Khachar.
	Rat,	Indúr,	Injúd,	Júbá.
	Mouse,	Nakanai,	Injúd ingini,	Mhoika júbá.
	Marmot,	...	...	...
	Rhizomys,	...	Injúr búnga,	Bóhá.

	English.	Kocch.	Bodo.	Dhimál.
ANIMALS, QUADRUPEDAL.	Lagomys,	...	...	...
	Hare,	Sasai,	Shésá,	Sosai.
	Porcupine,	Chéda,	Múdói,	Chéda.
	Squirrel,	Dál génora,	Mántáp,	Dál gounra.
	Flying squirrel,	...	...	...
	A herd,	Hánja, jhánk,	Phalwa,	Jhákwa.
	A flock,	Hánja,	Phalwa,	Jhákwa.
	Tusk,	Kúkúr dánt,	...	...
	Talon,	Angsá,	Asigúr,	Khúrsing.
	Muzzle,	Thatama,	Gúthútri,	...
	Horn,	Singh,	Gong,	Dáng.
	Hoof, entire,	Táp,	Yakhúng,	Táp.
	Hoof, cloven,	Khúrá,	Yakhúng,	Khúr.
	Tail,	Néngór,	Lánjai,	Météng.
	Mane,	Jhúl,	Báboï,	Jhúl.
	Fur,	Rom, Poshom,	Khaman,	Moïshú.
	Hair, animal,	Rom,	Khaman,	Moïshú.
	Hide, raw,	Khál,	Bigúr,	Chám.
	Hide, tanned,	Sábar,	...	Khál.
	Peltry, prepared furs,	...	...	...
13th, BIRDS.	A bird,	Pókhi,	Dou chen,	Jihá.
	Vultures, Vultur, Lin.,	Singni,	Sígún,	Sigún.
	Eagles, Aquila, Lin.,	Báj,	Dou léngá,	U'wá.
	Pernes or fishing eagles,	Hókós, kúrwa,	Dou phó,	Kúrwá.
	Falcons, Falco,	Báj,	...	...
	Hawks, accipiter,	Báj,	...	...
	Kites, Milvus,	Chíl,	Sila,	...
	Buzzards, Buteo,	Alichápra,	...	...
	Owls, all, Strix, L.,	Péchá,	Dou khú,	Péchá.
	Goat-suckers,	Bhirki,	Dou thúmphoï,	Thádar.
	Swallows and swifts,	Nák-kata,	Dou blúkhúr,	Nák-kata.
	Blue-throats or Eurystomus,	Són kowá,	Dou khatáng,	...
	Kingfishers, Alcedo, Lin.,	Mátchréngá,	Dou náthút,	...
	Bee-eaters, Merops, Lin.,	Patréngá,	Máthlanka,	...
	Hoopoes, Upupa, Lin.,	Bánia bóhú,	Dou khánjong,	...
	Sun-birds or Nectarines,	Madh chúsi,	...	...
	Trogons, Trogon,	...	...	...
	Horn-bills, Buceros,	Húkúl kúlli,	Dou ching, Dou wáng,	Lénjá.
	Barbets, Bucco,	...	Dou khún thúlo,	Hútúk tákí
	Thrushes, Turdus, Lin.,	Béswári,	Akaisikai,	...
	Chattering thrushes or Garrulax,	Sáth Bhai,	Golia sin khoudi,	Góïdiddi.
	Orioles or mango birds,	Haldiarám,	...	...
	Búlbúls,	Dómná,	Búlút,	...

	English.	Kocch.	Bodo.	Dhimál.
BIRDS.	Harewas or Chloropsis,	...	...	...
	Fly-catchers, Muscicapa, L., Macharias,	Thépi,	...	...
	Phanbúdi, Phúdki, or Tiny Sylvians, Sylvia antiq,	Choti pokhi,	Thóphleng,	Lati tipa.
	Dahils or Copsychus,	Duyal,	Khúrjéng,	...
	Syámas or Grillivora,	...	...	...
	Stone-chats or Saxicola Piddas, or Sikoulas,	...	...	...
	Wagtails, Motacilla, L., Khanjans or Dhoubinis,	Chitkón,	Phúrsi,	Chitkon.
	Tit-larks or Anthus Masaréchi,	Bharia,	Dou shibing,	...
	Butcher - birds, or Lanius, L.,	Chátók,	...	...
	Black ditto, or Edolians, Cuv.,	Jhénchú,	Phiringa,	Chéútiá.
	Cotton-birds, or Graucalus,	Kapaswa,	...	..
	Magpies, kitta,	...	Gúgligáng,	Thergogo.
	Jays, Garrulus,	...	...	...
	Crows, Corvus,	Kág, Kowá,	Dou khá,	Kowa.
	Grackles, or Mainas Gracula, Lin.,	Sáró,	Dou sári,	Sáró.
	Starlings, Sturnus, Lin.,	Khoksáro,	...	...
	Weavers, Báyas, Ploceus,	Chonch,	...	...
	Amadines, Amadina, Sw.,	Chúá páni,	Thúni, and Dousit,	Púni.
	Thick-billed finches, Pyrrhulines,	Ram goura,	...	...
	Common finches,	Goura, Chonch,	...	...
	Sparrows, Passer,	Géonrá,	Ghor Chókha,	...
	Finch larks or Pyrrhulanda,	...	...	...
	Larks, Alauda,	Khúpúria chilchilia,	...	...
	Parrots, Tóta,	Tota,	Báthó,	Tota.
	Parrakeets, Súgá, Palœornis,	Patani,	Pútani,	Noltia.
	Swinging parrakeets, Latkan Psittacula,	Laṭan Súá,	...	...
	Wood-peckers, Picus, Lin.,	Khúta káti,	Dou théna,	...
	Walking cuckoos or Mahokas, Phœnicophaus cum centropus, &c.,	Chokúl ding, Kéch ke chia, Dema chor,	...	...
	Black cuckoos or koils, Endynamys,	Kóil,	...	Búdhéng.
	Common cuckoos,	Cúcúá,	...	...
	Pigeons, common,	Páró,	Pario,	Parho.
	Pigeons, green, Vihago, Cuv.,	Hariwál,	Bájó,	Haritól.
	Turtle-doves,	Ghúgú,	Dou thó.	Ghúgú.
	Peacocks, Pavo,	Máir,	Dou tai.	Khonja.
	Pheasants, Phasianus,	...	...	...

	English.	Kocch.	Bodo.	Dhimál.
BIRDS.	Fowl, pheasants or Kaliches, Euplocomus,	...	Dou gúrút,	...
	Fowls, gallus,	Chórhá,	Dou mashar,	Kiá.
	Wild fowl,	Ban chorha,	Dou mashar,	Chá kiá.
	Domestic fowl,	Chorha,	Dou or Tau,	Kiá.
	Cock,	Múrghó,	Dou jola,	Dhángái kia.
	Hen,	Múrghi,	Dou jo,	Bhúndi kia.
	Chicken,	Chéngná,	Dou syá,	Kéé chan.
	Partridges, Perdix, Lin.,	Títhar,	Dou thitiri,	Tithíri.
	Quails, Coturnix,	Batoi, Bháti,	Dou bathar,	Múgúm.
	Three-toed quails or Láwás,	...	...	...
	Bustards, Otis,	...	...	...
	Indian Bustards or charaj,	Dáber,	Dou dáber,	Dáber.
	Œdicnemusaut or Carvánacks,	...	...	...
	Plovers, charadrius, Lin.,	Nitáli,	...	...
	Lapwings, Vanellus, Lin.,	Gángtitti,	Sótmár,	Gáng títi.
	Curlews, Numenius,	...	...	...
	Ibises, Ibisaut,*	Kákról, kadoghoka,	Kádo ghóka,	Kádo ghóka.
	Tantali,	...	...	...
	Demoiselles, Anthopoides,	Sáras,	...	...
	Cranes, grus,	Sáras,	...	...
	Storks, Ciconía,	Laglag,	...	...
	Adjutants or Leptoptilos,	Hárgíl,	...	...
	Jabirus or Mycteria,	Jhángil,	...	...
	Gaping storks, Anastomus,	Lóhójáng,	...	...
	Herons, Ardea,	...	...	..
	Little white herons or Egrets,	Bagla,	Dou bo,	...
	Sand-pipers, Tringa, Lin.,	...	...	...
	Stilts or Himantopus,	...	...	...
	Snipes or Scolopax,	...	...	...
	Gallinules or Water Hens,	...	...	...
	Jacanas or Parra,	Heóni,	...	...
	Spoonbills or Dábil,	...	...	...
	Flamingoes, Phœnicopterus,	...	...	...
	Gulls, Larus, Lin.,	...	...	...
	Terns, Sterna, Lin.,	Gángchila,	...	...
	Grebes, Fulica,	...	...	...
	Divers, Plotus,	...	...	...
	Pelicans,	Bhérú,	Naishaka,	...
	Corvorants,	Cowár,	...	...
	Geese, Anser,	Hángs,	Hángs,	Hangs.
	Ducks, Anas,	Hangs,	Hángs,	Hangs.
	Teal, Querquedula,	Gairi,	...	...
	Egg,	Dimá,	Dou doï,	Túí.
	Yolk,	Kúsmá,	Gúmó,	Kékalai.
	Shell,	Kholta,	Dou doikhon,	Kholta.
	Feather,	Pákhana,	Gáng,	Pakhana.
	Down,	...	Thúlá,	Múïshú.
	Plume or quill,	Khól,	Dou gáng,	...
	Beak, bill,	Thót,	Khougá,	Thótwa.

* Eupodotis v. Sypheotides.

	English.	Kocch.	Bodo.	Dhimál.
	Wing,	Déná,	Káng khong,	Dám.
	Tail,	Phéchú,	Lánjai,	Métóng.
	Nest, bird's,	Bhásá,	Bithop,	...
	Den, wild beast's,	Khor,	Múdúá,	...
REPTILES.	Amphibia or Reptiles,	...	...	...
	Alligator,	Kúmmír,	...	...
	Crocodile,	Thoná gúi,	...	...
	Tortoise, land,	Dúrá,	Khúbchúng,	Rúhá.
	Ditto, water,	Páni mátch,	Góltáp,	Ghúkút.
	Lizards, generic,	Khaklás,	Lámá khandai,	Chéndóó.
	Monitor or Góh,	Gúhí,	Múphó,	Koïyá.
	Snakes,	Sámp,	Jibo,	Púuhiá.
	Python,	Ajangor,	Jibo yút,	...
	Coluber,	Dhamna, Bórá,	Jibo danda,	Bóró.
	Cobra,	Gohoma,	Riál,	...
	Toad,	Kotarai,	Imbú chitro,	Kótrái.
	Frog,	Hólá,	Imbú bónglá,	Hólá.
FISH.	Fish, all,	Mátch,	Gná,	Hiyú.
	Carp,	Róhi,	Rúhi,	Rúhí.
	Mullet,	...	...	...
	Eel,	Bámúj,	Lángdúr,	Bámi.
	Sóran,	...	...	...
	Soulí,	Soul,	...	...
	Boáli,	...	...	...
	Ekdhónga,	Thóná,	KhＡng killi,	Thóna.
	Phalli,	Phalli,	Gná laibú,	Gáchí.
	Kúrsá,	Kúrsá,	Karsa,	Kúrsá.
	Chittal,	Chittal,	...	...
	Crustaceans,	...	...	...
	Crab,	Kákór,	Kan kharai,	Kihá.
	Prawn,	Níchá,	Gná thút,	Tánhia.
	Oyster,	...	...	...
	Cockle,	Gúzúri,	Syámak,	Chúdár.
	Mussel,	Sámbúk,	Larái,	Dúdúkri.
	Snail, any,	Syáltina,	Khórikata,	Lótét.
	Shelled snail,	...	Jinai khong,	Jhól téng.
	Nude snail,	...	...	Lótét.
	Shell, any,	...	...	Khóltá.
INSECTS.	Insects,	Póká,	Impho,	Póká.
	Beetle,	Dhandhania,	Khí brúma, Kibrútma,	Bhúndúri. Dhikuri.
	Fly,	Máchí,	Thampoï,	Túnhá.
	Gadfly,	Dáns,	Dángso,	Dohá.
	Spider,	Mákor,	Bémá,	Makra.
	Butterfly,	Chitti,	Kántéólá,	Chitti.
	Moth,	Kúkti,	Kánteólá,	Chitti.
	Bee,	Mohúmáchi,	Béré,	Shóá.
	Wasp,	Bhéméról,	Támri mára, Choréma,	Bághi.
	Hornet,	Bághi,	Béré khángrai,	Tokrá.
	Moschito,	Mosho,	Thámphoi gangjang,	Jáhán.
	Bug,	U'ras,	Urow,	U'rús.
	Louse,	Nakuni khia,	Théma, Tiphúá,	Khít.
	Flea,	Chotka,	Chútki,	Chutki.
	Grasshopper,	Pharing kúkti,	Gúmagrán,	Jháriák.

	English.	*Kocch.*	*Bodo.*	*Dhimdl.*
INSECTS.	Locust,	Théri kúkti,	Gúyong,	Jhariáp.
	Ant,	Nutipípara,	Mocha rám, Hasha brai,	Nhá múi.
	Termite,	U'ri,	Rai khún,	U'ri.
	Centipede,	Chiára,	Chélémlá,	Tamia.
	Scorpion,	...	...	...
	Earth-worm,	Chérá,	Khanchiri,	Dória.
	Intestinal worm,	Pét chéra,	Phila,	Chárá.
	Leech,	Jálúk,	Bédlou,	Chamdlá.
	Fish scale,	Aisha,	Gná bigúr,	Aisha.
	Fish fin,	Déná,	Gná gáng,	Bhír.
	Fish gill,	Kánkáshi,	Galphá,	Kan kashi.
	Spider's web,	Jálshi,	Béma dóng,	...
	Cacoon,	Thúshí,	Bithóp,	Thúshi.
	Caterpillar,	Póká,	Chikri,	Poka.
	Chrysalis,	Látá,	Bithop,	...
	Imago, insect,	Chitti,	Chikri,	...
	Honey,	Madhú,	Gódói,	Shárti.
	Wax,	Móm,	Múshúthá,	Púring.
	Beehive,	Chhát,	Bejélép,	Chatta.
	Fur,	Pasham,	Khomon,	Moïshú.
	Silk,	Résham,	Phát, Indi,	Résham.
	Wool,	Rom,	Khomon,	Moïshú.
VEGETALS.	Vegetabilia,	...	...	...
GRAINS.	Grains or Cerealia,*	Lókhi,	Lókhi,	Lókhi.
	Rice, dhán,	Dhán,	Mai,	Bháko óm.
	Rice, choul,	Choul,	Mairong,	U'nkhú.
	Rice, bhát,	Bhát,	Maikhom,	Om.
	Wheat,	Gohom,	Gohom,	Gohom.
	Barley,	Paira,	Phoira,	Poira.
	Rye,	...	...	...
	Buckwheat, Fagopyrus,	...	.	.
	Millets,	...	...	...
	Kúdrúm or Kúdrúva,	...	..	...
	Jowár or Karbi,	...	..	...
	Janéra,	...	...	...
	Bajara or Bájra,	...	...	...
	Kodo,	...	...	...
	Marúá or Marwa,	Marwa,	Thekoro,	Mándú,
	Tángan or Tangui,	...	...	...
	Kangani,	...	...	...
	Sámá,	...	...	...
	Chíní,	...	...	..
	Kodai,	...	...	...
	Makara or Makara-jál,	...	...	...
	Bhatwás,	...	...	..
	Pulse, Dáls,	Dál,	Kalai,	Kalai.
	Mattar or Pease,	Motor,	Shobaima,	Ghontál.
	Karau, ditto,	...	...	...
	Channa,	Bút kalai,	Bút,	Bút.
	Bút,	...	...	...
	Rébla or Rawla,	...	...	...
	Arhar or Rahar,	Arhal,	Khokléng,	Lahár.
	Khésari,	Khisiri,	Khisiri,	Khisiri.
	U'rid,	Thákori,	Thakori,	Thakori.

* Piddington's glossary of plants will give the English reader the usual Botanical equivalents; which, however, are too unsettled to induce me to postpone to them the native terms.

	English.	Kocch.	Bodo.	Dhimál.
	Kalai,	Músh,	Wásóng,	...
	Másh,	...	...	...
	Múng,	Múng,	Múkh kalai,	...
	Kúrthi or Kúlthi,	Kúlthi,	Kúlthi,	Kúlthi.
	Masúr,	Masuri,	Músuri,	Músuri.
	Mót or Móthi,	...	...	...
	Bhiringa or Bhring-ráj,	...	...	...
	Textile materials,—			
THREADS.	San,	Son,	Son,	Son.
	Pát,	Pátá,	Nárjai,	Pátá.
	Bháng,	Bháng,	Bháng,	Bháng.
	Múnj,	Mújá,	...	...
	Tisi or Alsi,	Tisi,	...	...
	Sómal,	Simla,	Syúmli,	Láshing.
	Kapás, the plant,	Kapás,	Khún pháng,	Kapai sing.
	Baróach,	...	...	...
	Mánwa or Múlwa,	Márwá pát,	...	...
	Resham,	Resham,	Indi,	Indi.
	Tasar,	...	Indi,*	Indi.
	Wool,	Poshom,	Khomon,	Muishú.
OILS.	Oil plants,	...	...	...
	Tori,	Túri,	Bishwár,	...
	Rái,	Rai,	...	...
	Sarsún,	Sórsyá,	Bishwár,	Jingshé.
	Tísi,	Tisi,	...	...
	Til,	Til,	Sibing,	Mééshé.
	Dána or Póst,	Posot,	Phosto,	Pós.
	Réndi,	E'nda,	E'nda,	E'ndi.
	Kúsúm,	Kúsúm,	Khúsúm,	...
	Nímb,	...	...	...
	Mohwa,	...	...	...
	Náril,	Náriyúl,	Nálikhor,	...
GREENS.	Greens,	Torkári,	Moikri,	Sár.
	Karþúza,	Khormúnj,	...	...
	Tarbúza,	...	...	...
	Kohara,	Kúmla,	Kháklú,	...
	Lowka,	Láhú,	Lou,	Láhú.
	Kaddú,	Kaddú,	...	...
	Khíra,	Swás,	Thai syúmú,	Thaishi.
	Kankara,	Bángi,	Thai béng,	...
	Karéla,	Kóïlla,	U'dashi,	Kórla.
	Sém or Shim,	Chima,	Gorshi,	Chénsé.
	Bokla,	...	...	...
	Lóba or Lóbia,	...	...	...
	Bórá,	Bórá,	Shobaima,	Ghonta.
	Chichinda,	Dúdhcósi,	I'lángi,	Dúdh cósi.
	Taróï,	Toroï,	Jinkha,	Toroï.
	Palwal,	Paral,	...	...
	Béngan,	Béngan,	Phánthou,	Béngan.
	Ninuá or Genora,	Ghérá,	Phalla,	Ghérá.
	Pálúng,	Pálúng,	...	...
	Pálag,	...	...	...
	Póï,	Póï,	Moï pharai,	Ghóng.
	Chouráyi,	...	...	...
TUBERS.	Roots, edible,	Kandmúl,	Thá,	Lin.
	Múng phalli,	...	...	...

* Wild silkworm, different species from that which yields Tasar.

	English.	*Kocch.*	*Bodo.*	*Dhimál.*
TUBERS.	Pékchi,	...	...	...
	Arwi,	Máná,	Máná,	Máná.
	Alú, potato,	Alú,	Biláti Thá,	Biláti Lin.
	Pind álu or Banda,	...	...	...
	Sakarkand,	Rangálú,	Thá gúni,	I'gá lin.
SPICES.	Spices and condiments, &c.,	Masála,	...	...
	Haldi,	Halad,	Haldói,	Yúngái.
	Adrak,	A'dá,	Haijóng,	Yónkhó.
	U'kh,	Kúsiyár,	Kúsiyar,	Kúsiyár.
	Tambákú,	Támkú,	Támkú,	Támkú.
	Paun,	Paun,	Phátai,	Paun.
	Gátch mirich, or Cayenne,	Morich,	Bánjalút,	Morchi.
	Large or Capsicum,	Bada, Morich,	Bánjalút thopa,	Bada. Morchi.
	Lahsún,	Roshan,	Páder, shambráng,	Roshan.
	Piáz,	Piáj,	Piági,	Tángó.
	Jírá,	Jira,	...	...
	Lóng,	Lóng,	Lóng,	Lóng.
	Iláchi,	Iláchi,	...	...
	Kálá mirich,	Golmorich,	Játi morich,	Golmorchi.
	Jowain,	Jowni,	Jowni,	Jowni.
	Jáiphal,	Jáiphal,	...	...
	Sómph,	Gwámúri,	Gwámúri,	Gwámúri.
	Sóṇt,	Sónt,	...	...
	Pípal,	Pipli,	Chimphrai,	Pipli.
DYES.	Dyes,	Rong,	...	...
	Níl,	Níl,	Níl,	Níl.
	Kúsúm,	Kúsúm,	Khúsúm,	...
	Haldi,	Halad,	Acho (plant),	Lúdhá.
	Túnd,	...	...	Tángwá.
	Munjit,	Manjit,	Mai jitti,	Mai jatti.
	Bakúm,	Bokom,	...	...
	A'l,	...	...	...
	Supári,	Supári,	Shúphári,	Ṣhúphári.
	Kath,	Kath,	Kwoïro,	Khair.
	Tésú or Téns,	...	...	...
	Géndá,	...	...	...
	Harra,	Harra,	Silikhá,	Horkóti.
DRUGS.	Drugs, &c.,	...	...	...
	Bikh (poison),	Bish,	Bish,	Ning.
	Bikhma,	...	...	...
	Singhia Bikh,	Singhia,	Singia,	Singi.
	Harina Bikh,	Harina,	Harina,	Harina.
	Dúdhia Bikh,	Dúdhia,	Rúh,	Túh.
	Téjpát,	Tejpát,	Théjpát,	Théjpát.
	Lal chandan,	Rakt chandan,	Chandan,	...
	Dhúpi chandan,	Dhúpi,	Chandan,	Chandan.
	Charaita,	Chirita,	Khábitítá,	Khábá.
	Jainti or Bhútkés,	...	...	...
	Jata mángsi,	Jata Mási,	...	...
TREES.	Trees, generice,	Gácch, Péd,	Pháng, Bóṇ pháng,	Sing.
	Sísú,	Sisrong,	Sisrong,	Sisrong.
	Sakwa,	Sál,	Sál,	Sál.
	Túnd,	...	...	..

	English.	*Kocch.*	*Bodo.*	*Dhimál.*
Trees.	Ságwan,	...	...	...
	Bábúl,	...	...	...
	Khair,	Khair,	Kwoiro,	Khair.
	Báns, common,	Báns,	Wá,	Pá sing.
	Báns, small,	Bish báns,	...	...
	Bént or Cane,	Bénth,	Raidong,	Rádhú.
	Champa,	Champa,	Champa,	Champa.
	Sómál,	Simla,	Syúmli,	Losing.
	Réndi, large tree,	...	...	...
	Mohwá,	...	...	...
	Sahajná,	Raikhanjan,	...	...
	Nimb,	Ním,	Ním,	Ním.
	Barr,	Bór,	Bór,	Bór.
	Pípal,	Pípol,	...	...
	Pákar,	Pakuri,	...	...
	Adambar,	...	...	...
	Palás or Dhák,	Panás,	Phalás,	Palás.
	Madár or Ekonia,	Madár,	Mándári,	...
	Jamalgota or Bhágréuda,	Kánikól,	...	...
	Síj or Euphorbia,	Sijú,	Bátho sijo,	Sijo.
	Nágphani or Cactus,	Nara sijú,	Maibúng-sijú,	...
	Asoka,	...	...	...
	Tál,	Tál,	Thál,	Tál.
	Khajúr,	Khajúr,	...	...
	Náril,	Nárél,	Nalikól,	...
	Súpári,	Supári,	...	...
	A'dhásúpári,	...	...	...
Fruit Trees.	A'm or Amba,	A'm,	Thaikjo,	Tórsé.
	Amrúd,	...	...	...
	'Sharífa,	...	...	...
	A'tta,	Atta,	...	...
	Katahar,	Kathal,	Khantal,	Dámshé.
	Barahar,	Bohor,	...	...
	Nárangi,	Santala,	Santara,	...
	Nímbú,	Jámír,	Cholonga,	Choishé.
	Bair,	Bobori,	Boigri,	Bágri.
	Tut,	...	...	...
	Imli,	Tétáli,	Tetali,	Tetáli.
	Kélá,*	Kollo,	Tháli, Laipháng,	Yómphi.

Parts of Plants.

English.	*Kocch.*	*Bodo.*	*Dhimál.*
Grain,	Lokhi,	Lókhi,	Lókhi.
Straw,	Púal,	Jigáp,	Natan.
Chaff,	Patán,	Gúbú,	...
Bran,	Ankári,	Gúndoï,	Akandi.
Stubble,	Nárá,	Jigáp,	Nara.
Husk,	Túsi,	'Júzai,	Túsi.
Pod, long,	Chéúr,	Chochá, Bejóng,	Thúkrá.
Round capsule,	Chéúr,	...	...
Ear of grain,	Shís,	Shís,	Shís.
Barb of ear,	Súngá,	Khisláng,	Súngá.
Stalk,	Gátch,	Bipháng,	Sing ?
Rind,	Chilka,	Bigúr,	Chónchá.

* For the mountains, mountainous species should be added or substituted, as Rhododendron, Oak, Chesnut, Pine, Cedar, Cypress, Alder, Willow, Birch, Magnolia, Cherry, Walnut, Paper-plant, Butter-tree, Camellia.

	English.	*Kocch.*	*Bodo.*	*Dhimál.*
PARTS OF PLANTS.	Pulp,	Másó,	Modom,	Bóhá.
	Core,	Sáns,	...	...
	Seed or stone,	Bichi,	Bigot,	Bichi.
	Flower-bud,	Kórhá,	Tropidong,	Kórhá.
	Flower,	Phúl,	Bibár,	Lhép.
	Pollen,	Bhúsóng,	Shúmú,	Dhúlá.
	Fruit,	Phal,	Bithai,	Sihá.
	Root,	Sikor,	Ródá,	Shikár.
	Bole or stem,	Solsol,	Gúdúi,	Górá.
	Bark,	Chál,	Bigor,	Chám.
	Wood or timber,	Manja,	Bónpháng,	Mánjá.
	Branch,	Dál,	Tálai,	Dáléng.
	Leaf,	Pát,	Lai, Bilai,	Lhábá.
	Grass kind,	Trin,	Taroi, gángsho,	Dinchanáimé.
	Creeper kind,	Néóshi,	Eóndong,	Léóshi.
	Air-plant kind,	Laut,	Rótt, Biád,	Alogrot.
	Reed kind,	Bátáli,	Khagra, Khámi,	Batali.
	Rush kind,	Hokola, Taranju,	Nangdorbilai, Tharai,	Hokola.
	Gum,	Atha,	...	...
	Glue,	A'thá,	...	...
	Nat, resin, of Pine,	Dhúná,	...	...
	Ditto, ditto, Saul,	Dhúná,	Dhúná,	Dhúná.
	Prepared extract, Pitch or Tar,	...	...	...
	Juice, any,	Ros,	Bidai,	Singkochí.
	Gáb or gluten,	Gáb,	...	...

NATURAL AND POLITICAL TIES.*

English.	Kocch.	Bodo.	Dhimál.
A man,	Beta choá,	Hiwá,	Wával.
A woman,	Beti choá,	Hinjou,	Béval.
An infant, sucking,	Chóá,	Galai,†	Chan.
A child, weaned,	Chengra, Chengri,	Gotho,‡	Dhámka-chan.
A mature man,	Gábhúr,	Jholou,	Whántéka.
A mature woman,	Gábhúr,	Sikhlou,	Whántéká.
A dry nurse,	Dái,	...	...
A wet nurse,	Dái,	Bima bátúl,	Mousi ámá.
A midwife,	Dai yáni,	...	...
A bride,	Kwoina,	Bihi,	Kaina.
A bridegroom,	Bór,	Bishai,	Bor.
A husband,	Bhatár,	Bishai,	Ké.
A wife,	Móghi,	Bihi,	Bé.
A widow,	Ránd,	Rándi,	Rándi.
A widower,	Rándrá,	Bálúndá,	Rándra.
An orphan,	Mouria,	Mouria,	Mouria.
A virgin,	Kumári,	Sikala,	Dháni.
A whore,	Nóti,	...	...
A whoremonger,	Láphandar,	...	...
A corpse,	Mórá,	Gathói,	Siká.
A sexton, burier or burner,	...	...	...
A mourner,	...	...	...

* These headings to the several parts of the matter should have been given throughout. I have subjoined them on the margin where deficient.

† All young. ‡ Human young only.

NATURAL AND POLITICAL TIES.

English.	Kocch.	Bodo.	Dhimál.
Parent,	Janam jata,	Bipha,	Aba.
Child,	Béta,	Bisha,	Chan.
Guardian,	...	...	...
Ward,	...	...	...
Minor,	...	...	...
Bastard,	Járwa,	Bipha yonga,	...
Adopted child,	Posh béta,	Dharam Bisha,	Poshya chan.
Heir,	Wáris,	Khúnigár,	Hárkhún.
Ancestor,	Pírhí,	Pirhi,	...
Descendant,	Choá réchoá,	...	...
A relation of blood,	Gótri,	Hárkhún,	Hárkhún.
Do. of marriage,	...	...	...
Kinsfolk or relatives of blood and marriage,	Kútúmbh,	Gúshti, Gouini manushí,	Gúshthí, Tai ko diang.
Own family or household,	Alabás,	Nóöni manushi,	Sáko gúthi.
Other folk, strangers,	Pórlóg,	Malaicho,	Bóömi.
A householder,	Giri,	Giri, Grá,	Giri, Grá.
An ascetic,	Bairági,	Houria,	...
Father,	Báp,	Aphá,	Aba.
Mother,	Má,	A'yá,	Amma.
Brother,	Bhai,	Bida,	Yolla.
Sister,	Bahin,	Bina nou,	Rima.
Son,	Bétá,	Bishá,	Chán.
Daughter,	Béti,	Bishú,	Chámdi.
Boy,	Chéngra,	Hiwa gotho,	Wájan.
Girl,	Chéngri,	Hinjou gotho,	Béjan.
Pat. grandfather,	Aju,	Abo,	Aju.
Grandchild,	Náthi,	Bichou,	Náthi.
Mat. grandfather,	Náná,	Abo,	Ajú.
Pat. grandmother,	Abo,	Aboi,	Ajai.
Mat. grandmother,	Náni,	Aboi,	Ajai.
Father's sister's husband,	Pisha,	Amai,	Pisha.
Father's sister,	Pisai,	Anoï,	Pisai.
Father's brother,	Jétho, Khúrá,	Ayong, Adoi,	Jétha, Dádo.
Brother's son,	Bhatíja,	Biyadóï,	Bhatijá.
Mother's brother,	Mámá,	Amai,	Mámú.
Mother's sister,	Máshi,	Madóï,	Moushí.
Sister's son,	Bháginá,	Banaicho,	Bhágina.
Brother's daughter,	Bháṭiji,	Biyá doï,	Bhátiji.
Sister's daughter,	Bhágini,	Biyá noï,	...
Paternal cousin,	Dádá, Bába,	Ada, Agai,	Dai, Yolla.
Maternal cousin,	Dádá, Bába,	Ada, Agai,	Dai, Yolla.
Father-in-law,	Bábáji,	Apha,	Júwá.
Son-in-law,	Jamai,	Bija madoi,	Mháwa.
Brother-in-law,	Sála,	Bibnáng,	Sála.
Sister-in-law,	Sáli,	Bibnáng,	Sáli.
Foster brother,	Dúdhia Bhai,	...	...
Foster sister,	Dúdhia Bahin,	...	...
Friend,	Sákhi,	Gúshthi,	Taikodiáng.
Enemy,	Bairi,	Bairi,	Bairi.
Neighbour,	Pasporsi,	Gyáti,	...
Stranger,	Noudhia,	Aláshi,	...
Patron,	...	...	...
Client,	...	...	...

	English.	Kooch.	Bodo.	Dhimál.
NATURAL AND POLITICAL TIES.	Partner in trade, &c.,	Lúdú, Bhágiára,	Rannai,	Bántha pahi.
	Fellow caste man,	Ekjatia,	Jóngni Bótó,	...
	Own country, natal soil,	Janam Bhúm,	Jongni raijo,	Tai ko rájyo.
	Fellow-countryman,	Désbhai,	Jongni raijoni mánushi,	Nal súkhá.
	Alien, foreigner,	Pordési,	Gúbún raijoni mánashi,	Borájyo-kodyúng.
	Host,	Ghorgribasth,	Barthán hodong,	Gwoipika.
	Guest,	Sohor,	Aláshi,	Cháliléhé.
	Traveller,	Porbásia,	...	...
	Master,	Múnib,	Grá,	Grá.
	Servant,	Chákor,	Arpho,	Chákor.
	Debtor,	Dháruá,	Dhárjáyá,	Dhárcbáika.
	Creditor,	Mahájan,	Dhárhoua,	Dhárpúká.
	Freeman,	Sádhín,	...	...
	Slave,	Bándá,	...	...
	Predial slave,	...	...	...
	Menial slave,	Bándá, Bándi,	...	...
	Born slave,	...	...	...
	Bought slave,	...	...	...
	Domestic servant,	Kamáïl,	Arpho,	...
	Male ditto,	Kamáïl,	...	...
	Female ditto,	...	...	...
	Mistress of house, manager,	Girthání,	...	...
	Steward, outhouse manager,	Déóniá,	...	...
	Sovereign,	Rája,	Raja,	Raja.
	Subject,	Praja,	Porja,	Porja.
	King,	Raja,	...	...
	Noble,	Kúlín,	...	...
	Peasant, bourgeois,	Dhékara,	...	...
	Gentleman,	Kúlín,	...	...
	Plebeian,	Dhékara,	...	...
	Landlord,	Giri,	Grá,	Giri.
	Tenant or lease-holder,	Mastájir,	Grá,	Giri.
PROFESSIONALS AND TRADESMEN.	Hunter,	Byádhi,	...	...
	Fisherman,	Mátchúá,	Mála, Jáluá,	Jáluá.
	Herdsman,	Gwál, Sapál, Majathi,	Gwál,	Gwál.
	Agricultural cultivator,	Kirsán, Chása,	Porja,	Porja.
	Gardener,	Máli,	...	...
	Hired labourer,	Kámla,	Bhéran boyo,	Bénihár.
	Ploughman,	Halwáhá,	Halwa,	Halwái.
	Merchant, wholesale,	Dhoni,	Máhájan,	Mahájan.
	Trader, retail,	Dokáni,	...	...
	Banker, money-dealer,	Sarráfi,	...	...
	Bankrupt,	Khángta,	...	...
	Manufacturer,	...	...	...
	Artisan, craftsman,	Mistrí,	Dágrá,	...
	Artist, liberal,	Silpiwár,	...	...
	Priest, cleric,	Pújak pátak,	Déóshi, Dhámi,	Déóshi, Dhami.
	Layman, laic,	...	...	...

PROFESSIONALS AND TRADESMEN.

English.	Kocch.	Bodo.	Dhimál.
Gúrú,	Gosain,	...	...
Chéla,	Bhogot,	...	...
Puróhit,	Púrohit,	Déóshi,	Déóshi,
Pújári,	Pújári,	Dhámi,	Dhámi.
Witch, male,	Dákin,	Híwa daina,	Dhaina.
Ditto, female,	Dákini,	Hinjou daina,	Mhái.
Sorcerer or magician,	Khot komi, Jádúgar, Jontri,	...	...
Diviner or augur,	...	...	...
Astrologer,	Jótshi,	...	...
Fortune-teller,	Nat, Bánd,	...	...
Exorcist,	Jhár phúnk kornia,	Ojha,	Ojha.
Clerk, scholar, man of letters,	Pondit,	...	...
Teacher,	Gúrú,	...	...
Learner,	Sish,	...	...
Minister of state,	Mantri,	Dewán,	Dewán.
Prime minister,	Múl mantri,	...	...
Finance ditto,	Díwán,	Díwán,	Díwán.
Law ditto,	Dharmádhikári,	...	...
Foreign ditto,	...	...	...
Envoy,	Dút,	...	...
Judge, lawyer,	...	...	...
Umpire, single,	Sális,	...	...
Jury, Pancháyat,	Pancháti,	...	Diámi.
Pleader, attorney,	Wókil,	Wokil,	Wokíl.
Plaintiff,	Phairádi,	...	...
Defendant,	Asámi,	...	...
Witness,	Gowa, Sáki,	I'sát,	I'sát.
Civilian,	...	...	...
Soldier,	Sipáhi,	Siphai,	Siphai.
Officer,	...	...	...
Private,	...	...	...
Commander-in-chief,	Sénapati,	...	...
Sailor, boatman,	Kéónia, Mallάh,	...	...
Physician,	Rójhá,	Ojhá,	Ojhá.
Surgeon,	...	...	...
Druggist,	Pasári,	Pakháli,	...
Poet,	Kabiráj,	...	...
Painter,	Málákór,	Máli,	Máli.
Architect,	...	...	...
Sculptor,	...	...	...
Musician,	Gáin,	...	...
Mason or house-builder,	Mistri,	Thávui,	Dárí.
Miner, quarrier for metal,	...	...	...
Stone quarrier,	...	...	...
Stone cutter or engraver,	...	...	...
Metallic engraver,	...	...	...
Smelter,	...	...	...
Bricklayer and maker,	Kúmhál,	Kúmhál,	Kúmhál.
Tile-maker,	...	...	...
Thatcher,	Chál,	Nukhúm lápgra,	Sádámka.
Carpenter,	Baróï,	Shútár,	...
Potter,	Kúmhár,	Khúmár,	Khúmár.
Smith,	Kámhár,	Khámár,	Kámár.
Ironsmith,	Kámhar,	...	...
Coppersmith,	Kámhar,	...	...

PROFESSIONALS AND TRADESMEN.

English.	Kocch.	Bodo.	Dhimál.
Brazier,	Kámhar,	...	...
Pewterer,	Thatári,	Thatári,	Thatári.
Bell-maker,	...	...	...
Gold and silver smith,	Bánia,	Bánia,	Bania.
Cutler,	Kámhár,	...	...
Cook,	Bhandári,	...	...
Barber,	Nowa,	Nowa,	Nowa.
Tailor,	Dorji,	...	...
Shoemaker,	Chúmár,	Chúmár,	...
Currier, tanner,	Chumár,	...	...
Miller,	...	...	...
Oilman,	Téli,	Téli,	Téli.
Dyer,	Rangsáz,	...	...
Confectioner,	Bowri,	Bhújári,	Bowri.
Butcher,	Kassai,	...	...
Baker,	...	...	...
Distiller,	Súndi,	Súṇdi,	...
Brewer,	...	...	...
Turner,	...	...	...
Cloth-printer,	...	...	...
Spinner,	...	Khúnlúdong,	Kapai kátika.
Weaver,	Tánti, Joláha,	Dágrá,	Dháwa thirka.
Basketmaker,	Hári, Dóm,	...	...
Cordwainer,	...	...	...

ABSTRACT FORMS OF ABOVE NOUNS.*

English.	Kocch.	Bodo.	Dhimál.
Carcase, animal,	Mórá,	Gothoï,	Síká.
Corpse, human,	Mórá,	Gothoï,	Síká.
Sex,	Ling, játí,	...	...
Male sex,	Pú ling,	...	...
Female sex,	Stri ling,	...	...
Age, how old,	Boïsh,	Boïsh,	Boïsh.
Birth, sheer,	Jonom,	Jonom,	Jonom.
Infancy,	Chóá bóïsh,	Gothoblá,	Dúdúám boïsh.
Childhood,	Chengra bóïsh,	Khat gúgúrblá,	Wájan boïsh.
Puberty,	Gábúr bóïsh,	Jholou slo,	Whánté boïsh.
Old age, decrepitude,	Búḍha boïsh,	Braibla,	Wáráng boïsh.
Youth,	Júán boish,	Gothobla,	Whánté boïsh.
Parturition,	Phorébá,	Upzidong,	Chanjónka.
Delivery, accouchement,	...	...	...
Baptism, naming,	Janam kúshti,	Múngdóna,	Mingtapika.
Weaning, weaned state,	Bhát chúáni,	Maikhamdóá,	Omcháka.
Toga virilis, coming of age, the mere fact,	...	...	...
Marriage, mere act,	Béhá,	Habba,	Béhoú.
Wedlock, state of,	Bibáhota,	...	...
Celibacy,	Abibáhota,	...	...
Virginity,	...	...	...
Whoredom,	Kosobgiri,	...	...
Divorce,	...	...	...
Courtship,	...	...	...

* That is, the nouns from p. 22, or Natural and Political Ties.

	English.	Kocch.	Bodo.	Dhimál.
ABSTRACT FORMS OF ABOVE NOUNS.	Betrothal,	Somond,	...	...
	Burial, mere act,	Máti dévá,	Goti phopnin,	Bhónóîpika.
	Cremation, ditto,	Jolává,	Goti syounin,	Médúká.
	Mourning, state of,	Chúá,	Bádúa,	Chúá.
	Progenitorship,	...	...	...
	Ancestry,	...	...	...
	Succession or line of inheritance,	...	...	...
	Relationship of blood,	Somond,	...	...
	Ditto, of marriage,	Somond,	...	...
	Ditto, of adoption,	Somond,	...	...
	Legitimacy, state of,	...	...	...
	Bastardy, ditto,	...	...	...
	Adoption, ditto,	...	...	...
	Status by birth,	Játi,	Játi,	Játi.
	Status by vocation,	Béwósa,	...	...
	Lineage, race, stock, sect, tribe, clan,	Bongs, kúl,	Bodo,*	Játi.
	Class, order of men,	Boron,	...	...
	Vocation, means of livelihood,	Rójgár,	Rojgár,	Rojgár.
	Profession, liberal art,	...	...	...
	Craft, art, mechanical,	Kárigari,	...	...
	Trade, commercial status,	Béópár,	Béphár,	Bépár.
	Service, menial,	Chákari,	Chákari,	...
	Friendship,	Dósti,	Lagúgaman,	Nálsúkha.
	Enmity,	Dúshmani, Bair,	Gasho bráp-dong,	Montahika.
	Neighbourhood,	...	...	...
	Partnership,	...	...	...
	Fellowship, any,	Sangat,	...	...
	Fellowship of caste,	Ekjátyata,	...	...
	Ditto of trade or craft,	...	...	...
	Freedom,	Sádhintá,	...	...
	Slavery,	Gólámi,	...	...
	Sovereignty, status or act,	Rájatri,	...	...
	Subjection, status,	Projapan,	...	...
	Nobility, gentry, status,	Kúlínta,	...	...
	Peasantry, bourgeoisie, ditto,	Ajáti, ka-minta,	...	...
	Nomade or erratic state,	Páikásht,	...	...
	Agricultural or fixed state,	Khodkásht, Grahasthi,	...	...
	Proprietary class, landed,	...	...	...
	Tenantry, status,	...	...	...
	Priesthood, status,	...	Dóóshi blá, Dhámi blá,	...
	Laic state,	...	...	...
	Ministry of state,	Mantrigari,	...	...
	Clerkship, scholarship, act or status,	...	...	...
	Guardianship,	...	...	...
	Pupilage, minority,	...	...	...

PROFESSIONS, DETAILS.

1st, RELIGION.	Religious administration,	...	...	...

* Own name of own race, *i.e.* Méçch.

	English.	Kocch.	Bodo.	Dhimál.
RELIGION.	Convocation, religious session,	Dharm Sobhá,	...	...
	Doctrine,	...	...	...
	Discipline,	...	...	...
	Rubric, ritual,	...	...	...
	Heresy,	...	...	...
	True faith,	...	...	...
	Miracle,	Aschorj,	...	...
	Calendar,	Pattra,	...	...
	Date,	Tárikh, Tithi,	...	...
	Lucky day,	...	...	...
	Unlucky day,	...	...	...
	Festival day,	Bhojer din,	...	...
	Fast day,	Upásaker din,	...	...
	Religion,	Níyom, Dhorom,	Ném nísht,	Ném nishtí.
	Sin,	Páp,	Páp,	Páp.
	Repentance, remorse,	Póstán,	Jingásió,	...
	Forgiveness, remission of sin,	...	...	...
	Purification,	Shúdan,	Udraibai,	Shúdhár jéhika.
	Purificatory rites,	Shúdh kirya,	Pharál chúibai,	Déójal pátia.
	Impenitence,	Ogyán,	Jinga siá,	Ogyán..
	Excommunication,	Ját máran,	Yét gárbai,	Játi sihí.
	Conscience,	...	...	...
	Salvation,	Rakyá,	Rakya,	Táïná.
	Damnation,	Nás,	Násti,	Nás.
	Religious rite or sacrament,	Korom kiryá, Bhos,	Bhós,	Kámpáká.
	Natal rites,	Jaman kírya,	Uptan bhos,	...
	Baptismal rites,	Nám korom,	Múngdono,	...
	Weaning rites,	Bhát chuáni,	Galaino maïkham dobai,	Cháuéómchapai.
	Toga virilis rites,	Chúra korom, Harinám,	...	...
	Marriage rites,	Bibáh kirya,	Habba bhos,	Bihou páká.
	Marriage procession,	Boiráti,	Boiráti,	Boiráti.
	Funereal rites,	Máran kirya,	Machou bhos,	Síka bhos.
	Ditto, procession,	Kathúlia,	...	...
	Ancestral rites,	Shrádh,	...	...
	Public worship at a temple,	Pújá,	Madai hodong,	Dír púja.
	Offering,	Porsad,	...	...
	Burnt-offering,	Hóm,	...	...
	Bloody offering or sacrifice,	Bali,	Thoi hóyú,	Hitti.
	Isht púja or domestic worship,	Isht púja,	...	...
	Kúl púja or ancestral penate worship,	...	...	...
	Prayer, petition to God,	Súharan,	Bátho súharan,	Waráng beráng sohoran.
	Thanksgiving, thanks to God,	Túti,	...	...
	Church service, prayers,	Pújá pát,	Madai hodong,	Dír púja.

	English.	*Kocch.*	*Bodo.*	*Dhimál.*
RELIGION.	Church service, preaching,	Pát,	...	...
	Witchcraft,	Dáhinpana,	Dáin hobba,	Dháin páká.
	Exorcism,	Jhár phúnk,	Ojhá nainu, Ojhá hobba,	Bhúpi, Náparaéli.
	POLITICAL ADMINISTRATION.			
2nd, POLITICS.	Treaty,	Dhorom patra,	...	...
	War,	Larai,	Danjalai,	Larai.
	Peace,	Salúk,	Misha mishi,	...
	Tax,	Khajana,	Khajana,	Khojana.
	Land-tax,	Khajana,	Khajana,	Khajana.
	House-tax,	Bhitari khajana,	...	...
	Capitation-tax,	...	Dau ganti, Bángda lekha,	Ghongwai.
	Customs, tax on external trade,	Músúl,	Ghát kouri,	...
	Tax on consumption, excise,	Abkári,	Súndini khajana,	Súndini khajana.
	Tax on fairs,	Gándi, Tola,	Gandi, Tola,	Gándi.
	Tax on manufactures, excise,	...	...	...
	Transit duty on internal trade.	Sáyar,	Ghát kouri,	Ghát ko kouri.
	Tribute from foreign states,	...	...	...
	Tax on office-bearers,	...	...	...
	JUDICIAL ADMINISTRATION.			
3rd, JUSTICE.	Adjudication of rights,	Hak, Nisáf,	Dharam bichár,	...
	Punishment of wrongs,	Sásti,	Sásti,	Sásti.
	Plaint,	Nálish,	Ardásh,	Ardásh.
	Answer,	Jawáb,	...	...
	Trial,	Tajvij,	...	...
	Proof,	Gawáhi,	Isátbla,	Isat.
	Oath,	Kasam,	Shómai,	Kirá.
	Ordeal,	Pórik,	Phorika,	Porik.
	Summons,	Talab,	Linghot,	Kaikó.
	Bail,	Jámini,	Jámini,	Jámini.
	Arrest,	Dhor pokor,	Homdong,	Rhim.
	Decree, sentence,	Húkum,	...	...
	Punishment, corporal,	Sajai,	Sájai,	Sásti.
	Fine,	Dónr,	Gúnakhár?	Chínára?
	Confiscation,	Sorbos,	Sorbos,	Sorbos.
	Hanging,	Phánsi,	Phánsi,	Phánsi.
	Decapitation,	Mátha kata,	Dángárú,	Pál.
	Imprisonment,	Kaíd,	Khot,	Kaid.
	Manacle, fetter,	Béri,	Biri,	Béri.
	Watch and ward, police,	Choukidári,	...	...
	Watchman,	Choukidár,	...	...
	Contract, legal,	Korár máda,	Khorál,	Khorál.
	Contract of hiring,	Bhára léva,	Bhára khoral,	Bhára ko khoral.
	Ditto of letting,	Bhára déva,	Bhára khoral,	Bhára ko khoral.
	Ditto of buying,	Kinna koul,	Baino khoral,	Chól ko khoral.
	Ditto of selling,	Bécha koul,	Phannokhoral,	Píko khoral.
	Ditto of exchange,	Bodoli koul,	Slainokhorál,	Só ko khorál.
	Ditto of carrying,	Bhára koul,	Bibánkhorál,	Bhár ko khorál.

	English.	*Kocch.*	*Bodo.*	*Dhimál.*
JUSTICE.	Contract of altering or manufacturing,	...	...	...
	Ditto of service,	Bochormári,	Bóchórche, khorál,	Báchor ko khorál.
	Wages,	Dormáha,	...	...
	Lease of land, the instrument,	Potta,	Phátá,	Potta.
	Verbal promise,	Koul,	Khogaino jachyá,	...
	Note of hand,	Rúkká,	...	...
	Bond,	Tammasúk,	...	...
	Inherited property,	Wársi Bhág,	...	...
	Own acquisitions,	Jóhútiári,	Johúntia,	Kang ko jokitya.
	Dower,	Dán, Dahéj,	Jophop táká,	Bewál ko táka.
	Appanage,	...	...	...
	Testament, will,	Dán potro,	...	...
	Gift, deed of,	Dán potro,	...	...
	Sale, ditto,	Kinna potro,	...	...
	Theft,	Chúri,	...	...
	Robbery,	Dákaiti,	...	...
	Housebreaking,	Sindh,	...	...
	Murder,	Khún,	Khún,	Khún.
	Battery,	Márdang,	Shojalaibú,	Dángshúka.
	Mayhem,	Gháil,	Phéjén,	...
	Adultery,	Chínára,	Dando,	Chinàro.
	Incest,	Horon,	Dando,	Chínára.
	Other illicit commerce,	Horon,	Dando,	Chínára.
	False witness,	Micha sáki,	Ongá Isat,	Máelká Isat.
4th, ARMS.	Military administration or art,	Shastrer bidya,	...	...
	Army, troops,	Fouj,	Phoudo,	Phoudá.
	Cavalry,	...	...	...
	Infantry,	...	...	...
	Artillery,	...	...	...
	Musket,	Bondúk,	Shilai,	Shilai.
	Cannon,	Tóp,	Thóp,	Tóp.
	Powder,	Bárúd,	Bárúj,	Bárúj.
	Shot or ball,	Gúli,	Gúli,	Góli.
	Sword,	Tarwál,	Torál,	Torál.
	Shield,	Dhál,	Dhál,	Dhál.
	Bow,	Dhanúk,	Jillit,	Dhanúk.
	Arrow,	Tír,	Bálá,	Tír.
	Quiver,	Thorko,	Thómka,	Thomká.
	Ensign, flag,	Nishán,	Nirshan,	Nirshina.
	Mail, armour,	...	...	...
	Spear,	Ballam,	Jóng,	Khápor.
	Battle,	Júјh,	Dán jalai,	Larai.
	Victory,	Jít,	Dé habai,	Jít.
	Defeat,	Hár,	Jén bai,	Hár.
	Conquest,	Dokhol,	Lá bai,	Dokhol.
	Pillage, plunder, prize,	Lút,	Lút,	Lút.

LITERARY ADMINISTRATION.

	English.	*Kocch.*	*Bodo.*	*Dhimál.*
5th, LETTERS.	Literature,	...	...	...
	Knowledge,	Gyán,	Gyán,	Gyán.
	Education,	Sikkhá,	Phoróng,	Dhírka

	English.	*Kocch.*	*Bodo.*	*Dhimál.*
Letters.	Language,	Bhákhá,	Khouráng, Rái,	Dóp.
	The alphabet,	Kophálá,	...	...
	A letter,	Akhór,	...	...
	A word,	Shobdo,	...	...
	A vowel,	Phala,	...	...
	A consonant,	Akhor,	...	...
	A sentence,	Kathá,	...	...
	Noun,	...	...	...
	Pronoun,	...	...	...
	Adjective,	...	...	...
	Verb,	...	...	...
	Ethics,	Níti,	...	...
	Politics,	Rájnítí,	..	...
	Arithmetic,	Gónti,	...	...
	Geography,	...	...	...
	Astronomy,	...	...	...
	Astrology,	...	...	...
	Medical science,	Baidáli,	...	...
	Grammar,	Byakoron,	...	...
	A continent,	...	...	...
	Island,	Májhati,	...	...
	Peninsula,	...	...	...
	Frontier,	Sim,	Sim,	Sim.
	Boundary, any,	Sim,	Sim,	Sim.
	Boundary mark,	Nishán,	Nírshan,	Nírshin.
	An epistle,	Lékhá,	Lékhá,	Lékhá.
	A seal,	Mohor, cháp,	Cháp,	Cháp.
	A signature,	Sóhi,	Múngdan,	Sohi.
	Reading and writing,	Lékhápori,	Nitno naino,	...
	A book,	Púthi,	Púthi,	...
	A pen,	Kolom,	Kolom,	Kolom.
	Ink,	Káli,	Kháli,	Káli.
	Paper,	Kágaj,	Khágaz, Lekhá,	Khágach.
6th	Parchment,	...	...	...
Navy.	Naval affairs,	...	...	...
	A ship,	Jáháj,	...	...
	A boat,	Nau,	Nau,	Náwár.
	A baggage-boat, large,	Ghórnau,	Jhák,	...
	A baggage-boat, small,	Sórónga,	Sorongo,	...
	A pleasure-boat,	Sorongo,	...	...
	A skiff or canoe,	Sorongo,	Sorongo,	...
	Hull,	Tóli,	Thálá,	...
	Keel,	...	...	...
	Head,	Agál dónga,	Agál dinga,	...
	Stern,	Pách donga,	Gor dinga,	...
	Hulk,	Náér tóli,	Toli,	Tholi.
	Mast,	Mastúl,	Khérká,	...
	Sail,	Pál,	Phál,	Pál.
	Oar,	Dáṇr,	Boithú,	...
	Rudder,	Háíl,	O'di,	O'di.
	A voyage,	...	...	...
	Freight or charges,	Náér bhára,	Náer bhára,	...
	Cargo or load,	Náér bojha,	Náer bhója	...
7th	Insurance,	Bíma,	...	...
Medicine. Diseases.	Medical administration or art,	Kavirájí,	...	...
	Disease,	Káhil,	Biád,	Túúka.
	Cure,	Arám,	Gabai,	E'lhé.
	Prescription,	...	...	...

	English.	Kocch.	Bodo.	Dhimál.
MEDICINE DISEASES.	Physic, the drug,	Dárú, Bóti,	Múli,	O'shar.
	A vomit,	...	...	...
	A purge,	Júláb,	...	...
	Blood-letting,	...	...	...
	Pulse-feeling,	Nári dékhibár,	Shór nainé,	Shorkhanka.
	Pulse,	Nárí,	Shór,	Shór.
	Dysentery,	Jhára róg,	Khinai biád,	Moidan gilka.
	Diarrhœa,	Lóhú jhára,	Thoï khiö,	Hiti moidan.
	Looseness, mere,	Jhára,	Khigobúyo,	Moidan.
	Fever,	Jór,	Lúmdóng,	Misha.
	Ague,	Jor,	Lúmdóng,	Misha.
	Hepatitis,	Koljar bish,	Bikha chádong,	Tumsing túúka.
	Asthma,	Séshi, Hapání,	Dhái,	Seshi.
	Pulmonary consumption,	Kás,	Khásúlá,	Shúká.
	Other consumption, general wasting,	Súkana,	Súkan,	Chopka.
	Belly-ache,	Pétér bish,	U'di chádong,	Héman túúka.
	Head-ache,	Máther bish,	Khóró chádong,	Púrin túúka.
	Ophthalmia,	Chókúr bérám,	Mokonháyá,	Mí túúka.
	Itch,	Chúlkáni,	Géchou chorop,	Khää ko túúka.
	Elephantiasis,	...	...	...
	Leprosy,	Kúḍhi,	Khuḍia,	Khuḍia.
	Dropsy,	Pánilágá,	Doïnáng,	Chiténghi.
	King's evil,	Karanmúl,	...	...
	Goitre,	Ghég,	Golóndo,	Golondi.
	Measles,	Khésara,	Lónthi,	Khésara.
	Small-pox,	Boson,	Bonthai, Bánsmaria,	Boson.
	Pox, Siphilis,	Bau ghává,	Noti garai,	Noti péchara.
	Piles,	Bindisór,	Oros,	Bindisor.
	Cholera,	Bhéd bómi,	Hómahómi, Thangan mara,	Tanka dhárá.
	Swoon or Syncope,	Jhánk,	Tai hapmo,	Chotbat né.
	Falling sickness,	Téúriá,	Téúriá,	Téúriá.
	Gravel stone in bladder,	Páthari,	Akhír,	Páthari.
	A wound or hurt,	Ghau,	Garai,	Péchara.
	A cut,	Kata ghau,	Garai,	Péchara.
	A bruise,	Thétáli ghau,	Khúgrúma,	Khara.
	A boil,	Dúmál,	Gúgúlá,	Yúmchá.
	A pustule,	Phúnsá,	Chithot,	Phúrkótá.
	A pimple,	Phútka,	Chithot,	Phúrkotá.
	A fracture of bone,	Bhángá,	Baibai,	Bhoiká.
	A dislocation,	Jóra lóra,	Jóra lódidong,	Jora léíka.
	A plaster,	Patti,	Múli bilai,	Tépáhika.
	An ointment or unguent,	Malham,	...	...
	A liniment,	...	...	...
	An amulet, charm, talisman,	Táviz,	Gou khás,	Oshor.
	Spell, incantation, bewitchment,	Khot korom, Jontor-montor, Móhon,	Dain hobba, Madai homdong,	Dhaina páka. Mhaidi lagaipi.
	Exorcism,	Jhár-phúnk,	Ojha hobba, Ojha naino,	Bhúpi. Ojha kám paka. Núpara eli.

	English.	*Kocch.*	*Bodo.*	*Dhimál.*
	Omen,	Lokshon,	Biphút,	Játra éli.
	Auspices,	...	...	...
	Second sight,	...	...	...
	Evil eye,	...	Khúga nángo, Mogon nángo,	Mí nojo.
	Palmistry or fortune-telling,	...	...	...
	Horoscope,	Jonom pattri,	...	...
USEFUL ARTS OR CRAFTS AND TRADES DETAILS.	Pestle,	Lodha,	Gotha,	Gotha.
	Mortar,	Síl,	Onthai,	U'nthúr.
	Bandage,	Bandhan,	Khátop,	Jinka.
1st, HUNTING.	Hunter's and fisher's craft,	Shikár,	Moïhónú,	Shikár.
	Game, the spoil,	...	...	...
	A noose or snare,	Jhónt,	Khóï,	Jhónt.
	A net,	Jál,	Jyé,	Jálé.
	A sling,	Rám dóri,	Dúngdúng,	Dihá.
	A pitfall,	Gádh,	Hákór,	Gádhó.
	A trap,	Dhórphí,	Dúrphí,	Dhórphí.
	Bird-lime,	A'thá,	A'thá,	A'thá.
2nd, HERDING.	Herdsman's craft,	Górú bháins pálan,	Maishúmúsbo púshya,	Diá pía poshika.
	Flock, Herd,	Jhánk, Hángá,	Phálú,	Jhákó.
	Fleece,	Poshom,	Khomon,	Moïshú.
	Breeding, act of,	Púshyá kám,	Poshini hobba,	...
	Shearing, ditto,	...	...	...
	Milking, ditto,	Chénká,	Sródóng,	Chepká.
	Churning, ditto,	Móhan,	...	...
	Milk-pail,	Kándia,	Khándia,	Khándia.
	Churn,	Ráhí,	...	...
3rd, AGRICULTURE.	Shears,	Kénchi,	Kháïs,	Khainch.
	Fodder,	Cháni,	Gángsho,	...
	Grass,	Ghás,	Gangsho,	Naimé.
	Hay,	Khar,	Jígáp,	Sónká naimé.
	Agricultural art,	Chásári,	...	...
	Grains, genericé,	Lókhi,	Lókhi,	Lokhi.
	Grasses, ditto,	Ghás, Trin,	Gáugsho,	Naimé.
	Oils, ditto,	Tél,	Thau,	Chúïtí.
	Dyes, ditto,	Rong,	Rong,	Rong.
	Textile stuffs, ditto,	Sútpát,	Khúndúng,	Sútó.
	Agricultural products,	Khétér jinis,	Arjún,	Léngko.
	Farming stock,	Grihasthér sáj,	...	...
	Cart, small,	Gárí,	Gárí,	Gárí.
	Waggon, large,	Bojhái gárí,	...	...
	Carriage,	...	...	...
	Harness,	Sáj,	Jhim,	Jing.
	Saddle,	...	...	...
	Bridle,	...	...	...
	Sack,	Dhúkúr,	Chálá,	Chálá.
	Basket,	Dhúkí,	Khádá,	...
	Pitchfork,	Tánrá,	Thárá,	...
	Winnow,	Kúlá,	Chongrai,	Rá.
	Flail,	...	...	...
	Sickle,	Káchi dau,	Káchí,	Káchí.
	Scythe,	...	...	...

	English.	*Kocch.*	*Bodo.*	*Dhimál.*
AGRICULTURE.	Mattock or pick-axe,	Khónti,	Khónti,	Khónta.
	Spade,	Kódál,	Kódál,	Kódál.
	Shovel,	Bédhá,	Bédá,	...
	Hoe or spud,	Dáhúki,	Doukhi,	Ghóngóï.
	Bill, Bill-hook,	Dáu,	*Chékhá,	*Ghóngóï.
	Plough,	Hal,	Hal,	Hal.
	Harrow,	Móï,	Móï,	Móï.
	Ploughshare,	Phalli,	Phalli,	Phalli.
	Ditto yoke,	Yongál,	Jongol,	Jongol,
	Ditto shaft,	Nángol,	Nángol,	Nángol.
	Ditto handle,	Múthia,	Múthi,	Múthi.
	Landed property or estate,	Milik,	...	...
	Freehold,	Milik,	...	...
	Leasehold,	Ijára, Jót, Gotch,	...	...
	Farm,	Ijára, Jot,	...	...
	Rent,	Khajana,	...	...
	Contract of rent,	Kábúlíyat,	...	...
	Metairie or Batái,	Adhiári bánt,	Phorjáni rannai,	Adhiá-ko-bánta.
	Horticultural art,	...	...	...
	Ditto products,	Sós,	...	Sós.
	Flower,	Phúl,	Bíbar,	Lhép.
	Fruit,	Phal,	Bithai,	Sibá.
4th, TRADE.	Merchant's craft,	Mahajani,	Béóphár,	Béópár.
	Merchandise or things in barter,	Mahajanér jinis,	Baiyá jinis,	Chol-ko-jinis.
	Bale of goods,	Mót,	Bíbáh,	Bókchá.
	Crane,	...	...	...
	Pulley,	...	...	...
	Lever,	...	...	...
	Capital or stock,	Púnji,	Ponji,	Ponji.
	Profits,	Monáfa,	Bishá,	Oléká.
	Price,	Dám,	Bhau,	Bhau.
	Market rate,	Bhau,	Nirik,	Rakam.
	Dearness,	Sastái,	Monga jái,	Jánka.
	Cheapness,	Mangái,	Géër jài,	Lénka.
	Barter,	Adol bodol,	Slijalai,	Sóska.
	Purchase,	Kinna,	Phan,	Chól.
	Sale,	Béchá,	Bái,	Pít.
	Banker's craft,	Sharáfi,	...	...
	Money, any,	Taká kóri,	Baina jinis,	Chol ko jinis.
	Coin,	Kóltaka,	Kóltaka,	Kóltáka.
	Credit, trust,	U'dhar,	Dhár,	Dhár.
	Silver coin,	Táká,	Taka,	Tháka.
	Gold coin,	Mohor,	Mohor,	Són móhor.
	Capital,	Púnji,	Púnji,	Púnji.
	Interest,	Biáz,	Bishá,	Oléhé.
	Loan, letting,	Korojdén,	Dhár lá,	Dhár rhú.
	Loan, borrowing,	Korojlén,	Dhár hot,	Dhár pí.
	Pawn or deposit,	Bandhak,	Bandha,	Bandha.
	Debit, side of account,	...	Bó hanáng go,	Rhúliká.
	Credit, side of account,	...	Imbé hanang go,	Pilika.

* The principal and almost only agricultural implement of the Mécch and Dhimál: a sort of bill.

	English.	*Kocch.*	*Bodo.*	*Dhimál.*
TRADE.	Debt,	Koroj,	Dhár,	Dhár.
	Payment,	Chúkti,	Jopbai,	...
	Shopkeeper's craft,	Dokání,	...	...
	Retail trade,	Páikári,	...	...
	A measure,	Náp,	Chúyo,	Dóng.
	A weight,	Toul,	Chúyo,	Dóng.
	Dry measure,	Dón,	...	...
	Wet measure,	Kánriá,	Háchúng,	Chóngbai.
	Measure of bulk,	Dón, káttá,	Dón, káthá,	Don, káthá.
	Ditto of extent,	Dighól,	Gallou,	Rhinka.
	Land measure,	Rassi,	...	...
	A span,	Tákor,	Khújála,	Takór.
	A cubit,	Háth,	Múché,	Khúr dóng.
	A yard,	Gaj,	Nálám,	Bátóng.
	A tolah,	Tolah,	...	...
	A chatak,	Chatak,	...	...
	A seer,	Sér,	Phól,	...
	A maund,	Man,	Mon,	...
	Scales or balance,	Tarázú,	...	...
	Steelyard,	Túl,	Thouli,	Túl.
	Manufacturer's craft,	Banái,	...	...
	Textile stuffs or cloths,	Tánter jinis,	Dáyá, Hi,	Sájá.
5*th*, ARTISAN-SHIPS.	Artisan's craft,	Kárigari,	...	...
	Implement, tool,	Mistrir hathiár,	Yágújú,	...
	Mason's craft,	Choporbandi,	Nóönúgra,	Sá dámká.
	A house,	Ghor,	Nóö,	Sá.
	A storey,	...	...	...
	Ground-storey,	...	...	...
	Mid-storey,	...	...	...
	Attics,	...	...	...
	Foundation,	...	...	...
	Wall,	Bárá, Táti,	Injúr,	Bérhéın.
	Roof,	Chhál,	Núkúm,	Cháli.
	Roof-tree,	Máról,	Mándáli,	Mándál.
	Supports,	Múli, Bówna,	Múddá,	Móling.
	Door,	Dúár,	Dwár,	Dúár.
	Window,	Khúrki,	...	...
	Staircase,	Móï,	Jákhlá,	Páhiri.
	Room or chamber,	Kóthari,	...	...
	Bedroom,	Sútibár ghar,	Mudunai, Nóö,	Jim ko sá.
	Cookroom,	Rándhon sála,	Nishing,	Gá ko sá.
	Sitting-room, guest-house,	Dándi ghor,	Mándo,	Choura sá.
	Verandah, portico,	Cháli,	Cháli,	Dháp.
	Necessary, cloaca,	...	...	...
	Outhouse,	Báhiri ghor,	Baira Nóö,	Bahira sá.
	Zenána,	Bhitar bári,	...	...
	Courtyard,	Ágina,	Chétbála,	Sáléng.
	Rule or measure,	Náp,	Mú,	Dóngsúlá.
	Plummet or level,	...	...	...
	Trowel,	...	...	...
	Hod,	...	...	...
	Lime cement,	...	...	...
	Clay ditto,	...	...	...
	Stone-quarrier's craft,	...	...	...
	Stone-graver's craft,	...	...	...
	Inscription on stone,	...	...	...

	English.	Kocch.	Bodo.	Dhimál.
ARTISANSHIPS.	Metal-graver's craft,	...	...	...
	Inscription on metal,	...	...	...
	A mould or die,	...	...	...
	A mallet,	...	...	...
	A graver,	...	...	...
	Miner's craft,			
	A mine,	...	...	...
	A vein,	...	...	...
	A flaw,	...	...	...
	A shaft or tunnel,	...	...	...
	A vent,	...	...	...
	Smelter's craft,	...	...	...
	Native ore,	...	...	...
	Metal, pure,	...	...	...
	Dross,	...	...	...
	Matrix,	...	...	...
	Bricklayer's craft,	Kúmháler kám,	Kúmhálni hobba,	...
	Brick,	I'nth,	I'nt,	I'nt.
	Tile,	Khapra,	...	...
	Paving tile,	...	...	...
	Roofing tile,	...	...	...
	Plain brick,	...	...	...
	Ornamental ditto,	...	...	...
	Brick mould,	...	...	...
	Tile mould,	...	...	...
	Smoothing implement,	...	...	...
	Carpenter's craft,	Barhoi, Sútár,	...	...
	Carpentry goods,	Barhóir jinis,	...	...
	Furniture, household,	Gharér jinis,	Nóóni jinis,	Sá ko jinis.
	A door-frame,	...	...	...
	A window-frame,	...	...	...
	A seat, any,	A'san, Pídha,	Kómplai,	Tákhim.
	Bench,	Chángrá,	Chángrá,	Chángrá.
	Stool,	Mórá,	...	...
	Table,	...	...	...
	A chest or box, large,	Sandúk,	Sandúk,	Sandúk.
	Ditto, ditto, small,	...	Iskádor,	...
	Chest of drawers,	...	...	...
	A drawer,	...	...	...
	A trencher or wooden platter,	Káthúá,	Káthúá,	Kathou.
	Bedstead,	Khát,	Khát,	Khát.
	Okli Músal to husk rice,	Chám gáhin,	U'lar gáin,	Shim khondi.
	Wooden utensil,	Káthér hatiyár,	...	...
	Haft or handle, any,	Dénthá,	Biphóng,	Dénthá.
	Knife haft,	Chúri dénthá,	Biphong,	Dénthá.
	Spade haft,	Kódáler déntha,	Biphong,	Dénthá,
	Plough haft,	Halér múthúá,	...	...
	Ditto body,	Halér dénḍa,	...	...
	A plank,	Phálá,	Phálá,	Phálá.
	A beam, large,	Chókrá,	Sál bónpháng,	Sili.
	A beam, small cross-beam,	Jhángi, Gól batti,	Sili,	Sili.
	A plane,	Lóndá,	...	...
	An axe,	Kúrál,	Rúá,	Dúphé.
	A drill or gimblet,	Bhávar,	...	...

	English.	*Kocch.*	*Bodo.*	*Dhimál.*
ARTISAN-SHIPS.	A turnscrew,	...	...	...
	A saw,	...	...	...
	A chisel,	Chouras,	Baithál,	Chouras.
	A hammer,	Háthúrá,	Dákbáli,	Danghaishúla.
	Potter's craft,	Kúmháler kám,	Kúmhánihobba,	Chokti bonai.
	Pottery goods, crockery, &c.,	Kúmháler jinis,	Kúmháni jinis,	Kúmhál ko jinis.
	A vessel, any,	Pátrá,	Yágójéng,	Bhándá.
	Earthen vessel,	Mátér bartan,	Háni gojeng,	Bhonoï ko bhánda.
	Wooden vessel,	Khatárbartan,	Bonphóngni-gójeng,	Khatáng ko bhanda.
	Metal vessel,	Dhátér bartan,	...	...
	Large earthen vessel to store grain,	Gózina,	Dábar,	...
	Water-jar, large,	Kólshi,	Taihú,	Kálshí.
	Ditto, small,	Básuna,	Tikli,	Básuna.
	Earthen cooking-pot,	...	...	...
	Earthen dish or plate,	...	...	...
	Potter's wheel,	Kúmháler chák,	...	...
	Shaper,	...	...	...
	Smoother,	...	...	...
	Glazing substance,	...	...	...
	Smith's craft,	Kámhári,	Kámárni hobba,	...
	Hardware, any,	Kámháler jinis,	...	...
	Ironware,	Lóhér jinis,	Shorrni jinis,	Chír ko jinis.
	Copperware,	Támbér jinis,	Thamáni jinis,	Tamba ko jinis.
	Brassware,	Pítaler jinis,	...	...
	Pewterware,	Kánser jinis,	Khasáni jinis,	...
	Chain,	Jinjári,	Jhinjári,	Jhinjari.
	Wire,	...	...	...
	Nail,	Jóli,	Khíli,	Khíli.
	Screw,	Péch,	...	...
	Hinge,	Kabja,	...	...
	Lock,	Tálá,	Cháki,	Tálá.
	Key,	Choráni,	Airi,	Choráni.
	Bolt or bar,	Dwárdévá láthi,	Dwár chúnaini louthi,	Dwár gip-ko-láthi.
	Hook,	Kántá,	Angthá,	...
	Bell,	Gháti,	Ghátá,	Ghánti.
	Iron vessel, large,	Kádhá,	Kharou,	Kádhá.
	Ditto, small,	Lúhia, kadhai,	Lohora,	...
	Copper vessel, large,	Dékchá,	Thámjang,	Thámjáng.
	Ditto, small,	Dékchi,	...	...
	Metallic cooking-pot,	Dékcha, Bogna, Batlohi,	Thou or Dou, Khánta, Lohara,	Tasala. Lóhia. Chokoti.
	Metallic dish,	...	...	...
	Metallic plate,	Tháli, Bhánda,	Thórsi, Kúrúi,	Tháli. Bhánda.
	Metallic drinking-cup,	Lóta, Ghóta, Bári,	Thikli, Lota,	Lota báti. Tukuri.
	A pot, any,	Hándi,	Dú,	Chokoti.
	A pot-lid,	Pórsún,	Shárai,	Dhakana.
	A spoon,	Háta,	Kárba,	Háta.
	A knife,	Káti,	Dábá,	Kathári.
	A fork,	...	...	...

	English.	Kocch.	Bodo.	Dhimál.
Artisanships.	Goldsmith's craft,	Bániér káj,	Bániani habba,	Baniá ko kam.
	Jewellery,	Gahana, Páta,	...	...
	A Janter,	...	...	...
	A blow-pipe,	Chúngi,	Wáchúng,	...
	A fan,	Pákbá,	...	...
	Nippers,	Chimta,	...	...
	Bellows,	Bháthí,	...	...
	Glow, red heat,	Tau,	Gúdúng,	Sá,
	Cutler's craft,	...	...	...
	Cutlery goods,	...	...	...
	Razor,	Khúr,	Khúr,	Chúrá.
	Scissors,	Kénchí,	Khánch,	Kénchi.
	Shears,	...	...	...
	Tweezers,	Chimta,	Léphó,	Chimti.
	Large knife,	Chúrá,	Dábá,	...
	Pocket-knife,	Chúri,	...	...
	Sword,	Tarwál,	Thorál,	Tórál.
	Dagger,	...	...	...
	Arrowhead,	Phól,	Blá, Dóng,	Khápór.
	Needle, large, packman's,	Súí,	Mohan,	Béndi.
	Needle, small,	Súi,	Biji,	Béndi,
	Thimble,	Angúshtán,	...	...
	Grindstone,	Sán,	Sán,	Sán.
	Emery,	...	...	...
	Barber's craft,	Khéóri,	Khorichimbai,	Púshám.
	Soap,	Sábón,	Chábon,	Chábon.
	Brush,	...	...	...
	Lather,	...	...	...
	Shaving, the act,	Khéóri,	Khori chimbai,	Pusham.
	Shaving head,	...	...	...
	Shaving beard,	...	...	...
	Nailparing,	Nángúl káti,	Asigúrhán,	Khúrsing chémi.
	Tailor's craft,	Dorjerkám,	Hishúgrá,	Dhábá joka.
	Thread,	Sútá, sútli,	Kúndúng or Dúng dúng,	Shúté.
	Wax,	Móm,	Múshátha,	Mom.
	Shoemaker's craft,	Chámárer kám,	Chámárni, habba,	Chámár-ko-kam.
	Shoemaking,	Júta banávan,	Jota godan,	...
	Shoemending,	Júta, songot koron,	Jota phósáp,	...
	Shoe,	Jóta,	Jota,	Jóta.
	Boot,	...	...	...
	Slipper or sandal,	...	Yápthóng,	Champhóï.
	Wooden shoe,	Khorong,	...	...
	Leather shoe,	Jota,	Jota,	Jota.
	Straw or grass shoe,	...	...	...
	Last,	Pharma,	...	...
	Awl,	Sútári,	...	...
	Cobbler's wax,	...	...	...
	Cook's craft,	Rándhon,	Chógrá,	Gáka.
	Boiling, the act,	Jhólan,	Chongwo,	...
	Roasting or grilling,	Bhunjan,	Yauvo,	...
	Frying,	Sénkhan,	Hangwo,	...
	Fireplace,	Akha,	Doudáp,	...
	Tongs,	Chimta,	Chimta,	Chimta.

	English.	Kocch.	Bodo.	Dhimál.
ARTISANSHIPS.	Poker,	Kalchúl,	...	...
	Currier's or Tanner's craft,	Chámárer kam,	Chamárui-hobba,	...
	Peltry goods,	Chámér jinis,	...	...
	Leather, any,	Chám,	Bigúr,	Dhálé.
	Tanner's vat,	Nádh,	Dábar,	Dábar.
	Tannin or bark,	Banda,	...	...
	Miller's craft,	...	Yúndúng.	Mháika.
	Grinded goods,	Písán,	Yúna jinis,	Mháika jinis.
	Flour or meal,	Atta, maida,	...	...
	Bran,	Bhúsi,	Béjéng,	Bhús.
	Mill,	Jánta,	...	...
	Windmill,	...	...	...
	Watermill,	...	...	...
	Handmill,	Jánta,	...	...
	Oilman's craft,	Téliér kám,	Telini hobba,	...
	Oilman's stores,	Téliér jinis,	Phiritni jinis,	...
	Oilpress,	Gyéch, Ghúni,	Góchá,	Ghání, H.
	Dyer's craft,	Rongdibár kam,	...	...
	Dyed goods,	Rongil jinis,	...	...
	Dyer's vat,	Nádh,	...	...
	Dyer's press,	...	...	...
	Dye, any,	Rong,	Rong,	Rong.
	Red dye,	Lál rong,	Gaja rong,	Jïka rong.
	Green dye,	Hara rong,	Khángshúr rong,	Nélpá rong.
	Blue dye,	Nil rong,	Gochoni rong,	Dúúka rong.
	Yellow dye,	Pila rong,	Gammo rong,	Yónka rong.
	Sugarmaker's craft,	U'kpíran,	Khúsyárphérét,	Kúsyárpérika.
	Goor,	Goor,	Mithai,	Mithui.
	Chíní,	Chíni,	...	...
	Misri,	Misri,	...	...
	Sakar,	Sakar,	...	...
	Ráb,	Náli,	Láli,	Láli.
	Sugar-press,	Gyéch,	Góchá,	Ghání.
	Confectioner's craft,	Bhújárer kám,	Ladúdágra,	Ládú bonaika.
	Sweetmeats,	Mithaï,	Gódóï,	Túúka jinis.
	Cake,	Malpúá,	Enkrong,	Bábór.
	Comfit,	Lai,	Húrúng,	Khoïláro.
	Lollypop,	Laddú,	Phétta,	...
	Butcher's craft,	Kassaiér kám,	...	...
	Flesh,	Masong,	Bidot,	Béhá.
	Garbage,	...	Chippika,	...
	Slaying-axe,	Garsá,	Lúmbri, Thungbri,	Dúpki.
	Cleaver,	Chépsá,	Phátháng,	Dábiá.
	Block,	Góri,	Dingri,	Dingri.
	Knife,	Kathari,	Dábá,	Kathari.
	Baker's craft,	...	...	...
	Bread,	Róti,	...	...
	Unleavened bread,	...	...	...
	Leavened bread,	...	...	...
	Dough,	Gandhan,	...	...
	Runnet or leaven,	...	...	...
	Distiller's craft,	Chúlávan,	Chounó,	Sááká.
	Spirituous liquors,	Modh,	Pitika,	Phatika.

	English.	*Kocch.*	*Bodo.*	*Dhimál.*
ARTISAN-SHIPS.	Still,	Bhatti,	Bháti,	Bháti.
	Receiver or boiler,	Bhatti,	Bháti,	Bháti.
	Condenser,	Adkar,	Daihú,	Dúkí.
	Cooler,	Nádh,	Dúbar,	Hindá.
	Funnel,	...	...	...
	Pipe,	Náli,	Nálá,	Nálá.
	Spirits made from grain,	Modh,	Pítiká,	Phatika.
	Do. from flowers,	...	...	...
	Do. from juices, like toddy,	...	...	...
	Brewer's craft,	Ubálan,	Chongno,	...
	Fermented liquor,	Katla,	Jóni jinis or Jó,	Yú.
	Brewer's vat,	Matka,	Dú,	Rööti.
	Washerman's craft,	Dhóbir kám,	...	...
	Soap,	Sábon,	Sábon,	Sábon.
	Tub,	Powna,	...	...
	Beater,	Mogdor,	...	...
	Block,	Phállá,	...	...
	Dirty clothes,	Maila kapra,	Gini Hí,	Mirhi Dhába.
	Clean clothes,	Safa kapra,	Hí gúphút,	Má mirhi dhaba.
	Turner's craft,	Kúndáíl,	Khúndáïn,	Kúndai katang.
	Turned goods,	Kúndáíl jinis,	Kúndaini jinis,	Kúndai ko jinis.
	A lathe,	Chouras,	Baithal,	...
	Clothprinter's craft,	Chapáíl,	...	...
	Printed goods,	Chápér jinis,	...	...
	Chintz,	Chínt,	Chít,	Chít.
	Coarse chintz,	Chínt,	Chít,	Chít.
	Fine chintz,	Chínt,	Chít,	Chít.
	A stamp,	Cháp,	...	...
	A press,	...	...	...
	Spinner's art,	Sútkátan,	Khúndúngluye,	Sútékátika.
	Spun goods,	Sútér jinis,	Khundungni jinis,	Súté ko jinis.
	Spinner's wheel,	Charkha,	Janthér,	Charkha.
	Thread,	Sút,	Khúndúng,	Súté.
	Skein,	Motha,	Lémchá,	Waina.
	Knitter's art,	Jabibanáíl,	Jókhana,	Chiting púíka.
	Knit goods,	Jaber jinis,	Jóni jinis,	Chiting.
	Weaver's art,	Banávan,	Hidáín,	Dhába thírka.
	Woven goods,	Banáíl jinis,	Danai jinis,	Thirka.
	A web or piece,	Tán,	Gangché,	Dhába.
	The warp,	Táná,	Gochong,	Táná.
	The woof,	Pétwan,	Géhén,	Pétwan.
	Fine cotton or mulmal,	Mulmal,	Rúbú Hí,	...
	Coarse do. or calico,	Gajbóri,	Hi shima,	...
	Fine woollen or broad cloth,	Banát,	Bánát,	Bánát.
	Coarser or malida,	...	...	...
	Coarsest or blanket,	Kómból,	Kúmbali,	Kámili.
	Hemp cloth or linen,	Bhángrá,	...	...
	Flax cloth or linen,*	...	...	...

* The Linum usitatissimum, Tsi, or Alsi, however common and good, is nowhere used in India save for oil.

	English.	Kocch.	Bodo.	Dhimál.
ARTISAN-SHIPS.	Sack-cloth of San or Pát,	Dhokrá,	Phátta, Chola,	Dhókra.
	Sail-cloth, finer, of San,	Jhálok, Mékhári,	Jhálok,	Jhálok.
	Silk or Satin, cloth,	...	Injini Hi,	...
	A loom,	Sájá,	Híchan,	Sája.
	A shuttle,	Mákú,	Mákú,	Mákú.
	A paddle,	Khút,	Górkhá,	Náchá naiti.
	A roller for winding web,	Kérkhí,	Gándai,	Dángda-lánga.
	Weaving, the act,	Banáil,	Dáin,	Thírká.
	Cord-wainer's craft,	Rasser banáil.	Doudong, Chádong,	Díhapeka.
	Cord or thick rope,	Dor, rassa,	Dóga, Doudong,	Bada-Dihá.
	Twine or thin rope,	Rossi,	Dóga múdúi,	Mhoika-Diha.
	Tow, any,	Pátá,	Phatta,	Páté.
	Oakum,	Bákél,	...	...
	Lint,	...	...	...
	Rags,	...	Hísri,	Tékadhábá.
	Paper-maker's craft,	...	...	...
	Paper made of bark,	Kágaj,	...	...
	Ditto of rags,	Kágaj,	...	...
	Bleacher's art,	...	...	...
	Basket-maker's craft,	...	Hépmá,	Púíká.
	Decorticating,	Máthán,	Sóin,	Koïkatang.
	The slip or strip peeled off,	Pátí,	Bishi,	Páti.
	Basket, open plat,	Changári,	Kho,	Dondora.
	Basket, close plat,	Dháki,	Dón,	Bhútúri.
	Basket, any,	Doura, Douri,	Dónkho,	...
	Deep closed basket,	Sapuri,	...	...
	Shallow open do.,	Dháki,	...	...
FINE ARTS.	Fine arts,	...	...	...
	Poetry,	Kavit,	...	...
	A poem,	Kavit,	...	...
	Metre,	...	...	...
	Rhyme,	...	...	...
	A distich,	...	...	...
	Painting, the art,	Chittrakári,	Málini habba,	...
	A picture,	Chobi,	...	...
	Light and shade,	...	...	...
	Perspective,	...	...	...
	Colouring,	...	...	...
	Human portrait,	Tazvír,	...	...
	Landscape,	...	...	...
	Colour-box,	...	...	...
	Easel,	...	...	...
	Brush,	...	...	...
	Pencil,	...	...	...
	Musical science,	Gávan bajávan ilm,	Rajápdam,	...
	Music,	Gávanbajáwan,	Rajápdam,	Léïka béïka.
	Musical note,	...	...	...
	The gamut,	...	...	...

	English.	Kocch.	Bodo.	Dhimál.
FINE ARTS.	Harmony,	...	...	...
	Melody,	...	...	...
	Vocal music,	Gáwan, Git,	Rajáp,	Léika.
	Instrumental music,	Bajáwan,	Dám,	Béika.
	A concert,	Nátch,	Músáyú,	Hyúká.
	A fife,	Báshi,	Chíphúng,	Múhari.
	A pipe,	Sahanái,	Phéngphá,	...
	A trumpet,	Túrhói,	Túrhoi,	Túrhoï.
	A drum,	Dhól, Nagara,	Nagara,	Dhól.
	Cymbals,	Kortál,	Khowawáng,	Jháil.
	A stringed instrument,	Sáringi, Dotára Bina,	Sénja, Dótára,	Sénja, Dotára.
	Sculpture,	Chinni,	...	...
	A stone statue, human,	Mánushermúrti,	...	...
	Ditto of a deity,	Devater múrti,	...	...
	An idol of clay,	Mátir múrti,	...	...
	Image, plaything,	Chóbi,	...	...
	Metallic idol,	Dhátuér múrti,	...	...
	Architecture, the science,	...	...	...
	A pillar or column,	Filpay, khamba Powa,	...	...
	A shaft or body,	...	...	...
	A capital,	...	...	...
	A basement,	...	...	...
	Entablature,	...	...	...
	Architrave,	...	...	...
	Frieze,	...	...	...
	Cornice,	...	...	...
	Façade,	...	...	...
	An arch,	...	...	...
	An arcade or colonnade,	...	...	...
	A dome,	Gúmbaj,	...	...
	A minár,	Minár,	...	...
	A minaret,	...	...	...
	A pent roof,	Bangaler Chat,	...	...
	A flat roof,	Sobsóir Chat,	...	...

NOUNS OF TIME.

English.	Kocch.	Bodo.	Dhimál.
Time,	Kál,	Khál,	Kál.
Eternity,	Anant kál,	...	...
Day,	Din,	Shán,	Nhitima.
Night,	Ráth,	Hórr,	Nhishing.
Morn,	Bérbhán,	Phújáni,	Rhima.
Noon,	Dóphór,	Sánjáphú,	Béla génka.
Eve,	Górúdhúkani béla,	Bili,	Bilémá.
Sunrise,	Súraj úday,	Shánangkhatbai,	Bélalóhika.
Sunset,	Súraj asti,	Shánang hopbai,	Bélahadéka.
Moonrise,	Chándúday,	Nókhábir khatbai,	Tálilohika.
Moonset,	Chándasti,	Nókhábir hapbai,	Tálihadeka.
A moment,	Pal,	...	...

English.	Kocch.	Bodo.	Dhilmál.
A minute,	Pal,	...	...
An hour,	Ghari,	...	...
A week,	Athóra,	...	...
A month,	Más,	Dán,	Máshá.
A year,	Bóchór,	Bochor,	Bochor.
A timepiece,	Ghari,	...	...
A date,	Tárikh, Tithi,	...	...
Sunday,	Déobár,	Déó,	Déó.
Monday,	Sombár,	Som,	Sóm.
Tuesday,	Mongolbár,	Mongol,	Mongol.
Wednesday,	Búdhbár,	Budh,	Búdh.
Thursday,	Bishtibár,	Bishti,	Bishti.
Friday,	Súkalbár,	Súkal,	Sukal.
Saturday,	Súnibár,	Súní,	Súni.
January,	Mágh,	Mágh,	Mágh.
February,	Phágún,	Phágún,	Phágún.
March,	Chaityo,	Choit,	Choit.
April,	Boisákho,	Boisákh,	Boisákh.
May,	Joith,	Jait,	Jait.
June,	Asár,	Asár,	Asár.
July,	Sáwon,	Sráwon,	Sáwon.
August,	Bhodor,	Bhodor,	Bhodor,
September,	A'sin,	Asin,	Asin.
October,	Kortik,	Kortik,	Kortik.
November,	Oghon,	Oghon,	Oghon.
December,	Pús,	Poush,	Poush.

Indeclinables of Time.

English.	Kocch.	Bodo.	Dhilmál.
To-day,	A'ji,	Dinai,	Náni.
To-morrow,	Kál,	Gábún,	Júmni.
Yesterday,	Páchila rój,	Miyá or Mía,	A'nji.
Previously,	A'gá,	Sigáng,	Lámpáng.
Now,	Elai,	Dánó, Dá,	E'láng.
Afterwards,	Páché,	Yúnó, Dénáng,	Nhúchó.
Always, ever,	Sodá,	Orai,	E'loú.
Never,	Konokálé nabín.	Orainegéyá,	Elou mántho.
Seldom,	Kónokóno bélá,	Hénobéla hónó béla,	Thóráng.
Often,	Báré báré,	Phélé phélé,	Ghaning gháning.
Sometimes,	Konokono bélá,	Héno béla Heno bela,	Thoráng.
Now, recently,	E'i kharai,	Dánó,	Idom Bólá.
Long ago,	Bhélé diné,	Gúbán choi,	E'shito.
When,	Jélá,	Jélai,	Jéla.
Then,	Sélá,	Sélai,	Kóla.
When?	Kónbéla,	Mábilai,	Hélou.
At once, together,	E'kchak,	Phakché,	Edo sáng.
Gradually, one by one,	Eké Eké,	Háshing,	E'mé Emé.
Slowly,	Dhíré,	Láshi láshi,	Dhíré.
Quickly,	Dhór,	Gakré gakré,	Dhimpá.
Instantly,	Sót,	Dánó,	E'láng.
Late,	Bilómé,	Yúnó,	Yérhé.
Early,	Jogoté,	Gakré,	Jogotáng.
Daily,	...	...	...
Weekly,	...	...	...
Monthly,	...	...	...
Yearly,	...	...	...
Once,	...	...	...

English.	*Kocch.*	*Bodo.*	*Dhimál.*
Twice,	...	...	...
Thrice,	...	...	...

NUMBERS.*

English.	*Kocch.*	*Bodo.*	*Dhimál.*
One,	Ek,	Man-ché,	E'-long.
Two,	Dú,	Man-gné,	Gné-long.
Three,	Tín,	Man-thám,	Súm-long.
Four,	Chár,	Man-bré,	Día-long.
Five,	Pánch,	Man-bá,	Ná-long.
Six,	Choi,	Man-dó,	Tú-long.
Seven,	Sát,	Man-sini,	Nhií-long.
Eight,	A'th,	...	Yé-long.
Nine,	Nou,	...	Kúhá-long.
Ten,	Das,	...	Té-long.
Eleven,	Egáro,	...	...
Twelve,	Báró,	...	...
Twenty,	Bís,	Chokai-bá, Thai-khon, Bisha-ché,	E-long Bisha.
Twenty-one,	Ekóïs,	...	...
Thirty,	Tís,	...	...
Forty,	Chálís,	Bisha-gné,	Gné-lóng bisha.
Fifty,	Pachás,	...	...
Sixty,	Sáït,	Bisha-thám,	Súm-lóng bisha.
Seventy,	Sohotor,	...	...
Eighty,	Assi,	Bisha-bré, Phanai-ché,	Diá-long bisha.
Ninety,	Nobbi,	...	...
One hundred,	Sou,	Bisha-bá,	Ná-lóng bisha.
One thousand,	Hájár,	...	...
Ten thousand,	Dashajár,	...	...
A lack,	Lakh,	...	...
A crore,	Krór,	...	...
First,	Pahilo,	...	...
Second,	Dósrá,	...	...
Third,	Tisrá,	...	...
Fourth,	Chouthá,	...	...
Fifth,	Páchín,	...	...
Sixth,	Chatín,	...	...
Seventh,	Sátín,	...	...
Eighth,	A'thín,	...	...
Ninth,	Nóhín,	...	...
Tenth,	Doshín,	...	...
A numeral sign or cipher,	A'nkhó,	...	...

NOUNS OF PLACE.

English.	*Kocch.*	*Bodo.*	*Dhimál.*
A place,	Thán, Jágah,	Núpthi,	Chól.
Presence,	Hájari,	...	...
Absence,	Ghairhájári,	...	...
A level,	Sóbsóïr,	...	...
A slope,	Hékakúra,	Khéngláp,	Chálgór.
Acclivity,	Chórti,	Gáná,	Tánka.
Declivity,	Lámti,	U'nkhat,	Khúka.
The centre,	Bích,	Géjér,	Májhata.

* The Méch prefix (man), and the Dhimál postfix (long), are sometimes omitted, and both are liable to variations, for which see Grammar.

English.	*Kocch.*	*Bodo.*	*Dhimál.*
The side,	Bógól,	Ging,	Jéngshó.
The corner,	Kóná,	...	...
The top,	Mathi,	Khró,	Púring.
The bottom,	Hént,	Khibo,	Léttá.
A nation or kingdom,	Ráïj,	Ráijo,	Rájyá.
A province or súbah,	Súbah,	...	...
A country or zillah,	Zillah,	...	...
A parish township or pagus	Bondor,	Bondor,	Bondor.
A guild-hall, trader's,	...	....	...
A town-hall, municipal court,	Prodháner-kachéri,	Mondolni-kachóri,	Mondol ko-sá.
A palace,	Rájbári,	Rájbári,	Rájbári.
A council-chamber,	Ráj sobha,	...	...
A temple or church,	Déótá thán,	Madainóö Báthoninoö,	Dírko sá.
A burial-place,	...	Goth oiphop Dongni núpthi,	Lípko-chol.
A burning place,	Sásán,	Gothoi syoudongni núpthi,	Dú-ko-chol.
A public office or court,	Kachérí,	Kachérí,	Kachérí.
Court of justice,	Adálater Kacheri,	...	...
Ditto of revenue,	Chákalér Katcheri,	...	...
A jail,	Phátok,	Bondon sálá,	Kót-sá.
A village court,	Prodháner Kacheri,	Mondolni Kacheri,	Mondol ko-sá.
A college,	...	...	...
A school,	...	...	...
A hospital,	...	...	...
A library,	...	...	...
A bank,	...	..	..
An arsenal for making arms,	...	...	...
A magazine for storing arms,	...	...	...
A fort,	Gorh,	Khót,	Killa.
A cantonment,	Chouni,	Siphai thána,	Siphai jomka.
A camp,	...	...	...
A warehouse, merchant's,	Kóthí,	...	...
A shop, retailer's,	Dókán,	Dokán,	Dokán.
A factory or workshop,	...	...	...
A smithy,	Márúï sála,	Khámárninoo,	Kámhár-ko-sá.
A tannery,	Chámárér thán,	...	...
A dye-house,	...	...	...
A distillery,	Bháttí khána,	Súndininoo,	Súndi-ko-sá.
A brewery,	...	...	...
A farmhouse,	...	...	...
A farmyard,	...	...	...
A granary,	Khalyán,	Kholto,	Khaniár.
A stack,	Khalyán,	Kholto,	Khaniár.
An inn,	Dándi ghor,	Mando, Noukháli,	Chourá sá.
A stable,	Ghórér ghor,	Gorainінoö,	Onhya ko sá.
A cow-house,	Góháli,	Gwálninoö,	Gwálli sá.
A dairy,	...	...	...
A sheepcote,	Bhérír sála,	Búrma gógra,	E'chá ko sá.
A pigstye,	Súarer khór,	Yóma yógrong, Yóma gógra,	Páyá ko sá.

English.	*Kocch.*	*Bodo.*	*Dhimál.*
A dwelling-house,	Ghor,	Nöö,	Sá.
A machán to watch crops,	Kúda,	Nöochá,	...
A cottage,	Khóprá,	Nöö,	Sá.
A hut,	Khopra,	...	...
A city,	Shohor,	...	...
A town,	Shohor,	...	...
A village,	Gáón, Bondor,	Phárá,*	Dérá.
A street,	Gali,	...	...
A square,	Chouk,	...	...
A road, high,	Pod, sorok,	Lámá,	Dámá.
A road, bye,	...	...	...
A footpath,	Dégór,	Degor,	Dégór.
An estate, the ubi,	...	...	...
A farm, ditto,	...	...	...
A garden,	Bágiche,	...	...
An orchard homestead,	Bári,	Bári,	Bári.
Flower-garden,	Phúl bári,	Bibar bári,	Lhèp ko sá.
Kitchen garden or kaleyard,	Ság bári,	Moikong-bári,	Sár bári,
Field, garden,	Khét bári,	Húbári,	Ling bári.
Field, any,	Khét,	Hú,	Ling.
Arable field,	Bhúmi bári,	Hú,	Ling.
Grass field, lea, or meadow,	Khouna, Rávana,	Phúthár,	Piá ling.
Hay field,	...	...	...
Fallow field,	Nótkhíla,	Hágrá,†	Lóngdhó.
Ridge,	Góhí,	...	...
Furrow,	Ghós,	...	...
Hedge,	Bédhá,	Chékhór,	Cháti.
Ditch,	Póri, Pághár,	Phoiri, khoui,	Ani.

INDECLINABLES OF PLACE.

Separately, apart,	Bégól, Alog,	Gúbún,	Bhináng.
Together, along with,	Lóg, éksáth,	Logoché,	E'dósáng.
Towards,	Tí,	...	Só?
Up to, to, unto,	Tako,	Chim or Sim,	Thiká. Thékapa.
As far,	Jéithé,	Jédong,	Jéso.
So far,	Séithé,	Sláp,	Kósó.
Beyond, over,	Pár,	Bát,	Pén.
In, at,	Té,	Sing, há, ou,	Tá.
On this side,	Yépár,	Imbé jing,	Yépár.
On that side,	Wúpár,	Hobe jing,	Wúpár.
On both sides,	Wárpár,	Yéjungwojung, Mébúbébújing,	...
About, around,	Agolbogol,	Jing jing, Mébú bèbú,‡	Chéngsho bhéngsho.
All round,	Cháro bhitti,	Chamcham,	Ora paring.
On, upon,	Pór,	Chou,	Rhútá.
Here, poz.	Hitti,	Jung, Imbohá,	Isho, Itá.
There, poz.	Hútti,	Hobóhá, Hujúng,	U'sho, U'tá.
Where?	Kúnti,	Mouhá, Bojong,	Hésho. Hetá.

* See note at p. 103. Phárá and Dérá are Hindi words.
† Hágrá, the waste, jungle; no fallow.
‡ Mébú bébú, here and there, corruption of Imbébú-hobebu, this side and that.

English.	*Kocch.*	*Bodo.*	*Dhimál.*
Where, } rel.	Eíthi,	Jérúno,	Jótán.
There, } rel.	Séíthi,	Byúno,	Kótán.
Where?	Kúnthí,	Bojúng, Mouka,	Hétá.
Everywhere,	Sokolthi,	Boiyaubo,	Ora páring.
Nowhere,	Konothi náhín,	Jirobo gèyà,	Hétabú mántho.
Hence,	E'ithé hatti,	Imboni phrá,	Ita song.
Thence,	Jéíthé hatti,	Hoboni phrá,	U'ta song.
Whence?	Kónthé hatti,	Bojong phrá, Mouni phrá,	Hota song.
Whence,	...	Jéjong,	Jóta sho.
Before,	A'g,	Shigáng,*	Láng, Lámpá.
Behind,	Pách,	Yúnó,*	Nhú chopa.
Between,	Bích,	Gézér,	Májhata.
Above,	U'par,	Chá,	Rhútá.
Beneath,	Tola,	Sing,	Léttá.
Near,	Nikot,	Khatai,	Chéngsó.
Far,	Dúr,	Gajáng,	Dúró.
Within,	Bhitiri,	Singou or sing,	Sáléng. Lipta.
Without,	Báhiri,	Bahirou,	Báhira. Sátáng.

Nouns of Quality and Condition, &c.

English.	*Kocch.*	*Bodo.*	*Dhimál.*
Health,	Arán,	Gakhrángblá,	Elkapàka.
Sickness,	Birám,	Jobrablá,	Máelkapáka.
Knowledge,	Gyán,	Gyán,	Gyán.
Ignorance,	Ogyan,	Gyáng géyá,	Gyan manthu.
Fatigue,	Thakái,	Méngbai,	Máka.
Rest,	Jírán,	Jirébai,	Maisháka.
Occupation,	Korom,	...	...
Leisure,	Jírán,	...	...
Liberty,	Chhútti,	Hógár,	Láppika?
Restraint,	Káid,	Howál,	Kaid.
Society,	Dósór,	...	...
Solitude,	...	...	...
Crowd,	Bhír,	...	Diáng jóm.
Strength, bodily,	Bal,	Baló,	Balo.
Weakness, ditto,	Nibal,	Balgéyá,	Bal mánthúka.
Ability, mental,	Búddhi,	...	...
Inability, ditto,	Kúbúddhi,	...	...
Power, general,	Sak,	Háyá or Háá,	Dóáng.
Powerlessness,	Nisak,	Haágai,	Dóáng mántho.
Lameness,	Léngrá pan,	Léngran matno?	...
Blindness,	Kana pan,	Kánan matno?.	..
Deafness,	Bahira pan,	Bénga slo?	...
Dumbness,	Gúngá pan,	Pháglá slo?	...
Stutter, stammer,	Thotala pan,	Tótla slo?	...
Wealth,	Dhón,	Dhón,	Dhón.
Poverty,	Nidhon,	Dhón géyá,	Dhón mánthúka.
Scarcity,	Akál,	Ankhál,	Akál.
Plenty,	Satti kál,	Satti kál,	Satti kál.
Famine,	Akál,	Ankhál,	Akál.
Drought,	...	...	...
Inundation,	Bán,	Bán,	Gódá.
Happiness, Pleasure,	Súkh,	Súkh,	Súkh.

* In place or time, as in English. So Dhimál.

English.	*Kocch.*	*Bodo.*	*Dhimál.*
Misery, pain,	Dúkh,	Dúkh,	Dúkh.
Beauty,	...	Machángan matno ?*	...
Ugliness,	...	Shapman matno ?	...
Straightness,	Sídhapana,	...	...
Crookedness,	Térápana,	...	...
Fulness,	...	...	...
Emptiness,	...	...	...
Heaviness,	...	Illitnan matno ?	...
Lightness,	...	Réchéngan matno,	...
Greatness,	Baḍáï,	Gédétnan matno,	...
Smallness,	Chotáï,	Múdóyan mato,	...
Length,	Lambáï,	Gallóvan matno,	...
Shortness,	Chótáï,	Gúchúman matno,	...
Depth,	Gáhir pana,	...	...
Shallowness,	...	...	...
Width,	Chouḍáï,	Gúáran matno,	...
Narrowness,	...	Géchépan matno,	...
Height,	U'cchái,	Gajóvan matno,	...
Lowness,	Níchai,	Gaháyan matno,	...
A round body,	Gol,	Tolot or Dolot,	...
A square,	Choukón,	Kóna manbré,	...
A triangle,	Tríkón,	Kóna manthám,	...
An angle or corner,	Kóná,	Kóná manché,	...
Area,	Paróst,	...	...
Circumference,	Bér,	...	...
Diameter,	Biás,	...	...
A half,	A'dhá,	Khou (ché-one),	E'phala.
A quarter,	Póá,	Khousilingche, (ché-one),	E'póá (ó one).
A third,	Tíháï,	Phán thám, Khou thám ?	...
A part, piece,	Túkrá,	Thúmá, Chóché,	Thúmá.
The whole,	Samúchá,	Bimaíno, Boibo ?	Támánóng.
Redness,	Lálí,	...	...
Whiteness,	...	...	...
Blackness,	...	...	...
Sound,	Sobd,	Shodop,	Hinka.
Noise,	Gondogol,	Gondogol,	Gondogól.
Silence,	Nibháva,	Dórshi,	Chípaká.
Echo,	Ghóng,	Chatta,	Chatta.
A cry, scream, human,	Shór, Púkár,	Gapchi,	Rhíkai.
A roar, bestial,	Dák,	Thétnú,	Dikhár.
A low, bovine,	Dódári,	Dodáya,	Dódai.
A bleat, sheep's,	Bhélbhéli,	Gapmo,	Mémai.
A bark, dog's,	Bhúnk,	Chúngno,	...
A whistle, man's,	Súskári,	Múshút,	Súskári.
A whistle, bird's,	Sitti,	Gapmo,	Khárka.
A hiss, snake's,	Súsári,	Nérú,	Phopal.
A mew, cat's,	Memári,	Gapmo,	Dhúí.
Savour or flavour,	Swád,	Gathou,	Táá.
Good savour,	Acha swád,	Gathou,	Elka Táá.
Bad savour,	Búrá swád,	Thouwá,	Máelka Táá.
Sweetness,	Mitháí,	Gadoï matno ?	...
Sourness,	Khátapan,	Gakhoï matno ?	...

* Machang for majang; so Dou for Tau, and Gorài for Korai: Euphonic.

English.	Kocch.	Bodo.	Dhimál.
Bitterness,	Khátapan,	...	...
Ripeness,	...	Gamánan matno?	...
Rawness,	...	Gathángan matno?	...
Soundness,	...	Ghám matno?	...
Rottenness,	...	Géchéó matno?	...
Odour, smell,	Gandh,	Manámo,	Nhámká.
Perfume,	Ácha gandh,	Manámo-madamo,	Elka nhámka.
Stink,	Búra gandh,	Manámo-khéchara,	Máelka nhámka.
Roughness,	Rúkhái,	...	...
Smoothness,	Chikonái,	...	...
Hardness,	Sakhti,	...	...
Softness,	...	...	...
Dryness,	Súkhápan,	...	...
Wetness,	Bhíjápan,	...	...
Juiciness, fruit,	Rosilta,	...	...
Sappiness, greenness, wood,	Gilápana,	...	...

Nouns of Motion—Things.

Appearance,	...	...	...
Disappearance,	...	...	...
Ascent,	...	Gadong,	...
Descent,	...	U'nkhat,	...
Advance,	Ága gaman,	...	...
Retrogression,	Páchè hatan,	...	...
Vibration, oscillation,	Hilat, Kámp,	Moudáng,	Phirka. Léóka.
Pressure by own weight,	Dáb,	Kichin,	Rhèpkà.
Depression, active,	Daban,	Náchin,	Rhép páká.
Compression, ditto,	Chíp,	Chíp,	Chíp.
Relaxation, loosening,	Dhilau,	Shóngrop,	Dhíl páká.
Increase, self,	Barhti,	...	Dhámé.
Decrease, ditto,	Ghotti,	...	Shímhé.
Addition, others,	Barháwan,	Phédétin,	...
Subtraction, ditto,	Shattávan,	Phúdúin,	...
Expansion, self,	Phútan,	Barsara,	...
Contraction, ditto,	Múnjan,	Khopjop,	...
Opening, others,	Khúlan,	Khéóin,	...
Shutting, ditto,	Bond koron,	Jokhlop,	...
Conjunction, self,	Sanjog,	Lagomano,	Lágal nénka.
Disjunction, ditto,	Bíyog,	Gúbúnslo,	Lakka.
Rupture, bursting, self,	Phút,	Gauwo,	Dheiká.
Fracture, breaking others,	Tórphór,	Chépai,	Bhóïka.
Melting, self,	Galán,	Gillin,	Galé hí.
Congealing, ditto,	Jamán,	Dakháin,	Jóm hí.
Melting, other's,	Galávan,	Gilí hóïn,	Galé páká.
Congealing, ditto,	Jamávan,	...	Jóm páká.

Nouns of Action—Persons.

Approach,	Nikot án,	Khatiou phoïn,	Jéngsholé.
Retirement,	Dúr ján,	Gajan thángin,	Dúré hadé.
Arrival,	Pohúnch,	Chobai,	Dhí.
Departure,	Prasthán,	U'nkhat,	Hadéká.
Entry,	Bhitor án,	Sing hap,	Saleng wáng.
Exit,	Báhir ján,	Báhir tháng,	Sátángólé.
Preservation,	Rakya,	Rákhi,	Báncha páká.
Destruction,	Nás,	Nás,	Nasht páká.
Injury, spoiling,	Bigáran,	...	...

English.	*Kocch.*	*Bodo.*	*Dhimál.*
A journey,	Játrá,	Játrá,	Játrá.
A stage or day's journey,	Monjil,	Shún chénilúma,	E'-nhí-ko-dámá.
Expedition, haste,	Táp,	Gakhri ?	Dhimpá.
Delay,	Dérí,	Dirong,	Bilombh.
A walk, the act,	...	...	...
A pace, stride,	Pau, kodom,	Agán ?	Títar.
A run, race,	Dour,	Khat,	Dháp.
A gallop, animal's,	...	...	...
A trot, ditto,	...	...	...
A leap, jump,	Phán,	Bát,	Tónka.
A hop, skip,	Kúd,	Bajalo,	Hyúká.
A kick,	Lát,	Jóyú,	Lát.
A scratch,	Achúran,	Khúró,	Rhaika.
A bite,	Kátan,	Wát,	Chíika.
A sting,	Bin,	Jó,	Chúka.
A blow of hand,	Már,	Shó,	Chour.
Ditto of stick,	Dáng,	Shó,	Dánghai.
A cut,	Katávan,	Háyú,	Pál.
A thrust or push,	Dhakél,	Nájérót,	Dhikaika.
A pull,	Kénch,	Búbú,	Tánika.
A cast or throw,	Phénk,	Gárhót,	Jhátéká.
A pinch,	Chim,	Khép,	Chim.
A laugh,	Hongsi,	Mini,	Lénká.
A smile,	Múshki,	Minislú,	Atoïsa lénka.
A weeping,	Rówan,	Gáp,	Khár.
A sneeze,	Chíkan,	Háchú,	Háchú.
A cough,	Khási,	Gújú,	Shú.
A gulp or swallow,	Dhók,	Grótché,	Níl.
A belch,	Dhékár,	Molong,	Hito,
A fart,	Pát,	Kíphoi,	Lí.
A spitting,	Thúk,	Mújú,	Thóp.
A chewing or mastication,	Chaboun,	Chouïn,	Rhé katang.
A talking,	Bólan,	Ráïn,	Dóp katang.
Talk,	Bóli,	Rái,	Dóp.
A kiss,	Chúmá,	Khódúm,	Chúmá.
Seeing, the faculty,	Dékhan,	Náïn,	Kháng katang.
Hearing, ditto,	Súnan,	Khónáïn,	Hinkatang.
Smelling, ditto,	Súngan,	Manamchúïn,	Nhú katang.
Tasting, ditto,	Chátan,	Chóláïn,	Déé katang.
Touching, ditto,	Chúïyan,	Dángnáïn,	Vér katang.
Pissing, the act,	Mútan,	Háshúin,	Chicho katang.
Shitting, ditto,	Hágan,	Khíyin,	Líshi katang.
Eating, ditto,	Khávan,	Jáïn,	Chá katang.
Drinking, ditto,	Píwan,	Lóngin,	Am katang.
Sleeping,	Sútan,	Múdúïn,	Jím katang.
Waking,	Jágan,	...	Chét katang.
Dreaming,	Soponkoron,	Símáng núïn,	Sopon kháng katang.
A dream,	Sopon,	Simáng,	Sopon.
Breathing,	Sansphékan,	Hángláïn,	Sánslho katang.
Breath,	Sáns,	Háng,	...
Sweating,	Pasíjan,	Galámin,	Bhim katang.
Sweat,	Pasina,	Galamdoï,	Bhimka.
Palpitation,	Kápan,	Mouin,	Phir katang.
Coitus, impregnation, generating,	Choda-chodi,	Khóïn,	Lú katang.
Conception in womb,	Gaubhári hón,	Bishúphúlin,	Hómángdhamkatang.
Digestion,	Pach,	Gílin,	Póch pà katang.
Indigestion,	Apach,	Gilya gáïn,	Póch mápa katang.

Nouns of Resemblance, Affirmation, &c., and of General Import.

English.	*Kocch.*	*Bodo.*	*Dhimál.*
Resemblance,	Sománta.	...	...
Difference,	Osomanta,	...	...
Identity,	E'ktá,	...	...
Otherness,	...	...	...
Doubt,	San déhi,	...	...
Certainty,	Nichoita,	...	...
Assent,	Kábúl,	...	...
Dissent,	Nákabúl,	...	...
Affirmation,	Sohi,	Ongo,	Jénghi.
Denial,	Inkár,	Ongá,	Májénghi.
Offer, tender,	Charáván,	Jáchiyu ?	Kórhú.
Acceptance,	Kabúl,	Ráyo,	Rhúká.
Rejection,	Nákabúl,	Ráyá,	Márhúká.
Aid, help,	Modot,	Chúmphá,	Moidhop.
Hindrance,	Horj,	...	...
Advice, counsel,	Prámús,	Sanjalaiyú,	Búddhipáká.
Difficulty,	Kathintá,	Gabráp,	...
Easiness,	Sohojtá,	Althói,	...
Expedient, contrivance,	Júgti,	Júgthi,	Júgthi.
Fitness,	...	Somaiyo,	Sobaiká.
Unfitness,	...	Somaiyá,	Má sobaika.
Danger, risk,	...	Gabráp,	Láchi.
Escape, safety,	...	Gówaché,	Bánchi.
Protection, refuge,	Saran,	Kirphát,	Soron.
Abandonment, desertion,	Tyág,	Nágár,	Tyág.
Change, mutation,	Bodol,	Slai,	Shóöka.
Immutableness,	Abodol,	Dá slai,	Má shóöka.
Luck, hap, fortune,	Bhág,	Bhág,	Bhág.
Good luck,	Sú bhág,	Gham bhág,	Elka bhág.
Bad luck,	Kú bhág,	Hammabhág,	Má elka bhág.
Accident, contingency,	Daiv', Gati,	...	...
Meeting, the act,	Milán,	Lagomano,	...
Parting, ditto,	Júda jávan,	Gúbún gúbún tháng,	...
Necessity, fate,	Daiv',	Dáiv',	Daivé.
Free-will,	Súchótan,	Gouini khúsi,	Tái ko khúsi.
Necessity, compulsion,	Jarúrat,	...	...
Choice, option,	Khúsi,	Khúsi,	Khúsi.
Residue, what left,	Báki,	A'drá,	Adrá.
Model, pattern,	Noksha,	...	...
Method, mode,	Doul,	...	...
Original,	Asal,	...	...
Copy,	Nakal,	...	...
Share, lot,	Bakra,	Bhág,	Bántha.
Prop, support,	Powá,	Thongtháng,	Powa.
Instrument,	Hathiár,	Gágújú,	Ghon goï.
Process,	...	...	...
Product,	...	...	...
Order,	Rítí,	Japdong,	...
Disorder,	Anrítí,	Chilai bilai,	...
Benefit,	Hit korom,	Khaichen bhal,	Jaiba elka.
Injury,	Dúsht korom,	Khaichen mando,	Jaiba ma elka.
Loss,	Háráil,	Gamaiyá,	Mhánhé.
Search,	Khój,	Naigro,	Bhóö.
Discovery,	Páwan,	Maibai,	Nónká.
Gain, advantage,	Lábh,	Bisha,	...

English.	*Kocch.*	*Bodo.*	*Dhimál.*
Loss, disadvantage,	Háni,	Loksán,	...
Question,	Sawál,	...	...
Answer,	Jawáb,	...	...
Promise,	Karál,	Kharál,	Karál.
Breach of promise,	...	...	...
Job, piece of work,	Kám,	Hobba,	...
Joke,	Thatta,	Sikrai,	Rouchi.
Knot,	Gánthi,	Gánthi,	Gánthi.
Cleft, crack,	Chír,	Gouwo,	Dhéiká.
Hole,	Gádha,	Hákór,	...
Quake,	Kámp,	Mou,	Phirka.
Earthquake,	Bhúi kámp,	Há mouwo,	Bhanóï phirka.
Point, } of weapon,	Gójá,	Góphát,	...
Edge, } of weapon,	Dhár,	Dhár,	Dhár.
Back, } of weapon,	Píthi,	Gédá,	Gándi.
Pair, mas et fœm,	Jórá,	Jórá,	Jórá.
Pair, sorted,	Jora,	Jórá,	Jórá.
Fee, douceur,	Inám,	I'lám,	I'lám.
Atom,	...	...	...
Inventory or list,	Férist,	...	...
A mark, any,	Chin,	Chin,	Chin.
A stain,	Dágh,	Dágh,	Dágh.
A label,	...	...	...
Errand of business,	...	...	...
Message, simple,	...	...	...
News, intelligence,	Khobor,	Khopor,	Khopor.
Essence,	Mánja,	Mánja,	Mánja.
Equilibrium,	...	...	...
Bias,	...	...	...
Excess,	Jyádati,	...	...
Deficiency,	Ghotti,	...	..
Sufficiency,	Bos,	...	...

Indeclinables of Affirmation, Quantity, Mode, &c., including Conjunctions and Prepositions.*

Perhaps,	Kún káló,	Mithia? Blá,	Nághé.
Certainly,	Kháti, Nichoi,	Ongthárgo,	Nichói.
Yes,	Hén,	Ongo,	Hé.
No,	Nanín,	Ongá,	Ahé.
General privative,	...	Géyá,	Mánthú.
Do not, verbal privative,	Ná Ná koris,	Dá, Dá khlúm,	Má. Má pá.
Wherefore, } rel. and correl.	Jéi táné,	...	Jéi páli.
Therefore, } rel. and correl.	Séi táné,	...	Séi páli.
Why?	Ki táné,	Mánó,	Hai páli.
Much,	Bhéléla,	Góbáng,	E'shúto.
Many,	Bhéléla,	Góbáng,	E'shúto.
Little,	Gútik,	Kitisi or Tisi,	Atóïsa.
Few,	Gútik,	Kitisi,	Atóïsa.
Less,	Kónék,	Kitisi,	Atóïsa.
More,	Arár, Phai,	Aro,	Aro.
Enough,	Bós,	Thúbai,	Jéhé.
More, } signs of comparison,	Tá té,	Binbo-shin,	O'kónhádóng.
Most, } signs of comparison,	Sabá té,	Boinobo-shin,	Sogimingko-nhádong.

* For more prepositions see Grammar, p. 75. Add thence Of, To, In, On, From. Many prepositions will be found under Indeclinables of Place.

English.	*Kocch.*	*Bodo.*	*Dhimál.*
As much,	Joto,	Jé chibang,	Jó jokho.
So much,	Toto,	U' chibang,	U'dong jokho.
How much?	Koto,	Béchi chibang,	Hé jokho.
How many?	Kiti,	Béchébá, Piché,	...
Too much,	Phai?	Gabáng?	Sópá.
Too little,	Olop,	Kitisi?	...
Very much, most,	Oti,	Boinobo-gabang shin,	Sokapé Sóká. Saiko sopa.
Than,	...	Shin or Sin, also Nó,	Nhá or Nhádong.
As,	Jémón,	Jirin,	Jédong.
So,	Témón,	U'rin,	Kódong.
Thus, poz,	Wéó mon,	Wo rin, Risha, Idi,	U'dong. Usáng.
How?	Kémón,	Bré,	Hésá.
Like, in manner of,	Jokho,	Púsá,	Bhaika.
Unlike, otherwise,	Ná jokho,	Dá púsá,	Má Bhaika.
Verily, indeed,	Thik thik,	...	...
Only, merely,	Kháli kéval,	Bánó,	...
As long,	Joto khún,	Jóché bon,	Jejokho bilombh.
So long,	...	Woché bon,	Sejokho bilombh.
Until,	...	...	Kola.
Because,	...	...	Konáng.
If,	Jékhón, Jédú,	Jélá,	...
Then,	Tékhón, Té,	Kola,	...
But,	Kintu,	Kintu,	Kintu ná.
And,	E'vong, O,	Bi, Ré? Bó?	E'dóng?
Also,	Aro,	Aro,	Aro.
Again,	Bárí,	Phin,	Nhé chota, Gnéchota.
Or,	Kí,	Ná,	Ná.
Both,	Dóno,	San-gne,* Man-gné,	Nhómi, Gnémi. Nhélong, Gnélong.
Either,	Káhóng,	...	Háshúng.
Neither,	Káhongná,	Bibo nangá?	Háshúng mantho.
Or not, otherwise,	Nátė,	Dáté,	Máté.
Hush!	Jhit már,	Shrithá,	Dhiká pá.
Lo!	Dékhék,	Nai hót, or Nái,	Kháng.
Hurrah!	Dhanyo dhanyo,	Khanomathai,	...
Alas,	Hai hai,	Habap,	Hai hai.
With, cum,	Dosor, sáthé,	Logo,	Dosa.
Without, sine,	Biné,	...	...
By, instrument,	Diyá,	Jóng,	Shó, Dong.
Except, unless,	...	...	...
Moreover, besides,	Aro,	Aro,	A'r.
Notwithstanding,	Táhón,	Toblábó,	...
According to,	Ba mójim,	...	...
Almost, nearly,	Atát,	Khatió, Háché,	Thorángi.
Quite, entirely,	Tamám,	Boinobo?	Dónghé.
Partially, in part,	Kúcch kúcch,	Khaiché,	...
Rightly, well,	Acha koria,	...	...
Wrongly, ill,	Mondo koria,	...	...
Violently,	Balibal,	Balohanáné,	Jormájor.
Gently,	Dhire dhire,	Láshi láshi,	...

* Sangné, two people; Mangné, two animals.

English.	*Kocch.*	*Bodo.*	*Dhimál.*
	PRONOUNS, PERSONAL.		
I,	Múí,	Áng,	Ká.
Thou,	Túi,	Naug,	Ná.
He, she, it, that,	Oní,	Bí,	Wá.
We,	Hámi,	Jong (chúr),	Kyél.
Ye,	Túmi,	Nang chúr,	Nyél.
They,	U'ni,	Bi chúr,	U'bal.
	POSSESSIVE PRONOUNS.		
Mine,	Mór,	Angni,	Káng.
Thine,	Tór,	Nangni,	Náng.
His, hers, its,	O'r,	Bini,	O'ko, wang.
Ours,	Hámaro,	Jongni,	King.
Yours,	Túmáro,	Nangshúrni,	Ning.
Theirs,	U'nnár,	Bichúrni,	U'balko.
	RELATIVE DEMONSTRATIVE PRONOUNS, &c.		
Self,	Áp,	Gouï ?	Tái.
Own,	Ápnór,	Gouïni, Bitháni,	Táiko.
This,	Yáhi,	Imbo,	Iti or Idong.
That,	Vóhi,	Hobo,	U'ti or U'dong.
Who, rel.,	Jé,	Jé,	Jéti or Jédóng.
Who, correl.,	Sói,	Bi? (He, it),	Sóti or Kodong.
Who?	Kái,	Chúr,	Héti or Háshú.
What, that which,	...	...	...
What?	Kí,	Má,	Hai.
Any,	Káhó, kóno,	Múngbo? *	Káibo.
All,	Sob,	Boino,	Saikó? Sogiming.
Anybody, Somebody,	Káhó,	Chúr,	Háshú.
Nobody,	Káho nahin,	Chúr óngá, Chúr géyá,	Má hashú. Háshúmanthuka.
Anything, Something,	Kúcch,	Jishláp, Mongbo,	Haidong.
Whoever,	Jéhí,	Jái,	Jédong kédong.
Like,	Sá, Món,	Púsá,	Bhaika ?
Like this, such,	E'món,	Ri púsá,	I'sáka.
Like that, such,	Wémón,	U'ri púsá,	U'sáka.
Like what?	Kémón,	Bré púsá,	Hésaka.
Other, another,	Áró,	Gúbún,	Bhináng.
	ADJECTIVES.		
Good,	Bhalo,	Ghám,	Elka.
Bad,	Mondo,	Hamma,	Má élka.
Virtuous, moral,	Púni, Dhormi,	Ghám,	Dharmi.
Vicious, immoral,	Pápi,	Hamma,	Pápi.
Religious,	Dhormi,	...	...
Irreligious,	Adhormi,	...	...
Penitent,	...	...	...
Impenitent,	...	...	...
Modest,	Lajúá,	Laji ganang,	Laji híka.
Impudent,	Niloj,	Laji yongá,	Láj mánthúka.
Hopeful,	Bhorósí,	Bórsa ganang,	Bhórsa híka.

* Múngbó, to things only.

English.	Kocch.	Bodo.	Dhimál.
Hopeless,	Nirási,	Bórsa géyá,	Bhorsa mánthúka.
Joyful, happy,	Horkit,	Khús,	Khús.
Sorrowful, unhappy,	U'dás,	Khús géyá,	Khús mánthúka.
Cunning,	Phaktia,	Phakta,	Phakta.
Candid,	Sídha,	Sódha,	Sódha.
Malicious,	Ghinábha,	Múgwino,	Chikaka.
Benevolent,	Doyasíl,	Wanjáno,	...
Envious,	Hinsok,	Mogon chanai,	Hiska.
Content,	San túshtit,	...	Hiska mánthúka.
Proud, vain,	Diphongi,	Dúnai,	Dim phúlla.
Humble,	Garíb,	Tháng jang,	Sójha.
Industrious,	Mahinati,	Mou chúno,	Kisri páka.
Idle,	A'lsia,	Alsia,	Alsia.
True,	Saccha,	Bobra,	Bobra.
False,	Jhúta,	Kholai,	Láppa.
Impatient, Passionate, hasty,	Rádh,	...	...
Placid, quiet, patient,	Dhír,	...	...
Merciful,	Doyasíl,	Wan gonáng,	...
Cruel,	Dúsht,	Wan géyá,	...
Brave,	Sáhosi,	Gíronga,	Mala chíika.
Cowardly,	Dórúk,	Gíkho,	Hatásia.
Constant, steady,	Sthír,	Ghoidária,	Gongouda.
Inconstant, Capricious,	Asthír,	Kholai,	Shát montina.
Wasteful, profuse,	Dhúlia,	Phútúa,	Khóï násia.
Niggardly,	Kírpini,	Kostia, khalé,	Koshói.
Kind, gentle,	Súsíl,	Ghám,	Dhílaka.
Unkind, harsh,	Kúsíl,	Hamma,	Chúkka.
Goodnatured,	Súsíl,	Gúroï, ghám,	E'lka.
Illnatured,	Kúsíl,	Hamma,	Má elka. Dóndúa.
Polite, wellbred,	Sishtácbári,	...	...
Rude, illbred,	Khada,	...	...
Obedient,	Maini,	Gíín ganang,	...
Disobedient,	O maini,	Gíín géyá,	...
Grateful,	...	...	...
Ungrateful,	...	...	...
Mad,	Págla,	Phagla,	Phagla.
Idiotic,	Pagla,	Phagla,	Phàgla.
Licit, morally,	Kortobya,	...	...
Illicit, ditto,	Okortobya,	...	...
Legal,	...	...	...
Illegal,	...	...	...
Physical or material,	Bhoutika,	...	...
Immaterial,	Aitmika,	...	...
Precise,	Thik thik,	...	...
Vague,	...	...	...
Hungry,	Bhúkil,	Yókidong,	Mhítúka.
Thirsty,	Piási,	Doï kángdong,	Chíám lihika.
Naked,	Nángta,	Hí géyá,	Dhába mánthú.
Clothed,	...	Hí gandong,	Dhába gúka vel hika.
Libidinous,	Kámi,	Cháltia,	Kokhoi hïka.
Gluttonous,	Pétú,	Jachográ,	Shopa cháka.
Drunken,	Sharábi,	Máthól,	Yú ámká.
Foul-mouthed, Abusive,	Múkhchór,	Khúga shápma,	Naika.
Alive,	Jíwat,	Gotháng,	Singlhoka.

English.	*Kocch.*	*Bodo.*	*Dhimál.*
Dead,	Mórá,	Gothoï,	Síká.
Sick,	Káhila,	Haiya, Jóbra,	Mádónka.
Healthy,	...	Gakhrúng,	Dónka.
Asleep,	Nindáil,	Múdú lángdong,	Ninda lékha.
Awake,	Jágil,	Sidi mondong,	Chétánka.
Mature,	Siáná,	Jholau,	Wháńtika.
Young,	Chéngór,	Gothoni, Galaini,	Chan híka.
Old,	Búdha,	Braï, Búroï,	Waráng. Beráng.
Strong,	Bali,	Balo grá,	Bal hika.
Weak,	Nibali,	Balo géya,	Bal mánthúka.
Free,	...	...	...
Confined,	...	...	...
Handsome,	Songot,	Mójáng,	Elka?
Ugly,	Baiya,	Shápmá,	Má elka.
Short, human beings,	Bángrá,	Gahái,	Bángra.
Tall, human beings,	Téngha,	Gajou,	Dhángá.
Fat,	Móta,	Gúphúng,	Dhámka. Chópka.
Thin,	Súkna,	Gaham,	Mboika.
Tired, weary,	Thakit,	Méng chóö,	Máïka.
Fresh, untired,	Athakit,	Méngyá gai,	Má máika.
Lame,	Léngra,	Khóra,	Kóhra.
Blind,	Kána,	Kána,	Kána.
Deaf,	Bahira,	Bénga,	Bahira.
Dumb,	Gúnga,	Ráin ónga,	Gúnga.
Alone,	Ekala,	Háshing,	Ekaláng.
Companioned,	Dosorér,	Lagolá,	Dosorhí.
Learned,	Gyáni,	Gyán ganang,	Gyán híka.
Ignorant,	Ogyáni,	Gyán géya,	Gyan mánthúka.
Wise,	Gyáni,	Gyán,	Gyán hika.
Foolish,	Ogyáni,	Gyán géyá,	Gyán mánthúka.
Poor,	Nidhoni,	Houria, thakageya,	Dhon mánthúka.
Rich,	Dhoni,	Dhon ganang,	Dhon hika.
Noisy, talkative,	Géngédia,	Phidua,	Phidua.
Silent,	Obola,	Ráyá, thándá,	Chíka páka.
Dirty,	Maila,	Gini,	Mírhí. Máchikan.
Clean,	Safa,	Gúphúr,	Chikan.
Married,	Biháta,	Noha jábai,	Mougia.
Single,	Akúmári, Akwári,	Jholou (mas.), Sikala (fœm.),	Dhóná.
Highborn,	Kúlín,	...	...
Lowborn,	Akúlín,	...	...
Dependent,	Porbos,	Malaini,	Bodós.
Independent,	Aponbos,	Gouini khusi,	Táides.
Taxed,	Málguzári,	Girini,	Girini.
Exempt,	Mááfi,	Máafi,	Máafi.
Designed,	...	...	...
Accidental,	...	...	...
Old,	Púrána,	Gozám,	...
New,	Náya,	Godám,	...
Present,	Hájir,	...	...
Absent,	Ghair Hájir,	...	...
Ready,	Tíyár,	...	...
Unready,	...	...	...
Scarce, rare,	Thora,	...	...
Common, vulgar,	Bohut,	...	...

English.	*Kocch.*	*Bodo.*	*Dhimál.*
Public,	...	...	...
Private,	...	...	...
Prosperous,	...	...	...
Unprosperous,	...	...	...
Saleable,	...	...	..
Purchasable,	...	...	...
Valuable,	Kímati,	...	...
Worthless,	Mond,	...	...
Habitual, usual,	...	...	...
Unusual, strange,	...	...	...
Similar,	Somán,	...	...
Dissimilar,	Asomán,	Gúbún,	Bhináng.
Same,	E'khí,	...	...
Different,	Júda,	Gúbún,	Bhináng.
Doubtful,	Sandéhi,	...	...
Certain,	Nichoi,	...	...
Deserted,	Chon,	...	Diáng mánthúka.
Frequented,	Bosot bári,	...	Diáng younka.
Easy,	Sohoj,	Altúá,	...
Difficult,	Kosor,	Gobráp,	Karákará.
Changeful,	Asthir,	Kholai,	Lapha.
Changeless,	Sthir,	Bobrai,	Bobrai.
Lucky,	Súbhágya,	...	...
Unlucky,	Obhágya,	...	...
Original,	Asali,	...	...
Copied,	Nokoli,	...	...
Methodical,	Doul sé,	Doul ganang,	Doul Híka.
Immethodical,	Andoul se,	Doul géya,	Doul manthúka.
Fit, suitable,	Láik,	Shomaiyo,	Sha baika.
Unfit,	Na láik,	Shomaiyá,	Másha baika.
Orderly,	Sári,		Sárika.
Disorderly,	Osári,	Chilai bilai,	Másárika.
Profitable,	Phalit,	U'daigo,	...
Unprofitable,	Ophalit,	U'daiyá,	...
Possessed, tenens,	...	Akhai ou,	...
Dispossessed, ousted,	...	Akhai ou géya,	...
Ornamented,	Rongíl,	Rong gonág,	Ronghíka.
Plain,	Súdha,	Rong géya,	Rong mánthúka.
Useful,	Phalit,	Hamsin,	...
Useless,	Ophalit,	Hammásin,	...
Quick moving, active,	Chálák,	Gakhrai mouin,	Dhimka chukka.
Slow moving, inert,	Gor chálák,	Généö mouin,	Má dhimka. Má chúkka.
Cheap,	Sosta,	Ghéér,	Lánká.
Dear,	Mhánga,	Mongo,	Jánká.
Pure,	Pabitor,	...	Chíkánka.
Impure,	Opobitor,	...	Mirhí.
Wholesome,	Pochya,	Gilinai,	Póch páka.
Unwholesome,	Nápochya,	Giliyá,	Poch má páka.
Edible,	Khábar,	Janaini,	Cháka.
Inedible,	Nakhábar,	Jáyáni,	Má cháka.
Manufactured, wrought,	Banail,	Daanai,	...
Raw goods,	...	...	...
Sharp-edged,	Chókha,	Gobbo,	Chúká.
Blunt,	Bhotora,	Bowa,	Má chúka.
Grinded,	Gúra,	Gandoï,	Tóölika.
Woven,	Banáil,	Shúnai,	Joka.
Spun,	...	Khúndóng,	...

English.	*Kocch.*	*Bodo.*	*Dhimál.*
Platted,	...	Hépnai,	Púïka.
Spacious, wide, ample,	Posár,	Gúwár,	Dhai dhaik.
Contracted,	Ato,	Gétchép,	Ato.
Moving,	Cholnir,	Thabaiyo,	Cholon hika.
Motionless,	Sthávar,	Thabaiyá,	Cholon mánthúka.
Figured,	Rúpit,	Rúpganang,	Rup hika.
Figureless,	Aurupit,	Rúp geya,	Rup mánthúka.
Luminous,	Ujjála,	Shrángni,	Phor phora.
Dark, obscure,	Andhkár,	Kómshini,	Chípka. Kitikitika.
Opaque,	...	Núyá,	Má dóöka.
Pellucid,	...	Núyó,	Dóöka.
Blazing,	Jolot,	Jong jong,	Tiïka.
Extinct,	Nibhal,	Komut bai,	Shéka.
The present time,	Bartamán,	Jáádong,	I'dong Béla.
The past,	Bhúta,	Japbai,	Jéhí.
The future,	Bhavish,	...	...
Right,	Dohina,	Nágdá, or A'gdá,	Dam.
Left,	Bain,	Nakchi,	Lédá.
Central,	Madhyika,	Géjér,	Mánjhika.
Lateral,	Pás,	Jiugni,	Aliká.
North,	Uttar,	Cha,	Dáhén.
South,	Dakshin,	Khlá,	Máhén.
East,	Púrab,	Sanja,	Núnhén.
West,	Poschim,	Shanáp,	Dinhén.
Passable, accessible,	Podit,	Pát lángá,	...
Impassable, Inaccessible,	Apodit,	Pát háyá,	...
Cultivated,	Jotáha,	Hú mouá,	Léng hika.
Uncultivated,	Unjotáha,	Hágráni,	Dinchaka.
Fruitful, rich,	Osár,	Gham,	Elka.
Barren, poor,	Ató,	Hamma,	Maelka.
Sandy,	Balúá,	Balani Hú,	...
Clayey,	Chik tháli,	Chik tháli,	Tyúka.
Calcareous,	Chúnaini,	...	...
Saline,	Núnia,	...	...
Muddy,	Kéchara,	Habdúni,	Kédóóka.
Dusty,	Dhúláha,	Hádrini,	...
Brakish water,	Núnia,	Shapma,	Máelka.
Fresh,	Mitha,	Gham, Majang,	Elka.
Flowing,	Bohonti,	Búyú,	Phaika.
Still,	Dhí,	Bilú, Dongo,	Máphaika.
Deep,	Móni,	Gatho,	Bhiló.
Shallow,	Alpho,	Thouá,	Kómka.
Windy weather,	Batásia,	...	...
Stormy,	Andhia,	...	...
Fine, fair,	Accha,	Majang, ghám,	Elka.
Cold,	Thanda,	Gúshú,	Tírká.
Hot,	Gorom,	Gúdúm,	Sááká.
Cloudy,	Méghér,	Nókháni,	...
Sunshiny,	Ghámér,	Syán dóngni,	...
Rainy, wet,	Pániér,	...	...
Dry, fair,	Bésh,	Nókhaháyá, gaini,	...
Moist, full of vapour,	Bhijá,	Gichi,	Jhakka.
Moist, sappy, green,	Gila,	Gotháng,	Sinka.
Juicy,	Rasáil,	Bidé gonáng,	Ros jénka.
Juiceless, dry,	Súkhá,	Bidé géyá,	Ros mánthuká.

English.	Kocch.	Bodo.	Dhimál.
Wet, } clothes,	Bhíja,	Gichi,	Jhakka.
Dry, } clothes,	Súkhá,	Grán,	Sinka.
Wooded, close, } land,	Jongoli,	Hágrá gonáng,	Dinchahika.
Naked, open, } land,	O'sár,	Dhai dhai,	Dhai dhaika.
Coloured,	Rongíl,	Rong gonáng,	Ika dáka.
Colourless,	Sádá,	Rong géyá,	Jéika.
Red,	Lál,	Gatchá,	Jika.
White,	Dhoula,	Gúphút,	Jéika.
Blue,	Níl,	Gotchóm,	Dúúka.
Green,	Hara,	Kháugshúr,	Nélpá.
Black,	Kála,	Gotchom,	Dúúka.
Yellow,	Píla,	Gúmmo,	Youka.
Sour,	Títá,	Gakhói,	Dákha.
Sweet,	Mítha,	Gadói,	Túäka.
Bitter,	Kaduva,	Gakha,	Khúka.
Ripe,	Pakka,	Gammang,	Minka.
Raw,	{ Kachha, Kancha,	} Gatháng,	Sinka.
Rotten,	Sara,	Géchéó,	Aika.
Sound,	Tája,	Ghám,	Má aika.
Stinking,	Kúgandhi,	Khéch ara,	Ma yokka.
Well-odoured,	Súgandhi,	Madamma,	Yokka.
Rough,	Korkoria,	Góbrá,	Khór souka.
Smooth,	Chikna,	Chil chil,	Chikan.
Hard,	Kaḍa,	Górra,	Korkorka.
Soft,	Norom,	Gúrói,	Norom.
Straight,	Sídhá,	{ Gotthong, Thong jong,	} Ghénka.
Crooked,	Béká,	Khónkra,	Kéóka.
Full,	Bhorti,	Tongo, Búnjá,	Bhélpá.
Empty,	Kháli,	{ Múngbo géyá, Géyá,	} Mánthúka.
Solid,	...	...	...
Hollow,	...	...	...
Heavy,	Bhári,	Gillit or Illit,	Lhíka.
Light,	Holka,	Réchéng,	Hómka.
Great,	Baḍo,	Gédét,	Dhámka.
Small,	Choto,	Múdói,	Mhoika.
Long,	Lámba,	Gallou,	Rhinka.
Short,	Choto,	Gúchúm,	Pótóka.
Wide,	Chowra, Osár,	Gúár,	Pachárka.
Narrow,	Tang, A'to,	Géchèp,	Chípka.
High,	U'cchá,	Gajou,	Dháugaka.
Low,	Nichá,	Gahái,	Bángrá.
Round,	Gól,	Tólótni,	Gótaka.
Square,	Chou konia,	Kóna manbréni,	Diá thúnika.
Angular,	Kónia,	Kóna manchéni,	E'long thúnika.
Broken,	Tútá,	Gójó,	Bhoika.
Entire,	Samúcha,	Bimainé,	{ Góthaka. Má bhoika. }
Porous,	...	...	...
Imporous,	...	...	...
Open,	Khúlá,	Khéwo,	Hóká.
Shut,	Bond,	Jókhlópmo,	Gibka.
Spread,	Asar,	Bodong,	Posárka.
Folded,	Goto,	Hútúmdong,	Jóm páka.
Expanded, blown, a flower,	} Phuta,	Bárshara,	Bárká.

English.	*Kocch.*	*Bodo.*	*Dhimál.*
Closed, shut, do.,	...	Khókjóp,	Chópka.
Tight,	Tántán,	Tánatán,	Tántán.
Slack,	Dhíla,	Gúrrún,	...
Loose, unsteady,	Larbaria,	Lúdo lúdo,	Léíka.
Fixed, firm,	Thir,	Gakhráng,	Kárkárka.
Cooked,	Rándha,	Gomon,	Minka.
Raw,	Kancha,	Gotháng,	Sínka.
Hairy,	Romáil,	Khomon gonáng,	Múíshú hika.
Hairless,	Cholchol,	Khomon géyá,	Múíshú mánthúka.
Feathered,	...	...	...
Scaly,	...	...	...

VÉRBS.

To do, ..	Konu, Koribar or Korinu,	Mouno, Khlámno, Khajámno,	Páli.
Not to do,	Na korinu,	Mouá gaino,!	Má páli.
To undo,	...	...	...
To do over again,	...	Mou phinno,	Nhéchúto pali.*
To shape, form, make,	...	Dááno,	Banaili.
To change, form, or alter,	Bodol korinu,	Baino, Slaino,	Shóóli.
To be (esse),	Hóbar,	Jááno,	Jéngli.
Not to be,	Na hóbar,	Jáä gaino,	Má jéngli.
To become,	Hóbar,	Jááno,	Jéngli.
To come to pass, happen,	Ásia poribar,	Jáá phoino,	Dhúli. Léténg wángli.
To create, god,	Sújibar,	...	...
To destroy, god,	Nasht korinu,	Nasht khlámno,	Nasht páli.
To be born,	Janam hobar,	Janam jááno,	Janam jéngli.
To give birth to, produce,	Janam dibar,	Gophaino, Uptan hotno,	Janam pili.
To deliver, accoucher,	...	...	...
To nurse, wet,	Dúdh khilibar,	Ábú dóno,	Dúdo ám páli.
To nurse, dry,	...	...	...
To live,	Jíbar,	Thángno,	Singlhóli.
To die,	Moribar,	Thóïno,	Síli.
To kill,	Mária phalánú,	Shithatno, Watno,	Shéli.
To grow,	Baḍibar,	Détno,	...
To decay, decline,	Ghotibar,	Brai lángno,	Waráng jéngli.
To be mature,	Syán hobar,	Jholau jááno,	Whántika jéngli.
To feel, be bodily sensible of,	...	Shútrúng khlámno: Disha khlámno,	Shúrti páli.
To perceive, mentally,	Chininú,	Shútrúng khlámno,	Shúrti páli.
To think,	Phóm korinu,	Mithino,	Phóm páli.
To desire,	Cháhinu,	Labaino: Gasho khajámno,	Khángli.
To remember,	Yád korinu,	Shútrúng khajámno,	Phém páli.
To forget,	Bhúlinu,	Bouno,	Nilli.
To learn,	Síkhinu,	Chúlóngno,	Dhírli.
To teach,	Síkha dinu,	Phúrróngno,	Dhír páli.
To educate,	Pátdibar or dinu,	...	...
To read,	Paḍbinu,	Chaláṅgno ?	Poṛhli.
To write,	Lékhinu,	Litno,	Lékhli.

* Nhéchúto from *gné*, 2, and *chót*, bout, turn, *dóbára* in Hindi. It should therefore be written Gnéchúto passim.

English.	*Kocch.*	*Bodo.*	*Dhimál.*
To sign,	Doskot korinu,	Doskot litno,	Cháp pili.
To seal,	Chàpinu,	Cháp thúno,	Cháp pili.
To sin,	Pap kónu,	Páp khajámno,	Páp páli.
To err,	Bhúlinu,	Bauno,	Bhúléli.
To revenge,	Bodol libar,	Bodol sophinno,	Bodol páli.
To forgive,	Mááf kónu,	Doya khlámno, Nágárno,	Doya páli.
To repent,	Patch kónu,	Jingá sino,	Patch taili.
To intend, purpose,	Mansúba korinu,	Gasho rákhina?	Mansúba páli.
To endeavour,	Ánthinu,	Jángi khapráno,	Kénkni tépli.
To persevere, continue doing,	Korté róbar,	Mouin tháno,	Púkaténg hili.
To desist from,	Thákibar,	Nágárno,	Láp páli. Lápli.
To enjoy, use,	Bhoginu,	...	...
To use, bring into use,	Kámot lagánu,	...	...
To disuse, lay by,	Chorinu, rákhinu,	Danno,	Láp pili.
To know, understand,	Bújhinu,	Mithino,	Géli.
To be ignorant of, not understand,	Na bújhinu,	Mithi gaino,	Má géli.
To cause to know, to explain,	...	Mithiya hotno?	Géli páli.
To believe,	Patiánu,	Ghám mithinu,	Sápli.
To disbelieve,	Na patiana,	Hammá mithinu,	Má sápli.
To doubt, hesitate,	Son déhi konu,	Ganogoto khlámno,	Dommo kommo pali.
To be sure,	Nichoi jánibar,	...	...
To make up mind, determine,	Taharounu,	...	...
To resemble,	Somán hobar,	Somán jááno,	Somán jéngli.
To differ,	Osomán hobar,	Dá somán jááno,	Ma soman jengli.
To compare,	Milajbar,	Rújúno,	Jora chá páli.
To cajole, wheedle,	Bhúr kánu,	Búr klaino,	Báng páli.
To please,	Khús korinu,	Khúsi khlámno,	Khús páli.
To displease,	Na khús korinu,	Khúsi khlamma gaino,	Mákhus páli.
To esteem,	Bodo máninu,	Máni chúno,	Mánéli.
To despise,	Chóto máninu,	Manyà gaino,	Má manéli.
To decry, run down,	Badnám kónu,	...	...
To deceive, mislead,	Bhúla kónu,	Bouhotno,	Nilli páli.
To persuade,	Manánu,	Rodongno,	...
To dissuade,	Báda dinu, Báran korinu,	Báda hotno,	Bádá pil.
To attend to, to heed,	Máninu,	Mánino,	Mánéli.
To neglect,	Ná máninu,	Mányá gaino,	Má mánéli.
To confirm,	Sábit koribar,	Kotha rákhinu,	Sábit páli.
To annul,	Rod koribar,	Ród khajámno,	Ród páli.
To allow, permit,	Hobar dibar,	...	...
To disallow, prevent,	Ná hobár dibar,	Báda hotno,	Báda pili.
To forbid, interdict,	Báda dinu,	Báda hotno,	Báda pili.
To succeed,	Parinu,	Háino : débáno,	Dóángli.
To be able,	Sakinu,	Hááno,	Dóángli.
To fail,	Ná párinu,	Hangaino, Jénno,	Má dóángli.
Not to be able,	Ná sakinu,	Háágaino,	...
To wonder at,	Acharaj mánuinu,	Ánkhá mánino,	Rhíwáli.
To approve,	Posin konu,	Phosin khlámno,	Posin pali.
To disapprove,	Ná posin konu,	Dá phosin khlámno;	Má posin páli,
To applaud, commend, praise,	Nigou korinu,	...	Posin páli.

English.	*Kocch.*	*Bodo.*	*Dhimál.*
To censure, blame,	Ninda konu,	...	Má posin páli.
To hiss, loudly decry,	Chíchi bolibar,	...	...
To cheer, loudly applaud,	Shábáshi korinu,	...	...
To cheer, comfort, cherish, protect,	Póshinu,	Posh khlámno,	Pósh páli.
To neglect, abandon,	Tyág korinu,	Nágárno,	Má posh páli.
To encourage,	Sahos dibar,	Bhorsa hotno,	Bhorsa pili.
To discourage,	U'dás koribar,	Gí hotno,	...
To abuse, revile,	Gáli dibár,	Raichúno,	Naili.
To frighten,	Dór khiláibar,	...	Láchili.
To be afraid,	Dor khilibar or khábar,	Giyúno ?	Láchi páli.
To tranquillise,	Sánt korinu,	...	...
To be tranquil,	Sánt hobar,	...	...
To brawl,	Jhogra korinu,	Náng jalaino,	Naishúli.
To brag, boast,	Badhai korinu,	Dúï láuo,	Gophï dopli.
To condole with,	Thátib dinu,	...	Thátib pili.
To annoy, vex, tease, irritate,	Dúkh dinu,	Dúk hotno,	Dúkh pili.
To love, feel affection,	Máya konu,	Wánchóno,	Doya páli.
To hate, feel malice,	Ghin konu,	Mógino,	Chika páli.
To hope,	Bhórsa konu,	Gironga jááno,	Bhorsá nénli.
To fear,	Hatás khábar,	Gíchíno,	Láchili.
To tell a lie,	Jhút bolinu,	Santha laino,	Mitcha dópli.
To tell the truth,	Sacch bolinu,	Thóngjóng raino,	...
To rejoice, *n.*,	...	Khúsi jááno,	Khúsi jéngli.
To grieve, *n.*,	...	...	...
To satisfy, *a.*,	...	...	...
To disappoint, *a.*,	...	...	...
To command order,	Húkam dinu,	Húkam hotno,	Húkam pili.
To countermand,	Báda dinu,	Báda hotno,	Báda pili.
To obey,	Hukám máninu,	Húkam manino,	Húkam mánéli.
To disobey,	Húkam ná máninu,	Húkam mánya gaino,	Húkam má mánéli.
To question,	Púchinu,	Songno,	Hilli.
To answer,	Jowáp dinu,	Rái douno,	Dopli.
To assent,	Kabúl konu,	Ongo raino,	Manóli.
To dissent,	Ná kabúl konu,	Ongá raino,	Má manóli.
To affirm,	...	Ongo raino,	...
To deny,	...	Ongá raino,	...
To speak, talk, say,	Bolinu,	Raino,	Dópli.
To repeat, say again,	Dobára bolinu,	Rái phinno,	Nhéchota, dópli.
To announce, tell, inform,	Khopor dinu,	...	...
To summon, call,	Dákibar,	Ling hótno,	Kaili.
To call out, shout,	Gondogol konu,	Hóchino,	Rhí kaili.
To accost, salute,	Saheb salamat konu,	Khúlúmno,	Dómli.
To invite,	Nyota korinu,	...	...
To visit,	...	...	...
To entertain guests,	...	...	...
To request, solicit,	Binti konu,	Binti khlámno,	Banti páli.
To beg alms,	Bhík mánginu,	Dán bíno,	Dán rhéli.
To refuse,	Ná dibar,	Dá hotno,	Má pili.
To ask, interrogate, inquire,	Jáchinu,	Songno,	Hilli.
To offer, tender,	Bhúrkibar.	Hotno,	Pili.
To accept,	Libár.	Láno,	Rhúli.
To reject,	Ná libar.	Dá láno,	Má rhúli.

English.	Kocch.	Bodo.	Dhimál.
To help,	Modod dibar,	Chúmpháno,	...
To hinder,	Horoj dibar,	Hómtano,	Ténkéli. Rhóli.
To advise, give advice,	Saláh dinu,	San jalaino,	Saláh pili.
To consult, ask advice,	Saláh mánginu,	...	Saláh rhúli.
To quarrel,	Jhogra konu,	Náng jalaino,	Nai shúli.
To be reconciled,	Milinu,	Bóng jalaino,	Láili.
To curse,	Sráp dinu,	Sráp hotno,	Sráp pili.
To bless,	Asirbád dinu,	Tháng baita raino,	Sing teng hili.
To forswear, renounce,	Kirya khái chári dinu,	Shomai lánáne nágárno,	Kirya cháteng láp pili.
To take oath,	Kirya khabar,	Shomai láno,	Kirya. Cháli.
To give oath,	Kirya khai dibar,	Shómailá hotno,	Kirya chápáli.
To swear falsely,	Jhúta kirya khabar,	Mitcha shomai láno,	Micha kirya cháli.
To preserve,	Báchá korinu,	...	...
To destroy,	Nosht korinu,	...	...
To hurt beings,	Chót dinu,	...	...
To injure, deteriorate goods,	Kharáb konu,	...	...
To benefit,	Bhalo konu,	Ghám khlámno,	Elka páli.
To wrong,	Búra konu,	Hamma khlámno,	Má elka páli.
To converse,	Bolinu,	Raino,	Dópli.
To be silent,	Chúp honu,	Srithánо,	Chikáli.
To silence,	Chúp korinu,	Srithá hotno,	Chika páli.
To make a noise,	Gondogol korinu,	Gondogol khajámno,	Gondogol páli.
To laugh,	Hásinu,	Minino,	Léngli.
To smile,	Múski hasinu,	Minisláno,	Atoïsa léngli.
To weep,	Rónu,	Gapno,	Khárli.
To moan,	...	...	...
To sob,	...	...	...
To squint,	Téra dékhinu,	Khónká naino,	Kéóká khángli.
To sneeze,	Chíkinu,	Háchúno,	Háchuli.
To cough,	Khásinu,	Gújúno,	Shúli.
To swallow,	Ghótinu,	Molongno,	Níli.
To belch,	Dhikar konu,	Gotno,	Dikáróléli.
To fart,	Pat korinu,	Kiphaino,	Lípaili.
To spit,	Thúk phálinu,	Mújúno,	Thópchi chibli.
To chew,	Chobibar,	Chouno,	Chobaili.
To bite,	Kátibar,	...	...
To kiss, give,	Chúma dibar,	Koudom hotno,	Chúma pili.
To kiss, take,	Chúma libar,	Koudom láno,	Chúma rhúli.
To copulate,	Choda chodi korinu,	Khoïno,	Lúli.
To cause to impregnate or cover, give male,	Jhág dibar,	Gúnáng hotno,	Dánkha tapipula.
To conceive in womb,	Gau bhári hobar,	Bisha phúlino,	Hémáng dhámli.
To digest in stomach,	Homjom konu,	Gilino,	Póch páli.
To lick,	Chátinu,	Chaláno,	Dééli.
To suck,	Chúsinu,	Chupno,	Chúüli.
To see,	Dékhibar,	Naino,	Khángli. Dóli.
To hear,	Súnibar,	Khanáno,	Hénli.
To taste,	Chákibar,	Cháláno,	Chákhili.
To smell,	Súngibar,	Srúk húno, Maunám chúno,	Nhúli.

English.	*Kocch.*	*Bodo.*	*Dhimál.*
To touch,	Chúbar,	Dángno : chétnaino,	Vérli.
To piss,	Mútibar,	Hásúno,	Chichóli.
To shit,	Hágibar,	Khíno,	Líshili.
To eat,	Khábar,	Jáno,	Cháli.
To drink,	Píbar,	Lúngno,	Ámli.
To cook,	Róndhón konu,	...	...
To sleep,	Sútibar,	Múdúno,	Jimli.
To wake, self,	Jágibar,	Sidi manno,	Chótámli.
To wake another,	Jágtá konu,	Phajáno,	Lhópáli.
To dream,	Sopon dékhibar,	Simáng naino,	Sopón dóli.
To breathe,	Sáns libar,	Hángláno,	U'kás rhúli.
To sweat,	Jhóshibar,	Galamno,	Bhémli.
To palpitate, tremble,	Kámpibar,	Modom mouno,	Phirli.
To make easy, facilitate,	Sohoj korinu,	Généö khajámno,	Hól páli.
To make difficult,	Kosor korinu,	Gopráp khlámno,	Kárákárá páli.
To risk, put in hazard,	...	...	...
To escape,	Báchinu,	Góno, gobaino,	Bán chili.
To save, deliver,	Rakhya korinu,	Gón hotno,	Báncbá páli.
To stay with, abide by,	Dosor robar,	Lagoché tháno,	Etánóng hili.
To desert, abandon, leave,	Tyág korinu,	Nágárno,	Bhináng hadóli.
To change, be mutable,	Asthir hobar,	Sláino ?	Shóöli.
To make, change, alter,	Bodol korinu,	Slái jalaino,	Shóö páli.
To meet, fall in with,	Bhétinu,	Lagomanno,	Dúsúli.
To part, go apart,	Júda génu,	Gúbún gúbún thángno,	Bhináng hadóli.
To come together,	Song ásinu,	Lagoché phoino,	Dósá léli.
To bring together,	Song lí ásinu,	Mislaino, Lagoché danno,	Miso laili.
To separate, segregate,	Júda korinu,	Gúbún gúbún khlámno,	Bhináng páli.
To crowd, make crowd,	Bhír korinu,	Mánushí phútúmno,	Díáng shóli.
To contrive, devise,	Júgti korinu,	Búddhi khlámno,	Búddhi páli.
To compel, constrain, oblige,	...	...	...
To leave, option,	...	...	...
To choose, take option,	...	...	...
To choose, select,	Chún koribar,	Sai khono,	Salténg chúmli.
To copy, imitate, pattern,	Nokol korinu,	Nokol khlámno,	Nokol páli.
To imitate, take off, mock,	...	...	...
To share out, distribute in shares,	Bántinu,	Ránno,	Bánta páli.
To produce,	Kamai konu,	U'ptan khlámno,	Kamai páli.
To consume,	Khoroch korinu,	Háni khlámno,	Bai páli.
To gain,	Náfa khábar,	...	Náfa cháli.
To loose,	Noksán khábar,	...	Naksán cháli.
To work, labour,	Kismot konu,	Habba mouno,	Léng kámli ?
To play, amuse oneself,	Khélinu,	...	...
To rest,	...	...	...
To be tired,	Thákinu,	...	...
To tire, another,	Tháka korinu,	...	...
To adorn,	Songot korinu,	Majáng khlámno,	Elka páli.
To disfigure,	Bérúp korinu,	Shápma khajámno,	Má elka páli.
To dress, self,	Kapra pinibar,	Hí gánno, Hí gúmnó,	Dhába gúpli.
To dress, another,	...	Hí gán hotno,	Dhába gúp páli.
To undress, self,	Kapra phálinu,	Hí khúno,	Dhába chibli.
To undress, another,	...	Hí khú hotno,	Dhábá chip páli.

English.	*Kocch.*	*Bodo.*	*Dhimál.*
To guide, direct,	...	Lámá dinthino,	Dáma dop pili.
To misguide,	...	...	Dámá awaili.
To lead,	Agot génu,	Sigouno, Sigang lángno,	Lampáng hadéli.
To follow,	Pacho ásinu,	Yúno phoino,	Nhú choleli.
To clasp, embrace,	Kól korinu,	Gobáno,	Báali.
To baptise, name,	Nám rákhibár,	Múng dóno,	Ming táli.
To wean,	An khilibár,	Abú nágár hotno,	Dúdú láp-páli.
To marry,	Bibah korinu,	Habba khlámno,	Béhé chumáli.
To divorce,	...	Hinjou nágárno,	Béwal-dú-pili.
To bury,	Máti dibár,	Phopno,	Libli.
To burn, corpse,	Phún kinu,	Shouno,	Dúüli.
To mourn, for dead,	...	...	...
To inherit,	Wársi bhág libár,	...	...
To acquire,	Kamainu,	...	...
To serve menially,	Chákori korinu,	...	...
To cheat, defraud,	Thaginu,	Chaléno ?	Chóléli.
To steal,	Chúri korinu,	Sikhou khouno,	Chúri páli.
To rob,	Dáká márinu,	Lúthino,	Dáka páli.
To murder,	Khún korinu,	Shithatno,	Khún páli.
To beat,	Pítinu,	Shúno,	Dánghaili.
To maim,	Ghäïl konu,	...	...
To commit rape,	...	...	...
To commit adultery,	...	...	...
To promise, give and take promise,	Korál korinu, dibár and libár,	Korál láno and hotno,	Korál pili and rhúli.
To impignorate,	Bandhak rakhinu,	Bandak hotno,	Bándá pili.
To redeem, pledge,	...	Bandak labono,	Bánda. U'láng páli.
To complain, tax with wrong-doing,	Nálish korinu,	...	...
To sue, legally,	...	...	...
To prosecute, ditto,	...	...	...
To examine, try legally,	Tajvij konu,	...	...
To prove, establish judicially,	Sábit konu,	...	...
To decide, decree, ditto,	Húkam dibár,	...	...
To sentence, condemn,	...	...	...
To fine,	Doṇr libár,	*Doṇr láno,*	*Doṇr rhúli.*
To punish,	Sásti dibár,	*Sásti hotno,*	*Sásti pili.*
To hang (per collum),	Phánsi dibár,	...	...
To imprison,	Kaid korinu,	...	...
To give physic,	Oshod dibár,	*Múli hotno,*	*Oshor am páli.*
To take physic,	Oshod libár,	*Múli láno,*	*Oshor amli.*
To bleed, let blood,	Phust libár,	...	...
To pay taxes,	Khajana dibár,	Khajana hotno,	Khajana pili.
To levy taxes,	Khajana libár,	Khajana láno,	Khajana rhúli.
To let,	Bhára libár,	Bibán láno,	Bhára rhúli.
To hire,	Bhára dibár,	Bibán hotno,	Bhára pili.
To appraise,	Bhou konu,	Bhou khlámno,	...
To cost,	Molinu,	Bhau jááno,	Dám jéngli.
To buy,	Kinibar,	Baino,	Chóöli.
To sell,	Béchibar,	Phanno,	Pilli.
To exchange, barter,	Bodol konu,	Slaino,	Shóli.
To calculate, reckon,	Gonti korinu,	Shyánno,	Gan hili.
To lend, money,	Dhár dinu,	Bináne hotno,	Dhár pili.
To borrow,	Dhár linu,	Bináne láno,	Dhár rhúli.
To owe,	...	...	...

English.	*Kocch.*	*Bodo.*	*Dhimál.*
To pay,	Chúkti korinu,	...	Dhár sújili.
To give credit,	...	...	...
To weigh,	Toulinu,	Chúno,	Dóngli.
To measure,	Nápinu,	Chúno,	Dóngli.
To build house,	...	Nóö lúno,	Sá dámli.
To quarry stone,	...	Onthai joukhono,	...
To make bricks,	I'nt párinu,	Ithá dááno,	...
To engrave on stone or metal,	...	...	...
To fuse, make melt,	...	Gíli hotno,	Gili páli.
To melt, self,	Galinu,	Gilino,	Giléli.
To mould, cast,	...	...	...
To manufacture,	Banaibár,	Dááno,	Thirli.
To dye,	Rong dibár,	Rong hotno,	Rong pili.
To grind (corn, &c.),	Písinu,	Yúnno,	Mhaili.
To give edge,	Bár dinu,	Bár hotno, Yúnno,	Bár pili. Laili.
To blunt edge,	...	Hútromno,	Bhoi páli.
To mine,	...	...	...
To smelt,	...	...	...
To refine,	...	...	...
To polish,	Chikon konu,	Gochong khajámno,	Rhíwa páli. Manjili.
To glaze, varnish,	Chikon konu,	...	...
To hammer,	...	Dúnó,	Tóöli.
To saw,	...	Chin khouno,	Chééli.
To sew, stitch,	Silai konu,	Shúno,	Jóóli.
To mend clothes,	...	...	...
To make clothes,	...	...	...
To weave,	...	Hí dááno, Dááno,	Thírli.
To spin,	Sút kátinu,	Khúndúng luno,	Katéli.
To knit,	...	Jéékháno,	Púïli.
To tan leather,	Sichíbar,	Chúngno,	...
To express sugar or oil,	Périnu,	Phérétno,	Péréli.
To shave,	Múndinu,	Chimno,	Kámli.
To bathe,	Snán konu,	Dúgwino,	Chéüli.
To wash clothes,	...	Chúno,	Phéli.
To dry clothes,	...	Lámno,	Shénli.
To cook,	Rondhon konu,	...	...
To roast,	...	Yóphránno, Youno,	Hóli.
To boil,	...	Chongno,	Khinli.
To fry or grill,	...	Hángno,	Hóli.
To bake,	...	...	...
To brew,	...	Chóngno,	Yú gaili.
To distil,	...	Chouno Jousouno,	Chúaili.
To turn with lathe,	...	...	...
To print cloth,	Chápibar,	...	...
To make rope,	...	Cháno,	Bataili.
To bleach,	...	...	...
To make basketry,	...	Hépno,	Gothaili.
To paint,	Ronginu,	Rong hotno,	Gabaili.
To sing,	Gáinu,	Rojápno,	Lééli.
To play music,	Bájá konu,	Damno,	Bééli.
To sculpture,	...	...	...
To cement, glue,	Sátinu,	Chitapno,	...
To paste,	Lépibár,	Léï hotno,	Léi pili.
To plaster walls,	Lépibár,	Litno,	Ló pili.

English.	*Kocch.*	*Bodo.*	*Dhimál.*
To breed, cattle,	...	Galai gophatno,	Pósh hili.
To fatten, ditto,	...	Gúphúng khlámno,	Dhám páli.
To feed, simply,	...	Jáhotno,	Chá páli.
To slaughter,	...	Danthatno,	Pálli.
To flay,	...	Bigúr khúno,	Dháló lhóli.
To shear,	...	Háchó gárno,	Chó hili.
To milk,	...	Dúdú chorotno,	Dúdú chópli.
To churn,	...	...	Móhéli.
To cultivate, agriculturally,	Khóti konu,	Shyám dáno,* Hú mouno,	Ling páli.
To dig,	Khan dibar,	Jouno,	Tóóli.
To plough,	Jótibar, chásinu,	Húmouno,	...
To harrow,	Héngá kona,	Moi hotno,	Moi pili.
To manure,	Sár dibár,	Sár hotno,	Sár pili.
To sow,	Chítibár,	Phúno, Gáino,	Dálli.
To reap,	Kátibar,	Háno,	Chééli.
To transplant,	Rópibar,	Gaino ?	Thiuli.
To weed,	Chikan phálinu,	Chékhá dángno,	Chalai upli.
To irrigate,	Síchinu,	Doï hotno,	Chí pili.
To desiccate,	...	Doï shátno,	Sháp pili.
To thrash,	Pítinu,	...	...
To winnow,	Súp korinu,	Shibno,	Om yápli.
To stack,	Kalián konu,	Húngno,	Jóm páli.
To germinate or sprout,	Phútinu,	Rojónó,	Yóli.
To grow,	Boḍhinu,	Gajo jáúno,	Hánli.
To flower,	Phúlinu,	Bárno,	Bárli.
To fruit,	Phalinu,	Thaino,	Shéli.
To ripen,	Pákinu,	Monno,	Minli.
To rot,	Saḍinu,	Chóóno,	Aili.
To blow, as wind,	Bohinu,	Bohino,	Báhili.
To blow, apply breath,	Phúkinu,	Chúno,	Mhúli.
To shine, as sun,	Chamkinu,	Gongno, Modinno,	Rhíwáli. Chilkáli.
To rain,	Bórsibár,	Nókhá háuo,	Wailéli.
To thunder,	Gargibár,	Khoromno,	Dúïli.
To lighten, flash, as lightning,	Chomkon korinu,	Múphlámno,	Rhíwáli.
To hail,	Páthar porinu,	Korthai gúklénno,	...
To snow,	Hém poḍinu,	Hém galaino,	Hém longli.
To freeze, congeal,	Jomibár,	Dákbákáno,	Jómli.
To thaw,	Gilibár,	Gilino,	Gáléli.
To burn, self,	Jólinu,	Wát júngno,	Tíli.
To burn, another,	...	Sou gárno,	Tí páli.
To glow, be of a glow,	Dáhakinu,	Wát jong balóno,	Lhóli.
To make glow,	Dah konu,	Wát chublouno,	Lhó páli.
To light, candle or fire,	Jolot konu,	Júng hotno, Lagaino,	Tíï páli.
To extinguish,	Nibhil konu,	Khúmatno,	Nibhaili.
To illumine, a room,	U'jjála konu,	Shráng khajámno,	Phara páli.
To darken, ditto,	A'ndhér konu,	Khámshi khlámno,	Dáp páli.
To flow, water,	Bohinu,	Bohi lángno,	Bahili.
To make flow, let off,	...	Bohi hotno,	Bahi páli.
To come,	A'sibar,	Phoino,	Léli.
To go,	Jábár,	Thángno,	Hadéli.
To remain,	Robár,	Tháno,	Hili.
To return,	Ghúribár,	Phoï phinno,	Gúrai hili ?

* To cut down the forest, a process equivalent among this people to cultivation.

English.	*Kocch.*	*Bodo.*	*Dhimál.*
To approach,	Logod ásinu,	Khatiou phoino,	Chóngsho hadéli.
To retire, go off,	Dúré jábár,	Gatchán thángno,	Bhinång hadéli.
To journey,	Játrá konu,	Jatra khlámno,	Játra páli.
To arrive,	Pohúnchino,	Srikhino, Chono,	Léli.
To depart,	Chalia génu,	Thángno,	Hadéli.
To enter,	Bhitor sonáinu,	Sing hopno,	Lipta wángli.
To go out,	Báhir nikalnu,	Bahir thángno,	Báhir oléli.
To make haste,	Jold konu,	Gakri khlámno,	Dhim páli.
To delay,	Bilombh konu,	Láshi láshi khlámno,	Bilomb páli.
To walk, as quadruped or man,	Béránu,	Thábaino,	Higilli.
To fly, as bird,	Uribár,	Birno,	Bhírli.
To creep, as insect,	Rénginu,	Mán baino,	Súrsúraili.
To pace or stride, as man,	Kodom konu,	Thabaino,	Higilli.
To run,	Dourinu,	Khotno,	Dhápli.
To run away, flee,	Bhágainu,	Khat lángno,	Khátli.
To gallop, horse,	...	...	...
To trot, ditto,	...	...	...
To leap,	Tirpanu,	Bátno,	Tónli.
To hop, skip,	Kúdinu,	Bájalono,	Hiá gili.
To kick,	Lát márinu,	Jónó,	Lát hili.
To scratch,	Achúránu,	Khúrchino,	Kháli.
To sting, as bee,	Binnu,	Júyúno,	Chúli.
To strike with hand,	Márinu,	Shúno,	Dáng haili.
To strike, beat, with stick,	Márinu,	Shúno,	Dáng haili.
To cut,	Kátinu,	Dáno, Háno, Phono,*	Pá pili.
To thrust or push,	Dhókánu,	Nágárétno, Chojaretno,	Dhé kaili.
To pull,	Tánnu,	Bónó,	Tán páli.
To catch, as thrown,	Dhorinu,	Chap khángno,	Bimli.
To throw,	Phenkinu, Dálinu,	Gár hotno,	Jhátéli.
To throw away,	Aphálinu,	Gar hotno?	Chipli.
To pinch,	Nóchinu,	Khépno,	Chim thaili.
To swim,	Porinu,	Santréno,	Nóïli.
To drown, sink, self,	Dúbinu,	Hapno,	Dúbili.
To make sink or drown,	...	Hap hotno,	Dúbi páli.
To stand,	Tháru honu,	Gochongno,	Jápli.
To fall,	Poribár,	Gataino,	Lóngli.
To make stand,	Thár konu,	Góchóng hotno,	Jáp páli.
To make fall or throw down,	Thélia phalánu,	Nákh laino,	Théliténg longpáli.
To sit down,	Bosinu,	Chóöno,	Yongli.
To get up,	Uthinu,	Jhi khángno,	Lhóli.
To lie down,	Ausánu,	Súnatno,	Auséli.
To take up,	Uthaibár,	Daikhangno,	Tothéli. Lhó páli.
To set down,	Rákhibar,	Danno,	Táάli.
To put, place, set in place,	Rákhibar,	Danno,	Táάli.
To fetch, bring,	Léásibár,	Lábono,	Chúmténg léli.
To take away,	Léjábar,	Lángno,	Chúm poli.
To carry, bear,	Bókibár,	Báno,	Phúli.

* Phono, to fell timber; Háno, to cut culinarily; Dáno, to cut generally.

English.	*Kocch.*	*Bodo.*	*Dhimál.*
To convey away, transport,	Bókléjábár,	Bálángno,	Phúchúmli.
To mount, vehicle,	Chorinu,	Yóng khatno,	Tángli.
To alight from,	Utarinu,	Gánó,	Khúli.
To climb, go up tree or hill,	Chorinu,	Yong khatno,	Tángli.
To descend, come down,	U'tarinu, Lámbibar,	Gáno,	Khúli.
To stay, stop, detain, *a.*	At kaibar chenkinu,	Thán hotno, Hop tano,	Táá páli.
To let go, suffer to depart, *a.*	Jábar dibár,	Thang hotno,	Háli pili.
To stop, stay, be staid, self, *n.*	Atkinu, Tókinu,	Thaptáno,	Táli, hili.
To hinder, impede, prevent, obstruct, *a.*	Chénkinu, Rokinu,	Homtáno, Thápta hotno,	Rholi. Táá páli.
To put a stop to, *a.*	Thám bhánu,	Thán hotno,	Rhóli. Táä páli.
To set a-going, *a,*	Cholon konu,	Tháng hotno,	Dingil pili.
To begin, have beginning,	N. Sharú hobar,	Hángno,	Mhoïli, Téngli.
To commence, make beginning,	A. Sharú konu,	Háng hotno, Moujenno,	Mhoï páli. Teng páli.
To end, have end,	N. Tamám hobar,	Japno, Khángno,	Hóïli.
To finish, perfect, complete, make end of,	A. Tamám koribar,	Mou japno, Jap hotno,	Hóï páli.
To have hold, possess,	Bós korinu,	...	...
To lack, want,	Obhág hobar,	...	...
To hold, retain, keep,	Rákhibar,	...	...
To cede, give up, relinquish,	Chárinu,	Nágárno,	Lháli.
To hold, have in hand,	Dhorinu, Rákhinu,	Akhaino, Rákhino,	Khúrtá rákhéli.
To grasp, hold forcibly,	Dhorinu,	Hômno,	Rimli.
To relax grasp,	Háth dhila konu,	Akhai phúrúnno,	Khúr dhila páli.
To let go, quit hold of,	Chári dinu,	Nágárno,	Lháli.
To dispossess, take forcibly, seize,	Kária libar,	Homno,	Ghinli. Rimli.
To take simply,	Libar,	Láno,	Rhúli.
To give, transfer by gift,	Dán konu,	Hotno,	Pili.
To transfer generally,	Dibar, Porbos sompibár,	Hotno,	Pili.
To receive, obtain, get,	Pábár, Libar,	Manno, Láno,	Nénli. Rhúli.
To acquire, earn, gain by own labour,	Kámápu,	Kamai khlámno,	Kámaili.
To find, discover,	Pánú, Pábár,	Manno,	Nénli.
To lose,	Harái konu,	Gómáno,	Mháli.
To search for,	Onsibár,	Naigrúno,	Bhóli. Rhéli.
To intrust with, commit to,	Sómpibár,	...	...
To conceal, hide,	Lúki rákhinu,	Hikmáno,	Mhó páli.
To reveal, disclose,	Pargot konu,	Dinthino,	Olé páli.

English.	*Kocch.*	*Bodo.*	*Dhimál.*
To cover, simply,	Dhákibár,	Khopno, Jokhlopno,	Thúmli.
To uncover,	Dháka phálinu,	Bót lápno,	Lá páli.
To lie hid, be hid,	Lúkibár, Chhipibar,	Khakmáno,	Mhóli.
To show oneself,	Nikalibár,	Núјáno,	Oléli.
To show, exhibit, display goods,	...	Dón thaino,	Dópáli.
To put up, put by,	Rákh chhorinu,	Chúk klápno,	Thúm pili.
To hoard, save, amass,	Songtibar,	Phútúmno,	Jom páli.
To spend, consume, use,	Khoroch konu,	Gárno, Háni khlámno,	Bai páli.
To waste prodigally,	...	...	...
To furnish house,	Sájanu,	Nóö chóno,	Sá lé páli.
To load, lade,	Ládinu,	Bá hotno,	Ladai páli.
To unload,	Bhár útárinu,	Yúngno, Thúngi khéóno,	...
To pack,	Mót bándhinu,	Thúngi kháno,	Jóm páli.
To unpack,	Mót khúlinu,	Thúngi khéóno,	Khaili.
To tie knot,	Gánthinu,	...	...
To untie knot,	Gánth kholinu,	...	...
To bind,	Bándhinu,	Kháno,	Jingli.
To unbind,	Kholinu,	Khóóno,	Khaili.
To tighten,	Bhíribar,	Garra khlámno,	Bhirili.
To loosen,	Dhíl koribár,	Rúnno Phúrúnno,	Dhil páli.
To erect, put up,	Khada kono,	Thúno, Pochongno,	Jap páli.
To pull down,	Pária phálinu,	Kúklaino,	Lóng páli.
To sheathe, weapon,	...	Chono,	Wháli.
To unsheathe,	...	Bokhóno,	Holi.
To mark,	Nishán dibár,	Chin hotno,	Chin páli.
To erase,	Métinu,	Khomatno,	...
To stain,	Dágh dibar,	Dágaino,	Dágéli.
To let in,	Bhitorásibár dibar,	Sing lá bono,	Lipta wángli pili.
To let out,	Báhir jábar dibár,	Báhir lá bono,	Báhir oleli pili.
To expel, drive out,	Nikálya dinu,	Tan hotno,	Olé páli.
To wring, wet clothes,	Nichóribar,	Chépno,	...
To wrench,	Aintinu,	Bophaino,	Thúrli.
To annex, add to,	Jodinu,	Jodinu,	Jom páli.
To denex, detach,	Alag konu,	Gúbún danno,	Bhináng páli.
To move, self,	Cholinu, Hilinu,	Thabáino, Mouno?	Léli.
To move, other,	Cholon-hilon-korinu,	...	Lé páli.
To remove, displace,	...	Gúbún nupthi lángno,	Bhináng chol. Lé páli.
To be stationary,	Thír hobár,	Gochongno,	Japli.
To make stationary,	Thír koribár,	Posongno,	Jap páli.
To appear, come in sight,	...	Núno,	Lhóli.
To disappear,	...	Hapno,	Dúbili.
To rise, sun,	Uday konu,	Chouno,	Lhóli.
To set, sun,	Asti konu,	Dédénno,	Dúbili.
To rise, ascend,	Uthinu,	Jhikhopno,	Lhóli.
To raise, lift,	Uthya kónu,	Boklopno,	Lló páli.
To sink, descend, *n.*	Dúbibar,	Hapno,	Dúbili.
To make sink, depress,	...	Chómno,	Dúbi páli.
To advance, go on,	A'gá jábar,	Douláugno?	Lámpáng hadóli.

English.	*Kocch.*	*Bodo.*	*Dhimál.*
To retrograde,	Páche ásibar,	Inslotno,	Nhucholi. Khángli?
To vibrate, shake, *n.*,	Hilibár,	Mouno,	Dailong lèli. Phirli.
To make shake, *a.*,	...	Champuno,	Léé páli. Phir páli.
To press, by own weight,	Dábinu,	Hap chono,	...
To compress, squeeze,	Chîpinu,	Chétno,	Répli.
To contain, hold in,	Sóndibár,	Chúno, Hapno,	Wángli?
To sustain, hold up,	Thámbhibár,	Thap tháno,	Tékili.
To stick, adhere, *n.*,	Lagibár,	Bi thángno,	Tépli.
To affix, attach, *a.*,	Sátibár,	Shithapno,	Té páli.
To come off, *n.*,	Uthinu,	Gúgáno,	Lháli.
To take off, detach, *a.*,	...	Botlapno,	Lhá páli.
To increase, self,	Badibar,	Détno,	Dhámli.
To make increase, add to,	Bodokonu,	Phédétno,	Dhám páli.
To decrease, self,	Ghotibár,	Dúïno, Shémno,	Shibli. Mhoili.
To make decrease, subtract from,	Ghotia horibar,	Phédúïno,	Mhoi páli.
To divide,	Khána kháni-konu,	Gúbún gúbún ránno,	Bánta páli.
To expand, self,	Phútinu,	Bárshráno,	Phútéli.
To open, other,	Khúlinu,	Khéöno,	Héli.
To close, self,	Múnjinu,	Khop jopno,	Chobli.
To shut, other,	Bond korinu,	Jókh lopno,	Gipli.
To exhale, evaporate, self,	Báph uthinu,	Khúndè khalángno,	Dhúá lhóli.
To exude, ditto,	Chùya podinu,	Bidé, yúng khatno,	Oléli.
To absorb, ditto,	Sósibar,	Chopno,	Chúli.
To sprinkle,	Chitanu,	Shátno,	Tirthira páli.
To moisten,	Bhijinu,	Phichino,	Jhá páli.
To soak,	Súsya khilibar,	Chi trono, Chi hapno,	Jhá páli.
To make dry,	Súkha konu,	Rán hotno,	Séng páli.
To be wet,	Bhijá hobar,	Gíchi jáäno,	Jháli.
To be dry,	Súkna hobar,	Ránno,	Séngli.
To filtrate,	Chénka konu,	Chogorno,	Chúaili.
To flash,	Chómkibar,	Chul gouno,	Rhiwáli.
To blaze,	...	Jong douno,	Méhtili.
To be extinct,	Nibhil hobar,	Gomatno,	Kombili.
To extinguish,	Nibhil korinu,	Khúmatno,	Nibhaili.

PROPER NAMES.

Dhimál Males.—Undo, Gúmbór, Jidbor, Dóda, Bhônda, Usóp, Endá, Méndú, Búmbai.

Dhimál Females.—Apchi, Dólóï, Sújóï, Salóï, Phirsóï.

Bodo Males.—Gijan, Moshto, Phabú, Birna, Jinkháp, Gongár, Theöphai, Laidar, Hajo, Gádar, Jónti, Gakháng, Nádong, Mélá.

Bodo Females.—Túlút, Mairi, Jijiri, Bújin, Khóm, Rondini.

PART II.—GRAMMAR.

ORTHOGRAPHY.

I MUST begin with the remark that I do not propose to say anything of the Kócch Grammar, which is wholly corrupt Bengálí. The reasons which have induced me to give the Kócch Vocabulary are stated elsewhere.* The following remarks will therefore apply solely to the Bódo and Dhimál languages—languages which, as it appears to me, have preserved to a wonderful extent their primitive raciness, both in vocables and in structure. Neither of them possesses, nor ever did possess, any alphabet or books, and I have consequently been left at liberty to apply to them any system of letters that might seem most advisable; for various reasons I have postponed the Nágari to the Roman, which latter I have, I hope, employed in a manner sufficiently conformable to that recognised by the Society,† except that, having no actual or prospective occasion to employ Arabic or Persian words or sounds, I have uniformly expressed the Indian *k* by the like English letter. The vowels are sounded as on the Continent of Europe and in Scotland—not as in England; and the graver or lengthened sound of each is denoted by an accent or mark above—thus *é*, a very long sound, in some rare instances, by reduplication as well as accent. A few sounds of this latter kind occur both in the Bódo and Dhimál languages, and in the former they subserve the important purpose of distinguishing the different senses of otherwise similar

* I have failed to get at the original and true speech of this race, whose ancient tongue is fast merging in Bengálí.

† For Mécch read Bôdo, *passim*. Mécch is a name imposed by strangers. This people call themselves Bodo, which, of course, is the proper designation. See note at Part III. Asiatic Society of Bengal, under whose auspices this essay was published.

words: thus, háno, 'to cut;' háäno, 'to be able;' jáno, 'to eat;' jáäno, 'to be.' Instances of this kind are rare in the Bódo, and rarer in the Dhimál language. The Bódo and Dhimál tongues have an easy and flowing enunciation, which is readily represented by our letters. Compound consonant sounds are rare—any such compounds as the Sanskrit ksha, &c., unknown—aspirates common.

The nasal *n*, denoted by me by a dot above the letter (*ṅ*), is fully as common as in U'rdú and Hindí, and is not unfrequently complexed into a harsher sound, which I have denoted by *gn*. Two concurrent vowels are always to be understood as a diphthong* with one blended and long sound, unless when the second vowel is doubly dotted (*ö*), and in these cases, which are common in Bodo and Dhimál, each vowel is to have a perfect and independent utterance. The naso-guttural French *é* is frequent in Dhimál, and has sometimes a prolonged and very harsh sound, which I cannot represent otherwise than by reduplication and accent, thus éécha, 'a goat.' *Y* is always a consonant. In Bodo *n* is often prefixed to words beginning with a vowel, as Akai Nakaï, and in this tongue the use of *ch* for *j*, of *t* for *d*, of *k* for *g*, are commutations constantly occurring, but deemed vulgarisms.

Articles.

There is no article, definite or indefinite, in the Bodo or Dhimál tongue. The demonstrative pronouns *this* and *that* usually, and the numeral *one* more rarely, stand in lieu of articles.

Substantives.

Nouns, like verbs, have only *one* regimen or mode of declension; nor is that single uniform mode perplexed with any refinements expressive of gender. Declension is accomplished not by inflection, of which, strictly speaking, there is hardly a trace, but by affixes, or rather post-fixes, analogous to the U'rdú and Hindí post-positions. Number is similarly expressed, that is, by post-positions. In Bodo there are clearly

Gender. Case. Number.

* I use three, *á* makes au, *é*, ai, and *ó*, ou, *e.g.*, hawfinch, *aye*, *aye*, *however*. See note at p. 82.

but two numbers, and I think also in Dhimál, though in the latter I have met with some vague traces of a dual, which further research may establish. In Bodo the word phúr, and in Dhimál the word galai, post-fixed simply to the noun, express the plural, thus, B., gotho, 'a child;' gotho phúr, 'children;' Dh., chan, 'a child;' chan galai, 'children.' These words have, I believe, no meaning whatever.

Gender. By turning to the Vocabulary it will be seen that the Bodo and Dhimál tongues both possess a great variety of substantive sexual terms, which usually suffice, as in English, to denote all that is needful in the distinction of sex among human beings. There are exceptions, however, to this rule; and then the defect of specific terms is supplied by periphrasis. Thus the Bodo tongue has no simple words equivalent to the English boy and girl, and the sex of minors is therefore expressed thus: 'man-child,' 'woman-child,' or híwá gotho, hinjou gotho. In Dhimál, wájan and béjan are simple and exact equivalents for 'boy' and 'girl.' The word chan, which properly means the young of all creatures, is likewise used in Dhímál to express 'boy,' in opposition to chamdi, or 'girl,' which last word affords the only and faint trace in Dhimál (none in Bodo) of that happy facility of converting male into female words, by mere variation of the terminal letter or syllable, which characterises U'rdú and Hindí. Sex among animals, generally, exclusive of human beings, is expressed in Bodo by the post-fixes jolá and jó, and in Dhimál by the prefixes dánkhá and mahani, equivalent to 'male' and 'female;' thus B., múshú *bos*; múshú-jolá, 'a bull;' múshú-jó, 'a cow.' Dh., piá, dánkhá piá, and mahani piá respectively. There are likewise in both languages a variety of specific terms expressive of sex among the domesticated and familiar animals, as in English and other languages. These may be found in the Vocabulary. They have no grammatical effect or character whatever, and this remark may be generalised or applied to the whole subject of gender in Bodo and in Dhimál.

The gender of substantives consequently has no influence at all on adjectives or on verbs.

Case. Cases in Bodo and Dhimál are formed entirely by postpositions. There is no inflection whatever. Cases are numerous; not less than nine were given to me. But all simple and direct languages which decline their nouns by means of pre- or post-positions have an almost unlimited field for the multiplication of cases. I apprehend that the companionative is a doubtful case, and that the ablative and instrumental are, normally, but one case, and also the dative and objective, and that on or upon is no case at all. In that event there would be only five cases, for the vocative seems wanting.

To form the plural it is merely required to supply the word phúr or galai in Bodo and Dhimál respectively, between the noun and the post-position.

All nouns substantive are declined according to the following example:—

English.	*Bodo.*	*Dhimál.*
N. A man,	Híwá,	Wával,
G. Of a man,	Híwáni,	Wával ko.
D. To a man,	Híwá no,	Wával éng,
Ac. A man,	Híwá kho,	Wával éng,
? On a man,	Híwá chou,	Wával ko rhúto,
Voc. O man!	Caret?	Caret?
Ab. From a man,	Híwáni phrá,	Wával sho,
Ins. By a man,	Híwá jong,	Wával dong.
Loc. In a man,	Híwá há or ou or nou,	Wával tá.
Comp. With a man,	Híwá lago,	Wával dosa.

Plural, híwá phúr, híwá phúr ni, &c., in Bodo; and in Dhimál, wával galai, wával galai ko, &c., as in the singular. Thus it appears that in Bodo *ni* is the sign of the genitive, *no* of the dative, *kho* of the objective, *chou* of the anonymous, *phrá* of the ablative, *jong* of the instrumental, *há* or *ou* or *nou* of the locative, and *lago* of the companionative; and that in Dhimál *ko, éng, éng, rhúto, sho, dong, tá,* and *dosa* are their equivalents. Number.

In Latin and other languages, prepositions govern a variety of cases. Post-positions are the equivalents of this part of speech in Eastern tongues and in the above declension. It appears that the Bodo phrá, equal to the Latin ab, and the Dhimál rhúto, equal to the Latin supra, govern the genitive, that is, require the sign of the genitive, even while occupying the place of the ablative in declensions. This is an anomaly, going far perhaps to prove that phrá and rhúto are not truly signs of case or declension, but rather post-positions in the general sense (like some of the others perhaps), that is, *not* signs of declension.

ADJECTIVES.

Adjectives in both these languages precede or follow the substantives, with all the simple directness of English and with no more effect on the grammatical structure; thus in Bodo, an
1 2 1 2 1 2 1 2
ugly son, shápmá bishá, an ugly daughter, shapmá bishú; a
1 2 2 1 1 2 2 1
good boy, híwá-gotho ghám, a good girl, hinjou-gotho ghám;
1 2 3 2 3 1 1 2 3
good child-ren, gotho-phúr ghám; the sport of good children,
2 3 1 1 2 1
ghám gotho-phúrni khél. In Dhimál, a naughty boy, má élka
2 1 2 1 2 1 2 3 1 2
wájan, a naughty girl, ma elka béjan; good child-ren, elka chan
3 1 2 3 2 3 1
galai; the play of good children, élká chan galai ko khél.
1 2 3 2 3 1
To naughty boys. Bodo. Hamma gotho-phúr no. Dhimál. Má
2 3 1
élka wájan-galai éng.

Nouns, substantive and adjective, of the simple forms abound in both languages, and both tongues are miserably deficient in abstract forms, whether derivative or primitive, such as childhood from child, greatness from great, and sex, age, &c. So nearly all compounds are wanting in these tongues, that is, that vast class of words which in Greek, Latin, and Sanskrit are formed either from a noun or verb compounded with privative, intensitive, qualitative, aggregative or disjunctive particles, or from two nouns or a noun and verb mixed; anarchy, astronomy, agriculture, nirvritti, pravritti, dwibháshya, vibritásih, hémáchal. Such words, as a class of terms, are wanting, though the means of forming them are forthcoming, and used to a small extent. These are points however which will be best explained by consulting the copious and carefully-constructed Vocabulary. Ellipsis is carried to a great extent, both as to nouns and verbs, sometimes with, sometimes without, the sanction of concurring vowels, and often in excess of what that

sanction would cover where it exists. Long-tailed words or sesquepedalians nor Horace nor Frere ever abhorred more heartily than do these simple races of men; and when three even short words come together without a verb, one of them, the central, is almost sure to be lopt and to lose the first syllable of a dissyllable; thus, taller than all, boinobo *jou* shin, for *gajou* shin, in Bodo;
1 2 3 3 1 2
and in Dhimál, *tai bééng* for *taiko béval éng*, to his own wife. Similar ellipsis takes place constantly among the verbs, especially in Dhimál, as hánká for hadéängká, 'I will go;' jenká for jéängká, 'I will be.'

There are verbal nouns both in Bodo and Dhimál, substantives formed from the root or imperative, and adjectives from the participle. There is likewise a very useful *privative* of general application in each of these tongues, which is the word géyá of the Bodo, and mánthó or mánthúka of the Dhimál. Ongá in the former tongue (yonga if a vowel precede it) has likewise a similar function, but of less currency; and this language has, further, a *possessive* of much value, called gonáng. All these are post-fixes, and separately viewed are adverbs rather than nouns; but in composition they form adjectives from substantives, and perhaps also one class of substantives from another; thus, from dhon, 'wealth,' we have dhongéyá or dhon mánthúka, 'poor, void of wealth,' respectively in Bodo and Dhimál; and, in the former tongue, from rai speech (from speak!) we have raïnóngá or raiyongá, 'dumb,' 'speechless:' also dhongonáng, 'wealthy, possessed of 'wealth.' Again, from dharam, justice, we have dharam-géyá vel mánthúka, 'unjust' and 'injustice'? and also, in Bodo, dharamgonáng, 'just.' I am not aware that adjectives in either language are ever transmuted into adverbs, as evly from evil, haughtily from haughty. Nor have I met with any instance of a diminutive, or the means of forming one, in either tongue.

I should add, before quitting the subject of nouns, that the Bodo attempt to form abstract nouns from the simple ones by means of the post-fixes matno, sló, and blá, with a slight change of the termination of the primitive word, and that they even affirm that of these post-fixes matno belongs more properly to things, sló and blá to beings. Thus, from gajou, 'tall,' is formed gajówan matno, 'tallness;' from majáng, 'handsome,' majángan matno, 'beauty;' from gotho, 'child,' gothobla or sló, 'childhood;' from gédét, 'great,' gédét nanmatno, 'greatness.' More samples of this formation may be seen in the Vocabulary, wherein however I have left most of the abstract nouns blanks, from doubts as to the authenticity of this method of filling those blanks; abstracts are very puzzling, yet it is indispensable to test the fact of their absence at all events. The Dhimáls make no attempt to form them, but fairly avow their unqualified astonishment that anybody should seek for such strange and useless words!

Comparison.

There are no distinct words in either of these tongues expressive of the degrees of comparison, like agathos, arión, aristos, bónus, melior, optimus; 'good,' 'better,' 'best:' nor any incrementory particles serving to the same end, such as the Sanscrit 'tar, tam;' the English 'er' and 'est,' and the Latin 'or' and 'ssimus.'

The comparative and superlative degrees are formed in Bodo and in Dhimál as in Hindí and U'rdú, by words expressíve of 'than that,' 'than all,' binbō shin and boinoboshin in Bodo, and oko nhádong, sogiming ko nhádong in Dhimál, according to the following example.

English.		*Bodo.*	*Dhimál.*
Tall,	Human beings.	Gajou,	Dhángá.
Taller,		Binbo gajou shin,	O'kó nhádong dhángá.
Tallest,		Boinobo gajou shin.	Sogiming ko nhádong dhángá, or dhángá saika.
Short,		Gabai,	Bángrá.
Shorter,		Binbo gahai shin,	O'kónhádóng bángra.
Shortest,		Boinobo gabai shin or sin,	Bángrá saika.

In the above examples Binbo is compounded of the inflected form of the word Bi, 'him, it, that,' and of the euphonic particle bó. Shin or sin is 'than.' Boinobo is compounded of the word boino 'all' and bó, 'as before.' In the Dhimál series oko is the inflected form of wá, 'him' or 'that' or 'it.' Nhádong is the indeclinable 'than.' Sogiming is 'all,' an adjective, and saika, I believe, an adverb equivalent to 'very,' 'most,' or the magis vel maxime of Latin. It will be seen that in the Bodo idiom the literal style is 'that or it great than' for the comparative, and 'all great than' for the superlative, whereas in Dhimál the Hindi and Úrdú idiom is followed, 'that than great'—'all than great.' I have already adverted to the elliptical manner of speech so popular with these races. In the above examples the Bodo constantly, almost invariably, drop the middle syllable of boinobo and the first syllable of gajou and of gahai. And in like manner, the Dhimál sink the second syllable of nhádong, and the middle syllable of sogiming. If my conjecture as to the Dhimál saika be correct, we shall have in one form of the Dhimál superlative a nearly exact equivalent of the English and Latin idiom very pious, most pious, magis pius, maxime pius, except that the adverb *follows* the adjective in Dhimál.

Pronouns.

The personal, possessive, demonstrative, relative, distributive, and reflective or egoïstic (self*) pronouns will be all found in the Vocabulary. The declension of the pronouns seems to be the least imperfect part of the structure of the Bodo and Dhimál tongues, and in the latter exhibits throughout marks of genuine inflection. The regimen is the same as that for the declension of nouns; but, as I have given the latter curtly, I will, at the risk of being tedious, give the declension of the pronouns more fully.

Gender affects it not: the numbers are two; the cases nine, as before.

English.	*Bodo.*	*Dhimál.*
N. I,	A'ng,	Ká.
G. Of me,	A'ng ni,	Káng ko.
D. To me,	A'ng no,	Kéng.
Ac. Me,	A'ng kho,	Kéng.
Voc. Oh me,	Caret?,	Caret?
Loc. In me,	Anghá, ou, nou,	Káng tá.
? On me,	Angni chou,	Káng ko rhúto.
Abl. From me,	Angni phrá,	Káng sho.
Inst By me,	Ang jong,	Káng dóng.
Com. With me,	Ang lago,	Káng doşa.

* This is wanting save in the possessive form 'own.'

The pluralising particle *chúr* is not usually applied to the first person, though always to the second and third; see on.

PLURAL.

N. We,	Jong,	Kyél.
G. Of us,	Jong ni,	King ko.
D. To us,	Jong no,	King eng.
A. Us,	Jong kho,	King eng.
V. O we!	Caret?	Caret?
Loc. In us,	Jong há, ou, nou,	King tá.
? On us,	Jong ni chou,	King ko rhútá.
Ab. From us,	Jong ni phrá,	King sho.
Ins. By us,	Jong jong,	King dong.
Com. With us,	Jong lago,	King dosa.
Thou,	Nang,	Ná.
Of thee,	Nang ni,	Náng ko.
To thee,	Nang no,	Néng.
Thee,	Nang kho,	Néng.
O thou!	Caret?	Caret?
In thee,	Nang há, nou,	Náng tá.
On thee,	Nangni chou,	Náng ko rhútá.
From thee,	Nangni phrá,	Náng sho.
By thee,	Nang jong,	Náng dong.
With thee,	Nang lago,	Náng dosa.
Ye,	Nang chúr,	Nyél.
Of you,	Nang chúrni,	Ning ko.
To you,	Nang chúrno,	Ning éng.
Ye, you,	Nang chúrkho,	Ning éng.
O ye!	Caret?	Caret?
In you,	Nang chur há, ou, nou,	Ning tá.
On you,	Nang chúrni chou,	Ning ko rhúta.
From you,	Nang churni phrá,	Ning sho.
By you,	Nang chúr jong,	Ning dong.
With you,	Nang chúr dago,	Ning dosa.
He, she, it,	Bí,	Wá.
Of him,	Bini,	O'kó, wánko.
To him,	Bino,	Wéng.
Him,	Bikho,	Wéng.
O he?	Caret?	Caret?
In him,	Bihá, ou, nou,	Wáng tá.
On him,	Bini chou,	Wáng ko rhúta.
From him,	Bini phrá,	Wáng sho.
By him,	Bini jong,	Wáng dong.
With him,	Bini lago,	Wáng dosá.
They,	Bichúr,	U'bal.
Of them,	Bichúr ni,	U'bal ko.
To them,	Bichúr no,	U'bal éng.
Them,	Bichúr kho,	U'bal éng.
O they!	Caret?	Caret?
In them,	Bichúr nou,	U'bal tá.
On them,	Bichúrni chou,	U'bal ko rhúta.
From them,	Bichúrni phrá,	U'bal sho.
By them,	Bichúr jong,	U'bal dong.
With them,	Bichúr lago,	U'bal dosa.

POSSESSIVE PRONOUNS, &c.

Possessive pronouns precede their nouns. Possessive and relative pronouns are seldom employed in the inflected forms of the personals, though these forms are common to both. Of the use of the relatives in any form the Bódo and Dhimál are very shy. Indeed, I doubt if their languages have any such words, though I have set down in the Vocabulary the evidently borrowed and seemingly perverted terms of others, and the misapplied ones of their own.

The interrogative pronouns 'who' and 'what,' they have, viz., Chúr and Má in Bódo, Háshú and Hai in Dhimál. These pronouns are declined after the general model of the personal ones.

DEMONSTRATIVE PRONOUNS.

As has been noticed, they serve for articles. Imbé is 'this,' and Hóbé 'that,' in Bódo; and in Dhimal *í* and *ú*, or, more formally, ídong, údong for 'beings,' ítá, útá for 'things.' Íbal, Úbal, signifying 'these' and 'those' in Dhimál, are considered the most express equivalents of the Bódo imbéchúr and hóbéchúr. Thus a good deal of difference is established between the third personal pronoun and the demonstratives, though ibál of the Dhimál is evidently but the correlative of the personal pronoun Úbal.* I proceed to exhibit the declension of the proximate demonstrative.

	SINGULAR.	
This,	Imbé,	I'.
Of this,	Imbé ni,	I'ko, Yángko.
To this,	Imbé no,	Yéng.
This,	Ímbé kho,	Yéng.
Oh this!	Caret?	Caret?
In this,	Imbé há, ou, nou,	Yáng tá.
On this,	Imbéni chou,	Yángko rhútá.
From this,	Imbéni phrá,	Yáng sho.
By this,	Imbéni jong,	Yáng dong.
With this,	Imbéni lago,	Yáng dosa.
	PLURAL.	
These,	Imbé chúr,	I'bal.
Of these,	Imbé chúrni,	Ibal ko.
To these,	Imbé chúr no,	Ibal óng.
These,	Imbé chúr kho,	Ibal óng.
Oh these!	Caret?	Caret?

* The demonstrative *ú* and the personal *wá* are probably the same word radically, Wá being but a vulgar pronunciation of U' vel Voh. The absence of an express third personal is so common in all languages that Smidt wittily observes—"I am No. 1, you are No. 2, and all others are nothing at all; that fellow or this, to wit, Ille, Iste."

In these,	Imbéchúr há, ou, nou,	Ibal tá.
On these,	Imbéchúrni chou,	Ibal ko rhúta.
From these,	Imbéchúrni phrá,	Ibal sho.
By these,	Imbéchúr jong,	Ibal dong.
With these,	Imbéchúr lago,	Ibal dosa.

Itá makes itáng and útá, útáng, in the dative singular; for the rest, these words, as well as idong, údong, are declined without change by means of the universal post-positions. So also the Bódo Hóbé, plural hobéchúr, follows the model of Imbé.

There are two great peculiarities in the use of the pronouns in these tongues; one is, that in both languages the pronouns frequently stand as the last word in the sentence, and this whether they be personal or possessive. The other peculiarity is confined to the Dhimál, and consists in the reduplication of the first and second persons* plural (we-ye) thus, from hinli, 'to laugh,' we have kyél hin *kyél*, 'we laughed,' nyél hin *nyél*, 'ye laughed.' Ubal hin, 'they laughed,' ceases to exhibit this characteristic mark. The possessive pronoun sometimes follows the governing noun, not usually. It will be observed from the above examples that the plural in most Bodo pronouns, and in many Dhimál ones, is formed by the respective postfixes chúr and bal. These are further distinctions between the declensions of the nouns and pronouns of these tongues.

NUMERATION.

The cardinal numbers extend only to 7 or 8 in Bódo, to 10 in Dhimál. Beyond these numbers the method of reckoning common to both people is by the Indian ganda and bísa, thus, 5 gandas are = 1 bisa or score, and 2 bisa = 40, 5 bísá = 100, and thus they contrive to reach the ne plus ultra of 200 or ten score. There are no ordinals in either tongue. The cardinal series is evidently the same in both tongues, and is derived from Tibet—the only instance of the kind I have noticed in their languages,† but I have not yet gone into comparisons of this sort, nor purpose to do so till I have

* Singular also. See on.

† 10 of the 60 words in Brown's List are identical in Dhimál and Tibetan; one in Bodo and Tibetan; 15 in Bodo and Gáró.

completed the whole contemplated series of Vocabularies for the Hills and Tarai, from the Bramapútra to the Káli or Ghágrá.

The following is the cardinal series of numbers, stript of their affixes.

English.	*Bódo.*	*Dhimál.*
One,	Ché,	E.
Two,	Gné,	Gné.
Three,	Thám,	Súm.
Four,	Bré,	Diä.
Five,	Bá,	Ná.
Six,	Dó,	Tú.
Seven,	Sini,	Nhíï.
Eight,	...	Yé.
Nine,	...	Kúhá.
Ten,	...	Té.

To these the Bódo *prefix* the particles San or Sá, Man or Má, and Thai, according as human beings, other animals and things, or money, are in question. The numeral, with these affixes, may either precede or follow the noun. Thus, Bihi[2] sáché[1], one[1] wife[2]; Híwá[2] sanché[1], one[1] man[2]; Búrmá[2] máché[1], one[1] goat[2]; Tháka[2] thai[1] ché, one[1] rupee[2];* Chokai manthám[1] ménda[3], 12 sheep or 3[2] gandas[1] of sheep[3].

The Dhimáls, again, have an immutable *postfix,* which is the word long, void of meaning like the Bódo prefixes. Thus *é* long is one, *gné* long two. This postfix is often omitted, as well as part of the noun to which the numeral is attached, with that love of ellipsis that has been already remarked on. Thus one day is properly *é* long nhítima; but the Dhimáls content themselves usually with Enhí. One man is Ediáng or Élong diáng; and thus it appears that in Dhimál the numeral always precedes the substantive. In Bódo, on the contrary, the numeral follows it or precedes it; generally the former.

* Chokai Vel Jokai, so Dou Vel Tou and Gorai Vel Korai. The mutation is no doubt euphonic and systematic, though the people are not aware of this, and generally prefer the harsher letters, I must say. The harsh sounds therefore are probably the more normal and appropriate. Thus Korai and not Gorai is the genuine Bódo commutative of the Hindi and Urdu Ghóra.

THE VERB.

Verbs express being, possession, or action. Those of the two former classes are very rare, or wholly wanting, in Bodo and in Dhimál. Those of the third class, if they belong to the primitive or simple type, are abundant. Verbs are divided by Grammarians into the active and passive, the transitive and intransitive or neuter, the personal and impersonal, the regular and irregular, the entire and defective, the compound and simple, the auxiliary and primary. Of these kinds, passives are formed in Bódo by means of the perfect auxiliary verb to be (jáäno) added to the root of the primary, which root is the imperative, second person singular. In Dhimál there is no passive voice, though there is a past participle (n̈ay, two) attached to the active voice, and in constant use as an adjective. A substitute for the passive voice is attempted to be found by the Dhimáls in a manner analogous to the Úrdú and Hindi idiom, according to which a man less frequently says, 'I have been beaten by my brother,' than 'I have *eaten a beating* from my brother,[2]' Bhaí[1] sé már[2] kháyá[3]. So the Dhimál says yollasho[1] dánghai[2] nénchábiká[3]. But the parallel is not complete, for nénchábiká is a compound, made up of nénli, to find, and cháli, to eat, so that the Dhimál idiom, literally rendered, is, 'I have found and eaten a beating from my brother.' Transitive and neuter verbs are, of course, common to both tongues; but neither, nor perhaps any language in the world, possesses the Úrdú and Hindí facility of transmuting the latter into the former, as úthná, úthána; chalna chalána, samajhná, samjhána, &c., *ad infinitum.* The only contrivance of this sort known to the Bodo and Dhimál languages is the compounding of the verb hotno, to give, in Bódo, and of the verb páli, to do, in Dhimál, with the root of the neuter verb, which it is proposed to make active; thus from hángno, to begin, n, comes háng hotno, to begin a, and from mholili n, mhoi páli; a in Bódo and Dhimál respectively. In Bódo, japno, to be finished, is made active by prefixing the imperative of the verb to do, thus moujapno. Of impersonal verbs I have nothing to say. Of reflected or deponent verbs I have found no trace. Verbs in general are very regularly conjugated according to *one* regimen, irregular verbs being rare in Bódo, and rarer in Dhimál. Jéngli, to be, is an irregular in Dhimál, as in so many other tongues. I scarcely know another instance in Dhimál; but in Bódo hotno, to give, háäno, to be able, phoino, to come, with some others, are irregular in one or more tenses. Of defective or fragmentary verbs, the Bódo auxiliary dong and dongman, equivalent, I apprehend, to the hún and thá of Úrdú and the hou and bhayou of Hindi, and the Dhimál auxiliaries, khíka, híká, and ángká, fragments of verbs of similar meaning with dongman, are samples. Compound verbs other than those already spoken of, whereby neuters are made active, are very rare, as I have already hinted under the head of nouns. Wherever they exist they are formed in the manner of neuters made active. The auxiliary verbs have been already mentioned, in part, as defectives. To those there spoken of we must here add the Bódo regular and perfect verb jáäno, to be, which is of the highest value, as the sole means of forming the passive voice, by postfixing its various inflections to the root of the primary verb in the active voice *Per se*, it is little used, the Bódo (and Dhimál) seeming to think that talk of mere existence is neither very profitable nor very intelligible. The Dhimál auxiliaries, khika, mhika, nhika, hika, ángká, are of the last importance, as forming the sole means of conjugating all verbs. From much inquiry through the medium of multiplied sentences—not of direct questions, which I found wholly futile and worse—I infer that the three first of the above five words are really one and the same, only varied for the sake of euphony, but upon principles too subtile for ready detection by a stranger; that all the three represent the *present* tense, indicative mood, of the fragmentary verb to be or to do;* that hika, the fourth word, represents the *past* tense of the same or a similar verb; and that ángká, the fifth word, stands in like manner for the *future* tense. These words are modified by genuine inflection,†

* Take the style of English conjugation as a help to appreciate this peculiarity, I do love, I did love, I will love.

† Is this inflection, after all, nothing more than the reduplicated pronoun

to suit the persons of the singular number, and the whole may be tabularised thus:—

SINGULAR.

1st. person, Ká khika : Ká mhika : Ká nhika : Ká hika : Ká ángká.
2d. person, Ná khina : Ná mhina : Ná nhina : Ná hina : Ná ángna.
3d. person, Wá khí : Wá mhí : Wá nhí : Wa hí : Waáng.

PLURAL.

1st. person, Kyél khi kyel :* K. mhi k : K. nhi k : K. hí k : K. áng k.
2d. person, Nyel khí nyel : N. mhi n : N. nhi n : N. hí n : N. áng n.
3d. person, Ubal khí : Ubal mhi : Ubal nhí : Ubal hí : Ubal áng.

The three first of these are apparently equivalent to the English verbal signs, 'do,' 'am;' the next to 'did,' 'was,' 'have,' 'had;' the last to 'shall,' 'will.' The student will find these remarks a key to the whole process of conjugation in Dhimál verbs. He has only to prefix the root of the verbs he wishes to conjugate to the above auxiliaries, and he at once obtains all of conjugation that the language exhibits; for the imperative or root, the infinitive and the participles, have, each and all, a single and inflexible form.

Should the conjecture hazarded in the foot-note of the last page prove well founded—and there seems every probability of its proving so—a very singular state of things would be the result; for we should then have the whole process of conjugation of Dhimál verbs accomplished by affixing an invariable auxiliary verb or verbal particle (viz., khí or hí or áng) to the root of the primary verb, with reduplication of the first and second pronouns, both singular and plural. Whether that particle or verbal fragment be really one or three, and whether significant or meaningless, are doubts which higher grammatical skill than I can pretend to, may go far to settle.† The people use their language with extreme carelessness, even in regard to those grand distinctions of time, the past, the present, and the future; and

added to the root, after the manner of the plural? Bopp says all personal inflection was originally pronominal, and Bunsen in his Egypt gives us samples from the oldest language on earth of pronouns used indifferently either as independent prefixes or as servile postfixes.

* The double pronoun is marked by its initial letter only, to save space.

† I am now satisfied that these so-called particles are fragmentary verbs like thá in Udú, and bhaya in Hindi, or 'do,' 'did,' 'will do' in English. 'Must,' 'ought,' &c., being invariable in form, are yet nearer approximations.

though I have stated, as the result of much investigation, that khí denotes 'the present,' hí 'the past,' and áng 'the future,' I cannot deny that I have often found the whole three employed promiscuously. Possibly, therefore, the three may prove to be only one, and even to have some connection with the perfect verb jéngli, to be analogous to that which seems to conjoin the fragmentary verb hún, thá, hou, bhayou, with the perfect verb hóná. Hí is often employed in the sense of the Úrdú hai, 'is;' as, for example, 'who is there?' Háshú[1] hi,[2] exactly equivalent to kón[1] haï[2]? rather kón thá? in the past tense. 'Who was it?' as if he were gone.* And though hí may be alleged to be a contraction of jéhi, which is deduced regularly from the perfect verb jéngli, 'to be,' yet, on the other hand, I see not any necessity for excluding the conjecture of an affiliated fragmentary verb consisting of hí solely, and khí and áng may possibly be of the same nature. That mhí and nhí are euphonic variations merely of khí I have no doubt whatever. Under the head of compound verbs I ought to have observed, that in Bódo such as express repetition or reiteration have the reiterative adverb placed in the *centre* of the *verb*, between its radical and inflected portions; thus, phoino, 'to come;' phoi-*phin*-no, 'to come *again;*' and that both in Bódo and Dhimál there is a useful set of quasi-compound verbs formed, as in Úrdú and Hindi, by verbs equivalent to their chukná and lagná. These are in Bódo, khángnó and lángnó; in Dhimál, hóïli and téngli. But whereas in the former tongues these accessary verbs are added sometimes to the imperative and sometimes to the infinitive of the primary verb (márchúka, honé laga), in the latter languages they are subjoined solely to the imperative, which in all four languages alike is likewise a verbal noun.

In most cultivated tongues there are several regimens for the conjugation of verbs, and under each regimen or model are comprised a great variety of moods and tenses, all which,

* The past tense is invariably used whenever the act is, or seems to be, over and passed.

as well as the numbers and persons of each tense, work changes upon the radical form of the verb, whether by inflective or auxiliary increment.

In Bódo and Dhimál there is apparently but one regimen for the conjugation of all verbs, which is accomplished by means of inflection in Bódo, of auxiliaries (immutable, verbal fragments) in Dhimál. This regimen exhibits great simplicity in both tongues, there being but three moods, the imperative, the infinitive, and the indicative,* and the last only admitting of a variety of tenses, which are limited to three, or, the absolute present, the absolute past, and the absolute or simple future. If a Bódo would express the time of the action with greater precision, he obtains an imperfect present by means of the auxiliary dong (thus, mou, 'do'; moudong, 'I am doing'); an imperfect past by means of dongman (thus, mou dongman, 'I was doing'); an emphatic past by means of the separate verb khángno, 'to be ended' (thus, mou, kar, khángbai, chúka, 'I have,' 'it is,' 'entirely done'); or else he marks decisively the three grand divisions of time, or any one of them, by *pre*fixing an adverb of time (dáno, 'now,' 'this instant'; sigáng, 'previously,' 'in the past'; yúnó, 'afterwards,' 'in the future'). Of these methods of marking time with precision, the last alone appears to be available to the Dhimáls, although the careless manner in which they employ their sole conjugational index of time (khika, hika, and ángká, supposed to represent respectively the 'present,' 'past,' and 'future') would seem to render further expedients more needful to them than they are to the Bódo. The Dhimál adverbs of time, corresponding to the Bódo ones just given, are éláng, lámpáng, and nhúcho respectively, and these likewise are placed before the verb as in the Bódo tongue. In Dhimál there is no passive voice; in Bódo the passive is formed precisely as in English; thus, shúno, 'to strike'; shú jááno, 'to be struck.' In Bódo, however, the auxiliary follows instead of going before the primary verb. There are two numbers, and three

* There are vague traces of a subjunctive mood in Mecch, formed by the postfix blá; thus, 'if I should go,' áng tháng blá. But in general the future indicative denotes contingency. 'Power' and 'will' are denoted by separate verbs, and 'duty' also.

persons in each number, both in Bódo and Dhimál. In Bódo number and person have no effect upon the verb, nor in Dhimál either, if, as conjectured, the second syllable of the Dhimál auxiliaries (khi*ká*, khi*ná*, khi, *et sic de cæteris*) be reduplicated pronouns, and not inflections. The imperative mood has but one tense and one *person* in both tongues, viz., the second person singular; and to this the negative is prefixed (dá in Bódo, má in Dhimál). In Bódo this proper verbal negative (mat in Úrdú) is nearly confined in its use to the imperative. In Dhimál it is as constantly applied to the infinitive, thus creating a very useful class of contrasted verbs (dóángli, 'to be able'; má dóángli, 'not to be able'; khángli, *velle*, 'to will'; má khángli *nolle*, 'not to will' or 'wish'). This function is discharged in Bódo by the general primitive géyá, contracted to gai, and put as usual between the radical and inflected part of the verb (háäno, 'to be able'; háä*ga*ino, 'to be *un*able'). This contrasted negative is likewise universally obtained in Bódo verbs by varying merely the terminal vowel, whether simple or diphthong ('Do you go or not?' Thangoná thang*á*? 'Will you go or not go?' Thángn*ai* ná thángá?). The infinitive mood has only a present tense, and there is nothing more analogous to gerund or supine than the three participles, viz., a present, a past, and a remote past; the extensive use of which in lieu of conjunctions and of relative pronouns is very characteristic of both tongues. The root of the verb, as already frequently noted, is the imperative, and it is peculiar to these tongues that they form all tenses and compounds from it, and seldom or never from the participles or infinitive. From this root, in Bódo, the present tense (indicative) is formed by adding ó (go, if a vowel precede) for all the persons of both numbers; the past by á (yá, if a vowel precede) or bai; the future by nai; the infinitive by nó; the present participle by in, the past participle (like the past tense) by á (yá, if a vowel go before); and the remote past participle by nánć.*

In Dhimál the inflective increments, as above enumerated, are either khí, impersonal, or khika, khina, khi for the three

* This last is equivalent to the kar ké of Urdú, aptly called the conjunctive participle.

persons; hí, impersonal, or hika, hina, hí; áng, impersonal, or ángká, ángná, áng; lí, katang, ká, téng.

The passive voice in Bódo is conjugated precisely as is the active, while in Dhimál there is no such thing as passive voice. In neither tongue is there anything like honorific tenses or phrases of any sort. We may now conclude the subject of verbs with some samples of conjugation.

English.	*Bódo.*	*Dhimál.*
Go!	Tháng,	Hadé,
Go not!	Dá tháng,	Má hadé.
To go,	Tháng no,	Hadéli.
Going,	Tháng in,	Hadé ka tang.
Gone,	Thángá,	Hadé ká.
Having gone,	Tháng náné,	Hadé téng.
I go,	Áng thángó,	Ká hadé khiká.
Thou goest,	Nang thángó,	Ná hadé khiná.
He goes,	Bi thángó,	Wa hadé khí.
We go,	Jong thángó,	Kyél hadé khí kyél.
Ye go,	Nang chúr thángó,	Nyel hadé khi nyel.
They go,	Bichúr thángo,	Úbal hadé khí.
I went,	Ang thángá or tháng-bai,	Ká hadé hiká.
Thou wentest,	Nang thángá or bai,	Ná hadé hiná.
He went,	Bi thángá or bai,	Wa hadéhí.
We went,	Jong thángá or bai,	Kyél hadéhí kyél.
Ye went,	Nang chúr thángá or bai,	Nyel hadéhi nyel.
They went,	Bichur thángá or bai,	Úbal hadé hi.
I will go,	Áng tháng nai,	Ká hadé áng ká.
Thou wilt go,	Nang tháng nai,	Ná hadé áng ná.
He will go,	Bi tháng nai,	Wá hadé áng.
We will go,	Jong tháng nai,	Kyel hadé áng kyel.
Ye will go,	Nang chúr tháng nai,	Nyel hadé áng nyel.
They will go,	Bichur tháng nai,	Úbal hadé áng.
Come!	Phoi,	Lé.
Come not!	Dá Phoi,	Má lé.
To come,	Phoino,	Léli.
Coming,	Phoi ïn,	Lé, katang.
Come,	Phoi yá,	Léká.
Having come,	Phoi náné,	Lé téng.
I come,	Áng phoigo,	Ká lé khiká.
Thou comest,	Nang phoigo,	Ná lé khiná.
He comes,	Bi phoigo,	Wá lékhí.
We come,	Jong phoigo,	Kyel lékhi kyel.
Ye come,	Nang chúr phoigo,	Nyel lékhi nyel.
They come,	Bichúr phoigo,	Úbal lékhí.
I came,	Ang phoi bai or yá,	Ká lé hiká.
Thou camest,	Nang phoi bai,	Ná léhi ná.
He came,	Bi phoi bai,	Wá léhi.
We came,	Jong phoi bai,	Kyel léhi kyél.
Ye came,	Nang chúr phoi bai,	Nyel léhi nyel.
They came,	Bichúr phoi bai,	Úbal léhí.
I will come,	Ang phoi nai,	Ká lé ángká.
Thou wilt come,	Nang phoi nai,	Ná lé ángná.

English.	*Bódo.*	*Dhimál.*
He will come,	Bi phoi nai,	Wá léáng.
We will come,	Jong phoi nai,	Kyel léáng kyel.
Ye will come,	Nang chúr phoi nai,	Nyel léáng nyel.
They will come,	Bichúr phoi nai,	Úbal léáng.
Eat !	Já,	Chá.
Eat not !	Dá já,	Má chá.
To eat,	Jánó,	Cháli.
Eating,	Jáyin,	Chákatang.
Eaten,	Jáyá,	Chákά.
Having eaten,	Jánáné,	Chá téng.
I eat,	Áng jágó,	Ká chá khiká.
I ate,	Áng jabai or jáyá,	Ká chá hiká.
I will eat,	Ang jánai,	Ká chángká (for chá ángka).
Speak,	Rai,	Dóp.
Speak not,	Dárai,	Má dóp.
To speak,	Raino,	Dópli.
Speaking,	Raiyin,	Dóp katang.
Spoken,	Ráyá,	Dópká.
Having spoken,	Rai náné,	Dóp téng.
I speak,	Ang raigo,	Ká dóp mhiká.
I spoke,	Ang raibai,	Ká dóp hiká.
I will speak,	Ang rainai,	Ká dóp ángká.
Be,	Jáä,	Jé.
Be not,	Dá jáä,	Má jé.
To be,	Jáäno,	Jéngli.
Being,	Jááyin,	Jéng katang.
Been,	Jááyá,	Jéngká.
Having been,	Jááunánó,	Jéng téng.
I am,	Áng jáágo,	Ká jéhiká.
I was,	Ang jaabai,	Ká higá hiká.
I will be,	Ang jáánai,	Ka jénká (for jé ángka).
Strike !	Shó,	Dáng hai.
Strike not !	Dá shó,	Ma dáng hai.
To strike,	Shúnó,	Dáng haili.
Striking,	Shú ïn,	Dáng hai katang.
Stricken,	Shúä,	Dáng hai ká.
Having struck,	Shónáné,	Dáng hai téng.
I strike,	Ang shógó,	Ká dáng hai khiká.
I struck,	Ang shúá or shúbai,	Ká dáng hai hiká.
I will strike,	Ang shonai,	Ká dáng hai ángká.
Be thou stricken,	Shó jáá,	...
Be thou not stricken,	Dá shó jáá,	...
To be struck,	Shó jááno,	...
Being struck,	Shó jááyin,	...
Having been struck,	Shó jaaya,	...
I am struck,	Ang sho jáágo,	...
I was struck,	Ang shó jáábai,	...
I shall be struck,	Ang shó jáánai,	...
Desire !	Labai,	Kháng.
Desire not !	Dá labai,	Má kháng.
To desire,	Labaino,	Khángli.
Desiring,	Labaiyin,	Kháng katang.
Desired,	Labaiyá,	Khánká.
Having desired,	Labainánó,	Kháng téng.
I desire,	Ang labaigo,	Ka kháng khiká.
I desire not,	Ang labai *gaigo,*	Ká *má* kháng khiká.
I am desiring,	Áng labai dong,	Ká eláng kháng khika.
I was desiring,	Ang labai dongman,	Ká lámpáng kháng khika.

English.	*Bódo.*	*Dhimál.*
I desired,	Áng labaibai,	Ká kháng hika.
I will desire,	Ang labainai,	Ka khángká (for kháng ángká).
Give,	Hót,	Pí.
Give not,	Dá hót,	Mápí.
To give,	Hótnó,	Pílí.
Giving,	Hotnin,	Pí katang.
Given,	Hotná, Húá,	Píká.
Having given,	Hotnáné,	Pí táng.
I give,	Ang Hóyú,	Ká pí khiká.
I gave,	Ang hotbai or húá,	Ká pí hiká.
I will give,	Ang hogon,	Ká pí áng ká.
Be able!	Háá,	Dóäng,
Be not able!	Dá háä;	Má dóáng,
To be able,	Hááno,	Dóángli (dóngli per ellipsin).
Being able,	Hááyin,	Dóáng katang.
Been able,	Hááyá,	Dóángká.
Having been able,	Háá náné,	Dóáng téng.
I am able,	Ang háágo,	Ká dóáng khiká.
I was able,	Ang Háábai,	Ká dóáng hiká.
I shall be able,	Ang Háánai,	Ká dóáng ángká (dóángká vulgo).

INDECLINABLES.

These highly useful parts of speech which give precision to all the others, whilst they connect them into well-knit sentences, are sadly deficient in the Bódo and Dhimál languages. Here more than any where, and almost only, I trace evidence of systematic borrowing and very clumsy assimilation. For the adverbs of place, time, quantity, quality, mode, and for the conjunctions the Vocabulary must be consulted; nor is there anything needful to be added in this place. Conjunctions of pure or unborrowed character are very rare * both in Bódo and Dhimál, and this circumstance, together with the habitual neglect of those post-positions which denote the cases of nouns, causes the sentences to hang very loosely together. Euphony, however, is studied, and the euphonic particles, which are the chief links of the construction, may be properly regarded as conjunctions. In Bódo the chief ones are, bo, no, ná, á, yá, má. All are postfixes and insignificant, except the last, which has an intensitive sense, as hágrá, 'a jungle,' hágrá má, 'a great jungle or forest.' In Dhimál there are fewer of these euphonic links of sentences, and indeed I remember distinctly but one, which is sá, and is void of meaning. Prepositions

* The want is cleverly evaded by means of the participles, à la Turque.

in these languages, as in others, govern various cases, of which some examples have been given, and more may be drawn from the subjoined sentences. Adverbs generally precede, but sometimes follow, the verb or nouns whose sense they qualify, and in close juxtaposition to which they are always found. I have met with no method of converting adjectives into adverbs, and this may account in part for the poorness of these tongues in indeclinables. Participles perform the function of conjunctions, as in Turki.

Sentences illustrative of the above rules of grammar and of the construction of the Bódo and Dhimál languages:—

Yesterday[1] I went[2] to the forest[3] to cut[4] timber[5]. To-day[6] I am[7] going to the jungle[8], to cut[9] grass[10]; and to-morrow[11] I shall[12] go to the village[13], to choose[14] a fit[15] site[16] for building[17] a house[18] on.

Bodo.—Miá[1] áng[2] thángá hágrámou[3], bóngphóng[5] phónó[4]. Áng diné[6] hágrou[8] thángdong[7] thúré[10] hánó[9]. Gábún[11] áng phárou[13] thángnai[12] núpthi[16] majáng[15] naino[14], jérúbo[18] nóökho[17] lúnó labaigo.

Dhimál.—Ánji[1] ká hadéhiká[2] bada dincha[3] tá, sing[5] pálli[4]. Náni[5] mhoiká[8] dinchá[7] tá hadéká (for hadékhiká), naimé[10] chéli[9]. Júmni[11] ká[13] dératá[12] hadéáng (ká), sá[18] dámli[17], elká[15] chol[16] (éng) khángli[14].

The big[1] boy[2] beat[3] the big[4] girl[5], till[6] she[7] began[8] to cry[9].

Bodo.—Híẉágotho[2] gedet*ná*[1] hinjougotho[5] gedet*na*[4] shúá[3], bini[6] phrá[7] gápmá[9] dongman[8].

Dhimál.—Bada[1] chan[2] badá[4] chámdéng[5] (for dióng) dánghaihí[3], kólá[6] wá[7] khárli[9] téngbí[8].

The large[1] pig[2] has given[3] six[4] young[5], three[6] males[7] and three[8] females[9].

Bódo.—[2]Yómá [1]gédé*tna* [5]yoshá [4]mádó (kho)* [3]góphaiyá; [6]má-thám [7]jólá; [8]matham [9]jó.

Dhimál.—[1]Badá [2]páyá [4]túlong [5]chan [3]jéhi; [6]súmlóng [7]dánkhá, [8]súmlong [9]mahani.

The girl is older than the boy, but the boy is taller than the girl.†

Bódo.—Hinjougotho*ä* gibï, híwá gothó*ä* gódóï; tóblábo hinjougo tho*no* híwágothó*ä* jou (for gajou) sin.

Dhimál.—Wával chan nhá (dong) bével chan síäná hí; tai béjan nhádong wájan dhángá hí (hi for jehi).

The horse is fatter than the cow, but the cow is less fleet than the horse.

Bódo.—Múshújo*no* gorai*ya* gúphúng shin; tóblábó múshújoNOBO‡ gorai gakhri sin.

Dhimál.—Píä nhádong óṅyhá gándi hi; tai píá nhádong óṅyhá chúkká hí.§

This pen is longer than that knife.

Bódo.—Imbé kalam hóbé dábá galou sin.

Dhimál.—Útá chúri nhádong ita kalam rhinká hí.

This pen is the longest of all.

Bódo.—Boino*bo mánino* imbé kalam galou sin dong.

Dhimál.—Sogiming nhá (dong) itá kalam rhinka.

What (is) your name?

Bódo.—Nangni your, mung*a* name, má what, *mung* name.

Dhimál.—Hai what, ming name, nangkó your's.

[1]When [2]you [3]called [4]me [5]I [6]was [7]within the [8]house, and [9]did not hear.

Bódo.—[1]Jélá [2]nang [4]ángkhó [3]linghotbai [5]áng [8]nóö [7]singou [6]jááb ai, [9]khanáyé.

* Sign of case, or elliptical omission, supplied within brackets.

† The comparative style not used in this member of the sentence, which literally means girl old, boy tall.

‡ Expletive particles marked by italics; double expletives by small capitals.

§ Literally, than the cow the horse fat, but than the cow the horse fleet.

1 2 3 4 5 6 8 7
Dhimál.—Jélá ná kaihiná kéng, ká higáhiká sáko-liptá.
9
Má hinhiká.*

Who is (there)? It is I.

Bódo.—Chúr dong. Ang dong.

Dhimál.—Háshú hí. Ká hiká.

It was so or thus. It is not so now; but it will be so again to-morrow.

Bódo.—Rísliá dongman. Dáno úripúsá géyá. Gábúnríshá jáá phin nai.

Dhimál.—Úsáng higáhi. Eláng úsáng mantló. Júmni úsáng nhéchuto jéáng.

Why say so? It is false!

Bódo.—Máno idi raigo. Óngá.

Dhimál.—Hai pálé úsáng dópkhiná. Micchá jéng (for jé áng).

As it was, so it is.

Bódo.—Jiring dóngman, úring dong.†

Dhimál.—Jédong higahi, kódong hí (for jéhi).

Will you go with me to the hills?

Bódo.—Nang ángjong hájóhá tháng nai.

Dhimál.—Ná káng dosa dángtá hángná (for hadéáng ná).

I will go. I will not go.

Bódo.—Áng thángnai. Áng thangá.

Dhimál.—Ká hánká (hadéángká). Ká má hánká.

Did you go with him? I did not go.

Bódo.—Nang bijong (lagoche together) thángá. Thángí.

Dhimál.—Ná wáng dosa haina (for hadéhina).

Má haiká (for hadéhika).

Is he here, or not?

Bódo.—Imbóhá jáágo, ná géyá.

Dhimál.—Ishó jéhí, ná máhi (má jéhí).

Is it so (fact), or not?

Bódo.—Óngó, ná óngá.

Dhimál.—Jéhí, ná májéhí. (Precisely, hast yá nést.)

Yesterday I was beaten by Birna for leaving the calves in the cultivation.

* Here is a sample of sheerly direct construction in Dhimál.

† Or, Jiring jáábai, úring jáágo.

Bódo.—Áng míá Birnáni ákhai* jong shojayá, húnou múshúgalai phúr (kho) hógárnáné. (Past participle *always* if the act be done.)

Dhimál.—Ká ánji Birnako khúrdong dáng hai nénchábi, léngtá píá ko changalai (éng) lappíká.

Alas! I was yesterday beaten without fault.

Bódo.—Chi! chi! míá áng dóshgéyá (*lámáno*) shójáyá.

Dhimál.—Hai! hai! dóshmánthó ká ánji dáng hai nénchá-hiká.

1 2 3 4 5
He was killed by a tiger, and when we went to look for his
6 7 8 9 10
remains, we found nothing but shreds of his clothes.

2 1 3 6 5
Bódo.—Mochájong wátjááäbai; jélai jong, bini bégéng nai-
4 10 9 7
grúno thángá, sélai hísrí bánó maná, mangbo máné [any thing (else) found not].

2 1 3 6
Dhimál.—Khúná dong chá nénchábí, jélá kyel wéngko hárá
5 4 10 7
bhóli hadéhi kyel, télá théká dhábá (éng) kyel nénhí kyel, aro [else], haidong [anything], mánthó [not].

The mouse was killed by the cat, and the cat was killed by the dog.

Bódo.—Injot*na* mouji jong wáthat jáyá, mouji*ä* choïma jong wát phin jáyá.

Dhimál.—Júhá ménkou sho shé nénchábi úthoï ménkou khíá dong shé nénchahi.

I struck him and he struck me, and thereon we fought.

Bodo.—Áng bikho shúá, biö ángkho shúá, yúnó jong khomjalábai.

Dhimál.—Ká wéng dánghai hika, wá kéng dánghai hí kólá kyel púchú hí kyel.

Having so said, he departed.

Bódo.—Rishá rainánó, thángbai.

Dhimál.—Üsáng dóp téng, hadéhí.

Having beaten his own wife, he fled for shame.

Bódo.—Gouini bihi (kho) shúnáné, lájin*ini* khat lángbai (or khatbai).

* Literally, by the hand of Birna; and so in Dhimál.

Dhimál.—Tai (ko) bé (wal) éng dáng haiká, léder téng khat ṇhi (nhi=khi or hí).

He goes laughing.

Bódo.—Minin minin thángdong.

Dhimál.—Lénkatáng lénkatáng hadékhi.

He comes crying.

Bódo.—Gap*m*in gap*m*in phoidong.

Dhimál.—Khárkatáng khárkatáng lékhi.

He goes speaking.

Bódo.—Raiïn raiïn thángo.

Dhimál.—Dópkatáng dópkatáng hadékhi.

Having come, he will speak.

Bódo.—Phoináné, rainai.

Dhimál.—Léténg *sá*, dópáng.

Having gone, he finished his business,

Bódo.—Thángnáné, hobbá (kho) moujapbai.

Dhimál.—Há (dé) téng *sa* kám jéhí.*

I shall be beaten to-morrow for not having finished the work.

Bódo.—Gábún áng shojáánai, máno, hobbá háágai.†

Dhimál.—Kám 'work,' (eng) 'the,' ma 'not,' páká 'done,' kónáng 'because,' ká ánji dánghai nénchángká (for chá ángká).

A beaten dog is good to nothing.

Bódo.—Sojáyá choïmá, mangbo 'any,' hobbá*no* 'work,' (for) údaiyá (údaiyá 'useless').

Dhimál.—Dánghai nénchaká khiá, haibo 'any,' kám ko 'use,' má 'not.'

Spoken words are quickly forgotten.

Written words are not soon obliterated.

Bódo.—Ráyá kothá, gakhri bou jáä bai litnai; kothá, gakhri gomatná.

Dhimál.—Dópká kothá, dhimpá nílká,‡ lekhika kothá, má§ páká (idiomatic ?).

Yesterday he came, but the work was done previously.

* A strong idiom if correct; literally, the work 'was,' fuit; so p. 93, chan jéhí for 'has produced young.'

† Literally, for 'why?' I was unable for the work.

‡ Nílká 'forgotten'; Mápáká 'not done.' I could not obtain the trace of a passive save the participle by any variety of questions.

§ Má páká is probably a contraction for níl má páká.

Bódo.—Bi míá phoiyá, kintú habba sigáng japbai.

Dhimál.—Ánji léhi 'came,' wá 'he,' kintú kám lámpáng hóïhí.

If I find him I will beat him.

Bódo.—Jélá áng bikho mano, ólá bikho, 'him,' shonai 'will beat,' áng 'I.'

Dhimál.—Jélá ká wéng nénangká, ólá wéng dáng haiángká.

Will you eat, or not?

Bódo.—Jánai, ná jáyá (or jáyá gai).

Dhimál.—Chángná, ná má chángná (chá ángná).

Will you sit down, or not?

Bódo.—Jòönai, ná jówá.

Dhimál.—Yóngángná, ná má yóngángná.

Will you speak, or not?

Bódo.—Rainai, ná ráyá gai.

Dhimál.—Dópángná, ná má dópángná.

Go quickly, Birnà is gone.

Bódo.—Thó (familiarly for tháng) gakhri, Birna * thángbai

Dhimál.—Dhimpá hadé, Bírná hadébí.

Go alone; I am going to the village.

Bódo.—Tháng nang háshing, áng thángdong pharou.*

Dhimál.—Ekélang hadé, ká dératá hadéángká.

I am not going to-day. I shall go to-morrow.

Bódo.—Diné áng thángá, Gábún thángnai.

Dhimál.—Náni ká má hánká (for hadéángka) júmni hadéángká.

He was false. He is true.

Bódo.—Santalén jáábai, Ghám jáágo.

Dhimál.—Micchá higábí, Élká jébi.

That boy is fat. That boy is very thin.

Bódo.—Imbé gotho gúphúng dong, Hóbé gotho gaham dong.

Dhimál.—Ídong chan dhámka hí, Údong chan chóp mhí (mhi = khí).

Father, and mother, and child.

Bódo.—Bi bipha, bi bima, bi bisha.

Dhimál.—Aba, ama, chan.

1. Eaten by a tiger.

* In these two instances the construction is as direct as in English, and would, I think, have been found so oftener if the Urdú questions had not told on the replies.

2. Ab homine stuprata.
3. Beaten by a hand.

Bódo.	*Dhimál.*
1. Mochá jong jájáyá.	1. Khúńásho chá nén chákά.
2. Hiwa joug khóï jáyá.	2. Wával dong lú nén chákά.
3. Ákhai jong shójáyá.	3. Khúr sho dánghai nen chákά.

Given things how shall I take back?

Bódo.—Hotnai jinis bré 'how,' láphinnai 'take back shall,' ang 'I.'

Dhimál.—Píká jinis hésá 'how,' nhéchuto 'back,' rhù 'take,' ángká 'shall I.'

Heard words why should I hear again?

Bódo.—Khanáyá kothá máno raiphinnai ('shall I hear,' future).

Dhimál.—Hinká kothá haipáli nhéchuto hin ang ká ('shall I hear,' future).

The man who told you so is your own friend.

Bódo.—Jai nangkho idi raibai, bí 'he,' gúshthi 'friend,' nangni 'yours.'

Dhimál.—Jai úsáng, dópmhi keng wái taiko 'own,' díáng 'man.'

The man[1] whom[2] you[3] seek[4] is dead[5].

Bódo.—Jékho[2] nang[3] naigrúgo[4] bí[1] 'he,' thóïbai[5].

Dhimál,—Jidongdíáng 'what man,' rhékhiná[3] kódóng[4] 'that,' díáng 'man,' síhi[5].

With what shall I plaster this wall?

Bódo.—Imbé injurá májong litnai.

Dhimál.—Ithai bérhém haiou lépángká.

What do you want? and what are you saying?

Bódo.—Bi 'and,' má 'what,' bídong 'wanting,' bi 'and,' ma 'what,' raidong 'saying' (conjunction repeated: so above).

Dhimál.—Hai rhékhiná, hai dópkhiná.

The nátch is begun, come and see it.

Bódo.—Moshá hángo, thángnáné 'having gone,' bikho 'it,' nai 'see.'

Dhimál.—Híäli ténghí, hátengsa 'having gone,' útáng 'it,' dó 'see.'

The nátch is over, I will not go.

Bódo.—Moshá khángbai, áng thángá.

Dhimál.—Híäli hoïhí, ká má hángká (hadéángka).

Having finished that job, he went to do the other.

Bódo.—Hobé habbá háánáné (or moujapnáné) gúbún hobba (kho) mouno thấng bai.

Dhimál.—Útá káméng hoipáténg, bhináng kám (eng) páli hadéhi.

He wished to go with us yesterday, but was not able. To-day he is able, and willing to go.

Bódo.—Bi jong jong míá thángno labai bai, háá (yá) gai; Diné hááyin, * thángno labaigo.

Dhimál.—Wá júmni king dosa háli (hadéli) kháng hí; má dónghi (dóánghi). Náni háli dóng katang, † wá khángkhi háli.

Are you able (to do it) or not?

Bódo.—Nang háágó, ná háágé (gé for gai).

Dhimál.—Ná dóáng khiná ná ma dánkhiná (dáng for dóáng).

From Siligóri to Dorjiling how many cós?

Bódo.—Siligori ni phrá Dorjiling chim, chéwá piché.

Dhimál.—Siligori sho Dorjiling thékapa hé cós.

How many sheep and goats in the pen?

Bódo.—Méndá *bo* búrmaiya nóönou béchébá.

Dhimál.—Méndá *wá* ééchá sákolipta hé jéhi.

Take it from the water, and throw it in the fire.

Bódo.—Doïni phrá bokhángnáne, waton gárshún.

Dhimál.—Chísho chumateng méntá húüpí.

In a large house two fires are better than one.

Bódo.—Nóö gédétnou doudap manché *no* doudap mangné ghámsin.

Dhimál.—Bada sátá élong ákhá dong (for nhá dong) gnélong ákhá *nú élang.* ‡

1 2 3 4 5 6 7 8 9
Take it from these naughty boys and give it to those good
10
girls.

* Thus, in every instance, the conjunction is evaded by the use of the participles.

† Literally, to-day being able, he wishes to go.

‡ Strong idiom: this word cannot translate: for ordinary use the word elka may take its place. Eláng is probably nothing but a jingle with elóng.

4 5 6 3 2
Bódo.—Imbechúr hámma hiwa gothophúrni phrá bĭkho
1 8 9 10 10 7
lánáné hobechúr ghám hinjoúgotho phúr (kho) hot.*

4 5 6 3 1 2
Dhimál.—Ídóng máélká wájan galai sho ghinténg wéng,
8 9 10 7
údóng elka béjan-galai éng pí.

Call all the children quickly.

Bódo.—Boi (no) bogotho (phúr) kho gakhri ling hot.

Dhimál.—Sogiming chan (galai) éng dhimpá kai.

Sáheb! this is our buffalo: give it to us and take it from them.

Bódo.—Giri! imbé jongni maisho jáágo. Jongno hot. Bichurni phrá bikho lá.

Dhimál.—Giri! Idong kingko díä, king éng pí, úbal sho ghinteng 'having seized,' rhú 'take.'

He took all the pigs from us, and gave them to Birna.

Bódo.—Boinobo yómá phúr (kho) bi jongni phrá láyáné, Birná*no* húá.

Dhimál.—Sogiming páyá (galai éng) king sho ghinténg, Birnéng píhi.

CONSTRUCTION.

I know not that anything need be added to the copious and careful particulars, the statement of which is just concluded. It has been my object to make that statement *perfectly adequate to the ends in view*, or a full illustration of these peoples as they are in themselves, and as they are in relation to one another, and to the larger group to which they belong. A few concluding remarks may, however, be expected from me; but to avoid useless repetition I must glance at the whole group of tongues which I purpose to examine. It has been already observed that the Bódo and Dhimál languages belong pretty evidently to the aboriginal Indian tongues of the pronomenalised type.† They seem to me to have retained to a remarkable degree their primitive character, so as

* The participle is used all along to avoid the conjunction. There is not one exception to this rule.

† See note at Part III., p. 105.

to constitute very valuable exemplars of the class of languages to which they belong; nor have I any doubt that further time would have enabled me to replace many of the Úrdúi or Hindí vocables to be found in the Vocabularies with others of indigenous stock. Such exotic words are surprisingly few, considering how long the Bódo and Dhimál people have lived in peaceful intercourse with the people of the plains on the one hand, and of the hills on the other; and, what is still more singular, is the broad distinction between the Bódo and Dhimál tongues as compared with one another, seeing that these people have lived for several generations, if not actually mixed (for their villages are separate, nor do they intermarry), yet in the closest apposition and intercourse. That the Kócch were originally an affiliated race, very closely connected with the Bódo and entirely distinct from the Hindus (Arian immigrant population using the Prákrits), I have no hesitation in saying. But since the beginning of the sixteenth century of our era, the Kócch have very generally abandoned their own in favour of the Hindu (and Moslem) speech and customs, though there be still a small section called Páni or Bábú Kócch retaining them. I failed to obtain access to the Páni Kócch, so that my Kócch Vocabulary exhibits little more than a mass of corrupted Prákrits. There are, however, some primitive vocables; and the Vocabulary, such as it is, has been taken in order to preserve a living sample (soon to disappear) of that process whereby the Arian and exotic are rapidly absorbing the non-Arian and indigenous tongues of India—tongues (the latter) which, if we make a general inference from the state of things in the hilly and jungly districts, wherein alone they are now found, must have been prodigiously numerous, when they prevailed over the whole face of the land; *unless*, indeed, the dispersion and segregation in holes and corners of the aboriginal population have given rise to that Babel of tongues which we now find.

Hill tribes. In the sub-Himálayas, between the Káli and the Tishta rivers, I know of the following aboriginal tongues and dialects:*—The Cisnivean-Bhótia, the Thaksia, the Pakia, the

* For a fuller enumeration see Trübner's reprint of my papers at pp. 13, 14, and 29, 30. See also papers on "The Broken Tribes," and on "The Vayu and Bahing," in J. A. S. of Bengal for 1857.

Sunwar, the Magar, the Gúrúng; the Múrmi, the Néwári, the Kíránti, the Limbú, the Lapchá, the Haiyú or Vayu, the Chépáng, the Kúsúndá, the Dénwár, the Dúrré, the Brámhú; the above in the hills. In the Tarai, extending our limits easterly to Assam, so as to include its south-west skirt, the Kócch, Dhimál, Rábhá, Gáró, Khyi or Khasia, Kachári or Mecch, or Bódo, Hájóng, Kúdi, Batar or Bor, Gangai, Kíchak, Kuswar, Thárú, Kébrat, Pallah, Amath, Maraha, Dhamúk, Dhékrá, besides those of hill-tribes located there long ago, and now very different from their confreres of the hills, such as Sringia Limbús, Dénwárs, Dúrrés, &c. What a wonderful superfluity of speech! and what a demonstration of the impediments to general intercourse characterising the earlier stages of our social progression! How far these languages, though now mutually unintelligible to those who use them, be really distinct, how far any common link may exist between them and the rest of the aboriginal tongues of India—so as to justify the application of the single name Tamúlian to them all—are questions which I hope to supply large means of answering, when I have gone through the hill and Tarai tongues of this frontier, as above enumerated. Be these points as they may, the Bódo and Dhimál tongues will be, I think, allowed to be genuine and highly-interesting samples of the aboriginal languages of the plains of India (whatever their source or connection, matters to be settled hereafter), as well as to furnish a good key to the moral and physical condition of the simple races using those tongues. What can be more striking, for example, than agriculture being expressed by the term 'felling' or 'clearing the forest;' than the total absence of any term for 'village,'* for 'plough,' for 'horse,' for 'money' of any kind; for nearly every operation of the intellect or will, whether virtuous or vicious; and, lastly, for almost every abstract idea, whether material or immaterial? Structurally viewed, these languages are distinguished by a frequent absence of inversion that is unwonted in Indian tongues;† by the peculiar use of the pronouns, particularly in Dhimál; by the special form and uses of the

* Arva in annos mutant et superest ager! See on.

† As will be seen, the *usual* structure of sentences is like that of Hindi and

privatives: by the loose cohesion of the sentences, resulting from a want of, and a contempt for, conjunctions, as well as a neglect of the signs of case and tense; by the conjunctive application of the participles; * by a want of precision arising from the paucity of adverbs, and also from the features just marked; by a passion for ellipsis, yet an attention to euphony; by extreme simplicity of structure; and, lastly, by the universal and exclusive use, in Dhimál, of fragmentary auxiliars in the business of conjugation.

Adam Smith long ago remarked, that original languages might be known from derivative ones, by those auxiliars and prepositions of the latter, whereby the complex inflections of the former are got rid of. It would be practically very convenient if we had any certain marks of this sort, serving to distinguish those two classes of languages; but it is difficult to suppóse the Bódo and Dhimál languages other than primitive; and yet if they *be* primitive, Smith's deduction from the languages of Europe cannot be allowed to have general validity.

Urdú; but, as already remarked, it must be borne in mind that the Urdú and Hindi medium of questioning should be allowed for as necessarily influencing the responses, which *therefore*, perhaps, exhibit too much inversion!

* In lieu both of relative pronouns and of conjunctions, thus, instead of 'go and bring,' we have 'going, bring,' and instead of 'he who brings,' 'he bringing.'

In the Vocabulary words will be found for most of these things and ideas; but they are all *borrowed* terms, the nature and sources of which the Indian reader will readily recognise, and see how clumsily and imperfectly they have been incorporated when any attempt at assimilation is made.

PART III.

ORIGIN, LOCATION, NUMBERS, CREED, CUSTOMS, CHARACTER AND CONDITION OF THE KÓCCH, BÓDO, AND DHIMÁL PEOPLE, WITH A GENERAL DESCRIPTION OF THE CLIMATE THEY DWELL IN.

IF we commence our researches into the aboriginal tongues and races of India in its north-east corner, or Assam, we find that province rich in such materials for inquiry. But the majority of the numerous aborigines of the mountains of Assam appear to belong to the simpler-tongued or Tibetan stem,* with which we have at present nothing to do. A line drawn north and south across the Brahmapútra, in the general direction of the Dhansri river, and continued southwards so as to leave Káchár within it or to the west of it, would seem not very inaccurately to divide the simpler from the more complex-tongued section of the Himalayan races. Possibly, indeed, some of the hill tribes to the north of the Brahmapútra, although within the limits of the former section, as above conjecturally defined, may yet be found to belong to the latter; † but to the south of that river, I think it is pretty evident that such is not the case, for the Káchárians, Khasias, and Gárós, are, in creed, customs, and languages, either identical with, or most closely affined to, the Bódo, while the Kúḍi, Rábhá, and Hájóng, if not rather nominal than real distinctions (Hajong, Hojai Kachari), are but branches of the great Bódo or Mécch family, whose

* I divide the Himalayan races primarily into two groups, distinguished by the respective use of simple or non-pronomenalised, and of complex or pronomenalised languages.

† In the Northern Hills also the Dhansri seems to demark the Alpine races of Tibetan origin (ending easterly with the Lhopa or Bhutanese) from the Daphlas, Akas, Bors, Abors, Mishmis, Miris, and others of apparently Chinese or Indo-Chinese stock.

proper habitat, be it remembered, is the plains and not the mountains. I should add that it is a mistake to suppose the mass of the population in the *valley* of Assam to be of Arian race. I allude to the Dhékrás or common cultivators of the valley, who, as well as the Kácháris and Kócch of that valley, are non-Arians, as is proved beyond a doubt by their physical attributes, and in despite of that Bengálí disguise of speech and customs which has misled superficial observers. The illustration of these Assamese races is, however, I believe, in better hands than mine; and I therefore shall proceed for the present more westward. Whoso should advance from Góálpára in Assam to Aliganj in Morang would, in traversing a distance of some 150 miles along the skirts of the mountains of Bhútán* and Sikim, pass through the country of the following aborigines of non-Arian extraction: the Kócch, the Bódo, the Dhimál, the Rábhá, the Hájong, the Kúḍi, the Batar or Bor, Kébrat, Pallah, Gangai, Marába, and Dhánuk, not again to mention the Kachárians separately, they being demonstrably identical with the Bódo, and so in future to be regarded, nor further dwelling now on the Khasias and Gáros than to observe that Buchanan notes them as parts of the population of Rangpúr in its old extent.† We may have more to say of the rest of these tribes hereafter. Many of them have abandoned wholly their own tongues and a deal of their own manners. But our present business is with the Kócch, Bódo, and Dhimál, and first with the first.

Kócch Location. In the northern part of Bengal, towards Dálimkót, appears to have been long located the most numerous and powerful people of non-Arian extraction on this side the Ganges, and the only one which, after the complete ascendancy of the Arians had been established, was able to retain or recover

* Bhútán recte Bhutant, 'the end of Bhót,' Sanskrit name of the country, which the people themselves call Lhó, but, like the Hindus, consider it an appendage of Bhot *v.* Tibet, of which the former is the Sanskrit and the latter the Persian designation. The native one is Bód.

† Fifteen in sixty words of Brown's Vocabulary are the same in Gáró and in Mécch, and the whole sixty or nearly so in Kachári and Mécch. Again, the Kacháris called *themselves* Bódo, and so do the Mécch; and, lastly, the Kachári deities, Sijú, Mairong, and Agráng, are likewise Mécch deities—the chief ones too of both people, to whom I restore their proper names. These are abundant proofs of common origin of Gárós also.

political power or possession of the open plains. What may have been the condition of the Kócch in the palmy days of Hinduism cannot now be ascertained; but it is certain that after the Moslem had taken place of the Hindu suzerainty, this people became so important that Abul Fazul could state Bengal as being "bounded on the north by the kingdom of Kócch, which," he adds, "includes Kámrúp." Hájo founded this kingdom towards the close of the fifteenth century or beginning of the sixteenth, and it was retained by his sovereign successors for nearly two hundred years.* In 1773 the Company's gigantic power absorbed the Kócch Ráj, which once included the western half of Assam on one side and the eastern half of Mórung on the other, with all the intervening country, reaching east and west from the Dhansri river to the Konki, whilst north and south it stretched from Dálimkót to Ghóraghát. In other words, the Kócch Ráj extended from 88° to 93½° east longitude, and from 25° to 27° north latitude, Kócch Bihar being its metropolis, and its limits being coequal with the famous yet obscure Kámrúp of the Tantras. Hájo's representative still exercises *jura regalia* in that portion of the ancient possessions of the family which is called Nij Bihár, and he and the Jilpaigori and Pángá Rajahs, together with the Bijni and Darang Rajahs, and several of the Lords Marchers of the north frontier of Kámrúp (Barúas of the Dwárs)—all of the same lineage—still hold as Zamindar Rajahs most of the lands between Sikim, Bhútán, and Kámrúp, as at present constituted, and a southern line nearly coincident with the 26° of north latitude. Sukla Dev of the Kócch dynasty divided the kingdom, and there seems to have been in later times a triple Sultanat fixed at Bihar, Rangamati, and Gauhati. The Rajahs of Gauhati and their kinsmen of Darang extended the Kócch dominion eastward to and beyond the Májuli or great island of the Brahmapútra. Hájó, the founder, having no sons, gave his daughter and heiress to a Bódo or Mécch chief in marriage; and to the wise policy indicated by this act (the policy of uniting the aborigines and directing their united force against intruders) was the founder of the Kócch dynasty indebted for his suc-

* Buchanan, Rangpur., vol. iii. p. 419, &c.

cess against the Moslems, the Bhútánese, and the Assamese.* Nevertheless the successors of Hájó speedily abandoned that policy, casting off the Mécch (Bódo) with scorn, and renouncing the very name of their own country and tribe, with their language, creed, and customs, in favour of those of the Arians, who, however resolutely they may eschew the aborigines whilst continuing obscure and contumacious, never fail to hold out the hand of fellowship to them when they become powerful at once and docile. In a word, Visva Sinh, the conqueror's grandson, with all the people of condition, apostatised to Hinduism; the country was re-named Bihár; the people Rájbansi; so that none but the low and mean of this race could longer tolerate the very name of Kócch, and most of these being refused a decent status under the Hindu regime, yet infected, like their betters, with the disposition to change, very wisely adopted Islám in preference to helot Hinduism. Thus the mass of the Kócch people became Mahomedans, and the higher grades Hindus: both style themselves Rájbansi. A remnant only still endure the name of Kócch, and of these but a portion adheres to the language, creed, and customs of their forefathers—as it were merely to perpetuate a testimony against the apostasy of the rest! The above details are interesting for the light they throw upon the *character and genius of Hinduism*, which is certainly an exclusive system, but not inflexibly so; and whilst it readily admits the powerful to the eminent status of Rajpút vel Kshatriya,† it is prone to tender to the humble and obscure no station above helotism—a narrowness of polity that enabled Buddhism not only to establish itself in the very metropolis of Hinduism (Bihar, Oude, Benares), but for fifteen to sixteen centuries ‡ (sixth B.C. to

* The Yogini Tantra denounces these three under the appellations of Plov,* Yavan, and Saumar, as the foreign scourges of the land. Buch. iii. 413. The Assamese (Saumar) alluded to are the Ahoms, who held upper Assam when the Kócch held lower and middle, but with ever-varying limits.

† Witness the Khas tribe of Nepal, as to which see "Essay on the Military Tribes," i. 37 aforegone.

‡ Sakya was probably born in 545 B.C., and died in 465, and that his creed was still flourishing in the eleventh century A.D. is proved by the then solemn repair of the great temple at Gaya. The persecution, however, was hot in the ninth.

* Pluh or Pruh is the Lepcha name of the Bhutanese, and may be the etymon of the Plava of the Tantras. The people of Bhutan call themselves Lhópá.

eleventh A.D.) to contest with it the palm of superiority. The Yogini Tantra very properly denominates the Kócch, Mlécchas or aborigines, the fact being imprinted in unquestionable characters on their non-Arian physiognomy, and also on the language and customs of their unconverted brethren. They are called Kavach * in the Tantra just named, Hásá by the Kácháris or Bódos of Assam, Kamál by the Dhimáls, and Kócch by the Mécch or Bódos of the Méchi, as well as by themselves where not perplexed with Brahmanical devises. Buchanan, who was furnished with every appliance for satisfactory research, and whose sagacity was not unworthy of his opportunities, estimated the numbers of the Kócch people twenty-five years ago at 350,000 nearly. I am not aware that any good census has since been taken, and I have failed to obtain a general estimate: but from much inquiry, aided by Major Jenkins, Dr. Campbell, and Permanand Acharj, I conclude that Buchanan missed a great many of them under the disguise of Islám, that cultivation has vastly increased since his time, that the Kócch abound throughout the northern part of Rangpúr, Púrnea, Dinajpúr, Mymansing and in all Kámrúp and Darang, as far as the Dhansri river, and that their numbers cannot be less than 800,000 souls—possibly even a million or million and quarter. In Assam they are divided into Kamthali and Madai or Shara, and Kolita or Kholta, and in Rangpúr, &c., into Rájbansi and Kócch—those of the Moslem faith everywhere dropping their ethnographic designation. Their first priests were Déóshi, their next, Kolita or Kholta, and their last, the Brahmans or Múllahs. Buchanan vouches that their primitive or proper language (as still used by the unadulterated remnant of the race) has no affinity with the Prákrits, and I can attest the entire conformity of the physiognomy of all, and of the creed and customs of this remnant with those of the other aborigines around them. I have already stated that I failed to get at the unconverted Kócch, and that my Vocabulary is that of the converted. Hereafter I trust to supply this desideratum,

* This is identical with Kócch, the difference being merely that of the Sanscrit and Prakrit forms of the same word.

Observe that this is the name of the extant Bodo and Dhimál priesthood, one of numerous proofs demonstrative of the affinity of all the three people.

and in the meanwhile I cannot do better than give Buchanan's unusually careful and ample account of the condition, creed, and customs of this people—which, being compared with my own subsequent statement of the condition, creed, and customs of the Bódo and Dhimál (of whom Buchanan says little or nothing), will satisfactorily demonstrate the affinity I have insisted on.

Kóćch. Status.

"The primitive or Páni Kóćch live amid the woods, frequently changing their abode in order to cultivate lands enriched by a fallow. They cultivate entirely with the hoe, and more carefully than their (Arian) neighbours, who use the plough; for they weed their crops, which the others do not. As they keep hogs and poultry, they are better fed than the Hindus; and as they make a fermented liquor* from rice, their diet is more strengthening. The clothing of the Páni Kóćch is made by the women, and is in general blue, dyed by themselves with their own indigo, the borders red, dyed with Morinda. The material is cotton of their own growth, and they are better clothed than the mass of the Bengalese. Their huts are at least, as good, nor are they raised on posts like the houses of the Indo-Chinese, at least not generally so. Their only arms are spears: but they use iron-shod implements of agriculture, which the Bengalese often do not. They eat swine, goats, sheep, deer, buffaloes, rhinoceros, fowls, and ducks—not beef—nor dogs, nor cats, nor frogs, nor snakes. They use tobacco and beer, but reject opium and hemp. They eat no tame animal without offering it to God (the gods), and consider that he who is least restrained is most exalted, allowing the Gárós to be their superiors, because the Gárós may eat beef. The men are so gallant as to have made over all property to the women, who in return are most industrious, weaving, spinning, brewing, planting, sowing—in a word, doing all work not above their strength. When a woman dies, the family property goes to her daughters; and when a man marries, he lives with his wife's mother, obeying her and his wife. Marriages are usually arranged by mothers in nonage, but consulting the

* The classic Zyth, ζυθον, beer without hops, as universal among the Aborigines is the absence of spirits or distilled waters.

destined bride. Grown-up women may select a husband for themselves, and another, if the first die. A girl's marriage costs the mother ten rupees—a boy's five rupees. This sum is expended in a feast with sacrifice, which completes the ceremony. Few remain unmarried, or live long. I saw no grey hairs. Girls who are frail can always marry their lover. Under such rule, polygamy, concubinage, and adultery are not tolerated. The last subjects to a ruinous fine, which if not paid, the offender becomes a slave. No one can marry out of his own tribe. If he do, he is fined. Suttees are unknown, and widows always having property can pick out a new husband at discretion. The dead are kept two days, during which the family mourn, and the kindred and friends assemble and feast, dance and sing. The body is then burned by a river's side, and each person having bathed returns to his usual occupation. A funeral costs ten rupees, as several pigs must be sacrificed to the manes. This tribe has no letters, but a sort of priesthood called Déóshi, who marry and work like other people. Their office is not hereditary, and everybody employs what Déóshi he pleases, but some one always assists at every sacrifice and gets a share. The Kócch sacrifice to the sun, moon, and stars, to the gods of rivers, hills, and woods, and every year, at harvest home, they offer fruits and a fowl to deceased parents, though they believe not in a future state. Their chief gods are Rishi and his wife Jágó. After the rains the whole tribe make a grand sacrifice to these gods, and occasionally also, in cases of distress. There are no images. The gods get the blood of sacrifices; their votaries, the meat. Disputes are settled among themselves by juries of Elders, the women being excluded here, however despotic at home. If a man incurs a fine, he cannot pay with purse; he must with person, becoming a bondman, on food and raiment only, unless his wife can and will redeem him."

The climate of north Bengal or Kócch (including the country of the people so called, and of the Bódo and Dhimáls) is too well known to require any particular notice. It is much less healthful than that of north Bihár, being infested with low fevers, which are either propagated from Climate.

the wilds north and east of it, or, more probably, generated on the spot by excessive moisture and vegetation in the very extensive tracts of waste, still unhappily to be found everywhere east of the Kósi river. West of that river, or in the ancient Mithilá, and modern north Bihár, the climate is as much more salubrious as cultivation is more diffused. The Saul forest everywhere, but especially to the east of the Kósi, is malarious to an extent which no human beings can endure, save the remarkable races which for ages have made it their dwelling-place. To all others, European or native, it is deadly from April to November. Yet the Dhimál, the Bódo, the Kíchak, the Thárú, the Dhénwár, not only live but thrive in it, exhibiting no symptoms whatever of that dreadful stricken aspect of countenance and form which marks the victim of malaria. The like capacity to breathe malaria as though it were common air characterises nearly all the non-Arian aborigines of India, as the Kóls, the Bhíls, the Gónds, who are all fine and healthy races of men, though dwelling where no other human beings can exist. This single fact is to my mind demonstration that the non-Arians have tenanted the wilds they now dwell in for many centuries, probably thirty, * because a *very* great lapse of time could alone work so wonderful an effect upon the human frame; and even with the allowance of centuries, the fact stands forth as one of the miracles of human kind, which those who can explain may sneer at the *other* amazing diversities worked by time and clime on that marvellous unit, the seed of Adam! The Bódo and Dhimáls, whom I communicated with, alleged that they cannot endure the climate of the open plains, where the heat gives them fevers. This is a mere excuse for their known aversion to quit the forest; for their eastern brethren dwell and till like natives in the open plains of Assam, just as the Kóls of south Bihár (Dhángars) do now in every part of the plains of Bihár and Bengal, in various sites abroad, and lastly in the lofty sub-Himálayas. The Kóls are indeed, as enter-

* There is "no cabalistic virtue" in thirty, as Mr. Lyell observes in reference to his theory of the fourfold division of Tertiary rocks. That number expressly is given, however, because about 3000 years back is the probable date of the immigration of the Arian Hindus.

prising as industrious, and they should be employed by every European who seeks to reduce and cultivate any part of the malarious forests of India.* But it must not be forgotten that the very same qualities of freedom from disabling prejudices, cheerful docility, and peaceable industrious habits and temper, which render the Kóls now so valuable to us, are the inherent characteristics of most of the aborigines, requiring only the hand and eye of a paternal Government to call them forth, as in the case of the Kóls. Ages of insolent oppression drove the aborigines to the wilds, and kept them there till their shyness of all strangers had become rooted and intense. But I can answer for the Bódo and Dhimál possessing every good quality of the Kóls in an equal or superior degree, and the Bódo have already shown us with what facility those qualities may be put in action for our benefit as well as their own.

The physical type of the Kócch, as contrasted with that of the Hindu, is palpable, but not so as compared with that of the Bódo and Dhimál. In other words, the physical type in *all* the non-Arians (of this frontier at least) tends to oneness. A practised eye will distinguish at a glance between the Arian and non-Arian style of features and form—a practised pen will readily make the distinction felt—but to perceive and to make others perceive, by pen or pencil, the physical traits that separate each group or people of Arian or of non-Arian extraction from each other group, would be a task indeed! In the Arian form (Hindu) there is height, symmetry, lightness, and flexibility: in the Arian face, an oval contour with ample forehead and moderate jaws and mouth; a round chin, perpendicular with the forehead; a regular set of distinct, and fine features; a well-raised and unexpanded nose, with elliptic nares; a well-sized and finely-opened eye, running directly across the face; no want of eyebrow, eyelash, or beard; and lastly, a clear brunet complexion, often not darker than that of the most southern Europeans. Physical type of all.

In the non-Arian form, on the contrary, there is less height,

* How comes it that the Deyrah grantees, whom the malaria disables through their peasantry, do not procure Dhángars or Kóls, who would answer thoroughly and exactly for the purpose in view? I speak from much experience.

less symmetry, more dumpiness and flesh: in the non-Arian face, a somewhat lozenge contour, caused by the large cheek-bones; less perpendicularity in the features to the front, occasioned not so much by defect of forehead or chin as by excess of jaws and mouth; a larger proportion of face to head, and less roundness in the latter; a broader, flatter face, with features less symmetrical but perhaps more expressive, at least of individuality; a shorter, wider nose, often clubbed at the end and furnished with round nostrils; eyes less, and less fully opened, and less evenly crossing the face by their line of aperture; ears larger; lips thicker; beard deficient; colour brunet, as in the last, but darker on the whole, and, as in it, very various. Such is the general description of the Indian Arians and non-Arians. With regard to the particular races of the latter, it can only be safely said that the mountaineers exhibit the Mongolidan or Turanian type of mankind more distinctly than the lowlanders, and that they have in general a paler, yellower hue than the latter, among whom there are some (individuals at least) nearly as black as negroes. Among the Kóls * I have seen *many* Orauns and Múndas nearly black; whereas the Larkas or Hós (says Tickell) are as pale, and handsome too, as the highest-caste Hindu. The Kócch, Bódo, and Dhimál are as fair as their Bengali neighbours on one side, and scarcely darker (especially the Bódo) than the mountaineers above them on the other side, and whom (the latter) they resemble in the latter style of their features and form, only with all the physiognomical characteristics softened down, and the frame less muscular and massive. The Kóls have a similar cast of face, and a very pleasant one it is to look upon in youth, exhibiting ordinarily far more of individuality, character, and good humour than the more regular but tame and lifeless faces of the Arian Hindus. For the further illustration of this point I beg to refer to the accompanying drawings and appendix, and proceed now from the Kócch tribe to the Bódo and Dhimál tribes, who occupy the entire northern and eastern

Bódo and Dhimál Location.

* Kól is an old and classical name, and the best I think for the great mass of aborigines intervening between the Bhils, the Gonds, and the Ganges—at least till we know them better. The Orauns, Múndas, Kóls proper, and Larkas, seem to be distinct, and the chief families or stirpes.

skirts of the Kócch country, between the open plains and the mountains, both of which sites, generally speaking, they avoid, and adhere to the great forest belt that divides the two, and which is, on an average, from fifteen to twenty miles broad. The Dhimáls, who seem fast passing away as a separate race, and whose numbers do not now exceed 15,000 souls, are at present confined to that portion of the Saul forest lying between the Konki and the Dhorla or Torsha, mixed with the Bódo, but in separate villages and without intermarriage. But the Bódo are still a very numerous race, and extend as foresters from the Súrmá to the Ḍhansri, and thence, viâ Bijni and the Bhútan and Sikim Tarai, to the Konki, besides occupying, outside the forest limits, a large proportion of central and lower Assam. In the divisions of Darang and Chatgari they constitute the mass of the fixed population: they abound in Chárdwár and Noudwár: in Nougáoṉ and Tularam's country they are the most numerous tribe next to the Mikirs and Lalongs; in Kámrúp next to the Dhékra and Kócch; whilst in the marches or forest frontier of the *north* from Bijni to Aliganj of Morung they form the sole population, except the few Dhimáls who are mixed with them; and in the *eastern* marches from Gauhati to Sylhet they are less numerous only than the Gárós, Rábhás, and Hajongs, not to mention that the two last, if not all three, are but Bódos in disguise. I look upon the Rábhá as merely the earliest and most complete converts to Hinduism, who have almost éntirely abandoned the Bódo tongue and customs, and upon the Hájóngs or Hojaí Kacháris of Nowgong, as the next grade in time and degree of conversion, who now very generally affect a horror at being supposed confreres in speech or usages with the Bódo, though really such. Nor have I any doubt that the Gárós are at least a more affiliated race, and no way connected with the monosyllabic-tongued tribes around them.* I do not, however, at present include the Gárós, or Rábhás, or Hájóngs among the Bódo, who are now viewed as embracing only the Méches of the west and the Kácháris of the east and south; and, so limited, this race numbers not less than 150,000 to 200,000 souls. An

* See note at page 106.

accurate general census seems out of question except for Assam, but the above enumeration is given as an approximate result of several statements obligingly supplied to me by Mr. Kellner, Mr. Scott, Dr. Campbell, and that enlightened traveller, Permanand Acharya. Thus the Bódo race extends from Tipperah and the country of the Kúkis on the south-east to Morung and the country of the Kíchaks to the north-west, circling round the valley of Assam by the *course of the Dhansri*, en route to the north, though Major Jenkins assures me that Bódos may be found even east of that river in the Assam valley. The latitude and longitude of the Bódo country are the same with those of the Kócch country, to speak without any affectation of a precision, the subject does not admit of, and thus we may say the Bódo extend from 25° to 27° north latitude, and from 88° to 93½° east longitude; and that the Dhimáls are confined to the most westerly part of this wide range of country, or that portion lying between the Konki and the Dhorla. My personal communications with these tribes were chiefly with those still found in all their primitive unsophistication on the banks of the Méchi river, and from much intercourse with these, during four months, I conclude that neither people have any authentic ancient traditions. Nevertheless the ancient connection of the Dhimáls with the west, and of the Bódo with the east, part of north Bengal, is vouched by the facts, that a tract of country lying between the Konki and the Mahananda is still called Dhimáli; and a still larger tract situated between the great bend of the Brahmaputra and the Gáró hills is yet called Méchpárá. The close connection of the Bódo with Kámrúp is further confirmed by the facts of the mass of the people being still found there, though under the name of Kachári, and by the intimate affinity of the Bódo speech and customs with those of the Gárós. The so-called Káchár Rajah is a new man and alien to the Bódo race, and so is the mass of the people of Káchár. But Túlarám is a Bódo, and the late Rajah of Karaibári another, and the Kalang dwár chief a third; and among the Lords marchers of the southern confines of Assam, others might once, if not still, be found; for when the keeping of the northern marches (towards Bhutan) was entrusted to the Kócch race, that of the southern dwárs or doors (towards Gáró and Nágá land) was committed to the Bódo tribe, that is, to its chiefs. It would not appear that any chief of Dhimál race now exists: but the scattered remnants of this race assure me that they once had chiefs when they dwelt as a united people in Morung, on the banks of the Kaval (Kamla), whence they removed to the Téngwá, and ultimately to and across the Konki, sixty years ago, in order to escape from Górkhali oppression. Of the few lately extant chiefs of Bódo race, the Karaibári Rajah's estate is transferred to the stranger, and the Kalang and Tularam chiefships are shorn of much of their "fair proportions." But in the days of Hajo, the Kócch founder, as well as in those of some of his more prudent successors, the Bódo seem to have had great political consequence, and if Hajo's descendants had steadily adhered to the wise maxims of their ancestor, their power might longer and more effectually have defied its enemies, whereas most of the Kócch Rajahs followed the illiberal Arian maxims of Viśwa Sinh, and thus the Bódo were driven back upon their beloved forests, retreats which, speaking generally, neither they, nor the Dhimáls, have since quitted, save in Assam. I proceed now to the consideration of the status, creed, and customs of the Bódo and Dhimál. Upon these points the two people have so much in common, that though I have myself gone through each particular separately in regard to each people, I shall spare the patience of my readers by aggregating what is common, and separating only what is particular, to the Bódo and Dhimál.

Condition.—The condition or status of the Bódo and Dhimál people is that of erratic cultivators of the wilds. For ages transcending memory or tradition, they have passed beyond the savage or hunter state, and the nomadic or herdsman's estate, and have advanced to the third or agricultural grade of social progress, but so as to indicate a not entirely broken connexion with the precedent condition of things; for, though cultivators, all and exclusively, they are nomadic cultivators, so little connected with any one spot that neither the Bódo nor Dhimál language possesses a name for village! Though dwelling in those wilds, wherein the people of

Status.

the plains (Ahírs and Gwállas) periodically graze immense numbers of buffaloes and cows, they have no large herds or flocks of their own to induce them to wander; but, as agriculturists little versed in artificial renovative processes, they find in the exhaustion of the worked soil a necessity, or in the high productiveness of the new a temptation, to perpetual movement. They never cultivate the same field beyond the second year, or remain in the same village beyond the fourth to sixth year. After the lapse of four or five years they frequently return to their old fields and resume their cultivation if in the interim the jungle has grown well, and they have not been anticipated by others, for there is no pretence of appropriation other than possessory; and if, therefore, another party have preceded them, or if the slow growth of the jungle give no sufficient promise of a good stratum of ashes for the land when cleared by fire, they move on to another site, new or old. * If old, they resume the identical fields they tilled before, but never the old houses or site of the old village, that being deemed unlucky. In general, however, they prefer new land to old, and having still abundance of unbroken forest around them, they are in constant movement, more especially as, should they find a new spot prove unfertile, they decamp after the first harvest is got in. † They are all in the condition of subjects (of Népál, Sikim, Bhútán, or Britain) having no property whatever in the soil they till, and discharging their dues to the Government they live under (Sikim, for example), 1st, by the annual payment of one rupee per agricultural implement, for as much land as they can cultivate therewith (there is no land measure); 2nd, by a corvée or tribute of labour for the sovereign and for his local representative. They calculate that they can raise thirty to forty rupees' worth of agricultural produce

* Arva in annos mutant et superest ager! So immutable is human nature that the descriptions applied to our ancestors in their pristine state are absolutely and most significantly true of similarly circumstanced races now abiding in the forest jungles of India.

† Such are the primitive habits still in use from the Konki to the Monásh, and which are most worthy of study and record, as being primitive and as being common to two people, the Bódo and Dhimál, though abandoned by the Kámrúpian and most numerous branch of the Bódo.

with one agricultural implement, so that the land-tax is very light; and the corvée is more irksome than oppressive. It requires them, on the Rajah's behalf, to quit their homes for three or four days, thrice a year, in order to carry burdens for him into the hills, whenever he has goods coming from the plains; but, on the representative's behalf, to work only on the spot. Four times a year they must help to till his fields; also to build or repair his dwelling-house; to supply him with fuel and plates (leaves) whenever he gives a feast; and, lastly, they must pay him one seer of cotton each year for every cotton field they have. Very similar is the condition, in regard to taxation, of the Bódo and Dhimáls under the Nepal and Bhútán Governments. Under the British, the permanent cultivators of the open lands of Kámrúp are subject to the usual burdens incidental to our rule, which they discharge with ease, owing to their industrious and orderly habits. Major Jenkins gives them the highest character, observing that—"they are a remarkably fine peasantry, and have very superior cultivation of the permanent kind." This is abundant proof of the docility of the Bódo, and strong presumptive evidence that their erratic habits and adhesion to the wilds, elsewhere, are the result of oppression, at least as much as of the bias of pristine custom. But as the Kámrúpian Bódo have abandoned with their erratic propensities a deal of whatever is most characteristic of them as a distinct race, I resume the delineation of them and of the Dhimáls, as still found in primitive simplicity between Bijni and Mórang. There they are migratory cultivators of a soil in which they claim no sort of right, proprietory or possessory, but which they are allowed to till upon the easy terms of a quit-rent and labour tax, because none others will or can enter their malaria-guarded limits. There is no separate calling of herdsman or shepherd, or tradesman or shopkeeper, or manufacturer or handicraft, alien or native, in these primitive societies, which admit no strangers among them, though they live on perfectly amicable terms with their neighbours, and thus can always procure, by purchase or barter, the very few things which they require and do not produce themselves.

To a person accustomed to the constitution of social bodies in India, whether Arian or Tamulian, it must seem nearly impossible that communities could exist without smiths, and carpenters, and potters, and curriers, and weavers, not to mention barbers. Yet of these helot craftsmen, whose existence forms so striking a feature of all Indian societies, and whose origin and status so much need * illustration, there is no trace among the Bódo or Dhimáls, though they live apart from all others, like the Khónds, Gónds, and Kóls, who *have* these aliens among them; and necessarily so, for their inaccessible position and predacious propensities would otherwise too often cut them off from all aid of craftsmen; whereas the Bódo and Dhimál, who dwell upon the plains, and on peaceful equitable terms with their neighbours, can always command such services, or rather their products in the markets. The Bódo and Dhimáls have no buffaloes, few cows, no sheep, a good many goats, abundance of swine and poultry, some pigeons and ducks. They have no need, therefore, of separate herdsmen, unless it were swine-herds, and these might be very useful in feeding their large store of pigs in the forest. But they have no such vocation among them, each family tending its own stock of animals, which is entirely consumed by that family, and no part thereof sold, though the proximate hill-men would gladly purchase pigs from them. But they love not trade nor barter further than is needful, and their need is confined to obtaining (besides rice) a few earthen and metallic culinary utensils, still fewer agricultural implements of iron, and some simple ornaments

* When we consider the indispensableness of the services of these craftsmen, it is remarkable that they should have continued to the present day in a helot or out-caste state, not only among the Arians but even among the non-Arians, not only in the plains but in the mountains. My belief is, that most of the non-Arians, on the Arian conquest, retired to the mountains and jungles, and that those who remained were reduced to helotism and became the artizans of Arian society, such as we now see them. Ages afterwards some of them passed into the fastnesses and wilds occupied by their non-Arian brethren, in freedom, and fierce defiance, for the most part, of their Arian enemies. These immigrants are the recent helot craftsmen of the Gónds, Khónds, and Kóls, such as we now see them, non-Arians in origin like the masters they serve, but from whom they fail to obtain better treatment than from the Arians. No common tie is recognised; and ages of freedom and of servitude have left no common trait of character.

for their women—all which are readily obtained at the Kócch marts in exchange for the surplus cotton and oil-seed of their efficient agriculture. Each man builds and furnishes his own house, makes the wooden implements he requires, and is his own barber, or his neighbour for him, and he for his neighbour. He uses no leather, and he makes basketry for himself and family, whilst his wife spins, weaves, and dyes the clothes of the family, and brews the beer which all members of it freely consume. Thus, all manufactures are domestic, and all arts. The Bódo and Dhimáls are generally averse from taking service with, or doing work for, strangers, whether as soldiers, menials, or carriers, though there are a few soldiers and servants at Dorjiling belonging to the Bódo race, who conduct themselves well in their respective capacities. Among their own communities there are neither servants nor slaves, nor aliens of any kind; and whilst their circumstances tend to perpetuate equality of means, neither their traditions, their religion, nor their usages sanction any artificial distinctions of rank. Though they have no idea of a common tie of blood, yet there are no diverse septs, clans, or tribes among them, nor yet any castes; so that all Bódo and all Dhimáls are equal—absolutely so in right or law—wonderfully so in fact. Nor is this equality the dead level of abject want. On the contrary, the Bódo and Dhimáls are exceedingly well-fed, and very comfortably clothed and housed; and so soon as you know them—for they are very shy of strangers—their voices, looks, and conduct all proclaim the absence of that grovelling fear and cunning which so shock one in one's intercourse with the people of Bengal, and the mass of whom are much worse fed, and distinctly worse clothed and housed, than either Bódo or Dhimáls. Equality.

Laws.—It having been already stated that these people are, and have been for ages, in the condition of subjects of foreign Governments, I need hardly observe that they have no *public laws* or polity whatever, nor even any traces of that village economy which so pre-eminently distinguishes Indian-Arian societies. Their habits are too simple and migratory to allow of the existence of the village system, with its train Laws.

of hereditary functionaries and craftsmen. They dwell in the forest in little communities, consisting of from ten to forty houses, which they are perpetually shifting from place to place. Each of these communities is, however, under a head called Grá by themselves, Mondol by their neighbours. To the foreign Government they live under their Grá is responsible for the revenue assessed, which he pays periodically to the Rajah's representative—the Choudri—in cowries or rupees, the only currency. He has no scribe, nor keeps any accounts, his simple explanations to the Choudri being verbal. To the Choudri he is answerable, likewise, for the keeping of the peace and for the arrest of criminals: but crimes of a deeper dye are almost unknown, and breaches of the peace very rare. Should a murder or robbery occur, the Choudri would take cognizance of it, assisted by three or four proximate heads and elders of villages, and report to the Rajah, from whom alone in such cases a decision could issue. With regard to his own community, the head of the village has a general authority of voluntary rather than coercive origin, and which, in cases of the least perplexity, is shared with the heads or elders of two or three neighbouring villages. Those who offend against the customs of the Bódo or Dhimál—that is, their own customs—are admonished, fined, or excommunicated, according to the degree of the offence; the village priest being called in, perchance, to give a higher sanction to the award. The same jury-like tribunal seems to have almost exclusive cognizance of *civil law*, or the usages of each people in regard to inheritance, adoption, divorce, &c. Marriage is rather a contract than a rite, and as such is dissoluble at the will of either party; and if the divorce be occasioned by the wife's infidelity, the price paid for her to her parents must be refunded by them. Dower is not in use, and women, in general, are deemed incapable of holding or transmitting property. All the sons get equal shares, nor is there any nice distinction of sons by marriage, adoption, or concubinage. Adoption is common and creditable, even if there be one son of wedlock: concubinage is rare and discreditable. Daughters have no inheritance nor dower, but if their parents be rich and give them marriage presents, such are held to be their own, and will be retained by them in the event of divorce. Neither Bódo nor Dhimál can marry beyond the limits of his own people; and if he do, he is severely fined. Within those limits only, two or three of the closest natural ties are deemed a bar to marriage. In the event of divorce, the children belong to the father, or the sons to the father and the daughters to the mother. If the husband take the adulterer in the fact, he may beat him and likewise the wife; but no more;* and thereafter, if he please, he may put his wife away, when she and the adulterer will continue to abide together as man and wife without scandal, but without marriage rite; or, if the husband please, he may pardon her, and frequently does so, should the offence have been the first, and committed with one of the tribe and not with an alien. Chastity is prized in man and woman, married and unmarried; and, as a necessary consequence, women are esteemed and respected, and divorce and separation rare, notwithstanding the bad footing upon which the custom or law of these nations sets the nuptial union. Siphilis is absolutely unknown among the Bódo and Dhimál—a fact that speaks volumes, and one that renders it scarcely necessary to add that any class of women, devoted to unchastity, is a thing for which their languages have no name, and their manners no place. Filial piety is not a marked feature in their character, nor perhaps the want of it. Sons, on marriage, quit the parental roof, and sometimes previously; but it is deemed shameful to leave old parents entirely alone; and the last of the sons, who by his departure does so, is liable to fine as well as disinheritance. Infanticide is utterly unknown, with every savage rite allied to it, such as human sacrifice, self-immolation, and others, too frequent among rude people. Daughters, on the contrary, are cherished, and deemed a source of wealth, not poverty; for every man must buy his wife with coin or labour, and 'tis very seldom that the price comes to be redemanded by the wronged and unforgiving husband. There is no bar to remarriage, and satti is a rite held in abhorrence.

* **Among the Parbattias of Nepal the wronged husband may, nay must, slay the adulterer.**

Learning. Of *learning and letters* the Bódo and Dhimáls are totally devoid, and always have been so. The numerals of the cardinal scale are only seven in the Bódo tongue, ten in the Dhimáls, and they have no ordinals at all. Beyond seven or ten they count by the Hindu ways of fours and of scores, and in this manner they can reckon to 200. Very few of the Bódo or Dhimáls have learnt to write the neighbouring Prákrits, but many can converse in them, particularly in the corrupt Bengálí prevailing from the Kosi to the Brahmapútra. To the segregated manner of life of the Bódo and Dhimáls, and to the practice of both people of marrying only within the pale of their own folk, I ascribe the present purity of their languages.

Religion. *Religion.*—The religion of the Bódo and Dhimáls is distinguished, like their manners and customs, by the absence of everything that is shocking, ridiculous, or incommodious. It lends no sanction to barbarous rites, nor does it hamper the commerce of life with tedious inane ceremonial observances. It takes less cognizance than it might advantageously do of those great sacraments of humanity, baptism, marriage, and sepulture, withholding all sanction from the first, and lending to the other two, especially marriage, a less *decided* sanction than the interests of society demand. The deplorable impediments to the business of society, occasioned by the Hindu (Arian) religion, are too well known to call for specification. But even some of the non-Arians are pestered with usages, under the guise of religion, which are alike injurious to health and convenience,* or are pregnant with cruelty.† From all such crimes and mischiefs the religion of the Bódo and Dhimáls is wholly free. With the most striking events or dearest ties of life it meddles little directly, confining itself almost exclusively to the propitiation of the superior powers by offerings and sacrifices. A Bódo or Dhimál is born, is named, is weaned, is invested with the toga virilis, without any intervention of his priest, who is summoned to marriages and funerals chiefly, if not solely, to

* Khasias. Robinson's Assam, p. 413, and Buchanan's Reports, vol. iii. p. 695.

† Gárós. Elliott. Asiatic Researches, iii. 29. Khónds. Macpherson's Reports and Taylor's Account, vide Madras Journal, No. xvi., and Calcutta Review, No. ix.

perform the preliminary sacrifice, which is indispensable to consecrate a feast, for no Bódo or Dhimál will touch flesh the blood of which has not been offered to the gods; and flesh constitutes a goodly proportion of the material of those feasts which solemnise funerals and weddings alike. The office of the priesthood is not an indefeasible right vested in a caste, nor is the profession at all exclusive. The priests are native Bódo or Dhimál, no way distinguished from the rest of the community, either before or after induction. Occasionally the son will succeed the father in this office, but rarely; and whoever chooses to qualify himself may become a priest, and may give up the profession whenever he sees fit. More than this, the Elders of the people may and do participate in the functions of the priesthood and even exercise them alone, so that it is not improbable there was a time when the civil heads of the community were likewise its ecclesiastical directors. This imperfect constitution of the clerical office has probably proved, upon the whole, a great blessing to these people by saving them from the trammels of *all* refined Paganism (Egyptian, Classic, Indian), though it has had the necessary ill effect of keeping their religious ideas in a state of extreme vagueness. I am not inclined to consider "the natural man" as a savage; and I have no hesitation in calling the religion of the amiable Bódo and Dhimáls the religion of Nature or rather, the natural religion of Man. It consists, clearly enough, of the worship of the most striking and influential of sensible objects—of the "starry host," and of the terrene elements—with a vague but impressive reference of the *powers* displayed by these sensible objects to an immaterial or moral source; unknown indeed, but still adored as Divine, and even as a divine Unity.* It is true that these latter conceptions are too vague to be denominated, strictly speaking, ideas proper to these people, much less positive tenets of their creed; and hence their languages have no word for God, for soul, for heaven, for hell, for sin, for piety, for prayer, for repentance. It is true that their gods are many, and are all void

Priesthood, p. 175.

* I refer the caviller to Pope's universal prayer, and to that famous fane of antiquity dedicated to the Unknown God.

of definite moral attributes (save when their own meaner passions of vanity and anger and grief are occasionally ascribed to them). But still, in the pre-eminence assigned, however vaguely, to one (or two) of these gods, we cannot deny to these simple-minded races the germ of a *feeling* of God's unity; and when they appeal to Him as the avenger of perjury, the sanctioner of an oath; we must acknowledge that the moral sentiments of their own nature irresistibly impel them to ascribe like sentiments to the Godhead. Now, in every serious matter of dispute that cannot be decided by testimony, usually so called; oaths and ordeals are had recourse to—and both as substitutes for, and not confirmatives of, evidence, according to the ancient Jewish (nay, universal) notions on this head. But oaths and ordeals are appeals to the moral nature of the Divinity: nor can it be denied that, though the practical religion of the Bódo and Dhimáls consists of idle offerings and sacrifices to trivial deities, supplications for protection from danger, and thanksgivings when it is over, accompany these offerings and these sacrifices, forming a part, how inconsiderable soever, of the religious rites of the people, as conducted by the priesthood. The priests, *or* the elders, superintend the administration of oaths and of ordeals: the priests *alone* direct and conduct those high festivals, which thrice a year are celebrated in honour of the Elemental gods, and once a year in honour of the household divinities; as likewise those occasional acts of worship which originate with more or less diffused, or individual, calamity. The calamities to which the Bódo and Dhimál stand most exposed are small-pox and cholera, which sorely afflict them; and drought, blight, and the ravages of wild elephants and rhinoceroses, from which their crops suffer not less. Diseases are considered to arise entirely from preternatural agency, and hence there are no medical men but a regular class of exorcists, who are a branch of the priesthood, and whose mode of relieving the possessed or sick will be described presently. They are called Ojhá, and are the sole physicians. Small-pox is the direst scourge of the Bódo and Dhimáls; next cholera (since 1818); next itch; then diseases of the intestines, as diarrhœa and dysentery; then fever; then goitre: diseases of the liver and lungs are very rare, and siphilis is unknown. The Bódo and Dhimál, though healthy races, are not long-lived nor prolific. Grey hairs are less common than in the hills or plains: sixty is deemed a great age: a family of eight or nine living children is hardly known; five or six alive is nearly the maximum, and two to four the mean. The hazards and the importance of agriculture to the Bódo and Dhimál are sufficiently indicated by their creed, the three chief festivals of which have almost exclusive reference thereto. Great as are the ravages committed on the crops by insects and wild animals, drought seems to be dreaded still more than either, so that among all the numerous gods, Jupiter pluvius, as typed by the rivers, commands a reverence second to none with the Dhimáls, second to one or two only with the Bódo. *All* the rivers between the Cosi and the Torsha are chief divinities of the Dhimáls—all those between the Konki and the Bar nadi, prime deities of the Bódo. Fire, however indispensable agriculturally for the clearing of the forest, is by no means equally reverenced; nor the earth, which yields all; nor the noble forest, so cherished, and so many ways indispensable; nor the mountains whence come these very rivers; nor even the sun and moon, which alone of the starry hosts are worshipped at all. All these deities are worshipped devoutly indeed, but none with such earnestness as the rivers: and yet the rivers flow too low to allow of their waters being turned to irrigation, so that it is as an index of copious rains, upon which exclusively Bódo and Dhimál crops are dependent, that the rivers are entitled to this reverence, though crossing as they do *so* frequently and *so* directly the route of communication through the country of these tribes, 'tis no wonder that they have unusually commanded attention. When I first obtained lists of the Bódo and Dhimál divinities, at once so numerous and so devoid of attributes, I was exceedingly perplexed what to make of these gods, how to render them at all intelligible to myself or others. But one key to the enigma was soon found in the Hindu pantheon—another in the best frontier maps, especially those of Rennell, where the rivers proved to be so many Dii majores. A third class of gods, and a very important and characteristic one, in regard to the Bódo more particularly, remained, however, for solution. These, following the people themselves, I have denominated the 'household gods,' because their worship is conducted *inter parietes.* 'National,' however, were the fitter term, for these are the original deities of the whole people; and though their worship be conducted at home, or in each house, the whole neighbourhood participates through the medium of the accompanying sacrifice and feast, and reciprocally at every householder's of the village, once a year in solemn pomp, and more frequently and quietly as occasion may require. Not to mention that these deities likewise share with the elemental gods the high triennial festivals above adverted to; for how ample soever the Bódo or Dhimál pantheon, their practical religion is as simple as their manners, and they dispose of their superfluous divinities by adoring them all in the lump! A good many of the household or national divinities of the Bódo are elemental gods, chiefly rivers. Báthó, however, the chief god of the Bódo, is not an elemental god; but he is clearly and indisputably identifiable with *something tangible*, viz., the Síj or Euphorbia, though why that useless and even exotic plant should have been thus selected to type the godhead I have failed to ascertain. Mainou or Mainong is the wife of Báthó, and equally revered with him; more I cannot learn of her. The supreme gods of the Dhimáls are usually termed Waráng-Béráng, that is, the old ones, or father and mother of the gods. They likewise are a wedded pair, whose proper names are respectively Pochima and Timai vel Timáng, of whom the latter is undoubtedly the Tishta river, and the former, I believe, the river Dhorla. The Bódo and Dhimáls have neither temple nor idol, and altogether their religion belongs to the same primitive era with their habits and manners, is void of offence or scandal, and if any judgment may be made of it from the manners and character of its professors, is not without beneficial influences.

I proceed now to some details upon this point, in which it will be necessary sometimes to speak separately of the Bódo and Dhimál religions, though so little essentially distinct. This general correspondence extends not merely to the entire substance and character of the religion, properly so called, of each people, but to all minor points connected therewith: for example, both people have but a vague notion of the existence or functions of those Dii minores called Genii, Fauns, Satyrs, and Sylvans by the classic ancients, and Fairies, Sprites, Gnomes, Ogres, &c., by our Gothic or Teutonic ancestors. Neither people is infested with the Gothic bugbear of ghosts, or with the Gothic and classic follies of magic, sorcery, divining, omens, auspices, astrology, or fortune-telling. On the other hand, both Bódo and Dhimál alike and devoutly believe in witchcraft, of which they entertain a deep dread, and likewise in the influence of the evil eye, though much less dreaded than witchcraft. Omens are very slightly, if at all, heeded by either.

THE CHIEF DEITIES OF THE *Bódo* *and* *Dhimáls.* Pantheon.

Bódo

The household or National gods or Noöni Madai:

- Báthó, chief god; Euphorbia, or Sij plant.
- Mainou, or Báthó Búrói, } wife of above.
- Agráng, male, relative of above pair.
- Khárgi, male.
- Ablákhúngar, male.
- Khoïlá, male, river?
- Manáshó, female. River Monás or Bonás.
- Bráli, male, river? styled Brai, or the ancient.
- Búli, female, river? styled the ancient, or Búrói.
- Khandaira, male, a Rajah.
- Jaman, male, Yama of Hindus.
- Kóngar, or Góngar, } male, Bhutanese Deity.
- Jishing, Mishing, } males.

The Doïni madai or River Deities:

- Dhórlabrai, mas., river, husband of Tishta.
- Dúdkosi, female, river.
- Tishta, ditto, ditto.
- Kangkai, ditto, ditto.
- Ménchi, male, river.
- Torsha, ditto, ditto.
- Jórdaga, ditto, ditto; the Jerdeckér R.
- Bálakhúngar, ditto, ditto; the Bálásan.

Dhimáls.

- Pochima, mas., father of the gods, the river Dhorla?
- Timai vel Timang, } fœm., mother of the gods; the Tishta river.
- Lákhim, fœm., sister of Timai, with some; Mahanada?
- Chímá, fœm., sister of Timai; the Kosi river.
- Konokchiri, fœm., feeder of Konki river.
- Kangkai, fœm., river Konki.
- Ménchi, fœm., river Méchi.
- Sonási, mas., the Soran river.
- Bonási, mas., the Boás or Doás.
- Dhúlpi, mas., the Dúbélly river.
- Danto, mas., styled the Old.
- Chádúng, mas., styled Rajah, son of Timai.
- Aphoï, mas., Rajah, son of Timai.
- Biphoï, ditto, ditto, ditto.
- Aphún, ditto, ditto, ditto.
- Káphún, ditto, ditto, ditto.
- Báphún, ditto, ditto, ditto.
- Shúti, ditto, ditto, ditto.
- Rong, mas.
- Aika, mas. et fœm., styled the Old.
- Tairúng, Túïrúng, } males, sons of Biphoi.
- Hili mahadói, Khúnchi mahadói, Khili mahadói, Airi mahadói, } Females all; wives of the 7 sons of Timai above given; appa-

Bódo	*and*	*Dhimáls.*

Bódo:

Máhámáyá, female. River Mahananda.
Dóïmá, Bráhmaputra ; fœm., Mater magna.
Chádúng.
Gédúng.
Brai Bhandári.
Jholou Bhandári.
Káthá, male, a Rajah.
Dípkhúngar.
Phorou khúngar.
} Sons of Tishta. (Chádúng … Phorou khúngar)
} The Döini madai or River Deities. (Máhámáyá … Phorou khúngar)

Shyánmadai, the Sun, Nokhábírmadai, the Moon. } male brothers.
Hámadai, the Earth, fœm.
Wátmadai, Fire, mas.

Hájó, Rajah, mas.
Ujan, ditto, ditto.
Bháti, ditto, ditto.
Phúlibar, mas.
Malibar, mas.
Súkra brai, mas., Súkra barói, fœm., } styled the Old, like several others.
Dhonkúvir, mas., Kátbákúvir, mas. } Hindu god of wealth.
} The Hájóni, Hágráui or forest gods. (Hájó … Kátbákúvir)

Khúmla brai, Khúmla búrói } The Kamla river, as mas. et fœm.
Kháti búr,
Chomkhábír,
Dhon bír, } The Champamati river.
} Males all. (Khúmla brai … Dhon bír)
Súnókhi,
Búnókhi, } The Soran river.
Anari.
Banari, } The Boás riber.
} Fœm. omnes. (Súnókhi … Banari)
} The Jaman Madai, or Dii minores. (Khúmla brai … Banari)

Dhimáls:

Birti mahadói,
Nilo mahadói,
Kálo mahadói, } rently Hindu deities, newly named or rather re-named by the Dhimáls.
Bólá, mas., the Sun.
Táli, fœm., the Moon.
Bhanói, fœm., the Earth.
Singko Dír, the forest gods.
Rá ko Dír, the mountain gods.
Chambochiri, fœm., the Champamati river.
Dávai chiri, fœm., river ?
Phúl chiri, ditto, ditto.
Rávai chiri, ditto, ditto.
Jívhánté,
Báwhánté,
Ráwhánté, } Males, styled the Young, whánté ; husbands of above Chiris.
Nitti,
Achár,
Ribhar, } Dii minores, male and female of each name, equivalent to the Bódo Jaman.
Dáta,
Bidáta, } Preside over nuptials.

Extra List of the Pantheon of the Bódos, of Assam and Kámúp.

Siju Gohain,* . . Same as Báthó.
Sásúng, . . . Male, great and malignant.
Róng chiklau, . .
Róng madai, . .
Bor gám, . . .
Sor gám, . . .
Pát bir, . . . } Spirits attendant on Sásúng, propitiated on occasions of sickness, death, or other calamity.
Hap búsa, . . .
Hap búsi, . . .

---

* Gohain is a mere corruption of the Prakrit Gosain, the Supreme ; Siju is the Sij vel Euphorbia, type of Batho.

Ranga tékla,		Spirits attendant on the god Hapbúsa and goddess Hapbúsi. Goats and fowls sacrificed to them.
Boja tékla,		
Moják̈ng Mojáng,		
Jang khalap,		
Jang khilip,		
Cháta bír,		
Matho bír,		
Khona khoni,		Dii minores, get fowls or eggs only in sacrifice.
Match langkhar,		
Jang khana,		
Jang khani,		
Búra Gorung,		Same as Búrha Gosain of the Kóch.
Khola Gorung,		Attendant spirit on last.
Raj phúsarú,		Male, a Penate.
Agráng kólia,		Agrang of prior list.
Khandab,		Fluviatile deities, malignant. Pigeons sacrificed to them.
Jol khúnjara,		
Jol khúnjari,		
Áyá, or Ai,*	Adopted Hindu gods.	Kámakhya.
Maknar,		Lakshmi.
Jomon,		Yama.
Jal kúvír,		Kúvír, Indian Pluto.
Thal kúvír		
Dhon kúvír,		

I know not that I can add anything worth preserving to the foregone list of the deities of the Bódo and Dhimál, save what will fall more appropriately under the head of rites and ceremonies. The list might have been considerably enlarged, but chiefly by importations from the Hindu pantheon; and as these consist of mere names, it seems sufficient to observe, once for all, that the Bódo and Dhimál have latterly adopted a good many of the Hindu goddesses, particularly the various forms of Durgá or Kálí, but without any of the rites appropriate to her worship, or even any images of her. The deities of the Bódo and Dhimál are divided into males and females, old and young; and the latter distinction is material, as indicating the relative rank and consideration of the gods: the ancient or venerable (Brai-Baroï in Bódo, Waráng-Béráng in Dhimál, according to the sex) are the Dii majores; the young (Khúngar vèl Jholou in Bódo, Whánté in Dhimál) are the Dii minores. It will be noticed that several of the deities bear the title of Rájah; and as one of these (Hájó) is a known historic person, it seems probable that this portion of the Bódo and Dhimál pantheon exemplifies the classic and Hindu practice of deifying the mortal benefactors of man-

* Unde Ai húnó, the great festival, presently to be described.

kind—in a word, apotheosis, or hero worship. Madai, in Bódo, is a general term, equivalent to Deity, Divinity; Dír and Grám are corresponding terms in Dhimál.

Religious rites.

Rites and Ceremonies.—The rites of the Bódo and Dhimál religions are entirely similar, and consist of offerings, sacrifices, and prayers. The prayers are few and simple when stript of their mummery; and necessarily so, being committed solely to the memories of a non-hereditary and very trivially instructed and mutable priesthood. They consist of invocations of protection for the people and their crops and domestic animals; of deprecations of wrath when sickness, murrain, drought, blight, or the ravages of wild animals, prevail; and thanksgivings when the crops are safely housed, or recent troubles are passed. The offerings consist of milk, honey, parched rice, eggs, flowers, fruits, and red-lead or cochineal; the sacrifices of hogs, goats, fowls, ducks, and pigeons—most commonly hogs and fowls. Sacrifices are deemed more worthy than offerings, so that all the higher deities, without reference to their supposed benevolence or malevolence of nature, receive sacrifices—all the lesser deities, offerings only. Libations of fermented liquor always accompany sacrifice—*because*, to confess the whole truth, sacrifice and feast are commutable words, and feasts need to be crowned by copious potations! Malevolence appears to be attributed to very few of the gods, though of course all will resent neglect; but, in general, their natures are deemed benevolent; and hence the absence of all savage or cruel rites. All diseases, however, are ascribed to supernatural agency. The sick man is supposed to be possessed by one of the deities, who racks him with pains as a punishment for impiety or neglect of the god in question. Hence, not the mediciner but the exorcist is summoned to the sick man's aid. The exorcist is called both by the Bódo and Dhimáls Ojhá, and he operates as follows. Thirteen leaves, each with a few grains of rice upon it, are placed by the exorcist in a segment of a circle before him to represent the deities. The Ojhá, squatting on his hams before the leaves, causes a pendulum attached to his thumb by a string to vibrate before them, repeating invocations the while. The god who has possessed the sick man is indicated by the exclusive vibration of the pendulum towards his representative leaf, which is then taken apart, and the god in question is asked what sacrifice he requires—a buffalo, a hog, a fowl, or a duck, to spare the sufferer? He answers (the Ojhá best knows how!) a hog; and it is forthwith vowed by the sick man and promised by the exorcist, but only paid when the former has recovered. On recovery the animal is sacrificed, and its blood offered to the offended deity. I witnessed this ceremony myself among the Dhimáls, on which occasion the thirteen deities invoked were Póchima or Waráng, Timai or Béráng, Lákhim, Konoksiri, Ménchi, Chímá, Danto, Chádúng, Aphóï, Biphóï, Andhéman (Aphún), Táto-pátia (Báphún), and Shúti. A Bódo exorcist would proceed precisely in the same manner, the only difference in the ceremony being the invocation of the Bódo gods instead of the Dhimál ones.

The *great festivals* of the year are three or four. The first is held in December-January, when the cotton crop is ready. It is called Shúrkhar by the Bódo, Haréjata by the Dhimáls. The second is held in February-March. It is named Wága-léno by the Bódo, who alone observe it. The Bódo name for the third, which is celebrated in July-August, when the rice comes into ear, is Phúlthépno. The Dhimáls call it Gávi púja. The fourth great festival is held in October, and is named Ai húnó by the Bódo—Pochima páká by the Dhimáls. The three first of these festivals are consecrated to the elemental gods, and to the interests of agriculture. They are celebrated abroad, not at home (generally on the banks of a river), whence attendance on them is called Hágron húdong or madai húdong, 'going forth to worship,' in contradistinction to the style of the fourth great festival, which is devoted to the household gods, and is celebrated at home. The Wágaléno or bamboo festival of the Bódo I witnessed in the spring of this year, and will describe it as a sample of the whole. Proceeding from Siligori to Pankhabárí with Dr. Campbell, we came upon a party of Bódo in the bed of the river within the Saul forest, or rather were drawn off the road by the noise they made. It was a sort of chorus of a few syllables, solemnly and musically incanted, which, on reaching the spot, was found to be uttered by thir-

Festivals.

teen Bódo men, who were drawn up in a circle facing inwards, and each carrying a lofty bamboo pole decked with several tiers of wearing apparel, and crowned with a Chour or Yakstail. Within the circle were three men, one of whom, with an instrument like this (__|_|__) in his hands, danced to the music, waving his weapon downwards on one side and so over the head, and then downwards on the other side and again over the head. He moved round the margin of the circle, in the centre of which stood two others; one a Deóshi or priest, and the other an attendant or servitor called Phantwál. The priest, clothed in red cotton, but not tonsured or otherwise distinguished from the rest of the party, muttered an invocation, whereof the burden or chorus was taken up by the thirteen forming the ring above noticed. The servitor had a water-pot in one hand and a brush in the other, and from time to time, as the rite proceeded, this person moved out of the circle to sprinkle with the holy water another actor in this strange ceremony, and a principal one too. This is the Déódá, or the possessed, who when filled with the god answers by inspiration to the questions of the priest as to the prospects of the coming season. When we first discerned him, he was sitting on the ground panting, and rolling his eyes so significantly that I at once conjectured his function. Shortly afterwards, the rite still proceeding, the Déódá got up, entered the circle, and commenced dancing with the rest, but more wildly. He held a short staff in his hand, with which, from time to time, he struck the bedizened poles one by one, and lowering it as he struck. The chief dancer with the odd-shaped instrument waxed more and more vehement in his dance; the inspired grew more and more maniacal, the music more and more rapid, the incantation more and more solemn and earnest, till at last, amid a general lowering of the heads of the decked bamboo poles, so that they met and formed a canopy over him, the Déódá went off in an affected fit, and the ceremony closed without any revelation—a circumstance which must be ascribed to the presence of the sceptical strangers; for it is faith alone that worketh miracles, and only among and for the faithful. This ceremony is performed annually by the Rajah of Sikim's orders, or rather with his sanction of the usages of his subjects, is addressed to the sun, the moon, the elemental gods, and above all to the rivers, and is designed to ensure health and plenty in the coming year, as well as to ascertain beforehand its promise or prospect through the revelations of the Déódá. With regard to the festival sacred to the national or home-bred (noöni) gods, called Aihuno by the Bódo, and Póchima páká by the Dhimáls, it is to be observed that the rite, like the separate class of deities adored thereby, is more distinctively Bódo than Dhimál. With both people the pre-eminence of water among the elements is conspicuous; but whereas the river gods of the Dhimáls have nearly absorbed all the rest, elementary or other, the household gods of the Bódo stand conspicuously distinguished from the fluviatile deities. The Póchima and Timang of the Dhimáls are one or both rivers; the Báthó and Mainang of the Bódo are neither of them rivers, and their interparietal rites are as clearly distinguished from the rites performed abroad to the fluviatile and other elemental gods. However, the rites of Báthó and Mainou are *participated* by deities of elementary and watery nature; and, on the other hand, the Dhimáls assert that Póchima and Timai have a two-fold character, one of river gods (Dhorla and Tishta), and one of supreme gods, and that they are adored separately in these two characters, the Póchima páká or home rite of October being appropriated to them in the latter capacity, or that of supreme gods. I have not witnessed the Póchima páká, and therefore speak with hesitation. The Ai* húnó is performed as follows. The friends and family being assembled, including as many persons as the master of the house can afford to feast, the Déóshi or priest enters the enclosure or yard of the house, in the centre of which is invariably planted a Síj or Euphorbia, as the representative of Báthó, who is the family as well as national god of the Bódo. To Báthó thus represented the Déóshi offers prayers and sacrifices a cock. He then proceeds into the house, adores Mainou, and sacrifices to her a hog. Next, the priest, the family, and all the friends proceed to some convenient and pleasant spot in the vicinity,

* Ai or Aya is the goddess Kámákyá or Kámrúp, vis genetrix naturæ, typed by the Bhaga or Yoni. See page 131.

previously selected, and at which a little temporary shed has been erected as an altar, and there, with due ceremonies, another hog is sacrificed to Agráng, a he-goat to Manásho and to Búli, and a fowl, duck, or pigeon (black, red, or white, according to the special and well-known taste of each god) to each of the remaining nine of the Noöni madai. The blood of the sacrifice belongs to the gods, the flesh to his worshippers; and these now hold a high feast, at which beer and tobacco are freely used to animate the joyous conclave, but not spirits, nor opium, nor hemp. The goddess Mainou' is represented in the interior of each house by a bamboo post about three feet high, fixed in the ground and surmounted by a small earthen cup filled with rice. Before this symbol is the great annual sacrifice of the hog above noted performed; and before this the females of the family, *once* a *month*, make offerings of eggs. For the males, due attention to the four annual festivals is deemed sufficient in prosperous and healthful seasons. But sickness or scarcity always begets special rites and ceremonies suited to the circumstances of the calamity, and addressed more particularly to the elemental gods if the calamity be drought, or blight, or devastations of wild animals; to the household gods if it be sickness. Hunters likewise and fishers, when they go forth to the chase, sacrifice a fowl to the Sylvan gods to promote their success; and, lastly, those who have a petition to prefer to their superiors conceive that a similar propitiation of Jishim and Mishim, or of the Chiris, will tend to the fulfilment of their requests. And this, I think, is nearly the whole amount of rites and ceremonies which their religion prescribes to the Bódo and Dhimáls; and anxious as I am fully to illustrate the topic, I will not try the patience of my readers by describing all that variety of black victims and white, of red victims and blue, which each particular deity is alleged to prefer; first, because the subject is intrinsically trifling; and, second, because the diverse statements of my informants lead me to suspect that the matter is optional or discretionary with each individual priest prescribing these minutiæ. I have mentioned the rude symbols proper to Báthó and Mainou. None of the other gods seem to have any at all, though a low line of kneaded clay attached to the Tháli that surrounds the sacred Euphorbia in the yards of the Bódo is said to stand for the rest of the divinities, who, as I have already said, are wont to be worshipped collectively rather than individually; and thus the sun, the moon, and the earth, though adored by Bódo and by Dhimál, have no separate rites, but are included in those appropriated to the elemental gods. Witchcraft is universally dreaded by both Bódo and Dhimál. The names of the craft and of its professors, male and female, will be found in the vocabulary. Witches (Dain and Mhái) are supposed to owe their noxious power to their own wicked studies, *or* to the aid of preternatural beings. When any person is afflicted, the elders assemble and summon three Ojhás or exorcists, with whose aid, and that of a cane freely used, the elders endeavour to extort from the witch a confession of the fact and the motives. By dint of questioning and of beating, the witch is generally brought to confession, when he or she is asked to remove the spell, to heal the sufferer—means of propitiating preternatural allies (if their agency be alleged) being at the same time tendered to the witch, who is, however, forthwith expelled the district, and put across the next river, with the concurrence of the local authorities. No other sorcery or black art, save that of witches, is known; nor palmistry, augury, astrology, nor, in a word, any other supposed command of the future than that described in the 'Wá galéno' as the attribute (for the nonce) of the Déódá or vates. The evil eye causes some alarm to Bódo and to Dhimál, who call it mogon nángo and mí nójó respectively, and who cautiously avoid the evil-eyed person, but cannot eject him from the community. The influence of the evil eye is sought to be neutralised by offerings of parched millet and eggs to Khoja Rajah and Mansha Rajah—Dii minores, who find no place in my catalogue, ample as it is. Moïsh madai, I am told, likewise claims a place in the Bódo pantheon, and a distinguished place too, as the protector of this forest-dwelling people from beasts of prey, and especially the tiger.

Priesthood.—The priesthood of the Bódo and Dhimáls is entirely the same, even to the nomenclature, which with both

Priesthood, p. 125.

people expresses the three sorts of clergy by the terms Déóshi, Dhámi, and Ojhá. The Dhámi (seniores priores!) is the district priest, the Déóshi the village priest, and the Ojhá the village exorcist. The Déóshi has under him one servitor, called Phantwál. There is a Déóshi in nearly every village. Over a small circle of villages one Dhámi presides, and possesses a vaguely defined but universally recognised control over the Déóshis of his district. The general constitution and functions of the clerical body have already been fully explained. Priests are subject to no peculiar restraints, nor marked by any external sign of diverse dress or other. The connection between pastor and flock is full of liberty for the latter, who collectively can eject their priest if they disapprove of him, or individually can desert him for another if they please. He marries and cultivates like his flock, and all that he can claim from them for his services is, first, a share of every animal sacrificed by him, and, second, three days' help from each of his flock (the grown males) per annum towards the clearing and cultivation of the land he holds on the same terms with them, and which have been already explained. Whoever thinks fit to learn the forms of offering, sacrifice, and accompanying invocation can be a priest; and if he get tired of the profession, he can throw it up when he will. Ojhás stand on the same footing with Dhámis and Déóshis. They are remunerated solely by fees; but into either office—priests or exorcists—the form of induction is similar, consisting merely of an introduction by the priests or exorcists of the neophyte to the gods the first time he officiates. One Dhámi and two Déóshis usually induct a Déóshi; three Ojhás an Ojhá; and the formula is literally that of an introduction—'This is so-and-so, who proposes, O ye gods! to dedicate himself to your service. Mark how he performs the rites, and, if correctly, accept them at his hands.'

Customs.

Customs.—Under this head I shall state the usages observed at births, naming, weaning, toga virilis, marriage, and death, aggregating what is common, and distinguishing what is peculiar, to the Bódo or Dhimáls. The customs of both people have a great similitude, owing to their perfect simplicity. They are derived, in fact, from nature, and nature as little strained by arbitrary devices of man as can well be. At births the mother herself cuts the navel-string, so soon as she has recovered strength for the act. No midwives are found, so that nature must do all, or the mother and offspring perish together. But deliveries are almost always very easy, and death in childbed scarcely known—a blessing derived from the active and unsophisticated manners of the sex. The idea of uncleanness occasioned by births, and by deaths also, is recognised; but the period of uncleanness and segregation is very short, and the purificatory rites consist merely of bathing and shaving, performed by the parties themselves. The infant is named immediately after birth, or as soon as the mother comes abroad, which is always in four or five days after delivery. There are no family names, or names derived from the gods. Most Bódo and Dhimáls bear meaningless designations, or any passing event of the moment may suggest a significant term: thus a Bhótia chief arrives at the village, and the child is called Jinkháp; or a hill peasant arrives, and it is named Góngar, after the titular or general designation of the Bhótias. Children are not weaned so long as their mother can suckle them, which is always from two to three years—sometimes more; and two children, the last and penultimate, are occasionally seen at the breast together. The delayed period of weaning will account in part for the limited fecundity of the women. When a Bódo or Dhimál comes of age, the event is not solemnised by any rite or social usage whatever. Marriage takes place at maturity, the male being usually from twenty to twenty-five years of age and the female from fifteen to twenty. Courtship is not sanctioned; the parents or friends negotiate the wedlock, though in so simple a state of society it cannot be but the parties have frequently met and are well known to each other. The Hindús wisely and decorously attach much discredit to the parent who takes a "consideration" for the grant of his daughter in marriage. No such delicacy is recognised by Bódo or Dhimál parents, who invariably demand and receive a price, which is called Jan in the language of the former, and Gándi in that of the latter people. The amount varies from ten to fifteen rupees among the Dhimáls, from fifteen to forty-five among the Bódo. I cannot learn the cause of the great difference. A youth who has no means of discharging this sum, must go to the house of his father-in-law elect, and there literally earn his wife by the sweat of his brow, labouring, more judaico, upon mere diet for a term of years, varying from two as an average to five and even seven as the extreme period. This custom is named Gabóï by the Bódo—Ghárjyá by the Dhimáls. It, of course, implies a good deal of intercourse between the betrothed youth and damsel prior to their nuptials; but from all I can learn, instances of opportunity abused are most rare. The legal nature and effects of the nuptial contract have been already explained under the head of Laws: what concerns fecundity, longevity, &c., under the head of Medicine, as a branch of religion. The marriage ceremony is little perplexed with forms. After the essential preliminaries have been arranged, a procession is formed by the bridegroom elect and his friends, who proceed to the bride elect's house, attended by two females specially appointed, to put red-lead or oil on the bride elect's head when the procession has reached her home. There a refection is prepared, after partaking of which the procession returns, conducting the bride elect to the house of the groom's parents. So far the same rite is common to the Bódo and Dhimál—the rest is peculiar to each. Among the Dhimáls, the Déóshi now proceeds to propitiate the gods by offerings. Dáta and Bídata, who preside over wedlock, are invoked, and betel-leaf and red-lead are presented to them. The bride and groom elect are next placed side by side, and each furnished with five pauns, with which they are required to feed each other, while the parents of the groom cover them with a sheet, upon which the Déóshi, by sprinkling holy water, sanctifies and completes the nuptials. Among the Bódo the bride elect is anointed at her own home with oil; the elders *or* the Déóshi perform the sacred part of the ceremony, which consists in the sacrifice of a cock and a hen, in the respective names of the groom and bride, to the sun; and next, the groom, rising, makes salutation to the bride's parents, and the bride similarly attests her future duty of reverence and obedience towards her husband's parents; when the nuptials are complete. A feast follows both with Bódo and Dhimáls, but is less costly among the former than among the latter—as is said, because the higher price paid for his wife by the Bódo incapacitates him for giving so costly an entertainment. The marriage feast of the Dhimáls is alleged to cost thirty to forty rupees sometimes, the festivities being prolonged through two and even three days; whereas four to six, rarely ten, rupees suffice for the nuptial banquet of a Bódo.

The Bódo and Dhimáls both alike bury the dead, immediately after decease, with simple but decent reverence, though no fixed burial-ground nor artificial tomb is in use to mark the last resting-place of those most dear in life, because the migratory habits of the people would render such usages nugatory. The family and friends form a funeral procession, which bears the dead in silence to the grave. The body being interred, a few stones are piled loosely upon the grave to prevent disturbance by jackals and ratels rather than to mark the spot, and some food and drink are laid upon the grave; when the ceremony is suspended and the party disperses. Friends are purified by mere ablution in the next stream, and at once resume their usual cares. The family are unclean for three days, after which, besides bathing and shaving, they need to be sprinkled with holy water by their elders or priest. They are then restored to purity, and forthwith proceed to make preparations for a funeral banquet, by the sacrifice of a hog to Mainou or Timáng, of a cock to Báthó or Póchima, according to the nation. When the feast has been got ready and the friends are assembled, before sitting down they all repair once again to the grave, when the nearest of kin to the deceased, taking an individual's usual portion of food and drink, solemnly presents them to the dead with these words, 'Take and eat: heretofore you have eaten and drank with us: you can do so no more: you were one of us: you can be so no longer: we come no more to you: come you not to us.' And thereupon the whole party break and cast on the grave a bracelet of thread priorly attached, to this end, to the wrist of each of them. Next the party proceed to the river and bathe, and having thus lustrated themselves, they repair to the banquet, and eat, drink, and make merry as though they were never to die! A funeral costs the Dhimáls from four to eight rupees—something more to the Bódo, who practise more formality on the occasion, and to whom is peculiar the singular leave-taking of the dead just described.

Arts. *Useful Arts.*—As already observed, the arts practised by the Bódo and Dhimáls are few, simple, and domestic. Agriculture is the grand and almost sole business of the men, but to it is added the construction and furnishing of the dwelling-house in each of the frequent migrations of the whole people. The boys look after the domestic animals. The women, aided by the girls, are fully employed within doors in spinning, weaving, and dyeing the clothing of the family, in brewing, and in cooking. The state of the arts will be sufficiently and most conveniently illustrated by a description of the house, household furniture, clothes, food, and drinks of the people, preceded by an account of the implements, processes, and products of agriculture.

Agriculture. The agricultural implements are an axe to fell the forest trees, a strong bill or bill-hook to clear the underwood and also to dig the earth, a spade for rare but more effectual digging, and lastly a dibble for sowing the seed. The axe is called Rúá by the Bódo, Dúphé by the Dhimáls. It is a serviceable implement of iron (the head) similar to that in use in the plains, where the head is bought; the haft being made at home. The bill, called Chékhá by the Bódo, Ghongóï by the Dhimáls, is a 'jack of all work,' like in shape to our English bill, but with the curved extremity or beak prolonged, and furnished with a straight downward edge of some three inches. It is of iron, of course, and purchased in the Kócch marts. The spade is the ordinary short bent one of the plains, where it is bought, and where it is called Kódál. The Bódo and Dhimáls use it but little, and have no name of their own for it. The dibble is a wooden staff about four feet long, made by the people themselves. It is like a stout walking-staff sharpened at the lower end. The process of culture, emphatically called 'clearing the forest,'* is literally such for the most part, and would be so wholly, but that several of the species grown being biennials, a field is retained over the first year, so that the second year's work consists merely of weeding and re-sowing rice amid the other standing products. The characteristic work is the clearing of fresh land, which is done every second year, and thus axes and bills clear away the wood. Fire completes what they have left undone, and at the same time spreads over the land an ample stratum of manure (ashes). The soil is worked nearly enough in eradicating the undergrowth of trees (for the lords of the forest are only truncated); so that what little additional digging is needed may be and is performed with the square end of the bill. 'Tis no great matter, and firing is the last *effectual* process. Amid the ashes the seed is sown by a dibbler and a sower, the former of whom, walking erect, perforates the soil in quincunxes by sharp strokes of his pointed staff (called Shómán by the Bódo, and Dhúmsi by the Dhimáls), so as to make a series of holes from one to two inches deep, and about a span apart; whilst the latter, following the dibbler, and furnished with a basket of mixed seeds, drops four to six seeds into each hole, and covers them at the same time. All the various produce raised is grown in this promiscuous style. Chait, Baisák, and half Jeth † comprise the season for preparing and sowing the soil. Sáwan, Bhádún, Kúár, and half Kártik,‡ that for gathering the various products, save cotton, which is not gathered till Pús-Mágh.§ The rest are reaped as they successively ripen: first, cucurbitaceous plants (Kóhara, Louka, Khíra, Kankara, Karéla); then greens (Sém, mattar, Béngan, Chichinda, Póï); then the several edible roots (Yam, Arwi, &c.); then the condiments (Haldi, Adrak, red peppers); then the millets and pulse (Marwa, Kúlthi, Úrid); then maize; next rice; then the mustards (Tori or Sarsún or Til); and last of all, cotton. The fields, which are much better worked in eradicating the jungle than

* See pp. 103 and 118 for more samples of the use of a full vocabulary in illustrating the condition of the people.

† March, April, and May respectively.

‡ July, August, September, and October respectively.

§ December-January.

those for which the Bengal plough performs the same office, are likewise as much better weeded; and how strange soever to mere English ears the huge mixture of crops may sound, this mixture does not greatly exceed the practice of Bengal, nor is it inconsistent with good returns, though there be no artificial irrigation whatever. The cotton is a biennial of inferior quality, but it is the main crop, and that from the sale of which in the plains the Bódo and Dhimáls look to provide themselves with the greatest part of the rice they consume; for their own supply is very inadequate. Nevertheless rice is usually spoken of as the crop next in estimation to cotton, though maize and even millet seem to contribute as much to the quantity of home-reared food. The rice grown is similar to the 'dry rice'—'the Ghaiá' of Nepal—the 'summer rice' of the plains. The other articles grown have all been enumerated above, save indigo, which, with the cochineal of the forest and madder procured from the hills, supplies the Bódo and Dhimáls with dyes. Arhar and a few more of the superior agricultural and horticultural products of the plains are occasionally grown by the Bódo and Dhimáls, whose chief products, however, are those given above, and of them not absolutely all in one field and year, though from twelve to fifteen are always there, and include a good supply of vegetables, condiments, and cerealea, but the last deficient in the article of rice, which is the principal grain eaten. Of vegetables, the favourites are Béngans, cucurbitacea, and roots (Thá vel Lin in their own tongues); of cereals, rice; of condiments, red peppers. Mustards are grown not for their oils, nor as stimulants, but merely for eating like parched pease. The oil-seeds are fried, and are relished in that state;* the young plants also are used as greens. The surplus seed is sold to the oilmen of the plains, neither Bódo nor Dhimál being wont to express oil, of which they consume little, and that only for cooking. Lights they use none (save on occasions of ceremony and of púja), but go to bed early, and sit by the fire—a splendid wood-fire—till then. The small quantity of oil used for cooking they buy in the adjacent marts of

* They are fried with greens, and of course yield up a good deal of their oil to flavour the vegetables.

the Kócch. The cotton crop and the surplus of the mustard crop are all the agricultural products which they sell any portion of. Cotton is habitually sold, the small portion only that is needed for clothing the family being reserved, which may be about one-fifteenth of what is raised. The domestic animals have been enumerated elsewhere, and must be spoken of again when we come to the head of Food. Agriculturally viewed, they are a dead letter, not even their manure being employed.

Upon the whole, the agriculture of the Bódo and Dhimáls is conducted with as much skill as that of their lowland neighbours; with skill much superior to that of their highland neighbours; and with pains and industry greatly above those of either highlanders or Kócches. The following details of what is raised by one Bódo cultivator, and consumed by himself, his wife, and three young children, imperfect though they be, will help to convey a just idea of his position; and those who care to compare it with the position of a peasant in the hills and in the plains will find the means of making such comparison in Appendix II.

Bódo peasant tilling $1\frac{3}{4}$ bigha with the spade.

PRODUCTS OR INCOME.

Dhán or rice in husk,	24 bisi = 12 maunds =	4	0	0
Cotton undressed,	16 bisi = 8 maunds =	32	0	0
Maize,	3 bisi = $1\frac{1}{2}$ maunds =	0	8	0
Millets and Pulse,	4 bisi = 2 maunds =	0	12	0
Condiments, dyes, & greens,	2 bisi = 1 maund =	4	0	0
Total Rupees,		41	4	0

EXPENSES.

Rice in husk, bought,	3 Pouthi = 48 maunds =	15	0	0
Salt bought,	18 Phol = 18 seers =	3	0	0
Cotton-field pujá,	=	1	0	0
Government tax,	=	1	0	0
Cotton-seed bought,	=	1	0	0
Ai huno festival,	=	3	0	0
Oil bought for worship and for occasional lights,	=	0	8	0
Sickness, fees to the Ojha,	=	4	0	0

Presents to sisters and friends who ask aid and make visits, ...	=	2 0 0
Ornaments for wife, ...	=	2 0 0
Fruits bought for self, wife, and children, .	=	2 0 0
Fish bought in rains when none can be taken in the forest, ...	=	1 8 0
Earthen vessels bought, . . . , . . .	=	0 8 0
Proportion of price of Chékhá or Bill, . .	=	0 8 0
Ditto ditto of Jong or spear, . .	=	0 8 0
Ditto ditto of metallic pots and pans,	=	0 8 0
Sundries, ...	=	2 0 0
Total Rupees, . .		40 0 0
Balance in favour, ...		1 4 0

It has been already mentioned that the Bódo and Dhimál peasant is liable to a corvee or labour tax, the items of which may be added thus—for the Rajah, 3 days thrice a year, or 9 days; for the Rajah's local representative, 6 days; for the village priest or Déóshi, 3 days—total, 18 days per annum. This is so much deducted from his resources, and may be stated at two * rupees in coin. A peasant of the plains using the plough will earn twice or even thrice as much as a Bódo or Dhimál, and yet, what with the wretched system of borrowing at 25 to 30 per cent., and the grievous extra frauds incidental to that system, he will not be nearly so well off. The Bódo or Dhimál, again, has abundance of domestic animals, and is, moreover, at liberty to eat the flesh of all save the cow; whereas the peasant of the plains has few, and of those only the goat that he can eat. And, lastly, the Bódo's industrious wife not only spins, but weaves and dyes all the clothes of the family, besides supplying it amply with wholesome and agreeable beer, whilst the peasant's wife in the plains does nothing but spin; and though this may diminish the cost of the family clothing, still it must be bought; nor will there be much thread to dispose it in free sale, apart from the clothier. The highland peasantry generally earn less than the Bódo and Dhimáls, and are proportionally worse

* If the Bódo pay one rupee of direct and two of indirect taxes, he will be nearly on a level, *quoad* public burdens, with the peasant of the plains.

off, though lightly taxed, and exempt from the curse of the borrowing system. The Néwár peasants of the great valley of Nepal—as industrious as the Bódo and Dhimáls—nay, more so—and more skilful too—earn more and retain more, notwithstanding the heavy *rent* they pay to their landlord, who pays the light tax or Government demand on the land. The particulars may be seen in the Appendix.

Houses.—The Bódo and Dhimáls build and furnish their own houses without any aid of craftsmen, of whom they have none whatever. They mutually assist each other for the nonce, as well in constructing their houses as in clearing their plots of cultivation, merely providing the helpmates with a plentiful supply of beer. A house is from 12 to 16 cubits long by 8 to 12 wide. A smaller house of the same sort is erected opposite for the cattle; and if the family be large, two other domiciles like the first are built on the other sides, so as to enclose an open quadrangle or yard. The houses are made of jungle grass, secured within and without by a trellis-work of strips of bamboo. The roof has a high and somewhat bulging pitch, and a considerable projection beyond the walls. It also is made of wild grass, softer than that which forms the walls. There is only one division of the interior, which separates the cooking and the sleeping portions of the house, which has no chimney or window, and but one door. Ten to forty such houses form a village, without any rigid uniformity or any defences whatever. Houses.

Furniture is very scant, consisting only of a rare bedstead, some sleeping-mats, a stool or two, and some swinging-shelves; and all of these are made at home. Household utensils are a few earthen vessels for carrying and holding water, some metallic cooking, eating, and drinking pots, and a couple of knives, to which we must add the spinning, weaving, dyeing, and brewing apparatus of the women. All the latter are of the simplest possible form and home-make. The earthen and metallic pots and pans are purchased in the Kócch marts. There are none of iron nor of copper; all are of brass or other mixed metals that are metallic, owing, it is said, to the dearness of iron and copper. There are no leathern utensils. Baskets of bamboo and of cane and ropes Furniture of grass are abundant, and of home-make by the men, who likewise haft all the iron implements they purchase abroad for agricultural or domestic uses. It has already been said that lights are dispensed with beyond what is afforded by an ample fire.

Clothes. *Clothes.*—With both people they are made at home, and by the women. The Bódo women wear silk procured from the castor-plant worm, which they rear at home in each family. The Bódo men and Dhimáls of both sexes wear cotton only. Woollen is unknown, even in the shape of blankets. The manufactures are durable and good, and not inconveniently coarse—in fact, precisely such as the people require; and the dyeing is very respectably done with their own cochineal, morinda, or indigo, or with madder got from the hills; but all prepared by themselves. The female silk vest of the Bódos possessed by me is 3½ feet wide by 7 long, deep red, with a broad worked margin of cheque pattern—and of white and yellow colours, besides the ground red—above and below. This garment is called Dókhana by the Bódo, and must be a very comfortable and durable dress, though it somewhat disfigures the female form by being pressed over the breast as it is wrapped round the body, which it envelops from the armpits to the centre of the calves. The female garment of the Dhimáls differs only in material, being cotton. It is called Bónha. The male dress of the Bódo consists of two parts—an upper and a lower. The former is equivalent to the Hindu Chadar or toga. It is called Shúmá, and is 9 to 10 cubits by 3. The latter, styled Gámchá, and which is 6 cubits by 2, is equivalent to the Hindu Dhoti, and after being passed between the legs is folded several times round the hips, and the end simply tucked in behind. The male dress of the Dhimáls is similar. Its upper portion is called Pátaka; its lower, Dhári; the whole, Dhába with this people; Hí with the Bódo. All cotton clothes, whether male or female, are almost invariably white or undyed. Neither Bódo nor Dhimál commonly cover the head, unless when the men choose to take off their upper vest and fold it round the head to be rid of it. Shoes are not in use; but a sort of sandals or sole-covers, called Yápthong vel Champhoï, sometimes are, and are made of wood by the people themselves. There are no other shoes. Ornaments are rare, even amongst the women, who, however, wear small silver rings in their ears and noses also, and heavy bracelets of mixed metal on their wrists. These are bought in the Kócch marts, and are quite simple in form.

Food.—The sorts of vegetable food have been already enumerated in speaking of agriculture. Rice is the chief article; wheat or barley unknown even by name, Ghiu or clarified butter is likewise totally unused and unnamed, and oil is very sparingly consumed for food. Salt, chillies, vegetables, plenty of rice, varied sometimes with maize or millet, and fish or flesh every second day, constitute, however, a meal which the poor Hindu might envy, washed down as it is with a liberal allowance of beer. Plenty of fish is to be had from December to February, both inclusive, and plenty of game from January to April inclusive, though the Bódo and Dhimál are no very keen or skilful sportsmen, notwithstanding the abundance of game and freedom from all prohibitions. They have the less need to turn hunters in that their domestic animals must supply them amply with flesh. They have abundance of swine and of poultry, and not a few of goats, ducks, and pigeons, but no sheep nor buffaloes, and cows are scarce. Milk is little used, but not eschewed, as by the Gárós it is. They may eat all animals, tame or wild, save oxen, dogs, cats, monkeys, elephants, bears, and tigers. Fish of all sorts, land and water tortoises, mungooses, civets (not cats!), porcupines, hares, monitors of enormous size, wild hogs, deer of all sorts, rhinoceros, and wild buffaloes, are amongst the wild animals they pursue for their flesh, and altogether they are abundantly provided with meat. Food.

Drinks and Stimulants.—The Bódo and Dhimáls use abundance of a fermented liquor made of rice or millet, which the former call Jó, the latter Yú. It is not unpleasant, and I should think was very harmless. Its taste is a bitterish sub-acid, and it is extremely like the Ajimana of the Néwárs of Nepal. Brewing and not distilling seems to be a characteristic of nearly all the Tamulian races, all of whom drink and make beer, and none of them spirits. The Bódo and Dhimál pro- Drinks.

cess of making this fermented liquor is very simple. The grain is boiled; the root of a plant called Agaichito is mixed with it; it is left to ferment for two days in a nearly dry state; water is then added *quantum sufficit;* the whole stands for three or four days, and the liquor is ready. The Agaichito plant is grown at home. Its root, which serves for balm, is called Emon. I have never seen it. Besides this beer—of which both people use much—they likewise freely use tobacco; but never opium nor hemp in any of the numerous preparations of both; nor distilled waters of any kind; and, upon the whole, I see no reason to brand them with the name of drunkards, though they certainly love a merry cup in honour of the gods at the high festivals of their religion. Among my own servants, the Bódo have never been seen drunk; the Moslems and Hindús several times excessively so.

Manners. *Manners.*—The manners of the Bódo and Dhimáls are, I think, a pleasing medium between the unsophisticated roughness of their highland neighbours and the very artificial smoothness of their neighbours of the plains. They are very shy at first; but, when you know them, are cheerful without boisterousness, and inquisitive without intrusion. Man's conduct to woman is always one of the best tests of his manners; now the Bódo and Dhimáls use their wives and daughters well, treating them with confidence and kindness. They are free from all out-door work whatever, and they are consulted by their husbands as their safest advisers in all domestic concerns, and in all others that women are supposed likely to understand. When a Bódo or Dhimál meets his parent, or one of the elders of the community, he drops his joined hands to the earth, and then raises them to his forehead; and if he be abroad, he says, 'Father, I am on my way;' to which the parent or senior answers, 'May it be well with you.' There is little visiting, save that which is inseparable from the frequent religious feasts and festivals, already sufficiently described; nor are amusements or pastimes for young or old common. Indeed, children or women seem to have none, and the men so little heed them that neither Bódo nor Dhimál tongue has a word of its own for sport, play, or game! The young men, however, have two games, which I proceed to describe summarily. In the light half of October, on the day of the full moon, a party of youths proceeds at nightfall from village to village, like our Christmas wakers, hailing the inhabitants with song and dance, from night till morn, and demanding largess. This is given them in the shape of grain, beer, and cowries, wherewith on their return they make a feast, and thus ends the pastime, which is called Harna-harni by the Bódo, and Harna-dháká by the Dhimáls. Again, in the dark half of the same month, when the wane is complete, the youths similarly assemble, but in the daytime, and dressing up one of their party like a female, they proceed from house to house and village to village, saluting the inhabitants with song and dance, and, obtaining presents as before, conclude the festival with a merrymaking among themselves. The Bódo name of this rite or game is Chórgéléno; the Dhimáls call it Chór-dháká. And now we shall conclude the subject of manners with a statement of the ordinary manner in which a Bódo or Dhimál passes the day. He rises at day-spring, and having performed the offices of nature and washed himself, he proceeds at once to work in his field till noon. He then goes home to take the chief meal of the day, and which consists of rice, pulse, fish or flesh (on alternate days), greens and chillies, with salt—never ghiu—seldom oil. He rests an hour or more at noon, and then resumes his agricultural toils, which are not suspended till nightfall. So soon as he has got home he takes a second meal with his family, then chats a while over the fire, and to bed betimes, seldom two hours after dusk. If the children be young, they sleep with their parents; if older, apart. The Bódo call their first meal Sanjúphúni inkhám; their second Bílíni inkhám. The Dhimál name for the first is Mánjbéla-chákâ; for the second Dilima-cháká. Wives usually eat after their husbands, children with.

Character.—The character of the Bódo and Dhimál, as will be anticipated from the foregoing details, is full of amiable qualities, and almost entirely free from such as are unamiable. They are intelligent, docile, free from all hard or obstructive prejudices, honest and truthful in deed and word, Character.

steady and industrious in their own way of life, but apt to be mutable and idle when first placed in novel situations, and to resist injunctions, injudiciously argued, with dogged obstinacy. They are void of all violence towards their own people or towards their neighbours, and, though very shy of strangers, are tractable and pleasant when got at, if kindly and cheerfully drawn out. The Commissioner of Assam, Major Jenkins, who has by far the best opportunities for observing them, *when drawn out of their forest recesses*, gives them, as we have seen, a very high character as skilful, laborious cultivators and peaceable respectable subjects; whilst that this portion of them want neither spirit nor love of enterprise is sufficiently attested by the fact, that when the Dorjiling corps was raised, two-thirds of the recruits first obtained were Bódo of Assam.* Neither the Bódo nor Dhimál, however, can be characterised, upon the whole, as of military or adventurous genius, and both nations decidedly prefer, and are better suited for, the homebred and tranquil cares of agriculture. They are totally free from arrogance, revenge, cruelty, and *fierté*; and yet they are not devoid of spirit, and frequently exhibit symptoms even of that passionate or hasty temperament which is so rare, at least in its manifestations, in the East. Their ordinary resource against ill-usage is immovable, passive resistance; but their common demeanour is exempt from all marks of the wretched alarm, suspicion, and cunning that so sadly characterise the peasantry of the plains in their vicinity, and which, being habitual, must be fatal to truth. The Bódo and Dhimál in this respect, as in most others, more nearly resemble the mountaineers, whose straightforward, manly carriage so much interests Europeans in their favour. Oppression and its absence beget these different phases of character. The absence of all petty trade likewise contributes materially to the candour and integrity of the Bódo and Dhimáls. Among all mankind, women, wine, and power are the great tempters, the great leaders astray. Now the Bódo and Dhimáls rise decidedly superior to the first temptation, are not unduly enslaved to the second, and, from the perfect equality and subject condition of the whole of them, are en-

* See also Griffith's Journals.

tirely exempted from the third. Power cannot mislead those who never exercise it; where women are esteemed, and no artificial impediments whatever exist to prevent marriage, women are a source, not of vice, but of virtue; and, lastly, where "honest John Barleycorn" is free from the dangerous alliance of spirits, opium, and hemp, I know not that he, even if assisted by the "narcotic weed," need be set down as a necessary corrupter of morals. True, the Bódo and Dhimál do not pretend to the somewhat pharisaical abstemiousness *or* cleanliness of the Hindús. But I am not therefore disposed, particularly on Hindú evidence, to tax them with the disgusting vices of drunkenness and dirtiness, though these, and obstinacy, *if any,* are the vices we must lay to their charge, as the counterpoise of many and unquestionable virtues. Peasant, be it remembered, must be compared with peasant, and not peasant with people of higher condition; and if the comparison be thus fairly made, it may perhaps be truly decided that the Bódo and Dhimál are *less* sober and *less* cleanly and *less* tractable than the people of the plains; *more* sober and *more* cleanly and *more* tractable than those of the hills. The Bódo and Dhimáls are good husbands, good fathers, and not bad sons; and those who are virtuous in these most influential relations are little likely to be vicious in less influential ones, so that it need excite no surprise that these people, though dwelling in the forest, apart from the inhabitants of the open country, are never guilty of blackmailing or dacoity against them, whilst among themselves crimes of deep dye are almost unknown. To the ostentatious hospitality of many nations whose violence against their neighbours is habitual they make no pretensions; but among their own people they are hospitable enough, and towards the stranger invariably equitable and temperate.

APPENDIX.

No. I.

Physical Attributes.

The physical characteristics of these races have already been summarily stated. But it is desirable to be more particular on this head. A young man named Bírna, a Bódo, has been selected to represent his nation, and through it the Dhimáls and Kócches also, for the traits of face and form are so nearly alike in all that neither pen nor pencil could satisfactorily set them apart.* Bírna is about twenty-one years of age (for, like a true Bódo, he knows not how old he is), so that we are obliged to give his age conjecturally. The mistake, however, cannot exceed a year or two.

His dimensions are as follows in English feet, inches, and quarters:—

	1st time.		*2d time.*	
Total height,	5	$3\frac{3}{4}$	5	$3\frac{1}{2}$
Crown of head to hip,	2	3	2	$2\frac{3}{4}$
Hip to heel,	3	1	3	1
Length of arm,	2	$3\frac{1}{2}$	2	$3\frac{3}{8}$
Length of foot,	0	9	0	9
Length of hand,	0	$6\frac{5}{8}$	0	$6\frac{7}{8}$
Greatest girth of chest,	2	$7\frac{1}{4}$	2	7
Greatest width across shoulders,	1	$2\frac{3}{4}$	1	$2\frac{3}{4}$
Girth of pelvis at hips,	2	3	2	5
Greatest width of pelvis, at hips, less,	0	11	0	$10\frac{1}{2}$
Greatest girth of head,	1	9	1	$8\frac{3}{4}$
Greatest length of head, chin to crown,	0	9	0	$9\frac{1}{4}$
Greatest width of head, across parietes,	0	$5\frac{3}{4}$	0	$5\frac{3}{8}$
Greatest girth of thigh,	1	$5\frac{3}{4}$	1	$5\frac{1}{2}$
Greatest girth of calf,	1	$1\frac{1}{4}$	1	$1\frac{1}{2}$
Greatest girth of arm,	0	9	0	$9\frac{3}{8}$

Bírna's colour is an olive or brunet, clear and pale as that of a high-caste Hindú. Though a stout youth, of twenty-one or more, he has not yet the least symptom of beard, and but a very faint show of moustache. He expects, he says, to have more or less of beard in five or six years, but shall carefully eradicate the stray hairs, *more majorum!* He has no want of eyelash or

* Pages 113, 114.

eyebrow, and the hair of his head is copious, straight, strong, and glossy. He has no hair on the chest, but as much as usual on the armpits and elsewhere. He is well made and stout enough, sufficiently fleshy, but without any striking muscular development. His calves, in particular, though not quite equal to those of the mountaineers, are very superior to anything of the sort to be seen amid the people of the plains. His legs are long in proportion to his trunk, but not awkwardly so, and his chest is finely formed, broad and deep. His head is well formed and well set on the shoulders, the great foramen having apparently a central aperture. There is no defect of cranial development anteally or posteally, and the skull is well shaped and round, though not so ample in the frontal region as in fine specimens of the Arian vel Caucasian family, and the face is larger in proportion to the head than in *such* specimens. The length of the head to that of the body is as one to seven nearly. If the features are not straight, or perpendicular, to the front, the want of right line is caused less by recession of the forehead or chin than by the advance of the jaws and lips, which are both large. The mouth is too wide and the lips too thick for beauty; but there is no ape-like or negro-like deformity, nor do the finely-formed teeth project forward. The chin wants the rounded projection of the Arian type; but it is not ill formed nor retiring. The forehead has sufficient height and breadth, though there are vague indications of contraction and backward slope as compared with very fine heads. The eye is sufficiently large and sufficiently well opened; but the cavity around it is too much filled with flesh, and the angles of the aperture have a tendency to obliquity, the outer one upwards and the inner downwards. The nose, sufficiently long and well raised between the eyes, has a good, narrow, straight bridge, but a somewhat thickened or clubbed extremity; and the nares are wide, inclining from the elliptic to the round shape. The ears are somewhat large, and stand rather apart from the head, but not remarkably so. The oval form to which the contour of the face inclines is broken by the projection of the cheek-bones, between which the face is noticeably wider than anywhere else, but only in a small degree; and, upon the whole, the ill effect of the somewhat large and quasi-Mongolian features is redeemed by their cheerful and amiable expression, though the human type indicated is clearly rather Mongolian than Caucasian.

No. II.

Production and Consumption of a Néwár Peasant of the Valley of Népál, cultivating with the spade seven standard ropini of Népál.*—1 *man*, 1 *wife, and* 3 *small children.*

Household Utensils and Agricultural Implements.

Iron pots and implements, domestic and agricultural.—1 Lóhyá or Tá-kyá; 1 lamp, Díp or Dallú; 1 spoon, Dárú or Dhouwo; 1 spade, Kúdál or Kú; 2 sickles, Hasuá or Íí; 2 spuds, Basuli or Kokaicha; 1 knife, Churi or Chú-pi; 1 cleaver, Pahasúl or Khúni,	2	13	6
Copper pots, domestic.—4 plates or Thàls; 1 drinking-pot, Lótah or Táhán-po; 2 cups or saucers for greens, &c., Katóra or Khola,	4	0	0
Earthen pots.—2 large vessels, Hándi or Kousi; 1 water-drawing, Méntá or Gópah; 1 to hold water, Gharra or Dhapa; 4 dishes, Parai or Bhégó,	0	2	0
Sundries.—1 Pestle and mortar, Silalora or Lohómá; 1 winnow, Dagara or Hásá; 1 broom, Jharu or Túphi; 1 rope, Dora or Lákhá khi,	0	6	3
1 sleeping mat, Chatai or Súkhú; 1 blanket, Kamal or Sángá,	1	1	0
Woman's weaving apparatus.—1 spinning-wheel, Charka or Yong; 1 cotton cleaner, Phatka or Tímá; 1 loom, Karigá or Tánjolong,	1	8	3

Production, annual.

5 Ropini of wet rice-land or ½ Lakhábú—1st crop, Málsi dhán, 20 múri = 40 man,	40	0	0
2 Ropini of dry rice-land or U'lábú—1st crop, Ghaiá-dhàn, 5 múri = 10 man,	8	0	0
Gleanings of both the above, Phúlówá, 10 Páthi = 1 man,	0	12	0
Second crops, or summer crops, Jari or Séé—Lakhábú Séé—Wheat, 2 múri = 4 man,	8	0	0
U'lábú Séé—Greens, roots, and red peppers, 1½ múri = 3 man,	3	0	0
Straw and bran of rice and wheat of all crops, 36 loads (mans),	2	8	0
Wages earned as a carrier in cold months,	24	0	0
Wages for odd jobs all the year round,	12	0	0
Total earnings,	98	4	0
Earnings from the soil,	62	0	0

* Four ropini equal one bigah, or thereabouts.

Monthly Expenses.

Rice for all the family, 17th páthi = 1 man 27 sér,	3	3	3
Salt for do. do., 2 mána = 1½ sér,	0	4	0
Oil, eating, do. do., 1 bokóché = ⅛ sér,	0	2	0
Tobacco, do. do., 1 bádháni = 1½ sér,	0	3	0
Greens, roots, red peppers, do., 2¾ páthi = 11 sér,	0	4	0
Fuel, Louna or Chúsí, 3 loads,	0	3	3
Lights (burn pine-sticks of own cutting),	0	0	0
Grain for brewing and distilling, 3¼ páthí = 13 sér, yielding 1 sér spirits, 10 sér of beer,	0	8	0
Daily luncheon, Jalpán or Diko,*	0	12	0
Per mensem,	5	7	6
Per annum,	65	10	0

Annual Expenses.

Twelvefold of the above expenses,	65	10	0
Landlord's rent on the Lakhábú, called Péón,	20	0	0
Do. do. on the Ulábú, do. do.,	4	0	0
N.B.—Second crops are rent free; landlord pays the land-tax.			
Government capitation or house tax, viz., sáwani, 0 1 6; phágú, 0 1 6; shri panchami, 0 0 9,	0	3	9
Government corvee or bíth, composition for,	0	12	0
Mendicant tax or Jógi pá,	0	0	6
Barber,	0	6	0
Wear and tear of implements and utensils,	1	11	0
Cotton to make clothes, 2 dhárni = 6 sér,	2	0	0
Total expenses,	94	11	6
Balance in favour,	3	4	6

Peasant of the plains (Azimgurh) cultivates 6 standard bighas with the plough. Family as before.

Agricultural Implements or Stock.

Two oxen for the plough,	16	0	0
One plough,	1	0	0
One harrow, &c.,	1	0	0
One Dúrmús or smoother,	0	2	0
One Kodál or spade,	1	0	0
Two Khúrpi or spuds,	0	2	0
Two Hasúá or sickles,	0	3	0

* Throughout these details the native terms have been given to secure accuracy and facilitate reference. The first term is Hindi; the second, Newari, a language so little known that the Hindi equivalent is added.

	Rs.	a.	p.
One Háthá or irrigating shovel,	0	4	0
One Doura or shovel,	0	1	3
One Páncha or rake,	0	1	6
One Akhana,	0	1	6
	19	15	6

Household Utensils.

Iron pots and pans, none,	0	0	0
Brass pots, 1 lótah, 1 thál,	2	4	0
Earthen pots for cooking, drawing and holding water,	0	8	0
Wooden utensils—Okli músal, to husk rice,	0	4	0
——— Plates, dishes, &c.,	0	7	0
Leathern utensils, Chalani, Súp, &c.,	0	2	0
Stöne utensils, pestle and mortar,	0	8	0
Two bedsteads,	0	7	0
One blanket,	1	0	0
Bed-clothes, Dohar, Chadar,	1	12	0
Wife's spinning-wheel,	0	4	0
	5	4	0

Annual Production.—Two fasals or crops, Kharíf and Rabbi—
Wet rice-land, three bighas.

First crop, kharíf—Dhán or rice, 20 mans,	20	0	0
Janéra, 8 mans,	8	0	0
Tángan, 1 man,	0	8	0
U'rid, 1 man,	2	0	0
Kaukari, 1 man,	0	12	0
Second crop, Rabbi—Wheat, 1½ bigha, 10 man,	13	5	3
	44	9	3
Sugar ½ bigha, 10 mans gúr,	25	0	0
Arhar, } 1 bigha mixed, { 8 mans,	8	0	0
Cotton, } { 4 mans,	8	0	0
Dry or wheat land, 3 bighas, 1 crop.			
Barley, 2 bighas, 20 mans,	20	0	0
Wheat, 1 bigha, 10 mans,	13	5	4
Straw, bran, &c., of all the crops, 80 kháchá,	14	0	0
Total raised,	130	10	8

Annual Expenses.

Government tax,	12	0	0
Interest at 25 per cent. on whole stock, raised on loan,	29	0	0
Seed,	8	8	0
Wear and tear of implements	1	0	0
Wagon or cart hire,	0	8	0
Cotton bought to make thread,	0	4	0
Pújas or worship,	5	0	0

Puróhit or family priest,	0	8	0
Weaver's charge for weaving wife's and children's clothes from own thread,	2	0	0
Wear and tear of pots and pans,	0	4	0
Repairs of house,	0	12	0
Earthen pots,	0	8	0
Physician,	0	8	0
Fees to miller,	1	0	0
Washerman, barber, smith,	2	0	0
Man's clothes bought,	4	0	0
	67	12	0

Monthly Expenses.

Barley for food, 3 mans,	3	0	0
Pulse, do., 20 sérs,	1	0	0
Salt and oil, 2 sér of each,	0	8	0
Tobacco, 2 sér,	0	4	0
Food of two oxen,	2	0	0
Flesh and fish for family,	0	8	0
	6	15	0
Per annum,	83	4	0
Total expense per annum,	151	0	0
Balance against,	20	5	4

Thus it appears that the productive energy of the Néwár, working with the spade upon the same extent of land or thereabouts, is to the productive energy of the Bódo working somewhat similarly—that is, without aid of plough—as 3 to 2; and to that of the peasant of the plains, using the plough, as 3 to 2 also. The Néwárs, indeed, are the best cultivators in Asia. 'Tis hard to compare the Bódo with them. I have no materials yet for comparison with the highlanders of Sikim, who, however, I know pretty well, cannot compete with the Bódo, whose productive energy exceeds that of the lowland peasant, aided by the plough, by one-seventh. With regard to the peasantry of the plains, it is very evident that it is not the weight of Government taxation which crushes them, but the borrowing system—the miserable habit of never laying by a sixpence—of living upon loans—annually taking up their whole stock from the capitalist at an interest never less, and often more, than 25 per cent., so that, as they say themselves, their life is spent in filling a vessel full of holes at the bottom, and beneath which is another *entire* vessel belonging to the usurer! The above details show that the Government tax is but one-eleventh of what the Azimgarh peasant raises from the soil; and also that the interest he annually pays is nearly (in fact fully) threefold of the public demand. Thus the poor peasant is perpetually plunged into difficulties such as the present account may fully explain, whereby it is seen that the annual deficit is equal to one-sixth of the annual gross produce raised by this cultivator. Now, look at the Bódo cultivator's account. Here is no debt; and small as the whole earnings are, I can testify that they suffice for such comfort as no peasant of the plains has any conception of. But the Bódo, it may be argued, is nearly exempt from taxation.* Look, then, at the Néwár peasant of Népál, whose burdens equal two-fifths of all he rears from the *soil*—one-fourth of whatever he annually produces by *all* his industrious toils. Nor does it in the least matter to the present question that what he pays is rent, not tax; for in the plains of India the Government stands in place of landlord, and if it did not, the peasant's position cannot be at all affected by the quarter or denomination of his payment, but only by its positive and relative amount, including *every* permanent charge, such as that incurred by the Hindu to those craftsmen whose services his scrupulosity and his indolence compel him to pay for. On the other hand, the simpler and more active habits of the Néwár peasant and his wife enable him to dispense with these craftsmen, and to add, besides, nearly a third to his agricultural income by labour apart from, and in excess of, that devoted to the soil. And thus the Néwár peasant, whilst living far more comfortably than the Hindú peasant—better fed, better clad, and better housed by much, yet never exceeds his income, and paying not a sous to the usurious capitalist, or rather loan-monger, whose *indirect frauds are as bad as his direct extortions*—can sustain cheerily legitimate agricultural burdens great as those I have recorded!

DARJEELING, *June* 4, 1846. B. H. HODGSON.

P.S.—I have said that I do not propose to go into comparisons till I have accumulated a large mass of materials. But I may mention, as a sample of the prospective fruits of this inquiry in reuniting the so long and so utterly scattered members of the Non-Arian family, that the identifying of the Gárós and Khasias (as well as of the Kacháris) with the Bódo is already nearly or quite established, and that points of arbitrary similitude in creed and customs and speech, indicating radical identity of race, are rapidly multiplying in relation to the aborigines of this frontier and those of South Bihar, viz., the Kóls or Dhángars.†

* It has been shown above that the real pressure of taxation is, in fact, equal in both cases.

† Since this paper was written, Mr. [now Sir Walter] Elliot of Madras has shown that the Gónd language of Séóni (north of the Nerbudda) is in vocables and structure very closely allied to Tamil; that is, to the typical speech of the Aborigines.

SECTION II.

ON HIMÁLAYAN ETHNOLOGY.

I.

COMPARATIVE VOCABULARY OF THE LANGUAGES OF THE BROKEN TRIBES OF NÉPÁL.

DARJILING, *October 4th*, 1857.

The Secretary of the Asiatic Society of Bengal.

SIR,—I have the honour to transmit to you herewith four series of Vocabularies of Himálayan tongues, comprising (in two parts), 1st, the languages of the broken tribes of the Central Himálaya; and, 2d (also in two parts), the several dialects of the Kiránti language, which likewise is proper to the same part of the chain, or, to be more specific, to Eastern Népál. The languages included in the two parts of these two papers are—

Broken Tribes.

1. Ḍahi or Darhi. Daḍhi.
2. Dénwár.
3. Pahi or Paḍhi.
4. Chépáng.
5. Bhrámu.
6. Váyu or Háyu.
7. Kuswár.
8. Kúsúnda.
9. Pákhya, *unbroken.*
10. Tháksya, *unbroken.*
11. Tháru.

Tribes of the Kiránti People.

1. Chamling or Ródóng.
2. Rúngchhénbúng. Bontáwa.
3. Chhingtáng. Bontáwa.
4. Nachhereng.
5. Wáling. Bontáwa.
6. Yákha.
7. Chourásya.
8. Kulung.
9. Thulung.
10. Báhing.
11. Lohorong.
12. Lambichhong. Wáling.
13. Báláli.
14. Sángpáng.
15. Dumi.
16. Kháling.
17. Dungmáli.

The arrangement and nomenclature of these, made some time back, are not quite correct, but they will serve the present end, and can be corrected when we come to particulars. At present it will suffice to say that 9 and 10 of the "broken tribes" cannot well be classed under that head, the Pákhya and Tháksya being still unbroken.

Of the Kiránti tribes, the value of the subdivisional names is not always equal. I have indicated this on the right hand. Thus, 2, 3, 5, as to language, &c., could be unitised under the common name of Bontáwa; and 5, 12, both classed first as Wáling, and then as Bontáwa, the larger aggregate. These minuter affinities are pretty well indicated by the dialects. I was obliged to begin in the dark as to what varieties of the language would be fittest for selection as dialects, and those I hit on were not always of equal value.

As samples of the broken tribes and of the great Kiránti people, I have lately selected for special study the Váyu of the one and the Báhing of the other. I shall forthwith submit these ample essays,* and then may find time to advert to some

* These also will be found in the sequel, but awkwardly blended by a common heading with the empirical comparative vocabularies of the languages of the broken tribes and of the dialects of the Kiránti language, which two latter also are similarly confused. Neither have anything to do with the complete analyses following them. The whole of the papers consist of—(1) comparative vocabularies of the languages of the broken tribes; (2) ditto of the dialects of the Kiránti language;

general considerations. If not, they will be found in the new essay on the "Physical Geography of the Himálaya" now issuing from the Calcutta press as No. XXVII. of Selections from the Records of the Government of Bengal.—I am, Sir, your obedient servant,

B. H. HODGSON.

---

(3) grammatical analysis of the Váyu tongue; (4) ditto of the Báhing tongue, (5) description of the Váyu people; (6) ditto of the Kiránti people, of whom the Báhing are a sept. The two first papers form the sequel of that long series priorly given with a view to furnish *primâ facie* evidence of the affinity of all the Túranians in and near India. But after these two papers had been completed, they were held back in order to that fuller style of investigation which is exemplified by papers 3 and 4. Suddenly, however, I found myself obliged to quit India; and then, deeming it wisest on the whole no longer to delay the publication of the several papers, I sent them all to press, and in my hurry forgot to erase from papers 1 and 2 certain hints for correction or addition which grew out of my increasing knowledge, but which, not having been worked out, should have been erased from these two papers before they were forwarded for publication. This, with my inability to correct the press, will explain what else might seem odd.

COMPARATIVE VOCABULARY OF THE LANGUAGES OF THE BROKEN TRIBES OF NÉPÁL.

English.	*Daḍhi vel Dahi.*	*Dénwár.*	*Paḍhi vel Pahi.*	*Chépáng.*	*Bhrámú.*	*Háyu, or Váyú.*	*Kuswár.**
Air	Batás †	Bátás	Phú-sá	Má-rú	A-sí	Hujum	Batás
Ant	Cheunta T-seu-n-ta	Cheu-ti T-seu-ti	Mig-za	Túl-ti	A-nap	Chiki-bulla	Kimili
Arrow	Kánr	Kánr	Bá-rá	Lá	Pá-rá	Sár	Sár
Bird	Chárí	Cháráï	Bú-khíncha Bu-khin-cha	Wá. Mó-á	Jyá-ling	Chín-chí	Chárí
Blood	Rágát	Ráktáï	Hí	Wé-í. W-í	Chí-wí	Ví	Rakti
Boat	Dúngo. Dun-go	Dúnga. Dun-ga	Dón-ga	Dún-gá	Dun-ga	Dun-ga	Dun-ga
Bone	Had	Had	Ku-sá	Rhu-s	Wot	Rú	Hadh
Buffalo	Bhainsa	Bhainsi	Mé-sá	Mí-syá	Bhai-sa	Caret	Bhainsa
Cat	Birálo	Mai-ni	Bhí	Bírál	Manzyi	Dána	Bírálo
Cow	Gai	Gai	Mó-sá	Mó-syá	Syá	Caret	Gai
Crow	Káwá	Kowa	Kó-kó	Kág. Ká	Káng-kang	Gá-gín	Kág-lé
Day	Din	Di-ni	Nhí-na-ko	Nyí. Ngí	Di-ná	Nu-ma	Di-ní
Dog	Kúkúr	Kú-kúr	Ku-ju. Ku	Kwí. Kúí	A-kyá	Urí	Ku-kol
Ear	Kán	Kán	Nhúa-puru	Né. Nó	Ká-ná	Nak-chú	Kán
Earth	Máti	Máto	Chá	Sá	Ná-sá	Kó	Mati
Egg	Anda	Dimba	Khén-ja	Wá-kúm. Lu-m	Hom	Chalung	Dimba
Elephant	Hathi	Hattí	Ki-si	Há-thi	Caret	Caret	Hathi
Eye	A'nkhí	A'nkhá	Mí-gi	Mi. Mi-k	Mi-k	Mé-k	A'nkhi
Father	Búbó	Bábá	Bá	Ba-bú	Ba-bâi	U'-pá	Bábáïk
Fire	A'-gé	Agi	Mí	Mé. Mí	Má-ï	Mé	A'ghi
Fish	Má-chha	Ma-chhe	Nyó-já	Nyá. Ngá	Ná-ngá	Hó	Jhá-in
Flower	Phúl	Phúl	Só-nó	Dó. Ró	A-wai	Púm-mí	Phúl
Foot	Gód	God	Lí	La	U'n-zik	Lé	Gor
Goat	Chág-ri Cha-g-ri	Chá-gár Cha-ga-r	Chá-lá	Mé-syá. Mí-chá	Mí-chha Mí-ch-ya	Chí-lí	Chá-gari Cha-ga-ri
Hair	Bár	Bár	Són	Mén	Syám	Sóng	Bár
Hand	Hát	Háth	Lá	Kút-t. Kú-t-pa	Bhi-t	Gót	Háth
Head	Múd	Mú-dek	Chhé	Tá-Tó-long	Ká-pá	Pú-chhi	Ká-pá
Hog	Sú-er	Sú-gúr	Phó	Pyá. Pyák	Pak-syá	Pög	Sú-ri
Horn	Sing	Sing	Mhú-ní	Ró-ng	U'-nyá. U'n-yú	Ru-ng	Sing-ek ‡

Horse	Ghóro	Ghóra	Sa-ro	Sé-rang	Caret	Caret	Ghóra
House	Ghar	Ghar	Chén	Tim. Kyim	Nam	Kim	Ghara
Iron	Phalám	Phalám	Né	Phalám	P*ha*iám	Ka-k ching	Phalám
Leaf	Pát	Páta	La-ti	Ló	Sou	Ló	Páta
Light	U'-jung	U'-jat	Ja-la	Sa-mo. An-gho Ang-ha	Caret	Dang-dang	Johan. Joha-n
Man	Má-nus	Má-nus	Man-che	Pur-si	Bal. Bar	Sing-tong Lon-cho	Gok-chái Chá-wái
Monkey	Banker	Bandar	Mú-ga	Yú-k	Pá-yúk	Phó-ka	Báner
Moon	Já-nhá Já-n-ha	Jyún	Nhí-bá	La-he. La-me	Chala-wani Cha-la-wa-n	Chó-lo	Jún
Mother	U'-yá	Am-báï	Mí	A-maí	A-maí	U-mé	A-mái
Mountain	Dán*d*a	Pa-khá	Tó-lhá	Rí-ás	Dán*d*a	Chyá-jú. Wa-ne	Pahár
Mouth	Mú-hú*n*	Mú-hú*n*	Mhú-r	Mó-tong	A-nám	Múk-chu	Mú-hú
Muschito	Kón-kón-ya	Ghú-suná	Pa-ti	Caret	A-mín	Eks'a-mék (Night-eye)	Pip-sa. Bhun-si
Name	Ná-yám	Ná-u	Nu-ng	Myéng	Min	Ming	Nou
Night	Ráto	Ráting	Chá-nákô Chan-ko	Yá	Caret	E'k-sá	Ráthi
Oil	Tél	Tél	Sú	Sáté. Lí-ko	A-sá	Kí	Tél
Plantain	Kéra	Kéra	Mó-syi. Mozyí	Mlé-sai. Mai-sé	Ung-syé	Rí-sá	Kéra
River	Khó-lá	Lá-rí	Khá-rá	Kyú. Gó-ro	Gú-dúl	Gang. Bimbo	Kó-si
Road	Pán-ya	Bát	Lóng	Lyám	U'm-má	Lóm	Bát
Salt	Nún	Nún	Chí-há	Sé	Chhá	Chíä	Nún
Skin	Chá-la	Chá-la	Chúg-ra	Caret	Caret	Kók-chó	Chá-la
Sky	Sa-ra-g	Sá-rá-g	Sá-rá-g	Sá-rá-g	Caret	Caret	Sá-rá-ng
Snake	Sámp	Sámp	Bí	Lú	Pái-gú	Hó-bú	Sámp
Star	Tí-ryá Tí-r-yá	Tá-rái	Nú-ng-gí Nung-gni	Ka-r	Caret	Caret	Tára-ï
Stone	Pá-thár	Do*n*-kho	Lhong-go Lho-ng-g-no	Báng	Kúng-bá	Lún-phu	Pathár
Sun	Gá-má	Gá-má	Su-je	Nyám	U-ní	Nó-mó	Súraj

* The Kuswár tongue is remarkable for having, though it has nearly lost its vocables, retained its grammar, which shows the affinity of the Kuswár to the Turkic group of tongues. The conjunct pronoun is suffixed to both noun and verb. See on page 170.

† It is almost needless to remark that in cloumns 1, 2, and 7 the vocables are mostly corrupt Hindi or Khas. The Dahis, Dénwárs, and Kuswárs are located in the Tarai, where the aboriginal tongues are being gradually superseded by Hindi, as they are in the mountains by Khas. But some retain a deal of their grammar—*e.g.*, Kuswár, as to which see the note at page 170.

‡ See note at page 170.

English.	Daḍhi vel Dahi.	Dénwár.	Paḍhí vel Pahi.	Chépáng.	Bhrámú.	Háyu, or Váyú.	Kuswár.
Tiger	Bág	Bág	Dhún	Já-ké-la and Já	Bú-máng	Bílo	Bághi
Tooth	Dánt	Dánt	Wá	Srék	Sú-a. S-wá	Lú	Dant
Tree	Rúk	Gátch	Sí-má	Si-ng. Sing-tak	Sim-ma	Sing-phung	Gátch
Village	Gáon	Gaon	Gón	Caret	Háng-dúng	Caret	Gáon
Water	Pa-tí	Kyú	Lú-khú	Tí	A'-wá	Tí	Pání
Yam	Pin-álu	Chó-yán	Sá-gí	Gó-í	Yá-k	Rá-pí. Chó-pi	Gé-ti. Bhyá-gar
I	Máï	Múï	Núng and Já	Ngá	Ngá	Gó	Má-ha
Thou	Taï	Tu-ï	Chhúng. Chhí	Náng	Náng	Gon	Tá-ha
He. She. It	U'	I'	Hó. U'	U'	U'	Mü. Wáthi. A'. I'	Hú-lo. Há-lo
We	Há mi	Hami	Já-di	Ngí-lum	Ní	Gókháta	Há-mi
Ye	Ta-he	To-ho	Chhá-di	Ning-lum	Núng	Góne-khata	Tú-mi
They	U'-nin	U'-ho	U'-si. Ho-si	Wó-mai	Hú-dú	Mïí-khata Kó-me. A'-mé	Hú-ri. Há-ri. Há-ring
My	Mé-ro	Mo-ra	Núng-gu. Já-gu	Ngá-ku	Ngá-ku	Ang or Ang-mu *	Má-ha-na Suffix, im
Thy	Téro	Tó-ra	Chhúng-gu	Náng-ku	Nang-ku	Ung or Ung-mu	Ta-ha-na Suffix, ir
His. Hers. Its	U'-ker	Wok-rak	Hong-gu H-wang-gu	U'-ku	U'-ku	A' or A-mu	Hú-lo-kara Suffix, ik
Our *	Ham-ro	Ham-rai	Já-gu	Ngí-ku	Ní-ku	Ang-ki or Ang-ki-mu	Hamára
Your *	Taha-ro	Caret	Chhá-gu	Ning-ku	Núng-ku	U'n-ni. U'n-ni-mu	Túmára
Their *	U'n-karo	Wal-ko	As-ya-gu. Asya-gu	U'-mai-ku	U'n-kú	A'khata A-khata mu	Háring-kara
One	E'k	E'k	Chhí or Chhi-gu	Yá-zho. Ya-z-yo	Dé	Kó-lú	E'k
Two	Dwi	Dwí	Ní or Ni-ng-gu	Nhi-zho. Nhi-z-yo	Ni	Ná-yung	Dwí
Three	Tin	Tin	Súng or Sung-gu	Sum-zho. Sum-z-yo	Swóm	Chú-yung	Tin
Four	Chár	Chár	Pi or Pi-ng-gu	Plóï-zho. Plo-ï-z-yo	Bi	Bí-níng	Chár
Five	Pánch	Pánch	Ngo or Ngo-ng-gu	Pú-ma-zho Pu-ma-z-yo	Bá-ngá	Caret	Pánch
Six	Cháh	Cháh	Khú or Khu-ng-gu	Krúk-zho K-ru-k-z-yo	Caret	Caret	Cháh
Seven	Sát	Sát	Nhé or Nhe-ng-gu	Chána-zho Cha-na-z-yo	Caret	Caret	Sát

Eight	A'th	A'th	Chyá or Chya-nggu	Prap-zho / Prap-z-yo	Caret	Caret	A'th
Nine	Nó ú	Nó-ú	Gún or Gung-gu	Taku-zho / Taku-z-yo	Caret	Caret	Nó-ú
Ten	Das	Das	Gí or Gi-ng-gu ‡	Gyí-b-zho / Gyi-b-z-yo	Caret	Caret	Das
Twenty	Bís	Bís	Ní	Caret	Caret	Caret	Bís
Thirty	Tis	Tís	Su*n*	Caret	Caret	Caret	Tís
Forty	Chális	Chálís	Pí í	Caret	Caret	Caret	Chálís
Fifty	Pachás]	Pachás	Ngé-é	Caret	Caret	Caret	Pachás
Hundred	Sou	So	Sá-chi	Caret	Caret	Caret	Sou
Of	Kó	I'k. Ak	Yá. Yágu	Kú	Kú	Mu. Mo. Mi	Ná. Kara
To	Lai	Ki	Yá-ta	Sáï	Tú	Caret	Láï
From	Nhé	Sú*n*	A'ng	I'	Jáng. Gáng	Khen	Bátho. Dékhi
With	Súï	I'*n*	Nang	I'	Chou	Nong	Sin
In. On	Yér. Hér	I'*n*	Gar-hi-né	Háng	Thá-chi	Bé	Kana
On. Upon	U'paré	U'paré	Caret	Caret	Gáï	Bé. Wane	Kana. Te. E'
Now	Yéhe	Akhan	Alaga;	Caret	Tha-chi	U'm-be	Já-khen
Then	Wóhe	Takhen	Wélhe	Caret	Wá-lhé	Mé-the	A'-khen
When	Káhe	Ka*n*hin	Gwé-thé	Caret	Kai-lhé	Há-ké	Ka-khen
To-day	A'ju	A'-ju	Tha-ra	Té-n	Ti-ya	Ti-ri	A'-ja
To-morrow	Kálú	Ka-lhi. Ka-l-hi	Kín-chi	Syáng	Wó-gai	Nú-kana	Kál-hi
Yesterday	Kálú	Ká-lú	Mi-zyé	Yón	Mi-lya	Tí-jong	Kal-hai
Here	I'-chi	Yé-ti	Thúgu-thá	Caret	Hí-di	I'-ne. I-the	Achi-na
There	U'-chi	Wo-ti	Hong-tha	Caret	Hú-di	Mí-ne. Wa-the	U'-chi-na
Where	Ká-chi	Ká-chi	Gu-thá	Caret	Ku-nai	Há-né	Ka-chi-na
Above	U'para	Akásai	Cho-gu-tha	Caret	Hú-khai	Wa-ne	U'para
Below	Hét	Hé-then	Ko gú-thá	Caret	Hu-mai	Hu-the	Hét
Between	Májhai	Majhen	Dári	Caret	A-sal	Mádúm-be	Manjhi
Without. Outside	Báhir	Báhir	Pen-há	Caret	Am-bu	Tongma. Lok	Báhir
Within	Bhitar	Bhítar	Doho*n*	Caret	Trka. Náng	Neng. Bék	Bhitar
Far	Tárho	Tar-hai	Ta-pa-le	Dyáng-to	Ka-lók	Ho-lám	Dú-re

* These are plurals. I subsequently found that some of these tongues have duals also, as well as separate pronominal affixes. See Váyu grammar in sequel for a sample.

† Ang=my; angmu=mine; and so of the others. See full treatise of Váyu in the sequel.

‡ Gu', affix of all the numerals, as of all the pronominal and other qualitives, is the minor of gender. The major is hma, as in Néwári, to which tongue Pahi is closely allied.

English.	Daḍhi vel Dahi.	Dénwár.	Paḍhí vel Pahi.	Chépáng.	Bhrámú.	Háyu, or Váyú.	Kuswár.
Near	Ná-gík	Yén-chi	Nhyár-ke	Lok-to	Ka-nyák	Khé-wa	Pas-yong
Little	Chút-hi	Chút-ek-pe	Bhá-chá	Caret	Són-bi	Ití-bang	Thóre
Much. Many	Dhérai	Dhéré	Chó-hóng	Jhó	Búd-he	Ching-ngak Sing-ye	Dhére
How much	Kat'-ha	Kat'-ha	Gu-ri	Caret	Ku-wa	Há-thá	Katak
As	Ja-sai	Já-nhé	Gé-ré	Caret	Jún	Háng-nga	Jásege
So	Wó-sai	Tá-nhé	Hé-ré	Caret	U'chi	Mé-má	Há-sege
Thus	Yé-sai	Ye-nhe	Yé-ré	Caret	Hé. Khháksá	I'-ma	I'-sege
How?	Ká-sai	Ka-nhe	Gi-re	Caret	Hé-tu	Húng-ngá	Ká-sege
Why?	Caret	Caret	Caret	Caret	Caret	Mis-pa	Kyú-hún
Yes	Hó	Té	Khyú[1]	Caret	Mó. Lik	Dik-sa. Nom	An. An
No	Hói-né	Boy-in	Má-khí	Caret	Mami. A-lik	Má. Ma-nom	Ná
Do not	Jún	Jú-nú	Mí-re	Caret	Man	Thá	Má-má
And	Ra. Pún	Sá. Şúá	Khá	Caret	Wóng	Lé	Gyú
Or	Tí	Láne. Né	Kí. Lá	Caret	Ké	Ki	Ná
Which. Jón	I'se-k	I'	A'rkhyá-gu	Caret	Hé-tu	Sú-do	Jé
Which. Tón	U'-se-k	U'	Hórkhyá-gu	Caret	Hó-tu	Mí-do	Húle
Which? Who? } Kon*	Kó-no	Kó-hik	Gú-gú. Gu-hmo	Caret	Hai	Sú	Ké
Something	Kyá-hú-je	Ki-chhu	Chala	Caret	Háng	Mís-che	Ké-hu
Somebody	Kólho-pun	Kó-lhu	Súnung	Caret	Súng	Sú-na	Ké-hu
Good	Niko	Sajhá	Bhing-gu-hma †	Pi-to	Gá-do	Nuh-'kámo Nuh'ka-mo	Bhala
Bad	Bón-thia	Bón-sajha	Ma-bhing-gu-hma	Pi-lo	Ma-dó	Maning-nuh-kamo	Nakhaja
Cold	Chíso	Chíso	Khu-khu-dha	Yés-to	Chíso	Khémta	Chíso
Hot	Tá-to	Ta-to	Kwá-gu-hma	Dhá-to	U'dúm	Jé-ta	Tá-to
Raw	Ká-cho	Caret	Ka-zhi-gu-hma	Caret	Pón	Chala-mo	Ká-cho
Ripe	Pá-ko	Caret	Bú-gu	Caret	Ki-míng	Mín-mo	Pá-ko
Sweet	Gúre	Gúryo	Chág-gu	Ním-to	Kyó-syá	Chin-ji-mo	Gúlyo
Sour	Syí-syé	Ko-ro	Pa-lu-gu	Ním-lo	Kyá-só	So-kim. So-ki-m	Ná-gúlyo
Bitter	Ti-ta	Ti-ta	Khá-ḳhá-dha	Caret	Kyá-khai	Khá-chim Kha-chi-m	Títo
Handsome	Rámro	Caret	Bángla-gu-hma	Dyáng-to	Ku-syén	Bing	Banaila

Ugly	I'nje-ramro	Caret	Bámala-gu-hma	Pi-lo	Má-syón	Mam-bing	Nakhaja
Straight	Sojhó	So-lar	Ti-pyúng-gu-hma	Dhím-to	Caret	Chéng-chéng-mo	Sójho
Crooked	Kwón-káro	Bán-ko	Phara-só-gu-hma	Dóng-to	Bán-go	Ko-ko-láng-mo	Bángo
Black	Kaj-ráro	Kár-da	Há-ku-gu-hma	Gal-to	Chi-ling	Khák-ching-mi	Kal-da
White	Góro	Goró	Túyú-gu-hma	Bhám-to	A'-bo	Dawáng-mi	Pán-dal
Red	Kak-ta-ro	Rak-ta-ro	Sí-dha-gu	Dú-to	Pháya	Lang-ching-mi	Píl-la
Green	Haryo	Harro	Wón-wón-dha	Phélto	Sik-sik	Girúng-mi	Hardiálo
Long	Lámo	Lámo	Tá-há-gu ‡	Caret	Kíwo. Alhok	Phín-ta	Lámo
Short	Chóti	Kháto	Púti-ha-gu	Caret	An-yak	Mam-phín-ta	Chóto
Tall } man	Dhénga	Algo	Tha-so	Caret	Alhok	Jóng-ta	Algo
Short } man	Nanar	Hócho	Khó-so	Caret	Anyak	Thó-thi	Hó-cho
Large	Bát-ko	Bat-ke	Hwongu-dha-gu	Bron-to	Alham	Hóng-ta	Bara
Small	Nání	Chot-ke	Chí-ja-gu Chigi-dha-gu	Mai-to. May-yo	A'-mi	Choh'-mi	I'bra
Round	Dallo	Dúmro	Gó-ná-gu	Caret	Dallo	Kúl-kúl	Dal-lo
Flat	Chep-to	Chep-to	Pherchya-kyen-gu	Caret	Nim-bu-le	Teng-teng	Sambh
Square	Char-konya	Caret	Pekúng-la-gu	Caret	Chárpatya	Caret	Chárpatya
Fat	Móto	Móto	Lhóng-hmo	Caret	Ki-chho	Lón-ta	Moto
Thin	Dúbró	Dú-bro	Gang-si-hma	Caret	Má-chho	Gér-*ta*	Khéngralo
Weariness	Thá-kin	Hadyaila	Nél-nu. Ngal-nu	Caret	Kitu-khwi	Jób	Caret
Thirst	Pias	Tirkha	Pyá-há	Caret	A'wáphang	Tí-daksa	Tirkha
Hunger	Bhú-kha	Bhúk	Ha. He-nu	Caret	U'yangkéhé	Sóksa	Bhók
Eat	Khóu	Khá-ik	Né	Jé-che. Jhí-sa	Chá	Já-che, *n.* Ja-ko, *a.*	Khá-ik
Drink	Pyú	Khá-ik	Tó-*in*	Túm-che. Tum-sa	Syá-ngá	Túng-che, n. Tung-ko, *a.*	Khá-ik
Sleep	Sút-uk	Sút	Dyú*n*	Em-che. Yem-sa	Ná-wa	Im'-che	Sut-ou
Awake	Chétas. Chet-as	U'th	Dó*n*	Tyok-che. Tyok-sa	Só-wa	Thá-im'-che Sis'-che	U'thou. Uth-ou
Laugh	Hans-uk	Rhyás. Rhi-as	Nhí-li	Nhí-s-che. Ǹhí-sa	Nú-ya	I'-sche. Yès-che	Hás-kou Hask-ou
Weep	Ró-uk	Há*n*	Khwé	Rhí-as-che. Rhi-a-sà	Há-pá	O'k-che	Da-ka-rou Da-ka r-ou

* Jon and ton, as well as kon, are Hindi and Urdu—languages very rich in relative and correlative terms. At first I got professedly equivalent terms in these Tartar tongues, but afterwards I saw reason to doubt their accuracy, as being contrary to the genius of these tongues—a point as to which see the full treatises on Váyu and Báhing in the sequel.

† For the affixes gu, hma, see note at the word "ten," supra. Dang and dha respectively are quasi-equivalents, sometimes substituted, more rarely added.

‡ Ta-ha-gu, quod (gu) longitudine (ha) magnum (ta). So púti-ha-gu is quod longitudine parvum (púti). Ha is the generic sign of long things.

English.	*Daḍhi vel Dahi.*	*Dénwár.*	*Paḍhí vel Pahi.*	*Chépáng.*	*Bhrámú.*	*Háyu, or Váyu.*	*Kuswár.*
Speak	Bórá-uk	Sa-rha	Lhá	Nhó-s-che. Nho-sa	Kha-lá-wa	It'. Dáwa-hot. Bót *	Bar-ou. Ghan-ou †
Be silent	Júnbora-uk	Júnsá-rhá	Sunán-chón	Caret	Má-pé. Má-khale	Thá-it. Gyúng-pon-che	Mámá-bor-ou. Mama-bor-ou
Come	A'-úk	An	Yá	Caret	Thá-yá	Phí ‡	A'be
Go	Já-úk	Já	Lá-són	Caret	Yé-ngá. Yen-ga	Láh'-lá	Ná. Ná-hin
Get up	U'th-úk	U'th	Dáïng-chon	Ching-sa	So	Y'ép-che	U'th-ou
Sit down	Bas-uk	Bas	Kujung-chon	Mús-che. Mu-sa	Mú-ká	Mós-che	Basou
Walk	Hid-uk	Chól	Gó	Whá. Whá-sa	Syó. Jéwa	Khók-che	Nón
Run	Dú-gar-uk	Dúgar	Kéng-gno. Ke-in-go. Ke-ng-go	Kí. Kísa	Gé-gwé-ya	Lúng-che	Dhou
Give	Di-hik	Dí-ik'	Bí-chhon	Bú-ï §	Pyú	Há-to	Dé-ik
Take	Lé-hik	Lé-ik'	Há-ya	Lé-ï	Thá-yo	Dó-ko	Né-ik
Strike	Thá-thá-ik	Már-ik'	Dá-chhon	Caret	Mó-tó	Toh'-po	Thá-tha-ik ‖
Kill	Káti-ik	Már-ik'	Pá-li	Caret	Sáto. Aprito. A-pri-to	Sísh-to. Yúk-to	Hirka-ik
Bring	An-ik	A'nhik'	Bú-yá	Caret	Kháï	Pish-to	An-ik
Take away	Léj-ik	Léga-ik'	Búlásón. Bú-lá-son	Caret	Yáng-gnó. Ya-n-go	Lák-to. La-k-to	Né-hin
Lift up	Bok-uk	Algá-ik'	Bú-gno. Bu-n-go	Caret	U-yo-gno. U-yo-go	Ré-ko	Alga-ik
Put down	Rák-uk	Dhár-ik'	Tí-gne. Tí-n-ge	Caret	Caret	Tá-ko	Thé-ik
Hear	Sún-kare	Sún	Nyú	Sáï	A-só-yo	Hón-ko. Thá-ko	Sunou
Understand	Bújh-kare	Bújh	Thú-í	Caret	Búz-dyú	Sé-ko	Bujhou
Tell. Explain	Ká-huk	Sa-rha	Kyén	Nhó-s-che	Chí-só-yo	Ish'-to. Boh'-to	Ghanai-ik

* Throughout the *Háyu column che suffix is the reflexive sign*; to, ko, vel po, the transitive; *it, hot'*, and *bot'* are contractions for i-to vel ish-to, ha-to, and bo'-*to*. *As nature suggests, in point of sense* both signs are applicable; thus, ish-che, speak to thyself, articulate; ish-to, speak to him, to some one; ha-s-che, give to thyself; ha-to, give to him. Sis-che, learn = teach thyself; sish-to, teach another. In the other tongues which are losing these niceties they are less clearly explicable. See Váyu grammar in sequel.

† Ou is the neuter or reflexive formative, as ik is the active; and added su makes the former passive—*e.g.*, from root ghan, to speak, ghan-au-mi, n, I speak, utter. Ghan-ou-su, m-mi, p., and ghanaimik-an, a., = ghana-im-ik-an, told I him or it, I told it or I told him.

‡ Phi is a sample of the primitive and neuter verb. There are several other samples in the other columns. See grammar in sequel.

§ I' vel ya of Pahi, Chépáng, and Bhrámú is the transitive or active sign, as in Néwári and Telugu, though unrecognised as such in either.

‖ Ik, it will have been seen, is the pronominal affix of the third person. The whole, and their application, may be given in this place:—

Baba-im, my father.	Saken-im, I can.	Thatha-im-ik-an, I strike (him or it, transitive).
Baba-ir, thy father.	Saken-ir, thou canst.	Thatha-ir-ik-an, thou strikest.
Baba-ik, his, her, anyone's father.	Saken, he, she, it, can.	Thatha-ik-an, he strikes.

Continuation of the Comparative Vocabulary of the Languages of the broken Tribes of Népál.

English.	*Kusúnda.*	*Pák'hya.*	*Thák'sya.*	*Tháru.*
Air	Kái	Bayálo	Nammar	Bayár
Amaranth, the grain	Bhartu	Bethyáng	Bhendo	Rámdáná
Ant	Pyai ki	Krímula	Naṭo	Doká
Arm	Táü bi	Hát, H. K.*	Yá	Hát
Arrow	Muyu	Kádha, H. K.	Tumé	Khándha
Barley	Jo	Jou, H.	Chíka	Jau
Bird kind	Kotau	Cháda, H. K.	Nom'ya	Chirai
Ditto, male	Gyá kotau	Bhályа cháḍa, K.	Nom'ya dhó	Chirai
Ditto, female	Gimi kotau	Pôthi cháḍa, K.	Nom'ya íso	Chirai
Bitch	A'gaigimi	Kyatáï chhowri	Nagamoma	Pilli
Blood	Uyú	Ragat, H. K.	Ká	Lohu
Boat	Wai. Wou	Dúga, K.	I saba	Náu
Boar	Yássgyá. Higyá	Baigan harra	Tili	Suwar
Boiled rice	Káddi	Bhát, H.	Bhát, H.	Bhát
Bone	Gou	Hád, H.	Nati	Hád
Boy	Tala sáï	Kéta, K.	Kala chája	Ketá
Buffalo kind	Mahi	Bhaínsa, H. K.	Mai	Bhaisa
Ditto, male	Máhi-gyá	Bhaínsaráugo, K.	Mai rágo	Bhaisá
Ditto, female	Máhigimi	Máu bhaínsa	Mai móma	Caret
Bull	Nogmwa gyá	Ballasádh, H.	Hméyese	Sáḍha
Cat kind	Birálo	Billo, H.	Nobar	Birála
Ditto, male	Birálo gyá	Dágo birálo	Nobar kho	Birála
Ditto, female	Birálo-gimi	Chháuri birálo	Nobar hmo	Birála
Calf, male	Nógmwachyáchigyá	Báchho, H. K.	Hméchaja	Báchhá
Calf, female	Nogmwachyáchi-gimi	Bad	Hmé chájasimo	Báchhi
Child kind	Gitasé. Chyáchi	Chhóra chhóri Kétakéli, K.	A'lópichám	Ladikábálá
Child, male	Gitasé	Kéta. Chhó ra, K. Nánu bálakha, H.	Kalachája	Laḍiká
Cow	Nokmwa gimi	Gái, H.	Hmémama	Gáye
Cock	Tab'gyá	Bhályakukuddo, K.	Caret	Mur'ga
Crow	Kaúwa H.	Kág, H.	Ghábráng	Kaúwa
Daughter	Taksé	Chhóri, K.	Chame	Béti
Day	Dina	Diüso, K.	Sar	Dina
Dog kind	Agai	Kyatáï	Nága. Nak'yu	Kútta
Dog, male	Agai gy'a	Kyatáï dango	Nak'yughyutya	Kútta
Ear	Chyáü	Kán, H.	Hna. Nha	Kán
Earth	Doma	Máto, H.	Sa	Máti
Egg	Góä. Gwá	Phul, K.	Chhyárkyaphúm	An'da
Elephant	Hátti gyá	Hátti, H.	Lam'bochhé	Háthi
Ditto, female	Hátti gimi	Mákuna, H.	Lam'bochhémhyo	Háthi
Ewe	Ghalogimi	Caret	Ghyúmama	Bheti
Eye	Chining	A'nkhá, H.	Mi	A'nkh
Face	Hángná	Mudhá, H.	Lí	Muhu
Father	Páï	Babaï	A'bo	Bábá
Fire	Já	A'go, H. K.	Hmé	A'gi
Fish	Gnása	Máchhá, H.	Trang gná	Machheri
Flower	Gipoán	Phul, H.	Ro	Phul
Fowl kind	Táp	Kukura, K.	...	...
Foot	Chán	...	Malethin male	Pángo góḍa
Fruit	Yegiyan	Phala, H.	Phum	Phar
Girl	Taksé	Keti, K.	Mrin	Laḍiki
Grain	Kadiyun	Caret	Caret	Anaj
Goat kind	Míjha	Boko, K.	Rámo	Chhegadi
Goat, male	Míjha gyá	Bòko, K.	Rámogyá	Chhegaḍi

* H. for Hindi, K. for Khas; see note at page 165. In the Tháru column I have not thought it worth while to indicate the endless borrowings. For the Kusúnda and Chépáng tribes, see J.A.S.B., or No. XXVII. afore cited.

English.	Kusúnda.	Pákh'ya.	Thák'sya.	Tháru.
Goat, female	Míjha gími	Bákhro, K.	Rámomá	Baghiya
Hair	Gyai-i	Ráwa	Chham	Bár
Hand	Gipan	Hatkela	Yáyáthin	Tar hatti
Head	Chipi	Manto	Ta	Mudi
Hen	Táp gimi	Kukhurako pothi, K.	Caret	Murgi
Hog kind	Hí. Yása	Har'ra	Tili	Suwar
Horn	Iping jing	Sing, H. K.	Ru	Sing
House	Báhi	Ghar, H. K.	Ghim	Ghar
Husband	Dúwói	Lóg nyá, K.	Mrinthin	Caret
Iron	Phalám	Khaḍar	Phré	Lóha
Leaf	Hák	Pát	Lhá	Pátá
Leg	Nawágichán	Godá	Phale. Bhalethin	God
Light	Jina íkya	Urt bátti	Muthnangmu	Anjoriyo
Maize	Makai	Ghóga	Makai	Makáya.
Man kind	Míh'yák	Manchha	Mli	Manhai
Ditto, male	Mih'ya dawái	Log nyá, K.	Pyung	Caret
Mare	Caret	Caret	Támáma	Ghoḍi
Millet or Konganī	Kwá chhó	Caret	Dhéya	Tágnun
Millet or Kodo	Mádyi. Mazyi	Kódo	Rangre	Madúwa
Monkey, male	Ugu	Bádar, H. K.	Pángdar	Bánar
Ditto, female	Ugu gimi	Bádarni, H.	Pángdarsyá	Bádari
Moon	Jun	Chan'drama-bel', H. K.	Láti gná	Chand'ra-majún
Mother	Máï	A'má	A'má	Mahatári
Mountain	Parbat	Páhár, H. K.	Yedadhyu	Par'bat
Mouth	Birgyád. Birgyang	Múkha, H.	Sung	Múkha
Mosquito	Caret	Pokha	Polorinaba	Mas
Name	Giji	Ná u, K.	Min	Ná u. Ji
Night	Ing gai	Ráti, K.	Mun	Ráti
Oil	Jing	Tel, K.	Chhigu	Tela
Old man	Caret	Caret	Khéba	Budhá
Old woman	Jigel. [Nogmwa	Caret	Khúgyu	Budhiyá
Ox kind	Nwágwá. Nógo.	Caret	Mekinba	...
Paddy, or rice in husk	Chhusum	Dhán, H. K.	Mlasam	Jadhan
Plantain	Mochá	Kela, H. K.	Tatung ro	Kera
Ram	Bhanták. Ghologya	Caret	Ghyu kidaba	Baigan-bhátá
Cleaned rice	Kádiyun	Caret	Mla	Chá ur
River	Gimmekoná	Khola, K.	Umdakyu	Kholá
Road	Won	Báto, K.	Ghyám	Rastá
Salt	Huk vi	Nún, H. K.	Chacha	Nun
Sheep kind	Gholo	Caret	Ghyu	...
Skin	Gitán	Chhála, H.	Dhi	Chám
Sky	Lágá i	Sarga	Mu	Caret
Snake	Tou	Sápa, H. K.	Pudhi	Sápa
Son	Tala sáï	Chhorá, K.	Jha	Taranggan
Star	Ing gai	Tárá, H. K.	Sar	...
Stallion	Caret	Caret	Ta	...
Sow	Higimi. Yásagimi	Baigani harra	Tili moma	Sugarni
Sun	Ing	Gháma, H. K.	Ghán gni. Saughini	Ra uda
Tiger	Dájá káüli	Bágha, H. K.	Ná	Bágha
Tooth	Toho	Dáta, H. K.	Gyo	Dáta
Tree	I'	Rukha, K.	Ghyung	Gáchh
Vegetable	Mál ghyák	Ság, H.	Dhap	Ság pattá
Village	Láháng	Gá u, H. K.	Hál	Ga won
Water	Táng	Páni, H. K.	Kya	Páni
Woman	Ning dai	Baigini	Mrin	Meráru
Wheat	Gabun	Gahun, H.	Karu	Gohun
Wife	Ningdaimyáhoa	Baig'ani	Mrínhmí	Jani
Yam	Byalougolandán	Caret	Hmau dáu	Hanmul
I	Chi	Ma	Ghyáng	Hang

English.	*Kusúnda.*	*Pákh'ya.*	*Thák'sya.*	*Tháru.*
Thou	Nu	Ta	Gna	Tong
He. She. It	I' si. It'. Tok'-pya? Gida	U'kya	Chana. H'mi	Utu
We two. Dual	Tok'jhig'na	Caret	Ghyangsi	Hángdu
Ye two	Nók'jhig'na	Caret	Gnísi	Tongdu
They two	Gidajhig'na	Caret	Hmi si	Unudu
We all. Plural	Chóbaki [ráki	Caret	Ghyang cha	Hang log
Ye all	Nokibaki Toga-	Caret	Gna cha	Tusal
They all	Gidabaki	Caret	Hmichá	Usal
Mine. My	Chíyi	Mero, K.	Ghyang ge	Caret
Thine. Thy	Níyí	Tero, K.	Gná ye	Caret
His. Hers. Its	Gidayí	Usai ko, K.	Hmi ye	Caret
Ours. Dual	Tokjhignayí	Caret —	Ghyang si ye	Hamarnu hye
Yours. Dual	Nokjhignayí	Caret	Gni si ye	Caret
Theirs. Dual	Gidajhignayi	Caret	Hmi si ye	Uduwonko
Ours. Plural	Takibakimida Chobakiyida	Caret	Ghyang cha ye	Hámlogkau
Yours. Plural	Nokibakiyida	Caret	Gna cha ye	Tahárasabake
Theirs. Plural	Gidabakiyida	Caret	Hmi cha ye. Hmi ye ke	Unakara
One	Goï sáng	Yek	Di	Yek
Two	Ghígna	Dúï	Gni	Dúï
Three	Dáha	Tin	Som	Tin
Four	Pinjáng	Chár	Bla	Chár
Five	Pagnangjáng	Pách	Gná	Páche
Six	Caret	Chha	Tu	Chha
Seven	Caret	Sát	Gnes	Sát
Eight	Caret	A'th	Bhre	A'th
Nine	Caret	Nau	Ku	Nau
Ten	Caret	Das (Hindi and Khas throughout.)	Chyu (Almost wholly Tibetan.)	Das
Twenty	Caret	Bis	Gniyu	Bis
Thirty	Caret	Tis, H. K.	Sombu	Tis
Forty	Caret	Chális, H.	Blibyu	Chalis
Fifty	Caret	Pachás, H.	Gnasyu	Pachas
Hundred	Caret	Saya, H.	Bhra	Sau
Of	Nata igin	Ko, H.	Chaye	Keha
To, *dat. and acc.*	La i, K.	La, T.	Dhyári	Keráke
From	Jáng jui	Báto, K.	Kyáche	Paidádekhalbat
By. Instrumental	A' i	Le, K.	Kau	Le
With. Cum.	Tángche	Saga	Gnáyero	Saga
Without. Sine.	Káuthá i	Bholi	A'robhoja	Náhiho i
In	Tái	Beli	Hísono	Bákinahi
Now	Ipwaji	Yeso	Ghyángchye	Amai. Abhai
Then	Nhu	Caret	Khaghángchye	Nabhai. Tabhai
When?	A'sahi	Caret	Tigni	Kabahu
To-day	Itwaji. Ipwaji	A'ja, K.	Námá	Aju
To-morrow	Gorak	Bhóli, K.	Tila	Kálhi
Yesterday	Binágá	Híjo, K.	Kemichuri	Byáhan
Here	Tau wa	Yétá, K.	Kesichosi	Yehara
There	Isága	U'ta, K.	Khatáikhanti	Uhara
Where?	A'naka	Kóta, K.	Tomi	Kánha
Above	Drasu ok	Hapra	Caret	Upara
Below	Tumái	Tala, K.	Masi	Tare
Between	Gijhágda	Májha, K.	Kung ri	Biche
Without. Outside	Bangjo	Báhira, K.	Phelori	Bahera
Within	Wáha	Bhitra, K.	Nhári	Bhitra
Far	Isinha	Táhi	Chari	Uhá
Near	Ista	Nesai	Nyese	Ihyá
Little	Dyoro	Yokai. Thokái	Ohipri	Thoro
Much	Mang gni	Mauti	Dan há	Bahut
How much?	A'sina	Kati, K.	Kang nya.	Ketaná
As	Natiya	Caret	Khajibá	Jaisan
So,	Nápawai	Caret	Khapribá khaju	Wunaisan

English.	*Kusúnda.*	*Pákh'ya.*	*Thák'sya.*	*Tháru.*
How?	Natuwan	Caret	Khajulába	Caret
Thus	Tantan	Caret	Ho alába	Há*n*
Yes	A'yábakiho	Hóhó, K.	Hin	Náhibá
No	A'yewá	A'sin	Aí	Náhi
Not. Prohibitive	Hyá	Na, H. K.	Kino	Rahare
And	Caret	Ra	Bikigang	Ká
Or	Caret	Caret	Howochuchhyáng	Ihe
This	Tá i. Ta.	Yehi. Yó, H.	Pa áug kyungpa	...
That	Issi. It	Wóhi. U', H.	Cha. Khapami	U
Which } Jón Who }	Hágim'ya hak, vel hag-it	Jimanchha	Khanángpémhi	Kunmanai
Which } Tón Who }	Nataim'ya hág-it vel hak	Jaunaman-chha, K.	Khajupémhi	Umanai
Who } Kón * Which }	Nátat	Kaunaman-chha, K.	Tá	Kaunmanai
What?	Nátáng	Kyá, H.	Khajupero	Ká
Anything	Nataum'ya hágit	Kehi bastu, H.	Khajang pemhi	Kunbastu
Anybody	Nataim'ya hak vel hyák	Kohimán-chhá, H.	Sabadhyángpá	Konamana
Good	Waiyaki	Báhiya. Ni-ko, K.	A'sbá	Niman. Bad-hai
Bad	Ka ingbarai	Ghatiyá. Behor	Na ásba	Tniman
Cold	Kháng go	Chiso, K.	Sim	Thandá
Hot	Bhrok	Táto, K.	Lhap	Chuhan
Raw	Ben	Kácho, K.	A'tehebá	Kácha
Ripe	Pakog	Páko, K.	Tyáhejiba	Pákal
Sweet	A'hál	Guliyo, K.	Koghibá	Mithá
Acrid, pungent (as red pepper, &c.)	Byá	Piro, K.	Swobá	Tin
Bitter	Kátuk	Tito, K.	Kambá	Tin
Sour	Dam tan	A'milo, K.	Kimbá	Khattá
Handsome	Waiyaimyá hák	Rámro, K.	Bastu. Mhik-yahepá	Besmanai
Ugly	A'ingbarai	Caret	Mhi ákyáhopá	Bauramani
Straight	Caret	Tersai, K.	Tananphirphai	Sojh
Crooked	Wáng káng	Báng go, K.	Yeba	Tat
Black	Páng sing	Kálo, K.	Maláng	Kariyá
White	A'sai	Séto, K.	Tarpa	Ujar
Red	Bá*n* ubá	Ráto, K.	Walá	Lál
Green	Hariyo, K.	Hariyo, K.	Phin	Hariyer
Long	Hwang gai	Lámo, K.	Hrimba	Lambá
Short	Poktok	Chhoto, K.	Rimba	Chhot
Tall } man	Phiyong	A'go, K.	Bauchhe*n*ba	Uchcha
Short } man	Poktok	Hocho, K.	Putulu	Nícha
Small	Hungkoi	Sánu, K.	Chángba	Chhot
Great	Wogonrái	Thúlo, K.	Théba	Mot
Round	Mang gni	Bátulo, K.	Ghighírba	Gola [bate
Square	Chárapáte, K.	Chárapálo	Bhilirchhówá	Chárakuna-
Round	Dallo, K.	Dallo, K.	Bhumríba	Dhela
Flat	Chyángkáng	Pátalo, K.	Pabapilhe	Pánarabang-pánang
Fat	Biji	Móto, K.	Dhum'wa	Mot
Thin	Gharáu	Háriyáko	Jyaíba	Dabar
Weariness	Balangba	Galelágyo	Bhalápji	Thákali
Thirst	Táp yáu	Pámitís, H. K.	Kejuphiji	Pipás
Hunger	Idáng	Bhok lágyo, K.	Phothanji	Bhok
Eat	A'm	Gáu. Khú-wa, H. K.	Lhila	Khai
Drink	Táng gonong	Piu, H. K.	Pi u	Piyal. Pilá-yaha
Sleep	Iptu (? Causal)	Saira, H.	Nhuko	Sutali

* See note aforegone at page 169.

English.	*Kusúnda.*	*Pak'hyá.*	*Thák'sya.*	*Thárú.*
Wake	Blengwoto	U'tha, H.	Réto	Uthali. Jagal
Do	Au ó. Au wo	Háribal	Lhaú. Lau	Kara
Do not	Anibil	Janahára	Thalaú	Nakara
Laugh	Nakyába	Hás, H.	Gnéto	Káhasal
Weep	Jháma ó	Sanchha	Táko	Káro ól
Be silent	Abágánebin	Chochira	Lhemthalo	Chupraho
Speak	Pwáktoba	Caret	Tyáto	Bolai
Do not speak	A'noktabin	Janabol	Tha tyáto	Nabol
Come	Agga	A'ija, K.	Khau	A'wá. Yánha
Go	Dá	Báija	Hero	Jájá
Remain standing	Loengwóto	Pakhanataba	Pranhogatu	Khadárahawa
Stand up, get up	Loengwóto	Utha, K.	Gnajurpa	Khadáhó
Sit down	Bhingwóto	Basa, K.	Túpa	Baith
Walk or move	Aban	Hat, H.	Hero	Chal
Run	Gorgowóto	Phalála	Gninahero	Dhába
Give	A'i	Deu, K.	Pino	Dada
Take	Má	La, K.	Bhakáu	Lala
Strike	Pungbógo	Kût, K.	Táü. Thopáti	Már. Maráu
Kill by cutting, cut down	Puwágo	Kát, K.	Thagothápáti	...
Kill anyhow, *i.e.*, destroy,	Wagdágo	Márideú, K.	...	Már
Kill with stone or other missile	Yuphwágo	Hán, K.	Prino	Kát
Bring	A'i	Lyályá, K.	Bhakau	Lyáre. Léáre
Take away	Wá	Láljá, K.	Bhoro	Léjáre
Lift up	Yúlinggwajo	Bok, K.	Thíthóuko	Uthá o. Lád
Put down	Gyag'mo	Bísa	Thano	Rákhare
Hear	Mang'bo	Suna, K.	Nagníno	Suna
Understand	Caret	Bujha	Ghau	Bujhare
Tell or relate	Wongdágo	Kaha, K.	Bhígho	Kahare
I beat	Ki-pomatanha-u	Man kut'chhu *	Gnajai toba	Hama marilá
We two beat. Dual	Tokjhignai pomatanhaï	Hamidwi kut'chau	Gnigni tobaká	Hamadunu marilá
We all beat. Plural	Tokkhágyai pomatanhaï	Hamiharu kut'chaun	Gnignichai tobomu	Raura márila
Thou beatest	Nupomatawa	Ta kut'chhas	Chyang chaitobá	Raura márila
Ye two beat. Dual	Nokjhegna pomatawa	Timidwi kut'chhau	Namágni tobamu	Rauradunu márila
Ye all beat. Plural	Nokkhag pomatawa	Timiharu kut'chhau	Namacha tobamu	Raurapangchanmárila
He, she, it beats	Gida pomatawa	U kut'chha	The tobamu	U márala
They two beat. Dual.	Gidajhigna pomatawa	Undwi kut'chha	Thamagni tobamu	Udunu márila
They all beat. Plural	Gidbki pomatawa	Unharu kut'chhan	Hmichaka tobamu	Unaloga márala
I am beaten	Tangda pungmatabahini	Malai kut'chha	Gnazir tobamu	Hamake márila
We two are beaten. Dual	Tokjhigai pomatabai	Hámidwilai kut'chha	Gnigni tobamu	Hamdunuké márila
We all are beaten. Plural	Tokhkádai pomatabai	Hámiharulai kut'chha	Gniri tobamu	Hámálogake márila
He, &c., is beaten	Gidodánigidai pungmataba	Uslai kuttachha	Caret	Woke márila
They two are beaten. Dual	Gidajhignaigi pungmataba	Unaidwilai kuttachha	Caret	Woduke márila
They are all beaten. Plural	Gidakhaigi pungmataba	Unharulai kut'chha	Caret	Wologanake márila

* The rest of this column is pure Khas or Parbatya, as also all the other words having the "K" subjoined. The corrupt Urdu or Hindi of Tháru is too palpable and incessant to need a mark. The Tháru tongue, like the Kócch and so many others of the Taraï from Hardwar to Assam, is fast merging in the proximate Arian tongues; and so also the Hill dialects into Khas.

COMPARATIVE VOCABULARY OF THE SEVERAL LANGUAGES (DIALECTS)
EASTERNMOST PROVINCE OF THE KINGDOM OF NÉPÁL, OR THE BASIN

English.	*Rodong, or Chámling.*	*Rúngchhénbúng.*	*Chhingtángya.*	*Náchheréng.*
Air	Hyú	Heek. Hak	Him'ma	Hí. I'
Amaranth	Lúng'ma	Chhénna. U-chen na *	Chhénna	Chípa nám
Ant	Chíkárépa	Sáchakáwa. Chikyang	Póngkharók	Chhámpalyú
Arm (see Hand)	Chhu	Chhuk. U-chho *	Muk	Hú ü. Hu hú
Arrow	Bhé	Bhyé. Bhé U'bhé*	Phésúk. Phesu k	Bé í
Barley	Yéwa dám. Wádám	Tongchhóng	Jáma. Jáwa	Chhóng kha
Bird kind	Wása	Chhóngwa	Wása	Chhó wa
Bird, male	Wása opá	O'pa chhóngwa	U'pa wása	U'pa chhó wa
Bird, female	Wása óma	O'ma chhóng-wa	U'ma wása	U'ma chhó wa
Bitch	Khlíma	O'ma kochuwa	U'ma kochuwa	U'ma haaga
Blood	Hí. Háa	Há. Héu	Há li	Hí
Boar	Opa bó. Húípa. Hwí pa	O'pa-bá. Yútpabá	U'pa phák	U pa bóó
Boat	Náwa	Náwa	Dóng' ga	Dúng' ga
Boiled rice or Bhat	Rón	Kok. Koo	Kok	Já. Rákojá
Bone (see horn)	Sar'wa. Sárú-wa †	Sá yúba. Yúwá. (Pí yúwa, cow's bone)	Sárúk wa	Tu prú.. Tu pru
Boy	Sorro*n* chha-chhá	Dú wachhachhá	Yém bichhá	Wáchchha chhá
Buffalo kind	Báhira. Maisi	Sángwa	Sá*n*gwa	Méisá. Meis
Buffalo, male	Um'pa maisi	O'pa sáng'wa	U'pa sángwa	Um'pa méisá
Buffalo, female	U'mma maisi	O'ma Sáng'wa	U'mma Sá*n*gwa	Um'ma méisá
Bull	Pí umpa	O'pa pít	U'papít	Wáchchha píya. Um'pa péya
Calf kind	Pí úmchhá	Pitchhá. Pih'chhá	Pitchil	Pími úmchhá
Calf, male	Pí úmpa úm-chhá ‡	O'pa pitchhá	U'pa pitchilé	Pími úmpa-chhá
Calf, female	Pí úmma úm-chhá	O'ma pitchhá	U'mma pitchilé	Pími úmma-chhá
Cat kind	Bé ra	Sur'ma. Minima	Púsú	Manima
Cat, male	Bé rapá	O'pá minima	U'pá púsú	U'mpá manima
Cat, female	Bé ramá	O'ma minima	U'mma púsú	U'mma ma-níma
Child	Chháchi. Yáyachhá	Chhá chi. Ma-nachhá	Chh'a che	Chhámú wa

* U prefixed is the pronominal definitive; ó of ópa and óma is the same. U' vel ó: eu is best; French eu in heure, beur.

† In this and the following columns the sá prefixed is the generic definitive (sá = flesh). Very generally words used singly must have the pronominal or the generic definitive. In composition both fall away, especially the latter; thus, "bone" of column 2 is úyúba or sáyúba, but cow's bone is pí yúba. In "skin" of this column the word is given in all three ways—hókwa, úhok'wa, and sáhok'wa.

‡ Pí úmpa úmchhá, literally cow, its male, its young (see the words for father and mothre,

OF THE CELEBRATED PEOPLE CALLED KIRÂNTIS, NOW OCCUPYING THE OF THE RIVER A'RUN, WHICH PROVINCE IS NAMED AFTER THEM, KIRÂNT.

Wáling.	*Yákha.*	*Chouras'ya.*	*Kúlung'ya.*	*Thulung'gya.*
Him'ma. Hak	Hig'wa phák Hik'gwa	Phúrim	Hik' pa	Iú
Chhénná	Magarm	Gósaráni	Lúng kúpa	Lúng kúpa
Chhíkyáng	Khelek. Khelem	Po urung'ma. Pwórum'm	Khá lem	Khálim
Chhuk	Muk	Lá	Húh, u	Lwá
Bó. Bhó	Pí si k'. Píshi k'	Bló	Béï. Bé í	Né plé
Tóng chhóng	Chí-cháma	Bóg já	Jéú. Chhóngki	Jéú. Jé ú
Chhong wá	Núa and Nwa-wachi	Chak bwa	Chhówa	Chakpu
A'po chhongwá	I'ba chhano-wachi	A'po chák bwa	Wápchhọ wa	Grok'pu-Chak'pu or Upap chakpu
A'ma chhong-wá	I'ma chhano-wachi	A'bomo chakbwa	Wámchhó-wa	Umam' chakpu
A'ma kwachu-wa	I'ma chha kwa-chúmá	Cháliníma. A bomóchâli	U'makhéba	Umám khlé ba
Hí. Há	He l'la. He l'wa	U' sú	Hí	Sísi
Bẹphá. Apo-khong	Ipáchha phák	A'po pá	Léma	U'pa bo
Dúng' ga	Dúng' ga	Ghág	Bo kho	Dúng' ga
Kok	Cháma	Hépa	Já	Jám
Sar'wa. Saí wa	Séng·khok' wa. Seng khog' we	Rúsú	Tapri. Tap rí	Sasar
Dú wachhá	Wéngpha pícha	U'chobéba	Wáchhachhá	Wes' chwe-chwéchwé
Sáng wa	Sán wa	Bé í so	Mési	Mési
A'pa sáng wa	I'pa chha sán wa	A'po be i so	Mési mipa. Um'pa mési	Upap mési
A'ma ṣáng wa	I'ma chha sán wa	A'bomó be i so	U'm'ma mési. Mési mima	Umám mési
Caret	I'pachha pík	A'po bíya	U'mpapi. Pímpa	Bénwa
Caret	Pikaïchwe	Bíya nunu	Pim'chha	Gaikam§ úchwé
	Pikaïchwe ípachhá	Apo bíya nunu	U'mpa pim'chhá	Gaikam upap-úchwe
	Pikaïchwe ímachha	Abomo bíya nunu	Um'ma pim'chhá	Gáikam úmam-úchwe
Mú nimá	Púsúma	Bir'mo	Biráli	Bir'má. Ubirma
Apa múnimá	I'páchhá pú-súma	A'po bir'mo	U'mpa biráli	Upáp bir'ma
Ama múnimá	I'máchhá pú-súma	A'bómó bir'mo	U'm'ma biráli	Umám bir'ma
Chháchi	Píchhá	Béba	Nukcha. Chhá-chháma man-chhámá. Cha-s-cha	Chwé chwé. (Málochém · chwéchwé, human young)

also used as sex signs, and the third possessive pronoun, conjunct form). As noted at "bone," words used singly must have almost always a definitive, pronominal or generic; and voce egg, umdí, uding, uthin, are samples of the one, as wádí, wadin, babangya, are of the other (wá, bá = fowl). In column 2, "day" has the pronominal definitive, while "face" omits it; in column 1 precisely the reverse is the case. This may indicate optional use; and in column 8 "egg" occurs in all three ways—that is, with either definitive, and without either. In regard to the words for father and mother, the pronominal definitive is indispensable.

§ Gaika borrowed; definitive 'm annexed.

English.	*Rodong, or Chámling.*	*Rúngchhénbung.*	*Chhingtángya.*	*Náchheréng.*
Cow	Pyu pa. Pí	Pit. Pih'	Pit	Pí
Cock	Wápá	Wápá. O'pa wápá	Rang gába	Wápá
Crow	Oúwá	Ká ga. Kah' wá. Gah' wá	Ghák wa	Gógok pá
Daughter	Márchha chhá. Chhachhha ma	Méch' chha chhá-chhá. U mech'-chhá chhá chhá	Méch'chha chha	Mímchha chhá
Day	Kholé	Ukholén	Nám	Mlépa
Dog-kind	Khlí	Kóchúwá	Kochúwá	Haga
Dog, male	Khlípá	O'pá kóchúwá	U'pa kochúwá	Haa ga
Ear	Nápro	Nába	Nárek	Nábá
Earth, little } Earth, whole }	Bókhá	{ Bákhá. Henk-hama	Khám	Baha
Egg	Dai. Da i	U díng. Wá dín	U thín	Dí i
Elephant-kind	Hátti	Háti	Háti	Háthi
Elephant, male	U'mpa hátti	O'pa háti	Upá háti	U'mpa háthi
Elephant, female	U'mma hátti	O'ma háti	Um'ma háti	Um'ma háthi
Ewe	U'mma bhéda	O'ma bhédá	Um'ma bhédá	Um'ma lúsa
Eye	Michak	Mak. Maák	Mak	Mik'sa
Face	Ugnálúng	Gnálúng	Gnálúng	Nábwa
Father	U'm' pa	Eu pa. U'pa. O'pa	U'pá	U'pa
Fire	Mi	Mi	Mi	Mi
Fish	Gnásá	Gná	Gnásá	Gná
Flower	Búngná	Búngwaí	Phúng	Bá
Fowl-kind	Wá	Wá	Wá	Wá
Foot (see leg)	Phílú	Langtemma. Wukhuro. U khuro	Láng	La. Lóphóma
Fruit	Báda. Yóda	O síwa	Síwa	Súsá
Girl	Chhámárchhá	Mechchhachhá-chhá	Máchchhachhá	Mim chhá chhá
Grain	Chá	Chámá	Kwak. Kok	Chám'ma
Goat-kind	Chhóng gara	Chhéng gara	Méndíba	Chhángara
Goat, male	U'mpa chhong gara	O'pa chhén gara	U'pá méndíba	U'mpa chhángara
Goat, female	U'mma chhong gara	O'ma chéng gara	U'mma méndíba	U'mma chhángara
Hair	Mus'ya. Twóng. Ta = head	Má a	Tang'phúkwa. (Tang = head)	Táä sám. (Táä = head)
Hand (see arm)	Chhúku phé-ma, arm flat	Chhúkhu phéma, arm, flat	Múk	Húú *
Head	Táklo. Tak lo	Táng. Eu táng †	Táng	Ták lo
Hen	Wáma	O'ma wáma	U'ma wa	Wámá
Hog-kind ‡	Bó	Bá. Yángbá, the wild	Phak	Bó ó

* Vowel repeated marks the pausing tone here and everywhere.
† Eu prefix is the same as ó and ú elsewhere, *e.g.*, oma, u bawá, u sanggo, &c.
‡ Abo-mo adds the male to the female designation. The two are in Tibetan bo-mo or ba-ma; in Lepcha, a-ben, a-mot.
§ Myek-chi, Myet-si, Burmese.

Wáling.	*Yákha.*	*Chouras'ya.*	*Kulúng'ya.*	*Thulungg'ya.*
Gái	I'machha pik	Bía. Bíya. A'mobía	Pí im'ma. Um-mapi	Gai
Wápá	I'páchhá wa	Bó gnápa	Wápá	Grókpupó
Gówá	A'h' gwá. A g wa	Gág bó	Gágáh' pó	Gápwa. Gá pó
Máchhá	Chíyá méch chhá	Tábe	Mimchhácbhá	Máschwéchwé. Mis'che chwé-chwé
Wo kholé. Námdíya	Leh' ni	Duk'so	Lépá	Némphú
Kótima. Ko-chuwá	Kóchúma	Cháli	Khé b	Khlébá
A'pa kochuwá,	I'pachhá ko-chuma	Chali gnápo. A'pochali	Um'pa khebá, Khémi pá	Upáp khlébá
Náphák	Náphák	Dóbú	Nóbwa, Nó bo	Nókphla
Pákhá	Khám	Kánski	Bóhó	Kwá
Dim	In. Wá ín. (Wa = fowl	Bábáng'gya. (Bá = fowl)	U'mdí. Wádí. Di. (Wa=fowl)	Dí í
Háthi	Hátti	Hátti	Hátti	Háti
A'pa háthi	I'páchhá hátti	A'po hátti	Háttimpá	Upáp háti
A'ma háthi	I'máchhá hátti	A'bómó hátti	Háttim'má	Umám háti
A'ma bhéḍa	I'máchhá bhénda	A'bómó bhéḍá	Bhédim' má	Umám bheḍa
Mak	Mik	Bisi	Muk'si §	Mik'si
Gná láng	Náchik	Kúli	Gnóbwa. Gnó bo	Kul
A'pá. Pápá	I'pa	A'po	Um'pá	Páp. U'páp
Mi	Mi	Mi	Mi	Mú
Gná	Gnásá	Gnósó	Gná	Gnósá ‖
Búng	Phúng	Phúri	Búng	Búng'ma
Wá	Wá	Bó	Wá	Pó
Lángkutóm	Lang tápi	Lósu	Lóng	Phémkhél ¶
Sángsí wa **	Ichá	Ching'chi	Sísí	Sísi
Máchhá	Méchchhá pi-chhá	Bicho bébá	Mimchhácbhá	Musche chwé
Chá	Chabák	Jáma	Chásúm	Má
Bákara	Méngthibak	Sángara	Chháng gara	Chhwánra
A'pa bákara	I'pachhá méngthibak	A'po sángara	Chháng garámpa	Upáp chhwán-ra
A'ma bákara	I'máchhá méngthibák	A'bomó sángara	Chháng garámma	Umám chhwánra
Táng múwa. (Tang = head)	Tángpháng'wa. (Tang = head)	Sóm	Múí. Tósúm. (Tó = head)	Sém. Swém
Chhúk	Múktápi	Lá	Húh'pháma	Lwáblém ¶
Táng	Tukh rúk. Tukhurúk. Tú khrúk	Phútiri	Tóng	Búi
Wáma	I'máchha wá	A'bomó bo	Wáma	Pwa. U'mam pwa Pó. Umam po
Bók. Phá. Khong	Phák	Pá	Bó o	Bwá. Bo

‖ Final sá vel só is the generic sign or definitive as used throughout this column (sá = flesh).

¶ Under "foot" and "hand," see and compare "leg" and "arm." To the names of the latter the sign of flat things is added to form words for the former.

** Sang = tree is the generic definitive.

English.	*Rodong, or Chámling.*	*Rúngchhénbúng.*	*Chhingtángya.*	*Náchheréng.*
Horn	Rúng. Tong. Umtong	Usang'ga	Sing' ga	Tá á*
Horse-kind	Ghódá, H	Ghódá, H	Ghódá, H.	Ghódá, H.
House	Khim	Khim	Khim	Khim
Husband	A'túmi. Túmi	Caret	Pápbo. A'túmi	Umtópo
Iron	Phalám	Phalám	Bánchhúwa	Phalám
Kid-kind	Chhong gara umchha	Chhén garachha	Méndíbachhá	Chhángara umchhá
Kid, male	Chhong gara umpáchhá	Chhén gara ópachha	Upa méndibachhá	Chhángara umpachhá
Kid, female	Chhong gara ummáchhá	Chhéng gara ómachha	U'ma méndibachhá	Chhángara ummachhá
Lamb-kind,	Bhédi umchhá	Bhéda umchhá	Bhédichha	Lúsa umchhá
Lamb, male	Bhédi umpachha	Bhéda opa chha	Bhédi upa chha	Lúsa umpachhá
Lamb, female	Bhedi ummachha	Bhéda oma chha	Bhédi uma chha	Lúsa ummachhá
Leaf	Lábo	Ubáwa euchha	Laphówa	Sam. Saa ma
Leg	Philú	Láng	Láng	Ló ó
Light	Námchha. Khawíya	Uláwachhámi, sam.	Khálámthá	Wújyálo
Maize	Makai	Makai	Makai	Bapsú sá
Man-kind	Mína	Mana. Ma a na	Mápmi. Mah'mi	Mína. Min
Man, the male	Soronchha. Soronchhá mina	Dú wachhá. [Mech-chhachha, woman chha homo] §	Pá	Wáchechhá
Mare	U'maghóḍa	O'ma ghóḍa	U'mma ghódá	U'mma ghódá
Millet (Kangani)	Phéro	Phésa	Phésa	Písa
Millet (Kódó)	Char'ma	Sámpícha	Sambok	Chérchá
Monkey-kind	Tóng bhú. Nó i	Héláwa	Héláwa	Pópa
Monkey, the male	U'mpatong bhú	O'pá hélíwa	U'pa hélíwa	U'mpa popa
Monkey, the female	U'mma tong bhú	O'ma hélíwa	U'mma hélíwa	U'mma popa
Moon	Ládípa	Ládíma	Láthíba	Láníma
Mother	U'ma. Umma	O'ma. U'ma. Euma.	U'ma	U m-ma
Mountain	Dánda	Bhar	Bour	Dánda
Mouth	Dyó	Dó	Thurum'	Gnócho
Musquito	Túngkáma	Lámkhútya	Twang gyómma	Súpyál
Name	Nang	Nang	Nang	Na
Night	Khósai	Ukhákhwái. Ukháko	Ukha khúit. Ukhakhuit	Umsyápa
Oil	Bóli	A'h'wa	Kiya	Tél
Old man	Páchha. Pachha kówa	Búdhá khókpa	Búdhapá	Passou
Old woman	Máchha. Machhakóma	Bhúdá khókma	Búdhimá	Massou
Ox-kind	Pí	Pit	Pik	Péh' yá‖
Paddy	Róng	Chá	Cháya	Rá á

* The vowel repeated represents the pausing tone, which, as also the abrupt tone, is very decided.

† Ōn (in Balali, ūn, vel ōun; in Lohorong, ōu) recalls Dhimalí, ōn-hya; and all the more in that so few of the Himalayan tongues have a word for horse.

‡ In Kid we have the form with genitive sign and definitive prefix. Here we have both dropt. With them the terms would run bheda-kam-uch (for um) chwe or bhera-kar-u-chwe.

Wáling.	*Yákha.*	*Chouras'ya.*	*Kulúng'ya.*	*Thulungg'ya.*
Khú úng táng. Atam'mi khak	Itáng'	Róso	U'mpitta. Pitta	Ráng. Um ráng
Ghódá	O'n †	Ghódá	Ghóḍa	Ghodá
Khim	Páng	Kúdú	Khim	Ném
Apa sang'	Wémphá	O' chó. Wó cho	Umtúppo. Túppo	Kha
Phalám	Chek chi	Phalám	Sél	Sél
Bákarachhachi	Menthúbaich-chya	Sángár núnu	Chhángarachhá	Chhwárakam uchwe
A'pa bákara-chhá	Ipáchhá men-thúbaichchya	Sángár táwa	Chhángarachhá-úmpá	Chhwárakam, uchwe úpah
Ama bákara-chhá	Imachhá men-thúbaichchya	Sángár tábe	Chhángarachhá-úmma	Chhwárakam uchwe úmam
Bhéḍáchhachi	Bhedaïchwe	Bhéda núnu	Bhedamchhá	Bhéḍáchwé ‡
Apo bheda-chhachi	Ipachha bhe-daïchwe	Bheda táwa	Bhedumpachhá	Bhedupapchwé
Amo bhera-chhachi	Imachha bhe-daïchwe	Bheda tábe	Bhedummachhá	Bhedumam-chwó
Sung'phák. Bá	Súm phák	Sáphá. Móli	Siba. Lá. Um bóa	Só blám
Láng	Láng	Lósu	Lóng	Khel
Wújyáló. Khá-dái —.	Wop'na	Dwám somo	Kodáta. Nám-chhowa. Mi-wal'ma	Hwah'wáya, sam.
Makai	Makaï	Groboma	Makai	Mákái
Mana. Mína	Yáp'mi	Múyo	Mis	Michyu
Adúwa. Dúwa	Wengpha	O'cho	Wáchchhá	Wáschwe
A'ma ghoḍa	Imáchha wón (ōn)	A'bomo ghoḍá	Ghodám ma	Umam ghoda
Phésa	Póya	Já	Pési	Sar
Sámpícha	Páng gyá	Charjá	Lísí	Lisér
Héláwa	Pubáng	Pokú	Púpwa	Núk'syu
Apa héláwa	Ipáchha pu-báng	A'po pokú	Púpwampá	Núk'syu upáp
Ama héláwa	Imáchha pu-báng	A'bomo pokú	Púpwammá	Núk'syu umám
Ládíma	Lá	Twasyál. To syal	Lá	Khlyé, Khlé
A'má	I'ma	A'mo	Ummá	Mám. Umám
Dánda	Kwángu	Kwáma	Tám' him	Bro
Twó. Do	Múláphu	Dúli	Gno	Si
Súpyál. Tokli.	Thokthoki láng	Gang'gayúmo	Kwongtholi	Mas
Nang	Ning	Di	Ning	Nang
Umkhakhú. Akhakhwi	Séh' ní	Domsá. Dwáng-príme. Dom-paíme	Sépa	Dum'ma. Dungma
A'h' wá	Kiwa	Tilyám	Khilám	Tel
Pásang	Tháp' pa	Gné wá	Manchám wá-chhá	Gná ú
Másang	Tháp' ma	Gné bé	Manchám mim-chhá	Gnámi
Caret	Pik	Bíya	Pí	Caret
Káya	Chám	Gárjá	Rá	Résépma (ma =grain)

But genitive ka is borrowed, and kam is = ka-um. See remarks on genitive signs in sequel (Bahing Grammar).

§ What bracketed was one of those hints for further research referred to in the first leaf, *supra*. See Waling, wherein duwa is man; duma, woman; or, with the definitive, aduwa, aduma.

English.	*Rodong, or Châmling.*	*Rúngchhénbúng.*	*Chhingtángya.*	*Náchheréng.*
Plantain	Gnósi *	Gnak'sí	Gnáklásí	Li gnáksi
Ram	U'mpa bhéḍa	O'pa bhéḍa	U'pa bhéḍá	U'mpa lúsa
Rice or choul	Charáng	Cháyóng	Chá srák	Síra
River	Wá hwái	Hongkú	Wáhóh' ma	Húng kwáma. Hung kóma
Road	Lám	Lám	Lámbo	Lám
Salt	Rúm	Yúm	Yúm	Ram
Sheep-kind	Bhédá	Bhéḍa	Bhéḍa	Lúsa
Skin	Húlépá	Hokwa. † Uhok'wa. Sa hok wa	Sáhok' wa	Sá hok
Sky	Nám	Námchok	Námchhuru	Nám chho
Snake	Púchho	Púchhám	Púchhá	Pu ú
Soil	Bóh'khá	Héngkháma	Tháng'pu	Thámpu
Son	Sorónchhachhá ..	Dúwachháchhá	Chhái	Wach'chha chhá
Star	Pitipya. Pitappa	Sáng gén	Chok chong i. Chok choi	Sangger'wa
Stallion	Umpa ghoḍá	O'pa ghoḍa	U'pa ghoḍa	U'mpa ghoḍa
Stone	Lúng'to	Lúng'ta	Lúnggwak' wa	Lú ú '
Sow	O'ma bó	O'ma bá	U'mma phák	Um'ma boö
Sun. Sunshine	Námliya. Nam	Nám	Nám	Nám
Tiger	Chábhá	Kiwa	Kibha	Dhing'trá
Tooth	King	Kang	Kéng	Ka a
Tree	Song púwa	Sang'táng	Sang'	Sá á
Vegetables	Ság	Limkhám chokkhám	Ságá	Sánkhai lúnkhai
Village	Túng má	Téng	Tén	Tyál
Water	Wá	Cháwá	Chú wá	Ka a wá
Wife	Mai. U mai	Mechchhachha	Méchchhá	Yúh' ú §
Wheat	Chhong. Námbo	Núh'chhong	Jáwá	Docher
Wood	Sang	Sáng	Sáng	Sou
Woman	Márchha	Méchchhachha	Máché	Mim'chha
Yam	Sóki	Sáki	Khí sú wa	Khí yok'sa
Young man	Wálalichhá	Phánta. Phántáchhá	Wánchábáng	Solò
Young woman	Klámáichhá	Káméchhá	Káméchchhá	Solome
I	Kágná. Ka. Ingka	Unka. Angka. Ang	A'ká	Kágná. Ká
Thou	Khana	Khana	Haná	A'ná
He, She, It ‖	Khú. Tyako Hyako	Oko. Moko. Euhyako. Euyauko	Mogo. Mogwa. Yoko. Mogo	Manka. Yáko
We. Plural inclusive	Kai. Ka í	Ungkan ¶	Kánaná. Kanga na	Ka i

* In all the words si vel chi vel cha is the generic sign for all fruits. So also cha vel já, = all grains, in the words for barley and rice: ma in Thulung (resepma).

† See notes at "calf" and "bone." U the pronominal, sá the generic definitive—*e.g.*, yu-a or sá-yúba, bone; sa or u-sa, flesh; hokwa or sa-hokwa, skin; heu or sa-heu, blood, and also u-heu; hokwa, skin; sá-hokwa, flesh-skin; sing-hokwa, tree-skin or bark.

‡ Sí = sa is the generic sign; kök = hok, vel hokwa, ante.

Wáling.	*Yákha.*	*Chouras'ya.*	*Kulúng'ya.*	*Thulungg'ya.*
Gnáksi	Chémokla	Bál chí	Li gnoksí. Li-gnoksi	Lég noksí
A'pa bhéḍa	Ipáchhabhéda	A'po bhéḍa	Bhéḍámpá (for Bhéḍa ampa)	U'pápvhóḍa
Cháyáng	Yáméchchhu	Sérá	Séri	Soar'. So ar'
Hong' ma	Hong'ma	Gúlo	Yo wá	Kúrkú
Lám	Lám' bu	Lám	Lám	Lám
Yúm	Yúm	Yok'si	Gúm	Yo
Bheḍa	Bheda	Bhéḍa	Bhéḍá	Bheda
Sáhok	Sáho wárik	Kwak' te. Kok' te	Soko wári	Kwok'si. Kok'-si.‡ Kok'te
Sag'ra	Táng khyáng	Dwám	Chhúburi. Net-wa. Neto	Dwámu
Puchháp. Púchham	Púchák	Bísa	Pu	Phú chyú
Bákhá	Khámbema	Kák'si	Thám'pu	Kwá
Chhá. Dúwa-chhá	Chyá. Chwe	Táwa	Wáchha chhá	Chye. Chwe. Waschhwe chwe
Sang gen ma	Chokchígi	Soru	Súngger	Swar
Apa ghodá	Ipáchha won	A'po ghoḍá	Gho dám'pa	U'pápghoḍa
Lúng-ták	Lúngkhok' wa	Lúng	Lúng	Lúng
Amopha. Khongmá	Imáchhá phák	A'bomo pá	Bwam má. Bo oma	U'mám bwá. Umam boö
Mámchho wa. Sunshine	Nám	Dwám	Nám	Nepsúng. Nem, sunshine
Dhí na rá. Dhínra	K'iba	Gúpso	Nári	Gúpsyú
Kang	Há. Háchi	Gúm'so	Káng	Lyú
Sang u	Ing tháp. Sing gaitháp	Sing	Thonám	Dhak'sa
Ságá	Phíyakhyú	Silim	Kháiyu	Ság
Teng	Ten	Del	Tel	Del
Chá wá	Máng chúwa	Ká-kú	Káú	Kú
A'masang'	Mechchhá	Bícho	Yuh' u §	Kha ‖
Cháyong' chhong	Chíchá ma	Caret	Docher	Jepser
Sang	Caret	Sing	Sing	Sáng
Adúmá	Mecchha yapmi	Bíchomúyo	Mim'chhá	Wo-chyú
Sá khí. Yák	Khe. Súchígwa	Rang'jabi	Khe	Balak'pu
Phang' ta	Wengchá	Sálá cho	Solo	Swálachwé
Kámechhá	Kime	Sálame	Solome	Twálame
Ingka. Angka	Ká	U'nggú	Kogná	Go
Háná. Khana	Ing'khi. 'N khi	Gnome. U'nu	A'na	Gána
Aya. Hayako. Moko	Khena. Yona. I'khi. Yona. Mona. Tona	Time. Yome. Yame	Náko. Múko. Netako	Hána
Iká. U'ká. Ing kai. Ingka ni	Kani	U'ng gúticha	Keká á, Ko i. Koni	Gokú

§ Yú is wife in Lepcha and in Tamil. U, ind. art., = 'a' prefix in those tongues, a-yú and ta-yú; tayú = u-yú or yú-ú. Yuh' for abrupt accent only.

‖ Kha = husband *or* wife. Husband *and* wife = Khábung'.

¶ This dual is one of the hints for emendation. Most of the dialects have a dual, and one with inclusive and exclusive forms of the first person. Note † p. 184 has them for the Rungchhen dialect. See on to grammars for the three persons of the dual.

English.	Rodong, or Chámling.	Rúngchhénbúng.	Chhingtángya.	Náchheréng.
We. Plural exclusive	Kai. Ka	Ungkanka	...	Kai ka
Ye. Plural	Khaini. Khana i	Khánánin. Khana na	Hánánina	A'nnimo. A na i
They. Plural	Hay i. Khu chu. Khu-i Tya i	Moko *	Yo go. Yo gwana. Mo go na	Yák mowa. Yako i. Ma ka i
Mine, disjunct.	Ang' ma	Ang'ko	A'kwa. A ko o	Angmi
My, conjunct.	A'. Ang	Ang	A'	...
Thine	Khámo	A'mko †	Hana. Háná-yakkwa	An mi. A'mmi
Thy	Ká	Am	...	Am
His, Hers, Its, disjunct.	Khúmo	Moso. Ya u so	Mogwasékkwa	Yákmi. Man-kami
His, Her, Its, conjunct.	U'. O'. Um. Ung	O. Eu vel U.	U'	U'. Um
Ours / Our	Imo. A'imo	A'inkwá	Kánúgnáikkwá	Wokimi. / Woki
Yours / Your	Khamo / Khaímo	A'mno	Hániyakkwá	Amnimowá
Theirs / Their	Khu i' mo / Khúmo	Myáúcho	Húngcheikkwa	Yákmomi
One	Aúra. Itto ‡	Eukchha. Eukpop. Eukta §	Thítta	I'bhou
Two	Hákara	Heuwang. Heu sa. Heu wa pop ‖	Híchche	Nísbhou
Three	Súm'ra	Súm ya. Sumpang. Sum ka pop	Súmche	Súk'bhou
Four	Lyúra	Láya. Lawang. La wa pop	...	Lik'bhou
Five	Gnára	Gnáya. Gnawang. Gna ka pop	...	Gnák'bhou
Six	Túk'karu	Túk-ya. Tukwang. Tuk ka pop	...	...
Seven	Raíkara	Bhángya. Bhangwang. Bhangka pop	...	...
Eight	Bhok'kara	Reya. Re wang. Reka pop	...	...
Nine	Kípura	Pháng ya wang pop	...	...
Ten	Lípura	Kipu. Kip. Dheukya. Dheuk pang. Dheukka pop	...	...
Twenty	...	Caret	...	...
Thirty	...	...	...	...

* Third pronoun, like nouns, transfers sign of number to adjective or verb.

† Dual, Ungka-cheua, exclusive; ungka-chi, inclusive: Khana-chi; Moko-chi, vel Okochi, vel Euyakochi, for the three persons of the dual.

‡ See and compare the table of numerals in the sequel.

§ Eukta is the separate unchangeable form; so also heusa, 'two,' and súmya, 'three.' Eukchha is the major and eukpop the minor of gender. To these chha and pop suffixes

Wáling.	*Yákha.*	*Chouras'ya.*	*Kulúng'ya.*	*Thulungg'ya.*
Kong kaika	Kani. Ka	...	...	Goi
Hánani	Inkhi ni. Ningkhi. 'Nkhi ni.	Gnometicha. Unu	A'ni. Ana i	Gáni
Haya ni. Háyák Mokoni	Ichi khi. I'khi ni. Yona ni	Tometicha	Nákoni	Hanommim. Hanom nu
A'ngpik	A'ga	Aleme	...	A'má
A'	...	A'	...	A'
Ampik	I'n gá	Ileme	A'mmi	Yemá
Am	...	...	...	I'
Hayek pik	I'gá. Yona ga, &c.	Gnemeleme	Nakwami	O'kam. Hanomkam
...	I'	...	Wa	U'
A'ngkapik	Aengá	Ikileme	Wokhimi	A'kima. Ikimá
Hayekkapik	Ning gá	Múyemleme	A'mnimi	Inimá
Káyankapik	Ichiga	Gono matichaleme	Kwachimi. Na kwachimi	Hanommikám
Aktai. Akta	Ik' ko	Kolo	Ubúm	Kwong vel Kong, humans. Kole, animals
Ni. Hasa. Hasak	Kichchi	Nik'si	Nih'chi	Níchi, humans. Nale, animals. Ni, root
Syum' ya k	Sum'chi	Súm'makha	Sup'chi	Syúm, humans. Sule, animals.
Lá ya k	Líchi	Phíbakha	Líchi	Blí. Bleule
Gná ya k	Gnáchi	...	Gnáchi	Gno. Gnolo
Túk ya k	Tuk'chi	...	Túk'chi	Ro vel Ru. Rule
...	Núchi	...	Núchi	Seren. Ser. Serle
...	Phang'chi	...	Rechi	Yen. Yet. Yetle
...	Yecchi	...	Bong'chi	Gú. Gale
...	I'bong. Ik' bong	...	Uk'bong	Kong'dyúm or Kwong dyum
...	Hí bong	...	Caret	Kong usang. Kwongusang
...	Súm'bong	...	...	Kwongusang-kodyúm

answer wang vel bang and pop of the other dialects. Wang and pop recall the numeral signs of Mikir. With reference to those of Kiránti, see and compare note ** of page 191 and note † of page 192; also Bahing grammar in sequel. Time was wanting to make out this point in regard to all the dialects; but in the Rungchhen it seems clear that in eu-k-ta, one, the 'ta' is radical, the 'eu' a pronominal definitive, and the 'k' a copula merely.

‖ These distinctions were not fully made out.

English.	*Rodong, or Chámling.*	*Rúngchhénbúng.*	*Chhingtángya.*	*Náchheréng.*
Forty	...	...	...	...
Fifty	...	...	...	...
Hundred	...	...	...	...
Of	Mi. Mo, pronoun. Mo', noun	No sign, genitive first of two nouns *	Caret. O, pronoun	Mi, pronoun
To, dat. and accus.	Caret	Caret	Lagi	...
From, out of	Dáká. Dano	Dángká	Gná	A'm
Towards	...	Yatni. Yatnung. Yatnung on level †	...	...
By, inst.	Wá	Ya. A'	Gná	A'
By, close to, near	Chakda, side in	Chakda, ditto	...	...
With, cum. Sáth in Hindi and Urdú	Pida	It' nan	Núng	Gnáng. Máng
Without, sine. Bina in Hindi	Madang	Madang. Mandang	Mángchi	Mąpgdi
In	Dá	Dá	Be. Pe	Pi
On, upon	Choda (top in)	Chokdo. Dungda	...	...
This, conj.	Hyáo	O' }	O'kó. Bago. Nago	U'nú. Angna
This, disj.	Hyáoko	Oko }	...	...
That, conj.	Tyá	Mo	Khókhó. Mogo.	Khán koú. Yakgna
That, disj.	Tyáko	Moko. Khokho ‡	...	...
Now, §	Wósara. Wospa	Hangde. Hande	Bágári	Ha
Then, §	Khónglo. Tespa	Khómló. Khollo	Uilhe	Khóntalo
When?	Délo	Démkhé	A'nám	A'dem
To-day	A'i. A'le.	A'ya. A'i	Páyam	A'se
To-morrow	Sén la. Sen lam	Mángkolén	Wárangda	Sála
Yesterday	A'se	A'khómáng	A'sinda	A'spa
Here	Wada	Oḍa	Báye. Báyétni	Ik. Yéksa
There	Túkhe. Tuku	Euhyana. Eudhako. Móda. Miyănung	Yótni	Méksa. Miyaya
Where?	Khoda	Kháda. Khádanung	Hókét	Háppa. Hápbále
Above	Dhala. Dhálo	Euchokda. Múdháni } far U'dháni } Euchongda. Eukhukda	Uténbe	Itwa ta. Itó ta
Below	Hila. Hwilúo	Múpúni. Uyuni	Móba	U' yúyu
Between	Mrá. Máru	Lúmda. Rádoa	U'rhábe	Umlam

* See notes to the Bahing Vocabulary further on.
† See voce He, page 206.

Wáling.	*Yákha.*	*Chouras'ya.*	*Kulúng'ya.*	*Thulungg'ya.*
...	Lígit	...	...	Naüsang
...	Gnágip'	...	...	Naüsang ko dyúm
...	Makuaibong	...	...	Gnosang
O	I'. Ga, pronoun	Caret. Lemá, pronoun	Mi, pronoun	Kam
Caret	A'	...	Caret	Caret
Pangkwa	Bwang	Logno	Gna. A'. Piká	Dang. Káng
Dáng ká	...	...	...	Honthyo
A'	Gná	Kho	A'	Ká
...	...	...	...	Phar'da
Pi. Edá. Inan	Núng	Bilo	Gámpi. Lo	Nung
Mochhi	Mánnúng. Metning	Sokho	Mándi	Mánthi
Inan. Da. Ida	Be. Songbe	Lo	Pá. Pi. Gopá. Pitú. Themtú	Ná. Dá. Dú. Deuda
...	...	...	...	...
O' gná. O'kó. Ipigna.	Khena. Ná. Námá. A'me	...	Ingkóng. Inkopi	Wó. Wóram Wo chi. Dl. Wo mim. Pl.
...	...	...	...	
Khógná. Khóko. Haya ya	Yóna. Yónámá. I'me	...	Múngkong. Nákong. Nakopi	Myó. Myórám. Hanúm
...	...	...	...	...
Isgháring	Akku	Bokkémse. Bokemmo	Wadolo. Wolló	A thá
Húlong	I'khóning	Ingyéló	Khodolo	Méhómlo
Dem'kha. Khínam	Hétning. Heh'ning	A'seló	Hádolo. Hádémiye	Hám syúká
A'ilo. A'yo	Hoh'yen	Tianso	Yése	Anep
Hámáye. Mangkolen	Wáng'di	Dis'na	Désa ah'	Díka
A'se. Akomang	A'chhén	Saiso	Is'pa	Básta
I'yák. Wada. Waya	Khé. Nákhé	Alo. Amna. Alvi	Yéksa. Ingkwápi	A'no. A'si. Asinda
Múyák. Modo. Moya.	Yóna. Yókhyá	Bhanala. Bhána. Gnóna	Méksa. Nakwápa. Náya	Háno. Hanopna
Khini. Kháda.	Héh'na. Hénnéhé	Thálo	Hápise. Hákwade	Báte. Bánte.
Itá. Adháni. Angyúni	Tó	Bháta. Imtóla	U'mdúptu. Métwáka. Metyoka	Deuda
Itú. Akhúkyu.	Mó	Bháya. Bhayola	U'mdhókpu. Núkka ah	Goyu
U'mrápe. Arádha. Adhung'ya	Ilúm	Khachi. Khachilo	U'mrápi	Théte

‡ O', Mó, conj.; Oko, Moko, disj.; all genders. Khokho, not present person, sort of relative.

§ Now and then are positive. See note at page 169.

English.	*Rodong, or Chámling.*	*Rúngchhénbúng.*	*Chhingtángya.*	*Náchheréng.*
Without, outside	Búng ya	Ubungya. Udungya. Huviya	Báhári H.	Pákhá
Within, inside	Kung ya	Ukonghud'ya. Ukông ya. Kongda.* Euhun'ya	U'kúmbe. Khim'-báyu	Khimgwa. Khimgo.
Far	Mokhá. Mise. Mose	Mángsa. Mangkhiyada. Mang	Mángnwa. Mangno	Chhíburu
Near	Gnan'. Gnan' ge. Nen ge	Nek-ta. Nekkhïda. Neék	Tanghe. Tangne	Caret
Little	Píchhe	Chi chí	Mih'mo	Chíchha
Much	Kébha	Bad dho	Dhéra. Bádhe	Antkhópa
How much?	Dúm no	Dém ye	A'suk	Dél
As, rel. Jaisa H.	Caret ...	Caret	Hókhyakkha?	Dákhtó?
So, corr. Taisa H.	Kyaskwa. Kyasokwa	Khóïnsa	Hún'gkhyakkha	Kh'ángtokgná
Thus, pos. Aisa H.	Tyaskwa ngó	Wóïnsa	Bákhyakkha	Antok gná
How, Kaisa H.†	Dáskwa. Dúsókwa	Khainsaki. Kháïnse	Hókhyakkha	Dákh'tó
Why?	Déma	Déna. Dene	Méchchhá	U'mú
Yes	Ou. Ai	Ang gna	Yé. Yét	Lé. Hó
No, negative	Aí na	Má áng	Máhá	Má. Má á
Not, privitive	I', suffix and infix.	Eu, prefix, and Nin, infix ‡	I', infix	I s-a, infix
Not, prohibitive	Mi. Mai. Dá	Man	Má. Thá	Nó
Also, And	Caret. Pini. Piti. Gno	Caret. Ning. Chháng	Yé. Nang. Yáng	Sa. Ló
Or	Wó	Hé	Yáng	Lé
Which } rel. Who } jón	Tyósó	Sáng	Hokkogó	A's
Which } corr.† Who } tón	Tyakwa. Chi	Khógná	Hoén	Khán
Which? kon, chhu	Só	Kháwa Sáng-yé	Hokkogó	A'snálé
What? kya, chhu	Dáko	Diyé	Thém	U'lé
Who? kon, su	Sa	Sáng	Hokkogo. Sáló	A's
Any thing, gugu, kucch	Dé-í. Dyeu. Nyú	Dichháng	Thém-yáng	Usa
Any body, guhma koi†	Isáma. Sóï	Sángchháng	Sáló-yáng	A'sa
Eat { dual { plural	Chó	Chó. Chacheu and Chachí, D. Chanum, Pl.	Chó-ha. Chó-a	Chú-u
Drink	Dúgnó. Dúgnu	Dúgnó. Dugnachu, D. Dugnanum, Pl.	Thú-wa. Thú-a	Dúngó
Sleep { dual { plural	Im'sa. Imsana	Im'sa. Imsachi, D. Imsanin, Pl.	Ip' sa	I'msa

* Final da = in, is a true post-position; but there are few such. Nouns in the possessive or locative replace in part or wholly. Here hud is a hole, and kong an interior, each word with the preposit. definitive inhering.

Wáling.	*Yákha.*	*Chouras'ya.*	*Kulúng'ya.*	*Thulungg'ya.*
Hibu. Bung-khúya	Caret	Bháná. Twala, Gota	Hochho. Pótél. Hachhópa	Chépnóa
Khim'ko. Akungya	Caret	Kudukwáya. Koya	Gópa	Góna. Ugwa ana
Máng'khaya	Mangdúna	Bhána	Chhúgri	Chhyubat
Mumikgná. Neh'yang	Ning'dáng	A'mna	Nén'kha	Gnépa
A'chichi. Achí	Misyháa	Chig'nápu	Chíchha. Gichha	Kichwe
Dhéráng. Bad-he	Pyág ha	Yétikhólse	Waddétwa. Wa-detto	Dhékóng
Tem. Dem	Ingkhóg ha	A'skwalo	Déïye. Déï	Hala. Hayu. Hamko
Hagné kagná	Irók ha	A'sijokcho	Dátúkwa	Heka. Hék-gnám
Múgnék	Ikhók ha	Imsimégná	Khúntúkwa	Mehomka. Mi-hópmá. O'-hópma
Múgnék	Naktog ha. Ná	A'msi mé	Wántwa. Wa-dómmó	Ohom
Hagnékagna	Náhók	A'si chokcho	U'dáim. Dáim	Hésaka. Heka. He
Déhá ná	Irók há. Irók	A' sé. A'má	Dái. Dátúkwa	Hágna. Hamta
Han *an*.. O'. A'	Ikhi	Time	Yé	Misi. Bú
Máin. Má ang'	Múnna. Im-únna	A'tti	Má	Méë
I', suffix	Ni. Nin, infix	A, prefix	I', infix. Ma, pre-fix	Ma, prefix
Má yé. Máï	An, prefix	A'. Nó	Na	Mé
Chha	Yó. A'ng.	Yó	Só	Nung. Bó
Hé	E	Ké	Yo	Dé
Kháú	Isá	Thámé	A sá	U'hém
Khógná	Ikhi	Emé	Kho	Myo
Kháú	I sá	Thámé. A'chú	A's. A'sdatukwa	Syú
Tikwa	I. E	A' má	U'so. U'i	Hám
Dei	Hétnámá. Hét ná	A' chú	A'sé	Syú. U'hém
Ti ikchhú	Ichá	A'má yé	U'so	Hambwa
A sakchhú	Isáchá	A' chú yé	Aso. A's	Syubwa
Cho	Cho	Jákátá	Cho	Pé
Dúgno	U'gnú	Túkátá	Dúng'gnu	Dúgná
Im' sa	Ip'sa	Glomtá	Im'sa	A'm's

† See note at p. 169. The second set of native terms is Newari; the first is Hindi or Urdu, *i.e.*, where there are two sets.
‡ Omko, white, ou-om-niuko, not white.

English.	*Rodong, or Chámling.*	*Rúngchhénbúng.*	*Chhingtángya.*	*Náchheréng.*
Wake	Púkalénda. Khrupsa	Púwalónta. Dl. chi. Pl. nin	Pógák	Póka
Laugh	Riya. Rya	I'yá. I'sa, chi, D. nin P.	Réta	Rhésa
Weep	Khápa	Khá-wa, chi—nin	Há-ba	Khápa
Be silent	Maichépda. Chyóma	Wáiwáiyút gna. Mancheháda, chi—nin	Wáyeb	Wáhe
Speak	Chéwa. Pul'sa	Chéwá. Kháng-méttú,* chi—nin	Ché-wa	Nína
Come	Bána	Bána, chi—nin	Thába	Táwa
Go	A'ta. Pung'sa	Khára, chi—nin	Khá-da	Khāta
Stand up	Púkalénda. Réta	Púwalónta, chi—nin	Yéba	Répa
Sit down	Yúgna. Hígna	Yúgna, chi—nin	Yúba	Tyúwa
Move, Walk	Póng sa. Lam-tya	Lám dúma. Bí ya-chi—nin	Phána	Lámdíma
Run	Wóna	Lwáya. Lóya, chi—nin	Ping'da	Bal'sa
Give { to me / to any	I'dóng. I'du	Púáng. Chang, D. Nang, P. Pú, chí—nin †	Púang. Pú	Pí a wa. Píyo
Take { from me / from any	Né. Púkji. Púdyu	Né.‡ Battu. Chu, D. num, P.	Khátta	Né. Beh yú
Strike	Chaí zyú. Chaí dyú	Mo u. Moa chu, D. Moa num, P.	Téna	Yop'sú
Kill	Sétyú	Séru. Sera chu, D. Sera num, P.	Séra	Sítu
Bring	Baizyu. Baidyu	Báttuki bana,§ chi—nin	Tháp ta	Béh' yu
Take away	Pugzyu. Púg-dyu (take and go)	Kháttuki khára (take and go), chi—nin	Kháttu khára. Kháttu lonta (take, get up)	Khé yu
Lift up, raise	Púku. Sandyu	Théntu. Thenta-chu, D. Thenta num, P.	Khúrá. Thédak	Théttu
Put down	Gnásyú	Yúng su. Sa chu, D. Sa num, P.	Yúng' su	Yúk' su
Hear	Yényú	Yénu. E'nu. Ena chu. Ena num	Khém sa	Yéna
Understand	Kámmú. Múï dyu	Mittu, chu—num	Pítta	Chí yu
Tell, relate	Rág'na	Yeng mettu. Khángmúsa? Khangmettu, chu—num	Chépta	Pú u
Good { dual / plural	Nyo. Krégne	Núwo.¶ Nuwo-chi, D. Manu-wo, P.	Núno	Nada. Nat. Natkhi
Bad	I'se. I'seko	Euwo. A'núninko. Euko. Euttko	It'no	Is'da
Cold	Chíso	Kéngko. Keng-mangwa	Rém no	Chhik' da

* Khangmettu = show, causal of Khang, to see.

† Púang, give to me, has dual chang and plural nang; pú, give to him, to any, has chi and nin respectively. Again, words ending in u, as battu, mó u, seru, change the u into a, and have chu, num, for dual and plural. "Give" and "take" are given as samples of that expression of the object which the genius of these tongues so rigidly demands (see on the Bahing grammar). If the verb, being adjective, cannot express the object, as né = take, then the sense is very limited; and, *e.g.*, I can only use né if I tender something at the time.

‡ D., Ne khanachi; P., Né khananin, Bontáwa.

§ Battuki bána = take and come.

Wáling.	*Yákha.*	*Chouras'ya.*	*Kulúng'ya.*	*Thulungg'ya.*
Thing' ta	Chéng' da	Búkátá. Sáistá	Poka	Báka
I'ya	Yúttucháya	Réndá réstá	Gésa	Rísá
Khá wa Wáyep	Hába Swák wáya	Khráptá Lihá	Khápa Wait wáya	Khrápda Líba
Chéwa	Chókta	Bákstá	Nèna	Jósa
Bána Khára Yé wa	A'ba Khyá Púgá	Pikátá Levástá Yámstá	Bána Kháta Thórépa	Bika Dak'sa Yép'da
Yúgna Biya	Yúgna Láma	Bákstá Háltá	Túwa Lámdúma	Gaínsa Lámdíya
Lóra	Lúk'ta	Prókátá	Búlsa	Wánda
Púang. Pú	Kapyáng. Pi-aug. Pi	Gaká. Góktá	Piyá. Piyú	Gwá áng. Gwáka
Nó. Báttu	Kwé. A'ktu. Kettu	Né. Paistá	Né. Kháú. Kháyu	Né. Briya
Mó-u	Mók'tu	Túptá	Kéru	Yalsa
Se'ru	Chénu. Sísu	Syáttá	Sétu. Khóksyu	Séda
Báttu	Ap'tu	Phittá	Báh' yu	Phída
Kháttu	Khéttu. Yang-khéttu	Léttá	Kháyu	Daú da
The'ntu	Khú. Théndu	Róttá	Póka	Phóká. Kwaksá
Yúng' su	Yúk'su	Chóptá	Yúksu	Jíla
Yénu	Khép'su	Thókátá	Yénu	Thyósa
Míttu	Míttu. Mettu?	Bimstá	Min'nu	Mim'da
Khouj su	Yok'méttu ‖	Sokátá	Póa	Sing'da
Nú. Khupunú. Amwa. I'	Núha	Dúcho	Nó. Nói. Nóyu	Nyúpa
Noúdhói. Aitpa	Nú nín ha	A'ḍúchó	Man'nói. Mánnó	Minyúpa
Waché yang	Ohíha	Chisó	Chhíke. Chía	Chhákpa

‖ Mettu is the general causative, and yok mettu = yengmettu of column 2, is cause to see, used for relate, make known, tell.

¶ The generic signs would seem to adhere to the numerals rather than to the qualitives, or than to both, as in Newari. Thus, in Rungchhen one good man is eukchha nuwo mana, literally, one head good of mankind, whereas in Newari it is chha hma bhing hma manu, of one head, good head of mankind. Again, one good knife is respectively eukpop nuwo chupi and chhagu bhinggu chupi. But note that these generic adjuncts of the numerals are much more clearly developed in Newari than in Kirânti. The dual and plural are always formed as in the samples given under "good" and "sweet." Of gender there is no mark in adjectives.

English.	*Rodong, or Chámling.*	*Rúngchhénbúng.*	*Chhingtángya.*	*Náchheréng.*
Hot	Kúrek'wa. Kúreko	Kúko. Ku mang-wa	Kú no	Sémí wa
Raw	Mo. Ummo	Wománg. U mang	U máng	Mápe
Ripe	Tupsáko. Mat-táko	Túmawo	Uthúbáï	Dú wák
Sweet	Lam'chho. Walye, Wa	Lémko. Lem chi, D. Ma lem, P.	Lém' no	Lém da
Sour	Súre	Sún chakwa	Súntá	Chochárpa
Bitter	Khí ke	Khá kwa. Khako	Khak' no	Khik' da
Handsome	Khan nya. Sangnya (to look at good)	Kháng núwo (to look at good)	Uchunúno (to look at good)	Khan náda (to look at good)
Ugly	Kháïse (to look at bad)	Khán euttko (to look at bad). Khangeuwo	Uchih' no. Uchui no (to look at bad)	Kháïsada (to look at bad)
Straight	Sójho, K.	Sójho, K.*	Cháng no	Séjhó
Crooked	Báng go. Koko dyú pa	Yék tu.* Uku-dak dak	Byángkruk	Báng-go
Black	Makchúma	Mák chakmá	Mákkachúkma	Mokchibpa
White	Páyón ma. Umpayonyon	Omko. Wóm-yáng. Wopi-yangma	Bathrúma	Umlók'pa
Red	Hípakíma	Hálalá mang. Hala chakma	Hálachékma	Hálálápa
Green	Hariyo, H. K.	Hariyo	Chak' la	Hariyo
Long	Kile	Akí bang. Amyet-pang. Metta	Keméh' no	Baïpa. Répa
Short	Inang kile. Pá-kile	Adúng-pang. Dúng-ta	Báun no	Yétebaipá. Chichhábaipa
Tall } man	Kile. Run'de	Kiyang. Kong-yang. Kwangta	Kéno	Bhái pa. Repa
Short } man	Inang kile. Pa kile	Simta. Simyang	Unno	Yétórépa. Ye-tebhaipa
Small	Inangko	U'chúk páng	Míkhá	A'msikholchó
Great	Kó. Mahipmá Mahippa	Utok pang. Ut-wapang	Thékhá	U'm dheppa. Yétikholchó
Round	Búplúngmá	Boptitiwo. Bopi-riri. Hitriri	Kalabok'bo	U'mkoldu. Púpúlpa
Square	Plangpáchimá	La ákúná, four corner	Cháraupátyá	Phéphé ya
Flat, depressed, compressed	Phlémpá	Phemdag wa. Phebda' wa. Phebdapma	Phémpédépmá	Phrémphrem ya
Level, as a plain	Tém má	Asémtontu. Atemma	U'sémtóndokto	U'mtélmá
Fat	Lété	Léyángko. Tok-pang.† Chhú-yangko. Chhuwo	U'sámtánó	U'mdhép pá Lidda
Thin	Pálété. Si-mámyo	Yomyangko. Ropyangko	Róng si	Ram dá
Weariness	Hó sá	Hóttáng	U' hottáng	Haya
Thirst	Wáimá	Wáit má. Wa-mitmá	Wáik má	Wámi má
Hunger	Sáká	Sá á. Súng sá wá	Sangsáwá	Saká á

* After noun or before.

† Tokpang, fat, is the same as útokpang, great, just above, and which answers to uchuk-pang, small. To-k and chu-k are the crudes = tú and chi of Newari, and eu, vol u, prefixed is the pronominal definitive, as pang suffixed is the generic one. The fact is, that Rungchhen applies its pronominal definitive equally to substantives (eu-pa, father; euma, mother), to adjectives (eu-tok, big; euchuk, small), to pronouns (eu hyaoko, that), and to numerals

Wáling.	*Yákha.*	*Chouras'ya.*	*Kulúng'ya.*	*Thulungg'ya.*
Kúyang	Kú ha	Táto	Hóke	Glyóglém
Umpáwa. Aamang	Núsúmha. Iuggrik	Krábó	Mámtumkhápa. Mamdúpa. Mópé	Uchákhli
Súm'sa. Tup'sa. Bhang'sa	Usáha. Túpsáha	Thichó	Tumkhápa. Dúpa	Thik'ta. Thókta
Lém. Lemya	Límha	Jijilúchó	Léma	Jijin
Súnta	Súá. Súha	Júrchó	Jujur	Jyúrpa
Khak	Khíka. Khigha	Kháchó	Khíke	Khópa
Khang' nú (to look at good)	Ichchúnúna (to look at good)	Ránchó	Gnáli núpa	Jyópa
Khán i (to look at bad)	Ichchúgnána (to look at bad)	A'ránchó (not handsome)	Gnáli ípa	Míjyópa
Séjho	Sójho, K.	Sojho, K.	Twáipa	Jóngpa
Bánggo	Yégékna. Yekyang	Ulgúmcho	Mantwáipa	Míjon'gpa
Mákchúma. Makchakchak	Mákhrúna	Khúchyámo	Gúgrúpa	Kékéma
Bóthrúma. Wompichichi	Phúna	Búbjóma	Wómlópa	Búbúm
Hárchhókma. Halachakchak	Phána	Lakachíma	Hálalápa	Lálám
Chak'la	Phína	Sisijókcho. Sisijoma	Gigípa	Gigim
Badhemet. Rhinbo	Kéna	Hik'bo. Yotihicho	Wadbháipa	Dhyúpa
Achimet	Lúklúk na	Ahikbó. Amsihicho	Chibhái ipa	Dókhóndhyúpa
Kiyáng	Kéná	Róbó. Rocho	Wadréppa	Yépa
Dúiyáng	Lúklúkna	A'róchó. Aro bo	Chireppa	Dókhón-yé pa
Achókpa	Mih' na	Yokka	Chisma	Kíchem
Atók'pa	Mákna	Khol bo	Dhéppa	Dókpu
Kalabókbók	Kákliktikara. Púkpukna	Khitiriri. Dolo	Júmjúmpa. Pulpúlpa	Púpúlma-
Layá khúktáng	Lichina yúsúk	Charkuné	Lih khónglá	Khikér-ma
Phimpichichi	Phékphékná	Plém plím mé	Phemphémpa	Plém plem má
Tómtú	Idém má	Koyogná	Tél má	Dhép dé
Chitpo. Badhépo. Léb yang	Yémnúbá	Khól bó	Léipá	Séuipá
Róng yang. Achitpó	Háchigókná	Yokká	Gamsipá	Jerpá
U' hottáng	Yáksyángná	Bál mé	Gúmó	Griúm dá
Wáik má	Wáitmáng	Dak khó	Wámmá	Kódá
Sáang sa wá	Sák	Krémkhó	Saká	Krúim

(eu-kta, one), and thus shows the extreme prevalence of that feature of the language. Our flexible, simply-structured English often assimilates to these Turanian tongues, more or less; and tok, eutok, eutok-pang may be compared to great, the or a great, the or a great one. A-myet-pang and a-dung-pang of column 2, and a-tok-pa and a-chuk-pa of column 5, are words formed precisely like the above. Elsewhere bo, po = ba, pa, is the formative, and again we have ko as in omko, leyangko, &c.

CONTINUATION OF THE COMPARATIVE VOCABULARY OF THE SEVERAL DIALECTS OF THE KIRÁNTI LANGUAGE.

English.	*Báhinggyá.*	*Lóhóróng.*	*Lámbichhóng.*	*Báláli.*	*Sángpáng.*	*Dúmi.*	*Kháling.*	*Dúngmáli.*
Air	Jú	Hiwá-bá Higwá-phak	Him-má	Húwápa Húwá-ma	Him-má. Heu	Húh'-ú Hu'-u	Jhúng	Heuk, Himma
Amaranth	Gósaráni	Mang gárá bújá	Mángrábúja Mangza	Mang-gar	Chípanám Chípanap	Lúng-kúpá	Lúng kúpá	Chhénná
Ant	Gága chimmo	Pong-khórók Yángkhrépa	Ya'-Khrépá Póng Khorok	Yá khlépa	Chhámphalú Champa-leu	Chiká-répú	Grákmó	Chig-yáng
Arm	Gú	Húk H.	Múk. Muh'	Húk. Huh'	Húh	Khúr or Khur-[bu	Khar	Chhúk. Chhu
Arrow	Blá	Phé. Thúklá Nóbé	Thuk-la. Phet Pheh'	Thuklá	Sébi	Númú-ú. No mo wo	Sélmó	Pó
Barley	Cho'-ja *	U'wa	Suchámа *	Chíchámа *	Chhóng-khá	Chóphu	...	Chhóng
Bamboo	Pálam, large Ri'cho, small	Báphú	Sak'pha. Sak-phaitangli	Bapho	Baphu	...	...	...
Bird-kind	Chik'ba	Sóng-wá	Nówa	Chhóng-wa	Chhón-wá	Sal-pa	Sal-po	Chhong-wá †
Bird, male	A'po chik'ba	U'm'pa Sóngwá or Umprúpa S. ‡	Nówá impá Im'pa nówa	O'pa chhong'-wa	U'mpa chhón-wá	U'pú vel Upyap salpú	U'páp salpó	U'mbhá chhong-wá
Bird, female	A'mo chik'ba	U'm'ma Song-wá or U'mm-ruma S.	Nówá imma Im'ma Nówa	Om'ma chong-wá	Ummá chhón-wá	U'mú U'myám salpú	U'mam salpó	U'mmá Chhong-wá
Bitch	A'mo khlícha	U'mmá húk'wá or Ummruma H.	Imma ókóchú	Om'makóchúma	U'mma ha-aga Umma hóga	U'mú vel U'm-yam khléb	U'mám Khlé-bá	Um'má kúti-má
Blood	Húsi	Hári	Háli	Héllu-wa. Hel-wa	Hí	Hí	Hí	Hí
Boar	A'po-po	U'mpá bág' or Umprupa bak'	I'mpa óphak Impa phak	Búcha (gelt) § Opa bak	Lámi bhá § Um'pa bhá	Télchyo. Tilú	Tél	Umbhá pák
Boat	Dúnga	Dúng'-ga	Dúng'-gá	Dúng-gá	Bakhon	Bákohpú. No	Pókham	Dun'ga
Boiled rice or Bhat	Mómara	Chám	Chámá	Chám	Ko	Jyá. Já	Já	Kvak. Koak
Bone, see Horn	Rísé Ri sye ‖	Syákówa ‖	Rúk'-wa Rú-k-wa	Sátuprú. Sa-tú-p-ru ‖	Tum'bu-rup Sá túmburú	Salú. Só ló	Solo	Súr-wá Sá-rú-wá

Boy	A'ta Wáisá bébáchá. Tá-wa Waisa táwa	Wátháppapasa Wadhampa pasa	Yém'-bachhá	Pih'-chhá. Wathakpachhá	Wáchohhachhá Man child	Pi'-dam. Lasbéchyo Langchúbú	Chwe-chwe Las-báchwe	Mir'chhachhá
Buffalo-kind	Mésé	Sán wa	Sáng-wa	Sáng-wa'	Mési	Més	Més	Sang-wá
Buffalo, male	A'po mésé	U'mpá Sánwá Umprupa S.	Impá sáng-wá	O'pá sang-wá	U'mpá mési	U'pú vel U'pyáp més	U'páp més	U'mbhá songwá
Buffalo, female	A'mo mésé	U'mmá sánwá Ummruma S.	Immá sáng-wá	O'mmá sang-wá	U'mmá mési	U'mú vel U'myam més	U'mám més	U'mmá songwá
Bull	A'po bing Bing	U'mpá pí Umprupa pi	Impá opit' Im'pa pit	O'pa pih'	U'mpa pih'	Bhai. U'pubí	U'chorpobhai	U'mchhosbá Umbha pit
Bow	Lí	Si gi	Rídang	Bíchhi	Bhí chi			
Calf-kind	Bingáta. Bingátamiátá	Pípasá	Pit' íchhá	Pih'-pachhá	Pich-chhá	Bípoúchú Gyaipo-úchyo	Gaikámuchésa	U'm'chhapit Pit' um'chha
Calf, male	Bing, ápoátáwa. Bing tá wa	Umprupa or U'mpá pípasa Pi' pasa	Im'pá opit-ichhá	O'pá pih'páchhá	U'mpá píchchhá	Bipoúchúúpú Gyaipoúchyoúpyáp	Gaipoúpápuchésa	Umbháchhapit
Calf, female	Bing' amoátámi. Bing tami	Ummruma or U'mmá pípasa Pi' masa	Im'ma opitichhá	O'mmá pih'pachhá	U'mmá pichchhá	Bípoúchúúmú Gyaipouchyoumyam	Gaipoúmámúchésa	Ummáchhapit
Cat-kind	Bir'ma	Myou ma	Múnumá	Mini-má	Mánimá	Birmá. Múni	Birme	Mánimá
Cat, male	A'po bir'ma	Umprupa myou ma	Impá-omúnuma	O'pá minimá	U'mpá mánimá	Upu múni. U'pyáp bir'má	U'páp bir'me	Umbhá mánimá
Cat, female	A'mo bir'ma	Umruma myou ma. U'mmá myouma	Immá-omúnumá	O'mmá minimá	U'mmá mánimá chí, Pl.	U'mú muni U'myám bir'má	U'mám bir'me	U'mmá manimá
Child-kind	Támitáwa Bébacha Bakechám Atamiáta **	Píasa chí (chi Pl.) Pasa	Chhá Chháchhí I'chha ¶	Pí-chhá Pa-chha	Chhá-chhe chhá	Chyóchyo	U'chyé	Chháche

* Já vel chá, and ma, generic sign. See Grain.

† No = Chinese Nyou and Sá vel Chá (whence song, chon, chong, and chik) are really synonymes of wá vel bá vel pá, and = bird. But the term when used alone is now commonly assigned to the bird of birds, the invaluable domestic fowl. Chinese t-sco-k = bird has the sa root: and k suffix is precisely = the Bahing k and the Lohorong, Balali, and Dangmali ng. The t prefix has endless parallels in Sifan, Himalaya, and Gyarung.

§ Búcha, Lámi = gelt male.

‡ Umpa vel umprupa for males, Umma vel umruma for females, passim.

‖ Sa Sí Sé syé, the generic sign. See Bone and Horn.

¶ Chha vel i'chha, shows the pronoun definitive, used or not at will.

** Ta = child, Ta wa boy, Ta mi girl, wa ta my, i-ta thy, á ta his, any one's child. Tamitawa is literally girl, boy; and atamiata his or her girl, his or her boy, used for children.

English.	*Báhinggyá.*	*Lóhóróng.*	*Lámbichhóng.*	*Báláli.*	*Sángpáng.*	*Dúmi.*	*Kháling.*	*Dúngmáli.*
Cow	A'mo bing	Pik. Pí úmma Ummruma pi'	Pih' Imma-o-pih'	Pih'. O'ma pih'	U'mma pí	Gyai. Bí	Gai, H.	U'mmá pit' *
Cock	Apo ba Sori-wába Sori wá	Wápa. Umprú-pa wá	Impa-wá Wá im'pa	Wápá	Wápá :	Koklup U'pú-phú	Koklap	U'mbhá-wá
Crow	Gá-gákba	A'rá-wá	Gáh'-wá. Gak-wa	A'ra'-wá	Ar'-wá	Gápo. Gagak	Gágakpo	Gah'-wá †
Daughter ‡	Támi. Mim-che bébacha	Mímium. pasa. Mennumma pasa	Méchchha-chhá	Mimáchhá-chhá	Mimáchachhá Mímachha	Mésbéchyo Mí chum	Melsimá-chyé	Méchichhá
Day	Nám'ti	Léntá. Len.	Ilémba (i prefix)	Létta	Lépa. Umlépa	U'nyol, Núlu	U'nyol	Lento. Lentok U'mléntok Umlénto
Dog-kind	Khlícha	Hú' wá	Kochú	Kóchúmá	Há-ága. Hoga	Khléb. Khl-i-bu	Khléb	Kúti-má
Dog, male	A'po khlichá	U'mpá hú wá Umprúpa hu'wá	Impá kochú	O'pá kochuma	U'mpa há-agá Um'pa ho-ga	U'pú. U'pyáp khléb	U'páp khléb	Umbhá kúti-má
Ear	Sámá-nyéú	Nábak. Nába	Noro	Naba	Naba	Nécho	Nécho	Náphak
Earth, the globe	Wáleko	Bá khá	Khamhangtang-ba	Bah'kha	Báhá	...	...	Wálikha
Earth, a little	Khápi	Bá-khá.	Khám	Bah'khamá	Báhá	Pok. Pu-khu	Pakh	Pakhha'
Egg	Dí Bá-dí, fowl egg	Wéh'-din. Wé-din	Thin. Ithin. Wá-thin	Wádin §	Dí	U'ttí. Ti	Phátté	U'mting. Ting
Elephant-kind	Hátti	Hátti	Hátti	Hátti	Bon-lan	Hátti	Hádi	Hátti
Elephant, male	A'po hátti	U'mprupa or U'mpá hátti	Impá ó hátti	U'pá hátti	U'mpá bon-ḷan	Upú. U'pyap hátti	U'páp hádi	U'mbhá hadi
Elephant, fem.	A'mo-hátti	Ummruma or Ummá hatti	Immá ó hátti	Umma hátti	Umma bon-lan	U'mú. U'myam hátti	U'mám hádi	U'mmá hadi
Ewe	A'mo bhéḍa	U'mruma or U'mmá bhéḍá	Imma ó bhéḍa	Umma bhéḍá	U'mma napchu-béma Nap-chu bema	U'myám bhen-di. Umú phépsú	U'mám didimá	Umma bheḍa
Eye	Míchi. (Mi chi da si D. Mi chi da P.)	Mik'. (Mi' chi D. and P.)	Mik. Mih'	Múik. Múh'	Mák. Múh'	Mas. Miksi	Mash	Mak

Face	Kúli	Gnáchyák. Gné chi'	Náphák	Gnácheh'	Gnába	Káphú	Káphí	Nyálung
Father	A'-po	Um pa	Impá ‖	O'pa	Um'pa	Upyap. Ipyáp Upú	Upáp	Umpa ‖
Fire	Mi	Mi	Mi	Mi	Mi	Mi	Mi	Mi
Fish	Gná	Gná sá ¶	Gnásá ¶	Gná	Gná	Gno	Gno	Gná
Flesh	Syé	Sá	Sá	Sá	Syá	...	...	...
Flower	Phúng	Búng	Phúng	Bung. Búng-wa	Bún-wa	Púmmá	Púngmá	Púng
Fowl-kind	Bá	Wá	Wá	Wá	Wá	Pho. Phú	Pho	Wá
Foot. See Leg	Kholi-blém ** blem = flats	Lang = leg Láng phokma	Temmaláng	Lák'phékma	Lán pháma	Syáb. Yú	Syál	Láng
Fruit	Sichí	Sing chási. Cha-si. Sí. Si'in comp.	I'sa. Sing ísa	Omchási	Chási	Bopsás	Phém-sas. Sas	Umsiwa
Girl	Támi. Ming'-chabébachá Atami	Minnúminapasá Masa	Méchchháchhá	Píchchhamímá-chhá	Mímachháchhá	Mésbéchyo. Mis-chumchú	Mélsemchye	Mechachhá

* Pit', pih', pik' of this series merely denote the abrupt tone with pi', perhaps also some slight dialectic differences, but the tone is very decided and the final consonant nearly merged in it.

† We have here another sample of the generic sign. See note at the word Millet. Wá vel Bá vel Pó is the class sign for all birds, and the specific name for crow precedes it, precisely as in Chinese, wherein, moreover, the specific name (aa) is identical with the Sangpang name. Thus tseok = bird and aa-tseok = crow. So also kai = fowl, whence Shan-kai, a pheasant. So also Shu = tree (our Dumi word, less the double prefix), whence Fung shu, a maple, and Poutei shu, a vine. In like manner kai = fowl is added to the specific names for egg, whence Kai-tan vel Kai-lun: and observe that here the two words, being treated as a compound like our fowl's egg, the genitive goes first, minus the mark of case, though kai be in fact as much a generic sign in this instance as in that of Shan-kai = pheasant; and in fact the generic sign may be prefixed or suffixed, and this whether it stand alone or be blended with the numeral. Thus, Shan = mountain. Myung, a proper name: whence Shan myung. So Yat ko yun, or Yun yat ko = a man, precisely as in Newari we say Chha hma manu, or Manu chha hma. In all these respects Chinese agrees entirely with our tongues.

‡ See Girl. There is no proper name for daughter. Own girl is used often. So also Son.

§ Ba Pha Wá vel Wé of Lóhóróng, Báláli, and the rest is the customary generic sign derived from the word for fowl. See notes at Bird and at Millet. In Dumi and Dungmali the U' vel Um prefix is not the same, but the ordinary articular prefix, as in U-pa, U-ma = father and mother. This prefix and its equivalents ka and ta are almost inseparable in Kassia, and scarcely less common in Gyarung. In the Kiránti tongues the ka and ta prefixes, so common elsewhere, are hardly found, and ú, having a sort of relational sense, has not been generalised into a sheer article. So in Khassia the Ka and U, elsewhere generalised, have taken a partitive sense = hic et hæc. It will be shown elsewhere that these special uses do not militate against the essential oneness of the particles in question, both as to origin and function. Thus U-pa, U-ma, vel O-pa, O-ma of these tongues are demonstrably = wo-po, wo-mo of Gyarung, which again has the synonymous forms ta-pe, ta-me = ka-pe, ka-me of Khassia, and Ta-ga-pa-n = father of Tamil, whose ta yu again = mother, is pure Lepcha, as is its alternative form a-yu. Ta-yu vel A'-yu, a mother or wife in Tamil and Lepcha, from the yú root for man, yu-n in Chinese and You-k in Burmese. Just so from the Rí root we have ta-g-ri in Lepcha and Ta-n-d-rí in Telugu (g-ri' in Bodo and Koch) for father, man. Ta-rí, ga-rí, ta-ga-rí = Ta-pa', ga-pá, ta-ga-pa'. G soft k, as d soft t.

‖ In none of the dialects can the pronoun definitive be omitted in father or mother. In Bahing, a change in the root as well as in the definitive occurs (apo for wapa). But this is limited to those two words. See Grammar in sequel. Apa, my father; ipo, thy father; apo, his, any one's father, a father. In Lóhóróng, ungpa is my father; ampa, thy, umpa, his father, a father.

¶ In these two, sá final is the generic sign.

** See note at Hand, page 179. Suffixes blem, pha, phek, phok, with or without the ma, are signs of flat things.

English.	*Báhinggyá.*	*Lóhróng.*	*Lámbichhóng.*	*Báláli.*	*Sángpáng.*	*Dúmi.*	*Kháling.*	*Dúngmáli.*
Grain	Jáma	Cha. Bujá	Cháma. Búja	Cháma	Cháma	Jyá	Já. Dyu vel tyu?	Chámcha Cha ma
Goat kind	Song'gara	Míthuba	Méndi	Míthibá	Chhán'-gara	Grot. Chan'-gur	Grodyú	Chhágar
Goat, male	A'po songgara	U'mpa míthubá or Umprupa mithuba	Im'pá oméndi	U'pa míthibá, ba a last sign like u k ape	U'mpá chháng-gará	U'pú. U'pyáp grot	U'páp grodyú	U'mbhá chhá-gar
Goat, female	A'mo songgará	U'mma Míthubá or Ummruma mithuba	Im'má oméndi	U'mmá mithibá	U'mmá chháng-gará	Umú. Umyám grot	U'mám grodyú	Ummá chhá-gar
Hair	Chám. [Súng of head] all	Tagna'. Mih' of head all and feather	Mung. Tang-phúkwa (tang = head)	Tagná. Chámi. Múng	M-wa. Támu sám (ta = head)	Dosúm. Usom (do = head)	Umarsam Dosamúsam	Mú-a
Hand, see Arm	Gúblem * arms flat	Húh'-phekma *	Temma-múk	Húphek'-ma	Huh'-pháma	Khar	Phlemkhar	Chhúk
Head	Píya	Tákhrok'. Ning-tang wa. Um-mruma	Táng	Tákh-lo	Tákhúlo	Dhong. Dakh-lok	U-dhong	Táng. Um-táng
Hen	Bá. A'mobá	Wámrúp'ma Wama	Wá imma. Im-ma wa. Wámá	Wámá. Wá-oma	Wámá. U'mma-wáma	Phyám. Phá-mu. Umuphú	Uphám	U'mmá-wá
Hog-kind	Po	Ba'. Bak'. Bag'	Phák	Báh'	Bhá	Po. Pwo	Po	Pák. Pa
Horn, see Bone	G-ro-ng Grong	Tang	Sínga	Sátáng †	Tán. Umtán	Grong. Gro	Ughrong	Khúkmútáng
Horse-kind	Ghoda. [Apo amo, m. & f.]	E'n. [Umprupa. Ummruma, m. & f.]	Ghoḍa	Yen. Eún	Phun yempa ‡	Ghoḍa H.	Ghora H.	Ghoḍa H.
House	Khim	Khim.	Khim	Khim	Khim	Kám. Kim	Kám	Khim
Husband	Wán-cha	Nupa, see wife	Yemba	Om dap'mi	Dhábmi. Um-dhabmi	A'dúmbo	A'dumbu	Pádúm
Iron	Syál	Chyak'-chí	Chyak'chí	Phálám	Sel. Syel	Sel	Caret	Caret
Kid-kind	Songara-atá-miáta §	Míthubapasá	Mendi-íchhá	Mithibami-up-chhá. Mithi-bampaccha	Chháng-gara-chhá	Grot-poúchyo	Grot poúchy-esá	Chhágarchhá
Kid, male	(A'po) songara-atáwa	Umprupa vel Umpa mithu-bápasá	Impá omendi-chhá	U'pa mithibámi-upchhá	U'mpa chháng-garachhá	Upú U'pyap grot-poúchyo	Grot poupáp-úchye	U'mbhá chan-garchhá

Kid, female	(A'mo) songá-rá-atami	Ummruma vel U'mmá mithu-bápasá	Immá omendi-chhá	U'má mithi-bámi-upchhá	Umma chháng-garachhá	U'mú U'myám grot-poúchyo	Grotpo umám-úchye	U'mmá chan-garchhá
Lamb	Bhedá atá-miata	Bheḍapasá	Bheḍá ichhá	Bheda pachha. Bheḍi upchha	Nap'chu bema-chha	Phepsia Bhendi poú-chyo	Didimo-úcehy	Caret
Leaf	Sopho Sá pha	Singbak' ‖	Láphák	Singbák.‖ Bák	Sánbá	Sapam. Sapho	Sapang. Sa-phung	Sum-pha
Light	Hwa	Nám-woge Námde	Kháte yú	Nam-oh'wa	Khásema	U'nel	Háhám	Khou. Sam
Leg	Kholi	Láng	Láng	Láng	Lán	Syál	Syál	Láng
Maize	Grele womo	Mákai K.	Makai	Makai	Múlung-bap	Makai	Bápsás	Makai
Man-kind	Múri. [Dual Muri daa si. Plural Muri daa]	Mina. Yápmi. Yapmichi D. and P.	Máh'-mi. Mah' mi chi	Mína chi D. no Pl.	Mína	Has	Hash	Mína
Man, male	Wáisa	Wáthappa. Wa-thangpa	Pá. Páchhi	Wathakpa. Wá-thappa	Wáchchhá	Las'be	Las'ba	Mírchha. Pá
Mare	A'mo ghoḍa	U'mmá én. Um-mruma en	Immá-o-ghoḍá	O'ma yen. Oma eun	Phún yemmá	U'myám ghoḍa	U'mám ghora	U'mmá ghoḍa
Millet (kan-gani)	Bására	Píya	Peya	Phesá	Phísá	Bú-o. Bu-hu	Bú-o	Phesá ¶
Millet (kodo)	Chárjá	Pánke	Sámbo	Kháwá	Lang-chá	Lújá	Laújá	Sambíchá
Monkey-kind	More. Mooryo	Púbáng	Kubáng	Pubáng	Popán	Nús. Nuksu	Nús	Násá
Monkey, male	A'po more	Umprupa. U'm-pa pubáng	Impa o kubáng	U'pa pubáng	U'mpa popán	U'pyáp nús	U'páp nús	U'mbhá nasa
Monkey, fem.	A'mo more	Ummruma. U'mmá pubáng	Immá o kubáng	U'mma pubáng	U'mma popán	U'myám nús	U'mam nús	U'mmá nasa
Moon	Lá	Lá	Ládí-ba	Lá	Lá	Lúmyámtu. Lu	Lyá	Ládíma. La-dipma

* Blem and phek are always, but ma suffix not always, added. See note at Hand.

† Sá generic mark, see Flesh. In compounds it is dropt, *e.g.*, kis-a-táng, deer's horn. Column 4 has the generic definitive, and columns 5, 7, the pro-nominal one.

‡ E'n, yen, eun, passim, is horse. In Sangpang, phúnpa, phunma, mark the sexes. See note at Horse, p. 180.

§ A tá mas.; atami fæm.; both = our kids or kid kind; apo = átá, repeated in male, and amo = atami, in female.

‖ Sing. generic mark, see Wood.

¶ The sá final of this series, as well as the chá vel já of the next series of words, is the generic sign for all grains. It will presently be shown in detail that this fundamental characteristic of Tartaric modes of speech is common (like most others equally normal and essential) to Chinese with all the neighbouring languages of Tibet, Himalaya, Indo-China, and the islands. The word "egg" presents another sample, and the word "plantain" yet another, wa = fowl, and sí = fruit being the respective generic signs.

English.	*Báhinggyá.*	*Lóhóróng.*	*Lámbichhóng.*	*Báláli.*	*Sángpáng.*	*Dúmi.*	*Kháling.*	*Dùngmáli.*
Mother	A'mo *	Umma	Ima	U-ma	Má. Umma	Myám. Umyam	Mám. U'mám	U'ma. Umma
Mountain	Serte. Kongkú	Sani. Kongku	Sáng-gú	Yák-phú	Bhúri	Caret	Udhám	Caret
Mouth	Syeu	Yá	Yá-si	Yá	Gno	Kwom. Ko-m	Kwom	Twó
Musquito	Seupyel. Sip-yel	Bhúsuná K.	Tong-geng-wa	Khasuk'ma. Lamkhútia	Tokli-há*n*. Ba-hauma	Sapal	Sapal	Kong kon'gma
Name	Ning	Ning	Ning	Nang	Na*n*	Nang	Nang	Nang
Night	Tyúgnáchi	Sen, compare san ap Lepcha	Isembá. Semba	Setta	Sepá. Umsepá	U'senyám	U'senám	U'mkhákhú. Khákhúi
Oil	Gyá-wa	Kewa	Kiya	A'h'wá	Khil'lam	Khí-lem	Khilam	A'h'-wá
Old man	Gná-wa	Thap'pa	Páhúba. Hú, root sex repeated	Tháp-pá	Pásang. Pasy-ung	Páchhá	Páchhá	Táppá
Old woman	Gná-mi †	Thap'má	Má húma	Thap-má	Másang. Masy-ung. Masy-ung ma	Máchhá	Máchhá	Táp-má
Ox-kind	Bing	Pí	Pih'. Pit	Pih'	Pí	Bí	Bhai	Pit
Paddy	Bura	Cham	Chá-yák	Chámang	Chá	Ryá	Ré	Kárá
Plantain	Grámuchí	Cháng-mak' (si added or not ‡)	Gnáklá-bu	Gnák lásí ‡	Gnálásí ‡	Legnásí ‡	Legnáksi ‡	Gnáksi ‡
Ram	A'po bheḍa	Umpa bheḍa	Im'pa ó bheḍa. Impa bheḍa	O'pa bheḍa. Bheḍa pa	Namchubepá. Umpá náp-chu-bema	U'pyáp bhe*n*dá	U'páp didimo	Caret
Rice or chaul	Seri	Sí-a	Chásák	Síya	Síra	Syor. Syar	Bé'-ser	Chásrák. Chasra
River	Gúlo §	Yú wa. Hong'-ma. Díhongma	Wáyá	Hong'-ma	Hokoma. Hong-koma	Rú	Yó. Ká-wá	Hong-ma
Road	Lám	Lám. Lam'-phú	Lámbo	Lam	Lam	Lám-daú	Lám-dó	Lám
Salt	Yúk'si	Yúm	Yúm	Yúm	Rúm	Raṃ	Ram	Yúm
Shade, shadow	Bála	Nami dungwa sáwa	...	...	...	...	...	...
Sheep-kind	Bheḍá	Bheḍá	Bheḍá	Bheḍa	Napchúbe. Nap'chu	Bhe*n*dá	Didimo	Caret
Skin	Kok'si. Kok-syu	Sáhok' ‖	Sáhok'-wa ‖	Sá-ho'	Sáhok'-wa ‖	Saká	Saká	Hok-wa. U'mhokwa. Sa hokwa ‖

Sky	Dwá mún	Námtrúngma	A'tto.¶ Nám-chhiri	Nám	Ninámbobi. Nám'chho. Nánu	Nám-tú	Dhám	Nám
Snake	Búsá	Pú-se. Pusema	Pú	Pú	Pú	Bheï	Bheï	Púchháp
Soil	Wáleko. Khápi	Bah'kháma. Ba'kha	Khámhángtám-ba.** Kham	Bah'-kha	Caret	Pok	Caret	Wáli-khá
Son = child	Tá-wa ††	Wátháp pa pasá	Yembachhá, male child	Wáthapchhá. Wathakpachh	Wáchohháchhá	Lasbéchyo	Tárápáchye	Mirchháchha
Star	Só-rú	Sánge. Sáng-gemmá	Chokchong-gi	Súng-emmá	Sáng-geun	Song-ger	Song-gar	Sáng-genmá
Stallion	A'po ghoḍa	Umprupa én. Umpá	Impá ó ghoḍá	O'pá yen	Umpa phun yempa. Phún-yempá	U'pyáp ghoḍá	Upáp ghorá	U'mbhá ghoḍá
Stone	Lúng	Lúng kong-wa. Lingkáwá	Lúng. Lúngo. Lung-ok'wa	Lu'ko'wa	Lúng	Lúng	Lúng	Lúng-tá
Sow	Khomi, when old. A'mopó	U'mmá bág. Ummruma bak	Immá ó-phág. Phak' imma	Oma bak'. Bak'-mi óma	Khon'-ma. Um-ma bha	Khóm	Khóm	U'mmá pak
Sun. Sunshine	Nám	Nám	Nám	Nám	Lonpá	Nám	Nám	Námchhon'g-wa (sky bird)
Tiger	Gúpsá	Kiba	Kíba	Keuba	Kípa	Nyor	Nyor	Khíbhá
Tooth	Khleú	Kéng	Keng	Kéng	Kán	Gnúlo. Ang'lo	Gnálu	Kang
Tree	Sing. Dhyáksí	Sin'g táng-dák. Sim mak	Sin'g-itángli ‡‡	Sin'tenda	Tup-sáng	Topshú	Dhyáksá	San'g-pu
Plant	A'pum	Tangda	Tangli §§	Tenda=vegetal.	Um-po ‡‡	...	...	...
Vegetables, greens	Caret	Khen	Sing phá ó lúng-pháo	Phikhen	Khá-h'-yú	Ság	Gilokvái	Limkhan-chokkhún

* Ama my mother, amo any mother, so a pa, apo. Last=Hayu upa and Sontal apú a-ma my, i-mo thy, a-mo his, mother. See father. The pronominal definitive is indispensable in all the dialects.

† Gnawa, gnami, agrees with tawa, tami, boy and girl, as to the position of the sex-signs; but in columns 5, 6, and 7 that position is reversed, while in column 3 the sign is put both before and after. Such freedom of style is frequently met with. ‡ Si = fruit, the generic sign.

§ Gúlo recalls khóla of the Khas tongue, and Dihong of next column reproduces exactly the proper name of the great river of Asam. See "XXVII. Records of Government of Bengal," page 94.

‖ Sa, generic sign (see Flesh); sa bok, skin; sing hok, bark; sa = flesh; sing = tree (see it and notes at pages 176 and 182).

** First is soil as it lies = Newari ban; second, a little separated.

¶ A'tto = above and sky.

†† My son, wa ta; thy son, i tá; his son, á tá. Tá and táwá = son; tá mi = daughter.

‡‡ Sing i tangli, literally tree or wood, its plant = ligneous plant. See Fruit.

§§ Tangli = vegetalia = ma Newar and pó of Sángpáng—*e.g.*, oak = wai-po. Its seed, wai-si; Pó, trees; Sí, fruits; Khí, roots; Syápa = potatoes; syápa khí, potato *root*; syapa khi-m-po = potato plant. Sing itangli, wood-yielding plant; phúng itangli, flower ditto. Raka itangli, grass ditto; ísa tangli, fruit ditto. Sí-ma, Swá-ma, Ghaí-ma Newári. A'púm Bahing, Sing ápum, Phúng ápum, Síchi ápum.

English.	Báhinggyá.	Lóhóróng.	Lámbichhóng.	Báláli.	Sángpáng.	Dúmi.	Kháling.	Dúngmáli.
Roots	Caret	Nam khi	...	Caret	Khíyá	...	...	...
Village	Dyal [pu	Gán wá	Ten	Ten	Té	Dél	Dél	Tén
Water	Pwá-ku. Bwá-	Yo-wá	Chú-wá. Wét	Kúng-wá	Wá. Kán-wá	Kú	Kú	Cháh'-wa
Wife	Ming	Nú-má	Mechchha	Númá	Yú	U'meï. Meï	U'may	Mádúm
Wheat	Choja *	U' á. Chhong	...	Chíchámá	Don-cher	Docher	Docher *	Chhong
Woman	Min-chá	Menúmmá	Máchhi	Memchhá	Míma-chhá	Mes-bé	Mespá	Umma
Wood	Sing	Sing	Sing	Sing	Sang	Sang	Sang	Sang
Yam	Rébe. Swo kokti	Námkhe. Súa. Khibre	Nángkhi	Khú	Khi	Ki	Sás-ros	Sakhi
Young man	Swalachá	Wenchá	Wángchabáng	Weh'-chhá	Sanlan	Sáláchyo	Sáláchye	Wángchhá
Young woman	Swá-lamí	Láng-mé	Kám-rum-mé	Lángna-mé	San-lan-me	Sálá me	Sáláme	Mechhábang
I	Gó	Kágná. Ká	Kágná. Ká	Kágná. Ká	Kágná	U'ng. A'ng-gnu	U'ng	Ang'-ka. Ing'-
Thou	Ga	Háná. A'ná	Khháná	A'ná	A'ná	In. A'nu.	In	Hána [ka
He, she, it	Harem. Igo-Mogo	Mo-nu. Mi. Mo	A'ko. Yona. Mona. Toma†	Mo. Kho	Moko. Meko	Mam. Yákam. Momi	Tam. Mam. Yákám	Múgo
We, dual inclusive	Gosí	Káchí	Kánchhí	Káchí !	Káchí	I'chí	Ichi. Inchi	Anchákáche, che suffix
We, dual exclusive	Gosúkú	Káchíka	Kánchhígna	Káchíká. Kachiga	Káchíká	O'chú	O'chá. Anchú	In'kachága
Ye, dual	Gasi	Hánáchí Anachi. Hanchina	Khánachhí	Anáchí	A'náchí	Yechí	Yechi. A'nchí	Hánache
They, dual	Harémdáa si	Igachi. Mochi. Máháchi. Mogochi	Yona chhi. Mona chhi. Tona chhi. Oukha chhi. Ako chhi	Khochi hippáng. Mochi-hippáng	Mókóchi. Mekochihippong	Yákám-sú. Ummi	O'msa	Mu. Makhache. Moko chi
We, plural inclusive	Go-í	Káni	Káni	I'kin	Káyí. Kaye	Iki. Inki	I'k	A'nkán. Inkan
We, plural exclusive	Gokú	Káning-ka	Káni-gná	I'kká	Kani. Kákíká	O'gne. A'ngkú	O'k	I'nkán-ga
Ye, plural	Gáni	Hanina. Aniná Kang-ná	Khánáni	Anin	A'náni	A'nni	Yen	Hánánin
They, plural	Haremdaa	Míháná. Mihachi	Oukha. A'okhá. Yokhá. Mokha. Tokha	Khochi. Moch	Mekoni. Mekochi	Yákám hám. Mam hám	Am ham	Mú kha. Makhá

My	A'.‡ Wa	U'ng	Ang. U'ng. Um	U'ng. Um	An	O'	A'	Ang
Mine	Wáke	Kágnámi	Kákhá	Kángmi	Anami	O'po	A'po	Ang-bi
Thy	I'	A'm	A'. Am. An	A'. A'm. A'p	A'm	A'	I'	A'm
Thine	I'ke	Hánámi	Khánákhá	A'mmi	A'mmi	A'ppo	I'npo	A'm-bi
His, her, its, attributive	A'. Haremkeá	Um	A'ko-im.§ I'm	Mom. Khom U'. O'. Up	U'm. Mek'um	Mom. U'	Yákám. U'	I'gem. Mogom
His, hers, its, predicative	A'ke. Haremke	Momi. Meyemmi. Igomi	Yonágnákhá. A'kognákhá	Momi. Khomi	Mekomi	Mompo	Yákámpo	Igámbí. Mogom-bí
Our, dual inclusive	I'si	Káchim. En'chi	Kánchhi	Káchim	U'chú	I'-chi	I's	Angchu. A'ncha
Ours, dual inclusive	I'sike	Káchími. Enchi	Kánchhikhá	Kachim-mi	U'chúmi	I-chi-po	I'chipo	Ang. A'nchabi
Our, dual exclusive	Wási	Káchikám. Ung chi	Kánchhigná	Káchigám	A'n chú	O-chu. An chi	O's	Ang. A'nchaga
Ours, dual exclusive	Wásike	Káchikámi. Ung chimí	Kánchhigná-khá	Káchigám-mi	A'n chúmi	O-chupo. An-chipo	O'chúpo	Ang. A'ncha-ga-bi
Your, dual	I'si	Amchi. A'náchim. Anchinam	Khana chhi	A'náchim	A'm chú	Yechi. A'nchi	Yés	Amcha
Yours dual	I'sike	Anchinámi. Amchimi	Khánachhikhá	A'náchim-mi	A'm chúmi	Yechipo. A'n-chipo	Yechipo	Am. Kanchábi
Their, dual	A'si. Haremdosike	Máháchim. Umchi	Akochhi. A'ukháchhigná-khá-inchhi	Kho-chim. Michim. Mochihippáng chim	Mekohippángchim	Yakam supo. Momni. Umni.	U'n-sú. U' Amsa	Mugum. Mukhacha-cha
Theirs, dual	A'sike	Máháchimi. Umchimi	Akochhi kha A'ukháchhignakhá	Michimmi. Mochihippáng-mi. Kho chim mi	Mekochihippángmi	Yakam su. Momnippo. Umnipo.	Yákám-súpo Amsapo	Mukhacha-bi
Our, plural inclusive	I'kke	Kánim. Enni	Káni	I'king	Yé	I'nki. Iki	I'k	A'n-ga
Ours, plural exclusive	Ikke	Káni-mi	Kánikhá	I'kim-mi	Yémi	I'nkipo. Ikipo	I'kpo	A'n-bi
Our, plural inclusive	Wakke	Káninkám. Ungni	Kánigná	I'kkám	Angká	Angkú. Ok	O'k	A'ng-ga

* Suffix já vel chá, vel ché of this series is the generic sign, derived from the name of all grains. See note at Millet.

† The third pronoun and its equivalents, the demonstratives, are apt to be very minutely specific, expressing not only proximity or remoteness, but also every position, as above, below, on a level with, &c.

‡ A only with the words for father and mother. Wa for all others. See Father, p. 197.

§ His tree is not good, my tree is good. Akoim sing itangli nuyuk nin kha; kákhá'-ng sing itangli nu yuk kha.

English.	*Báhinggyá.*	*Lóhóróng.*	*Lámbichhóng.*	*Báláli.*	*Sángpáng.*	*Dúmi.*	*Khaling.*	*Dúngmáli.*
Ours, plural, exclusive	Wakke	Káninkammi	Kánignákhá	I'kkám-mi	Angkámi	Angkúpo. Ok-po	O'kkam	A'ng-gabi
Your, plural	I'ni	Amni. Hánnam Haninam	Khánani	A'nim. A'ninim	A'mnú	Anni	Yén	Amga
Yours, plural	I'nike	Hannam-mi. Háninámi	Khánnanikhá	A'nim-mi	A'mnúmi	Annipo	Yénpo	Kán-bi
Their, plural	Haremdaake. Ani	Um chi. Mihachim. Igachim	A'okhá	Mochim. Khochim	Me-ko-chim	Mamhám	Yákám. U'	Mugum ga. Makhá-úm-cha
Theirs, plural	Ditto	Umchimi. Mihachim-mi. Mahachimmi. Igachimi.	A'okhákhá	Mochim-mi. Khochimmi	Meko-chimmi	Manhámpo	Yákámpo	Makha-bi
One	Kong. Kwong (unchanged all) *	Yekko, hic hæc hoc, things and animals	Thili, n.† Thi bang, men only	Ik'kú ‡ unchangeable	Itta, n.§ Euli. Eukla-pang	Mamhámpo Táu. Tá-wa (Ta Burmese)	Tau. Tá-wo (Ta Burmese) Thi Lam	Ak'po, m. (po =pang bang)
Two	Niksi	Hich'chi, n. Hippang, m. and f.	Hich'chi. Hippang	Hich'che	Hich'chi. Hissali. Hisala pang	Sak'pu	Sakpo	Híchi
Three	Sám	Sum-chi, n. Sumpang, m. and f.	Súm'chi. Sum bang	Súng'-che	Súm'chi. Samkali. Sumka la pang	Súk'-po	Súkpo	Sum'chi
Four	Lé	Líchi. Ríchi. Li-bang	...	Líji	Lákkabo. Lakkali. Laka la pang	Bhyál	Bhál	Líchi. Richi
Five	Gno	Gnáchi. Gnabang	...	Gnáji	Gnákabo. Gnakali. Gnaka la pang	Bhúong. Bhwong	Bhong	Gná-chi
Six	Rúkka	Túk-chi. Tuppang	...	Túk'chi	Túkkábo. Tukkali. Tu ka la-pang	Rá wong = pong, m.	Ré	Túk'-chi
Seven	Chan ni	Nú-chi. Nu vang	...	Núji	Núkkabo. Nakkali. Nu-k kala pang	Ré	Tár	...

Eight	Yá	Yé-chi. Ye-pang	...	Yéchi	Rekabo. Rek-kali. Re-k-kala pang	Rí	Rin	...
Nine	Ghú	Báng-chi. Bang-pang	...	Báng'ji	...	...	Ghú	...
Ten	Kot dyum	I'p'pong, hic, hæc, hoc	Ippong, m. n. f., all gen., see 2	I'p'pong	...	...	Taḍham	...
Twenty	Kwong'asing	Ní bong	...	...	...	...	Khál-taú. Kál. Taú-khál	...
Thirty	Kwong asing-kot' dyum	Sum bong	...	...	...	...	Taḍhamkhál-taú	...
Forty	Ní pachi	Rik' pong	...	...	...	...	Khál sákpo	...
Fifty	Ni pachi-kot' dyum	Gná-k'-pong	...	...	...	...	Khál sákpo-taúdham	...
Hundred	Gno asing = 5 score	Ippon'g pong	...	...	...	...	Khál bhong	...
Of	Ké. Kem dim (Omitted except when used disjunctly) ‖	Mi. (Ditto)	I. Khá. Im. Gná ka	'M. Mi	Mi	Pó	Pó	Bi. U'm
To	...	...	...	...	...	...	...	...
From, local	Ding	Báng. Páng	Behong	Páng. Pí	Piká	Biká	Bíká	Bang. Iban'gá
From, personal	Ke ding. Keng	Ditto		...				
By, inst.	Mi	E'. Yé.	Gná	Gná	A'	A'. Gná	A' -	A
With, cum	Núng	Núng.	Lok	Lúng	Pí	Bí. Ke	Póbi. Kólo	Bit'pi. Náng
Without, sine	Mán-thí (not is: Burmese thi)	Meddin'g ¶	Mángchhi	Medding	Mand. Mán	Mánthine. Mandi	Máng-thá	Mánchhi
In. Within	Dí. Bóre. Gware. A'gwáre	Be. Bí	Bé	Pí. Chápíttu	Pí	Yó. Bi	Bí	Pí. Yá

* For Bahing numerals see full treatise of sequel, and for the other dialects see and compare those aforegone, p. 333 *et seq.*

† Lí for one, chi for rest, is neuter: bang for men only, animals are neuter. Thili is the minor, Thibang the major.

‡ Kú, unchanged, hic, hæc, hoc; chi, things and animals; bang, men.

§ Sangpang, euli-pi, one cow, hisali-pi, two cows, samkali-pi, three cows, and so of all animals. Euklapang mina, one man, hisalapang mina, two men, samkalapang mina, three men. Itta is the separate unchanging form.

‖ See references afore made ad vocem and Grammar in sequel.

¶ Not is. Compare mandong of Gyarung and maan of Newari, both with same sense.

English.	*Báhinggyá.*	*Lóhóróng.*	*Lámbichhóng.*	*Báláli.*	*Sángpáng.*	*Dúmi.*	*Kháling.*	*Dúngmáli.*
On, upon	Tóre. Taure	Wettú. Songpi. Sokbe. Langbe	Temdú	Chápittú	Chhopi	Cho-tu. Tyú. Teyo	Tí	Chokpi. Chokyá
Under, beneath	Háyula. Pumai	Khukmemu. Hongpikmu	...	...	...	...	...	...
Now	Yekhoná, yé this khona timé	Hog'nok' Honok. Igorokloonok'	Hálik	Hogno	Otolo. Wotolo	Tholo	A'nagná	Ighári
Then *	Mekhona †	Moklona.‡ Wanok. Morok' lona'k	U'ndena	Múdoklo	Khotolo. Kholo	Melo	Mebelo	U'ghári
When?	Gyána	A'nám. Hánám	Hembína	Hádemlo	Hallo	Hélo	Hebelo	Khinám
To-day	A'na	A'yu	Hálok	Isin	Yése	A'nyol	A'nyalo	A'-i
To-morrow	Dil'la	Weng-dá	Wáring	Selmá	Sélámá	Dis'yá	Disá-á	Hámá-yóung
Yesterday	Sanam'ti	A'-seï. A'sen A'-sye	A'sen	Yé-má	A'-thépá	A'meski	A'miske	A'-sé
Here	Yákáre. E'ke. Yeke	Igobe. Igiyú. Kiyú. Igi	Nábe. Nate	Kobi. Koyú	Nopyá. Nopi	Tébi	Tábi. Tábigná	Ibi. Yák
There	Nekare. Méke. Hare	Miyú. Mobe Hákiyu	Yó	Mobi. Moyú	Meni. Mopyá	Yákámbi	Yakámbi	Háyeyá. Múhyák
Where?	Gyála A juju di	Hángbe. Hámpe	Hetne	Hápábi. Hápáng	Há-pi	Khebi	Khábi	Khíbi. Khíbiyá
Above, up	Hát'yu Apiye di	Songpittú. Mittu. Mito	Itemdu. Tó	Múttú	Mitáni	Túkálá	Túká	Háté dá
Below, down	Háyu.§ Apum di	Khúkmemo. Mih'-mú	Ikhúk-bé-Mó	Múh'-mú	Mú-yúni	Yúkálá	Yúká	U'ngkhok-morábi
Between	A'lyo. Aleu-da	Lúmbe. Lúmpi	Ilúm-bé	Májhábi. Luh'pi	Ammrápi	Májhábi	O'lipphíbi	U'mrá. U'm-Kúbú-yá
Without, outside	A'to-la	Song-bé U'ng-phú	A'yó	Pákha yú	Amkonpó	Ghobai. Ghoyo	Pátel	
Within, in, inside	A'gwádi Agwa la ‖	Hongsiyú	Ichhite	Hoksyúyú	Hoptán	U'tong	Ugo-ya	U'm-kong-ya
Far	Brába. Hare	Wó. Miyo	Mánglok	Tárho	Chhúsi	Chhyú	Chhy-úpá	Máng. Mángkhá-yá
Near	Neng-tha Pumbi	Nen. Ningtáng	Tang-neklok	Netá	Neti. Yúbhi	Mebigná	Népham	Nek. Nektáng

Little	*Ká-chi*	*Mig'-mo*	*Míyo*	*Mechhúk*	*U'ttú-chhe*	Tibichyo	Tibiche	A'chichi
Much	Yáko	Dhe-rok. Dilik. Kh'wa. Chopmo	Badhebák	Dúklo	O'tto. Wotto	Thobe	Thebe gole	Ninám-má
How much?	Gísko	Yeh-wa	Caret	Aptoklo	Dáhile	Hebe	Hebe	Tem
As, rel.*	Caret	Mantok'. Caret	Caret	Caret	Caret	Caret	...	...
So, correl.	Mekho	Mado-knok	Natte	...	...	...	...	...
Thus, correl. and positive	Yekho. Me kho	Idok. Mo-dok	Natte-khá	Kodokpá	O'tá	Temphem	Támphém	Igne-go
How?	Gekho	Mantok	Hende-khá	A'pto	Yán-táko	Hemphem	Hemphem	Tete
What like	Gekhom	Mantok'ye	...	...	...	...	...	...
Why?	Mar'cho. Mar'tha	Imang-musi Manthong	Thimmá	U'khálo	Yán pi	Mápúne	Mábi	Tená
Yes	Moko	Yé	Yé	Hegne	Yé. Inchhúng. Ingná	Anmá	Gó. A'm'má	Han-an. Gó. Imchang bá
No, negative	Máh'-á	Caret	Máhá. Mále	Hé-gnane	Máná	Mo-ó	Ma-an	Mán. Jé. Soh'
No, privitive	Dekho. Ma Man, prefix	Ni, suffix	Nin, suffix	Ni, infix	Man, prefix. I'si, suffix	Ma, prefix	Ma, prefix Dokhai, prefix	I', suffix
Not, prohibitive	Ma, prefix	E', prefix	Ang—n (ang before; n after the word)	Ná	Na	Mú	Mó	Man'-to
And *	Caret	Caret	Lá. Chhá	...	...	...	...	...
Also	Yó	Sá. Song	...	Sáng	Sang	Yó	Núng-yo	Chhang
Or	Ki. Caret	Dú. Dó	A'		Lé	Yé	Yé	Hé
This	Yam. Yem	I'go	Ná. Nárok	Kó-ó ¶	Noko. Nokog-ná	Tem. Temgna. Tami	Tomgná	Igo
That	Myám. Mem Harem	Mo **	Y'oná. Yonarok A'ko	Mo-ó	Moko. Mokog-ná	Momi. Yákam. Yakamgná	Mámgná	Mgú-o
Who or which, relative	Caret	Caret	Caret	...	...	...	...	...

* See note aforegone, p. 169. The now and then at this place are positive.

† Hona=time. ‡ Lonok=time.

§ Go down, Ha-yu lawo. Go up, Hat-yu lawo. Come up, ku wo. Come down, yu wo. Come on level, pí wo. Go on, go back, gnalla lawo, nótha lawo. Come in, Khim gware piwo. Come out, átola piwo. See full treatise in sequel.

‖ A' gwa di = its inside in. A gwá la, its inside to. So á tó la, its exterior to. A púm di, its base in, A' juju di, its top in.

¶ The vowel repeated denotes the pausing accent.

** Yem neu, this is good; mem má neu, that is not good, *Báhinggyá*. Mó-nú, that is good; ígo-nú, this is good; nú-ní, not good, *Lóhóróng*.

English.	*Báhinggyá.*	*Lóhóróng.*	*Lámbichhóng.*	*Báláli.*	*Sángpáng.*	*Dúmi.*	*Kháling.*	*Dúngmáli.*
Who or which, correl.	Mém=that	Caret	U'ndok	Khosá. Khosálo	Khogná	Mom	...	Há-go
Who or which? interrogative	Syú. Seú	A'sá	Sé-ong	A'sálo. A'sá	Asá. Asále	Syúgo. Syú	Khám	Ság. Khigo
What?	Mara	Imang	Thíya	U'kha	Yen	Mimgna	Mang ga	Tigo
Anything	Máráye	Imáng-sáng	Thíchhá	U'k-háng	Yon sáng	Máng-yó	Máng-yó	Tichhang
Anybody	Syúye	A'sá-sáng	Síchhá	A'sáne	A'sá sáng	Syúyo	Súi-yo	Ságchhang
Eat { dual { plural	Báwo. Jáwo Já se, D. Já *ne*, Pl.	Cháé. Cho-ye. Chai' che, D. Chái ne, P.	Choh'. Chasa chu, D. Cha-sa num, P.	Chó. Cha chi, D. Cha nin, P.	Chó. Chó chu, D. Cho num, P.	Jyu	Jyú-ye. Kúye	Chóye
Drink	Túgno Túse, D. Túne, Pl.	Dúng-é * Dun-gache, D. Dungane, P.	Thúgna. Thugna chu, D. Thug-nanum, P.	Dúgno. Dugna chi, D. Dugna nin, P.	Dugnu. Dúgnú chu, D. Dugna-num, P.	Tíngne	Tyung'-ye	Túgne
Sleep	Ip'po. Ipse, D. Ipine, Pl.	I'me. Imache, D. Immane, P.	Im'sa. Imsachi, D. Imsa ni, P.	Ipcha. Ipchasi, D. Ipchá nin, P.	Ipsa. Ipsa chi, D. Ipsa ni, P.	Am'si	Am'si	Im'se
Wake	Bokko Bokse. D. Bokine, Pl.	Cheno. Póge. Póglénte	Poga. Pogachi, D. Poga ni, P.	Polit'. Polita chi, D. Polita nin, P.	Thittá-chi-ni. Chi, D. Ni, P.	Phúge	Phúk'ye	Phú-ge
Laugh	Ríso. Rische, D. Ri'sini, Pl.	Yichae. I'chóye. Ichare. Icha-che, D. Icha-ne, P.	Risa'. Risa chi, D. Risa ni, P.	Yúcha. Yúcha chi, D. Yúcha nin, P.	Ghísá. — chi, D. — ni, P.	Réche	Réche	Ríge
Weep	Gnokko. Gnokse, D. Gnokine, Pl.	Hábe. Habache, D. Habáne, P.	Hába. Haba chi, D. Haba ni, P.	Khába. Khaba, chi, D. Khaba, nin, P.	Khápá,—chi-ni	Gnoke	Gnoke	Khá-be
Be silent	Libabwakko. Liba-bwak se, D. Liba-bwaki ne, Pl.	Chichú-ye. Chi-chuyache, D. Chichayane, P. Yonga. Yonga che, D. Yonga ne, P.	In'che'-nán. Inche'nan'chi, D. Inche'nan'-nin, P. —	Chíchu-wet. Chichuwetech, D.' Chichu-wetennin, P.	Wai-wai-túwa —chi-ni	Líbámo	Leba	Máncheptáye

Speak, n. utter	Boh'-ho. Bwó-kko. Bwok-se, D. Bwokine, Pl.	Yám-múse. ——sa che, D. ——sa ne, P.	Chega. Che ga chi, D. Che ga ni, P.	Púklús. Puk-lusa chi, D. Puklusa nin, P.	Niná,—chi-ni	Jé	Jeye	Ché bé
Come	Pi-wo Ráwo. Pí se, D. Pi ne, Pl.	Dábe. —a che, D. —a ne, P.	Thába. Thaba chi D. Tha-ba ni, P.	Dába. Daba chi, D. Da-ba nin, P.	Báná,—chi-ni	Pú	Paú-ye	Túbe
Go	Láwo. Láse, D. Láne, Pl.	Kháde. —a che, D. —a ne, P.	Kháda. Kháda chi, D. Khada ni, P.	Kheda. Kheda chi, D. Khe-da nin, P.	Khátá,—chi-ni	Khochche	Kho-che	Khá-de
Stand up	Ráppo. Rong-so. Rap'she, D. Rapine, P.	Yébe. Ye-poge. —a che, D. —a ne, P.	Poklonda. Yé-bá. —chi, D. —ni, P.	Yópok. Yóba. Ye po ka chi, D. Ye po ka nin, P.	Ripá,—chi-ni	Rípha	Rep-ye	Rebe
Sit down	Nísyo. Nis-che, D. Nisine, P.	Péne. —a che, D. —a ne, P.	Yúgná. Yugna chi, D. Yugna ni, P.	Péh'-yúsa. Pe-yusa chi, D. Peyusa nin, P.	Túwá,—chi-ni	Mó	Gnáche	Yú-gne
Walk or move	Gwakko. Gwakshe, D. Gwakine, P.	Lámdúme. ——a che, D. ——a ne, P.	Phana. Laoma. —chi, D. —ni, P.	Dúma. Be. Duma chi, D. Duma nin, P.	Lándúma. Bi, —chi-ni	Lámthúlo	Lámthúye	Lámtúme
Run	Wánno. Wan-she, D. Wan ne, P.	Píne. —a che, D. —a ne, P.	Pin'da. —chi, D. —ni, P.	Phína. Phina chi, D. Phina nin, P.	Bhúsa,—chi-ni	Ghúre	Ghúre	Róde
Give { to me † / to any }	Gïyi. Giwo. Gise, D. Gine, P.	Pígne. Pitte. —a che, D. —a ne, P.	Piráng, ching D. ning, P. Pira, chu, D. nu, P.	Pigná. Pittu. —a chi, D. —a nin, P.	Pián,—chi-ni. Píyú,—chi-ni	Bigná. Bi	Bignáye	Píyáng-ye. Piye
Take { from me‡ / from any }	Né, immut-able. Lato. Já-po. Bla-wo	Naye. Labe	Kó. unchanged. Thepta	Ná. Khettá	Né. Kháyú	Né. Khátn	Caret	Né. Kháye
Strike	Tyú-po. Tipo. Tip she, D.§ Ti pi ne, P.	Lóme. (Dúbe, by craftsman.) Lo ma chi. Lo mam ne	Tena	Lomu	Yosu. Kíru. Yop'-su	Klen'de	Yál'ye	Nó-re, sing. Nor chie, dual. Nor numye, pl.

* Mette is the general causative Hence dungmette is cause to drink; immette, cause to sleep; poğmette, cause to wake (from pógò), &c.

† Give to me, gíyí. Give to him, to any one, gíwó. For an explanation, see aforegone, p. 190. Also grammars in sequel. In column 3, píráng, give to me, makes dual ching and plural ning. Pira, give to him, to any, dual chu and plural nu.

‡ See note at p. 190, or full treatise of the sequel. Bahing grammar.

§ See full treatise on Bahing in the sequel. Tyuppo vel teuppo is the right form. The vowel is = French eu in peur, heur or English u in pure, azure.

English.	*Báhinggyá.*	*Lóhóróng.*	*Lámbichhóng.*	*Báláli.*	*Sángpáng.*	*Dúmi.*	*Khaling.*	*Dúngmáli.*
Kill	Sáto. Sa ti she, D. Sa ti ne, P.	Sede (causal of siye, die). Its causal sed mette. Se da che, D. Se dam ne, P. Thapta	Sera	Sedú	Situ	Sede	Sede, sing. Se chi, dual. Se snaye, pl.	Sede, S. Sede chie, D. Ser numye, P.
Bring	Pito. Rato.* Pi ti se, D. Pi ti ne, P.	Láḍuppo (take and come). Laḍuppa che, D. Laḍupam ne, P.	Tháp-ta	Dáppu. Yang-dáppu	Báh'-yu	Píde	Pide, S. Pí chíe, D. Pí-snaye, P.	Tág'-we, S. Tag wechíe, D. Tag nu-mye, P.
Take away	Láto.† La ti se, D. La ti ne, P.	Lahette (take and go), or Lakhetta. La-khette che, D. Lakhettam ne, P.	Khátta. Chi khette, beings. Yi khette, beasts. La khette, things	Yákhettu	Kháh'-yu	Ḳhotte	Khátte, S. Khatte chíe, D. Kho snaye, P.	Khá-de, S. Kháde chíe, D. Kháde ningye, P.
Put down	Tyullo vel Teullo. Jilo. Jil se, D. Jil ne, P.	Yúk-se. — sa che, D. — sam ne, P.	Yúng-sá	Yúk-su	Yú-su	Tú. Tyú	Gnánde, S. Gnande chíe, D. Gnandi niye, P.	Yúng'se, S. Yung'si chíe, D. Yung'-su num'ye, P.
Lift up	Rok-to. Rok ti se, D. Rok ti ne, P.	Thepoge. The-lente. —— a che, D. —— am ne, P.	Koba. Koplota	Thettu	Thettu	Thende	Thende, S. Thende chíe, D. Thende snaye, P.	Thende, S. Then'de chie, D. Then'de num'ye, P.
Do	Páwo. Pá se, D. Pá ne, P.	Muse. Lette. — a che, D. — am ne, P.	Númda	...	Mó	Mú	Múyè, S. Mú-íye, D. Mú-níye, P.	Mú-yé, S. Múchíe, D. Múnum'ye, P.
Make	Páwo. Pa se, D. Pa ne, P.	Dube. Tonge. Ache, D. Amne, P.	Ditto	...	Ditto	Ditto	Ditto	Tú-be, S. Tú-ba che, D. Túba num'ye, P.
Make not	Má pawo	Edúbe. E'tónge	...	...	...	...	...	...

Hear	Ni-no. Ni-nishe, D. Nin'ne, P.	Kheme. —— a che, D. —— am ne, P.	Khemsa	Yé-nu	Yénu	Ní	Níye, S. Ni-iye, D. Na niye, P.	Yé-ne, S. Yen'che, D. Yenanum'ye, P.
Understand	Mim-to. Mim tise, D. Mim tine, P.	Mitte. —— a che, D. —— am ne, P.	Mim'-da	Míttu	Mit'nu	Momsi	Mam'de, S. Mi miye, D. Mam naye, P.	Mih'-ye, S. Mih' yechie, D. Mih'-ye-num'ye, P.
Tell or relate	Sogno, utter. Sodi, to me. Sodo, to any‡	I'se. —— a che, D. —— am ne, P.	Tumlúsa	I'su	Pá-yu	Blet'te, b Le-t'te	Blátte, b. La-t'-te, S. Blatte-chi, D. Blatte-sna, P.	Lú-ye, S. Lú-chíe, D. Lu-numye, P.
Good { dual / plural	Nyú-ba. Ny-úba daa si, D. Nyúba daa, P.	Nú-ye. Nuk chia, D. Nuk miha, P.	Núyu-kkha	Nú-ne. Nup	Ní	Nyúpa	Nyúpa	Nú, S. Nú-chíe, D. Man'nú, P.
Bad	Mányú-ba. Manyuba daa si, D. Ma-nyuba daa, P.	I'sa. Phenna. —— chia, D. —— miha, P.	Núyuk-ninkha. Gnasi yukha	I'sáne. Isa'p. Núnine	I'si	Múnípa. Mú-myúpa	Mányúpa	I', S. I'chíe, D. Mayí, P.
Cold	Chhik'-ba. Chhikpa daa si, D. Chhik-pa daa, P.	Yep se. Yempa. Yemukye. —— chia, D. —— miha, P.	Chíyúkha	Ipchhiyúne	Chhíki	Chhú	Chhak'pa	Kéng, S. Keng'chíe, D. Má-keng', P.
Hot	Gle-glem. Gleglem daa si, D. Gle-glem daa, P.	Kúse. Kú. Kukchiá, D. Kuk miha, P. Kuse	Kúyu. Kúyú-kha	Kúne. Kú	Háki. Púti	Wál. Hai	Glogloma	Kú, S. Kú-chíe, D. Makú, P.
Raw (green)	Achekhli. Achekli daa si, D. Ache-kli daa, P.	Men tum pa. Mákam'-pa. Men chia, D. Men miha, P.	Hing-lí. Hinglíkha	Mátúpti	Man'-dú. Manduwako. Mansetnáchi. Mántúmako	U'súta	U'súta	Ummáng, S. Ummáug'-chie, D. Umangne, P.

* Causal of pi-wo, to come. See full treatise in sequel.

† Láwo, go; látyo, take away, *i.e.*, cause to go; lápátyo, cause to take away. Newari, hon, go; wonke, causal; yenke yon, take away; causal, yenke byu, give to take away.

‡ See note at page 191, or full treatise of the sequel. Bahing grammar.

English.	*Báhinggyá.*	*Lóhóróng.*	*Lámbichhóng.*	*Báláli.*	*Sángpáng.*	*Dúmi.*	*Khaling.*	*Dúngmáli.*
Ripe	Ming'-ta. Jita. Mim-ba. Jiba. —daa si, D. —daa, P.	Dumem'-pa. Tu mem'pa	Thúyú yekha. Thu-yu	Túmap = Tu-m-pa	Setnáchi. Tu-mako. Dú-wakó	Mis'te	Dham'pa	Túm'sá, S. Tum'sa chíe, D. Ma tum'sa, P.
Sweet	Jijim. —daa si, D. —daa, P.	Lim'pa. Lim-ni, neg. Limte, ——chia, D. ——miha, P. [Lim uk gna, Lim ti ne, I am sweet.*]	Lim-yu-kha. Lem-yú	Lim	Límí	Lem	Lempá	Lem, S. Lem' chíe, D. Ma lem', P.
Sour	Jyúr-ba. —daa si, D. —daa, P.	Sin'ta. Lim ni † ——chia, D. ——miha, P.	Sú-yu-kha	Sit'tu	Chúri	Jújúr	Jhár'pa	Sún, S. Sun' chíe, D. Ma sun', P.
Bitter	Ká-ba. —daa si, D. —daa, P.	Khikta. Khik'-ka. [Khik gna, Khik ti gna, verbal.*] Khik chia, D. Khik miha, P.	Khik'-yu-kha	Khy-u-kúp. Khe u kúp	Khíki	Khepa	Khápa	Khak, S. Khak' chía, D. Ma-khák, P.
Handsome	Rim'-ba. —daa si, D. —daa, P.	Kam-núye ‡ —chia, D. —miha, P.	U'chunú-yu-kha	Khen-núng	Khánní	Bhan'gpa = bhing-lma	Bhang pa	Khán-nu, S. Khannú chíe, D. Khan-manú, P.
Ugly	Márim'-ba. —daa si, D. —daa, P.	Kamísa ‡	U'chu núyuk nin. Uchu-gnasi yukha	Kheh'-yúg. Khen ni núng	Kháísi	Mú-bhang'pa	Mábhán'gpa	Kha-í-kha-ik' pu, S.
Straight	Dyom'ba.	Lúng-kúye. Cheng-ye. —chia-miha.	Sori. Sorikha	Lúng-ku	Toh'-ño	Dan'ta	Dhvaípa	Cháng
Crooked	Mádyom'-ba. Gung gung me,	Kho-kho. O'ok' ye	O'krik'-pa. Bang'krik'pa	Khok khok-pugu	Toh'-noná	Khráda	Gúng-gúngma	Okrokrak'ch

Black	Kyá-kyám. — daa si, D. — daa, P.	Máik' ye. Máiye. chia-miha	Má-yukkha. Mak-yuk	Mákthro-pa	Máó. Máka-chik'-pa	Mak'chupu	Kekem	Mákchácha, S. Makchák' pa chí, D. Makchak chak chíye, P.
White	Bu-bum'	Bihá. Bíye	O'm-yuk'-kha. Om-yuk	Béye-pa	Om'ban-lonpa	Bubum	Bu-bum	Om, S. Om-chi, D. Ma-on'gache, P.
Red	Lá-lám. — daa si, D. — daa, P.	Hár'rá. — chia, D. — miha, P.	Wára-wába	Ha lá-pa	Halalápa	Halála	Halálám	Hárchhop'-chho, S. Harchop'-chho kachí, D. Har-chop'chho makat' ka chíe, P.
Green	Gígím	Phíye	...	Phiphí-pa	...	Wálu	Gigí-ma	Mak'po keke, S. Mak'po-keka-ka chí, D. Makpo keke makat-kechíe, P.
Long	Jhoí-ba	Kéye. Kibe	Ke-yú-k. Ké yuk'-kha	Kepa	Máipa	Song-pa	Song'-pa	Ki. Kigo, S. Ki cha-go, D. Maki-gochíe, P.
Short	Dyakhojhoíba. Dekhojhoíba. — daa si, D. — daa, P.	Taks'ye. Tyáksu. — chia, D. — miha, P.	Wun yu-k. Wunyuk'-kha	Ték-sip	Duïpa. Dwípa	Tibichyám	Dokháisong'-pa	Tun. Tungo, S. Tun'-chíe, D. Matun'go-chíe, P.

* What is bracketed refers to the further researches previously adverted to. The verbs were quoted to show the participial nature of so many of the qualitives—a point as to which see the analyses of the Váyu and Babing tongues in the sequel.

† Lim-ni = sweet not; khik-ni = bitter not.

‡ Kam (recte kang) nuye, good to look at; kam ísa, bad to look at. In most of the other dialects the construction is the same, *e.g.*, úchu nuyukha; uchu-nuyuk nin vel uchugnási yukha. Nin vel guási is negative.

English.	*Báhinggyá.*	*Lóhóróng.*	*Lámbichhóng.*	*Búláli.*	*Sángpúng.*	*Dúmi.*	*Khaling.*	*Dúngmáli.*
Tall (high)	Lá-ba	Keye	Ké-yu-k. Ke yuk'-kha	Kí byép	Otto-rípiko	Song'pa	Song'-pa	Badhemego, S. Badhe-mechágo, D. Bádhe-meme-ka-chí, P.
Short (low)	Dyákholába. Dekho lába	Taksye. Mim'mu. Míh'-mu	W*un*-yuk'-kha. W*un*-yu-k	Ták-sip'	Uttuchhe-rípiko	Tibichyom	Dokháisong'-pa	Tungo, S. Tun'chágo, D. Matun'-gochíye, Pl.
Small	Kachim	Mi sy u ma. Misup'-pa Mi su k'-pa. Misu-yukha	Michi yuk'-kha. Michi-yuk	Mépa-chhá (small child)	Tuchheppa	Tibichyom	Tibichem. Yakhe	Umchuk'pang or Chuk, S.* Chukche-chi, D. Machuk'-kache, P.
Great	Gnolo — daa si, D. — da, P.	Dhe-a. Deha. —chia-milha	Theuyuk'-kha. Theu ya-k'	Dhé-pa	Um-dhep'pa	Gholpa	Ghálpa	Dhígo. Dhí, S. Dhí-chí, D. Madhik' chi, P.
Round, circular	Khíkhírme	Wengwengma. Tong-kuye	Tong-yuk'-kha. Tong-yuk	Wángwang pa. Wáng-wáp	Khíkhírko	Khokhor'ma	Khákhárma	...
Round, spherical	Pupul'-me	Pum pumma. Pum pumye	Kák'lik-lik'kha	Puk luk-luk	Phuphul'ko. Pupul'ko	Pupul'mu	Papal'ma	Um-pop, S.* Um-pophí-chi, D. Um-popchíye, P.
Square	Lepataye	Rik' suk ye	...	...	Líkapáta	...	Bhálchyusko	Rik'tum, S.
Flat, compressed, depressed	Plem plem'me	Phekphek'-ma	Ranrankha	Phek phek-pa	Phem phem'-ko	Phlem phlem'-me	Phem phem-me	Phepchidák-da, S. Phep' chidak'da-kachí, D. Phep'chi dak'da ma-makat go-che, P.

Level, as a plain	Dyom -ba. Adeb'de	Tem'-ma	Tenlang tong-yuk. Tenlang-ton'kha	Caret	em'-ma	Udel'mo	Dhoípa	Légó. Um-témma, S. Lego hichi. Hichi lègo, D. Légo-chíye, P.
Fat	Seneuba (flesh good†.) Gnolo	Yám-nuye	Isamtai mekha	Yám'nu Dhé-pa	Lítiko	Léï.	Senupá	Dhi }
Thin (lean)	Kachim. Ryam'ba	Yám-ísa	Reksu reksukha	Mépa-chá	Romiko	Róm	Jyor'pa	Chuk }
Weariness	Bál	Yáktáng	Su-a	Yák'ta. Yák	Ho yán	Ghrum'ma	Ghrí-ma	Mího
Thirst	Bwaku dwaktu	Wait'má	Wait'ma	Waíme	Wám'ma	Kumána	Kunur'. Ku-nuu'	Cháómit'ma
Hunger	Solimi	Sák'	Sák	Ságe	Sáka	Só-a	Só-o	Ságá

* See note at the word Fat, p. 192, and compare the adjectives here and there throughout.

† Sé neuba, flesh good, who is well fleshed. So yam núye is abounding in fat (yam). Yam isa, bad in fat, low in flesh.

END OF THE COMPARATIVE VOCABULARIES.

III.—GRAMMATICAL ANALYSIS OF THE VÁYU LANGUAGE.

A.—VÁYU VOCABULARY.*

1. *Nouns Substantive.*

English.	*Váyu.*
Air (wind)	Hójum
Affection, love	Chhánsa
Abuse	Jesi
Abode	Múlúng
Agriculture	No word
Agriculturist	Kóduvi. Víkpóvi
Amaranth (grain)	No word
Aqueduct	Dunri. Tilóm
Ankle	Léthulung
Arm—all	Gót
Arm—fore	Gót
Aunt, paternal	Nini
Aunt, maternal	Yeng-yeng
Ant	Chíkibula
Anus	Pó-ching
Arrow	Blo
Axe	Khoyóng
Alder-tree	Lichhing
Bag. Basket	Guh'mi †
Barley	Sáká
Bamboo	Pholo
Bark of tree	Sing kokchho
Back	Sónti
Backbone	Gátachu
Belly	Muli (organ). Bimli (whole
Beast, quadruped	No name
Box, chest	No word
Bat-kind	Pòkcheún
Bird-kind	Chinchi
Bird, male	Loncho chinchi
Bird, female	Mescho chinchi
Bird, young	Bengáli chinchi
Beer	Soe. Swe
Bread	Pipra
Bitch	Mescho úri
Birch-tree	Toura
Bed	Blem'chum'
Bedchamber	Imlung ‡
Bedtime	Imsing ‡
Bee	Singwo
Blacksmith	Got thutvi. Khakchingtuvi
Blood	Vi
Buttocks	Petuna
Battle, fight	Pat
Boat	Dunga
Bear	No word
Beard	No word
Boar	Loncho pok
Body	Chho
Burden, load	Khuli
Bone	Rú
Breast	Ripcha
Breast, nipple	Chuschu
Bow	Liwo
Bowman	Liwo-wo
Bottom, lowest part	Hutti
Boy	Loncho, choo. Tawo
Buffalo-kind	Mechho
Buffalo, male	Loncho mechho
Buffalo, female	Mescho mechho
Buffalo, young	Mechho choh'mi or cho'-mi mechho
Bull	Loncho gai (see Ox)
Breath	Hemchi
Branch, bough	Rámá
Brother	Bólo, elder. Bálu, younger
Brethren, uterine	Bolungcho
Calf	Gai cho'mi
Calf, male	Lóncho gai cho'mi
Calf, female	Mescho gai cho'mi
Can, cup	Boguna
Cart	No name
Cat-kind	Dána
Cat, male	Loncho dána
Cat, female	Mes'cho dána
Cat, young	Cho'mi dána
Carpenter	Sing chuk'vi
Cheek	Gwong-gwong
Chestnut-tree	Se'lu
Chin	Kumching
Child-kind	Choo.§ Tamtáwo-Bokvi
Child, male	Táwo ‖
Child, female	Támi ‖
Clay	Nakchyongkó
Cloth	Jéwa
Cloth, cotton	Rowa jéwa
Cloth, woollen	Belisong jéwa
Clothes, raiment	Jéwa
Cloud	Kowál
Cold (frigor)	Jungsa

* This analysis is divided into (A) a vocabulary and (B) a grammatical portion; but both are so framed as to bear on the structure of the language and to dispense with a separate array of rules.

† The h thus marked h' denotes the abrupt tone, which is of very frequent occurrence. The h is often omitted, as cho'mi, little; to'po, strike; cho'no, the nose, &c.

‡ Im is the verb to sleep, and lung and sing are affixes of place and time respectively, but useable only with verbs, with which, however, they form very many useful terms—*e.g.*, múlúng = abode.

§ The repeated final vowel marks the pausing tone, which is as common as the abrupt tone.

‖ Tá is the crude, = Sontal and Uraon Dá, and wo, mi, are the suffixes of gender.

English.	Váyu.
Colour	No word
Cane (calamus)	Dí
Cock	Loncho khocho *
Cousin, paternal	Bo'lu
Cousin, maternal	Bálu (see Brother)
Cow	Gai
Cough	Khwen khwen
Copper	No name
Cowherd	Gai túuvi
Cotton	Rówa
Crow	Gágín
Daughter	Támi
Daughter-in-law	Choyongmi
Dance	Hóli
Day	Núma. Nómo
Dust	Pínko
Darkness	Kwung-kwung
Death	No word
Desire, wish	Daksa
Deer	Kéchho
Dispute	Phwé
Dog	U'ri
Dog, male	Lôncho úri
Dog, female	Mes'cho úri
Dog, young	U'ri cho'mi
Dog, wild	Ghárímu uri. Béne úri
Dream	A'múng
Drink	Túntáung
Earth, the	Kó
Earth, a little	Kó
Ear	Nók'-chun'g
Egg	Chálung
Elephant	Háti
Elephant, male	Loncho háti
Elephant, female	Méscho háti
Ewe	Méscho béli
Eye	Mék' (abrupt tone)
Eyebrow	Mék' kwúyu
Elbow	Koko-chus'-chu
Evening	Nomothipsing
Exorcist	Bálung
Earthquake	Dukku
Face	Gnáru
Feather	Chínchi swám (= bird hair)
Feast, festival	No word
Father	U'pú
Father-in-law	Chákhi
My father	Ang úpú
Thy father	Ung úpú
His father	A' úpú Wáthim úpú. I'nung úpú. Minung úpú
Her father	The same

English.	Váyu.
Its father	The same
Fever	Jun'gsa
Fair, market	Inglungthamlung (buying and selling place)
Fear	Ramsa. Ram
Ferry	Theklung. (Lit. crossing place)
Fire	Mé
Fire-place	Phulung
Field, arable	Wík. Vík
Finger	Blemen
Finger-nail	Demen, got demen
Fellow-countryman	Angki mulung-wo-mi. Angki namsang-wo-mi
Fellow-tribeman	Angki thoko-wo-mi †
Fish	Ho
Fist	No name
Flavour, taste	No name
Flesh	Kwún. Kon
Flint	Bo-chha lumphu
Flour	Mádi
Flea	Ri'michhing
Flower	Pung'mi
Ford	Theklung
Fly	Jáma
Food	Játáng
Fog	Kow-al
Fowl-kind	Khocho, or Khwocho
Fowl, wild	Rikkho
Fowl, male	Loncho khocho
Fowl, female	Mescho khocho
Fowl's egg	Chálung. Kho-chalung
Foreigner, m. and f.	Gyetinam'sang-wo-mi ‡
Forehead	Tángláng
Filth, dirt	Penki
Foot	Lé
Form	Nárung
Forest	Vik. Ghári
Fruit	Sé. Sí
Frog	Boyukwong. (Khwocho is toad)
Garlic	No name
Girl	Támi. Méschochoo.§ Cho'-mi
Glue, cement	No word
Grandfather	Kiki
Grandmother	Pipi
God	Caret (Bhem Sen is the usual object of adoration)
Gold	Heldungmi. (Lit. the yellow)
Goat-kind	Che'li

* Kh uttered like kw, deep in the throat.

† Angki thoko is our tribe; angki namsang, our smell; angki múlúng, our dwelling-place. Therefore the suffixes wo, mi, here form derivative substantives, like countryman from country. So also li-wo-mi, male and female archers, from li, a bow; and hengong-wo-mi, a male and female of the Newar tribe (page 240 in the sequel). But in tá-wo-mi, boy and girl, from tá, a child, these suffixes are mere signs of gender. Again, in choti-wo-mi, strong, from choti, strength, they form adjectives from abstract substantives. See and compare the several uses in the sequel.

‡ Gyeti namsang wo, literally one of another smell. It answers to angki namsang wo, one of our own smell, supra.

§ Choo is probably cho'wa, a male child, and cho'mi, a girl, answering to tá-wo and tá-mi. But cho'mi is now chiefly used for a little one, and rather adjectively than substantively.

English.	*Váyu.*
Goat, male	Loncho cheli
Goat, female	Mescho cheli
Goat-herd	Cheli tunvi
Grain	Jomsit
Groin	Chhlágalúng
Hammer	Topchyang
Hammerer	To'vi *
Hand	Gót
Handle	Lut*kh*chyáng (English th)
Spade handle	Chukha lut*h*chyáng (English th)
Hair	Swom
Hair of head	Puchhi swom
Hair of body	Dukhu swom
Herdsman	Gaimechho-tunvi
Head	Púchhi
Heart	Thum
Heel	Konteng
Hail	Bopum
Hemp	Lapchhyo
Hen	Mescho khochi
Hip	Gangpangrú
Hope	No word
Hoof, cloven, solid	Khokhek
Hog-kind	Pok'
Hog, male	*Lon*cho pok'
Hog, female	Mescho pok'
Hole	Hom (like kh). Hom-lung
Hoe, spade	Chokhá
Husk	Ingsu
Hook, peg	Khondu
Horn	Rúng
Horn, goat's	Che'li rúng
Honey	Singwo khudu
Horse-kind	No name (Goḍa used)
House	Kém
Home, dwelling-place	Mu-lung
Hunger	Suk'sa
Husband	Rócho
My husband	Ang rócho
Thy husband	U'ng rócho
Her husband	I'nung rócho. Minung rócho. Wáthim rócho. A' rócho
Instrument, Implement	Póchyáng
Intestines	Chyot
Iron	Khakchhingmi (Lit. the black)
Jaw	Rá
Joint	Thulung
Juice	Bulung
Knife	Yukchyang
Knee	Khokáli
Knot	No name
Kitchen	Khoklung

English.	*Váyu.*
King	Pogú
Lamp, torch	Tuphi
Language, speech	Dábo. Dávo
Lip	Kumching
Leaf	Ló
Tree's leaf	Sing ló †
Leather	Kokchho
Leg—all	Ló
Leg—true	Poktólo
Light, lux	Dáng-dáng
Lightning	Dángdáng bíkup
Life	Hémchi (breath)
Liver	Ding
Louse	Be'mere
Lungs	Iot'
Loom	Punc'hyáng
Load	Kholi. Khúli
Maize	Mákai, H.
Master	Mó
Mark	No name
Market	Inglung thamlung ‡
Mason	Kem povi
Mankind	Singtong
Man, male	Lo*n*cho
Man, female	Mes-cho
Man, adult	Bangcho, male. Bangmi, female
Maker, doer	Povi
Madder	Láru
Mare	Mes-cho goḍa
Mill, hand	Rechyáng
Mill, water	The same
Millet (kangni)	Levi
Millet (kodo)	Dusi
Millet (juwar)	De*n*som
Millet (sama)	Náwáli
Milk	Dúdú, H.
Mist	Kokcho (cloud)
Manner, mode, way	Bá
Monkey, Macacus	Phoka
Monkey, Semnopithecus	Phoka
Measure	Pokchyáng
Medicine	No name
Mind	Thum
Moon	Cholo
Month	Cholo
Music	Dumku
Mother	U'mu
My mother	Ang úmu
Thy mother	Ung úmu
His, her mother	I'nung úmú. Minung úmú. Wáthim úmu. A' úmu
Mountain	Chhágu
Mountaineer	Chhájuwo. Chhajube mut'vi §

* Topchyáng is the instrumental, and to'vi the agentive participle. See grammar in sequel.

† Tree alone is singphum. See it and the note there.

‡ Buying and selling place.

§ Chhaju-wo-mi, male and female mountain-eer. Chhaju be mutvi, one (m. or f.) who dwells in the mountains. So also in sequel at native of the plains. Mutvi, the participle of mú, to dwell, has the pronoun inherent, and can be used, like every other word of the sort, as adjective or substantive.

English.	*Váyu.*	*English.*	*Váyu.*
Mouth	Mukchu	River	Bingmu
Moustache	Mukchhu swom *	Rivulet	Gáng
Moschito	Kánánáng	Root	Rochhing
Morning	Nomoloksing	Rust	Kéü (pausing tone)
Mouse	Chuyu	Rudder	No word
Nipple	Chúschu	Road	Lom
Noise	Sangma	Rope	Dámla
Neck	Chhidi	Roof	No name
Name	Ming	Rhododendron	Thán-kapu'li
Night	Eksa. Yeksa	Salt	Chia, culinary. Jikhom, other
Net	No name		
Needle	Pichyáng. Chuschung	Silence	Giwon
Nose	Cho'no	Spade. Spud. Hoe.	Chokhá
Nostril	Cho'no humlung †		
Navel	Sólipun'g	Spear	No word
Oar	Yo'king	Shape, form	Náruug
Oil	Kí	Sheep-kind	Beli (Bhenglung is the Barwal)
Oak-tree	Chyakphen		
Odour, smell	Namsang	Spirits (distilled)	Buko'ha
Onion	No word	Spindle	Chingchyáng
Ox-kind	No word. (Gai is now used)	Spinner	Chingvi
		Skin	Kókchho
Ordure	Epi. Yepi	Skull	Puchhí rú
Pain	Yánsa	Shoe, sandal	Khokhek
Palm of hand	Penteng	Sole of foot	Lé pengteng
Penis	Tholu	Seed	Rú (bone)
Place	Lúng (in composition with verbs only)	Sieve	Yáyáng
		Sleep	I'mpi
Plant	Levi	Sail of boat	No name
Pleasure	Bong	Sand	No word
Plough	Rukchyang	Spittle	Cheku
Ploughman	Rukvi. Rukcho-wo-mi ‡	Silver	Dawángmi. (Lit. the shining, the white)
Plain	Tengteng	Sport, play	No word
A native of the plains	Tengteng-wo-mi. Tengtengbe mutvi	Sisterhood, the	Nunung-cho
		Sister	Nunu, elder. Díyu, younger
Plate, dish. Platter	Tálung		
		Sitting chamber	Múlung
Parent	Phokvi. Bok'pingvi §	Spider	No name
Plantain	Risa	Smith	Khakching tovi
Pine (tree)	Thong chhing	Snake	Hóbu
Pepper	No name	Sky	Nomo (sun)
Potter	Ko-chonvi	Son-in-law	Jánwai
Peach	Powanse ‖	Son	Táwo
Priest	None. (Pater familias performs the part)	My son	Ang táwo
		Thy son	Ung táwo
Ram	Loncho-beli	His, her son	A' táwo. Wathim táwo. I'nung táwo. Minung táwo
Rat	Chuyu		
Rain	Nánum		
Rains, the	Nánum tokvínúma ¶	Shoulder	Pháka
Rice in husk	Bojá	Shepherd	Beli túnvi
Rice, unhusked	Chhán'ga	Side	Yákaju. Khuk
Rice, boiled	Ham	Star	Khwámen

* Mukchhu swom = mouth hair.

† Place where nose is perforated.

‡ Wo is masculine suffix; mi, feminine = hal-wala-wali of Hindi.

§ Phokvi, who begets, a parent, answers to bokvi, who is born, a child. Phok, the transitive, is formed normally from bok, to be born, the neuter. Both take the common transitive formative, pingko; and hence bokpingko = phokko, and, at pleasure, phokpingko, which is a double causal in the sense of to cause to be born, or a single in that of cause to beget. This tallying of transitive and causal and this making of double causals are Dravidian traits common, like many more traits, to Váyu and to Kiránti, not to add more of our Himal tongues.

‖ Sé = fruit, generic sign, as phum is for trees.

¶ Literally, rain-pelting days, or rainy season.

English.	Váyu.
Summit, top	Wani
Snow	Lirí
Steam	Hilili
Smoke	Kulu
Strength	Choti
Song	Kwom
Sow	Mescho pok'
Sun	Nomo, Numa
Sunshine	Lo-gáng
Sunrise	Nomo-loksing
Sunset	Nomo-thipsing
Still	Bukcha pochyáng
Stone	Lu*n*phu
Stomach	Muli (the organ)
Shade, shadow	Veli
Straw	Khisti
Sword	No name
Tail	Mú*n*
Testicle	Chálúng (egg)
Tiger	Bílu
Thigh	Phekteng
Thirst	Tídaksa
Tooth	Lú
Turmeric	Si*n*phi
Toe	Lé blémen
Toe-nail	Lé démen
Tongue	Lí
Time	No name. (Sing in composition with verbs)
Thread	No word
Thunder	Nómosangma *
Thief	Khútumún
Theft	Khutu
Tree	Singphum † (Phum in composition)
Tree bark	Sing kokchho (= tree leather) †
Uncle, paternal	Pongpong
Uncle, maternal	Kuku
Urine	Chipi. Chepi
Man's urine	Singtong chipi
Goat's urine	Che'li chépi
Vein	Vichho lom
Vegetable, wild herbs and roots	Chokphi setung
Vetch, pea	No word
Village	No word (Mulung = dwelling-place, is used)
Victuals	Játáng
Vice, sin	No word
Voice	Sángma

English.	Váyu.
Summer	Jekhom núma
Storm	Kungjum
Valley	No word
Vulva	Juju
Wall	Khoksu
Water	Tí
Water spring	Tí vok lung
Drinking-water	Dakmung tí ‡
Cooking-water	Khoschyang tí
Washerman	Up'vi
Washing-water	Upchyang tí
Weight (instrument)	Poke'hyáng
Weight, heaviness	No word
Wife	Romi
My wife	Ang romi
Thy wife	Ung romi
His wife	Wathim romi. A' romi. Minung romi. I'nung romi
Dual: Our wife	Angchi romi, excl. Ungchi romi, incl.
Dual: Your wife	Ungchi romi
Dual: Their wife	A'chi-romi § or A'- or Wáthim- or Minung- or I'nung- } nakphum romi
Plural: Our wife ‖	Angki romi, excl.
Plural: Our wife	Ungki romi, incl.
Plural: Your wife	Unni romi
Plural: Their wife	A' khata-romi. I'nung khata-romi. Wathim khata-romi or Minung khata-romi
Wax	Dikphi
Wheat	No name
Winter	Jungsa nomo
Wizard	Jochháng póvi
Witchcraft	Jochháng
Witch	Jochháng povi
Wealth	Penku. Gosta
Weaver	Jeva pungvi
Weed, grass	Moksa
Woman	Mescho
Wood	Sing
Wool	Beli swom
Work	No word. Kam is used.
Wound	Buma
Wrist	Gót thulúng
Year	Thong

* Nomosangma, one word; literally, sky sound.

† See tree's leaf, where also sing only is used. So also in branch of tree, root of tree, flower or fruit of tree. Newari is the same, si hau = sing lo. With the entire tree of all sorts phum is suffixed, as risa phum, plantain-tree = kéla má, Newari.

‡ Khoschyang is the instrumental and dakmung the infinitival form. See Grammar. Both these sorts of words are used as adjectives constantly. Note how nicely the more active agency of the water in cooking is discriminated.

§ The possessive m, mu, is repeated or not, and given either with the pronoun or with the numeral, thus: "of them the two the child" is Wathim nakpom cho'mi or Minung nakpo cho'mi.

‖ Wife or wives is the same. The plural sign khàta is seldom or never added to the noun when the pronoun conveys the sense, or when the verb conveys it, *e.g.*, mescho imchimen, the women sleep.

2. *Pronouns.*

English.	*Váyu.*
I, ego	Go
Thou	Gón
He, she, it	Wa'thi. Mi. I'.
We two incl. excl.	Gonakpo
Ye two	Gonchhe *
They two	I' nakpo. Wathi nakpo.* Minakpo
We all incl. excl.	Gokháta
Ye all	Góne. Gónekháta
They all	Mikháta. Wáthikháta. I'kháta.
This	I',† all three genders
That	Wáthi, Mi, ditto
These, dual	I' nákpo : m. and f. I' náyung : n.
These, plural	I' kháta : m. f. n.
Those, dual	Wáthi nakpo. A' nakpo. Minákpo, m. f. Wathi náyung, &c. n. ‡
Those, plural	Wáthikháta, Mikháta } all genders
Self, selves	None
Myself, thyself, himself	None
Own, my, thy, his own	None
Any, some (koi) person	Su; Suna, D. Su nákpo, Pl. Sukháta or Susu; m. and f. subs. and adj.
Any, some (kucch) thing	Mische : n. subs. only. Mische náyung, D. Mische khata or Mische Mische, Pl.
Many, much	Chhinggnak } m. f. n. subs. and adj. and adv.
Few, little	Yanggnak } m. f. n. subs. and adj. and adv.
How much, many	Hátha } m. f. n. subs. and adj. and adv.
So much, many	Mitha
All	No word
The whole	Khiri. Khulup in numbering
Half	Phak : com. gen. subs. and adj. Bá, adj. only

English.	*Váyu.*
Which, What, Who, Relative, of all genders, subs. or adjectival, and	Hánung, subs. and adj. Hánung nakpo, m. f. : Hanung nayung, n. : Dual
Which? What? Interrogative, relative, Which of several exhibited persons or things : subs. adj. m. f. n.	Hánung hánung or Hanung khata, Pl. : m. f. n. : inter. and relative ‡
Who?	Su. Suna, m. f. Suna nakpo, Dual. Susu, Suna suna or sukhata, Pl. m. and f. : subs. and adj.
Whoever	Sunado
What?	Mische, n. : subs. Mische náyung, Dual. Mische khata. Mische mische, Pl.
Whatever	Mischeda
Either	I' ki wathi. I' ki mi
Both	Nakpo, m. f. Nangmi, f. § Náyung, n.
Several	No word
My	Ang } all three genders
Thy	Ung } all three genders
His, her, its	A' Wáthim I'nung Minung } all three genders
Dual: Our	Angchi. excl. Ungchi. incl.
Dual: Your	Unchi
Dual: Their	I'nakpum. ‖ Minakpum. Wáthim nakpum. A' nakpum or A'chi
Plural: Our	Angki, excl. Ungki, incl.
Plural: Your	Unni
Plural: Their	A' kháta. Wathim kháta. Minung kháta. I'nung kháta
Mine	Ang mu

---

* Chhe, the dual sign of 2nd pronoun, is not used with 1st and 3rd. The numeral two (nakpo) is substituted.

† I', this, and mí, that, have the pausing tone. I sometimes represent it by doubling the vowel, ií, mií.

‡ *E.g.*, Hánung gothato'pungmi miī nómi, the hand with which I struck pains me; literally, what hand with I struck that pains. However much the Tartar tongues eschew relative pronouns, they still can and do use them in this way; and Newari, which is one of the simpler Himalayan tongues, herein agrees with Váyu, which belongs to the complex class. So also you can say for "call the man who has come" Hánungdo dongmi miī khamto, or, more usually, Phista khamto.

§ See numerals. Nakpo, m.; Nangmi, f.; Náyung, neuter, is no doubt the proper form. But these signs are passing out of use, and nakpo is now often used for all persons, male or female.

‖ I nak pum, or Inung nakpo, or Inung nakpum. The possessive nung is peculiar to the demonstratives, which it distinguishes from the adverbs of time and place. Inungmu or minungmu, of him. Inhemu, minhemu, of here, of there. Ithemu, mithemu, of now, of then.

	English.	*Váyu.*
	Thine	Ung mu
	His, hers, its	A' mu. Wathim mu. Minung mu. I'nung mu
Dual	Ours	Angchimu. excl. Ungchimu. incl.
	Yours	Ungchimu.
	Theirs	A'chimu. Wáthim nak pomu. Minung nak pomu. I'nung nak pomu.
Plural	Ours	Angchimu. excl. Ungchimu. incl.
	Yours	Unnimu
	Theirs	Wathim khátamu. Mi khátamu. A' khátamu.* A' khátamu, or rather Minung khāta mu. Inung khāta mu.

3. *Adjectives.*

	Crude.	*Affixes.*
Good	Noh'ka	wo m., mi f., mu n.†
Bad	Máng noh'ka	wo m., mi f., mu n.
	Chek pángsing	wo m., mi f., mu n.
Cunning Deceitful	Máng pingvi	m. f. no affix
Candid Truthful	Diksa hotvi Noh'kathum gotvi	m. f. no affix
Malicious Benevolent	Yángsa hávi Bóng havi	ditto
Industrious Idle	Kam povi Hanvi. Mutvi Kam máng povi	ditto (No affix, being participles, like all of the same form that follow; m. and f.‡)
True	Diksa	wo m., mi f., mu n. Diksa = truth
	Diksa hotvi	no affix; participial
False	Mang diksa	wo m., mi f., mu. n.
	Diksa máng hotvi	no affix (participial)
Passionate, hasty	Risi bukvi	m. f. (participial)
	Risi not'vi	no affix (participial)
	Risi ——	wo m., mi f. Risi is anger
Placid, patient	Máng risi bukvi vel notvi	m. f.; no affix
	Mang risi ————	wo m., mi f.
Cowardly	Rāṉvi Ram not'vi	m. f. no affix (participial)
Brave	Mang ránvi Rammá not'vi	(participial)
Constant-minded Unchangeable	Wonvi	ditto (participial)
Inconstant Changeable	Máng wonvi	ditto (participial)
Wasteful, profuse	Hokcho	wo m., mi f.
	Ho'vi	m. f.; no affix; participial
Niggardly	Kháli	wo m., mi f.; no neuter

---

* I or inung, that is, the genitive sign, is repeated at pleasure. Nung and ni, as well as m and mu (and also mi), are genitival and inflexional. Inung, of this person; ini, of this place.

† Wo and mi for rationals; *mu* for other beings.

‡ True adjectives are rare; most are participles (see on to grammar). In participles the relative pronoun inheres. They can be used as adjectives or any substantives without any affix beyond their own signs (vi ta tang). Thus hónvi, literally who obeys, is used for obedient and for the obeyer. Adjectives that are not participles, if used in the latter way, should have the wo, mi, mu affixes, but need them not if used in the former way—*e.g.*, noh'ka loncho, a or the good man; but ka of noh'ka is probably formative from noh', to be good. Possessive mú also makes adjectives from substantives, as chhomu, bodily, from chho, the body; thummu, mental, from thum, the mind; chhinji, sweetness, chhinjimu, sweet.

	Crude.	Affixes.	
Kind, gentle	Yáṉsa mánghávi	no affix	participial
Unkind, harsh	Yáṉsabávi	no affix	
Obedient	Honvi	m. f.; no affix	
Disobedient	Mánglyonvi	no affix	
Mad, idiotic	Thumnasidumta	no affix	
Licit	Pátáng, n.	no affix	
Illicit	Máng pátang	ditto	
Bodily, physical	Chhomu	genitival, n. Chho is body; thúm, mind	
Mental	Thummu		
Hungry	Suksa	wo m., mi f. Suksa is hunger	
	Suksa metvi	m. f.	participial
	Suksa meta	no affix	
Thirsty	Tidaksa	wo m., mi f. Tídaksa is thirst	
	Tidaksa metvi	m. f.	participial
	Tidaksa meta	no affix	
Naked	Gunangsenti	wo m., mi f., mu n.	
	Luphta	m. f. n.; no affix	participial
Libidinous man	Loncho daksa metvi	m.; no affix	
Libidinous woman	Mescho daksa metvi	f.; no affix	
Gluttonous	Chhing gnakjovi	m. f.; no affix	
Drunkard, drunken *	Chhing gnaktunvi	ditto, ditto	
Foul-mouthed	Jit'vi	m. and f.; ditto	
Abusive	Jisi	wo m., mi f. Jísi is abuse	
Alive	Kenki	wo m.,† mi f., mu n.	
	Gotvi	m. f.	Participial; no affix of gender
Dying	Met'vi	m. and f.	
Dead	Me'ta	m. and f.	
Sick	Met'kenvi	m. f.	
Sickening	Máng phat'vi	m. f.	
Sick, sickened	Met kinta	m. f.	
Healthy, healthful	Phatvi	m. f.	
Sleepy, asleep	Íṉvi. Impi yot'vi		
Healthful	Imta. Impi yos'ta		
Wakeful, waking	Si'vi. Bok'vi		
Awake, intr.	Sipta. Bokta		
Awakened, tr. and causal	Sipta. Sip pingta		
	Pokta. Pok pingta		
Young	Cho'mi	m. f. n.; no affix ‡	
Youthful	Ithijila (= small)		
Mature, in prime of life	Bang-cho	m.; cho affix ‡	
	Bang-mi	f.; mi affix ‡	
Old, aged	Chokta	m. f. n.; no affix; participial	
Strong	Choti	wo m., mi f., mu n. and com.	
	Choti notvi vel khotvi	m. f. n.; participial	
Weak	Mang choti	wo m., mi f., mu n.	
	Mang choti kotvi	no affix; participial	
Confined	Thikta	m. f. n.; no affix	particip.
Free, freed	Teshta	m. f. n.; no affix	

* Drunken = drunk, cannot be applied to a being any more than eaten, though beaten, seen, &c., can. The inherence of the passive sense in the past participle generally is the reason why the present participle of transitives is aoristic. Tunvi is he who drinks or drank. Tunta is what is drunk.

† Wo, vo, and mi for masculine and feminine of rationals; mu for irrationals, but often used for all, as a sign of common gender.

‡ The words bangcho, bangmi, and bingcho, bingmi, are now commonly used as substantives; and to make them adjectives they take the forms, bangchowo, bangchomi, bingchowo, bingchomi. So also rocho, romi. The words cho'mi and ithijila, small; nyesi, new; and tering, ready, are, like noh'ka, good, true adjectives, needing therefore no affix. Such addition, if made, has the same effect as that of adding wála, wali, to qualitives in Hindi.

	Crude.	*Affixes.*	
Handsome	Bing-cho	m.	rationals *
	Bing-mi	f.	
	Bingmu	n. and c.; bestials	
Ugly	Mang bing-cho	mi f., mu n.	
Tall, high	Jongta	m. f. n.	no affix
Short, low	Mang jongta	ditto	
Great, big	Honta	ditto	participial
Small, little	Cho'mi Ithijila	See note *	
Fat, fattened	Lonta	ditto	
Thin, thinned	Gerta	m. f. n.	no affix
Tired, weary	Jyopta	m. f. n.	no affix
Fresh, not tired	Mang jyopta	ditto	
Lame	Khokhappovi	m. f. n.	all participial
Lamed	Mang khokvi	no affix	
Blind, blinded	Mang yenvi	m. f. n.	
Deaf	Mang thatvi	m. f. n.	i.e., rationals & beasts
Dumb	Mang hot'vi	m. f. n.	
Alone, solitary	Chháling	cho m., mi f., mu n. and com.	
Companioned	Kácho gotvi	m. f.; no sign	
Wise	Juk'vi. Set'vi	m. f.; no sign	
Foolish	Mang jukvi. Mang setvi	ditto	participial
Learned	Lista	m. f.; no sign	
Ignorant	Máng lista	ditto	
Rich	Got'vi	m. f.; no sign; participial	
	Pe*n*khu	wo m., mi f., no, n. Pe*n*ku is riches	
Poor	Mang gotvi	no affix; participial	
	Mang pe*n*khu	wo m., mi f.	
	Pe*n*khu mang gotvi	m. f.; participial	
Noisy, talkative	Dávo povi † Hotvi Itvi Botvi	m. f.; no sign participial	
Silent	Giwo*n* ponvi †	m. f.; no sign	
Dirty	Penki	wo m., mi f., mu, n. and com. Pénki is dirt	
Clean Cleansed	Penki notvi Wota Penki mang notvi.	m. f. n.; no sign; participial	
Married	Ro-cho ‡	m.	or Rochowo
	Ro-mi	f.	Rochomi
	Ro-cho-gotvi, f.; Romi gotvi, m.	participial	
	Bia pota, m. f.		
Not married, single	Máng rocho	m.	or Mang rochowo-mi
	Máng romi	f.	
	Biá máng pota	c.	no affix
	Ro-cho-romi máng gotvi		
Taxed	Phengvi	m. f. n.	participial
Exempt	Máng phengvi		

* See note ‡ on previous page.

† From páko and pónche respectively. See grammar.

‡ Rocho and romi are so generally used substantivally for man and wife that there is some hesitation about the adjectival use of them, though "cho" and "mi" as suffixes are demonstrably equivalent to wo, vo, and mi. Still, as they are somewhat obsolete, the latter are often now superadded, bing-cho-wo = pulcher, bing-cho-mi = pulchra. Other words of the same form, as bangcho, adult or an adult, are also used in the same two ways, viz., bancho, bangmi, and bangchowo, bangchomi. Compare lon-cho, a man, and mes-cho, a woman, among the substantives. Bo-chho = the white-bodied, a white man, is quite a different affair.

	Crude.	*Affixes.*
Old	Yukháng Mithong	wo m., mi f., mu n. and c.
New	Nyesi	wo m., mi f., mu n. and c. See note at Bangcho
Ready, prepared (clothes, food, &c.)	Chusta Minta	n.; no sign; participial
Unready, not ready	Máng chusta Máng minta	
Ready	Tering	wo m., mi f., mu n. See note at Bangcho, p. 223.
Unready	Máng tering	wo m., mi f., mu n.
Common, abundantly procurable	Lingtang. Chhing gnák *lingtáng*	m. f. n.; no sign; participial
Scarce, rarely procurable	Yáng gnák lingtang	
Public, assert, revealed, patent	Khunta	
Private, secret, concealed, latent	Khista	
Successful Prosperous	Hokvi * Hokta Hoktang	m. f. n.
Unprosperous Unsuccessful	Máng hokvi Máng hokta Máng hoktang	
Saleable	Thámtáng	m. f. n.
Sold	Thamta	m. f. n. — no affix; participial
Purchaseable	Ingtáng	m. f. n.
Purchased	Ingta	m. f.
Similar	Tot'vi	m. f. n.
Dissimilar	Máng tot'vi.	m. f. n.
The same	Kwongmu † Kwong nárungmu	genitival, all genders
Different	Gegemu	
Another	Gyetti. Gyeti	see note at Bangcho
Easy	Mang chamta, m. f. n.	past participles; no sign
Difficult	Chamta, m. f. n.	
Changeful	Jýapvi	participles pr. and f.; m. f. n.; no sign
Changeable	Jyaptang ‡	
Changed	Jyapta	p. part.; no sign
Changeless	Mang jyapvi	pr. and fut. participles; no affix
Unchangeable	Mang jyaptang	
Unchanged	Mang jyapta	
Orderly, set in order	Tophta (Tosta)	m. f. n.; participial — no affix
Disorderly, disordered	Khulim khulim pota	m. f. n.; participial — no affix
Having, possessed of, tenens	Got'vi. Tovi	m. f.; participial; no affix
Dispossessed Ousted Not having	Mang got'vi Mang gota Mang tota Thosta	m. f.; participial; no affix
Ornamented	Bing chopota	m. f.; participial
Plain	Máng bing chopota	

* Hok', a neuter verb, is the source.

† Kwongmu comes from kwong, one; and narungmu, from narung, form. In these, especially in the latter, the possessive sign is needed. Not so in *gégé* and gyéti, which are pure adjectives. See note at p. 223.

‡ These agree as being derived from intransitive verb jyapche. Jyapvi, who or what changes; jyaptang, who or what is wont or liable to change.

	Crude.	*Affixes.*	
Useful	Kammu, genitival	Kampovi, m. f. / Kampachyang, n.	no affix; participial
Useless	Mang kammu / Kam máng povi / Kam máng páchyáng	negatives of Kammu; no affix; participial	
Quick-moving, active	Plakvi	m. f.; no neuter	
Slow-moving, lazy, inert	Gatvi	m. f.; no neuter	
Wholesome, eatable	Játáng	n.	
Unwholesome, uneatable	Máng játang	n.	
Manufactured-wrought	Pota	n.	
Unwrought	Máng pota.		no affix
Sharp	Ye'vi	n. (verb yep')	
Sharpened	Yepta. Yeppingta.		
Blunt	Gnumvi	n. (verb Gnun)	
Blunted	Gnuta. Gnut'pingta		
Grinded	Reta	past participles	
Woven	Pungta		
Spun	Chingta		
Platted	Pungta		
Spacious, wide, ample	Byengta		
Contracted, narrow	Máng byéngta		
Moving, capable of motion	Duk'vi	m. f. n.	participial
Movable, capable of being moved	Thuktáng	m. f. n.	
Motionless, n.	Máng dukvi	m. f. n.	
Moved, a.	Thukta	m. f. n.	
Moved, n.	Dukta	m. f. n.	
Immovable	Mang thúktáng	no affix; participial	
Figured	Nárung	wo m., mi f., mú n. and com. Narung is form	
	Nárung notvi	no affix; participial.	
Figureless	Nárung má notvi		
	Máng nárung	wo m., mi f., mu n.	
Figurable	Nárung pátang / Nárung hátang	no affix; participial	
Unfigurable	Nárung máng pátang / Nárung máng hátang		
Luminous, Shining	Dang dang mu	mu affix; genitival	
	Dang dang dumta / Dang dang notvi	no affix; participial	
Illumined	Dang dang pota		
Illuminated	Dang dang thumta		
Illuminable	Dáng dáng má pátáng		
Dark, obscure	Kung kung mu	mu affix; participial	
	Kung kung no'ta		
Darkened	Kung kung pota / Kung kung thumta	no affix; participial	
Flaming	Navi, candle		
Burning-self	Jotv'i, fire		
Kindled-self	Náta josta		
Kindled, Lighted, Inflamed } other	Náta. Josta * / Nat' pingta / Jot' pingta. Dupta		

* One great defect of this language (largely participated by the cognate tongues and even by English) is rendered peculiarly observable in its adjectives, owing to their being so very commonly the same with its participles. The defect is this, that all sorts of verbs (neuter, reflex, and transitive), and even the various forms of the same verbal root, are confounded in the participles; that is, they take identical forms as participles, though the senses be often

	Crude.	*Affixes.*
Burnt, consumed by fire	Yemta, general Umta, a corpse	
Burning, in process of destruction by fire	Yemvi	
Extinguishing self, going out, dying (flame)	Met'vi	no affix ; participial
Extinguished self, gone out	Me'ta	
Extinguished by other, put out	Met'pingta. Sishta	
The upper, superior	Lonkha *	cho m., mi f., mu n.
The lower, inferior	Yonkha	cho m., mi f., mu n.
Right	Jájá-mu	
Left	Khánjá-mu	
Central	Mádum-mu	
Eastern	Nomo loklung-mu	genitival. Mu is the genitive case sign
Western	Nomo thiplung-mu	
Northern	Liriphum-mu Lonkha-mu	
Southern	Yonkha-mu	
Passable or accessible	Khoktáng Khokmung	no affix ; participial no affix ; infinitival
Impassable	Máng khoktáng Máng khokmung	negatives of two preceding
Cultivated (soil)	Rukta. Dota	
Uncultivated	Máng rukta. Máng dota	
Cultivable	Ruktang. Dotáng	
Uncultivable	Máng ruktang. Máng dotáng	no affix ; participial
Fruitful, rich (soil)	Hokvi	
Barren, poor, sterile	Máng hokvi	
Sandy	No name	
Clayey	Chotáng	no affix ; participial
Calcareous	Chunmu	
Saline	Jikhommu	
Muddy	Pes-chyongmu	mu affix ; genitival
Dusty	Penkimu	
Brackish (water)	Jikhommu	
Fresh	Dáktáng (desirable) Chhumta (sweet)	
Flowing	Gik'vi	
Still	Máng gikvi	
Deep	*Kh*osta †	no affix ; participial
Shallow	Máng *kh*osta	
Windy } weather Stormy }	Hojumpovi	

very different. Thus náche, kindle thyself or be kindled, and náko, kindle it, and náto, kindle it for him, all alike give návi and náta; and as there is no separate form of the agent, návi is also the kindler. Pains are taken by the multiplication of roots to keep the several sorts of action distinct; but the further distinctions of active, intransitive, and transitive action are lost in the participles by defects of structure in the language. Thus sishta is self-killed and killed by another, and náta is self-kindled or kindled by another, though nát-pingta, the causal, may be used to express the latter sense. The defects of English aggravate those of Váyu. Thus a lamp that has been lighted, while it burns, is a burning lamp or lighted lamp, though the last word seems to infer what is past. In Váyu you can similarly say návi or náta tuphi, though návi (trans.) be also the lignter, not the lighted. In English you cannot say the lighting lamp for the lamp that is kindled and burning. In Váyu you cannot use the word burning, which is appropriated to destruction by fire.

* Lonkha, yonkha, like jaja, khanja, which come next, can be used without any affix.

† See note at p. 242, and conjugations of verbs in the Grammar. Khosta, nasta, is the true form, and so rista, rotten, infra, and musta, seated, and wasta, abandoned, &c. &c.

	Crude.	*Affixes.*
Fine, fair	Noh'kamu vel nohka	see note at p. 224
Cold	Jungsamu	1, 3, genitival; 2, participial
Hot	Jeta. Jekhommu	
Cloudy	Kokohhomu. Kokchho not'vi	1, genitival; 2, participial
Sunshiny	Logángmu	genitival
	Logáng katvi	participial
Rainy, wet	Nánummu	genitival. Nanum is rain
	Nánum tok'vi	
Dry, fair	Nánummáng tok'vi	no affix; participial
Moist, full of vapour	Kowál not'vi	
Moist, sappy Green (wood)	Chhá'lángmu	genitival; mu affix
Juicy (fruit)	Bulummu	genitival; mu affix
	Bulum notvi	participial; no affix
Juiceless, dry	Bulum má notvi	
	Sosomu	
	Máng bulummu	
Wooden	Singmu	mu affix; genitival
Leathern	Kokchhomu	
Stony, made of stone	Lumphumu	
Stony, stone-bearing	Lumphu notvi	
Wet (clothes)	Ná'ta. Nasta *	no affix; participial
Dry	Dungta. Bo'ta. Sunta	
Wooded (land)	Thimthimmu	genitival; mu affix
Open, naked	Lákalákamu	
Coloured	Chikta. Blekta	no affix; participial
Colourless	Máng chikta	
	Máng blekta	
Colourable	Chiktang	ditto ditto
Fit to be coloured	Blektang	
Red	Lángchhing	wo m., mi f., mu n.
White (thing)	Dáwáng	wo m., mi f., mu n.
White (man)	Bochho	wo m., mi f.
Black	Khakchhing	wo m., mi f., mu n.
Blue	No name	
Green	Girung	wo m., mi f., mu n.
Yellow	Heldung	wo m., mi f., mu n.
Sweet	Chhingjimu	mi affix; genitival
Sour	Juta (from Juto, make sour)	
Bitter	Khúta (from Khúto, make bitter)	no affix; participial
Ripe, ripened	Minta. Jishta	
Ripening	Minvi. Jitvi	
Raw	Chháláng	wo m., mi f., mu n.
Rotten	Rista. Wonta	no affix; participial
Sound, fresh	Mang rista. Máng wonta	
Coarse	Hokhro	wo m., mi f., mu n.
Fine	Nápi	wo m., mi f., mu n.
Rough	Hokhro	wo m., mi f., mu n.
Smooth to touch	Liku	wo m., mi f., mu n.
Smooth to eye	Likyep	wo m., mi f., mu n.
Polished	Likyep pota	no affix; participial
Unpolished	Likyep má pota	
Straight	Cheng-cheng	wo m., mi f., mu n.
Crooked	Kojuláng	wo m., mi f., mu n.
	Kwonghhet	wo m., mi f., mu n.

* See note (†) on previous page.

	Crude.	*Affixes.*
Full, filled	Phul	wo m., mi f., mu n.
	Damta	no sign, m. f. n.
Empty	Poláng	wo m., mi f., mu n.
Self-emptied	Poláng no'ta vel dumta	no affix; participial
Emptied by another.	Poláng pota	
Causal of the last	Poláng pápingta	
Solid	Phul *	wo m., mi f., mu n.
Hollow	Poláng	wo m., mi f., mu n.
Heavy	Lista	no affix; participial
Light (levis)	Oksáng	wo m., mi f., mu n.
Great	Honta (size or rank)	no affix; participial
Small	Cho'mi (size and rank) Ithijila (young)	see note at p. 223
Long	Phinta	n. (No affix; participial)
Short	Máng phinta	n.
Wide	Byengta	ditto
Narrow	Máng byengta	ditto
High	Jongta	all genders
Low	Máng jongta	ditto
	Tésre	wo m., mi f., mu n.
Angular	No word	
Round	Teltel	wo m., mi f., mu n.
Spherical	Kulkul	wo m., mi f., mu n.
Pointed	Kyerkyer	wo m., mi f., mu n.
Edged	Ye'vi. Yepta	no affix; participial
Broken } round things	Reta (self)	
Burst } round things	Kheta (by other)	
Broken, long things	Jekta (self) Chikta (by other)	
Torn	Jekta (self) Jita (by other)	
Split	Chita †	
Entire	By negative prefix to all or any of the above seven words	
Porous	Jot'vi	no affix; participial
Imporous	Máng jot'vi	
Opening	Hovi	
Open	Hota	
Shutting	Thikvi	
Shut	Thikta	
Spread	Chhyásta ‡	
Folded	Khosta	
Expanded, blown (flower)	Bo'ta	
Expanding (ditto)	Bot'vi	
Closed, shut = not expanded (ditto)	Máng bo'ta	
Unblown, not blowing	Máng bot'vi	
Tight	Khwásta	
Slack	Woso. Wosomu	
Loose, unsteady Shaking Shakable	Hokvi. Hoktang	
Fixed, firm	Dosta ‡	
Unshakable	Dot'pingta	

* Phúl, póláng, and tésrè may all be used without affix, and therefore may be added to the small number of primitive qualitives; also wóso, slack, infra.

† These six are nearly equal to Urdu and Hindi túta, tóra; phúta, phóra; phata, phara.

‡ See on in Grammar.

	Crude.	Affixes.
Unshaking	Máng hoktang Máng hokvi	no affix; participial
Cooked	Khosta	
Boiled	Tibe khosta	
Roasted	Sonta } Mebe khosta *	
Grilled	Chota }	
Hairy	Swom gotvi Swom mu	genitival
Hairless	Swom má got'vi Máng swommu	1, 4, participial; 2, 3, genitival
Feathered	Chinchi swommu Chinchi swom notvi	
Falling (on ground)	Rukvi	m. f.
Falling (from aloft)	Dukvi	m. f. n.
Fallen	Rukta. Dukta	
About to fall Ready to fall	Ruktang. Duktang	
Falling (tree)	Likvi	
Fallen (tree)	Likta	
Felling (man) ...	Photvi	
Felled (tree)	Phosta	
About to be felled	Phostang	
Rising. Standing	I'vi. Buk'vi	
Erect. Risen	Ipta. Bukta †	
Raised. Made erect	Ippingta. Bukpingta. Pukta ‡	
Lifted up, aloft	Reta. Guta	
Put down	Tóta	no affix; participial
Sitting	Mutvi	
Seated, self	Musta (Muphta)	
Seated by other	Mut'pingta	
Lying down. Recumbent	Likvi	m. f. n.
Laid down. Reclined	Likta (self)	
Prostrated. Laid down	Likpingta (by other)	
Wakened } n. and a. Awake }	Sipta	
Awakened, causal	Sippingta	
Waking	Sipvi	
Wakening	Sippingvi	
Sleeping	Imvi	
Asleep	Imta	
Sleepy	Impi yot'vi	
Put to sleep	Impingta	
Foreign	Gyeti namsang	wo m., mi f., mu n.§
Home-bred, of one's own race	Angki namsang Angki thoko	wo m., mi f., mu n. wo m., mi f., mu n.
Written	Blekta	no affix; all participles save those in mung, which are infinitival
Read	Lista	
Desirous	Yotvi, dakvi	
Desired	Yosta, dakta	
Desirable	Yostang, yot'mung Daktang. Dakmang	

* Mè bè khosta, literally cooked in or with fire; and ti' bè khosta, cooked in or with water.

† Ipta if previously seated, bukta if lying down.

‡ From neuter buk, transitive puk = bukping; and double causal pukping, formed like bukping. These are all normal traits. See on to Grammar.

§ Literally of another smell, smelling differently from one's own folk. See note at p. 217.

	Crude.	Affixes.
Eaten	Jota *	
Drank	Tungta	
Loving	Chhauvi	no affix; all participles save those in mung, which are infinitival
Loved	Chhanta	
Amiable, fit to be loved	Chhantang	
Payable	Phentang. Phengmung	
Paid	Phengta	
Well odoured	Noh'ka namsang	wo m., mi f., mu n.
Stinking	Máng noh'ka namsang	wo m., mi f., mu n.
Tibetan	Chhugong	wo m., mi f., mu n.
Nepalese	Hengong	wo m., mi f., mu n. see note at p. 241
Of the plains of India	Gágin	wo m., mi f., mu n.
Woollen, made of wool	Beliswommu	n.; mu affix; genitival
Woolly, wool-bearing	Beliswom notvi	m. f.; no affix; participial
Wooden, made of wood	Singmu	n.; mu affix; genitival
Timber-bearing, woody	Singnot'vi	n.; no affix; participial
Golden	Heldung-mi, f. ?	genitival; mi affix; adjectives or substantives
Iron, adj. made of iron	Khakchhing-mi, f. ?	
Silver, adj. made of silver †	Dáwáng-mi, f.	
Hairy, made of hair	Swommu	n.; mu affix; genitival
Hairy, bearing hair	Swom not'vi	m. f.; no affix; participial

COMPARISON OF ADJECTIVES.

As great as he	Wathim báhamu honta
Greater than he	Wathim khen honta
Greatest of all	Ini khata- ‡ Mini khata- } khen honta, or Sabim khen-honta
As small as she	Wathim- Minung- } báhamu cho'mi
Smaller than she	Wathim- Minung- } khen cho'mi
Smallest of all	Inung khata- Minung khata- } khen cho'mi, or Sabim khen-cho'mi
Very great	Chhing gnák honta
Very small	Chhing gnák cho'mi
Very cold	Chhing gnák khimta
Very hot	Chhing gnák jeta, or jikhommu
Cold	Khimta
Colder	Ini- Mini- } khen khimta
Coldest	Ini- Mini- } khata khen khimta, or Sabim khen khimta
Hot	Jeta, Jekhommu
Hotter	Ini- Mini- } khen jeta, or jekhommu
Hottest	Ini- Mini- } kháta khen jeta or jekhommu, or Sabim khen jeta

* The English senses of the participles eating and drinking must be variously expressed by the participles, infinitive, and gerunds, thus, Don't hinder the eating man, Jovi or jovi singtong thá thikto. By dint of eating, or by excess of eating, he will get ill, Jáhe jáhe nómi (no to be ill and to be). Eating is better than drinking, Tungmungkhen jámung noh'ka. By drinking to excess he got intoxicated, Chhinggnak tungtungha vimi. Drinking water, Dakmungtí.

† These last three words mean literally the yellow, the black, and the shining or white. Very much as in English, they are of the same form as substantives and adjectives. They appear to be regarded as feminines, because they have the feminine suffix formative, or mi.

‡ I' and Mi the demonstratives make ini, inung, mini, minung, for casus constructus; but as khata, the plural sign, seldom admits of inflexion, the sign of the genitive, which is required by the preposition, is attached to the pronoun in singular, sometimes to both, inung khatam. Newári agrees so far that in all the construct cases it rejects the plural sign. Thus ji-ping, we; wo-ping, they, make ji-mi, wo-mi, ours, theirs.

4. *Numerals.*

	SEPARATE.	MASCULINE.	FEMININE.	NEUTER AND COMMON.
1.	Kolu	Kom-pu *vel* Kwong-pu	Kwomi *vel* Kwongmi	Kolu
2.	Ná-yung	Ná-k-pu	Náng-mi	Náyung
3.	Chhu-yung	Chhu-k-pu	Chhung-mi	Chhu-yung
4.	Bli-ning	Bli-k-pu	Bli-ng-mi	Bli-ning
5.	U'-ning	Ung-pu ?	Um-mi ?	U'-ning
6.	Chhu-ning	Caret	Caret	Chhu-ning

NUMERAL COLLECTIVES.

5. Kolu got' khulup=one hand entire, or five fingers.
10. Náyung got' khulup=two hands entire, or ten fingers.
15. Náyung got' khulupha kolu got' khulup=two hands, plus one hand. Náyung got' khulupha bá khulup=two and a half (bá) of the whole hands.
20. Le got' khulup=hands and feet or fingers and toes complete.
20. Cholók=a score, also kolu cholok.
40. Náyung cholok=two score.
60. Chhuyung cholok=three score.
80. Blining cholok=four score.
100. Uning cholók=five score, or Kolu got' cholok=one hand of scores.

ORDINAL NUMBERS.

There are none such. No first, second, third, &c.

ADVERBIAL NUMBERS.

No firstly, secondly, thirdly, &c.

Once	Kóphi	And so on to 100 by adding "phi," a turn or bout, to the numerals.—The interrogative particle "ha" can be similarly used. How many times? Há-k-phi. Phi is the crude of the verb to come, thus Kó-phi =one coming, &c.
Twice	Nakphi	
Thrice	Chhúkphi	
Four times	Blikphi	
Five times	Kolugot khulup-phi	
Ten times	Náyung got khulup phi	
Twenty times	Le got khulup phi or cholop phi	

NUMERATION OF WEIGHTS.

1. Koti.
2. Nakti.
3. Chhukti.
4. Blik ti.
5. Ukti or Kolu got khulup ti.

NUMERATION OF DAYS.

1. Ko buk'.
2. Na buk'.
3. Chhu buk'.
4. Bli buk'.
5. Ubuk, or Kolu got khulup buk'.

Remark.—The adverbials are declinable like the cardinals, and may be regarded as compound substantives, which should therefore in strictness be put in the locative case, thus, kophe phíne, come ye all at once. But this nicety is little regarded, and kophinakphi la'lam is=he went once or twice. So Newári has as the equivalents of the above chha ko lang wá and chháko niko wana. In general the adverbs, when not gerundial, are subject to declension like the nouns.

---

5. *Adverbs.*

ADVERBS OF TIME.

To-day	Tiri
To-morrow	Nukun
Yesterday	Tenchong
Day after to-morrow	Niha

Day before yesterday	Nithibuk
This year	Tin thong. Íthongè
Last year	Ninganung. Mithongè
Year before last	Chhukthongnung
Year before that	Blikthongè
Coming year	Ningahe
Year after that	Chhukthongè
Year after that	Blikthongè
Now	Abo. Íthe. Umbe } ithi-hè = in this, and mithi-he
Then	Mithe } = in that (time) *
When? When	Hákhe. Hákhanúng. Interrogative and relative
Since when?	Hakhanungkhen
By and by	Omop'hè. Later. Omhè
Instantly	Wáliga
At once	Kophe (Kophi hè)
Before, priorly	Hubong, Honko
After, in composition	Khen
Afterwards	Nungna
Since	Hakhanungkhen
Till, until	Bong
Till now / Hitherto	Umbe bong. Ítham bong. Abo bong. Abonung bong
Till then	Mithanung bong. Mithong bong. Mithe bong
Till when?	Hakhe bong. Hakhanung bong
From when?	Hakhekhen. Hakhanungkhen
Formerly, long ago	Mithong. Hóṉko
At present / Now-a-days	Tiri nukún
Whilst	Not'he (in the being)
Henceforth / Hereafter	Ithekhen. Umbekhen. Abokhen. Tirikhen. Ithongkhen
Thenceforth / Thereafter	Mithekhen. Mithongkhen. Mithongnunkhen
Ever	No word
Never	Hákhele
Often	Giri giri
Sometimes	Kophi nak'phi
Early (shortly) / Soon (quickly)	Plak'plak'ha (literally, having hastened)
Late (slowly)	Gat'gat'tha (literally, having loitered) †
At night, in the night	Eksahe. Eksa nung. Yeksa-nung-he
In the day	Numa nung. Numa he
All day	Numa khiri
Daily	Hátha numa
At sunrise	Nomo loksinghe
At cockcrow	Khochho oksinghe
At dawn	Dángdáng dumsinghe
At sunset	Nomo thipsinghé
At dusk	Kungkung dumsinghé
At nightfall	Eksa dumkhen
From night till morn	Eksakhen nomolok bong
Noon	Khángse numa
Midnight	Khángse yeksa
Till noon	Khángse numa bong
At noon	Khángse numa he
To-morrow morning, to-morrow at dawn	Nukun dáng-dáng dum he

* See note (*) at next page.

† Gerunds constantly, as here exemplifie supply the lack of adverbs (see on to conj. of adverbs in sequel); more rarely, nouns in the ablative or instrumental case, *e.g.*, chotihe, forcibly.

Yesterday night	Tenchong eksa	
Yesterday at night	Tenchong eksa dum he	
In two or three days	Nak buk'chhuk buk'he	
In one or two days	Kwong buk'nak buk'he	
In three or four days	Chhuk buk blik buk'he	
How long?	Hákbuk'	
At once, at one time	Kophe	Ko-phi, &c., are regarded as compound substantives in the nominative case. In the locative, kophe, &c., best agree with our idea of adverbs. But they are used in either case. All are regularly declinable. Phó, verbal root, to come, occur.
Once	Kophi	
Twice	Nakphi	
Thrice	Chhukphi	
Four times	Blikphi	
How often	Hakphi	
Again	Gessa	

ADVERBS OF PLACE.

Here and there	I'thá dokhá	
Hereward	Inirek. Inungrek. I'tha	
Thereward	Minirek. Dokhá. Minungrek. Wathimrek	
Here	Inhe	
There	Wáthe. Minhe *	
Where?	Hánhe	Used also relatively, and minhe correlatively. So also the interrogative of time
Hence	Inikhen	
Thence	Minikhen. Wáthimkhen. Minungkhen	
Whence?	Hánikhen. Hánungkhen	
Which way	Hánung lom	
By what way?	Hánung lom khen	
By that way	Wáthim lom khen	
By this way	I lom khen	
This far	Inibong. Inungbong	
That far	Minibong. Minungbong. Wathimbong	
How far	Hánibong. Hanungbong	
By that way	Mi.† Wáthi lom khen	
Near	Khe'wa	
In the near	Khe'wabe	
From the near	Khewakhen	
Far	Kho'lam	
In the far	Kho'lam be	
From the far	Kho'lamkhen	
To, up to, the far	Kholam bong	
How far?	Hátha kholam	
Thus far	Inhe bong	
How near?	Hátha khewa	
This near	I'tha khewa	
That near	Mitha khewa	
Nearer	Inikhen-khewa. Minikhen-khewa	
Nearest	Minung khâta khen khewa	
Very near	Chhing gnák khewa	
Rather near	Yang gnak khewa	
Further	Inikhen-kholam. Minikhen-kholam	
Furthest	Inung khátakhen-kholam. Minung khátakhen kholam	

* "In," the locative, has two forms, bé and é or hé. Wathé = wathi-he and minhe = mini-he, in that; so wanhe = wani-he, in the top. Again, in the hand, eye, head, fire, is bé; gotbe, mekbe, puchhibé, mebe. In the house is kemé, and in the tree, singphum-é. The present gerund has hé, phit-hé; also nung, phit-nung. The words for place and time, or "lung" and "sing," cannot be used with pronouns, only with verbs (mu-lung = place of sitting; lok-sing = time of rising); and hence now and then, here and there, are but in this or that. There is no real difference between the two. The inflective signs ni and nung are equally applicable to both.

† Mini or Minung lomkhen and Wathim lomkhen are the inflected phases of the term. They are as usual and more correct.

Rather far	Yang gnak kholam
Very far	Chhing gnak kholam
Down	Yonkha
Up	Lonkha
Above	Wanhe (wani-he, in the top)
Below	Huthe (huti-he, in the bottom)
From above	Wánikhen
From below	Hutikhen
From top to bottom	Wánikhen hutim bong
Under, by under way	Hutikhen. Kuḍi kha
Over, by the top	Wánikhen. Kha khakha
Towards	Rek
Upwards, towards the top	Wánim rek
Downwards, towards the bottom	Hutim rek
Between, in the midst	Mádumbe. Madumna
From between	Madum khen
By the middle	Mádum na
By the midway	Mádum lom
On the right	Jájá be
On the left	Khánja be
From the right	Jájá khen
From the left	Khánjá khen
Towards the right	Jájá rek
Towards the left	Khánjá rek
Out	Tong ma
In	Bhitari
Through Across	Thekthekha (crossing) Kuḍikha (undering) Madumna (midways) Khak khakha (overtopping) *
On this side	Imba
On that side	Hómba
On both sides	Imba homba
From this to that side	Imba khen homba bong
Round	Vinvinha (literally, having rounded
Before	Honko
Behind	Nungna
Aside, at, or on the flank	Khukbe
To the side	Khukrek
By the side	Khukkhen
Face to face Opposite	Kakpháng
Abreast	Chelchelha. Kwongha
Straight	Kakpháng
Onwards	Chyeng chyeng ha
Forwards, on	Honko
Backwards, back	Nongna

ADVERBS OF MANNER, CAUSE, QUALITY, QUANTITY, ETC.

How?	Hágna. Hágnáhá. Hánung báha
Thus, in this way	I'mbá. Inung báha
Thus, in that way	Mimhá. Minung báha
Why?	Mischepá
How much?	Háthá. Hayung, n.

* All these save the third are gerunds of past time, and therefore should be Englished, having crossed, &c. A verb must succeed, as, thekthekha la'lam, he went through. Gerunds not only thus express the modes of action, but they link the several members of the sentences, replacing the conjunction "and." Intrinsically relative (conjunctive) participles make up the rest of those links, precisely as in the Dravidian languages.

How many?	Hakpu, m. f.
As much	Hátha? Háyung? Caret
So much	Mitha
As many	Hakpu, m. f.
How often?	Háthápbi. Hakphi
How great?	Hátha honta
How small?	Hátha chomi. Hátha ithijila
Well, rightly	Bingchoha. Bincho báha
Ill, badly	Máng bingchoha. Máng bingcho báha
Neither well nor ill	Bing chole má máng bing chole má
Wisely	Sit'sit'ha. Juk'juk'ha
Foolishly	Máng sitsithá. Máng jukjukhá
Hungrily	Suksa met'met'há
Thirstily	Tidaksa met'há or met-met'há
Angrily	Risihá. Risi not'ha. Risibukbukha
Gladly, or Joyfully	Bongbongha, or Bongnibong
Willingly	Yot'yot'ha. Yot'ni yot'.* Thumba. Thumsengha
Unwillingly	Máng yot'yot'há. Máng thumha. Máng yot ni yot. Máng thumsengha
Strongly	Chotihá
Weakly	Máng chotihá
Gently	Pomha. Pomhana
Noisily	Tamtamha. Tamnitam
Silently	Giwonha
With blows	Topnitop
Evenly, straightly	Chyengchyengha
Unevenly, crookedly	Kwonchyángving chyángha
Much, a great deal	Chhing gnák
A little ..	Yáng gnák
Neither more nor less	Chhing gnák le má yánggnák le má
More	Khapkhapha
Most, very much	Chhinggnák khapkhapha
Less	Yáng yáng ha
Least, very little	Chhing gnák yáng yáng ha
Again (afresh)	Gessa
Back (the same)	Liplipha
Thoroughly	Chhinggnák
Completely	Khuluphá. See Numerals
Partially	Ithi
By halves	Phakha
Heavily	Lid'lid'ha
Lightly	Oksangha
Tightly	Khwát'khwat'ha
Slackly	Wóso-wóso-hà. Woso báhà
Greatly, Increasingly	Chhinggnákhà
Trivially, Decreasingly	Yánggnákhà
In cowardly way	Ramram ha
Boldly	Máng ramram ha
Modestly	Khot'khot'há
Impudently	Máng khot'khot'ha
Secretly	Khita báha. Khit'khit'ha
Openly	Khunta báha. Khun-khunhà
Hastily	Plak plakha. Waliga
Slowly	Gat'gat'ha. Pomhana.
Jestingly	Wásong pápaha. Wásong pánipá

* Yotniyot is the iterative form of the verb, as is bongnibong, above, and tamnitam, below. Yotyotha, &c., is the ordinary gerundial form.

Seriously	Diksa pápáha
Mortally	Met'bong
Skin deep	Kokchho bong
Together	Kolube.* Ko'na
Separately	Gégé gégé
Singly	Kwongpu kwongpu, m.
One by one	Kolu kolu, n.
Solitarily	Chhále chhále
Afoot	Khokkhokha (literally, having walked)
On horseback, or mounted	Changchangha (literally, having mounted)
Truly	Diksa pápáha
Falsely	Máng diksa pápáha
Similarly	Tot'tot'ha. Kolu báha
Differently	Máng tot'tot'ha. Máng kolu báha
Look upwards, up	Lonkha chusto
Look downwards, down	Yonkha chusto
Look forwards	Kakphang chusto. Honko chusto
Look backwards	Nongma chusto
Look here and there	I'tha dokha chusto

DECLENSIONAL SIGNS.

G. Mu, ni, nung; ni and nung to pronouns only. If two substantives come together the sign is usually omitted, and the first in the genitive

D. None

Ac. None

Abl. Khen, with inflexion if pronoun

Inst. Há, without inflexion in any case

Loc. Bé, hé, é. Both commonly used with; the latter always if the governed word be a pronoun

Soc. Nung

——	Up to, as far as	Bong	with usually; always if pronoun
——	Towards	Rek	
——	On, upon	Wanhè†	
——	Off, under	Huthè	

---

6. *Prepositions.*

At this time	I'the (itha-hé)
At that time	Mithe (mitha-hé). Wáthe (wathi-hé)
At this place	Inhe (ini-hé). I'tha
At that place	Min-he (mini-hé). Dókha ‡
In this year	I'thong-he
In a little time, shortly	Omop, he
By and by, after a little more delay	Omhé
During, pending this year	I'thong not'he
Pending his coming	Wáthimáng phitbong
At home	Kém-é
At our house	Angki kemé
In the house	Kémé

---

* Kolube, literally in one, means in one place. Lung, the affix of place, can be used only with verbs.

† Wanhè = wani hè, in the top; húthè = húti hè, in the bottom. See declension in Grammar, and where, by the way, these "signs" should have stood.

‡ I'tha, dókha = idher, udher; inhé, minhé = ihán, uhán, or hither and thither, and here and there; the first with less of rest and definiteness. As already noted, the words for time and place (sing and lúng) can only be used in composition with verbs, *e.g.*, mulung, abode; nomoloksing, morning.

English	Váyu
In the wilderness	Ghári-bé
In my hand	Ang got bé
In, at Darjiling	Darjiling-é
Go into the house	Keme la'la or kem bhitar beklá
In me, thee, him	Angbé, ungbé, minúugbé
Come into the house	Kem bek'
Go into the house	Kem beklá *
Go into the water	Tibe beklá
Come out of the water	Ti khen lok'
Inside the house	Kemmu bhitari. Kemé
Outside the house	Kemmu tongma
Out of the house	Kem tongma
Come from the outside of the house	Kemmu tongma khen bek
Come out from the house	Kem khen tongma lok
Come out from inside or within the house	Kem bhitari khen lok
Go with me	Ang nung la'la
Sit by me	Ang be musche
Come near me	Ang khéwa phí
Sit beside me	Ang khuk be musché
Sit on my knee	Ang bimli be musché
Sleep in his bosom	Á bimli be imche
Put on my shoulder	Ang pháka be cho'ko (chokko)
Put in or on the fire	Me be táko
Put on (above) the fire	Mé wanhe táko
Take from off the fire	Mé wanikhen thosto
Put on, upon, the table	Mech wanhe táko
Take from off the table	Mech wanikhen thosto
Get on the horse / Mount the horse	Ghorabe chyánche
Get off the horse / Dismount from the horse	Ghora khen lische
Put on the horse (goods)	Ghoramu wanhe (*or* senti be) táko
Take from off the horse	Ghora wani (*or* senti) khen loko
On the head	Puchhibe. Puchhi wanhe
Under the feet	Le huthe
Put cap on head	Puchhi be topi chupche. Puchhi wanhe topi chupche
Put straw under thy feet	U'ngle huthe-khisti táko
From above the head	Puchhi wanikhen
From below the feet	Le hutikhen
On the head } touching	Puchhi wanhe
Under the feet } touching	Lé huthe
Above / Higher than } the head } not touching	Puchhi khenlonkha †
Beneath / Under / Lower than } the feet } not touching	Lé khen-yonkha †
Above the mouth is the nose / Below the mouth is the chin	Múkchhyu wanim rék cho'no ; múkchhyu hutimrek kamching

* Observe that bek is come in; bekla, go in. La thus added to other verbs expresses fromness. Bek is enter, consequently the borrowed bhitari is superfluous.

† Lonkha and yonkha refer mainly to the course of the water in this mountain country, and to relative position on a hill slope.

To, up to, as far as	Bong
As far as him	Inung-bong
To, as far as, Nepal	Nepal bong
Towards Nepal	Nepal rek
North of Nepal	Nepal khen liriphumbe
Near Nepal	Nepal khewa
Far from Nepal	Nepal khen kholám
Towards night	Eksa dumhe
Cruel toward his children	Ang tamtawo rek yáṉsa povi
Sit above me	Angkhen loṇkha musche
Sit below him	Minung khen yonkha * musche
Between us two	Ungchi mádumbe
On me (touching)	Ang wanhe
Under me (touching)	Ang huthe
The water comes from above and goes below	Lonkhá rek khenti yumi, yonkha rek giklam
On the top of the hill	Chhúju puchhibe or wanhe
In the mid ascent of the hill	Chhúju madumbe
At the base of the hill	Chhúju phumbe or huthe †
From top of hill	Chhúju wanikhen
From middle of hill	Chhúju madumkhen
From base of hill	Chhúju hutikhen
He dwells above me	Ang khen lonkha muschem
He dwells below me	Ang khen yonkha muschem
Sit on me	Ang wanhe musche
Pressed under me	Ang huthe napta
Underneath the chair	Chouki huthe
Lower than the chair (in position)	Chouki khen yonkha
Put under the table	Mech huthe or hutibe táko
Take out from under the table	Mech hutikhen thosto
Go through the door	Kámung khen lokla
Go through the hole	Hom kuḍikha, or Hom madumbe thekla
Go through the river (wading)	Gang thek thekha la'la
Go over the river (by boat)	Gang thek thekha la'la
Go over (by over) the couch	Khát lumlumha la'la
Go under (by under) the couch	Khát homlung khen lok'la or kuḍikha la'la
Come with me	Ang nung phi
Go without me	Ang má nosa la'la
Strike with force	Chotiha to'po (toppo)
Strike without force	Choti máng khot'khot'ha to'po (toppo) ‡
Sit before me	Ang honko musche
Sit behind him	Ánungna musche
Before-behind the door	Kámung-honko-nungna
Opposite, in front of, vis-à-vis	Kakpháng
Sit at my side, on my flank	Ang khuk be músche
Towards the side	Khuk rek

* See note (†) on previous page.

† Púchhi bè, in the head, top = wanhè ; phum bè, in the base = húthè.

‡ Literally, strength not having put forth strike ; and of course the precedent term can be expressed similarly, though there the noun in the instrumental case is preferred to the gerund.

Before nightfall	Eksa mádumsa
After nightfall	Eksa dumkhen. Eksa dumdumha
At nightfall Just as night falls	Eksa dumhe
Since dawn	Nomoloksing khen
Since I came	Ang phit' khen
After my arrival	Ang dong khen nungna
After to-morrow	Nukun khen
By nightfall Up to night Until night	Eksa bong. Eksa dum bong
Towards night	Eksa let'he
Towards dawn	Dang dang dumhe
At dawn	Nomo lokhe
During the night	Eksa nung
While it was night	Eksa not'nung
By the time I arrive	Ang dongsinghe
Before my arrival	Ang dong singkhen honko
After my coming	Ang dong singkhen nungna
Round about the house	Kemmu thelim phoksit'
About the house	Kemkhukhe itha dokha
In the middle of the village	Mulungmu mádumbe
On this side the river	Gangmu imba or Gang imba
On that side the river	Gang homba
He pierced him through the body	Chho chepchepha sastum
Go by the door	Kámung lomkhen la'la
At a distance from the house	Kem khen kholám
Near to the fire	Mé khewa
Near me	Ang khewa
After that	Minung nongna
Before that	Wáthím honko. Minung honko
Instead of that	Inung let'chhing
In lieu of him	Inung jyapchhing. Minung jyapchhing
For the sake of me	Ang lisi. Ang dulí khen
For the love of me	Gochhan chhanha
On this side of, short of, not so far as, the house	Kem khen imba or Kemmu itha
On that side of, or beyond, the house	Kem khen homba or Kemmu dokha
Far from the house	Kem khen kholám
With a house, *i.e.* having	Kem not'he or got'he. Kem not'nam. Kem not'khen
Without a house, wanting	Kem máng not'he. Kem máng nosa. Kem máng not'khen
With me, accompanying	Ang nung
Without me, leaving	Go wat'wat'ha. Angmá nósa
For the purpose of, on account of, the house	Kem lisi
In the middle of the house	Kem má dumbe
Even with the table, on level with table	Mech nungteng tengha
Through the house	Kem kudikha. Kemmu mádumna or mádum khen
Through the thigh	Phekteng sat'sat'ha or mádumna
With a will (*bon gré*)	Bong ni bong. Bongbongha. Bonghá
Without, against the will (*mal gré*)	Máng bongbongha. Máng bongha
Willy, nilly	Bongha máng bonghá

In spite of her husband	Rocho máng-honhonha *
For the love of her husband	Rocho chhan-chhan'ha
After the manner of the Newars	Hengong-wo báha †
In the form of a fish	Ho nárungmu
After the manner of the Tibetans	Chhogongwo báha
In the guise of a Tibetan	Chhogongwo narungbe or nárunghá

7. *Conjunctions.*

And	No such word
Also, likewise	Ló. Nung
Or	No word. Ki is used
Nor	Máng (not)
Nor this, nor that	Íï máng, mú máng (ii, mii, the pausing tone)
Moreover	Mekhen
Besides	Wánikhen
In excess of	Wanhe
Than (comp.)	Khen
As	Hágnado
So	Mimha
As, so	Ímha. Mimha
As well as	Hágnado noh'ka
As ill as	Hágnado máng noh'ka
But	No word
Nevertheless, Notwithstanding	No word
Though, yet	Mithele ‡
If	Sa. Nam, with present tense. Phen,§ with preterite
If not, Unless, Except	Can only be used with a verb; máng nosa, if there be not; mápo nam, if he do not
Whether or not	Nole má nole
In the meanwhile	Íthe
Thereon, upon that	Mithe
To wit, that is to say	Id'he. It h
Because, Since, As	Mischepá
Wherefore, For this cause	Ipánung
Therefore	Mipánung
For that cause	Wáthi pánung

Yes (assent), No (dissent)	No words
Verbal negative	Máng (prefix)
Verbal prohibitive	Thá (prefix)

* Literally, husband not having obeyed; and the next is husband loved—the usual gerundial style.

† Hengong means what in India is called a banghy, and hengongwo is Indicè banghywala. In the plains every one so carries burdens; in the hills the Newar tribe only; and therefore the other hill tribes, who seldom have proper names for their neighbours, denominate the Newar tribe from that circumstance—*e.g.*, the Khas, who call the Newars nhól boknya, a term having the precise sense of hengongwo. Of chhogong, just below, I could not learn the sense; but the name for a Tibetan is formed precisely like that for a Newar.

‡ Passionate, yet good; or, though passionate (he is), not harsh or cruel, risiwo mithele noh'ka or risibuk'vi mithele yánsa máng povi.

§ If I come or shall come, phignonam; if I had come, phisung phen. See Grammar.

Noun primitive	Máng. Má (prefix)
Alas! Bravo! Hurrah!	No words

8. *Verbs.*

Cause, tr.	Phá-(s)-to.* Pingko (see on †)
Cause not	Thaphá-(s)-to. Thá ping
Be born, n.	Bok'
Cause him to be born, tr.	Bok ping ko. Also phoko, which see
Cause thyself to be born or to be born for thyself	Bok pingche
Cause me to be born, &c.	Bokpingsung
Beget or give birth to	Pho'ko (phok-ko, conj. xi.)
Beget or produce me or for me ‡	Phoksung
Beget or produce for thyself	Phokche
Beget for another	Phokto
Cause to beget or to be begotten or produced	Phokpingko
Cause thyself to beget or to be begotten for thyself	Phok pingche
The same for another	Phokpingto
Cause me to beget or to be begotten	Phok pingsung
Be not born	Thá bok'
Cause not to be born	Bok' tká ping
Beget not or give not birth to	Thá phok'
Beget not for self	Thá phokche
Beget not for another	Thá phokto
Beget not for me	Thá phokgno
Live, n.	Gó
Live not	Thá gó
Cause him to live	Got'pháto (phasto). Got'pingko
Cause me to live	Got'pingsung. Got'phassung
Cause thyself (or for thyself) to live	Got'pingche. Got phasche,
Cause to live for him, for his sake	Gotpingto. Got phasto
Do not cause to live	Got thá phá'to. Got thá ping
Do not cause thyself to live	Got thá pinche. Got thá phásche
Die, n.	Met'
Die not	Thá met'
Cause to die	Met'pingko
Enable to die	Met'phá'to (phasto, conj. vii.)
Cause thyself to die	Met'pingche
Cause me to die	Met'pingsung
Cause not to die	Met' thá ping. Met' thá phá'to (phasto, conj. vii.)
Cause not thyself to die	Met' thá pinche. Met' thá phasche
Kill, tr.	Sisto. Sissung. Sische (conj. vii.)

---

* The "s" is essential, as proved by the whole conjugation, which see at pages 290 ff. Nevertheless, in the imperative, as spoken, the sibilant is replaced by an abrupt tone or accent, thus represented, pha'to. As the comparative strikes the keynote to the whole conjugation, its proper form needs much care. In the Grammar I have spared no pains to be correct. To it I refer, merely noting here that in verbs of the 7th conjugation, to which phasto belongs, the abrupt tone stands for a dropped sibilant, which must be restored; and that in conj. viii. and xi. it stands for a dropped consonant, identical with the consonant of the root, and which must be similarly restored. Thus, for to'po we must write toppo, and for pho'ko, phokko, &c. &c.

† These two verbs are used to make causals. Pingko and phásto are often identical; at other times, more or less discriminated in a way that may be best appreciated by a sample. Thus, khut pingko is cause to steal, and khut phasto, make a thief of.

‡ See note at page 261.

Kill thyself or for thyself, or do thou thyself kill, int.	Sische
Cause to kill or be killed	Sit' pingko
Cause thyself to kill, or to be killed, or to be killed for thyself	Sit' pingche
Cause him to kill or be killed for another	Sit' pingto
Kill me or for me	Sissung
Kill me not or do not kill for me	Thá sit gno
Cause me to kill or be killed, or for me	Sit pingsung
Cause not, &c.	Sit thá pinggno
Be, n.	Nó
Be not	Thá nó
Cause to be	Not' pingko
Cause to be for self	Not' pingche
Cause to be for me or me to be	Not' pingsung
Cause it to be for him	Not' pingto
Do not cause to be	Not' thá ping
Do not cause me to be or it to be for me	Not' thá ping gno
Because, n.	Dum
Because not	Thá dum
Cause to become	Dum pingko. Thumto
Cause to cause to become	Thum pingko
Cause me or for me to become	Thum sung
Cause thyself or for thyself to become	Thumche. Dum pingche
Be able, ac. intr.	Phásche. Wonche
Enable, tr.	Phá'to. Phásto. Wonto
Cause to be able or to enable	Phát pingko. Won pingko
Do, perform, make, tr.	Páko (conj. x.)
Do not	Thápo
Do for me	Pásung *
Do not for me	Thá págno
Do for self	Pánche
Do not for self	Thá pánche
Do for him	Páto
Do not for him	Thá páto
Do me, passive	Posung *
Do self (see Grammar)	Ponche
Cause to do or to be done	Pápingko
Cause me to do or to be done to me or to do or be done for me	Pápingsung
Cause thyself to do or be done to or for thyself	Pápingche
Cause to do or to be done to, for another	Pápingto
Keep doing, intr.	Pánapá nó. Pápáha musche
Cease doing. Desist, intr.	Wásche
Cease doing it, tr. Desist from it	Wá' (s) to (conj. vii.)
Suffer, endure } bodily	Ronche } These two reflex verbs serve to convey the only and very vague idea of passivity.
Submit thyself } bodily	
Brace thy mind to sufferance	Wonche }
Observe, take heed of, examine, think, intr.	Chusche. Chikche.
Observe it, take heed of it, think of it, tr.	Chuphto (Chusto). Chikto
Observe me or for me	Chussang. Chiksung
Cause to observe or to observe it, or it to be observed, tr.	Chut pingko. Chik pingko
Cause to observe or to be observed for thyself or thyself, intr.	Chut pingche. Chik pingche

* See remarks on the verbs Páko, Táko, and Jáko.

English	Váyu
Cause me to observe or me to be observed, quasi passive	Chut pingsung. Chik pingsung
Understand, intr.	Sēsche
Understand it, tr.	Sēko
Cause to understand or to be understood	Sē pháto (phasto)
Understand me or for me *	Sēsung
Understand thyself or for thyself, or simply understand	Sēche — conj. x.
Understand it for him or on his account	Sēto
Understand not	Thá sēche
Understand it not	Thá sē
Remember, intr.	Chikche
Remember it, tr. (see Observe)	Chikto
Remember not	Thá chikche
Remember it not	Thá chikto
Do not cause to remember or to be remembered	Thá chik phá'to (phasto, conj. vii.)
Forget, intr.	Mángche
Forget it, tr.	Mángto (conj. vi.)
Forget me or for me	Máng sung
Forget me not	Thá máng gnó
Forget thyself.(=err)	Mángche
Forget not thyself or do not thou forget	Thá mángche
Forget him or it	Mángto †
Forget him not	Thá mángto
Cause to forget (=deceive) or to be forgotten	Máng pingko. Máng phá'to (phasto)
Cause me to forget or to be forgotten	Máng pingsung
Cause thyself to forget or to be forgotten	Máng pingche
Cause him to forget or to be forgotten on a third party's account, or cause it to be forgotten by him	Máng pingto (pingkto). (Doubly objected transitive)
Desire, n. and p.	Dak' ‡
Desire it or make him desire	Dakto
Cause to desire or to be desired (per alterum, haud per se)	Dak pingko. Dak phá'to (phasto)
	Thā dak ping. Thá dak phá'to (phásto)
Do not cause to desire or to be desired	Dak pingsung
Cause me to desire or be desired	Dak pingche
Cause thyself to desire or be desired	
Cause him to desire or be desired on another's account, or him to desire it	Dak pingto (pingkto)
Love or love it, trans.	Chhánto
Love thyself or love simply, intr.	Chhánche
Love me, p.	Chhánsung
Love him, tr.	Chhánto
Love not	Thá chhánche
Love not it or him	Thá chhánto
Cause to love or to be loved	Chhán phá'to (phasto). Chhán pingko
Cause me to love or to be loved	Chhán pingsung. Chhán phassung
Cause thyself to love or be loved	Chhán pingche. Chhán phásche

* The word, when used in the latter sense, *with* lisi, on account of, is frequently put in the transitive form ang lisi seko, understand it for me. The alternative results from the imperfect development of the voices.

† Compare the transitive and causal transitive. Verbs in tó have no form = Sénto, Páto, &c., or the transitives in ko. The transitives in pó have this form, thus topo has topto; ipo, ipto; pipo, pipto, *&c.*

‡ Dak, like Bot: tell is used rather as a passive than active. Its form is passive: its sense both apparently. Dak gnom, I desire or am desired. Daksungmi, I desired or was desired. In Khas, Newári, &c., it is much the same.

Cause him to love or be loved on another's account	Chhán pingto. Chhán phá'to (phásto)
Hate or hate it, trans.	Chekto
Hate thyself or hate simply, intr.	Chekche
Hate me, p.	Cheksung
Hate him or for him (see note voce forget)	Chekto
Cause to hate or to be hated	Chek phá'to (phasto). Chek pingko
Cause thyself to hate or be hated	Chek pingche. Chek phásche
Cause him or it to hate or be hated for another's sake, or him to hate it	Chek pingto. Chek phásto
Be modest, n.	Khó
Cause to be modest	Khót' phá'to (phasto). Khot' pingko
Laugh, ac. intr. (ride, Latin)	Yische
Laugh at, tr. (irride, ditto)	Yisto. Yissung. Yische (conj. vii.)
Cause to laugh	Yit'phá'to (phásto). Yit pingko
Weep, n.	Ok
Weep for, tr.	Okto
Cause to weep	Okphá'to (phásto). O'k pingko
Dance, intr. and tr.	Holi páṉche, intr. Holi páko, tr.
Sing, intr. and tr.	Kwom páṉche, intr. Kwom páko, tr.
Hope	No such word
Fear, n.	Ram
Fear not	Thá ram
Frighten, tr.	Ram pingko. *Kh*am to (Arabic kh)
Frighten not	Ram thá ping. Thá *kh*am to
Frighten me	Ram pingsung. *Kh*amsung
Frighten thyself	Ram pingche. *Kh*amche
Cause to frighten or be frightened	*Kh*am pingko
Cause me to frighten or to be frightened	*Kh*am pingsung
Cause thyself to frighten or be frightened	*Kh*am pingche
Cause him or it to frighten or be frightened for another's sake	*Kh*am pingto
Tremble, ac. intr.	Hokche
Cause to tremble by own act or make him tremble, tr.	Hokto. Hoksung. Hokche (conj. vii.)
Cause to tremble through another's agency or cause him to be made or to make to tremble	Hok pingko
Tremble not	Thá hokche
Make him not tremble	Thá hokto
Cause him not to be made to tremble or to make tremble	Hok thá ping
Be good, n.	Noh'ka dum or poṉche
Make good, tr.	Noh'ka thumto or pako *
Make thyself good, intr.	Noh'ka thumche or páṉche
Be glad or gladden thyself, ac. intr.	Bongche
Gladden, tr.	Bongto
Gladden me	Bongsung
Gladden thyself or cause thyself to be gladdened	Bong pingche
Cause him to gladden or to be gladdened	Bong ping ko
Cause him to gladden or to be gladdened on another's account	Bong ping to
Cause me to gladden or to be gladdened	Bong pingsung

* Neuter dum becomes normally transitive thum. Both alike can take the causative pingko, and double causals like thumpingko can be made at pleasure.

Be not glad	Thá bongche
Gladden not	Thá bongto
Be sad, vexed, or sadden thyself	Thukche
Sadden, vex, tr.	Thukto
Cause to sadden or to be saddened	Thuk phá'to (phasto). Thuk pingko
Cause thyself to be saddened	Thuk pingche
Cause to sadden or to be saddened in lieu of or on another's account	Thuk ping to
Cause not, &c. &c.	Thuk'thá ping. Thuk thá ping to
Speak, utter, n.	Hot'. Dávo pánche
Utter not	Thá hot'. Dávo thá pánche
Utter thyself or for thyself, intr.	Hosche (the s like English th)
Do thou not utter for self	Thá hosche
Utter in lieu of another, or for him	Hophto (hosto)
Utter not for him	Thá hophto (hosto, conj. vii.)
Cause to utter or to be uttered	Hot' pingko
Speak to, tell, narrate, talk to, tr.	Ishto. Chhisto. Dávo páko
Speak to me, tell me or for me	Ishsung. Chhissung. Bo'sung * (Bo'to, the transitive, is lost)
Speak to thyself or tell it for thyself	Ishche. Chhische
Cause to tell or to be told	It'pingko. Chhit'ping ko. Dávo pá-ping ko
Cause not to tell or not to be told	It thá ping. Chhit' thá ping. Dávo pá thá ping
Tell on his account, tell his tale	Dávo páto (conj. vi.)
Tell on my account, tell my tale	Dávo pásung
Let speech be had	Dávo ponche
Tell on your own account, tell your own tale	Dávo pánche
Cause his tale to be told for him	Dávo pá pingto
Cause thy own tale to be told	Dávo pá pinche
Cause my tale to be told	Dávo pá pingsung †
Be silent or let silence be, n.	Giwon ponche
Silence, tr.	Giwon páko
Cause to silence	Giwon pá pingko
Silence me	Giwon posung ‡
Silence thyself	Giwon pánche
Silence him on another's account or for another	Giwon pato
Call. Summon, tr.	Rángto. Khámto
Summon me or for me	Rangsung. Khamsung
Summon for thyself	Rangche. Khamche
Shout, vociferate, intr.	Tamche. Sángma-panche
Shout to, for him	Tamto. Sángma-páko
Learn (=teach thyself), intr.	Lische } Conj. vii.
Teach or teach him, tr.	Listo } Conj. vii.
Read, intr.	Lische } Conj. vii.
Write it, tr.	Blekto (conj. vi., p. 126)
Write for thyself or write simply	Blekche
Cause to write	Blek pingko
Ask, question, tr.	Jiko } Conj. x.
Ask for self, or ask simply, or ask thyself	Jiche } Conj. x.
Ask for me, or me	Jisung } Conj. x.

* This last root, bot', to tell, is only used as a passive. Bot'gnom, I am told; Bosungmi, I was told.

† All these three are used actively also. Cause him to tell his tale; cause thyself to tell thine; cause me to tell mine.

‡ Compare Dávo pásung. This refers to the agent, do thou make speech for me, whereas Giwon posung refers to silence as governing the verb, let silence prevail for me. See remarks on the verbs Páko, Táko, and Jáko. They show signs of a true passive struggling into existence against the genius of the language.

Ask it for him	Jito
Ask it not, tr.	Thá ji
Ask not, intr.	Thá jiche
Ask not for me or me	Thá jigno
Ask not for self	Thá jiche
Ask not for him	Thá jito
Answer or answer him, tr.	Chhisto
Answer self or for self or answer simply	Chhische
Answer me or for me	Chhissung
Answer him or for him	Chhisto
Beg, intr.	Biche (see Buy)
Beg it, tr.	Biko } Conj. x.
Beg me or for me, p.	Bisung } Conj. x.
Beg for thyself, intr.	Biche } Conj. x.
Beg it for him, tr.	Bito
Approve, like, intr.	Yosche
Approve it, like it, tr.	Yophto (yosto)
Cause him to approve or to approve it, or it to be approved	Yot'phá'to (phasto). Yot'pingko
Approve not	*Thá yosche*
Approve it not	*Thá yot'*
Approve me or for me	Yossung
Approve thyself or for thyself	Yosche
Approve him or approve for him	Yophto (yosto, p. 137)
Cause me to approve or be approved	Yot'pingsung
Cause thyself to approve or to be approved or cause it to be approved for thyself	Yot'pingche. Yot'phásche
Cause it to be approved or cause him to approve it	Yot pingko
Cause it to be approved for him	Yot pingto
See, intr.	Yengche. Chusche
See it, tr.	Yengko.* Chuphto (chusto)
See thyself or for thyself	Yengche
See for him	Yeng to
See me or see for me	Yengsung
Cause to see or be seen	Yeng phá'to (phasto). Yeng pingko
Cause thyself to see or be seen, or to be seen for thyself	Yeng pingche
Cause to see or be seen for him	Yeng pingto
Show, intr.	*Kh*unche †
Show it, tr.	*Kh*unto. } Conj. vi.
Show me or for me	*Kh*unsung } Conj. vi.
Show thyself or for thyself	*Kh*unche } Conj. vi.
Show for him	*Kh*unto } Conj. vi.
Cause to show or be shown	*Kh*un pingko. *Kh*un phá'to
Cause thyself to be shown or to show	*Kh*un pingche
Cause me to be shown or to show	*Kh*un pingsung
Hide, ac. intr.	Kinche
Hide it, tr.	Khiko. Khiche. Khisung (conj. x.)
Hide thyself (lie hid)	Kinche
Cause thyself to lie hid	Kin pingche
Let me hide myself	Kin sung yu
Cause him to lie hid	Kin pingko
Cause me to lie hid	Kin ping sung
Cause it to be hid	Khit'pingko

---

* Yengko conjugated like pingko, which see in Grammar.
† The underlined *Kh* has a harsh Arabic sound.

Cause thyself to be hidden or cause it to be hidden for thee	Khit'pingche
Hide me	Khisung
Cause me to be hid	Khit'pingsung
Cause it to be hid for him	Khit'pingto
Hear simply or hear thyself, intr.	Thásche
Hear it, tr.	Tháko. Tháche. Thásung (conj. x.)
Cause thyself to hear or be heard	Thát'pinche
Cause him to hear or be heard	Thát'pingko
Hear me	Thásung. Ang dávo tháko
Cause me to hear or be heard	Thát'pingsung.
Hear not	Thá thasche
Hear it not	Thá thá
Hear not me	Thá thá gno
Cause me not to hear or be heard	Thá thát'ping gno
Taste, ac. intr.	Homche
Taste it, tr.	Hompo (conj. ix.)
Taste for thyself or thyself	Homche
Taste for him	Homto
Taste for me or taste me	Homsung
Cause to taste or to be tasted	Homping ko
Blow, apply breath, intr.	Hosche } Conj. vii.
Blow it, apply breath to it, tr.	Hosto }
Smell, ac. intr.	Námche
Smell it, tr.	Nampo (conj. ix.)
Smell for thyself or thyself	Námche
Smell for him	Námto
Smell me	Námsung
Cause to smell or to be smelt	Námping ko
Cause to smell or to be smelt for him	Námping to
Smell not	Thá námche
Smell it not	Thá nám
Smell me not	Thá ná (m) mo
Cause me to smell or be smelt	Námpingsung
Cause thyself to smell or be smelt	Námpingche
Touch, ac. intr.	Dusche
Touch it, tr.	Duphto (dushto)
Cause to touch or to be touched	Dut'ping ko
Cause thyself to touch or be touched	Dut'pingche
Cause it to touch or be touched for him	Dut'ping to
Touch me or for me	Dú-s-sung (dussung, vii.)
Touch me not	Thá dut'gno
Eat, ac. intr.	Jánche (see Buy) *
Eat it, tr.	Jáko (conj. x.)
Eat not	Thá jánche
Eat it not	Thá jó
Eat me	Josung (see Posung)
Eat for me	Jásung
Eat for thyself or do thou thyself eat, or eat thy own share	Jánche
Eat for him or eat his share	Játo
Eat not me	Thá jogno
Eat not for me	Thá jágno
Feed, tr.	*Kh*wá-s-to † (khwasto, conj. vii.

* Whenever the action terminates in self, or returns to self, the reflex form is used ; and jancho is eat; jako, eat *it*. So ingche is buy ; ingko, buy it. Compare the Hungarian analogous forms.

† *Kh* = harsh, guttural Arabic.

Feed thyself, intr.	*Kh*wásche
Feed not, tr.	Thá *Kh*wát'
Feed thyself not	Thá *Kh*wásche
Feed me	*Kh*wá-s-sung. Khwassung
Feed me not	Thá *Kh*wat'gno
Cause to feed or to be fed	*Kh*wát' pingko
Cause thyself to feed or be fed	*Kh*wát pingche
Cause it to feed or be fed for him	*Kh*wát pingto
Cause me to feed or be fed	*Kh*wát pingsung
Drink—water	Ti dak'
Drink not—water	Ti thá dak'
Cause to drink or to be drank—water	Ti dak'pingko
Cause not to drink or be drank—water	Ti dak'thàping
Drink—beer, spirits, ac. intr.	Tun̲che } See note at Eat and at Buy,
Drink it, beer, &c., tr.	Tun̲ko } further on
Drink not, beer, &c.	Thá tun̲che
Drink it not, beer, &c.	Thá tun̲'
Cause to drink or to be drank	Thun̲to or Tun̲pingko *
Cause to cause to drink or to be drank	Thun̲pingko
Don't cause to drink	Thá thun̲to
Don't cause to cause to drink or be drank	Thun̲ tháping
Don't cause to cause thyself to drink or to be drank	Thun̲ thápingche
Don't cause him to drink it, or it to be drank by him in lieu of another	Thun̲ thápingko
Drink me	Tun̲ sung
Drink not me	Thá tun̲ gno
Cause me to drink or to be drank	Thun̲sung
Cause me not to drink	Thá thun̲ gno
Vomit, ac. intr.	Lipche
Vomit it, tr.	Lipto. Li'po (lippo)
Cause to vomit	Lip'pingko
Sleep, ac. intr.	Imche
Sleep not	Thá imche
Cause to sleep	Im pingko. Hómpo
Cause not to sleep	Im thá ping. Thá hém
Cause thyself to sleep	Hem che
Help to put him to sleep	Hem to
Help to cause him to be put to sleep	Hem ping to
Cause thyself to be put asleep	Hem ping che
Wake, n.	Buk'. Sipche
Wake not	Thá buk'. Thá sipche
Awaken, tr.	Po'ko (pu'kko).† } Pukko (conj. xi.) Sipto } Sipto (conj. vi.)
Awaken not	Thá puk'. Thá sipto
Cause to awaken or to be awakened	Puk'pingko. Sip pingko
Cause thyself to be awakened or to awaken	Puk'pingche
Cause me to be awakened or to awaken	Puk'pingsung
Awaken me	Puk'sung
Awaken me not	Thá puk'gno
Awaken thyself or do thou thyself awaken him	Puk'che

* See note aforegone at Parent, page 219. Neuter tun makes transitive thun, as neuter ki, lie hid, makes transitive khí, hide. The double causals are thunpingko and khípingko. So pukpingko infra.

† O and u, like e and i, are hardly separable.

Awaken for him	Puk'to (conj. vi.)
Awaken not for him	Thá puk'to
Dream, intr.	Ámung yengche
Dream it, tr.	Ámung yengko
Dream not	Ámung thá yengche
Dream it not	Ámung thá yeng
Cause to dream or to be dreamt	Ámung yengping ko
Cause thyself to dream or be dreamt of	Ámung yengping che
Fart, ac. intr.	Peshche
Fart at, tr.	Peshto
Shit, n.	Dak'. Epidak
Shit it, upon it, tr.	Dakto. Epidakto
Piss, minge, intr. n.	Chepidak. Cheche
Piss it, on it, imminge, tr.	Chepidakto. Cheto
Kiss—give or take (osculor), tr.	Chugup páko
Cause to kiss or be kissed	Chugup páping ko
Cause thyself to kiss or be kissed	Chugup páping che
Kiss me	Chugup posung
Kiss me not	Chugup thá pogno
Kiss him for me	Chugup pásung
Kiss him for him	Chugup páto
Kiss (coe), tr. ...	Hepto (conj. vi.)
Cause to kiss or be kissed	Hep pingko
Cause thyself to kiss or be kissed	Hep pingche
Kiss me	Hepsung
Cause me to kiss or be kissed	Hep pingsung
Kiss not	Thá hepto
Kiss me not	Thá hepmo
Sneeze, ac. intr.	Khikche
Sneeze not	Thá khikche
Sneeze at or make sneeze	Khikto. Khi'ko * (khikko)
Do not sneeze at or make sneeze	Thá khikto
Cause him to sneeze at or him to be made or to make to sneeze	Khik pingko
Cause not, &c.	Khik thá ping
Do thou make me sneeze, &c.	Khiksung
Cause me to be made to sneeze, &c.	Khik pingsung
Do not sneeze at me or do not make me sneeze	Thá khikgno
Cause thyself to be made to sneeze, &c.	Khik pingche
Cause not thyself to be made to sneeze or to sneeze or be sneezed at	Khik tháping che
Spit, ac. intr.	Tokche
Spit at, on, tr.	Tokto. To'ko * (tokko)
Cause to spit or to be spat at	Tok pingko
Cause to spit or be spat at on another's account	Tok pingto
Spit on me or make me spit	Toksung
Cause me to spit or to be spat at	Tok pingsung
Cause yourself to spit or to be spat on	Tokpingche
Belch, ac. intr.	Garat pánche
Belch at, tr.	Garat páko
Cause him to belch or to belch at or to be belched at	Garat pápingko
Belch me or for me	Garat posung

* Khi'ko and to'ko, like li'po, vomit it, are falling out of use because of the homophones; but they are the true forms, and the others refer to a third party. See the word Exchange.

Belch him or for him	Garat páto
Cause me to belch or be belched at	Garat pápingsung
Cause him to belch or to be belched at on another's account	Garat papingto
Cough, ac. intr.	Khwen̲ khwen̲ pán̲che
Cough at, tr.	Khwen̲ khwen̲ páko *
Cough me, cause me to cough by own agency	Khwen̲ khwen̲ posung or pásung
Cause me to cough or to be coughed at through another's agency	Khwen̲ khwen̲ papingsung
Cause thyself to cough or to be coughed at through same	Khwen̲ khwen̲ pápingche
Hiccup, ac. intr.	Tukum pánche
Yawn, intr., tr.	Wakum pán̲che, intr. Wakum páko, tr.
Cause to yawn	Wakum pápingko
Cause me to yawn	Wakum pápingsung
Cause thyself to yawn	Wakum pápingche
Do thou thyself cause me to yawn	Wakum posung. Wakum thá po
Do not thou cause me to yawn	Wakum thápogno
Yawn not, intr. and tr.	Wakum thá pán̲che
Lick, ac. intr.	Popche
Lick it, tr.	Po'po (poppo, conj. viii.)
Cause to lick or be licked	Pop pingko
Lick me or for me	Popsung
Lick thyself or for thyself	Popche
Lick it for him	Pop to
Cause me to lick or be licked	Pop pingsung
Cause thyself to lick or to be licked	Pop pingche
Cause him to lick or be licked	Poppingko
The same, on account of, or in lieu of, another	Poppingto
Suck, a. intr.	Pipche
Suck it, tr.	Pi'po (pip-po, conj. viii.)
Suck me or for me	Pipsung
Suck thyself or for thyself	Pipche
Suck it for him	Pipto
Cause to suck or to be sucked	Pip pingko
Cause me to suck or be sucked	Pip pingsung
Cause thyself to suck or be sucked	Pip pingche
Cause him to suck or be sucked	Pip pingko
Bite, tr.	Chi'ko (chik-ko, conj. xi.)
Bite not	Thá chik'
Cause to bite or to be bitten	Chik pingko
Cause not to bite or be bitten	Chik thá ping
Bite me	Chik sung
Bite me not	Thá chik gno
Bite thyself	Chikche
Bite him	Chi'ko (chikko, conj.)
Bite it for him	Chikto
Cause me to bite or be bitten	Chik pingsung
Cause me not to bite or be bitten	Thá chikping gno
Cause thyself to bite or be bitten	Chik pingche
Cause him to bite or be bitten	Chik pingko
The same on another's behoof	Chik pingto

* Hence you can say in active intransitive, khwe*n* khwe*n* pachungmi, I coughed = I made myself cough; in the transitive, khwe*n* khwe*n* pakungmi, I coughed at him, very often used for "I made him cough," which is properly khwe*n* khwe*n* páping-kungmi; and in the passive, khwe*n* khwe*n* posungmi, I was coughed = was made to cough, which latter is more nicely expressed by khwe*n* khwe*n* pasungmi, showing also the active agency.

Kick, tr.	The*sh*to (Eng. *th*). Thesto
Kick not	Thá thet'
Kick me	Thé (s) sung
Kick me not	Thá thet' gno
Kick thyself or kick simply	The*sh*che
Kick not thyself or do not kick	Thá the*sh*che
Kick him	Theshto
Kick him not	Thá thet'
Cause to kick or to be kicked	Thet' pingko
Cause me to kick or be kicked	Thet' pingsung
Cause thyself to kick or be kicked	Thet' pingche
Cause him to kick or be kicked	Thet' pingko
The same on another's behoof	Thet' pingto
Strike, tr.	To'po (top-po, conj. viii.)
Strike not	Thá top'
Strike thyself	Top che
Strike me	Topsung
Cause him to strike or to be stricken	Top pingko
Cause thyself, &c.	Top pingche
Scratch, tr.	Phokto
Scratch thyself	Phokche
Push, shove, tr.	Thēko. Thēsung. Thēche (conj. x.)
Push not	Thá thé
Pull, tr.	Khinto
Pull not	Thá khinto
Walk, ac. intr.	Khokche
Walk not	Thá khokche
Walk it or cause it to walk, thou thyself	Khokto
Walk it not	Thá khokto
Cause to walk or to be walked by another's agency	Khok pingko
Walk me thyself, cause me to walk or be walked, by thy own agency	Khoksung
Cause to cause me to walk or be walked, or have me walked	Khok pingsung
Cause thyself to walk or be walked or have thyself walked	Khok pingche
Run, intr.	Lúnlá. Lún
Run not	Thá lunlá *
Run it, cause it to run, thyself	Lunto
Cause it to be run by another	Lunpháto (phasto). Lun pingko
Cause me to run or be run	Lunphásung
Cause thyself to run or be run	Lunphasche
Run away, flee, intr.	Rulá. Ru
Cause to flee	Ruto. Rut'pingko
Creep, intr.	Hobu báha khokche = walk like a snake
Jump, hop, intr.	Tuche (see note at Eat, p. 248)
Jump it or make it jump, tr.	Tūto. Tū sung. Tūche (conj. vi.)
Cause to make jump	Tupingko
Leap, intr.	Hopche
Leap it, tr.	Hopto (conj. vi.)
Cause to leap	Hop pingko
Fly, n.	Bon
Cause to fly	Bonpingko (phasto)

* Lun without the lá makes the passive lungnom, which being also the neuter form, lun lagnom, from lunla, is preferred to express the neuter sense, though lá also makes lagnom. See note at p. 238 supra. Lun is run; lunla, run away, run from me, that is; for flee is another word.

Enable to fly	Bonphâto
Swim, intr.	Hánche
Swim it thyself or cause it to swim by, thy own act	Hánto (conj. vi.
Cause it, him, to swim by other's agency, or have it swam	Hánpingko
Swim me, cause me to swim or make me swim (thyself)	Hánsung
Cause me to be made to swim by another's agency	Hánpingsung
Cause thyself to swim or be swam	Hánpingche
Wade, ac. intr.	Thekche
Dive } Sink } ac. intr. = sink thyself	Thamche
Sink it, make him dive, by thy own agency	Thamto (conj. vi.)
Cause to make dive or sink by other's agency, or have it sunk	Thampingko
Bathe = bathe thyself, intr.	Denche
Bathe him	Dento
Cause him to bathe or to be bathed	Denpingko
Wash, intr. = wash thyself, only body	Upche
Wash him	Upto (conj. vi.)
Cause him to wash or to be washed	Up pingko
Dress, ac. intr. = dress thyself	Chupche. Wásche
Dress it or him	Chupto. Wásto
Cause it to dress or be dressed	Chup pingko. Wat'pingko
Dress me	Chupsung. Wassung
Dress thyself	Chupche. Wásche
Undress (thyself), intr.	Lusche
Undress it or him	Luphto (lusto, see Conjugation)
Undress me	Lussung
Cause it to undress or to be undressed	Lut'pingko
Don't undress it or him	Lut'thá ping
Be naked, n.	Gunang senti dum or ponche
Denude thyself, ac. intr.	Gunang senti pánche
Denude him	Gunang senti páko
Denude me	Gunang senti posung (pásung)
Denude it for another	Gunang senti páto
Cause to denude or be denuded	Gunang senti pápingko
Cause thyself to denude or be denuded	Gunang senti pápingche
Cause me to denude or to be denuded	Gunang senti pápingsung
Cause me not to denude or to be denuded	Gunang senti thá páping gno
Be hungry, n.	Suksamet'. Suksametvidum
Make him hungry or cause him to be made hungry	Suksa met'pingko not'pingko
Make me hungry or cause me to be made hungry	Suksa met'pingsung
Make thyself hungry or cause thyself to be made hungry	Suksa met'pingche
Be thirsty, n.	Tidaksa met', or Tidakvi dum *
Make thirsty	Tidaksa met' pingko
Make me thirsty or enable me to make or be made thirsty	Tidaksa met' pinsung
Make thyself thirsty or cause thyself to make or be made thirsty	Tidaksa met' pingche

---

* Any state of body that continues or is to come, like thirsty, sleepy, is expressed by the active participle—if it be supposed complete, like asleep, by the past or passive participle, thus impi yotvi is sleepy; impi yosta, asleep. Met=die, and suksa met'=die of hunger; tidaksa met'=die of thirst, or literally, of want of water.

Be not hungry	Suksa thá met'
Make not hungry	Suksa met' thá ping
Be not thirsty	Tidaksa thá met'
Cause not to thirst	Tidaksa met' thá ping
Be sleepy=cover sleep, n.	Impi yot' or yosche. Impi yotvi dum
Make sleepy	Impi yot' pháto. Impi yotvi thumto
Make not sleepy	Impi yot thá pháto. Impi yotvi thá thumto
Be cold (being), n.	Jumsa met'
Be cold (thing)	Khimche
Make cold (being)	Jumsa met' ping Do. do. pháto (phastó)
Make cold (thing)	Khimto
Make not cold (being)	Jumsa met' thá ping Do. do. pháto (phasto)
Make not cold (thing)	Thá khimto
Be warm, n.	Jekhom ponche
Warm him or it	Jeto. Jekhom páko
Warm thyself	Jeche. Jekhom pánche
Cause thyself to be warmed or to warm him	Je pingche
Cause him to be warmed or to warm another	Je pingko
Warm me	Je sung
Cause me to be warmed or to warm another	Je pingsung
Be dirty (become), n.	Penki or Penkimu dum (become) Penki or penkimu no (be)
Dirty thyself, intr.	Penki or penkimu pánche
Dirty it, tr.	Penki páko
Dirty it for him	Penki páto
Cause to dirty or to be dirtied	Penki papingko
Be clean, n.	Wota dum
Be not clean	Wota thá dum
Clean thyself, intr.	Wota pánche and woche
Clean it, tr.	Woto. Wota páko
Clean it for him	Wota páto
Clean not thyself	Thá woche
Clean it not	Thá woto. Wota thápo
Be angry, n.	Risi bok'
Make angry, tr.	Risi phokto or pho'ko (phokko, conj. xi.)
Abuse, revile, tr.	Jishto
Cause to revile	Jit'pingko
Abuse thyself	Jishche.
Abuse me	Jishsung
Quarrel, n.	Phwe
Cause to quarrel	Phwet' phá'to (phásto)
Cause me to quarrel or be quarrelled with	Phwet' phásung
Cause thyself to quarrel or be quarrelled with	Phwet' phósche
Cause him to quarrel or be quarrelled with	Phwet' pháto (phásto)
Be friendly Be united or reconciled, intr.	Tosche * Totnachhe, D. Toschine, Pl.
Make friendly Unite Reconcile, tr.	Tophto (toshto)

* The genius of these tongues requires such a phrase as "be reconciled" to be set down in the dual or plural. So also fight, &c.

Cause to unite or to be united	Tot' pingko
Be not united = unite not yourselves	Thá tosche. Thá totnachhe, D. Thá toschine, P.
Unite not, tr.	Thá tot'
Fight, n.	Pat. Patnachhe, D. Patchine, P.
Cause to fight or to be fought	Pat pingko
Cause not to fight or to be fought	Pat thá ping
Cause me to fight or be fought with	Pat ping sung
Cause thyself to fight or be fought with	Pat ping che
Cause him to fight or to be fought	Pat ping ko
Be victorious, n.	Then
Make him victorious	Thento
Cause to make victorious	Then pingko
Make thyself victorious	Thenche
Make me victorious	Thensung
Cause me to be made victorious	Thenpingsung
Conquer him, tr.	Wonto *
Conquer thyself	Wonche
Conquer me	Wonsung
Cause him to conquer or be conquered	Wonpingko
Ask aid to conquer thyself	Wonpinche
Cause me to be conquered or to conquer	Wonpingsung
Be conquered Succumb, n.	Yáng. Yánglá (see note at Run)
Cause to succumb by thy own act	Yángto
Cause to succumb through another's agency	Yáng pingko
Cause me to succumb by thy own act	Yángsung
Cause me to succumb through another's agency	Yáng ping sung
Work, trans.	Kám páko
Work for self, do own work	Kam pánche
Work for him, do his work	Kam páto
Work for me, do my work	Kam pásung
Cause to work or be worked	Kam pápingko
Cause thyself to work or thy work to be done	Kam pápingche
Cause to work for him or his work to be done	Kam pápingto
Play = amuse thyself, intr.	Hánche (s'amuser)
Make him play or do thou thyself amuse him, tr.	Hánto (amuser)
Cause him to be made to play or have him amused (per alterum)	Hánpingko
Play with me	Ang nung hánche †
Amuse me	Hánsung
Cause me to be amused	Hánpingsung
Be tired, n.	Jyop' ‡
Make tired or tire it	Jyopto
Tire thyself	Jyopche
Tire me	Jyopsung

* The comparison of the roots then and won will show how these tongues attempt to fend off the equivoques resulting from imperfectly developed grammar. Wonto is used as a neuter with transitives, and phasche (not wonche) replaces it with neuters, Top won tungmi, I can strike; Im phaschungmi, I can sleep.

† Literally, amuse thyself with me, along with me. The sense is quite different from that of hánsung, in which I am solely the amused party.

‡ From jyop comes the Newari jyápu, a labourer, though one tongue has lost the noun, the other the verb! See Twist.

Cause me to be tired or to tire	Jyop pingsung
Cause thyself to be tired or to tire	Jyop pingche
Cause him to be tired or to tire	Jyop pingko
Be rested, take rest, rest thyself	Nekche
Rest it, give rest	Ne'ko (nek-ko, conj. xi.)
Cause to give it rest	Nek'pingto
Cause thyself to have rest	Nekpingche
Do thou give me rest	Neksung
Cause me to have rest	Nek pingsung
Take not rest	Thá nekche
Give not rest	Thá nek'
Move, n.	Duk'
Move it, trans.	Thukto. Duk' pingko *
Cause it to be moved or have it moved	Thukpingko
Be still, move not	Thá duk'
Make still, move it not	Thá thukto
Be quick, ac. intr. = quicken thyself	Plakche
Quicken, tr.	Plakto
Cause to quicken or to be quick	Plakpingko
Do thou quicken me	Plaksung
Cause me to be quickened	Plakpingsung
Cause thyself to be quickened	Plakpingche
Be slow, be dilatory, delay, n.	Gá
Cause to be slow or delay it	Gát'pingko
Stay, stop, stop thyself, intr.	Thikche
Stay him, stop him, tr.	Thikto
Cause him to be stopped or to stop him	Thik pingko
Let him depart	Lat'pingko
Be intoxicated, n.	Vi
Intoxicate, tr.	Vit'pháto (phasto). Vit'pingko
Tell the truth	Diksa hot, n. *Diksa ishto, tr.*
Cause to speak truth	Diksa hotpingko. Diksa itpingko
Tell falsehood	Mang diksa hot' Mang diksa ishto Buḍhia háto
Cause to lie	Buḍhia háṇpingko
Believe, obey, tr.	Honko
Cause to believe or obey, or to be obeyed	Họnpingko
Disbelieve, disobey	Thá hon
Forbid, tr.	Dávohá thikto (literally, stay by speech)
Prevent, tr.	Thikto
Present, offer, tr.	Cho'-ko (chokko, conj. xi.)
Offer not	Thá chok'
Accept, intr.	Doche } Dōko, dōche, dōsung (conj. x.)
Accept it, tr.	Doko }
Accept it for self	Doche }
Accept it for him	Doto
Accept not or refuse	Thá doche
Accept it not or refuse it	Thá dó
Choose, select, tr.	Lu'ko. Lukko. Luksung. Lukche. Lukto
Cherish, protect, tr.	Tunko
Cherish thyself or thy own	Tunche
Cherish me	Tunsung
Cause me to be cherished or to cherish	Tunpingsung
Abandon, neglect, leave, tr.	Wá'to (wásto, conj. vii.)

* Neuter duk makes normally transitive thuk=duk pingko, and double causal thuk pingko. Elsewhere the aspirate of the transitive is omitted in a seemingly identical word.

Confine, imprison, tr.	Thikto
Set at liberty, tr.	Testo. Tesche. Tessung (conj. vii.)
Have, intr.	Gosche.* Ungbe penku nó or dum
Have not, want	Thá gosche. Ungbe pen̲ku thá nó or thá dum
Cause him to have	Got'pingko. Wáthim bepen̲ku-thumto
Cause not to have	Thá got ping. Wáthim be pen̲ku thá thumto
Give, trans.	Háto. Mumto
Give me or to me	Hásung. Mumsung
Give to or for thyself	Hán̲che.† Mumche
Give to him or for him	Háto. Mumto, vi.
Give not	Thá háto. Thá mumto
Cause to give or to be given	Hápingko. Mumpingko
Cause not to give or not to be given	Há thá ping or Thá há ping
Give it back, return it to him	Lipto (see Take back)
Cause to return or to be returned	Lip pingko
Give again (more)	Gessa háto
Take, intr.	Lasche. Doche ‡
Take it, tr.	Lasto. Doho. (Dōko, see Accept)
Take for thyself, *i.e.*, appropriate	Lasche. Doche
Take it for him	Lashto. Doto
Cause to take or be taken	Lakpíngko. Dot pingko
Take it back, quasi, return it to self	Lipche (see Give back)
Save, preserve, cure, him (life)	Cholko
Save, cure thyself	Cholche
Save me	Cholsung
Destroy (life)	Sishto (see Kill)
Keep, preserve (thing)	Táko (see Keep)
Spoil (thing)	Nasi páko
Be handsome	Bingcho dum.§ Bingmi dum
Make handsome	Bingcho thumto. Bingmi thumto
Adorn	Bingcho páko
Adorn thyself	Bingcho pán̲che
Adorn him	Bingcho páko
Adorn it for him	Bingcho páto
Adorn her	Bingmi páko
Grow, animal plant, n.	Jongche. Hon (khon). Liche
Grow it or cause to grow, tr.	Jongto. Honto. Lito
Decay, n.	Ri. Rila
Decay it or cause to decay	Rito. Ripingko
Be adult or mature	Bangcho dum. Bangmi dum §
Make mature	Bangho páko
Steal, tr.	Khūko (conj. x.)
Steal for thyself	Khūche
Steal for him, for another	Khūto
Cause to steal or be stolen	Khū pingko ‖
Steal not	Thá khu

* Ung be pénku no, dum ; thee in wealth be, become.

† Compare "Take." The pronominalisation of the Váyu verbs prevents a good deal of that difficulty which the Turanians generally experience in furnishing simple equivalents for the words "give" and "take," because the genius of the languages exacts on all occasions a rigid attention to the results of action, the objective as well as subjective results. Different roots, or different modifications of the same roots, must necessarily convey the idea involved in each case.

‡ See remark at Buy. The result of taking is appropriation by self. Hence the intr. verb.

§ Final cho and mi are proper to the sexes. See Adjectives.

‖ Khū phá'to (phasto), make a thief of him.

Cause not to steal or be stolen	Khū thá ping
Deceive, cheat, tr.	Mángpingko (see Forget)
Deceive thyself	Mángpingche
Deceive not	Thá mángping
Deceive me	Máng pingsung
Cause me to be deceived	Máng pá pingsung
Accompany, intr.	Ko'na la'la. Minung khokche
Leave, quit, tr.	Wás'to
Remain with, intr.	Ko'na musche
Sit=seat thyself, intr.	Musche (S'asseoir)
Seat, tr.	Muphto (Mushto, conj. vii.)
Cause to seat or to be seated	Mut'pingko
Cause thyself to be seated	Mut'pingche
Sit not	Thá musche
Seat not	Thá mut'
Cause not, do not cause, to sit or be seated	Mut'thá ping or Thá mut'ping
Stand, intr.	Ipche=erect thyself
Make stand	I'po (ippo) = erect it or him (conj. viii.)
Make stand for another	Ipto=erect it for him
Cause to make stand, to be erect	Ippingko
Stoop, intr.	Khungche
Make stoop, tr.	Khungto
Cause to make stoop	Khung pingko
Lie down, intr.	Likche. Likla. Lik.
Lay down, make lie down	Li'ko (Lik-ko, conj. xi.)
Cause to be laid down or to lay down	Lik pingko
Get up, if recumbent	Buk' (see Wake)
Get up, if sitting	Ipche (see Stand)
Remain standing, intr.	Ipipha musche
Fall, on ground, n.	Ruk'. Ruk'la.
Cause to fall, ditto	Ruk'pingko
Fall from aloft, n.	Duk'. Duk'la
Make fall or throw down or let fall	Tu'ko (Tukko), tuksung, tukche, tukto. Duk pingko *
Do not make fall	Thá tuk'. Duk' thá ping
Get on, mount, n.	Chángche
Mount him, cause to mount	Changto
Get off, dismount	Lische, n. Listo, tr.
Put down. Place. Put, tr.	Táko
Put down or place for me	Tásung
Ditto, ditto, for self	Tánche
Ditto, ditto, for him	Táto
Lift up, raise † from ground, tr.	Rēko (conj. x.), without force. G'uko, gukko (conj. xi. ‡), with force.
Lift up for self	Reche. Gukche
Ditto, ditto, for him	Reto. Gukto

* Neuter duk makes normally transitive and causal tuk. See and compare Bahing, in the sequel. Both tongues alike make double causals in the same way. Compare "Move," p. 412, *ante*.

† Raise on the ground is i'po = erect it or him, as ipche is erect thyself = sit up or stand up. For get up, to a sleeping man, you say sipche; to a sitting man, ipche; to one lying down, buk'. Rise, as respects beings, is ipche or buk' therefore; but as respects the heavenly bodies, the equivalent term is lok' = appear. Specialisation is the soul and body of these tongues, which remedy defects of grammar by multiplication of terms, so as to fend off mistakes in the best way available (see note on Kuko). Quoad falling, ruk' and duk' apply to beings only. The word for things is lik'.

‡ Rēko, like dōko and chhūko, belongs to the tenth conjugation, which has the pausing tone; gu'ko, recte gukko, to the eleventh, with an abrupt tone.

Lift up for me	Resung. Guksung
Throw, tr.	Jupto, jupsung jupche
Catch with open hand or spread cloth, tr.	Dōko (conj. x.)
Catch with open hand for self	Dōche
Ditto, ditto, for him	Doto
Catch by grasp, tr.	Chhūko (conj. x.)
Ditto, ditto, for self	Chhūche
Ditto, ditto, for him	Chhūto
Keep, tr.	Táko (see Put)
Snatch from, tr.	Láto, lásung, lánche (conj. vi.)
Throw away, tr. Squander, tr.	Hopto
Squander your own	Hopche
Be near, n.	Khewa nó. Khewá pónche
Approximate thyself	Khewa pánche
Approximate it	Khewa páko
Be distant, intr.	Khosche. Khólámdum
Distance him, tr.	Khot'pháto. Khólám thúmto
Distance thyself	Khot'phasche
Bring, trans.	Pishto } conj. vii.
Bring me or for me	Pishsung } conj. vii.
Bring thyself or for thyself	Pishche } conj. vii.
Bring him or for him	Pishto } conj. vii.
Fetch, comp.	Bálá (= to bring go)
Fetch it	Pishto (bálá has no trans.)
Fetch it for me or fetch me	Básung
Fetch for thyself or do thou thyself fetch	Bánche
Fetch for him	Báto ?? (obsolete trans.)
Cause to fetch or be fetched	Bá pingko
Take away, tr.	Lakto (conj. vi.)
Take yourself off or take it away for thyself	Lakche
Cause to take away or to be taken away	Lak pingko
Send, tr.	Pingko (conj. x.)
Send it for thyself }	Pingche
Do thou thyself send or send thy own }	Pingche
Send it for him or on his account, or send his things	Pingto
Send me or for me	Pingsung
Send him or it	Pingko
Cause to send or be sent	Ping pingko. Ping phato (phasto)
Carry, bear, trans.	Kūko* (conj. x.)
Carry it for thyself	Kūnche
Carry it for him	Kūto
Carry it for me or me	Kūsung
Cause him, it, to carry or to be carried	Kūpingko
Cross over, act. intr. or ref.	Lumche †
Cross it over, tr.	Lumto
Cross under	Kuḍikhalala
Cross it under	Kuḍikha latpingko
Hold, take in hand, tr.	Kuko (see Carry)
Grasp, tr.	Chhūko, chhūche, chhūto (conj. x.)

* Kūko, like all transitives of its class, gives both the active and passive of 3d person, preterite; thus, kukum, he carried or was carried. But what we must call the passive has no imperative. From yu, to descend, you can indeed form kuyu, let thyself or him be carried. In the causal form of the verb both senses of the imperative are conveyed, and hence the causal form is often to be regarded as the only representative in these tongues of the passive; as, for example, in Newári.

† Lumche is cross yourself over, as lakcha (below, voce depart) is take yourself off.

Hold up, support, tr.	Dōko (see Catch)
Let it fall or let it be fallen	Liklayu
Fall, n. (things only)	Lik'la. Lik
Throw down, tr.	Li'ko (likko), liksung, likche, likto
Enter, n.	Bek'
Cause to enter	Phekto, pheksung, phekche
Admit. Insert, tr.	Bek pingko
Issue, n.	Lok'
Cause to issue, expel, drive out	Lokto, loksung, lokche. Lokpingko
Ascend, go up, n.	Bek'
Ascend, come up, n.	Jok'
Descend, go down, n.	Yonkha la'la. Yu lá
Descend, come down, n.	Yu'
Cause to ascend or to be ascended	Bek'pingko. Jok'pingko
Cause to descend or to be descended	Yonkha lat pingko. Yut' pingko
Arrive, n., here, there	Dong. Dongla *
Cause to arrive, tr.	Thongto
Depart, n.	Lakche † (see Take away)
Precede, n.	Honko ponche
Follow, n.	Nongna ponche
Attend on, n.	Ko'na ponche
Appear = show thyself, n.	Khunche
Make it, him, appear	Khunto (conj. vi.)
Cause to make appear	Khunpingko
Disappear, n. = hide thyself, or lie hid	Kniche
Make disappear, make hid, or make lie hid	Khiko. Khiche. Khisung. (conj. x.) Kinpingko
Cause to make disappear	Khit'pingko
Make disappear thy own person or goods	Khische
Make disappear for another	Khisto
Make me disappear	Khissung
Be lost / Lose, n.	Damla. Dam
Lose it, tr.	Thámpo, thamsung, thámche, thámpto
Cause to lose it	Thampingko
Lose it not	Thá thám
Cause it not to be lost or cause him not to lose it	Thám tháping
Search, tr.	Hōko.
Search not	Thá hō (Conj. x.)
Search me or for me	Hōsung (Conj. x.)
Search for thy own or for thyself, or do thou thyself search	Hoche (Conj. x.)
Search for him, for his, on his account	Hoto (Conj. x.)
Search not for him	Thá hōt (Conj. x.)
Find, tr.	Lénko (see conj. of pingko)
Find not	Thá leng
Cause to find or to be found	Leng pingko
Find me or for me	Leng sung
Find for thyself or thy own	Leng che
Find for him	Leng to
Cause to find for me or me to be found	Leng pingsung
Cause to find for self or thyself to be found	Leng pingche
Cause to find for him or him to be found	Leng ping to

* Dong is arrive here; donglu, arrive there. Lá added implies fromness. So yú is descend here; yulá, descend there. Neuter dong makes transitive thong, as bek makes phek and (at p. 256, voce "move") duk, thuk.

† Lakche = va-t-en in French. Lá, to go, is the root.

Begin, n.	Tesche
Begin it, tr.	Testo (conj. vii.)
Cause it to begin or be begun	Tet pingko
Continue	The root is repeated with the substantive verb to show continued action, as gik nagik nomi, it is flowing and flowing. Topna top nognom, I am striking
End, n.	Chusche
End it	Chuphto (chusto)
Cause it to end or be ended	Chut pingko
Come, n.	Phi (see On)
Cause him, it, to come or to be come	Phit'pingko
Cause me to come or to be come	Phit'pingsung
Cause thyself to come or be come	Phit'pingche
Cause him to come or to be come	Phit pingko
Cause him to come on another's account	Phit pingto
Come not	Thá phi
Cause not to come	Phit thá ping
Go, n.	La'la (iterated root)
Cause to go	Lat'ping ko
Go not	Thá la'la
Do not cause to go	Lat thá ping
Get out of the way	Khikche
Clear the way. Make get out of the way	Khikto
Clear the way for me	Khiksung
Wait, ac. intr.	Rimche
Wait for, expect, tr.	Rimto
Wait for me	Rimsung
Wait for him	Rimto
Cause to wait	Rimpingko
Arrive, (1) here, (2) there	(1) Dong. (2) Dongla *
Cause to arrive	Dong pingko. Thongto †
Depart, n.	Lokla
Dismiss, tr.	Lokto
Return, intr.	Lishche
Make return, tr.	Lishto
Increase in height, n. = grow	Jongche. Jongta dum
Heighten it	Jongto
Heighten me. Make me grow	Jongsung
Increase, in bulk, n., or Increase thyself = grow	*H*onta dum *H*onche ‡
Increase it, tr., in bulk, tr.	*H*onto (hard h), or *H*onta thumto.
Increase me in bulk	*H*onsung
Increase in length, n.	Phinche. Phinta dum
Lengthen it	Phinto. Phinta páko
Lengthen me	Phinsung
Decrease of all sorts, n.	Yáng. Yánglá
Decrease it	Yáng pingko
Add to, tr.	Khapto, khapche, khapsung
Deduct from, tr.	Yángto, yángche, yángsung
Cultivate (land), tr.	Vik ye' ko § (Yekko, conj. xi.)
Cultivate it for me or my land	Vik yeksung

* So also Bek' = enter, is *come* in, and Bek'la is *go* in.
† Thongto gives normally the double causal thongpingko.
‡ Italic *H* is a guttural. The two phrases are synonymous.
§ This word means "clear the jungle," and alone suffices to show the state of the country and of the people.

Cultivate it for him or his land	Vik yekto
Cultivate for self	Vik yekche
Dig, tr.	Dūko (conj. x.)
Dig for self Dig thy own	} Dūnche
Dig for him, dig his field	Dūto (conj. vi.)
Dig me, for me, my field	Dūsung
Cause to dig or be dug	Dū pingko
Cause thyself to dig or cause thy own field to be dug	Dū pingche
Cause him to dig for another, or another's field to be dug for him	Dū pingto
Cause me to dig or my field to be dug, or (if the field spoke) me to be dug	Dū pingśung
Dig not	Thá dū
Cause not to dig	Dū thá ping or Thá dū ping
Plough, tr.	Ru'ko (Ruk-ko, conj. xi.)
Plough for self	Rukche
Plough for him	Rukto
Plough for me, or (if the field spoke) plough me	Ruksung
Plough not	Thá ruk'
Plough not for self or plough not thy own field	Thá rukche
Cause not to plough or be ploughed	Thá ruk' ping
Sow, tr.	Chho'ko (chhok-ko) chhoksung, chhokche, chhokto (conj. xi.)
Cause to sow or be sown	Chhok'pingko
Cause not to sow, or be sown	Chhok'tháping
Sow for me or sow me *	Chhok'sung
Sow me not or sow not for me	Thá chhok'gno
Transplant, tr.	Luphto (Lusto) lussung, lusche (conj. vii.)
Transplant not	Thá lut'
Cause to transplant or to be transplanted	Lut'pingko
Reap, tr.	Peshto, pessung, pesche
Reap not	Thá pet'
Cause to reap or to be reaped	Pet'ping ko
Cause not to reap or be reaped	Pet'thá ping
Gather, pluck (flowers), *not* greens, tr.	Tūko, tūsung, tūnche, tuto { tūko and sōko are of conj. x.
Gather not	Thá tū
Gather (cotton) Pluck (fruit) } tr.	Seko, sēsung, sēnche, seto
Gather not (cotton)	Thá sē
Gather (greens), tr.	Peshto (see reap)
Pluck up by roots, tr.	Photo phosung, phonche
Eradicate not	Thá photo
Fell—tree, tr.	Phōko, phōsung phōche (conj. x.)
Fell not—tree	Thápho
Breed cattle, tr.	Tunko, tunsung, tunche, tunto
Breed not	Thátun
Slaughter cattle, tr.	Sisto (kill). Yukto (cut)
Graze, intr. and tr.	Gupche, intr. Gupto, tr.
Flay or decorticate, tr.	Tá'ko (takko), taksung, takche, takto (conj. xi.)

* Sow me (what the seed would say) is the true grammatical sense. But the other i widely, nay alone, in use, the constructio ad sensum still overruling the grammar.

Flay not	Thá tak'
Peel fruit	Keko, kesung, keche, keto (conj. x.)
Shear, tr.	Ye'ko (yekko), yeksung, yekche, yekto (conj. xi.)
Shear not	Thá yek'
Buy, ac. intr.	Ingche *
Buy it, tr.	Ingko, ingsung, ingche, ingto
Cause to buy or be bought	Ing pingko
Buy it not	Thá ing
Buy not for him	Thá ingto
Buy me or for me †	Ingsung
Do thou thyself buy it or buy it for thyself	Ingche
Buy it for him	Ingto (Ingkto) ‡
Buy it	Ingko
Sell, tr.	Thamto
Cause to sell or to be sold	Thampingko
Sell me or for me	Thamsung
Sell thyself or for thyself, or thy own	Thamche
Sell him, it, or for him or his	Thamto
Sell not	Thá thamto
Exchange or change, ac. intr.	Jyapche (see Buy)
Exchange it	Jya'po (Jyap po, conj. viii.)
Exchange me or it for me	Jyap'sung
Exchange it for him	Jyap'to ‡
Exchange not	Thá jyap'che
Exchange it not	Thá jyap'
Exchange it not for him	Thá jyap'to
Exchange me not or not for me	Thá jyapmo
Lend, tr.	Pénku háto, hásung, háṉche
Borrow, intr.	Pénku lasche (see Buy), lassung, lasto
Pay debt, tr.	Theṉgko, phengsung, phengche, phengto
Pay not	Thá pheṉg
Count, tr.	Hito, hisung, hinche, hito (conj. vi.)
Count not	Thá hito
Measure or weight, tr.	Po'ko (pokko), poksung, pokche, pokto
Weigh not	Thá pok'
Plaster, tr.	Súto, súsung, súṉche. Súto (conj. vi.)
Make house, tr.	Kem páko
Make clothes, tr.	Jéwa piko, pisuṉg, piṉche, pito
Make not clothes	Jéwa thá pi
Make clothes for me	Jéwa pisung
Make for self	Jéwa píṉche
Make for him	Jéwa pito
Spin, tr.	Chingko, chingsung, chingche, chingto §
Spin not	Thá ching

* See Eat and Take, and Exchange and Drink, &c. In every act, of which the result returns to self, this form is preferred to the transitive. The French tongue affords a good clue.

† I have already said that buy me seems to be the truer sense, whence the passive ingsungmi, I was bought. But in the class of transitives to which ingko belongs, ingsungmi is also the present and future tense of the active voice, viz., I buy it or will buy it. Ingche, the intransitive, gives ingchung mi in both tenses, I buy (*i.e.*, will buy) and I bought.

‡ This form solves the difficulty as to two transitive signs following a verbal root, and enables me often to reach the primitive monosyllabic type of words—a thing of the highest import to special and general philology. [This note should stand, if at all, as a mere query.]

§ Chingko and pungko are conjugated like pingko, which see in the sequel.

Weave, tr.	Pungko, pungsung, pungche, pungto *
Weave not	Thápúng
Sew, tr.	Piko (conj. x.)
Sew not	Thá pí (conj. x.)
Grind, tr.	Réko, résung, rénche, réto
Work mine, tr.	Khání dúko (dig)
Work iron, tr.	Khakchingto'po (beat) topsung, topche, topto
Work wood, tr.	Sing chu'ko (chukko) (plane) chyuksung, chukche, chukto
Work clay, tr.	Kō chyáko (knead) chyásung, chyásche, chyáto (conj. x.)
Cook, tr.	Khōko, khōsung, khosche, khōto (conj. x.)
Be cooked = be ripe, be prepared, n.	Min, minko, minche, minto
Boil, tr. (see Cook)	Khóko
Boil not	Thá khó
Roast, tr.	Súnko. Like pingko
Ditto for me	Súnsung
Ditto for self	Sunche
Ditto for another	Súnto
Gril, fry, tr.	Chūko, chūsung, chūnche, chūto (conj. x.)
Cut, tr.	Yukto (conj. vi.)
Cut not	Thá yukto
Cut me or for me	Yuksung
Cut thyself or for thyself	Yukche
Perforate, tr.	Sasto, sasche, sassung (conj. vii.)
Pierce (being), tr.	Chhepto, chhepche, chhepsung
Tear, tr.	Jito, jisung, jinche, jito (conj. vi.)
Tear thy own, tear for thyself, tear thyself	Jinche
Split, tr.	Hakto. Chi'to chisung, chiche, haksung, hakche, hakto
Break, tear (long things), tr.	Chi'ko (chik'-ko), chiksung, chikche, chikto
Break it, in pieces	*K*heto, *k*hesung, *k*henche (conj. vi.)
Burst it (round things), tr.	*K*heto, *k*hesung, *k*henche (conj. vi.)
Be broken or be burst, n.	Jik'. Jiklá. Kélá or Ré
Brew, tr.	Swe pophto, possung, posche, posto
Distil, tr.	Bukchápáko
Filtrate. Deficate, tr.	Chi'po (chippo), chipsung, chipche, chipto
Be sharp, n.	Yep
Sharpen, tr.	Yep'pingko. Chho'po. Chho'ppo gives chhopsung, chhopche, chhopto
Be blunt, n.	Gnun
Blunten. Make blunt, tr.	Gnúto, gnúsung gnúnche (conj. vi.)
Shake, tr.	Hokto, Hoksung, hokche (conj. vi.)
Move, n.	Duk'
Move it, tr.	Thukto, thuksung, thukche (conj. vi.)
Be still, n. (= move not)	Thá duk'
Make still, tr.	Thá thukto
Contain or hold (= Be contained and contain it)	Vek, vekche, n. Vekto, tr.

* Chingko and pungko are conjugated like pingk.

Make contain or cause to be contained	Vek pingko
Retain, sustain, tr.	Dōko. Doche. Dosung (conj. x.)
Retain, intr.	Donche
Cause to retain	Dot'pingko
Ooze out, n.	Jot'
Make ooze out	Jot'pingko
Stop it oozing out	Rúto, rúsung, rún̲che (conj. vi.)
Be full—belly (fill own belly), intr.	Tamche
Fill it—belly, tr.	Tamto, tamsung, tamche, tamto
Be full—vessel	Chin̲che. Dam. Phul dum
Fill it—vessel	Damto, dampingko, Phul páko, Chinko
Be empty, n.	Póláng dum
Empty it, tr.	Póláng páko
Shine, as sun, n.	Kák'. Chok'
Flow, as water	Gikla. Dengla. Gik'. Deng *
Cause to flow	Gik pingko. Deng pingko
Blow, as wind, intr.	Hujum pon̲che
Grow, as tree, ac. intr.	Liche
Cause to grow, or grow it	Lito, lisung, liche, lito
Decay, rot, n.	Rila. Méla
Make decay	Rit' pingko. Met' pingko
Flower, n.	But'
Cause to flower	But' pingko
Fruit, n.	Sé
Cause to fruit	Set'phá'to (phasto), vel pingko
Be ripe, n.	Min
Ripen, tr.	Minko, minsung, minche, minto
Ripen it for him	Minto
Be raw, n.	Chhálang-no-dum †
Make raw, tr.	Chhálang páko, posung, pán̲che, páto
Be cold (things only), intr.	Khimche
Make cold, tr.	Khimto, khimsung, khimche, khimto
Be hot, intr., n.	Jéche. Jekhomdum or pon̲che
Heat it, tr.	Jéto. Jekhom páko. Jeto gives jesung, jen̲che, jeto (conj. vi.)
Be luminous, n.	Dang dang dum or pon̲che
Make luminous	Dang dang páko
Be dark, n.	Kung kung dum or pon̲che
Darken it, tr.	Kung kung páko
Light it (candle), tr.	Náko, násung, náche, náto
Light, intr. (Be lighted)	Náche
Kindle it (fire), tr.	Du'po (duppo), dupsung, dupche (conj. viii.), dupto. Josto, jossung, josche, josto
Kindle / Be kindled / Kindle thyself } n. or ac. intr.	Josche. Dupche
Burn, *i.e.*, destroy by fire, tr.	Yemto, yemsung, yemche, yemto
Be burnt (=go burnt), n.	Yemla
Burn thyself or burn it for self, ac. intr.	Yemche
Burn, corpse, tr.	Umto, umsung, umche, umto (conj. vi.)
Bury, corpse, tr.	*Kh*umpo, khumsung, khumche, khumto
Melt, n.	Yekla (see Run)
Melt it, tr.	Ye'ko (yekko; see Cultivate, conj. xi.)
Cause to melt	Yek pingko

* Lá added merely conveys the additional motion of fromness.
† Nó=be. Dum=become.

Congeal, n.	Ningla.* Nengla
Congeal it, tr.	Ningto. Nengto
Congeal thyself	Nengche
Congeal me	Nengsung
Cause to congeal	Ningpingko
Share out, apportion, tr.	Pleko, plesung, pleche (conj. x.), pleto
Bring together, collect, tr.	Ko'na páko. Hupto
Collect for thyself, intr.	Hupche
Collect for me or me, p.	Hupsung
Separate, tr.	Gégé páko
Divide, tr.	Thúto, thusung, thunche
Scatter, tr.	Hampo
Join, what broken, tr.	Thuphto (Thusto) thussung, thusche (conj. vii.)
Disjoin, undo, tr.	Chháko, chhásung, chháche, chháto (conj. x.)
Mix, tr.	Khunto, khunsung, khunche
Unmix, tr.	Thoto, thosung, thonche (conj. vi.)
Save (money), tr.	Hupto, hupsung, hupche (conj. vi.)
Squander, tr.	Hopto, hopsung, hopche (conj. vi.)
Spread, tr.	Poko, posung, poche. Hámpo, hámsung, hámche
Fold, tr.	Khóko, khósung, khóche
Be shut, intr., or shut thyself	Thikche
Shut it, tr.	Thikto (conj. vi.)
Be open, open for thyself, intr.	Honche †
Open it, tr.	Honko, like pingko
Press, squeeze, compress it, tr.	Napto (conj. vi.)
Compressed be, or compress thyself or compress with own hand	Napche (conj. vi.)
Depress, tr.	Phimto (conj. vi.)
Be depressed, depress for thyself	Phimche (conj. vi.)
Express, tr.	Pelto (conj. vi.)
Be expressed, intr.	Pelche (conj. vi.)
Turn over carefully, tr.	Lo'ko (Lok-ko), Loksung, Lok-che, Lok-to
Turn topsy-turvy. Put in disorder	Khúlim, khulim, páko
Spread in sun to dry (grain), tr.	Blento or Bento, blensung, blenche
Roll up, tr.	Ku'ko (Kukko), kuksung, kukche, kukto (conj. xi.)
Unroll, tr.	Chháko, chhasung, chhache, chhato (conj. x.)
Be loose, be slack, n.	Woso dum. Woso ponche
Loosen, slacken, tr.	Woso páko, posung, pánche, páto
Be tight	Khwa, s., ta dum
Tighten thy own or for thyself	Khwásche
Tighten, tr.	Khwá, s., to khwassung, khwasche (conj. vii.)
Cause to tighten	Khwat'pingko
Gird thy loins, a. intr.	Kikche
Bind, tr.	Pángto, pánsung, pánche. Wampo, wamsung, wamche, wamto
Unbind, tr.	Chháko (see Unroll)
Pack, tr.	Khuli páko
Unpack, tr.	Khuli chháko
Load, tr.	Ku pingko
Unload, tr.	Khuli táko, tosung, tánche (conj. x.), táto

* E and i, like o and u, are constantly commuted.
† Thikche and honche, shut thyself, and open thyself, addressed to the door.

Put on, tr.	Cho'ko (chokko), choksung, chokche, chokto (conj. xi.)
Take off, tr.	Luko, lusung, luche, luto (conj. x.)
Take off (from fire)	Yo'po, yoppo, yopsung, yopche, yopto (conj. viii.)
Put in, insert, tr.	Kheko, khesung, kheche, kheto (conj. x.)
Take out, tr.	Thophto (thosto), thossung, thosche (conj. vii.)
Pour in, tr.	Kheko, khesung, kheche, kheto (conj. x.) Chosto, chhossung, chhosche (conj. vii.)
Catch as poured in, tr.	Doko, dosung, doche (conj. x.)
Pour out on ground, tr.	Lukto
Suspend, tr.	Chisto, chissung, chische. Veko, vesung, veche, veto
Take down what suspended, tr.	Luko, lusung, luche, luto (conj. x.)
Take hold of, tr.	Chhuko, chhusung, chhusche, chhuto (conj. x.)
Quit hold of, tr.	Teshto, tesche, tessung (conj. vii.)
Throw, tr.	Jupto, jupsung, jupche
Catch as thrown, tr.	Doko, dosung, doche, doto
Stay, stop, intr.	Thikche
Stay it, stop it, tr.	Thikto
Stop me	Thiksung
Let go, tr.	Lat'pingko
Enable to go, tr.	Lat'pháto (phasto)
Be clean, n.	Wóta dum. Wóche
Make clean, tr.	Wóto, wósung, wóche (conj. vi.)
Wash—things only, tr.	Chhunko
Wash thy own, intr.	Chhunche
Wash me or mine, p.	Chhunsung
Rub or rub it, tr.	Khisto
Rub thy own or rub simply, intr.	Khische
Rub me or mine	Khissung
Be polished	Liku poṉche
Polish it, tr.	Liku páko
Polish it for thyself	Liku páṉche
Cover, tr.	Rumto. Supto
Cover thyself	Rumche. Supche
Cover me	Rumsung. Supsung
Uncover, tr.	Hoṉko, hongsung, honche, hongto
Uncover thyself or thy own	Hongche
Shoot, with arrow, gun, tr.	Wo'po (wop-po). Wopsung, wopche (conj. viii.)
Shoot me or for me	Wopsung
Shoot thyself or for thyself	Wopche
Shoot it for him, tr.	Wopto
Stone, hit with stone, tr.	Chásto, chassung, chasche
Wring its neck, tr.	*Khi*'po (khippo), khipsung, khipche, khipto
Wring not its neck	Thá *khip*'
Wring clothes, tr.	Pelto, pelsung, pelche
Wring not clothes	Thá pelto
Twist rope, tr.	*Khi*'po * (Khippo, conj. viii.)
Untwist rope, tr.	Chháko (see Loosen)
Resemble, be like	Tosche. Totvi dum

* In Newari Khipo is used only substantively, a rope. Just so the root kai means the hand and to grasp in Telegu and Tamil, but to grasp only in Newari. Whosoever will *thus* search may discover the true extent, quoad words, of Turanian affinities, not otherwise. See Tire.

Cause to resemble or liken simply	Tophto (tosto). Totvi páko
Cause to cause to resemble, or cause to liken	Tot'pingko
Be unlike	Máng totvi dum
Make unlike	Máng totvi páko
Be white, n. (things, animals)	Dáwáng dum. Dáwáng ponche
Be white (rationals only)	Bochho dum, ponche
Whiten it, tr.	Dáwáng páko
Whiten him, tr.	Bochho páko
Whiten me	Dáwáng, or bochho, posung
Whiten thyself or it for thyself, or do thou thyself whiten him or it	Dáwáng, or bochho, pánche
Whiten it for him	Dáwáng páto
Be ripe (fruits)	Jí
Make ripe (ditto)	Jíto, jisung, jínche
Be ripe (grains)	Min
Make ripe (ditto)	Minko, minsung, minche, minto
Be wet or wet thyself	Ná'-che (nasche) (conj. vii.)
Wet it	Ná'to, nasto, nassung, nasche (conj. vii.)
Cause it to be wetted	Nat'pingko
Be dry (things only)	Dung
Dry it	Dung pingko
Dry it in sun	Boko or bloko,* blosung, blosche, blosto
Dry it at fire	Sungko, sungsung, sungche, sungto
Be flavoursome	Chhumche
Flavour it, tr.	Chhumto, chhumsung, chhumche
Be sweet, n.	Chhinji,† dum or ponche
Sweeten it, tr.	Chhinji, thumto or páko
Be sour	Jusche
Make sour	Justo
Be bitter	Khásche
Make bitter	Khásto, khasto, khassung, khasche (conj. vii.)
Be knotted, intr.	Rupche
Knot it, tr.	Rupto
Be great, n.	*H*on (Khon)
Make great, tr.	*H*onto. *H*onta thumto
Be heavy, intr.	Lishche. Lishtadum
Make heavy, tr.	Lishto. Lit pháto
Be light (levis)	Oksáng dum
Make light, tr.	Oksáng páko
Be hard, intr.	Chamche
Harden it, tr.	Chamto, chamsung, chamche
Cause to harden or to be hardened	Champingko
Be soft	Nalcho dum
Soften it, tr.	Nalcho pako
Be crooked	Khokche. Khokta dum
Crook it, tr.	Kho'ko. Khokko, khoksung, khokche khokto Khokta thumto

9. *Adverbs and Prepositions compared.*

Come, n.	Phi'
Come in	Bhitarí phi'. Bek'

---

* Every initial labial followed by a vowel admits ad libitum of an interposed liquid, thus boko vel bloko and so bekto vel blekto = write. I may here add that v and y are constantly used both to keep apart concurring vowels and to facilitate the utterance of initial vowels.

† For chhinji, sweetness, read chhinjimu, sweet.

Come out	Tongmaphi'. Lok'
Come back, to rear	Nongna phi' or ponche
Come on, to front	Hanko phi'. Honko ponche
Come up	Lonkha or Wanhe phi'. Jok'
Come down	Yonkha or Huthe phi'. Yu' *
Come back=return	Khálip phi' or Lische
Come again	Gessa phi
Come once	Kophi phi
Come twice	Nakphi phi
Come thrice	Chhukphi phi
Come four times	Blikphi phi
Come at once or in one place or together	Kolube phi
Come at once, at one time	Kophe phi
Come near	Khewa phi
Come close	Ko'na phi
Come apart	Gege phi
Come far away	Kholám phi
Come with	Ko'na phi
Come with me	Ang nung phi
Come alone	Chhále phi
Come without me—thee—him	Angmá nosa phi'. Ungmá nosa phi'. Ámá nosa phi
Come towards me—thee—him	Ang rek phi'. Ung rek phi'. Wathim rek phi
Come up to me, as far as my position	Ang bong phi
Come as far as this—that	I'nung bong phi. Minung bong phi'
Come quickly	Wáliga phi
Come slowly	Pomba or Pombana phi'
Come by and by, after awhile	Omophe phi'
Come silently	Giwonba phi'
Come noisily	Tamnitam phi'
Come early	Honko phi'
Come at sunrise	Nomoloksinge phi'
Come at sunset	Nomo thip singhe phi'
Come late	Nongna phi'
Come loiteringly	Gá'gát'ha phi'
Come over—by top	Wani phi'. Wanim khen phi'. Khakkhakha phi'
Come under—by under way	Hutti phi. Hutim khen phi'
Come through, between	Mádumna phi
Come across	Thekche phi † or Thek thekha phi
Come to this—that side	Imba phi. Homba phi
Come constantly	Phina phi ponche
Come sometimes	Kophi nakphi phi
Come ever	No such phrase
Come never	Hákhele ‡ thápbi'
Never come again	Hákhele gessa thaphi
Come by this side	Inikhen phi
Come by that side	Mini—wathim—khenphi
Come to the right	Jájábe phi
Come by the left	Khánja khen phi
Come from the west	Nomothip lung khen phi
Come to the east	Nomolok lung be phi
Come towards the east	Nomolok lung rekphi

* The words yū, jok', lok', bek, carry the sense of the adverbs, and would always be used. I have retained phi' to force the expression of separate adverbs as far as possible.

† Equal "to cross and come," that is, crossing come=having crossed come, thek thekha phi. The gerund of present time, thekhe, is never used on such occasions.

‡ Hákhele can only be used with the negative, like jamais in French.

Come towards the west	Nomothiplung rekphi
Go towards the plains	Gágin mulungrek la'la
Go as far as Nepal	Nepal bong lá'lá
Give a little	Yánggnák háto
Give much	Chhinggnák háto
Give secretly	Khinta báha háto
Give openly	Khunta báha háto
Give gladly	Yot'yot'ha or bong ni bong or bong-bongha háto
Give sulkily	Máng yot'yot'ha-háto
Give to-day	Tiri háto
Give mutually	Háhá, pánachhe, pochhe, Duals
Give continually	Hánahá páko
Strike forcibly	Chotiha to'po
Strike gently	Pom hana to'po
A house	Kem
Of a house	Kemmu
To a house	Kem
A house	Kem (no dat. or acc. sign)
In a house	Kem be
From the house	Kem khen
By (inst.) the house	Kem ha.
Inside / Into } the house	Kem bhitari
Outside / Out of } the house	Kem tongma
As far as house	Kem bong
Towards the house	Kem rek
Before the house	Kem honko
Opposite, in front of, the house	Kem kakphang. Kemmu bimli be *
Behind the house / To the rear of house	} Kem nongna. Kem senti be
On, upon, the house	Kem wáni be
Above the house	Kem khen lonkha
From upon house	Kem wáni khen
Beneath house	Kem hutti be
Below the house	Kem khen yonkha
From under house	Kem hutti khen
Near the house	Kem khewa
Far from house	Kem khen kholám
At the house	Kem be
On account of house	Kem mu lisi
In lieu of a house	Kem mu let'chhing
Through the house	Kem mu mádumna
Beyond the house	Kem wathe or kem homba
To right of house	Kem mu jájá
To left of house	Kem mu kháuja
On this side the house	Kem mu imba or kem imba
On that side the house	Kem mu or kem homba
From this side the house	Kem inikhen. Kem imbam khen.
From that side the house	Kem wathí khen. Kem mini khen. Kem hombam khen
With (having) a house	Kem not'he. Kem got'he.
Without (wanting) a house	Kem má not'he. Kem má got'he

* Kem mu bimli be = house of front in; kem senti be = house-back in.

B.—VÁYU GRAMMAR.*

I. *Declension of Pronouns.*

PERSONALS. SINGULAR.

N.	I, Go.
G.	of me, Ang, conjunct = my.† Angmu, disjunct, = mine
D. / Ac.	to me / to } Gó. No sign
L.	{ in, at / into, me } Ang be
Ab.	from me, Ang khen
Ins.	by me, G'há (go-ha)
Soc.	with me, Angnung
Priv.	without me, Ang má nosa‡

DUAL.

N. Gó nakpu, m. f. Gó náyung, n. § Or Gó nakpu, m. Go nangmi, f. Go nóyung, n.

CONJUNCT.

G. Angchi, excl. Ungchi, incl.

DISJUNCT.

G.	Angchimu, excl. Ungchimu, incl.
D. Acc.	Gonakpu, m. f. Gonarguug, n.
L.	Angchi, be, excl. Ungchi be, incl.
Ab.	Angchi khen, excl. Ungchi khen, incl.
Ins.	Gó nakpu ha or or Ghá nakpu ha
Soc.	Angchi nung, excl. Ungchi nung, incl.

PLURAL.

N. Gó khάta

CONJUNCT.

G. Angki, excl. Ungki, incl.

DISJUNCT.

G.	Angkimu, excl. Ungkimu, incl.
D. Ac.	Gó khάta. No sign
L.	Angki be, excl. Ungki be, incl.
Ab.	Angki khen, excl. Ungki khen, incl.
Ins.	Go khata ha or gha khata ha
Soc.	Angkinung, excl. Ungkinung, incl.

---

* Observe that this examination of the Váyu tongue, like the following one of the Bâhing tongue, is divided into (I.) a vocabulary and (II.) a grammatical portion, but that both are so constructed as to complement each other in illustrating the structure of the languages in question.

† Ang, the constructive form of *gó*, means my before a substantive or qualitative used substantively, but before a transitive participle it means me or of me, *e.g.*, ang tovi, who beats me, or the beater of me. Yet ang topchyáng is my club, topchyáng being the neuter form of tovi, used as a noun.

‡ There is no proper privative participle, nor, consequently, case. Ang má nosa or gó má nosa = if I be not, I not being, or my not being (present). In Khas, *man* na bhai; in Newari, ji ma dusa.

§ Nakpo, náyung is the second numeral which is gendered when used apart, but doubtfully I think, and still more so when used as a dual sign. I find, however, nakpu, nangmi, nayung, for the three genders. Also hic et hæc nakpu.

SECOND PERSON.

N.	Gon.
G.	Ung, conjunct., = thy. Ungmu, disjunct., = thine
D. Acc.	Gon. No sign
L.	Ung be
Ab.	Ung khen
Ins.	Gon ha
S.	Ung nung

DUAL.

N.	Gonchhe
G.	Ungchhi, conj. Ungchhimu, disj.
D. Acc.	Gonchhe. No sign
L.	Ungchhi be
Ab.	Ungchhi khen
Ins.	Gonchhe ha
Soc.	Ungchhi nung

THIRD PERSONAL.

N.	Wathi. All three genders
G.	Wathim, conj. Wathimmu, disj.
D. Acc.	Wathi. No sign
L.	Wathim be
Ab.	Wathim khen
Ins.	Wathi ha
Soc.	Wathim nung.

DUAL.

N.	Wathi nakpu, m. Wathi nangmi, f. Wathi nayung, n. c. See note aforegone
G.	Wathim nakpum, conj. / Wathim nakpumu, disj. } m. Wathim nangmim, conj. / Wathim nangmimu, disj. } f. Wathim nayung, conj. / Wathim nayungmu, disj. } n. and c.
D. Acc.	Wathi nakpu, m. Wathi nangmi, f. Wathi nayung, n. and c.
Loc.	Wathim nakpumbe, m. Wathim nangmi be, f. Wathim nayung be, n. and c.
Ab.	Wathim nakpum khen, m. Wathim nangmim khen, f. Wathim nayung khen, n. and c.
Ins.	Wathi nakpu ha, m. Wathi nangmi ha, f. Wathi nayung ha, n. and f.
Soc.	Wathim nakpum nung, m. Wathim nangmim nung, f. Wathim nayung nung, n. and c.

PLURAL.

N.	Wathi kháta, m. f. n.
G.	Wathim khatam, conj. Wathim khatamu, disj.
D. Ac.	Wathi khata.
Loc.	Wathim khata be.
Ab.	Wathim khata khen.
Ins.	Wathi khata ha.
Soc.	Wathim khata nung.

NEAR DEMONSTRATIVE.

N.	Í.* All three genders.
G.	Inung, conj. Inungmu, disj.

---

* Í, this, and mí, that, have the pausing tone which I sometimes represent by doubling the vowel, i i, mi i. The abrupt, as well as the pausing tone, is well developed in Váyu, and also in Kiranti, notwithstanding the pronomenalised, euphonic, and compounding character of the languages.

D. Ac. I'. No sign.
Loc. Inung be.
Ab. Inung khen.
Ins. I'ha.
Soc. Inung nung.

DUAL.

N. Inakpu, m. Inangmi, f. Inayung, n. and c.
G. Inakpum, conj. } m.
Inakpumu, disj. }
Inangmim, conj. } f.
Inangmimu, disj. }
Inayung, conj. } n. and c.
Inayungmu, disj. }
D. Ac. Inakpu, m. Inangmi, f. Inayung, n.
L. Inung nakpumbe, m. Inung nangmimbe, f. Inung nayung be, n.
Ab. Inung nakpum khen, m. Inung nangmim khen, f. Inung nayung khen, n. c.
Ins. Inak poha, m. Inangmi ha, f. Inayung ha, n. and c.
Soc. Inung nakpum nung, m. Inung nangmim nung, f. Inung nayung nung, n. c.

PLURAL.

N. I'khata. All genders.
G. Inung khatam, conj. Inung khatamu, disj.
D. Ac. I'khata.
Loc. Inung khata be.
Abl. Inung khata khen.
Ins. I'khata há.
Soc. Inung khata nung.

REMOTE DEMONSTRATIVE.

N. Mí.* All genders.
G. Minung, conj. Minungmu, disj., &c., as in the last.
Interrogative and distributive pronoun, m. f. Who? Any one. Some person. Su or Suna. Subs. and adj.
N. Sú. Suna.
G. Súm. Súnám, conj. Sumu. Sunamu, disj.
D. Ac. Sú. Suna.
Loc. Súbe, Sunabe.
Abl. Súkhen, Sunakhen.
Ins. Suha, Sunaha.
Soc. Sunung, Sunanung.

DUAL.

N. Su or Suna nakpu, m. Su or Suna nangmi, f., &c., as before.

PLURAL.

N. Sú or Sunakhata, as before.
Interrogative and distributive pronoun, n. What? Any or something.
N. Mische.
G. Mischem, conj. Mischemu, disj., &c.

DUAL.

N. Mische nayung, &c.

PLURAL.

N. Mische khata, &c.
Relative, interrogative, and distributive pronoun and pronominal adjective which, what, who.

---

* See note (*) on previous page.

N. Hánung, m. f. n.
G. Hánung,* conj. Hánungmu, disj., &c.

DUAL.

N. Hanung nakpo, m. Hanung nangmi, f. Hanung navung, n.

G. Hanung nakpum, m. / Hanung nangmim, f. / Hanung nayung, n. } conj.

Hanung nakpumu, / Hanung nangmimu, / Hanung nayungmu, } disj.

And so on, like wathi, except that hanung has no inflexional shape (itself being inflexional). Hence it has hanung nakpo and hanung khata where wathi has wathim nakpo and wathim khata. And this is likewise the case with the possessive pronouns, all of which, though but genitives of the personals, are regarded as independent, and declined like the personals.

Thus also are declined the interrogative and relative of number and quantity, with its correlative, or Háthá, Mitha = how much or many? and so much or many. Thus also the adverbs of time and place, Inhe, here, Wathe and Minhe, there; Hanhe, where? Íthe or Umbe or Abo, now; Míthe, then; Hákhe, when? with all the rest of the adverbs that are not gerunds.

Observe that these adverbs are derived from the demonstratives in the locative case. But where Í, Mí, and Wathi, the pronouns, take the inflexional m, or nung (whence come inungmu and wathimmu = his), the corresponding adverbs have no inflexional mark, but remain immutable, only adding the declensional signs m or mu, be, khen, &c.; and thus we have ithamu and inhemu, of here, and ithakhen, inhekhen, from here, and abomu, of now, abokhen from now, not abommu, abomkhen.

Observe also that the conjunct possessives (genitives of the personals) are indeclinable, but that the disjunct are declinable like the personals. Ang, ung, wathim inung, minung, are inflexional forms merely, therefore angkhen = from me. But angmu is a possessive pronoun proper, whence angmukhen-be-ha = from mine, in mine, by mine.

2. *Declension of Nouns (Substantive).*

I. Substantives Proper.

Lóncho, a man, m.

N. Lóncho
G. Lóncho, conj.† Lónchomu, disj.
D. Ac. Lóncho
L. Lónchobe
Ab. Lónchokhen
Ins. Lónchoha
Soc. Lónchonung

DUAL.

N. Lóncho nakpo ‡

---

* The conjunct form of the genitive of this pronoun has no sign, being marked by position alone, as when two substantives meet is always admissible. Hánung is itself a genitive = of whom, of which, *e.g.*, hanung got ha = of which (and which) hand; hanungmu = whose, apart, or in reply; hanungmu got = the hand of whom; hanung got = which hand.

† The first of two substantives is by position alone a genitive, as loncho got, the man's hand. But apart, it must have the sign, as lonchomu, the man's.

‡ Generally in the Himalayan languages, the dual and plural signs are eschewed in regard to substantives proper, except where ambiguity would arise from omitting them. In regard to appellatives and qualitives used substantively, as all may be, these signs are always annexed, and also those of gender, because such words (and pronouns of the third person also, to which the same rule applies), unlike the former, tell nothing of themselves on these points. Váyu, however, freely applies its dual and plural signs and its sex signs, where it has any, to all nouns and pronouns, though the structure of its verb renders such use of the dual and plural signs superfluous, *e.g.*, béli imchimem, the sheep are sleeping. Newari, though void of such help, lacks a dual and plural of neuters.

G. Lóncho nak pum,* conj. Lóncho nak pumu, disj.
D. Ac. Lóncho nakpo
Loc. Lónchonak pube
Abl. Lóncho nakpukhen
Ins. Lóncho nakpuhá
Soc. Lóncho nakpu nung

PLURAL.

N. Lónchokhata †
G. Lónchokhatam,* conj. Lóncho khatamu, disj.
D. Ac. Lóncho khata
L. Lóncho khabe
Abl. Lóncho khata khen
Soc. Lóncho khata hung

Thus also is declined the feminine noun mescho, a woman; the epicine noun singtong, mankind; and all such without reference to gender. Neuters also are similarly declined. But I add a specimen—

Sing, wood, a neuter.

N. Sing
G. Sing, conj. Singmu, disj., &c.

DUAL.

N. Náng sing (náng is a contraction of Náyung), or
Sing nayung
G. Nang sing, conj. Nang singmu, disj., &c.

PLURAL.

N. Sing khata
G. Sing khata, conj. Sing khatamu, disj., &c.

2d. Participles used substantively. (*Remark.*—When they are used adjectively, which they all are to a great extent, they precede the noun, and are immutable like all other adjectives.)

Tó'vi, he or she who beats, the beater, m. and f.

N. Tó'vi, m. f.
G. Tó'vi, conj. To'vimu, disj.
D. Ac. Tó'vi, &c.

DUAL.

N. Tó'vi nakpu, m. Tó'vi nangmi, f.
G. Tó'vi nakpu, m. conj. Tó'vi nangmi, f. conj. Tó'vi nakpumu, m. disj.
Tó'vi nangmimu, f. disj., &c. as before.

PLURAL.

N. Tó'vi khata, m. f.
G. Tó'vi khata, conj. To'vi khatamu, disj., &c., as before
Topchyáng, neuter of the above, what one strikes with, as club, stick, &c.
N. Topchyáng
G. Topchyáng, conj. Topchyángmu, disj., &c.

DUAL.

N. Nang topchyáng.
G. Nang topchyáng, conj. Nang topchyángmu, disj., &c.

PLURAL.

N. Topchyáng khata
G. Topchyáng khata, conj. Topchyáng khatamu, disj., &c.

---

* We should rather read nakpu and khata for the reason given in a prior note. Yet my informants, though they never apply the genitive to the conjunct form of this case in the singular, do so in the dual and plural.

† See note (‡) on previous page.

So also Topta, who or what has been beaten, m. f. n., with the requisite adaptation of nakpu, nangmi or náng (náyung) in the dual.

3d. Qualitives used substantively, *e.g.*,
Khakchhing-wo, m.
Khakchhing-mi, f.
Khakchhing-mu, n. and c.
} =the black one, being or thing.

This and all the like are declined as above. And so also are the qualitives which substitute the formative "cho" for "wo" in the masculine, as bang-cho, a mature man; bing-cho, a handsome man, &c. The feminines of these are in "mi," as in the last. They have no neuters in this form, but they can superadd the usual m. f. n. signs, as bang-cho-wo, a mature man; bang-cho-mi, a mature woman; bang-cho-mu, a mature thing; and then of course they have the complete hic, hæc, hoc of gender.

4th. The numerals, inclusive of the adverbial ones.

5th. Derivative qualitives formed from abstracts, as Daksa-wo, the covetous man; daksa-mi, the covetous woman, from daksa, covetousness. Choti-wo, the strong man; choti-mi, the strong woman; choti-mu, the strong thing, from choti, strength. Suksa-wo, the hungry man; suksa-mi, the hungry woman, from suksa, hunger; and all such.

6th. Nominal as well as pronominal genitives, which, with the m or mu formative, are all treated as distinct substantives, *e.g.*, singmumu, the wooden one. (*Remark.*—The cacophonous iteration of the mu (though often truncated in the second syllable, singmum), owing to the coincidence of the genitival and formative signs, makes the use of such words rare when a possessive case meaning must be assigned to them. They are used, however, freely in all other cases.)

7th. Simple or compound words indicating one's country, profession, or avocation, and the like, and which are not expressed participially,* form yet another class of substantives, as Chhugong-wo=a Bhotia, or native of Tibet; Chhugong-mi, a Bhotini, or female of Tibet; Héngong-wo (m.); Hengong-mi (f.), a male and female of Nepal proper; Gyétimnamsang-wo-mi, a male and female stranger or foreigner; Rukcho-wo-mi, a male and female ploughman; Bóchhó-wo-mi, a male and female European (white-body); Gáginmulung-wo-mi, a male and female of the plains. In short, nouns of whatever sort (and the above enumeration has been made here, though not strictly germain to declension, expressly to show the various sorts of nouns and their mode of construction), and pronouns also, wherever used substantively or disjunctly, and therefore declinable, all follow the above single form of declension. And, on the other hand, every noun and pronoun when used conjunctly, that is, preceding a substantive which is thereby qualified, is always indeclinable, and, for the most part, altogether unchangeable, having no expressed grammatical affections whatever, the signs of genders being neglected in use even where they exist. Indeed, qualifying and qualified words seem to be as much as possible regarded as constituting a single compound term; and, the more effectually to ensure this, one of the two elements (the one that goes first in the compound) is customarily truncated; thus rísa, a plantain, and singphum, a tree, make rísaphum; and topmung, to strike, and rámum, I fear, make toprámum. And so also the inflexional forms of the personal pronouns which are used as qualifying or adjectival words, are to be regarded as quasi agglutinated and perfectly immutable prefixes of the substantive, entirely distinct from the correspondent pronouns of the possessive kind, which latter stand apart and are liable to declensional changes after the above model, like all other qualitives used substantively or disjunctly.

* The participles (in vi, ta, and táng), being inherently relative, assume a substantival character without the necessity of affixing the usual appellative formatives in wo vel cho and mi, though these may be superadded, if to mark the sex of the agent be specially required. Thus to'vi, the striker, the he or she who strikes, is not only an adjective, as to'vi ta'wo, the beating boy, but an independent noun, the beater. Nevertheless, would you specify the sex, you can say to'vi-wo, the male striker, and to'vi-mi, the female striker.

VAYU VERBS.

First.—Conjugation of neuters, conjugated from the sheer root.
Verb *Phi*, to come.

Infinitive Mood.

Affirmative.—Phit'mung, to come or to have come, aoristic.*
Negative.—Máng phit'mung, not to come, &c.

Gerunds.

Phit'he } Present. Coming { Phit'he, with verbs in present tense.
Phit'nung } { Phit'nung, with verbs in preterite.
Phit'hephit'he, or Phit'nung phit'nung, continuative present.
Phit'phit'ha. Past, having come.
Phit'singhe. Present or Future, when coming.
Phit'khen. Past, after coming, after having come.

Participles.

Phit'vi. Present and future, who or what comes or will come. Also the comer substantival.
Phis'ta. Past, who or what has come or came.
Phit'táng, Verbal nouns, Phit'chyang, Phit'lung, Phit'sing, } These forms, expressing respectively *passive* futurity or fitness or habit, and instrumentality, locality, and time, are hardly or not at all useable, save with verbs more or less transitive. See on to them in sequel.
N.B.—The medial t' and s' are merely enunciative, not formative.

Imperative Mood.

Singular.	*Dual.*	*Plural.*
Phi	Phichhe	Phine
	Negative.	
Thá phi	Thá phichhe	Thá phine

Indicative Mood.

Future tense, used also for present.

	Singular.	*Dual.*	*Plural.*
1.	Phignom	Phi chhokmi, excl.	Phíkokmi, excl.
		Phi chhikmi, incl.	Phíkem, incl.
2.	Phími	Phi chhikmi	Phínem
3.	Phimi	Phi chhikmi	Phímem

Preterite tense.

	Singular.	*Dual.*	*Plural.*
1.	Phísungmi	Phí chhongmi, excl.	Phi kikóngmi, excl.
		Phí chhingmi, incl.	Phí kikengmi, incl.
2.	Phími	Phí chhem	Phínem
3.	Phími	Phí chhem	Phímem

Subjunctive Mood.

Present tense.

	Singular.	*Dual.*	*Plural.*
1.	Phigno } nam or sa	Phi chhoknam, excl.	Phi koknam, excl.
		Phi chhiknam, incl.	Phí kenam, incl.
2.	Phi-nam-sa	Phi chhiknam	Phine nam
3.	Phi-nam-sa	Phi chhiknam	Phime nam

---

* The infinitive is also used adjectively, and is nearly the same as the participle in "tang," *e.g.*, phitmunglom or khokmunglom, a way to go by, an accesaible road; khoktanglom, a walkable road, a road fit for walking.

Preterite.

1. Phisung phen	Phí chhong phen, excl. / Phi chhing phen, incl.	Phí ki kóng phen, excl. / Phi ki keng phen, incl.
2. Phí phen	Phi chhe phen	Phi ne phen
3. Phí phen	Phi chhe phen	Phi me phen

INTERROGATIVE MOOD.

Present tense.

Singular.

1. Phigno ki má
2. Phí ki má
3. Phí ki má

And so on, as in the subjunctive; that is, the terminal m or mi is dropped, and ki má, = or not, is added in lieu of the subjunctive signs, nam or sa and phen.

NEGATIVE MOOD.

There is no separate negative verb.

The affirmative verb is conjugated with má, the particle of negation, before it, Má phi gnom, Má phi sungmi, &c.

POTENTIAL MOOD.

Singular.

1. Phit' phas chungmi
2. Phit' phas chem
3. Phit' phas chem

For all tenses, phasche being aoristic except in dual and plural. Phasche, the reflex form of the verb phá, is conjugated with the root phi to express power. For phasche see im'che in sequel, or 5th conjugation.

PRECATIVE MOOD.

Singular.

Present.	*Preterite.*
1. Phi gnó yu	Phisung yu
2. Phi yu	Phi yu
3. Phi yu	Phi yu

Drops the final m or mi of the ordinary verb, and substitutes for it the immutable verbal participle yú.

Another form of the precative mood, equivalent to that which is usually joined with the imperative in English (let me come, come thou, let him come, &c.), is formed by compounding the infinitive of the main verb with the verb to give, used as an auxiliary, thus (omitting the 2d person, or imperative proper, which never can be mixed with any other mood):

Singular.	*Dual.*	*Plural.*
1. Phimsung hásung	Phimung háchgong	Phimung hátikong
3. Phimung háto	Phimung hátochhe	Phimung hátome

The first ordinary form of the precative may be best rendered in English by O! that I may or might come, &c.; this, by, let me come, let him come, &c., literally, give me to come, give him to come, and so on for the dual and plural according to the model of transitives in "to" in sequel.

OPTATIVE MOOD.

Singular.

1. Phit' dakgnom	Phit' daksungmi
2. Phit' dakmi	Phit' dángmi
3. Phit' dakmi	Phit' dángmi

And so on throughout the verb dak, to desire or want, which see in sequel. The root of the primary verb is prefixed.

Remark.—Duty, necessity, and propriety, as well as desire, are expressed by this mood, often in the impersonal form, mihi oportet vel decet, thus, go phit dakmi, I must, I ought to, come, it is necessary or proper for me to come; you can also say, go phitmung noh'ka, it is good for me to come.

INCHOATIVE MOOD.

Singular.

1. Phit' teschungmi
2. Phit' teschem
3. Phit' teschem

And so on, according to the paradigm of intransitives in che; this mood being constructed from the root of the main verb and the reflex form of the verb to begin.

FINITIVE MOOD.

Singular.	
1. Phit' chuschungmi	And so on, as before noted, chusche being the reflex form of the verb to end.
2. Phit' chuschem	
3. Phit' chuschem	

CAUSAL MOOD.

Present.	*Preterite.*	
1. Phit' pingsungmi	Phit' ping kungmi	And so on, for dual and plural, throughout the verb pingko, which see. The root of the primary verb is prefixed.
2. Phit' pingmi	Phit' ping kum	
3. Phit' pingmi	Phit' ping kum	

CONTINUATIVE MOOD.

Present tense.

Singular.	*Dual.*	*Plural.*
1. Phína phit'nognom	Phína phit'nochhokmi Phína phit'nochhikmi	Phína phit'nokokmi Phína phit'nokem
2. Phína phit'nonum	Phína phit'nochhikmi	Phína phit'nonem
3. Phína phit'nomi	Phína phit'nochhikmi	Phína phit'nomem

Preterite.

1. Phína phit'nosungmi	Phína phit'nochhongmi Phína phit'nochhingmi	Phína phit'nokikongmi Phína phit'nokikengmi
2. Phína phit'nonum	Phína phit'nochhem	Phína phit'nonem
3. Phína phit'nomi	Phína phit'nochhem	Phína phit'nomem

RECIPROCAL MOOD.

Present tense.

1. Phina phit'pánchung-mi	Phina phit'pánachhokmi Phina phit'pánachhikmi	Phina phit'páchikokmi Phina phit'pachikem
2. Phina phit'pánchem	Phina phit'pánachhikmi	Phina phit'páchinem
3. Phina phit'pánchem	Phina phit'pánachhikmi	Phina phit'páchimem

Preterite.

1. Phina phit'pánchung-mi	Phina phit'pánachhongmi Phina phit'pánachhingmi	Phina phit'páchikongmi Phina phit'páchikengmi
2. Phina phit'pánchem	Phina phit'pánachhem	Phina phit'páchinem
3. Phina phit'pánchem	Phina phit'pánachhem	Phina phit'páchimem

Remark.—Of the above two the first mood is formed by the root repeated with intervening reflex sign, and the substantive verb nó, to be. The second is formed by the same treatment of the root and the reflex form of the verb pá, to do, for which see conjugation V. The second, or reciprocal mood, is hardly useable in the singular number.

According to this paradigm of the neuter verb to come, are conjugated also the verbs gá, to be dilatory; jí, to ripen (fruit); rí, to rot; sé, to fruit; gó, to live; yú, to descend; ví, to be intoxicated; phwé, to quarrel; and, in a word, all words presenting a sheer root in the imperative, and which are all neuters. Essentially the same is the conjugation of neuters having added to the sheer root a conjunct and now (quoad force or meaning) obsolete consonant,* which consonant, however, according as it is labial, guttural, or dental, occasions some slight variations in the form of conjugation. Nasal endings make no change (*e.g.*, dong gnom, dongmi dongmi). I subjoin a sample of each variation.

Second.—Conjugation of neuters with a conjunct guttural, dak', to desire (da-k).

* Compare the so-called "euphonic additions" to the root in the cultivated Dravidian tongues.

INFINITIVE MOOD.

Affirmative.	Dakmung,	ut supra.
Negative.	Máng dakmung,	

Gerunds.		*Participles.*		
Dak he	ut supra.	Dakvi		ut supra.
Dak nung		Dakta		
Dak he dak he		Daktang		
Dak dak ha		Verbal nouns		
Dak sing he		Dak chyang	not useable.	
Dak khen		Dak lung		
		Dák sing		

The negative of all is formed as in the infinitive, máng dak he, máng dak vi, &c.

IMPERATIVE MOOD.

Singular.	*Dual.*	*Plural.*
Dak'	Dakchhe	Dángue
	Negative Imperative.	
Thá dak	Thá dakchhe	Thá dángne

INDICATIVE MOOD.

Present Tense.

	Singular.	*Dual.*	*Plural.*
1.	Dak gnom	Dak chhokmi, excl. / Dak chhikmi, incl.	Dak kokmi, excl. / Dak kem, incl.
2.	Dakmi	Dak chhikmi	Daknem
3.	Dakmi	Dak chhikmi	Dakmem

Preterite.

1.	Daksungmi	Dak chhongmi / Dak chhingmi	Dak'ki kongmi, or Dáki kongmi / Dak'ki kengmi, or Dáki-kengmi
2.	Dángmi	Dak chhem	Dak nem or Dángnem
3.	Dángmi	Dak chhem	Dakmem

This conjugation changes the radical k into ng, and lengthens the vowel.

The other moods as before.

Thus are conjugated buk', to get up; bok', to be born; bek', to enter; lok', to issue, to appear; gik', to flow; kák', to shine (sun); chok', to glow (sun); jik', to be broken; jok', to come up; duk', to fall from aloft; ruk', to fall on ground; ok', to weep; hok', to be prosperous; juk', to be wise, and all such words, as also the compounds épidak, cacare, chépi dák, mingere, tídak, to be thirsty.

Third.—Conjugation of neuters with a conjunct labial (m or p): I. in m. Dam to be full and to be lost, or to fill and to lose in the intransitive senses.*

Infinitive and participles as before.

IMPERATIVE.

Affirmative	Dam	Damche	Damne
Negative	Thá dam	Thá damchhe	Thá damne

---

* The Váyu neuter and passive conjugations coincide, and the expressions often tally with the equivalent English ones, as dámi, it is lost, and it is filled or full—that is, self-lost and self-filled. But the Váyu reflex verb, like the French, can express the latter meaning otherwise, viz., by damchem, which is equivalent to dámi, used neutrally. Dam lá lam is another equivalent form, answering literally to khógayá in Urdu, though Váyu never forms its passives like Urdu.

INDICATIVE MOOD.

Present Tense.

1. Dámum (Dammum)	Dam chhokmi, excl. / Dam chhikmi, incl.	Dámpopmi / Dámpem
2. Dámi	Dam chhikmi	Damnem
3. Dámi	Dam chhikmi	Dámem

Preterite.

1. Dam sungmi	Dam chhongmi, excl. / Dam chhingmi, incl.	Dámpi kongmi / Dámpi kengmi
2. Dámi	Dam chhem	Damnem
3. Dámi	Dam chhem	Dámem

This conjugation changes gnom into mum and kokmi, kem into popmi, pem, besides lengthening the vowel.

The other moods as before. In subjunctive, dámonam, damnam, damnam. Thus also conjugate ram, to be afraid, dum, to become, &c.

II. in p. Jyóp, to be tired.

IMPERATIVE.

Aff. Jyóp'	Jyop'chhe	Jyómne
Neg. Thá jyop	Thá jyop'chhe	Thá jyóp'ne

INDICATIVE.

Present.

1. Jyop' mum	Jyop chhokmi, excl. / Jyop chhikmi, incl.	Jyoppopmi / Jyoppem
2. Jyop'mi	Jyop chhikmi	Jyopnem
3. Jyop'mi	Jyop chhikmi	Jyopmem
1. Jyop sungmi	Jyop chhongmi / Jyop chhingmi	Jyópikongmi / Jyópikengmi
2. Jyómi	Jyop chhem	Jyómnem
3. Jyómi	Jyop chhem	Jyómem

This conjugation changes p into m and lengthens the vowel. *As in the last* kokmi, kem becomes popmi, pem.

Other moods as before. Subjunctive has jyop'monam, jyop'nam, jyopnam, jyopsung phen, jyóm phen, jyóm phen.

Thus also conjugate thip, to set (sun), yép, to be sharp-edged, &c.

Fourth.—Conjugation of neuters with conjunct dental (t).

Hot', to utter, talk.

Infinitive and participles and gerunds as before.

IMPERATIVE MOOD.

Singular.	*Dual.*	*Plural.*
Aff. Hot'	Hoschhe	Hóne
Neg. Thá hot'	Thá hoschhe	Thá hóne

Indicative Present.

1. Hot' gnom	Hoschhokmi, excl. / Hoschhikmi, incl.	Hot'kokmi / Hot'kem
2. Hot'mi	Hoschhikmi	Hot'nem
3. Hot'mi	Hoschhikmi	Hot'mem

Preterite.

Singular.	*Dual.*	*Plural.*
1. Hosungmi	Hoschhongmi / Hoschhingmi	Hotikong mi / Hotikeng mi
2. Hónmi	Hoschhem	Hónem
3. Hónmi	Hoschhem	Hónmem

This conjugation changes the t into n, and retains the t before the *plural kokmi kem, which are unchanged.* It lengthens the vowel as usual.

Thus conjugate pat', to fight; met', to die; but', to flower, &c.

Remark.—The verbs dung, to be dry; dong, to arrive; then, to win; yáng, to lose or decrease; min, to be ripe; hon, to be big; bon, to fly; lun, to run, and all others ending in a nasal (n or ng) follow without change the sheer root paradigm or phi aforesaid.

5th.—Conjugation of reflex or active intransitive (including also some neuters) verbs in che, that is, which have this (the only) reflex sign added to their root in the imperative, which always strikes the keynote to the several conjugations, always having the formative affix whenever there is one.

Im, to sleep.

INFINITIVE MOOD.

Aff.	Immung.	To sleep or to have slept	aoristic
Neg.	Máng immung.	Not to sleep, &c.	

Remark.—Í-mung is as often used as immung; so that i may possibly be the root, not im.

Gerunds.		*Participles.*		
Im he	ut supra	Imvi (invi)		ut supra
Im nung		Imta		
Im im há		Imtáng	not useable	
Im sing hé		Verbal nouns		
Im khen		Imchyáng		
		Imlung		
		Imsing		

Negatives as in infinitive; that is, by prefixing máng.

IMPERATIVE MOOD.

Singular.	*Dual.*	*Plural.*
Aff. Imche	Im náchhé	Imchiné
Neg. Thá imche	Thá imnáchhé	Thá imchiné

Indicative Present.

1. Imchungmi	Imnachhokmi / Imnachhikmi	Imchikokmi / Imchikem
2. Imchem	Imnachikmi	Imchinem
3. Imchem	Imnachikmi	Imchimem

Preterite.

1. Imchungmi	Imnáchhongmi / Imnachingmi	Imchikongmi / Imchikengmi
2. Imchem	Imnachhem	Imchinem
3. Imchem	Imnachhem	Imchimem

Thus are conjugated all reflex verbs whatever having the che sign, whether they be primitive or derivative (and all transitives can be so* commuted), as chikche, to remember; mángche, to forget; lische, to learn; musche, to sit; ipche, to get up; khokche, to walk; pipche, to suck; sipche, to wake; lipche, to vomit; popche, to lick; ki*n*che, to lie hid; lunche, to run; dé*n*che, to bathe; upche, to wash oneself; tesche, to begin; chusche, to end; khwé*n*khwé*n* pá*n*che, to cough; khikche, to sneeze; liche, to grow (plant only); gosche, to be rich; vekche, to contain; dosche, to sustain or hold up; du*n*che, to dig for

---

* Consequently every transitive has a reflex form or middle voice as well as an active and passive; but as the middle voice in transitives always tallies with the above paradigm, which includes many verbs originally, and some that are solely intransitive, with some neuters even, it must suffice to give it here once for all. The verbs enumerated will show that this conj. in "chi" is very comprehensive, and admits of many fine shades of meaning. Thus, lische, to learn, means to teach thyself, opposed to listo, to teach another. Again, not only functional action, but any of which the effort returns to the agent, as in buying and taking, must be primarily expressed in this form, *e.g.*, ingche, is buy; ingko, buy it—a Hungarian trait.

oneself; phasche, to be able; wónche,* to master oneself, be patient or firm; bongche,* to be happy; giwón pónche, to keep silence; rusche, to flee away; kwompánche, to sing; yángche, to decrease or lose; jonche, to grow or increase (animal only); yukche, to cut oneself; sische, to kill oneself; tánche, to put for oneself; senche, to know oneself or to know simply; hánche, to give to oneself; phokche, to beget or give birth to for oneself; ingche, to buy; jyápche, to exchange; khwásche, to tighten oneself; *kh*wásche,† to feed oneself; túnche, to drink; jááche, to eat; chénche,‡ to piss; topche, to beat oneself; yosche, to like, &c. &c.

Remark.—These verbs are aoristic in fact, though in the dual and plural they are obliged to accommodate themselves to the inflexible forms of those numbers; and such (by and by will be seen) is the case also with the aoristic transitives in "to." The reflex duals and plurals, however, always retain their own special signs, or na and chi, which are interchangeable for the sake of euphony, na being preferred to chi in the dual to prevent cacophonous repetition of the ch.

6th.—Conjugation of transitives in "to" not having a precedent sibilant.

The verb Há, to give.

INFINITIVE AFFIRMATIVE.

Hámung, to give or to have given, aoristic.

INFINITIVE NEGATIVE.

Máng hámung, not to give, &c.

GERUNDS.

Há he	Present, giving	With main verb in present or future
Hánung §		With main verb in preterite
Háhe háhe Hánung hánung	Continuative present, continually giving	
Háhá ha	Past, having given	
Há singhe	Present or future, when giving	
Há khen	Past, after having given, after giving	

PARTICIPLES.

Hávi	Who gives or gave or will give, aoristic. The giver
Háta	Past (passive), who or what has been given. The given
Hátáng	Future passive, what will be given, what customarily given, what fit to be given

VERBAL NOUNS.

Háchyáng	Expresses the instrument, as háchyáng gót, the hand that gives. It is also used substantively in a neuter sense; thus, topchyang, a hammer. Hammerer is to'vi
Hálúng	Expresses the place; hálúng, the place of giving
Hásing	Expresses the time; hásing, the time of giving

The negative of gerunds, participles, and verbal nouns is expressed, as in the infinitive, by the prefix máng, máng háhe, máng hávi, &c.

IMPERATIVE MOOD.

	Singular.	*Dual.*	*Plural.*
Aff.	Háto	Háchhe	Háne ‖
Neg.	Thá háto	Thá háchhe	Thá háne

* Tesche gives teshto, set free; wonche gives wonto, in composition only be able. See note (*) p. 285.

† *Kh* is the Arabic guttural.

‡ Chénche of this sort from chént.

§ *E.g.*, hábè lágnom, I go giving; hánung la' sungmi, I went giving. Having given, I went, is háháha la' sungmi.

‖ Here, when the occurrence of the first transitive gives occasion to note the thing, let us

Dual and Plural of Object.

*	Dual. Hátochhé	Give to them two
*	Plural. Hátomé	Give to them all
	Negative. Thá hátochhé, D.	Thá hátome, P.

INDICATIVE MOOD.

Present or future.

Singular.	*Dual.*	*Plural.*
1. Hátungmi	+Háchhokmi, excl.	Hátikokmi, excl.
	+Háchhikmi, incl.	Hátikem, incl.

Dual and Plural of Object.

* 1. Hátungchhem	I give to them two	
* 1. Hátungmem	I give to them all	
2. Hátum	+Háchhikmi	+Hánem
* 2. +Hátochhem	Thou givest to them two	
* 2. +Hatomem	Thou givest to them all	
3. +Hátum	Hátochhem	+Hátomem
* 3. +Hátochhem	He gives to them two	
* 3. +Hátomem	He gives to them all	

Preterite.

1. Hátungmi	Háchhongmi, excl.	Hátikongmi, excl.
	Háchhingmi, incl.	Hátikengmi, incl.

Dual and Plural of Object.

* 1. Hátungchhem	I gave to them two	
* 1. Hátungmem	I gave to them all	
2. Hátum	+Háchhem	+Hánem
* 2. Hátochem	Thou gavest to them two	
* 2. Hátomem	Thou gavest to them all	
3. +Hátum	+Hátochhem	+Hátomem
* 3. +Hátochhem	He gave to them two	
* 3. +Hátomem	He gave to them all	

NEGATIVE MOOD.

Singular Indicative Present.

1. Má hátungmi 2. Má hátum 3. Má hátum	Dual and plural in like manner, merely by prefixing the negative particle má. *N.B.*—Háto and all other transitives of its class are essentially aoristic. See remark aforegone.

INTERROGATIVE MOOD.

Singular Indicative Present.

1. Hátung ki má 2. Háto ki má 3. Háto ki má	Dual and plural in like manner, and all the rest of the verb also; that is, cut off the final mi or m and substitute ki má.

---

observe, once for all, that the singular, dual, and plural, coming first in the conjugation, denote the agents; the dual and plural coming afterwards, the objects. In Váyu, as in Babing, the complete fusion of all agents and objects with the action is the chief peculiarity of these tongues, indicating their close affinity with the Ho, Sontal, and Munda tongues. In the passive voice the position of agents and objects is reversed, if not necessarily, at least usually (see on to p. 286). Owing to the inseparability of actors and action, it results, first, that in the ordinary conjugation many forms are common to the active and passive voices; second, that certain special forms are needed (see p. 287) to eke out all the varieties of conjugation.

* The starred and bracketed portions express the peculiar forms of this language.

The mark + before any form signifies that it belongs also to the passive, which see. The difference is expressed in such cases by the use of the separate prefixed pronouns in the instrumental case for the active; in the objective or accusative case for the passive, or g'ha, gonha, wathiha, and go, gon, wathi for the three persons singular, and so on for dual and plural.

Potential Mood.

Singular Indicative Present.

1. Há wóntungmi 2. Há wóntum 3. Há wóntum	and so on through the rest of the verb; wónto, to can, being conjugated like háto, the root of which is prefixed merely (wónto is used with transitives, and phásche with intransitives).

Optative Mood.

Singular Indicative Present.

1. Há dakgnom 2. Há dakmi 3. Há dakmi	and so on through the rest of the verb dak, to wish or want, as before given. The root of the main verb is prefixed as before.

Precative Mood.

That I may give.

Singular Indicative Present.

1. Hátung yu 2. Háto yu 3. Háto yu	and so on, after the manner of the interrogative mood as to the main verb, to which is added the immutable verbal root expressive of wish in the nature of prayer, hátung yu=o! si mihi accedat dare.

Remark.—The solicitive form, let me give, let him give, há hásung, há háto, is seldom used owing to the iteration of the same root in two different senses.

Subjunctive Mood.

Present.	*Preterite.*	
1. Hátung nam	Hátung phen,	and so on for dual and plural
2. Háto nam	Háto phen	
3. Háto nam	Hato phen	

Continuative Mood.

1. Há na há nógnom,* 2. Há na há nónum, 3. Há na há nómi,	and so on, as in the neuter verb phí.

Reciprocal Mood.

1. Há na há pánchungmi,† 2. Há na há pánchem, 3. Há na há pánchem,	and so on as before, with reflex of the root pá, to make, conjugated like im-che.

Causal Mood.

Imperative.

	Singular.	*Dual.*	*Plural.*
Aff.	Há píngko	Há píngchhe	Há píngne
Neg.	Há thá píng	Há thá píngche	Há thá píngne

Indicative Present.

1. Há píngsúngmi 2. Há píngmi 3. Há píngmi	and so on, according to the form of conjugating the transitive verb píngko, which see in sequel, and to which the root of the main verb is prefixed when causation is expressed.‡

---

* The reflex form of the verb mu, to sit, imperative musche, is often used in this sense, há na há muschungmi, muschem, muschem, &c., like imche. So Newári has biye chona = I sit giving, I remain giving.

† The transitive form of pá, to do, is sometimes preferred to the reflex, Háhá pángmi, pómi, pómi, &c. See conjugation x.

‡ Causal verbs have all the complete forms of conjugation proper to primary verbs; and,

PASSIVE VOICE.

Imperative Mood.

	Singular.	*Dual.*	*Plural.**
Aff.	Hásung Give thou me †	Háchhong Give thou us two	Há kí kóng Give thou us all
Neg.	Thá hágno	Thá háchhok	Thá há kók

Dual and Plural of Agent.

*	
Hásúng chhé	Do ye two give me
Hásúng né.	Do ye all give me
Thá hásúng chhé Thá hásúng né	The negative forms

Indicative Mood.

Present.

Singular.	*Dual.*	*Plural.*
1. Hágnom = gives to me	+ Háchhokmi, excl. + Háchhikmi, incl. = gives us two	Hákókmi, excl. Hákém, incl. = gives us all (subaudi ille vel iste)

Dual and Plural of Agent.

* 1. Hágnochhem	Give me they two (or ye two)	
* 1. Hágnomem	Give me they all	
2. Hámi	+ Háchhikmi	+ Hánem
* 2. Hámi	Give thee they two	
* 2. Hámi	Give thee they all	
3. + Hátum	+ Hátochhem	+ Hátomem ‡
* 3. + Hátochhem	Give to him they two	
* 3. + Hátomem	Give to him they all	

Preterite.

Singular.	*Dual.*	*Plural.*
1. Hásúngmi	* Hachhongmi, excl. Hachhingmi, incl.	Hakikongmi, excl. Hakikengmi, incl.

Dual and Plural of Agent.

* 1. Hasungchhem	Gave to me they two (or ye two)	
* 1. Hasungmem	Gave to me they all (any)	
2. Hámi	+ Háchem	+ Hánem
* 2. Hámi	Gave to thee they two	
* 2. + Hámi	Gave to thee they all	
3. + Hátum	+ Hátochhem	+ Hátomem

---

as they are constituted by transitives, they take, like transitives, the reflex and passive and double objective forms, being conjugated from pingche and pingsung and ping (k) to, as well as pingko. The reflex of háto is hánche, conjugated like imche; the quasi passive is hásúng, for which see On. Háto has no doubly objected form. Itself expresses give it to him or give him.

* These are all of the object, those of the agent coming afterwards. See note ‖, p. 283. Gives me (not to me) = I am given, &c.

† Observe that in the passive I, the speaker, am the object (therefore me is better than to me); in the active intransitive or middle voice, self, the spoken to; in the active transitive, he, she, it, the spoken of. Hence há-sung, há-n-che, há-to, as the bases of the whole system of conjugation.

‡ The forms marked with a cross precedent (+) are common to both voices. See Active. There is no infinitive of this quasi passive. The causal transitive which carries a passive as well as active sense has it: thus hámung, to give; hápingmung, to be given; more properly, to cause to give. So Newári has biye, to give, bíyeke (ke the causal sign) to be given or cause to give. Newári has no other semblance even of a passive. Váyu, with its suffixed objective forms of the pronoun, has, as above seen. But this again is weakened by the special restriction of the suffixes; thus hánum, gives or gave to thee, *I only* and no other.

* The star and bracket as before explained.

* { 3. + Hátochhem Gave to him they two
   3. + Hátomem Gave to him they all }

A second passive may be formed by the passive participle and substantive verb, of clear meaning, but eschewed owing to the relative sense inherent in the participles.

Indicative Present Singular.

1. Háta nógnom
2. Háta nónum
3. Háta nómi

And so on through the verb Nó, to be, an irregular verb which is given in the sequel. *Remark.*—To this responds hávi nógnom of the active voice.

Passive potential.

(I can be given)

Present singular.

1. Há wóngnom
2. Há wónmi
3. Há wóntum

Preterite.

1. Há wónsungmi
2. Há wónmi
3. Há wóntum

And so on through dual and plural, the passive of wónto being conjugated like that of háto.

Passive Precative.

(That I may be given).

Present Singular.

1. Hágnoyu
2. Háyu
3. Hátoyu

Preterite.

1. Hásungyu
2. Háyu
3. Hátoyu

And so on through dual and plural, according to the passive forms of háto less the final mi or m, which is dropped, and the immutable verbal particle yú subjoined.

Remark.—Observe that in the potential mood, as in the causal below, the expression of the passivity is transferred from the truncated main verb, which shows only its crude root, to the secondary verb.

Passive Causal.

(I cause to be given, or to give).

1. Há pínggnom	Present.	1. Há píngsúngmi	Preterite
2. Há píngmi		2. Há píngmi	
3. Há píngmi		3. Há píngnum	

And so on through dual and plural, following the conjugational forms of the passive voice of the verb píngko, to send, which see.

Passive Subjunctive.

If I be given.

1. Há gno nam	Present	1. Hásúngphen	Preterite
2. Há nam		2. Há phen	
3. Háto nam		3. Háto phen	

Like the precative, only substituting the subjunctive participles for the single precative one. And the interrogative mood of the passive merely substitutes the participle of interrogation or kimá, hágnoki má, &c.

Special Forms.

Active or passive = agents objective.

1st.—I to thee.

Hánum	Give or gave to thee I only	aoristic
Hánochhem	Give or gave you two I only	
Hánonem	Give or gave to you all I only	

2d.—Thou to me.

γHágnom	Givest to me thou (or he)	Present tense*
γHagnochem	Give to me ye two (or they two)	
Hagnomen	Give to me ye all only	

* The forms preceded by the mark γ are not special, but are repeated here to illustrate such as are special. Compare the whole with those of the Peruvian language of America apud Markham, p. 397. There are slight differences indicating diverse degrees of decomposition, but the resemblance in substance and principle is wonderful. I commend it to those who so dogmatically tell us it is not legitimate philology to heed such coincidences.

γHásungmi	Gavest to me thou	Preterite
γHásungchhem	Gave to me ye two	
Hásungnem	Gave to me ye all	

Thus are conjugated all transitives in "tó" that have the root only precedent, as wóto, to cleanse; láto, to snatch away; chíto, to split; jito, to tear; phóto, to eradicate; chéto, immingere; ríto, to cause to rot or rot it; líto, to cause to grow, or grow it; hito, to count; jeto, to heat; kheto, to break; súto, to plaster; gnúto, to blunt; ruto, to staunch; thutó, to divide; wóto, to cleanse; &c. The verbs with a "p" before the sign, as lipto, to vomit; upto, to wash; hopto, to squander; jupto, to throw; napto, to compress—change the p into m in the plural imperative and in the second person plural preterite, as namne, do ye all compress, and namnem, ye all compressed. Those with a "k" before the sign, as thiktó, to shut; khikto, to cause to sneeze—change the k into ng, as thingne, do ye all shut, and thingnem, ye all shutted it. No other precedent letter makes any change, save the sibilant to, which we shall next proceed, as forming a different conjugation. Meanwhile conjugate as above, hanto, to cause to swim; thunto, to drink; thumto, to sink; dento, to bathe; another (not self); yangto, to make yield; khunto, to reveal; lumto, to transport; khungto, to make stoop; yángto, to decrease; bongto, to please; mangto, to cause to forget or to forget him; phimto, to depress; khámto, to summon; *kh*amto, to frighten; thento, to cause to win; yemto, to burn; umto, to burn corpse; wó*n*to, to win, to be able* pélto, to wring or extract juice; tamto, to cry out; damto, to fill, &c., &c.

Seventh conjugation of verbs in "to" having a precedent sibilant (always palpably felt in the reflex, sometimes not so in the transitive, wherein something like an abrupt tone, however, indicates in such cases its latent presence, or else a sound like English th or ph, as phá'to, múphto, hóthto for phásto, músto and hósto. But observe, there is no true tone as in the eighth and eleventh conjugations (to'po and pho'ko), and the real euphonic intercalary letter is the sibilant s).

The verb Sí, to kill.

INFINITIVE.

Aff.	Sit'mung, to kill, to have killed	aoristic
Neg.	Máng sit'mung, not to kill	

Gerunds.		*Participles.*	
Sit'he	ut supra	Sit'vi	ut supra
Sit'nung		Sista	
Sit'he sit'he		Sistang	
Sit' sit'ha			
Sis' singhe			
Sit' khen			

VERBAL NOUNS.

Sischyáng	ut supra
Sitlúng	
Sitsíng	

Their negatives are formed by prefixing máng—mángsit'he, mángsit'vi, &c.

IMPERATIVE.

	Singular.	*Dual.*	*Plural.*
Aff.	Sisto	Sischhe	Sitne
Neg.	Thasit	Tha sischhe	Tha sitne

Dual and Plural of Object.

* Aff.	Sistochhé	Do thou kill them two
	Sistome	Do thou kill them all
* Neg.	Thá sit'chhik	Kill not them two
	Thá sit'me	Kill not them all

* This neuter sense of wo*n*to is restricted to its use as a compound, and it is so used only with transitives. With intransitives the reflex form of phá, to be able, is employed; top wo*n*tum, he can beat; imphaschem, he can sleep.

Indicative Present.

Singular.	Dual.	Plural.
1. Sinmi *	+ { Sischhokmi, excl. / Sischhikmi, incl.	+ { Sitkokmi, excl. / Sitkem, incl.

Dual and Plural of Object.

* { 1. Sinchhem	I kill them two	
{ 1. Sinmem	I kill them all	
2. + Sitmi	+ Sischhikmi	+ Sitnem
* { 2. Sischhikmi	Thou killest them two	
{ 2. Sitmem	Thou killest them all	
3. + Sitmi †	+ Sischhikmi	+ Sitmem

Dual and Plural of Object.

* { 3. + Sischhikmi	He kills them two
{ 3. + Sitmem	He kills them all

Preterite.

1. Sistungmi	+ { Sischhongmi, excl. / Sischhingmi, incl.	+ Sistikóngmi, excl. / + Sistikéngmi, incl.

Dual and Plural of Object.

* { 1. Sistungchhem	I killed them two	
{ 1. Sistungmem	I killed them all	
2. Sistum	+ Sischhem	+ Sónem ? Sitnem ‡
* { 2. Sistochhem	Thou killedst them two	
{ 2. Sistomem	Thou killedst them all	
3. + Sistum	+ Sistochhem	+ Sistomem
* { 3. + Sistochhem	He killed them two	
{ 3. + Sistomem	He killed them all	

Negative Mood.

Of the Idicative Singular.

Present.	Preterite.
1. Má sinmi	1. Má sistungmi
2. Má sitmi	2. Má sistum
3. Má sitmi	3. Má sistum
&c.	&c.

Interrogative Mood.

Present.	Preterite.
1. Sinki má	1. Sistung ki má
2. Sitki má	2. Sistó ki má
3. Sitki má	3. Sistó ki má

---

* Another form = sinmi, sitmi, sitmi, is sitvi nognom, sitvi nonum, sitvi nomi, and so on, formed by active participle and substantive verb.

† Compare with sinmi, sitmi, sitmi, the correspondent syána, syáta, syáta of Newári. The root (si, sá vel syá) and the augments (n and t) are alike and alike disposed, that is, the augment following the root. So also in both tongues the augment of the second and third person, or t, constitutes the passive in all three persons, si-t-gnom ; sí-t-mi, sí-t-mi = Newári syá-ta, syá-ta, syá-ta. The si-t of the one is precisely the sya-t or sha-t of the other, the t being that mark of action, apart from one's own, whereby the passive (with the help of the separate prefixed objective pronoun in both tongues alike) is denoted. And yet these two languages have all the superficial marks of wide contrariety and opposition. In the vocabulary I have pointed attention to identical roots or words used verbally in one of these tongues, substantively in the other, or of which the one has the primitive, the other the derivative. What I would imply is that identical roots and constructive principles may be found in this family of tongues where one would least expect to find them.

‡ Sénem, like séno in the imperative, must be an error, though insisted on to me. Séko, to know, gives sénem and séne regularly, as sisto, to kill, gives sitnem and sitne. In the intransitives we have respectively senche and sische.

Potential Mood.

Aoristic.

1. Sit wón̲tongmi 2. Sit wón̲tum 3. Sit + wón̲tum	And so on, like háto, which also is aoristic in singular, though in dual and plural it is tensed and also in the passive voice.

Optative Mood.

Present.	*Preterite.*	
1. Sit + dakgnom	1. Sit + daksungmi	&c., like dak aforegone
2. Sit + dakmi	2. Sit + dáugmi	
3. Sit + dakmi	3. Sit + dáugmi	

Precative Mood.

That I may kill.

Present.	*Preterite.*	
1. Sin yu	1. Sistung yu	&c., as in the uncompounded verb
2. Sit yu	2. Sisto yu	
3. Sit yu	3. Sisto yu	

Subjunctive Mood.

Present.	*Preterite.*	
1. Sinnam	1. Sistungphen	and so on, as in the uncompounded verb
2. Sitnam	2. Sistophen	
3. Sitnam	3. Sistophen	

Continuative Mood.

Present.	*Preterite.*	
1. Sit'nasit' nógnom	Sit'nasit' nósúngmi	and so on, conjugating the auxiliary after the model of phi.
2. Sit'nasit' nónum	Sit'nasit' nónum	
3. Sit'nasit' nómi	Sit'nasit nómi	

Reciprocal Mood.

1. Sit'nasit' pán̲chúngmi 2. Sit'nasit' pán̲chem 3. Sit'nasit' pán̲chem	&c., after the model of imche, which, like all intransitives in che, is aoristic

CAUSAL VERB.

As before in all respects.

See Háto.

PASSIVE VERB.

Imperative Mood.

	Singular.	*Dual.*	*Plural.*
Aff.	Sissúng	Sischhóng	Sisti kóng
Neg.	Thá sitgnó	Thá sischhók	Thá sit kók

Dual and Plural of Agent.

*Aff.	Sissungchhé	Do ye two kill me
	Sissungné	Do ye all kill me
*Neg.	Thá sitgnochhé	Do ye two not kill me
	Thá sitgnoné	Do ye all not kill me

Indicative Present.

Singular.	*Dual.*	*Plural.*
1. Sit gnom	+ Sischhokmi, excl.	+ Sit kókmi, excl.
= kills me (subaudi ille vel iste)	+ Sischhikmi, incl.	+ Sit kém, incl.
	= kills us two	= kills us all

Dual and Plural of Agent.

* {	1. Sit gnochhem	Kill me they two (or ye two)	
	1. Sit gnomem	Kill me they all	
	2. + Sitmi	+ Sischhikmi	+ Sit'nem
* {	2. Sitmi	Kill thee they two (or we two)	
	2. Sitmi	Kill thee they all (or we all)	
	3. + Sitmi	+ Sischhikmi	+ Sitmem

Dual and Plural of Agent.

* {	3. + Sischhikmi	Kill him they two (or ye two)
	3. + Sitmem.	Kill him they all

Preterite.

1. Sissungmi	+ Sischhóngmi, excl.	+ Sistikóngmi, excl.
	+ Sischhíngmi, incl.	+ Sistikéngmi, incl.

Dual and Plural of Agent.

* {	1. Sissungchhém	Killed me they two (or ye two)	
	1. Sissungmém	Killed me they all	
	2. Sinmi	Sischhem	Senem? Sitnem
* {	2. Sinmi	Killed thee they two (or we two)	
	2. Sinmi	Killed thee they all (or we all)	
	3. Sistum	Sistochhem	Sistomem
* {	3. Sistochhem	Killed him they two	
	3. Sistomem	Killed him they all	

The negative mood prefixes má as in active voice.

The interrogative mood drops the final m or mi, and substitutes ki má, as in active voice.

The potential mood is conjugated by the passive form of the secondary verb wónto.

Present and Future.	*Preterite.*	
1. Sit'wóngnom	1. Sit'wónsúngmi	and so only conjugating like passive of Háto
2. Sit'wónmi	2. Sit'wónmi	
3. Sit'wóntum	3. Sit'wóntum	

Optative mood precisely as in the active voice, dakgnom, meaning I desire and I am desired, and the passive expression being removed from the truncated main verb.

PRECATIVE MOOD.

Present.	*Preterite.*	
1. Sit' gno yu	1. Sissung yu	and so on, by dropping final m or mi of the passive, and substituting immutable precative particle yu
2. Sit' yu	2. Sin yu	
3. Sit' yu	3. Sisto yu	

The subjunctive mood resembles the above, taking only its own signs in lieu of yu, the precative sign.

CAUSAL.

Present.	*Preterite.*	
1. Sit ping gnom	1. Sit pingsungmi	and so all through the passive forms of the verb pingko, which see at p. 304
2. Sit pingmi	2. Sit pingmi	
3. Sit pingmi	3. Sit pingkum	

According to the above paradigm of sisto, conjugate also pisto, to bring; khisto, to rub;† khwasto, to feed; phasto, to enable (pha'to); chásto, to hit with stone (chá'to); *kh*wásto (khwá'to), to tighten; dosto, to sustain for another (dophto); jisto, to revile; musto, to seat (muphto); testo, to set at liberty or cause to begin (te*th*to); thesto, to kick (the*th*to); chusto, to finish it (chuphto); chisto, to suspend;

* Brackets and stars before the repeated numbers (answering to three persons of verb), and the crosses (+), as before explained.

† Kh of khisto is a very peculiar sound, verging upon a vague th or hard h or Sanscrit ksh; *kh* is hard Arabic, without the least vagueness, as in *kh*wasto, to tighten.

isto, to tell; risto, to rot it; josto (jopto), to kindle; chhisto, to relate (chhi'to); wásto, to abandon; yosto, to approve, like; násto, to wet (ná'to); lusto (luphto), to transplant; thos'to (thophto), to take out; tosto (tophto), to reconcile, to unite; lis'to, to teach and to return; pes'to, to reap; lás'to (la*th*to), to take for another; &c., &c. *N.B.*—The intercalary sibilant varies to sh, ph, and English th. It is least obscure with the vowel i; most so with the vowels á, u, and ó.

SECOND FORM OF THE PASSIVE.

INFINITIVE MOOD.

Aff. Sista	nót'mung, to be / dúmung, to become	killed	
Neg. Sista	máng not'mung / máng dúmung	not to be / not to become	killed

Gerunds.

Sista nót'he, dúmhe
Sista not'nung, dumnung
Sista not'not'há, dumdumba
Sista not'singhe, dumsinghe
Sista not'khen, dumkhen
} *ut supra*

Participles.		*Verbal Nouns.*	
Sista not'vi or dumvi	ut supra	Sista not' or dum-chyang	ut supra
Sísta no'ta ór dumta		Sista not' or dum-lung	
Sista no'táng, dumtáng		Sista not' or dum-sing	

Negatives by máng prefixed.

IMPERATIVE PRESENT.

	Singular.	*Dual.*	*Plural.*
Aff.	Sista { nó / dum	Sista { nóche / dumche	Sista { nóne / dúmne

Neg. By prefixed particle thá.

INDICATIVE PRESENT.

1. Sista	nógnom / dúmum	And so on according to the paradigms phi and dam
2. Sista	nónum / dúmi	
3. Sista	nómi / dúmi	

Remark.—This form of the passive has a correspondent active form, sit'vi, nógnom vel dúmum, and both are singularly free from doubt as to the sense, and singularly correspondent with our English idiom, I am killing, I am killed, the phrases being in effect, I am the killer and I am the killed.

But, owing to the inherence of the relative sense in the participles, these forms are eschewed. The following correspondent forms in Khás and Newári are equally available in those languages, and equally eschewed for the same reason.

KHAS.

Active.	*Passive.*
1. Hánnya hún	Hányako hún
2. Hánnya hós	Hányako hós
3. Hánnya hó	Hányako hó

NEWARI.

1. Ji syáhmakhá, or jú	Syánahmakhá	kha or júlo *
2. Chha syáhmakha, or jú	Syánahmakha	
3. Wó syáhmakha, or jú	Syánahmakha	

* Kha and jú are substantive verbs in Newári, whereof the former is immutable, and the latter becomes júlo in the preterite.

Special Forms of Action between the two first Persons.

First form, I to thee.

S.	Sit'num	Kill or killed or will kill thee (I only)
D.	Sit'nochhem	Kill or killed or will kill you two (I only)
P.	Sit'nonem	Kill or killed or will kill you all (I only)

Second form, Thou to me.

S.	γSit'gnom	Killedst or wilt kill me thou (or he)	Present and Future
D.	γSit'gnochhem	Kill or will kill me ye two (or they two)	
P.	Sit'gnonem	Kill or will kill me ye all only	
S.	γSit'sungmi	Killedst me thou (or he)	Preterite
D.	γSit'sungchhem	Killed me ye two (or they two)	
P.	Sit'sungnem	Killed me ye all only	

8th. Conjugation of transitives in po not having a nasal (n. ng. m.) before it.

The verb Top', to strike (potius, tó).*

Infinitive Mood.

Aff. To'mung }
Neg. Máng to'mung } aoristic

Gerunds.		*Participles.*	
Top'he	ut supra	To'vi	ut supra
Topnung		Topta	
Toptopha		Toptang	
Topsinghe		*Verbal Nouns.*	
Topkhen		Topchyáng	
		Toplung	
		Topsing	

Negatives of all by prefixed máng.

Imperative.

	Singular.	*Dual.*	*Plural.*
Aff.	To'pa (toppo)	Topchhe	Tomne
Neg.	Tha top	Tha topche	Tha tomne

Dual and Plural of Object.

*Aff.	To'pochhe	Do thou strike them two
	To'pome	Do thou strike them all

Negatives.

*Neg.	Thá topchhik	Kill not them two
	Thá top'me	Kill not them all

Indicative Present.

1. To'mi †	+ Topchhokmi, excl.	+ To' popmi, excl.
	+ Topchhikmi, incl.	+ To' pem, incl.

---

* The root is properly tó, equal to tá vel dá of Chinese, Newári, Sontal, and thá, the same aspirated, of Kuswar. The crude root may be tó, but the whole conjugation proves that we must here write top' and toppo for the imperative, whence dual top-chhe and plural tom-ne. The substitution, in speaking, of an abrupt tone for the reduplicated consonant in this conjugation recurs in conj. xi., p. 242, while conj. x. has the pausing accent.

† It is very noticeable that the verbs in po have no mark of the first person singular of present tense, so generally contradistinguished from the second and third, or all other persons. Even Newari preserves this distinction—dáye, dáyu, dáyu (in the past, dáyá, dálá, dálá).

Dual and Plural of Object.

* {	1. Tomchhem	I strike them two	
	1. Tomem	I strike them all	
	2. To'mi	+ Topchhikmi	+ Topnem
* {	2. Topchhikmi	Thou strikest them two	
	2. To'mem	Thou strikest them all	
	3. + To'mi *	+ Topchhikmi	+ To'mem
* {	3. + To'pchhikmi	He strikes them two	
	3. + To'mem	He strikes them all	

Preterite.

1. To'pungmi	{ + Topchhongmi, excl.	+ To'pikongmi, excl.
	+ Topchhingmi, incl.	+ To'pikengmi, incl.

Dual and Plural of Object.

* {	1. To'pungchhem	I struck them two	
	1. To'pungmem	I struck them all	
	2. To'pum	+ Topchhem	+ Tomnem
* {	2. To'pochhem	Thou struckest them two	
	2. To'pomem	Thou struckest them all	
	3. + To'pum	+ To'pochhem	+ To'pomem
* {	3. + To'pochhem	He struck them two	
	3. + To'pomem	He struck them all	

Negative by prefixed má.

Optative mood by conjugating the verb to desire suffixed to the unchanging form top' of the main verb.

INTERROGATIVE MOOD.

Present.	*Preterite.*	
1. Tom' ki má	To'pung ki má	&c., by dropping the mi or m final and substituting ki má
2. + Top' ki má	To'po ki má	
3. + Top' ki má	+ To'po ki má	

Subjunctive by substituting nam in present, and phen in past, for the interrogative ki má.

POTENTIAL MOOD.

Present and Past (aoristic).

1. Top won̲tungmi	&c., as in Háto and Sishto potentials
2. Top won̲tum	
3. + Top won̲tum	

PRECATIVE MOOD.

Present.	*Past.*	
1. Tom yu	1. To' pungyu	&c. &c.
2. + Top yu	2. To' poyu	
3. + Top yu	3. + To' poyu	

CONTINUATIVE MOOD.

Present Tense.

1. Top ná top nognom †	and so on, conjugating the auxiliary verb nó after the manner of phi, in dual and plural.
2. Top ná top nonum	
3. Top ná top nomi	

---

* Tomi with the prolonged tone, instead of the abrupt one, means he places, whereas to'mi is he hits. The former comes from táko = place; the latter from to'po = hit.

† Top ná top muschungmi (from musche, to sit) may also be used = dáya chona of Newári. So also the reciprocal can be expressed by top ná top pángmi, or the transitive, which, moreover, is apt to blend in sense with the continuative. So also you can express the habitual present tense by to' vi nognom, literally, I am the striker.

RECIPROCAL MOOD.

Present.

1. Top ná top páṇchungmi 2. Top ná top páṇchem 3. Top ná top páṇchem	and so on, conjugating páṇche after the model of imche.

CAUSAL VERB.

As before in all respects. See prior samples.
Cause to strike, top'pingko (see trans. in ko, p. 304).

PASSIVE VERB.

IMPERATIVE MOOD.

	Singular.	*Dual.*	*Plural.*
Aff.	Top sung =Hit me	Top chhong =Hit us two	To'pi kong =Hit us all
Neg.	Tha topmo	Tha topchhok	Tha to'pok

Dual and Plural of Agent.

*Aff.	Top sungchhe	Hit me ye two
	Top sungne	Hit me ye all

Negatives.

*Neg.	Thá topmochhe	Hit me not ye two
	Thá topmone	Hit me not ye all

INDICATIVE MOOD.

Singular.	*Dual.*	*Plural.*
1. To' mum =hits me (sub-andi, he)	+Top chhokmi, excl. +Top chhikmi, incl. =hits us two	+To' popmi, excl. +To' pem, incl. =hits us all

Dual and Plural of Agent.

*	1. To' mochhem	They two (and ye two) hit me	
	1. To' momem	They all hit me	
	2. +To' mi	+Top chhikmi	+top nem
*	2. To' mi	They two (and we two) hit thee	
	2. To' mi	They all (and we all) hit thee	
	3. +To' mi	+Top chhikmi	+Topmem
*	3. +Top chhikmi	They two (and ye two) hit him	
	3. +Top' mem.	They all hit him	

Preterite.

Singular.	*Dual.*	*Plural.*
Topsungmi	+ Top chhongmi, excl. To'p chhingmi, incl.	+ To'pi kong mi, excl. To'pi keng mi, incl.

Dual and Plural of Agent.

*	1. Top sung chhem	They two (or ye two) struck me	
	1. Top sung mem	They all struck me	
	2. To' mi	+Top chhem	+Tom nem
	2. To' mi	They two (or we two) struck thee	
	2. To' mi	They all struck thee	
	3. +To' pum	+To' pochhem	+To' pomem
+	3. To' pochhem	They two struck him	
	3. To' pomem	They all struck him	

---

* The brackets and the initial crosses (+) refer, as before explained, to forms of the verb scarcely reconcilable with our ideas of conjugation, and yet not easily separable from such as are so, *and* to forms common to the active and passive voices; see further on for another view of the subject.

The optative mood is precisely similar to the optative active. The negative mood is formed, as before, by merely prefixing the particle of negation, or má.

INTERROGATIVE MOOD.

	Present.	*Preterite.*	
1.	To' mo ki má	Topsung ki má	Dual and plural by dropping m or mi final and substituting the interrogative form
2.	+ Top ki má	Tom ki má	
3.	+ Top ki má	+ To'po ki má	

Subjunctive mood by substituting nam and phen for ki má, according to tense.

POTENTIAL MOOD.

	Present (or Future).		*Preterite.*	
1.	Top wongnom	1.	Top wonsungmi,	and so on, conjugating with the passive of wonto like the passive of hato
2.	Top wonmi	2.	Top wonmi,	
3.	+ Top wontum	3.	+ Top wontum,	

PRECATIVE MOOD.

	Present.		*Preterite.*	
1.	To'mo yu	1.	Top sung yu	Dual and plural as in the indicative, substituting yu for the final m or mi
2.	+ Top yu	2.	Tom yu	
3.	+ Top yu	3.	+ To'po yu	

CAUSAL VERB.

Formed as before with the passive of pingko * added to top'. Top pinggnom, &c., top pingsungmi, &c. Like the above paradigm of roots in 'po are conjugated also chi'po, to defecate; wo'po, to shoot; i'po, to raise (make get up); du'po, to kindle; khi'po, to make rope; pi'po, to suck; po'po, to lick; yo'po, to take off; chho'po, to sharpen, and all others having no consonant but an abrupt tone (standing for truncated p) before the transitive sign.†

A second form of passive is constructed from the past participle and the auxiliary verb, as aforenoticed, thus—

1.	Topta nognom ‡	&c., according to the model of sheer neuters (see phi).
2.	Topta nonum	
3.	Topta nomi	

SPECIAL FORMS.

I.—I and thou.

S.	Top num	I (only) strike or will strike or struck thee	Aoristic.
D.	Topnochhem	I (only) strike or struck you two	
P.	Top nonem	I (only) strike or struck you all	

II.—Thou and I.

S.γ	Top'mum	Thou strikest or wilt strike me	Present and future.
D.γ	Top' mochhem	Ye two strike or will strike me	
P.	Top' monem	Ye all strike or will strike me	
S.γ	Top sungmi	Thou struckedst me	Preterite.
D.	Top sungchhem	Ye two struck me	
P.	Top sungnem	Ye all struck me	

Ninth.—Conjugation of transitives in po having a nasal (m. n. ng.) before it.

The verb Hom, to taste.

INFINITIVE MOOD.

Aff. Hommung, to taste or to have tasted.§ Aoristic.

---

* For conjugation to pingko, see pp. 304 f.

† As already remarked at p. 293, this merged consonant must be restored before the conjugation can proceed.

‡ See prior verb at p. 292. Here we have for Váyu active and passive to'vi nognom and topta nognom = Khas kutnya hon and kutyako hon and dahma kha, dáya'hma kha, of Newári.

§ Also used quite like an adjective hommung ti, drinking or palatable water, water fit for tasting or being tasted.

Neg. Máng hommung, not to taste or to have tasted.

GERUNDS.

Hom he Hom nung	Present. Tasting	With main verb in present or future. With main verb in preterite.
Hom hom há	Past. Having tasted.	
Hom sing he	Future or present. When tasting.	
Hom khen	Past. After tasting. After having tasted.	

PARTICIPLES.

Honvi or homvi	Who tastes, did or will taste. Aoristic.
Homta or hompta	What is or has been tasted. Past and passive.
Homtáng or homptáng	What will be tasted, what is usually tasted, what fit to be tasted. Future passive.

VERBAL NOUNS.

Hom chyáng	Expresses the instrument as homchyáng li, the tasting tongue. It is also used substantively hom chyáng, the taster (organ, not man).

Hom lung expresses the locality, external to self.
Hom sing expresses the time of tasting.

The negative forms of all the above are made by prefixing the privitive particle máng.

IMPERATIVE MOOD.

	Singular.	*Dual.*	*Plural.*
Aff.	Hompo	Homchhe	Homne
Neg.	Thá hom	Thá homchhe	Thá homne

Dual and Plural of Object.

* Aff.	Hompochhe	Do thou taste those two.
	Hompome	Do thou taste them all.

Negatives of the above.

* Neg.	Thá homchhik	Do not taste those two.
	Thá homne	Do not taste them all.

INDICATIVE MOOD.

Present Tense.

I. Hom sungmi	+ Hom chhokmi, excl. + Hom chhikmi, incl.	+ Hom popmi, excl. + Hom pem, incl.

Dual and Plural of Object.

* I. Hom sungchhem	I taste them two.	
I. Hom sungmem	I taste them all.	
2. + Hom mi	+ Hom chhikmi.	+ Homnem.
* 2. Hom chhikmi	Thou tastest them two.	
2. Hom mem	Thou tastest *them all.*	
3. + Hom mi	+ Homchhikmi.	*+ Homnem.*
* 3. + Homchhikmi	He tastes them two	
3. + Hommem	He tastes them all	

Preterite.

I. Hom pungmi	+ Hom chhongmi, excl. + Hom chhingmi, incl.	+ Hompi kongmi, excl. + Hompi kengmi, incl.

Dual and Plural of Object.

*	1. Hom pungchhem	I tasted them two	
*	1. Hom pungmem	I tasted them all	
	2. Hom pum	+Hom chhem	+Hom nem
*	2. Hom pochhem	Thou tastedst them two	
*	2. Hom pomem	Thou tastedst them all	
	3. +Hom pum	+Hom pochhem	+Hom pomem
*	3. +Hom pochhem	He tasted them two	
*	3. +Hom pomem	He tasted them all	

Negative mood by prefixed má.

Optative mood by conjugation of the verb dák suffixed to the root (hom) of the main verb, hom dák gnom, &c.

Interrogative mood by dropping final mi or m and substituting the interrogation form ki má, thus—

	Present.	Preterite.
1.	Hom sung ki má	Hom pung ki má
2.	+Hom kimá	Hom po ki má
3.	+Hom kimá	+Hom po ki má

Subjunctive mood by substituting nam in the present and phen in the past for ki má; thus, hom sung nam, if I taste; hom pung phen, if I had tasted, &c.

Potential mood by conjugating the aoristic transitive wonto after the root hom.

PRECATIVE MOOD.

	Present.	Preterite.	
1.	Hom sung yu	Hom pung yu	thus merely substituting the precative particle for the interrogative
2.	+Hom yu	Hom po yu	
3.	+Hom yu	+Hom po yu	

CONTINUATIVE MOOD.		RECIPROCAL MOOD.	
Hom na hom nognom	&c., as before	Hom na hom pá̱nchungmi	&c., as before
Hom na hom nonum		Hom na hom pá̱nchem	
Hom na hom nomi		Hom na hom pá̱nchem	

CAUSAL.

By conjugating the root hom with the causal verb pingko, as before.

PASSIVE.

IMPERATIVE MOOD.

	Singular.	Dual.	Plural.
Aff.	Hom sung	Homchhong	Hom pi kong
Neg.	Thá hommo	Thá homchhok	Thá hom pok

Dual and Plural of Agent.

*	Aff. Hom sungchhe	Do ye two taste me
*	Aff. Hom sungne	Do ye all taste me
*	Neg. Thá hommochhe	Do ye two taste me not
*	Neg. Thá hommone	Do ye all taste me not

INDICATIVE MOOD.

Singular.	Dual.	Plural.
1. Hom mum	+Hom chhokmi, excl.	+Hom popmi, excl.
	+Hom chhikmi, incl.	+Hom pem, incl.

Dual and Plural of Agent.

*	1. Hom mochhem	They two (or ye two) taste me
*	1. Hom momem	They all taste me

	Singular	Dual.	Plural.
	2. +Hommi	+Hom chhikmi	+Homnem
		Dual and Plural of Agent.	
*	2. Hommi	They two (and we two) taste thee	
*	2. Hommi	They all (and we two) taste thee	
	3. +Hommi	+Hom chhikmi	+Hommem
*	3. +Hom chhikmi	They two (and ye) taste him	
*	3. +Hom mem	They all taste him	
		Preterite.	
	1. Hom sungmi	+Hom chhong mi, excl.	+Hompi kongmi, excl.
		+Hom chhing mi, incl.	+Hompi kengmi, incl.
		Dual and Plural of Agent.	
*	1. Hom sungchhem	They two (or ye two) tasted me	
*	1. Hom sungmem	They all tasted me	
	2. Hommi	+Homchhem	+Homnem
*	2. Hommi	They two (or we two) tasted thee	
*	2. Hommi	They all (or we two) tasted thee	
	3. +Hompum	+Hom pochhem	+Hom pomem
*	3. +Hom pochem	They two tasted him	
*	3. +Hom pomem	They all tasted him	

NEGATIVE MOOD.

Is formed, as in active voice, merely by prefixing the privative particle má.

OPTATIVE MOOD.

Concurs with the same in the active voice, dák having an active and passive sense, and the neuter form dakgnom being also the passive form dakgnom, I desire or am desired; the latter sense transferred to root. With the synonymous verb yot', to like, the voices can be distinguished, yosto being the active transitive and yosung the passive; hence we have as optative active and passive.

Active Voice.		*Passive Voice.*	
1. Hom yonmi	*Present tense.* I like to taste.	1. Hom yotgnom	*Present tense.* I like to be tasted.
2. Hom yotmi		2. Hom yonmi	
3. Hom yotmi		3. Hom yostum	
1. Hom yostungmi	*Preterite.*	1. Hom yossungmi	*Preterite.*
2. Hom yostum		2. Hom yonmi	
3. Hom yostum		3. Hom yostum	

INTERROGATIVE MOOD.

Simply by dropping m or mi final and substituting ki má.

SUBJUNCTIVE MOOD.

Simply by dropping the mi or m and substituting nam for present and phen for past tense: hommonam, homsungphen, &c.

POTENTIAL MOOD.

By conjugating the passive of wonto, as before, added to the root hom.

PRECATIVE MOOD.

By dropping the final m or mi, and substituting yu: hommo yu, homsung yu, &c.

CAUSAL MOOD.

As before, by pingko added to the root.

Thus are conjugated námpo, to smell; thampo, to lose; *kh*umpo, to bury; hempo, to cause to sleep; hámpo, to spread; and all similar words. So also are conjugated all transitives in ko having a nasal before them (n or ng), as pingko, to send; chinko, to spin and to fill; puṇko, to weave; hóṇko, to uncover; honko, to obey; chhuṇko, to cleanse; túṇko, to drink spirits and to cherish; suṇko, to dry at fire; lenko, to find—only that the terminations dependent on the transitive change with that sign, and as hompo makes hompopmi hompem, so pingko makes pingkokmi pingkem. See pingko conjugated at p. 304.

N.B.—The nasal is n or ng, *e.g.*, lenko vel lengko, to find and see.

SECOND FORM OF THE PASSIVE.

Hompta nognom Hompta nonum Hompta nomi	&c., as before, throughout the auxiliary verb

SPECIAL FORMS.

I.—I and thou.

S.	Homnum	I (only) taste or will taste or did taste thee	Aoristic
D.	Hom nochem	I (only) taste or tasted you two	
P.	Hom nonem	I (only) taste or tasted you all	

II.—Thou and I.

S.γ	Hommum	Thou (or he) tastest or wilt taste me	Present and Future
D.γ	Hom mochhem	Ye two (or they two) taste, &c., or will taste me	
P.	Hom monem	Ye all taste or will taste me	

Preterite.

S.γ	Hom sungmi *	Thou (or he) tastedest me	Preterite
D.γ	Hom sungchhem	Ye two (or they two) tasted me	
P.	Hom sungnem	Ye all (only) tasted me	

Tenth.—Conjugation of transitives in ko not having any consonant nor any abrupt tone between the sign and the root.†

The verb Tá, to place.

INFINITIVE MOOD.

Aff.	Támung	Aoristic.
Neg.	Máng támung	

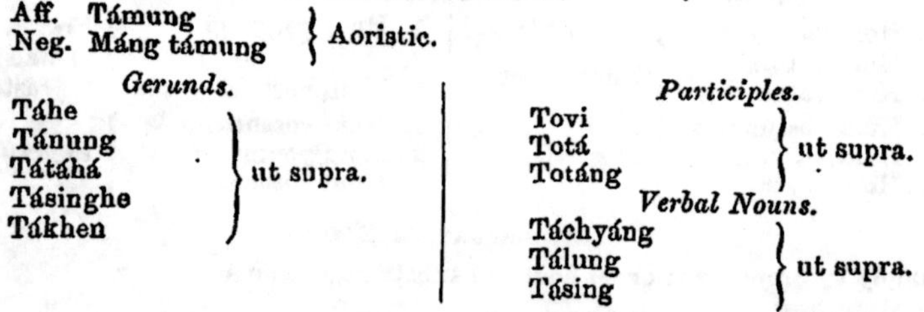

Gerunds.

Táhe Tánung Tátahá Tásinghe Tákhen	ut supra.

Participles.

Tovi Totá Totáng	ut supra.

Verbal Nouns.

Táchyáng Tálung Tásing	ut supra.

Negatives of all by máng prefixed.

IMPERATIVE MOOD.

	Singular.	*Dual.*	*Plural.*
Aff.	Táko	Táchhe	Táne
Neg.	Thá to	Thá tochhe	Thá tone

---

* The mark γ placed before some of these forms indicates that they are included in the more ordinary forms of conjugation. They are repeated here for illustration. The change of sense in dual and plural of preterite shows, in conjunction with the whole system of conjugation, how restive the language is under these trammels.

† There is not only no abrupt accent or tone, but there is an equally forcible pausing tone. Conj. viii. and xi. have the abrupt tone, not to add also conj. vii. The present conjugation only has the pausing tone. Both tones need close attention for sense sometimes as well as grammar, *e.g.*, to'vi and to'mi, with the abrupt tone, mean the striker and he strikes; with the pausing tone to'övi, to'öme, as here, they mean the placer and he places. Perhaps I ought to have so written the latter.

Dual and Plural of Object.

Aff.	Tákochhe	Put down them two
	Takome	Put down them all
* Neg.	Thá tochhik	Put not down them two
	Thá tome	Put not down them all

INDICATIVE MOOD.

	Singular.	*Dual.*	*Plural.*
1.	Tángmi *	Tá chhokmi, excl.	Tákokmi
		Tá chhikmi, incl.	Tákem

Dual and Plural of Object.

*	1. Tángchhem	I put down them two	
	1. Tángmem	I put down them all	
	2. + Tomi	+ Tochhikmi	+ Tonem
*	2. Tochhikmi	Thou putest down them two	
	2. Tomem	Thou putest down them all	
	3. + Tomi	+ Tochhikmi	+ Tomem
*	3. + Tochhikmi	He puts down them two	
	3. + Tomem	He puts down them all	

Preterite.

	Singular.	*Dual.*	*Plural.*
1.	Tákungmi	Tá chhongmi	Tákikongmi
		Tá chhingmi	Tákikengmi

Dual and Plural of Object.

*	1. Tákungchhem	I placed them two	
	1. Tákungmem	I placed them all	
	2. Tákum	Táchhem	Tánem
*	2. Tákochhem	Thou puttest down them two	
	2. Tákomem	Thou puttest down them all	
	3. + Tákum	+ Tákochhem	+ Tákomem
*	3. + Tákochhem	He put down them two	
	3. + Tákomem	He put down them all	

Negative mood by prefixed má.
Optative mood by dak conjugated after the tá root, as before given.
Interrogative mood by cutting off final mi or m and substituting the querying formula ki má.
Subjunctive mood by like truncation, and substitution of nam for present and phen for past tense.
Potential mood by conjugating wonto after the root tá.
Precative by the immutable particle yu substituted for final mi, m.
Causal by conjugating pingko added to root.

CONTINUATIVE MOOD.

1. Tá nátá nognom
2. Tá nátá nonum
3. Tá natá nomi

and so on, conjugating the substantive verb nó, to be, after the model of phi, to come, and prefixing the iterated root with na interposed

RECIPROCAL MOOD.

	Singular.	*Dual.*	*Plural.*
1.	Tá natá pánchungmi	Tá natá pánachhokmi	Tá natá páchikokmi
		Tá natá pánachhikmi	Tá natá páchikem
2.	Tá natá pánchem	Tá natá pánachhikmi	Tá natá páchinem
3.	Tá natá pánchem	Tá natá pánachhikmi	Tá natá páchimem

And so on, for the preterite, after the model of imche and all reflex verbs in che.

---

* Also tovi nognom, as elsewhere explained.

This is formed by the reflex of the verb pá, to do, which is pánche added to the iterated root as before. The construction ad sensum, which is the chief rule of this tongue, restricts the reciprocal mood in use to the dual and plural.

PASSIVE VOICE.

IMPERATIVE MOOD.

	Singular.	*Dual.*	*Plural.*
Aff.	Tosung	Tochhong	Tokikong
Neg.	Thá togno	Thá tochhok	Thá tokok

Dual and Plural of Agent.

*Aff.	Tosungchhe	Do ye two place me
	Tosungne	Do ye all place me
*Neg.	Thá tosungchhe Thá tosungne	Place me not, ye two, ye all

INDICATIVE MOOD.

	Singular.	*Dual.*	*Plural.*
1.	Tognom	Tochhokmi Tochhikmi	Tokokmi, excl. Tokem, incl.

Dual and Plural of Agent.

* 1. Tognochhem	They (or ye) two place me	
* 1. Tognomem	They all place me	
2. +Tomi	+Tochhikmi	+Tonem
* 2. Tomi	They two (and we) place thee	
* 2. Tomi	They all (and we) place thee	
3. +Tomi	+Tochhikmi	+Tomem
* 3. +Tochhikmi	They two (and ye) place him	
* 3. +Tomem	They all place him	

Preterite.

1. Tosungmi	Tochhongmi Tochhingmi	Tokikongmi, excl. Tokikengmi, incl.

Dual and Plural of Agent.

* 1. Tosungchhem	They two (or ye) placed me	
* 1. Tosungmem	They all placed me	
2. Tomi	Tochhem	Tonem
* 2. Tomi	They two (or we) placed thee	
* 2. Tomi	They all (or we) placed thee	
3. +Takum	+Takochhem	+Takomem
* 3. +Tákochhem	They two (or ye) placed him	
* 3. +Takomem	They all placed him	

NEGATIVE MOOD.

By prefixing má merely.

OPTATIVE MOOD.

Tá dakgnom, &c., as in active voice.

Tá ping dakgnom (the last as a neuter) seems to be more correct, but is eschewed; though dakgnom, if allowed to be a passive, could hardly, one would suppose, create the passive sense in the main verb in either form of this mood.

INTERROGATIVE MOOD.

Togno ki má	Tosung ki má	and so on, dropping the final
To ki má	To ki má	m, mi, and substituting the
+To ki má	+Táko ki má.	interrogative ki má

SUBJUNCTIVE MOOD.

As in the interrogative, but substituting nam in present and phen in past tense for the interrogatory form.

POTENTIAL MOOD.

Tá won gnom Tá won mi +Tá wontum	&c., like the passive of háto aforegone. Here also the passive sense lost in the truncated root is transferred to the secondary verb. Taping wonchungmi, I am able to be put down, is also admissible

CAUSAL MOOD.

Tá ping chungmi Tá ping chem Tá ping chem I am put down by my own will, &c.	Tá ping gnom Tá ping mi Tá ping mi I am set down by another's will, &c.	&c., by the reflex or passive causal of pingko, conjugated like imche and hompo respectively

CONTINUATIVE MOOD.

Tá natá pognom Tá natá pomi Tá natá pomi	&c., the iterated root conjugated with the passive of the verb pá, to do, which agrees with tá, to place

Thus are conjugated jáko, to eat; páko, to make; tháko, to hear; náko, to kindle; chháko, to loosen; chhuko, to seize; doko, to catch; khiko, to hide; dúko, to dig; seko, to understand; reko and guko,* to lift up; khoko, to cook; boko, to dry; and all others having a nude root before the ko sign. But observe that táko, jáko, and páko change their á into ó, as in the aforegone paradigm, whereas the rest suffer no such alteration. All alike take a half nasal before the intransitive sign che. It has already been remarked that transitives *in* "ko" having a nasal before the sign, as pingko, to send, are conjugated like transitives in po with a similarly-placed nasal; but as pingko is the great former of causatives, I give it before closing the conjugations, observing by the way that the root ping, which is merely nasalised pi, seems to explain the Dravirian causative sign.

Second Form of the Passive.

1. Tota nognom 2. Tota nonum 3. Tota nomi	&c., as before.

SPECIAL FORMS.

I.—I to thee.

S.	Tonum	I (only) placed or will place thee	Aoristic
D.	Tonochhem	I (only) placed or will place you two	
P.	Tononem	I (only) placed or will place you all	

II.—Thou to me.

S.γ	Tognom	Thou (or he) placest, &c., me	Present and Future
D.γ	Tognochhem	Ye two (or they two) place me	
P.	Tognomen	Ye all (only) place me	

Preterite.

S.γ	Tosungmi	Thou (or he) placed me	Preterite
D.γ	Tosungchhem	Ye two (or they two) placed me	
P.	Tosungnem	Ye all placed me	

---

* Guko is error; for it is not gúüko with the pausing tone proper to this conjugation, but gu'ko (recte gukko) with the abrupt tone; and therefore gu'ko belongs to the next conjugation. But add to this, kuko, to carry; hoko, to search; pleko, to share out; luko, to take off; piko, to sew; doko, to accept; kheko, to insert; veko, to suspend; poko, to spread; biko, to beg; theko, to push or shove.

IMPERATIVE.

	Singular.	*Dual.*	*Plural.*
Aff.	Pingko	Pingchhe	Pingne
Neg.	Thá ping	Thá pingchhe	Thá pingne

Dual and Plural of Object.

*Aff.	Pingkochhe	Do thou send them two
	Pingkome	Do thou send them all
*Neg.	Thá pingchhik	Dual
	Thá pingme	Plural

INDICATIVE PRESENT.

	Singular.	*Dual.*	*Plural.*
	1. Pingsungmi	+ Pingchhokmi + Pingchhikmi	+ Pingkokmi + Pingkem

Dual and Plural of Object.

*	1. Pingsungchhem	I send them two	
	1. Pingsungmem	I send them all	
	2. + Pingmi	+ Pingchhikmi	+ Pingnem
*	2. Pingchhikmi	Thou sendest them two	
	2. Pingmem	Thou sendest them all	
	3. Pingmi	+ Pinchhikmi	+ Pingmem
*	3. Pingchhikmi	He sends them two	
	3. Pingmem	He sends them all	

Preterite.

	1. Pingkungmi	+ Pingchhongmi + Pingchhingmi	Pingkikongmi + Pingkikengmi

Dual and Plural of Object.

*	1. Pingkungchhem	I sent them two	
	1. Pingkungmem	I sent them all	
	2. Pingkum	+ Pingchhem	+ Pingnem
*	2. Pingkochhem	Thou sendest them two	
	2. Pingkomem	Thou sendest them all	
	3. + Pingkum	+ Pingkochhem	+ Pingkomem
*	3. + Pingkochhem	He sent them two	
	3. + Pingkomem	He sent them all	

PASSIVE VOICE.

IMPERATIVE MOOD.

Aff.	Pinsung	Pingchhong	Pingkikong
Neg.	Thá pinggno	Thá pingchhok	Thá pingkok

Dual and Plural of Agent.

*Aff.	Pingsungchhe	Do you two send me
	Pingsungne	Do you all send me
*Neg.	Thá pingsungchhe	Thá pingsungne

INDICATIVE MOOD.

Present Tense.

1. Pinggnom	+ Pingchhokmi + Pingchhikmi	+ Pingkokmi + Pingkem

Dual and Plural of Agent.

*	1. Pinggnochhem	They two send me	
	1. Pinggnomem	They all send me	
	2. + Pingmi	+ Pingchhikmi	+ Pingnem

* { 2. Pingmi	They two send thee	
2. Pingmi	They all send thee	
3. +Pingmi	+Pingchhikmi	+Pingmem
* { 3. +Pingchhikmi	They two send him	
3. +Pingmem	They all send him	

Preterite.

1. Pingsungmi	+ { Pingchhongmi Pingchhingmi	+Pingkikongmi +Pingkikengmi

Dual and Plural of Agent.

* { 1. Pingsungchhem	They two sent me	
1. Pingsungmem	They all sent me	
2. Pingmi	+Pingchhem	+Pingnem
* { 2. Pingmi	They two sent thee	
2. Pingmi	They all sent thee	
3. +Pingkum	+Pingkochhem	+Pingkomem
* { 3. +Pingkochhem	They two sent him	
3. +Pingkomem	They all sent him *	

Eleven.—Conjugation of transitives in "ko" having an abrupt tone (equal iterate sign) between the sign and the root.

The verb phó (phok'),† to beget, or give birth to.

INFINITIVE MOOD.

Aff. Phok mung
Neg. Mang phokmung

Gerunds.	*Participles.*	*Verbal Nouns.*
Phokhe	Phokvi	Phokchyáng
Phoknung, &c.	Phokta, &c.	Phoklung
		Phoksing, &c.

IMPERATIVE MOOD.

Aff.	Pho'ko (phokko)	Phokchhe	Phongne
Neg.	Thá pho'ko (phokko)	Thá phokchhe	Thá phokne

Dual and Plural of Object.

*Aff.	{ Pho'kochhe	Do thou beget two
	Pho'kome	Do thou beget all
*Neg.	{ Thá phokchhik	Do not beget two
	Thá phokme	Do not beget all

INDICATIVE MOOD.

Singular.	*Dual.*	*Plural.*
1. Phongmi	{ Phokchhokmi, excl. Phokchhikmi, incl.	Phokkokmi, excl. Phokkem, incl.

Dual and Plural of Object.

* { 1. Phongchhem	I beget them two	
1. Phongmem	I beget them all	
2. Phokmi	Phokchhikmi	Phoknem
* { 2. Phokchhikmi	Thou begett'st them two	
2. Phokmem	Thou begett'st them all	
3. Phokmi	Phokchhikmi	Phokmem
* { 3. Phokchhikmi	He begets them two	
3. Phokmem	He begets them all	

* Thus are conjugated all verbs in "ko" preceded by a nasal, n, or ng, *e.g.*, all those cited at p. 211 f., or lenko, chenko, honko; and to these add phengko, to play; pungko, to weave; ingko, to buy, &c.

† Phok' is clearly the right rm. See note at p. 242.

Preterite.

1. Pho'kungmi	Phokchhongmi, excl. Phokchhingmi, incl.	Phokikongmi, excl. Phokikengmi, incl.

Dual and Plural of Object.

* 1. Pho'kungchhem	I begot two	
* 1. Pho'kungmem	I begot all	
2. Pho'kum	Phokchhem	Phongnem
* 2. Phokochem	Thou begott'st two	
* 2. Phokomem	Thou begott'st all	
3. Pho'kum	Phokochhem	Phokomem
* 3. Phokochhem	He begot two	
* 3. Phokomem	He begot all	

Reciprocal continuative, &c., compound with phok and the verbs nó and pánche, as before.

PASSIVE VOICE.

No infinitive gerunds or participles save in the causal form, phokpingmung, phokpinghe, phokpingví, &c.*

Imperative Mood.

	Singular.	*Dual.*	*Plural.*
Aff.	Phoksung	Phokchhong	Pho'kikong.
Neg.	Thá phokgno	Thá phokchhok	Thá pho'kok

Dual and Plural of Object.

Aff.	Phoksungchhe	Do ye two beget me
	Phoksungne	Do ye all beget me
Neg.	Thá phoksungchhe	
	Thá phoksungne	

Indicative Mood.

Singular. 1. Phokgnom 2. Phokmi 3. Phokmi *Preterite.* 1. Phoksungmi 2. Phongmi 3. Phongmi	Dual and plural and agento-objective as in the last conjugation, only substituting phok for tó, of which the latter shows the tá root, internally modified; and the former, the iterate transitive sign, elsewhere suppressed, here brought forward, for phok-gnom and phongmi both depend on pho'-ko being really phok-ko.†

Thus are conjugated tá'ko, to decorticate; kho'ko, to crook; pu'ko, to awaken; chi'ko, to bite; ne'ko, to give rest; Ju'ko, to choose; li'ko, to lay down or thrown down; cha'ko, to put upon, to make come up; ye'ko, to shear or clear the ground for cultivation; chho'ko, to sow; po'ko, to weigh or measure; chu'ko, to plane wood; lo'ko, to turn over; gu'ko, to raise forcibly; cho'ko, to offer; ruko, to plough, &c. Observe that in all these the latent iterate sign of the imperative, whose presence is only indicated by the abrupt tone (ta'ko), is preserved in the conjugation, whence from a common crude, or tá, to place and to decorticate, comes all the difference of tángmi, tomi, tomi and tángmi takmi, takmi in the indicative, whilst in the preterite there is only the difference of the abrupt accent, tákungmi, tákum, tákum, and ta'kungmi, ta'kum, ta'kum. The change of vowel is confined to the three verbs tako, jako, and pako. All other transitives in "ko" conjugated from the sheer root as Sé-ko, understand it, follow the paradigm of táko, less that change of vowel; as imperative Sé-ko, se-chhe, Se-ne, indicative, séngmi, sémi, sémi, &c. Compare with the transitives in 'ko, as above, those in 'po, as to'po, aforegone. Both follow the Dravirian rule of iteration, only disguised for the sake of euphony.

---

* This holds as to all the conjugations. But observe that the participles in tá and táng (2 in 3), though ranged under the active voice, are essentially passive.

† There can be no doubt than in all the verbs of this conjugation, as in all of the eighth, the dropped consonant must be restored, yet not so as to obliterate the tone which in those two conjugations is as decidedly of the abrupt kind as in conj. x. of the pausing kind; and, for example, táko (recte takko), here, is táko (táäko), apud conj. x.

Twelfth.—Conjugation (of Irregulars).

Lá, *to go.*

IMPERATIVE MOOD.

	Singular.	*Dual.*	*Plural.*
Aff.	Lá'la	Lá'chhe	Láne
Neg.	Thá lá'la	Thá lá'chhik *	Thá láne

INDICATIVE MOOD.

Singular.	*Dual.*	*Plural.*
1. Lágnom	Lá'chhokmi, excl. Lá'chhikmi, incl.	Lá'kokmi, excl. Lá'kem, incl.
2. Lá'lam	Lá'chhikmi	Lánem
3. Lá'lam	Lá'chhikmi	Lámem

Preterite.

Singular.	*Dual.*	*Plural.*
1. Lá'sungmi	Lá'chhongmi, excl. Lá'chhingmi, incl.	Lá'kikongmi, excl. Lá'kikengmi, incl.
2. Lá'lam	Lá'chhem	Lánem
3. Lá'lam	Lá'chhem	Lámem

Thirteenth.—Conjugation (of Irregulars).

Nó, *to be.*

PRESENT INDICATIVE SINGULAR.

1. Nógnom 2. Nónum 3. Nómi or Nóm	The residue is quite regular (see 1st conjugation), as also in the above verb, and indeed the dual and plural of all verbs whatever are nearly immutable, as will have been seen

Remark.—Both the above have an abrupt tone or obscure t' before the gerund, participle, and verbal noun signs, as lat'he; not'he; lat'lat'ha, not'not'ha; lat'vi, not'vi; la'ta, no'ta, also in the infinitive, lat'mung, not'mung.

Fourteenth and *Fifteenth.*—Conjugations (of Irregulars), being those of the verb lá, to go, as used in combination with other verbs.

I. With transitives as top', to beat.		II. With neuters, as im, to sleep.	
Indicative Present		*Indicative Present*	
Singular.		*Singular.*	
1. Top lángmi	Dual and plural, as in the uncombined verb lagnom, &c.	1. Im lagnom	Dual and plural are in the separate verb
2. Top lam		2. Im lam	
3. Top lam		3. Im lam	
Preterite.		*Preterite.*	
1. Toplasungmi		1. Im la sungmi	
2. Top lam		2. Im lam	
3. Toplachem		3. Im lam	

IMPERATIVE.

Topla	Imla

Remark.—In every conjunction of verbs the first loses the infinitive sign, and is used in the crude state, whence the peculiar transfer of passive expression to the subordinate verb, as before illustrated. But to this, háto, in the sense of let, is an exception,—thus, let me strike, is topmung hasung; and topmung hánum, I let thee strike.

The above fifteen conjugations, with their accessories (see bracketed portions), exhibit the whole scope of Váyu conjugation. But a reference to them will show that it has been necessary, whilst striving to accommodate our forms to the genius

* See first conjugation of neuters conjugated from the crude root.

of this language, to interpolate into the transitives certain forms expressive of both agent and object, and likewise to append to the passive certain other forms which have been necessarily set apart from all the conjugations; not to mention the perpetual coincidence of active and passive forms. It may now be of use to exhibit the whole matter of conjugation in another shape seemingly more accommodated to the genius of the language, and which, though exhibiting a deal of repetition, will be found convenient for comparisons when we proceed to the Kiránti language, a language still richer than the Váyu tongue in pronominal combinations with the verb, and wherein, consequently, many of the mere iterations of the following diagram will take distinct shapes; whence we may infer that decomposition has proceeded a good deal further in the Váyu language than in the Kiránti tongue.

The verb *já*, to eat.

Imperative Mood.

Singular.

Eat thou.

1. Jánche, self, as agent or object, eat simply.
2. Jáko, it or him
3. Játo, his or for him
4. Jákochhe, them two
5. Játochhe, their two
6. Jákome, them all
7. Játome, their all
8. Jósung, me
9. Jásung, mine
10. Jochhung, us two
11. Jáchhung, our two
12. Jókikong, us all
13. Jákikong, our all

Dual.

Ye two eat.

1. Jánachhe, selves
2. Jáchhe, it
3. Jáchhe, his, for him
4. Jáchhe, them two
5. Jáchhe, their two
6. Jáchhe, them all
7. Jáchho, their all
8. Jósungchhe, me
9. Jásungchhe, mine
10. Jóchhung, us two
11. Jáchhung, our two
12. Jókikong, us all
13. Jákikong, our all

Plural.

Ye all eat.

1. Jánchine, selves or simple action (functional)
2. Jáne, it
3. Jáne, his, or for him
4. Jáne, them two
5. Jáne, their two
6. Jáne, them all
7. Jáne, their all
8. Jósungne, me
9. Jásungne, mine
10. Jóchhung, us two
11. Jáchhung, our two
12. Jókikong, us all
13. Jákikong, our all

Indicative Mood.

Present and Future.

Singular.

I eat or will eat.

1. Jánchungmi, self, as agent or object
2. Jángmi, it, him
3. Játungmi, his, or for him
4. Jángchhem, them two
5. Játungchhem, their two
6. Jángmem, them all
7. Játungmem, their all
8. Jónum, thee
9. Jánum, thine or for thee
10. Jónochhem, you two
11. Jánochhem, your two
12. Jónonem, you all
13. Jánonem, your all

Dual.

We two eat or will eat.

1. Jánachokmi, excl. / Jánachhikmi, incl. } selves
2. Jáchhokmi, excl. / Jáchhikmi, incl. } it
3. Jáchhokmi-chhikmi, his, for him
4. Jáchhokmi-chhikmi, them two
5. Jáchhokmi-chhikmi, their two
6. Jáchhokmi-chhikmi, them all
7. Jáchhokmi-chhikmi, their all
8. Jómi, thee
9. Jáchhokmi, thine
10. Jóchhikmi, you two
11. Jáchhokmi, your two
12. Jónem, you all
13. Jánem, your all

Plural.

We all eat or will eat.

1. Jánchikokmi, excl. / Jánchikem, incl. } selves
2. Jákokmi, excl. / Jáhem, incl. } it
3. Játikokmi, excl. / Játikem, incl. } his, for him
4. Jákokmi-kem, them two
5. Játi-kokmi-kem, their two
6. Já-kokmi-kem, them all
7. Játi-kokmi-kem, their all
8. Jomi or Jokokmi, thee
9. Jákokmi, thine
10. Jóchhikmi, you two
11. Jákokmi, your two
12. Jónem or Jókokmi, you all
13. Jánem or Jákokmi, your all

Singular.

Thou eat'st or wilt eat.

1. Jánchhem, self
2. Jómi, it
3. Játum, his, or for him
4. Jóchhikmi, them two
5. Játochem, their two
6. Jómem, them all
7. Játomem, their all
8. Jognom, me
9. Jágnom, mine
10. Jóchhokmi, us two
11. Jómi, our two
12. Jókokmi, us all
13. Jákokmi, our all

Dual.

Ye two eat or will eat.

1. Jánachhikmi, selves
2. Jóchhikmi, it
3. Jáchhikmi, his
4. Jóchhikmi, them two
5. Jáchhikmi, their two
6. Jóchhikmi, them all
7. Jáchhikmi, their all
8. Jógnochhem, me
9. Jágnochhem, mine
10. Jóchhokmi, us two
11. Jáchhokmi, our two
12. Jókokmi, us all
13. Jákokmi, our all

Plural.

Ye all eat or will eat.

1. Jánchinem, selves
2. Jonem, it
3. Janem, its, his
4. Jonem, them two
5. Janem, their two
6. Jonem, them all
7. Janem, their all
8. Jognonem, me
9. Jagnonem, mine
10. Jochhokmi, us two
11. Jáchhokmi, our two
12. Jokokmi, us all
13. Jákokmi, our all

Singular.

He eats or will eat.

1. Jánchhem, self
2. Jómi, it
3. Játum, his, for him
4. Jochhikmi, them two
5. Jatochhem, their two
6. Jomem, them all
7. Játomem, their all
8. Jómi, thee
9. Jómi, thine
10. Jochhikmi, you two
11. Jachhikmi, your two
12. Jonem, you all
13. Jomi, your all
14. Jognom, me
15. Jagnom, mine
16. Jochhokmi, excl. / Jochhikmi, incl. } us two
17. Jáchhokmi-chhikmi, our two
18. Jokokmi-kem, us all
19. Jákokmi-kem, our all

Dual.

They two eat or will eat.

1. Jánachhikmi, selves
2. Jochhikmi, it, him
3. Jatochhem, his, its
4. Jochhikmi, them two
5. Jatochhem, their two
6. Jochhikmi, them all
7. Játomem, their all
8. Jómi, thee
9. Jómi, thine
10. Jóchhik, you two
11. Jochhikmi, your two
12. Jonem, you all
13. Jochhikmi, your all
14. Jognochhem, me
15. Jagnochhem, mine
16. Jochhokmi, excl. / Jochhikmi, incl. } us two
17. Jáchhokmi-chhikmi, our two
18. Jokokmi-kem, us all
19. Jakokmi-kem, our all

Plural.

They all eat or will eat.

1. Jánchimem, selves
2. Jomem, it
3. Játomem, his, its, for him
4. Jómem, them two
5. Játomem, their two
6. Jómem, them all
7. Játomem, their all
8. Jómi, thee
9. Jómi, thine
10. Jóchhikmi, you two
11. Játomem, your two
12. Jonem or Jomem, you all
13. Jánem or Jatomem, your all
14. Jognomem, me
15. Jagnomem, mine
16. Jochhokmi, excl. / Jochhikmi, incl. } us two
17. Jachhokmi-chhikmi, our two
18. Jokokmi-kem, us all
19. Jakokmi-kem, our all

Preterite Tense.

Singular.

I ate.

1. Jánchhungmi, self, own
2. Jákungmi, it, him
3. Játungmi, his, for him
4. Jákungchhem, them two
5. Játungchhem, their two, or for them two
6. Jákungmem, them all
7. Jatungmem, their all, or for them all
8. Jónum, thee
9. Jánum, thine, or for thee
10. Jónochhem, you two
11. Jánochhem, your two, or for you two
12. Jónonem, you all
13. Jáonem, your all, or for you all

Dual.

We two ate.

No.	Form	Meaning
1.	Jánachhongmi, excl. Jánachhingmi, incl.	selves, own
2.	Jáchhongmi, excl. Jáchhingmi, incl.	it, him
3.	Jáchhongmi, excl. Jáchhingmi, incl.	his, for him
4.	Jáchhongmi, excl. Jáchhingmi, incl.	them two
5.	Jáchhongmi, excl. Jáchhingmi, incl.	their two, or for them two
6.	Jáchhongmi, excl. Jáchhingmi, incl.	them all
7.	Jáchhongmi, excl. Jáchhingmi, incl.	their all, or for them all

8. Jómi, thee
9. Jáchhongmi, thine, for thee
10. Jóchhem, you two
11. Jáchhongmi, your two, or for you two
12. Jónem or jáchhongmi, you all
13. Jánum or jáchhongmi, your all, or for you all

Plural.

We all ate.

No.	Form	Meaning
1.	Jánchhikongmi, excl. Jánchhikengmi, incl.	selves, own
2.	Jákikongmi, excl. Jákikengmi, incl.	it, him
3.	Játikongmi, excl. Játikengmi, incl.	its, his, for him
4.	Jákikongmi, excl. Jákikengmi, incl.	them two
5.	Játikongmi, excl. Játikengmi, incl.	their two, or for them two
6.	Jákikongmi, excl. Jákikengmi, incl.	them all
7.	Játikongmi, excl. Játikengmi, incl.	their all, or for them all

8. Jómi, thee
9. Jákikongmi, thine, or for thee
10. Jóchem or jákikongmi, you two
11. Játikongmi, your two, for you two
12. Jónem, or jákikongmi, you all
13. Jánem, or játikongmi, your all, for you all

Singular.

Thou at'st or didst eat.

1. Jánchhem, self, own
2. Jákom, it, him
3. Játum, his, for him
4. Jákochhem, them two
5. Játochhem, their two, or for them two
6. Jákomem, them all
7. Játomem, their all, or for them all
8. Jósungmi, me
9. Jásungmi, mine, for me
10. Jóchungmi, us two
11. Jáchungmi, our two, or for us two
12. Jókikongmi, us all
13. Jákikongmi, our all, for us all

Dual.

Ye two ate.

1. Jánáchhem, selves, own
2. Jáchhem, it, him
3. Jáchhem, its, his
4. Jáchhem, them two
5. Jáchhem, their two, for them two
6. Jáchhem, them all
7. Jáchhem, their all, for them all
8. Jósungchhem, me
9. Jásungchhem, mine, for me
10. Jóchhungmi, us two
11. Jáchhungmi, our two, for us two
12. Jokikongmi, us all
13. Jákikongmi, our all, for us all

Plural.

Ye all ate.

1. Jánchinem, selves, own
2. Jánem, it, him
3. Jánem, his, its
4. Jánem, them two
5. Jánem, their two, for them two
6. Jánem, them all
7. Jánem, their all, for them all
8. Jósungnem, me
9. Jásungnem, mine, for me
10. Jóchhongmi, us two
11. Jáchhongmi, our two, for us two
12. Jókikongmi, us all
13. Jákikongmi, our all, for us all

Singular.

They ate.

1. **Jánchhem, self, own.**
2. **Júkum, it, him**
3. **Játum, his, for him**
4. **Jákochhem, them two**
5. **Játochhem, their two, for them two**
6. **Jákomem, them all**
7. **Játomem, their all, for them all**
8. **Jósungmi, me**
9. **Jásungmi, mine, for me**
10. **Jóchhongmi, excl. / Jóchhingmi, incl.** } **us two**
11. **Jáchhongmi, excl. / Jáchhingmi, incl.** } **our two, for us two**
12. **Jókikongmi, excl. / Jókikengmi, incl.** } **us all**
13. **Jákikongmi, excl. / Jákikengmi, incl.** } **our all, for us all**
14. **Jómi, thee**
15. **Jákum, thine**
16. **Jóchhem, you two**
17. **Jáchhem, your two, for you two**
18. **Jónem, you all**
19. **Jánem, your all, for you all**

Dual.

They two ate.

1. **Jánachhem, selves, own**
2. **Jákochhem, it, him**
3. **Játochhem, his, its**
4. **Jákochhem, them two**
5. **Játochhem, their two, for them two**
6. **Jákochhem, them all**
7. **Játochhem, their all, for them all**
8. **Josungchhem, me**
9. **Jásungchhem, mine**
10. **Jóchhóngmi, excl. / Jóchhingmi, incl.** } **us two**
11. **Jáchhongmi, excl. / Jáchhingmi, incl.** } **our two, for us two**
12. **Jókikongmi, excl. / Jókikengmi, incl.** } **us all**
13. **Jákikongmi, excl. / Jákikengmi, incl.** } **our all, for us all**
14. **Jómi, thee**
15. **Jákum / Jákochhem** } **thine**
16. **Jóchhem, you two**
17. **Jáchhem, your two, for you two**
18. **Jónem, you all**
19. **Jánem, your all, for you all**

Plural.

They all ate.

1. **Jánchimem, selves, own**
2. **Jákomem, it, him**
3. **Játomem, his, its**
4. **Jákomem, them two**
5. **Játomem, their two, for them two**
6. **Jákomem, them all**
7. **Játomem, their all, for them all**
8. **Jósungmem, me**
9. **Jásungmem, mine**
10. **Jochhongmi, excl. / Jochhingmi, incl.** } **us two**
11. **Jáchhongmi, excl. / Jáchhingmi, incl.** } **our two, for us two**
12. **Jókikongmi, excl. / Jókikengmi, incl.** } **us all**
13. **Jákikongmi, excl. / Jákikengmi, incl.** } **our all, for us all**
14. **Jómi, thee**
15. **Jákum, Jákomem, thine**
16. **Jóchhem, you two**
17. **Jáchhem, your two, for you two**
18. **Jónem, you all**
19. **Jánem, your all, for you all**

Remark.—The whole of the above forms will, by and by, be seen to exist distinctly in the Báhing dialect of Kiránti, and nearly all in the Bontáwa and Kháling dialects. In Váyu the principle is the same, and many of the forms exist; wherefore we must conclude that the others have been lost; or shall we say that the process of development was stayed in mid course? The more anomalies, the more instruction; and it is necessary to put so new and peculiar a matter in several lights in order to judge of it truly. So that, instead of apologising for the above almost interminable details, I shall proceed to subjoin a comparison of Váyu and Quichua, the latter from Markham, ut supra, cit.

	Quichua.	*Váyu.*
	I. I—thee.	
S.	I love thee, Munaiki	Chhánum
P.	I love you, Munaikichik	Chhánochhem, D. / Chhánonem, P.
S.	I loved thee, Munarkaiki	Chhánum
P.	I loved you, Munarkikichik	Chhánochhem, D. / Chhánonem, P.
	II. He—thee.	
S.	He loves thee, Munásunki	Chhanmi.
P.	He loves you, Munasunkichik	Chhánchhikmi, D. / Chhánem, P.
S.	He loved thee, Munasukanki	Chhanmi
P.	He loved you, Munasukankichik	Chhánchhem, D. / Chhánem, P.
	III. Thou—me.	
S.	Thou lovest me, Munahuanki	Chhángnom.
P.	Thou lovest us, Munahuankichik	Chhánchhokmi, D. / Chhánkokmi, P.
S.	Thou lovedst me, Munahuarkanki	Chhánsungmi.
P.	Thou lovedst us, Munahuarkankichik	Chhánchhongmi, D. / Chhánkikongmi, P.
	IV. He—me.	
S.	He loves me, Munahuanmi	Chhangnom.
P.	He loves us, Munahuanchik	Chhánchhokmi, excl., D. / Chhánchhikmi, incl., D. / Chhánkokmi, excl., P. / Chhánkem, incl., P.
S.	He loved me, Munahuarka	Chhánsungmi.
P.	He loved us, Munahuarkanchik / Munahuarkaiku	Chhánchhongmi, excl., D. / Chhánchhingmi, incl., D. / Chhánkikongmi, excl., P. / Chhánkikengmi, incl., P.

Remark.—Chhan, to love, in Váyu=Muna, in Quichua, is not a good word for comparison because of its being of the aoristic class of transitives in "to." In a tensed verb the resemblance to Quichua would have been more apparent. On the other hand, I have given the Váyu dual as well as plural, because its dual formative or chhik is almost identical with the Quichua plural sign or chik, whilst the plural one differs, and nothing is more certain than that these signs are apt to mingle and the dual to fall out of use.

By referring to the above paradigm of the verb já, to eat, it will be seen that the Váyu has many other forms expressly representative of the agent and object, and therefore more significant than some of those here collated with the Quichua forms. In Váyu the only forms which in the present state of the language refuse entirely to mix in the stream of conjugation are those which express the action passing from me to thee and no other. One cannot help imagining a system of conjugation with suffixed pronouns thus—

Ha, to give.		Tó, to strike.	
Singular.	*Plural.*	*Singular.*	*Plural.*
1. Hagnóm	Hákem / Hágnem	1. To'mum	To'pem / To'mem
2. Hanum	Hánem	2. Topnum	Topnem
3. Hatum	Hámem / Hátem	3. To'pum	To'mem / To'pem

But the following explanations of the senses of the leading series of these forms which is real (the subordinate is wholly hypothetical) will show how utterly such a notion would mislead.

1. { Hágnom, gives to me thou or he any single person.
Hákem, gives to us any one in all numbers.

1. { To'mum, beats me thou or he any one in singular number.
To'pem, beats us any one in all numbers.

2. { Hánum, gives to thee I only. Hámi, for any other giver.
Hánem, gives to you all any save I. Hánonem, for me as the giver.

2. { Topnum, beats thee I only. To'mi, for any other beater or beaters.
Topnem, beat you all, any save I, in all numbers.

3. { Hátum, gives to him thou or he or any single person except me. Hátungmi, for me.
Hámem. No such word.
Hátomem, gives to them any person or persons except me. Hátungmen, for me.

3. { To'pum, { struck him any single person but me. Topungmi, for me.
strikes him, the present tense is to'mi.
To'mem, strikes them all any person whatever.

Háto, to give, being aoristic hátum, is equally present and preterite. But top, to strike, has for the present tomi, which moreover serves for all three persons alike in the singular number.

Thus it appears that num and nem alone offer the appearance of uniformly inflected personal suffixes, and that even in regard to these, the singular and plural *senses* are diametrically opposite.

But there are other complications resulting from the plurality of agents or of patients which account at once for the specialities of the above explanations and of those which follow. Thus :—

1. Hágnom, gives to me any single person.
2. Hágnochhem, give to me any two persons.
3. Hágnonem, give to me ye all only.
4. Hágnomem, give to me they all only.

In the preterite hásúng takes the place of hágnóm; and with the verb top', to beat, we have only the euphonic change of gnom to mum, the residue being alike for both verbs; thus we have—

Present.	*Preterite.*
1. To'mum	1. Topsungmi
2. To'mochhem	2. Topsungchhem
3. To'monem	3. Topsungnem
4. To'momem	4. Topsungmem

If to the above crowding of agents and patients round the action we add the fact that the distinction of activity and passivity in the action itself is almost lost at the very corner-stone of the whole structure of conjugation—because the sign of action, kat' hexoki-n, viz., its having an object, is precisely that which denotes at once the transitive verb and the passive voice, *e.g.*, há-to, give to him; há-tu-m, he is given and he gives—we shall at the same time perceive how difficult it is to make these languages conform to our notions of conjugation (see and compare Tickell and Philipps, voce Sontal), and shall also be prepared to hear that a system at once so complex and so incomplete has been very generally cast aside either wholly (Newári, Lepcha, Bodpa, Malayalim, Burmah, Malay); or in part (other Dravirian, Dhimáli, Namsangnaga, &c.); and in this or that particular mode, one group of tongues rejecting the dual (Dravirian cultivated); another, the sex signs (Himálayan complex);* a third, the whole system of conjunct pronouns (Himálayan simple† and those above cited); whilst the attempt to blend with the action agents as well as patients, and both in the dual and plural numbers, has been maintained only by Kiránti and some Oceanic tongues, the Váyu, Sontal, &c., being now restricted to a duality and plurality on one side only, viz., that of the agents or that of the objects. The Váyu can express (like the Sontal) several agents and one patient, or several

* The complex Himalayan tongues are Limbu, Kiránti, Háyu, Kuswár, Súnwar, Dhimáli, Bhrámu, Chepáng, Kusunda, &c.

† The simple or nonpronominalised are Newári, Thumi, Pahi, Múrmi, Gúrung, Mágar Khas (mixed), Lep'cha, Pálusen or Syár'pa (Serpa), Bodo, &c.

patients and one agent, but not a plurality of both. The Kiránti can express a plurality of both. But neither the one nor the other has effected the same sort and degree of amalgamation of its conjunct pronouns in the case of its nouns as well as verbs, as the Himálayan, Kuswár, and the Ugrofinnic tongues generally have done, which all alike have perfectly blended suffixes for both; whilst the Kiránti, with an equal fusion in both cases, prefers the method of prefix for the nouns;* and the Váyu, following the same Dravirian order of arrangement, has not reached the same completeness of development in *this* respect (therein further agreeing with Dravirian), though more in others. It has a perfectly separate set of possessives for combination (áng, úng, á vel ú); but to the noun has got blended inseparably the third of these (ang-upa, ung-upa, a-upa or wathim u-pa), and thus a euphonic combination of the whole with the nominal root has been prevented, as in Bodo, which, however, as well as Váyu, can and occasionally does use as perfectly fused† prefix forms as the Kiránti, and sometimes both the disjunct and conjunct prefixually, and Dhimáli likewise.‡ From the verb, Bodo, like Malayalim and several Nilgiri tongues, has dropped the pronoun; Dimáli, like Tamil, Uraon, and Male, has kept it; in Váyu, as in Sontal and Hó, the phenomena are complex. (See note at the end of the article, further on, on the Kiránti tribe. Double pronominalisation affines our Váyu and Kiránti to Hó and Sontal, but different positions of the pronouns differences them. The fact of having them and this different use of them—what worth? See Poole on Egyptian J.R.A.S., p. 313; also the analogy with Quichua noted by me.)

I refer to the head of pronoun for some more remarks on this subject. In the meanwhile, and in conclusion of the topic of Váyu conjugation, I beg to suggest attention to the following collation of actives and passives of the several types in the third persons of the present (or future) and preterite.

---

* á-pa, my / i-po, thy / á-po, his } father | tib-ú, I / tib-í, thou / tib-á, he } strike

	Compare Sontal		and Kuswar.	
Wherewith	apu-ing	dal-eng aing	baba-im	thatha-im-ik-an
	apa-m	dal-me-am	baba-ir	thatha-ir-ik-an
	apa-t	dal-e ai	baba-ik	thatha-ik-an

†

Bodo.	*Váyu.*	*Dhimáli.*	*Its Verb.*
a-pha	am-pa	ka-pa	dengkhi-ka
na-pha	um-pa	na-pa	dengkhi-na
bi-pha	a-pa	wa-pa	dengkhi

‡ The full pronominal forms with the nouns are:—

Bodo.	*Váyu.*	*Dhimáli.*			
angni apha	ang upa	kang apa	or	kang ka-pa	Which last quite agrees with Kuki
nangni apha	ung upa	nang apa		nang na-pa	
bini-apha, or	wathim upa	oko apa		eko wa-pa	
nangni napha					
bini bipha					

COLLATION OF VOICES IN SINGULAR NUMBER.

		Present Tense.			*Preterite Tense.*		
		Transitives in "to." *Yemto*, to burn.					
I.	Active	1. Yemtungmi	2. Yemtum	3. Yemtum	1. Yemtungmi	2. Yemtum	3. Yemtum
	Passive	1. Yemum	2. Yémi	3. Yemtum	1. Yemsungmi	2. Yémi	3. Yemtum
		Transitives in "to," preceded by sibilant. *Sishto*, to kill.					
II.	Active	1. Sinmi	2. Sitmi	3. Sitmi	1. Sishtungmi	2. Sishtum	3. Sishtum
	Passive	1. Sitgnom	2. Sitmi	3. Sitmi	1. Sissungmi	2. Sinmi	3. Sishtum
		Transitives in "po." *Wopo*, to shoot.					
III.	Active	1. Wo'mi	2. Wo'mi	3. Wo'mi	1. Wo'pungmi	2. Wo'pum	3. Wo'pum
	Passive	1. Wo'mum	2. Wo'mi	3. Wo'mi	1. Wo'psungmi	2. Wo'mi	3. Wo'pum
		Transitives in "po," preceded by a nasal. *Hómpo*, to taste.					
IV.	Active	1. Homsungmi	2. Hómi / Hoṇmi	3. Hómi / Hóṇmi	1. Hompungmi	2. Hómpum	3. Hómpum
	Passive	1. Honmum	2. Hoṇmi	3. Hónmi	1. Homsungmi	2. Hó*n*mi	3. Hómpum
		Transitives in "ko." *Pako*, to do.					
V.	Active	1. Pángmi	2. Pómi	3. Pómi	1. Pákungmi	2. Pákum	3. Pákum
	Passive	1. Pógnom	2. Pómi	3. Pómi	1. Pósungmi	2. Pómi	3. Pákum
		Transitives in "ko," preceded by a nasal. *Pingko*, to send.					
VI.	Active	1. Pingsungmi	2. Pingmi	3. Pingmi	1. Pingkungmi	2. Pingkum	3. Pingkum
	Passive	1. Pinggnom	2. Pingmi	3. Pingmi	1. Pingsungmi	2. Pingmi	3. Pingkum

Infinitives and Participles of the above.

I.	Active	Yémung (yem'mung)	Yé*n*vi	Yemta	Yemtang
	Passive	Yempingmung	Yempingvi	Yempingta	Yempingtang
II.	Active	Sitmung	Sitvi	Sishta	Sishtang
	Passive	Sitpingmung	Sitpingvi	Sitpingta	Sitpingtang
III.	Active	Wo'mung (wopmung)	Wo'vi	Wopta	Woptang
	Passive	Woppingmung	Woppingvi	Woppingta	Woppingtang
IV.	Active	Hómung (hommung)	Hónvi	Hónta	Hóntang
	Passive	Hómpingmung	Hómpingvi	Hómpingta	Hómpingtang
V.	Active	Pámung	Póvi	Pótá	Pátáng
	Passive	Pápingmung	Pápingvi	Pápingtá	Pápingtáng
VI.	Active	Pingmung	Pingvi	Pingta	Pingtang
	Passive	Pingpingmung	Pingpingv	Pingpingta	Pingpingtáng

A Specimen of the Váyu Language.

Ang ming Páchya nom. Ang thoko Váyu nomi (or Gó Váyu gnom) Khásakhata Háyu itkem. Ungki dávo be Váyu ischikem.* Go jekta dumsungmi. Hátha bong dumsungmi ghá má sengmi. Lé got kulup chhuyung † wanikhen. Dhankuta mu khakchhing puchhum chupvikhata póguha háta vik páchikokmi. Ang kó má nom. Ang távo Gajraj Thápa nung nomi. Gonha kóphe nakphe inang munang wathi yengkum. Wathim nárung gonha blektum. Wathim chho le pókum. Honko á thum rámi. Captánha thúm hánung hónpingkum. Ang dávo lit'nung blining chólo chupsit khen inhe gó gonha mutpingkum. Dávo chinggnak chamchem. Gon sénche. Ungjitá dávo ghá chitnum. Ang thumbe ithaji nómi gonha wálige latpinggnom. Angki thóko kósi blingmu homba imba muschikokmi (our tribe, *we*). Népál kháral khen Támbakósi bong muschikokmi. Gókháta Awal be mutvi máng nokokmi. Kúswár, Bótia, Dénwár, Awal be mutvi nonem. Awal mu ramsa ha gáng khéva má muschikokmi. Vik máng póvi, ghádimu chokphi sétung jóvi, kem má póvi thóko Kusúnda, Chépáng báhamu chhúju puchhibe má muschikokmi. Angkimu kem nomi, vik le nomi; págnamu vik nom, memha, mákai, dósi, pháphár, bója, lévi, rówa, mása, sákha, góhún, láru, livi vik nom. Angki múlung kólube, Héngongwo báha. Lapcha, Limbu báha máng jáhe, chháju mádúmbe gadhá páhe, muschikokmi. Chháju púchhibe bója má lichem, jomsitmu ming mische le má nom. Hánung bong jomsit lichem minung bong lat'lat'ha muschikokmi. Ghákhata ha ruklung be rukkokmi, duklung be dukkokmi. Phalámtú'vi, singchuk'vi, kóchònvi angki thok be má nómem. Kampáchyáng, bingchopáchyáng gyétim gót khen ingchikokmi. Angki kem angki gót há páchikokmi. Angki wáschyáng angki vik sétang rówa khen rómekhatá há dúri chinchingha jéwa púngmem. Váyukhata khakchhingpuchhum póvi (or chupvi) má nómem. Mische pá gyéti namsangmu séva má pómem. Jéwa Héngongwo gót khen rangai pómem. Lónchokhata dáwángmi jéwa wáschimem. Meschokhata rangai póta wáschimem Angki mulung ithijila nomi. Náyung gót kulupha bàkulup khen chholup † (or lé gót kulup) bong múphta chháju mádúmbe itha dókha hamta nómem

---

* Here the inclusive form of the pronoun (ungki) and of the reflex voice of the verb Isto, to denominate (ischikem), are used; literally, in our own tongue, we call ourselves. In the preceding sentence, if itkem be not error, it is the inclusive also, but of the passive voice: we are called, *i.e.*, all of us Váyus are called Háyu by the Khas. But isto, which is both neuter and transitive, carries to a maximum the peculiarities of the three voices of Váyu verbs.

† Phrases of numeration. See Vocabulary.

(or hamchimem). Angki kem chhálung singha póta, diha wamta húnglúng kóha róta, khistiha supta, gége gége páchimem. Kembhitari náyung kuna nochhikmi; kólu, imlung; kólu khó'lung. Táwokhata, támikháta gégé tá má hokmi. Bangchodum khen biak pachikokmi. Náyung got kulup ha bá kulup khen lé gót kulup * bong pénku háhá ha rome ingchikokmi. Pénku phen mang wontike nam rome upu kembe lat'lat'ha, kam pápáha, phengkokmi. Mische má pápáha me'ta singtong kóbe *kh*umpopmi. Khócho, puk, chéli, béli, méchho, jachikokmi, Gai, bhálu, phóka, má jákokmi. Singwo, khúdu, dúdu, chálung, jákokmi. Sóve tungchikokmi, bukchhale tungkokmi (note the two forms of the verb). Sóve, angki póta, chinggnak tungkokmi. Bukchha, gyétim gót khen ingta, yanggnak tungchikokmi. Angki chhobe má blekchikokmi. Nokchhung saschikokmi, mescho le, lóncho le. Bálung khen gyéti suna le má dakkokmi. Angki chólvi Bálung. Gyéti suna le má nom. Váyu thoko mu singtong sunaha Brahman Lama má honmi (or honmem, indefinite). Gyétim lom má khokchikokmi. Angki vik hákhele má watkokmi. Upo met'khen táwokhata ha chhinggnak yanggnak má pápáha lingmem. Támikhata ha mische le má lingmem. Imhamu dáwo dévi angki májhua nomi. Inung wanikhen póvi suná le má nom. Angki thóko gyétim gót be lásta, yangta thóko, náti tolgong † bong yangmi. Finis.

TRANSLATION.‡

My name is Páchya. I am a Váyu. The Khas tribe call us Háyu, but our own name is Váyu. I am an old man. I don't know how old; above sixty. I am a cultivator of land assigned by the Rája to the soldiers of the Dhunkuta regiment. I have no land of my own. My son is in the service of Captain Gajráj Thápa. You saw him here often, and drew his portrait and measured him. He thought that very queer, and was a little alarmed. But the Captain reassured him, and he consented. I have been here four months to help you to learn our language. It is very difficult. You must judge of all. I can only answer your questions. I hope you will soon let me go home. Our people dwell in the basin of (or along the course of) the Kósi river from near the valley of Nepál proper to the Tamba Kósi. We are not Áwalias (people inured to malaria or áwal). The Áwalias dwell in the valley of the river, and are called

---

* A phrase of numeration. See Vocabulary.

† A phrase of measure. See Vocabulary. It is equal to two handfuls.

‡ Take notice that this sample of the Váyu language likewise reveals the location, status, &c., of the people. Therefore revert to it when you come to the article on the Váyu tribe.

Kuswar, Bótia, Déuwar, &c. We can't live there by reason of the malaria. Nor do we dwell on the hill summits like the Kúsúnda and Chépáng, who never cultivate, but live on wild herbs and fruits and never build houses. We have houses and cultivate the soil, growing maize and kódo and buckwheat, and rice, cotton, millets, barley, wheat, and madder. We are fixed cultivators, like the Néwárs, not migratory ones like the Lepchas, Limbus, and others. We occupy the central parts of the hill slopes, which we cut into terraces. Rice won't grow on the tops, nor any sort of grain. We go up as high as grain will grow. We use the plough or the spade, according to the nature of the site we occupy. We have no craftsmen, smiths, carpenters, or potters—of our own tribe. We buy utensils and ornaments from others. We build our own houses, and our women spin and weave the home-grown cotton of which they make our clothes. None of our race are soldiers, nor do we ever take service (menial). The Néwárs dye for us, if we need it; but the men wear plain clothes. Those of the women are sometimes dyed. Our villages are very small, usually fifteen to twenty houses scattered along the hill-sides. Our houses are built of rough timber, plastered and thatched with grass. Two rooms in a house—one for cooking and the other for sleeping. We have no general dormitory for all the grown girls or boys of the village. We marry at maturity, buying our wives. A wife costs fifteen or twenty rupees. If we have no money, we earn her by labour in her father's house. We bury our dead without any ceremonies. We do not tattoo our bodies. Our ears we bore occasionally. We have no priest but the exorcist, who is also our only physician. None of our tribe follow the bráhmans or lamas. We abide by our own creed and customs. We eat fowls, pigs, goats, sheep, buffaloes. Not oxen, bears, or monkeys, but honey, milk, eggs. We drink beer and spirits. Much of the former, as it is home-made; little of the latter, because we must buy it. Our law of inheritance gives equal shares to all the boys, and no share to the girls. Our head villager decides our disputes. We never appeal from him. Our tribe is a broken one, and is reduced to very inconsiderable numbers.

END OF ANALYSIS OF THE VÁYU LANGUAGE.

IV.—ANALYSIS OF THE BÁHING DIALECT OF THE KIRÁNTI LANGUAGE.

A.—Báhing Vocabulary.

Nouns Substantive.

Aír (wind), Jú
Affection, Dwakcho
Abuse, Waita. Khícho
A'bode, Bwagdikha
Adulterer, Ryamnipo
Adulteress, Ryamnimo
Agriculturist, Byangsikokba
Amaranth (grain), Gósuráni
Aqueduct, Kúlo. Pwálám
Ancle, { Khóli míchi / leg joint }
Arm-all, / Arm, fore, } Gú
Article, thing, Grókso
Aunt-pat, / Aunt-mat, } Momo
Anger, Sókso
Ant, Gágáchingmo
Anus, Dyála
Arrow, Blá
Ax, Khá
Alder-tree, Búrsi
Bag, Sálamá
Basket, Bainso
Barley. No name. Jou is used
Bamboo, Pálám (all). Rikcho (small)
Bark of tree, Singkokte
Back, Ching
Back-bone, Chinreúsyé
Belly, Kója
Beast, quadruped, { Lékhólithiba / Lékhólimigwákba }
Being, animal, Samthíba
Box, chest. No word
Bat kind, Pákati
Bat, { male, A'po pákati / female, A'mo pákati / young, Pákati átámi }
Birth. No name
Bird kind, Chikba
Bird, { male, A'po chikba / female, A'mo chikba / young, Chikbaatámi }
Beer, Gnási
Bread, Shéblem
Birch-tree, Phyékulima
Bed, Bló'cho
Bed-chamber, Ipdikha
Bed-time, Ipcho béla
Bee, Syúra (wasp, Yúkuwá)
Blacksmith, Teupteu'le
Blood, Húsi
Buttocks, Késidyála
Battle, fight, Mócho
Boat, Dúnga
Bear, Wam
Beard, Shéö sóng, mouth hair; or Yóli swón,* chin hair
Boar, A'po po
Body, Ram
Burden, load, Kúra
Bone, Reusye
Breast, Kúchü
Breastnipple, Neucheu
Bow, Li
Bowman, Lícha, m.† Límicha, or Lícha-nima, f.
Bottom, lowest part, Háyu
Boy, Táwa
Buffalo kind, Mésyéu
Buffalo, { male, A'po mésyeu / female, A'mo mésyeu / young, Mésyeu átámi }
Bull, Bing, A'po bing
Boundary, Rélu
Breath, Sam
Branch of tree. No word
Brother, { Lo'ba, younger / Yáwa, elder }
Brotherhood, / Brethren, } Lo'babum
Brother-in-law, Cháiwa. Wadyalcha
Calf, { male, A'po bing átámi / female, A'mo bing átámi }
Can, cup, { Pú. Dáchom / Grokso (thing) / Pwákutúcho grokso (water to drink vessel) }
Cart. No word
Cat-kind, Birma
Cat, { male, A'po birma / female, A'mo birma / young, Birma átámi }
Carpenter, Sing chokba
Cheek, Chocho
Chestnut tree, Syéli

---

* Sóng vol swón vol Swóm. The broad ó passes into wá and the final nasal is vague.
† As from li comes lícha, so from koja, the belly, kojacha, a glutton; and from khyim, a house, khyimcha, a householder, &c., &c.

Chin, Yéoli. Yoli
Child-kind, Tá. Gikba. Táwa. Támitáwa
Child, {male, Táwa, / female, Támi,} Gikba, m. f.*
Children, Tádau. Táwatámi
Clay, Phélemkhápi
Cloth, Wá'
Cotton cloth, Linkhi wá
Woollen cloth, Unke wá
Silken cloth. No word
Clothes, raiment, Wá
Cloud, Kuksyal
Colour, Moba
Cold (frigor) {Junamti (weather). / Jú (wind).
Companion, Wárcha
Claw, nail, talon, Gyáng
Cane (calamus), Gúri
Cousin {Pat. / Mat.} Gnwápsya
Cow, A'mo bing
Cough, Sheúkhé
Copper. No name
Cowherd, Bing theulba
Cotton, uncleaned, Linkhi
Cotton, cleaned, Rúwa
Courage. No word
Crow, Gagákpa
Daughter, Támi (girl)
Daughter-in-law, Dyalmi
Dance, Síli
Day, Namti
To-day, A'na
Dust, Dyerbakhápi (flying earth)
Darkness, Namring
Desire, wish, Dwakcho
Ditch. No name
Deer, Kísi
Deer, {male, A'po kísi / female, A'mo kísi / young, Kísi átámi
Door, Lapcho
Disease, illness. No name
Dispute,† Mocho? Khícho? Infinitives
Dog kind, Khlicha ‡
Dog, {male, A'po khlícha / female, A'mo khlícha / young, Khlíchá átámi
Death. No name
Dream, Gná'mo
Drink, Tu'mé. Tuchome
Drunkard, Dukba. Túba

Dyer, Ryákba
Earth—the, / Earth—a little,} Khápi
Ear, Sámaneu. (See Nose)
Egg, Dí. Bádi (Bá = fowl)
Elephant. No name
Echo, Thololamstikha
Enemy. No name
Ewe, A'mo bhéra
Eye, Michi
Eyebrow, Kur'mi swon'g
Eyelash, Michi swon'g
Elbow, Nyaksi
Exorcist, Jamcha
Earthquake, Khrínyam
Evening, Namtheuba
Face, Kúli
Feather, Chikbaswong (= bird-hair §)
Feast, / Festival,} Khoúmá
Father, A'po
Father-in-law, Yeppa
My father, A'pa
Thy father, I'po
His, her, its father, A'po
Fever, Júsara (ague)
Fair, / Market,} Jyapdikha ledikha, = buying and selling place
Fear, Níma. Gníma
Ferry, Hamba glúdikha
Fire, Mí
Fireplace, Mímudíkha. Bwakal
Field, arable, Rú. Byángsi
Finger, Brepcho
Finger-nail, Gyáng. Brepchogyáng
Fellow-countryman, {Dwábo dyelkem / Dwábo dyel dimmuryu ‖
Fellow-tribeman, {Dwábo thokkem / A'dwábo thokkem
Fish, Gná
Flavour, taste, Bró
Flesh, Syé
Flint, Chichilung
Flour, Phúl
Flea, Chukbe
Fence, Khor
Floor, Khápi (earth)
Flower, Phúng
Ford, Pwáku hambag ludikha ¶
Fly, Sheúmo
Food, Jáwáme. Jáchome. Participles **
Fowl-kind, Bá

---

* Gikba, literally, who is born, answers to Kikba, who begets or gives birth to, a parent. The inherency of the relative pronoun in the participles is normal, as in the mode of making transitive and causal verbs out of neuters.

† Khícho, verbal, mocho, practical, dispute.

‡ Khicha is Newári. The insertion of a labial is a common trick of these tongues. See note on Háyu verbs.

§ Quill is Básyurima.

‖ For suffixes kom, dim, see pp. 323, 325, 330; ke and di are prepositions; final m, mè is a possessive and formative. Qualitives and infinitives which take it can be used substantively. Instrumental participles are formed from the infinitive by it, and are usable as nouns of either kind, *e.g.*, jachome = food and edible.

¶ Literally, water (of) far side issuing place.

** Jáwáme, what he eats. Jáchome, what any one eats, an edible substance. See on to Conjugations.

Fowl, { male, Swáreúwabá
female, Chwongkameubá
young, Bukballo }
Fowl, wild, Sábala bá
Fowl's egg, Bá dí. Báädi *
Foreigner, Wángmedyeldim. Wángmedyelke
Fist. No word
Forehead, Kúpi
Filth, dirt, Ríku
Foot, Kholi blem †
Form, Moba
Forest, jungle, Sábala
Fruit, Síchi
Frost, Phúrsa
Frog, Krúkrú
Friend. No name
Garlic. No name
Ginger, Peúrim
Girl, Támi
Glue, cement, Kyapcho
Glutton, { Kojacha, m.
Kojachanima, f. ‡ }
Grandfather, Kíkí
Grandmother, Pípí
Grandson, Chácha
Granddaughter, Cháchánima
God, a god. No name
Gold, Syeúna
Goat-kind, Swongára, Sóngara
Goat, { male, A'po swongára
female, A'mo swongára
young, Swongára átámi }
Goat-herd, Swongára theulba
Grass, Jim
Grain, Jámá
Ghee, butter, Gyáwa (oil)
Groin, Téchi
Hand, Gublem †
Handle, Rísing
Spade handle, Rúkokchom rísing §
Hair, Swóng
Hair of héad, Cham
Hair of body, Swóng
Herdsman, Bing mésyeu-theulba
Heaven, Dwámu (sky)
Head, Píya
Heart, Thim. Theum. (French eu)
Heat, Haúlo. Haúnám
Heel, Cheuncheu leú
Hail, Músi
Hammer, Thyakchóme §

Hammerer, Thyakba
Hemp, Grá
Hen, A'mo bá
Hip, Khólimichi, or Jilamíchi
Hope. No word
Hoof, { whole
cloven } Gyakseuleú
Hog-kind, Pó
Hog, { male, A'po pó
female, A'mo pó
young, Pó átámi }
Hole, Gwályum
Hoe spade, Kokchóme §
Husk, Phíra
Hook peg, Cháchóme §
Horn, Grong
Goat's horn, Swongára ágrong (goat, its horn)
Honey, Syúra. Shúra
Horse-kind, Ghóra
Horse, { male, A'po ghóra
female, A'mo ghóra
young, Ghóra átámi }
House, Khyim
Householder, { Khyimcha, m.
Khyimchanima, f. }
Home, Bwágdíkha
Hunger, Sóli
Husband, Wancha
My husband, Wá wancha
Thy husband, I' wancha
Her husband, A' wancha ‖
Instrument, } Rúpachóme §
Implement, } Grokso. Rúpáchogrókso
Infant, { Bébacha, m.
Bébachaníma, f. }
Ice. No name
Intestines, Chisye
Iron, Syál
Jaw, Ka'kám
Joint, Míchi
Juice, Pwaku (water)
Knife, { Be'tho
Chwarchom § }
Knee, Pokchi
Knot, Khingna (pp.)
Kitchen, Kidikha ¶
King, Ho'po. Hwáng
Lamp, torch, To'si
Language, speech, Ló
Lip, Shéo-kokte (mouth leather)
Leaf, Swáphó

---

* See note § of next page.

† See leg and arm. To the words for these the signs of flat things (blem) is added to make names for foot and hand.

‡ Kojachanima, a female glutton. So khyimchanima, a housewife. See householder: and so also of all formatives in cha, koja = belly, khyim = house.

§ These and many more such are participles of the instrument or object, or of fitness, formed from the infinitives, or, less the m, mó, suffix, themselves infinitives. They can all be used as substantives or as adjectives.

‖ Wá, I', A', are the pronominal prefixes of nouns and suffixes of verbs, a thoroughly Dravirian trait and a fundamental. Here is a sample of the suffixes ú the first person = ur, wa, or o. { Jyul—ú I; Jyul—í Thou; Jyui—á He } put or place.

¶ Ki'dikha, literally, cooking-places, from the root ki', to cook, and dikha, place; but usable only as a suffix of verbs, like lung in Váyu.

Tree's leaf, Sing swápho
Leather, Kokte (skin)
Leg-all, Kho'li
Leg-true (tibia), Phóphól
Liar, Limochalba
Light (lux), Haúhaú
Lightning, Ploksa
Life, Sam (breath)
Liver, Ding
Louse, Túsyar
Lungs, Syeúporeú
Loom, { Wápachogrokso / Toblosing. Wápáchome
Load, Kúra
Lowlands, Dhepte
Lowlander, { Dheptecha, m. / Dheptechanima, f.
Mat, Thárkimo blócho
Maize, Greleuwámo
Master, Ho'po. Hwáng
Mark, Syancho
Market, Jyapdikhalédíkha
Mason, Khyimpába
Mankind, Múryeu
Man, { male, Wainsa / female, Mincha / young, A'tami. Muryeu ata*
Maker, doer, Paba. Pabba
Madder, Deu
Mare, A'mo ghora
Marriage, Grochyer
Mill, hand or water, Khuruwa
Millet (kangani), Básara
Millet (kodo), Chárjá
Millet (juwár), Binkhumá
Millet (sáma), Sáma
Milk, Neucheu
Mist, Kuksyal
Manner, / Mode, way, } Khó
Monkey (all), Moreu
Measure, the instrument, Khapcho
Medicine. No name.
Mind, Theum
Moon, Taúsaba. Lá
Month, Lá.
Morning, Didila
Music, Tapcho
Mother, A'mó
My mother, À'ma
Thy mother, I'mo
His, her, its mother, A'mo

Money (copper), Lálajima
Mountain, Syerte
Mountaineer, { Syértecha, m. / Syértechanima
Mountain products, Syértedim†
Mouth, Sheö
Moustache, Sheöswón
Muschito, Syúpyél
Mouse, Yeu
Nipple, Neúcheú (milk)
Noise, Syanda
Neck, Sheureu (French eu)
Name, Ning
Night, Tóugnachi
Net. No name
Needle, Léumje
Noon (day), Nam-helscho
Nose, Néu (French eu)
Neighbour, Kwaudaubwakba
Nostril, Neu'lam (nose—way)
Navel, Sheupum
Oar. No name
Oil, Gyáwa
Oak-tree, Sóbusársi
Odour, smell, A'rí. Rí‡
Onion. No name
Ox kind, Bing
Ox, { male, Bing. Apobing / female, A'mo bing / young, Bing átámi
Ordure, Khli
Man's ordure, Muryukhlí or Muryuákhli
Tiger's ordure, { Gupsa khli or Gupsa ákhli§
Pain, Deúkha, H.
Palm of hand, Gublem ágwalla (hand, its palm)
Penis, Bli
Place, Díkha‖ (in composition of verbs chiefly)
Plant, Wába, P.
Pleasure, Gyérsi
Plough, Jóchome
Ploughman, Jóba, P.
Plain, Dyamba
Plainsman, / Lowlander, } Dyambácha, m. / Dyambachanima, f.
Plate dish, / Platter, } Pú
Parent, Kíkba, p. ¶
Plantain, Grámochi
Plantain-tree, Grámochi sing

---

* Wainsa and Mincha are used substantively and adjectively. Not A'támi. Man's child or human child is Muryuatami = man, his child. Better átá or átáwo: see Child. Tami is used for the young of all animals.

† Syerte-di-m, mountain in of. See note ‖ at p. 321.

‡ Here, as often elsewhere, we have a noun used indifferently, with or without the pronominal definitive. Many instances have occurred in the foregone comparative vocabularies. Let a word imply relation of any sort, as of odour to an odorous body; and even if, by standing alone, it be liable to misconstruction, it must have the definitive pretty much, as in English the article is needed to separate nouns from verbal imperatives; *e.g.*, a cut from cut, a smell from smell.

§ In the first of these two forms of expression the two words are regarded as a compound; in the second we have the ordinary genitival style: man, his ordure; tiger, its dung.

‖ *E.g.*, Ip dikha, sleeping-place = bed-chamber. Kidikha, cooking-place = kitchen.

¶ To this answers Gikba = child; or who begets and who is born.

Plantain fruit, Grámochi sichi
Pine (tree), Tósi
Pepper (black). No name
Palate, Kókolyam
Pepper (red), Dukba
Potter, Khápi yalba
Peach, Khwómalchi
Peach-tree, Khwomalchi sing.
Peach fruit, Khwomalchi sichi
Price, Thing
Priest, Nokso
Poison, Ning
Point, Jeujeu or Juju
Ram, A'po bhéra
Rat, Yéu (French eu)
Rain, Ryá-wá
Rains, the, Ryáwa namti
Rib, Chakh yamreusye
Rice, unhusked, Búra
Rice, husked, Shéri
Rice, boiled, Mómara
River, any, Gúlo
Root, Syángri
Rust, Gári
Rudder. No word
Road, Lam
Rope, Grá
Roof, Khyimpú
Rhododendron, Twaksyel
R. —— tree, Twoksyel sing
R. —— flower, Twoksyel phung
R. —— fruit, Twoksyel síchi
Salt, Yuksi
Silence, Lícho
Spade, spud, hoe, Rúkókchome (= ground-digger)
Spear, Hóchóme
Shape, form (and colour), Móba
Sheep-kind. No name. Bhéra used
Spirits (distilled), Héna
Spindle, Panchom
Spinner, Panba
Skin, Kokte
Skull, Piya réusye
Shoe, sandal, Khólidi paschong
Seed, Wáchyár
Sieve, Ríyangma
Sleep, Ip'thi
Sail of boat. No word
Sand. No word
Spittle, Ríchukú
Snot, Neukhlí = nose-filth
Silk. No word
Silver. No word
Sport, play, Chamcho (inf.)
Sister, elder, Yáwa; younger, Loba, see Brother
Sisterhood, Yába loba bum

Sister-in-law, Wadyelmi
Sitting chamber, Bwagdíkha
Spider, Bájeringmo
Smith, Teupteulé. Teupteucha
Snake, Búsa
Servant, { Wáli, m. / Wálinima, f. }
Soldier, Kyakyamkhusiba
Sky, Dwamu
Son-in-law, Dyalcha
Son, { my Wá—tá * / thy I'—tá / his A'—tá } see Child
Shoulder, Balam
Shoulder-joint, Bálám míchi
Shepherd, Bhéra theulba †
Side, Chákhyam, Pum
Star, Sorú
Summit, top, Gnári. Juju. Agnari. Ajuju
Snow, Phúmu
Summer, Hau-namti = hot or heat day
Sweat, Gwaulau
Storm, Gnolojú (= great wind)
Steam, Sam (breath)
Smoke, Kúni
Strength, Sokti
Song, Swálong
Sow, A'mo po. Khomi
Sugarcane, Byar ‡
Sun, Nam
Sunshine, Nam
Sunrise, Namdhapcho
Sunset, Namwamcho
Still, Hechopú
Stone, Lung
Stomach, Koja
Shade, shadow, Bala
Straw, Jim (grass)
Sword, Bétho (knife)
Shield. No name
Tail, Méri
Testicle, Kollosíchi
Tiger, Gupsa
Thigh, Jíla
Thirst, { Pwákudwakcho / Pwákudwaktimi }
Thumb, Bombo
Tooth, Khleu (French eu)
Tobacco, Kuni
Turmeric, Byu'ma
Toe, Khólibrepcho
Toe, great, Kholi bombo
Toe—nail, Gyang
Tongue, Lyam
Time. No name. Béla used
To-morrow, Dilla
Thread, Sále

---

* Wa ta-wo, my son; Wa tami, my daughter; Wa ta, my child. Ta is child = Sontal and Uraon Dá. But ta is used also for son, as sa is child and son in Burmese, which language has also the mi suffix—sami, a girl = tami Bahing and Hayu.

† Bhera is, of course, borrowed. It is very strange that few of the Himalayan languages have names for sheep, or ox (bos), or horse.

‡ Sugar is Byar apwaku = juice of cane; literally, cane, its juice.

Thunder, Buk'bu
Thief, { Kuncha, m. / Kunchanima, f.
Theft, Kunchaniwa
Tree, Sing. Dhyáksi
Tree—bark, Sing kokte. Dhyaksi kokte
Tribe, Thok
Uncle, pat. Popo
Uncle, mat. Kuku
Urine, Charnika *
Man's urine, Murynáchárnika
Goat's urine, Swongara acharnika
Vein, Sagra
Vegetable, Cheúle pále
Vetch, pea, Kyangyalyangma
Village, Dyal
Villager, { Dyalpau, m. / Dyalpaunima, f.
Victuals, Jáchome †
Vice, sin. No word
Voicé, Syanda (sound)
Valley. No word
Vulva, Twárchi
Wax, Khóye
Wound, Bánám
Wool, Bhéda swón
Wall, A'tha. Antha
Weaver, Wápába
Water, Pwáku
Water-spring, Pwáku blo
Walnut, { tree, Phoro sing / fruit, Phoro sichi
Wife, Ming
Wrist, Gublemmichi
Work, Ru
Wizard, Krákrá
Witch, Krákránima
Witchcraft, Krákrániwa
Widow, Khlúmi
Widower, Khlúwa ‡
Whore. No name
Whoremaster. No name.
Wealth, Grokso
Wing (bird's), Báphlem (bá = fowl)
Witness, Kwóba. Tába
Year, Thó
Yesterday, Sanamti
Yeast. No name

ADJECTIVES.

Good, { Neuba, § m. and c. gender / Neubanima, f.
Bad, Ma neuba. Negative
Deceitful, Cunning, } Hánba, m. and c. / Hánbanima, f.
Candid, { Má hánba. Neg. / A'je. Ajebwakba
Malicious, { Deukha giba, m. c. / Deukha gibanima, f.
Benevolent, { Gyersi, { pába, m. c. / pabanima, f.
Industrious, { Pába, m. c. / Pábanima, f.

---

* Múryu or muryeu á chárnika, man his urine; songára á charnika, goat its urine.

† Jachome, literally what fit to be eaten or usually eaten. Participle of the object. See note at p. 327.

‡ Wa and mi are suffixes of gender. The formative suffix cha is equivalent to wa in words like lí-cha, a bow man; kún-cha, a thief, &c. The feminine of wa is mi; of cha is micha, as koja-cha, a glutton; koja micha, a female glutton; or it is nima, as kun-cha, a thief; kun-chanima, a female thief. Pau and pó are also masculine signs, whereof the former makes its feminine by adding nima; the latter by changing the po into mo, as dyal-pau, a villager; dyal-paunima, a female villager; ryamni-po, an adulterer; ryamni-mo, an adulteress.

The participial suffix ba, which also makes nouns of the agent, and gives qualitives a substantival character, as thyak-ba, a or the hammerer; neu-ba, a or the good one, is another masculine suffix which takes nima for its feminine.

But participial nouns in ba are often regarded as of all genders, and when used adjectively, as all can be used, they take no sign of gender, or number, or case. They precede the substantive, which they qualify in their crude form, as neuba wainsa, a good man; neuba wainsadau, good men; neuba wainsake, of a good man.

The inherent relative sense of the participles enables them to dispense with any formative, but if it be specially necessary to express gender, such words, when used as nouns, can take the wa and mi sex signs, and also the signs of number, always supposing that their use is substantival.

Dravidian participles are formed from the gerunds (fide Caldwell), and need a formative to give them the relative and participial sense. Such is not the case with Kiránti participles, though these when used substantively often take the m, me, formative, and always if the participles be of the impersonated kind. See Verbs.

Observe that the Vocabulary throughout is so constructed as to be a clue to grammar as well as to vocables.

§ Participial, like most of the following. See and compare the verbs neu, to be good; neu-gna, neu-ye, neu, I, thou, he, am good; neu-ba, who or what is good, all genders; dual, neubadausi; plural, neu-badau. Neu = it is good, is the root of the verb and noun. So Newari bhing, which has ji bhing, chha bhing, wo bhing, for the three persons, and bhing—hma-gu for major and minor of gender, and bhing hma, nihma, and bhing ping, for dual and plural. But note that Newari repeats the gender sign (hma) with both qualitive and numeral (bhing-hma, ni-hma) in the dual, while in the plural it omits it wholly, substituting for the sign of gender that of number, or ping = dáá in Bahing. What is said of Váyu qualitives holds generally true of Kiránti ones, viz., there are few proper or primitive ones. Most are participles, such as all those ending in ba, siba, na, and chome. The possessive suffix m, me, forms adjectives from substantives and nouns from verbal infinitives. So also the suffixes kem and dim make adjectives from substantives.

Idle, { Chwancha, m. / Chwanchanima, f.
True, or truth-speaking, } A'je. A'je bwakba, m. c. / A'je bwakbanima, f.
False, or false-speaking, { Limo.* Limo bwakba, m. / Limo. Limo bwakbanima, f.
Passionate, hasty, } Soksa, bokba, m. c. / Soksa bokbanima, f.
Placid, patient, Soksa má bokba. Neg.
Cowardly, { Níba, m. c. / Níbanima, f.
Brave, Má níba. Neg.
Constant-minded, Unchangeable, } Theumjásiba, m. / Theumjásibanima, f.
Inconstant, Changeful, } Theum májásiba. Neg.
Wasteful, profuse, } Wárba, m. c. / Wárbanima, f.
Niggardly, { Kákáchyákba, m. n. / Kákáchyákbanima, f.
Kind, gentle, { Theum neuba, m. c. / Theum neubanima, f.
Harsh, unkind, Theum máneuba. Neg.
Obedient, { Bíba, Bísiba, m. c.† / Bíbanima, Bísibanima, f.
Disobedient, Má bíba. Má bísiba
Masculine, Wainsake, Feminine, Minchake, } Genitival both
Mad, idiotic, A'theum má neuba
Sane of mind, A'theum neuba
Licit, Páchome, m. f. n.
Illicit, Má páchome
Bodily, Ramke, Mental, Theumke } Genitival, both of these; com. gender‡
Hungry { Sóleumi byakba, m. c. / Sóleumi byakbanima, f.
Thirsty, Pwáku dwaktimi byakba
Naked, { A'klancho bwakba, m. / A'klancho bwakbanimá, f.
Clothed, { Phísiba, m. c. / Phísibanima, f.
Libidinous (man), Ming dwakba, m.
Libidinous (woman), Wainsa' dwakbanima, f.
Gluttonous, { Kojacha, m. / Kojamicha, f.
Drunkard, Dhékong- { tuba, m. / tubanima, f.
Drunken, { Dukba, m. c. / Dukbanima, f.
Foul-mouthed, Abusive, { Khíba, m. c. / Khíbanima, f.

Alive, Living, { Blenba, m. c. / Blenbanima, f.
Dying, Byakchopaba
Dead, { Byakba,§ m. c. / Byakbanima, f.
Sickening, Sick, } Rícho- { paba, m. c. / pabanima, f.
Sickened, sick, { Ríbá, m. c. / Ríbánima, f.
Getting well, Swáchopába
Got well, { Swába, m. c. / Swabanima, f.
Healthy, { Neuba, m. / Neubanima, f.
Made well, Swápáng
Strong, { Sokticha, m. / Soktimicha, f.
Weak, { Soktimáthíba, m. / Soktimáthíbanima, f. / Sokti manthim, c.
Sleepy, { Myelchopába, m. / Myelchopabanima, f.
Asleep, { Myelba, m. / Myelbanima, f.
Waking, Syainscho- { pába, m. c. / pabanima, f.
Awake, Syains- { siba, m. c. / sibanima, f.
Awakening, Syainsipába
Awakened, Syainsipána
Young, A'kachíme, Youthful, Yáke, } m. f.
Adult, { Swolacha, m. / Swolami or Swolamicha, } f.
Old, aged { Gná-wa, m. / Gná-mi, f.
Handsome, { Rimba, m. f. n. / Rimsokpa, m. / Rimsongma, f.
Ugly, { Má rimba, / Má rimsokba, / Má rimsongma, } Neg.
Tall, high, { Lába, com. gen. and m. / Lábanima, f.
Short, low, { Dékho lába, m. and n. / Dékho lábanima, f.
Great, big, { Gnólo, m. and n. / Gnólonima, f.
Small, Akachime. Yáke.¶ See Young
Fat, { Syéneúba, m. and n. (well in flesh) / Syéneúbanima, f.
Thin, { Ryamba, m. and n. / Ryambanima, f.

---

* Limo, m. and f., can be used alone for false.

† Bíba is the transitive, bísiba the intransitive form. See Verbs.

‡ See p. 330 of Sequel, also the note and references at p. 321, *supra*.

§ Byakchopaba is literally who makes to die, and so of all similar words; but the form is doubtful, and in general the participle in bá, which is ao'istic, is used in neuter verbs exclusively to express both senses of dying and dead, sickening and sick, the preterite participle being regarded as an appendage of transitives only.

¶ These two words are samples of adjectives proper. Such are very rare in this tongue, wherein the qualifying words are mostly participles, usable, too, substantively, like those formed by the affixes cha and wa. This is another Dravidian trait; and the rarity of proper adverbs and prepositions, and the use of gerunds in lieu of the one and of nouns in lieu of the other (see Adverbs and Prepositions), are two more such traits, to be added to those elsewhere set down.

Tired, { Bálba, m. and n.
Weary, { Balbanima, f.
Untired, { Má balba, } Neg.
Fresh, { Má balbanima, }
Lame, { Sokopá, m. n.
{ Sokopánima, f.
Lamed, Sokopápána, c.
Blind, { Má kwoba, m. n.
{ Má kwobanima, f.
Blinded, Má kwobapana
Deaf, { Má nimba, m. and n.
{ Má nimbanima, f.
Deafened, { Má nimbapana, m. n.
{ Má nimbanimapana, f.
Dumk, { Má bwakba, m. n.
{ Má bwakbanima, f.
Deaf and dumb, { Glaúd-wa, m. n.
= idiotic, { Glaúdwanima, f.
Alone, solitary, *Gícha or A'gícha, m. f.
Companioned, { Wárcha thiba, m. n.
{ Wárcha thibanimá, f.
Wise, { Jókba. Teuba. Mimba, m. n.
{ Jokbanima. Teubanima. Mimbanima, f.
Foolish, Májokba. Máteuba. Mámimba. Neg.
Learned, { Parepába, m.
{ Parepábanima, f.
Ignorant, Má pare pába
Rich, { Thíba, m. n.
{ Thíbanima, f.
Poor, { Má thíba, m. n.
{ Má thíbanima, f.
Talkative, { Bwakba, m. n.
{ Bwakbanima, f.
Silent, Líba bwakba, m. c.† (silent who remains)
Dirty = black, Kekem, m. f. n.
Dirtied, { Kekempana, m. c.
{ Kekemnimapana, f.
Clean = white, Bubum, m. f. n.
Cleansed, { Bubumpana, m. c.
{ Bubumnimapana, f.
Married, { Gróchya dyumba, m.
{ Gróchya dyumbanima, f.
Unmarried, { Gróchya mádyumba, m.
{ Gróchya mádyumbanima, f.
Taxed, { Chóba, m. Chóbanima, f.
{ Chóchome, n.
Exempt, { Má chóba. Má chóbanima.
{ Má chochome. Neg.
New, Aninta, m. f. n.
Old, worn-out, Amaisam, m. f. n.
Ready, prepared, { Theumna (finished)
{ Mingba } (dressed as
{ Kina } food)
Unprepared, { Má theumna, } Neg.
Unmade, { Má mingba, }
{ Má kina }

Ready, { Rimsiba (adorned), m. c.
{ Rimsibanima, f.
Unready, { Má rimsiba, m.
{ Má rimsibanima, f.
Common, abundant, Táchome, n.
Rare, scarce, Má táchome. Neg.
Public, apert, patent, Kwóchome
Private, latent, not to be seen, Khleuchome
Successful, { Neupába, caus. pres. part.
Prosperous, { Neupana, cau. past. part.
{ Neupachome, c. f. p.
Unprosperous, { Má neupaba, } Neg.
Unsuccessful, { Má neupana, }
{ Má neupachome, }
Saleable, Léchome, p. f.
Sold, Lena, p. p.
Purchasable, Jyapchome, p. f.
Purchased, Jyamna, p. p.
Similar, { Deuba, m. n.
Resembling, { Deubanima, f.
Dissimilar, Má deuba. Má deubanima
The same, { Myemme or } (that very one)
{ Myemgno, } m. f. n.
Other, different, Kwagname. Wangme, m. f. n.
Easy, doable, Páchome, p. f.
Difficult, not doable, Má páchome
Changeful, { Phasiba,‡ p. n.
Changeable, { Phaschopaba, p. n. (about to change)
Changed, { Phásiba (self)
{ Phána (other, tr.)
About to be changed, Pháchome
Caused to be changed, Phásipána, c. ref. Phápána, c. tr.
Orderly, set in order, { Má hulsiba, n.
{ Má hulba, tr.
{ Má limsiba, n.
{ Má lipba, tr.
Disordered, { Hulsiba, n.
Disorderly, { Hulna, tr.
{ Limsiba, n.
{ Limna, tr.
Liable to disorder, { Hulchome
About to be disordered, { Lipchome
Having, possessing, { Thiba, m. c.
tenens, { Thibanima, f.
Not having, { Má thiba, m. c.
Wanting, { Má thibanima, f.
Ornamented, { Rimba, n.
Adorned, { Rimsiba, refl.
{ Rimpana, tr.
Plain, { Má rimba
{ Má rimsiba
{ Má rimpana
Useful, Sichome, p. f. tr. §
Useless, Má sichome, Neg.
Quick-moving, active, { Grukba, m. c.
{ Grukbanima, f.

---

* I, thou, he, am alone, is wá'gícha bwagna, í'gícha bwangé, a'gícha bwa = my, thy, his oneliness is or remains.

† The root bwá, to be (sit) and to speak, can hardly be distinguished in the participles.

‡ Be changed, is phaso = change thyself; change it, is pháto. The former gives for participles phásiba and phaschopaba = what changes or is about to change; and the latter, phábá, the changer, and phána, the changed.

§ Participles of the object (see Conjugations), and usable equally as substantives or as adjectives, *e.g.*, jachome is victuals or food at p. 325, while here it is edible or wholesome.

Slow-moving, lazy, inert, Má grukba, Neg.
Wholesome, eatable, Jáchome *
Unwholesome, Májáchome
Manufactured, wrought, Pána
Manufacturable, Páchome *
Sharp, Héba, n. p.
Sharpened, Hépána, tr. p.
Blunt, Má héba
Bluntened, Má hépána
Grinded, Khrina
Grindable, Khrichome
Spun, Pánna
Woven, Pána
Platted, Pána
Spacious, wide, ample, Bhyappa
Contracted, narrow, Má bhyappa
Moving, capable of self-motion, Dukba, † n. part. m. f.-n. Dukbanima, f.
Movable, capable of being moved, Dukchome, tr. p. f.
Motionless, Má dukba, m. n.
Immovable, Má dukchome, tr.
Moved,‡ self, Dukba
Moved, other, Dungna
Caused to be moved, Dungpána
Figured, self, Rám dyumba
Figured, other, Rám dyumpána
Figurable, Rámdyum pachome
Unfigurable, Rámdyum má pachome
Luminous, shining, Chyarba (self), n.
Self-illumed, Chyarsiba, refl.
Illumed by other, Chyarpána
Illuminable, Chyarpachome
Dark, Namrikba
Darkened, Namringpána
Flaming, burning self, Hoba (fire and candle)
Kindled, Inflamed, Made to flame, } Hopána
Kindleable, Inflammable, } Hopáchome *
Burning, in process of being consumed by fire, Deupba
Burnt, consumed by fire, Deumpána
Consumable by fire, Deumpachome *
Extinguishing (self), going out, Byakba
Extinguished by another, Byangpána
The upper, superior, Háteungme, m. f. n.
The lower, inferior, Háyungme ‡
Right, Jumrolame
Left, Perolame
Central, Alimbudime
Eastern, Namdhapdikhalame
Western, Namwamdikhalame
Northern, Háteulame
Southern, Háyulame

Passable, Accessible, } Gwakchome *
Impassable, Mágwakchome
Cultivated field, Jóna
Culturable, Jóchome *
Uncultivated, Ma jóna
Uncultivable, Má jóchome
Fruitful, rich (soil), Neuba (good)
Barren, sterile, Má neuba
Sandy. No word
Clayey, Phélépheleme
Calcareous, Chunnungme
Saline, Yuksinungme
Muddy, Kyelchome
Dusty, Byerbakhapinungme
Brackish (water) Yuksinungme
Fresh, Sweet, { Túchome / Néuba / Broba
Flowing, Gwakba
Still, Má gwakba
Deep, Gleumba
Shallow, Má gleumba
Windy, stormy (weather), { Júnam § / Júkhime / Júkhitame
Fine, fair, Neuba
Cold, { Junamme / Júmi byangme / Júkhitame
Hot, { Haulomi / Haulomi byangme / Haulau dyumme
Sunshiny, Namneume
Cloudy, Koksyalbwalme
Rainy, Ryáwayume
Cold (water), Chikba
Hot (water), { Gleugleum, conj. / Gleugleum-me, disj.
Moist, sappy green (wood), A'pwákunungme
Juicy (fruit), A'pwakunungme
Juiceless, sapless, A'pwákumanthime
Wooden, Singke
Woody, timber-bearing, Wooded, } Singdhyaksibwagdikhá
Stony, made of stone, Lungke
Stony, stone-bearing (place), Lung bwagdikha
Iron, made of iron, Syelke
Iron-producing, Syelgiba
Leathern, made of leather, Kwoksyeuke, Kokseke
Skin-bearing (animal), Kwoksyeu thiba. Kokse thiba
Wet, Dry, } clothes, &c., { Moba / Sheuba
Wooded (country), { Sabala bwakba / Sabala bwakdikha

---

* See note § at p. 327.

† The participle of neuter verbs is single and aoristic; dukba is changing and changed, et sic de cæteris.

‡ Hateu, top, above; háyu, below, bottom.

§ Wind and windy, and cloud and cloudy, &c., are confounded usually like "cold" in English, which is both substantive and adjective. So also Heat and Hot.

Open, A'klauchom (naked)
Jungly, Sábala dyumme
Coloured, { Ryansiba, self / Ryangna, by other }
Caused to be coloured, Ryangpána
Colourless, { Bubum (white) / Má ryangna / Má ryangsiba }
Colourable, Ryakchome
Red, Lalam *
White, Bubum
Black, Kyákyám
Blue. No name
Green, Gigim
Yellow, Womwome
Sweet, Jijim
Sour, Jeujeum †
Bitter, Kaba
Ripe, Jiba
Ripened, { Jiba, n. (self) / Jipana, tr. (other) }
Raw, Achekhli
That is raw, Achekhli bwakba
That is made raw, Achekhli pana
Rotten (flesh, fruit, &c.), Jyipba
Rotten (wood, &c.), Chyamba
Coarse, / Fine, } No words
Rough, Khwárbekhwárbem
Smooth, Phélephélem
Polished, Phélephélem
Unpolished, Má phélephélem
Straight, Dyomba
Crooked, { Gukba / Gung-gung, or / Gung-gungme }
Full, Dyamba
Filled, Dyampána
Empty, A'shéti
Emptied, A'shétipána
Solid, Dyamba
Hollow, A'shéti
Heavy, Hyalba
Light (levis), Hamba
Great, Gnolo
Small, Yáke
Long, Jheúba
Short, Má jheúba
Wide, Bhyakba
Narrow, Má bhyakba
High, Lába
Low, Má lába. Dékholába
Angular, Kona-bwakba
Round, Khirkhirme
Spherical, Pulpulme
Pointed, Jeujeume ‡
Unpointed, Má jeujeume

Edged, Hé'ba
Unedged, Má hé'ba
Broken, / Burst, } { round / things, } Bukba, Pwongna
Broken (long things), Jikba. Jingna
Torn (cloth, &c.), { Jiba.§ n. / China, tr. }
Split (wood), { Yésiba, int. / Yéna, tr. }
Entire, by negative prefix to all the above
Porous, Chapba
Imporous, Má chapba
Open, Hongsiba
Opened, Hongna
Opening, about to open, Hongschopaba
Shut, Tyangsiba
Shutted, Tyangna
Shutting, about to shut, Tyangschopaba
Spread, { Hamsiba, n. / Hamna, tr. }
Folded, { Plemsiba, n. / Plemna, tr. }
Expanded, blown (flower), Boba
Caused to blow, Bopána
Expanding, about to expand, Boschopaba
Closed, shut = not expanded, Má boba
Tight, Khimsiba, n.
Tightened, Khimna, tr.
Loose, Thyelvim
Loosened, Thyelvim pána
Unsteady, loose, or / Shaking, } { Má jásiba / Má jána }
Fixed, firm, { Jásiba, n. / Jána, tr. }
Cooked, Kina
Boiled, Pwákumikina
Roasted, Gryamna
Grilled, Cheuna
Hairy, Swo*n* thiba
Hairless, Swo*n* má thiba or Swo*n* manthi
Feathered, Swo*n* thiba
Unfeathered, Swo*n* má thiba or Swo*n* manthi
Rising or risen (sun), Dhapba
Setting or set (sun), Wamba
Issuing, coming out or come out (being), Gluba
Entering or entered (being), Woba
Falling (being), Dokba, n.
Fallen, Dokba, n.
About to fall, Dokchopaba
Falling (thing), U'ba
Fallen (thing), U'ba
Rising (being), Rapba
Remaining, risen or standing, Rapsobwakba
Risen or stood, Rapba. Rapso bwakba

---

* Lálam adjectival. Lalamme substantival = Newári, Hyáwun and Hyáwúngtu, and lál, lál wala of Hindi, or red and the red one. So Bubum and Bubumme Gigim and Gigimmo, &c. The affixes jokpa (m.) and jongma (f.) are often substituted for me in reference to colour, kyakyajokpa, the black.

† Jeujeum, literally pointed, acute, sharp, from Jeujeu (French eu), a point.

‡ Jeujeu vel juju is apex, point, top; pulpul is a sphere, and Khirkhir, a round but not spherical body.

§ Bukba, jikba, as participles of neuter verbs which are aoristic, wear the form of present participles, and as adjectives mean breaking as well as broken, &c.

Raising, Rampaba
Raised, { Ramna, tr. / Rampana, caus.
Putting down (man), Jyeulba *
Put down (things), Jyeulna
Sitting, Bwakba. Nisiba
Seating, Bwang paba. Ni paba *
Seated, Bwápána. Nina
Lying down, Glesiba, Ipba*
Laid down, { Glesiba Ipba, n. / Glesipana Impana, tr.
Waking, Syai*n*siba
Waked, Syai*n*siba
Awakening, Syai*n*sipaba *
Awakened, Syai*n*sipana
Sleepy, Myelcho dwákba
Asleep, Myelba
Sleeping, Myelba *
About to sleep, Myelchopaba
Domestic, home-made, Dwábodyel dim
Foreign or foreign made, Wangmedyel dim
Rustic, Dyelpo, m. f.
Loving, Desirous, Desiring, } (being), { Dwakba, m. / Dwakbanima, f.
Lovable, Desirable, } Dwakchome *
Written, Ryangna
Read, Parepana
Eaten, Jana
Drank, Túna (pausing accent)
Payable, Chochome *
Paid, Choona (pausing accent)
Well-odoured, A'rineubame †
Stinking, Arimaneubame
Having odour (thing) or smelling (man), } Namba
Belonging to a Tibetan or native of Tibet, } Leuchake, m. / Leuchanimake, f.
Tibetan, or produced in Tibet (thing), } Leuchadyeldim / Leuchadyelke, m. ‡
Nepalese, native of Nepal. No name
Belonging to a highlander or native of hills } Syértichake, m. / Syértenimake, f.
Highland thing, { Syertedim, or / Syertedyeldim
Of person of the plains, } Dheptechake, m. / Dheptechanimake, f.
Produce of plains, Dheptedim

European (person), { Bubum-ramcha, m. / Bubum-ramchanima, f.
European (goods), Bubum-ramthiba dyeldim
Woollen, made of wool, U'nke
Woolly, wool-bearing, U'nthiba
Hairy, made of hair, Swo*n*ke
Hairy, hair-bearing, Swo*n*thiba
Iron, made of iron, Syalke
Golden, Syeunake
Silver, made of silver, Chándike
Wooden, made of wood, Singke
Woody, full of trees (place), Dhyaksi-bwagdikha
Jungly, full of jungle, Sábálá bwangdikha
Eye-having (being), Michi thiba
Foot-having (being), Kholi thiba
Wealthy (being), Grokso thiba
Wealthy (place), Grokso-bwagdikha
Grain-having (man), Búra thiba
Grain-producing (field), Búra neudikha
Grain-abounding (place), Búra bwangdikha §

Comparison of Adjectives.

Great, Gnolo
As great as this, Yam khwome gnolo
Greater than this, Yam ding gnolo
Greatest of all, Haupe ding gnolo
Very great, Thé gnolo
Small, Káchim. A'káchim
Small as this, Yam khomekáchim
Smaller than this, Yamding káchim
Smallest of all, Haupe dingkáchim
Very small, Thé káchim
Cold, Chikba
Colder, Yam ding chikba
Coldest, Haupe ding chikba
Very cold, Thé chikba
Hot, Gleuba
Hotter, Yam ding gleuba
Hottest, Haupe ding gleuba
Very hot, Thé gleuba

Numerals.

Cardinals.

One, Kwong
Two, Niksi
Three, Sam

---

* All these, and numberless others ending in ba, siba, na, or chome, are participial. See further on. The relative pronoun inheres, and the use is adjectival or substantival.

† Me, m. affix, is a formative of all three genders = hma, gu of Newári, save that these are major and minor of gender. Mé, like hma, gu, attaches to all qualitives used substantively superadded to the gender sign, as gná-wá, gwa-mi = old (man and woman), whence gnáwame, gnámime = the old ones, male and female. So swalo-cha-mi = mature, male and female, whence swalocháme, swalomime.

‡ Ke (or kem, see p. 321) is the general sign of relation when one substantive only is used. When two are expressed, the second takes the á prefix (his, her, its), unless the relation be local, and then dim (diem = in of) is used instead of the á; *e.g.*, band of man, muryu á gu; rice of bazaar, bazar dim shéri. (See Grammar.)

§ Bwangdikha = the place where is; dikha usable only with a verb; bwang from bwakesse in loco.

Four, Lé
Five, Gno
Six, Rukba
Seven, Channi
Eight, Yá
Nine, Ghú
Ten, Kwaddyum
Eleven, Kwaddyum kwong,
= ten (and) one
Twelve, ,, niksi
Thirteen, ,, sam
Fourteen, ,, lé
Fifteen, &c., ,, gnó
Twenty, A'sim, = a score } Kwong ásim, = one score
Twenty-one, A'sim kwong, = a score (and) one { Kwong ásim kwong, = one score and one
Twenty-two, A'sim niksi. Kwongásim niksi
Thirty, Kwong ásim, kwong áphlo = one score, one its half
Thirty-one, Kwong ásim, kwong áphlo kwong, = one score, one half (and) one
Thirty-two, Kwong ásim, kwong áphlo niksi, = one score, and one half and two
Forty, Niksi ásim = two score
Forty-one, Niksi ásim kwong
Forty-two, Niksi ásim niksi
Fifty, Niksi ásim áphlo, = two score (and) its half
Fifty-one, Niksi ásim áphlo kwong
Fifty-two, Niksi ásim áphlo niksi
Sixty, Sam ásim
Seventy, Sám ásim áphlo, = three score (and) a half
Eighty, Lé ásim
Ninety, Lé ásim áphlo
One hundred, Gnó ásim, = five score
One hundred and one, Gnó ásim kwong
One hundred and two, Gnó ásim niksi, = five score (and) two
Ordinals. None

ADVERBIALS.

Once, Kwábálá
Twice, Nip pálá
Thrice, Sap pálá
Four times, Lep pálá
Five times, Gnó pálá
Six times, Rú pálá
Seven times, Chá pálá
Eight times, Yá pálá
Nine times, Ghú pálá
Ten times, Kwaddyum pálá
Firstly, Secondly, } Wanting, save as they coincide with the last

NUMERAL ADJUNCTS.

They are doubtfully ascribable to this tongue, or falling so fast out of use that what remains is a mere fragment. I shall illustrate by comparison with Newári, in which these generic signs are undoubtedly normal and in full use. Báhing, like Newári, has no division corresponding to the fully-developed gender, m. f. n. It has not even, as Newári has, a division correspondent to the logical gender, or beings and things, which is equivalent to the major and minor of gender in the plural of Dravirian nouns and verbs also.

English.	*Newári.*	*Báhing.*
Beings / Things	Hma / Gú	Li?
Rationals	...	...
Brutes	...	...
Vegetalia / Plants	Má	A'pum
Timber trees	Sima	Sing
Soft trees or grasses	Má	A'púm
Logs	Ká	...
Weapons / Implements	Pú	Syal
Pairs	Jú	...
Flowers	Phó	Lí
Fruits	Gó	Bwom
String of animals	Tya. Jhó	Chyarchyar
Heap of things	Dón. Púcha	Khumna
Herd of animals	Batháng	...
Days	Nhu	Kha

In the use of these signs first comes the numeral, then the sign, and then the thing or being specified, *e.g.*, Newári, Chha ma si ma, Báhing, Kwong sing ápúm = one (timber) tree.

Chha má singhali má, N.; Kwo ápúm, Séli ápúm, B., = one chestnut tree.

Swó nhu nhi, N.; Sam kha namti, B., = three days. Nigo santola si, N.; Ni bwom santola sichi, B., = one orange.

Chhapukhwón, N.; Kwosyal bétho, B., = one sword. Chhago singhali si, N.; Kwobwom seti sichi, B., = one chestnut fruit.

PRONOUNS.

Singular.

I, Gó
Thou, Ga
He, she, it, Harem, yam, myam

Dual.

We, inclusive, Gósi
We, exclusive, Gósuku
Ye, Gási
They, { Harem dausi* / Yam dausi / Myam dau

* For dausi, dau, read daüsi, that is, short a or soft a, with the pausing tone.

Plural.

We, inclusive, Góï
We, exclusive, Góku
Ye, Gani
They, { Harem dau * / Yam dau / Myam dau }
This, Yam } All genders ; no sign
That, Myam }

Dual.

These, Yam dausi
Those, Myam dausi

Plural.

These, Yam dau
Those, Myam dau
Self, Daubo (Dwabo)

Dual.

Dwabo dausi

Plural.

Dwabo dau
Myself, Wadaubo
Thyself, I'daubo
His, her, itself, A'daubo

Dual.

1. { Wasi daubo, exclusive / Isi daubo, inclusive }
2. Isi daubo
3. Asi daubo

Plural.

1. { Wake daubo, exclusive / Ike daubo, inclusive }
2. Ine daubo
3. Ane daubo

Any, some, person, Seú ; subs. and adj., m. and f.

Dual.

Seudasi

Plural.

Seu dau
Any, some, thing, Mára : subs. only : n.

Dual.

Múra dausi

Plural.

Mára dau
Another, Kwágnáme

Dual.

Kwágnáme dausi

Plural.

Kwágnáme dau
Many or much, Dhékong : subs. adj.: m. f. n.

No dual or plural.

Few. Little, Dékho : subs. adj.: m. f. n.
The same, Myem

Dual.

Myem dausi

Plural.

Myem dau
How many? } Gisko, { subs. adj.: m. f. n.
And how much? }
As many, much, Gisko, } ditto
So many, much, Metti, }
All, Hwappe, ditto
Half, A'kwáphala, ditto
The whole, Hwappe Haupe
Who? inter. { Seu. Singular, subs. adj. m. and f. / Seu dausi. Dual / Seu dau. Plural }
Who? rela.† { Gyem, sing. subs. adj. m. f. n. / Gyem dausi. Dual / Gyem dau. Plural }
Who? correl. { Myem, sing. subs. adj. n. / Myem dausi. Dual / Myem dau. Plural }
What? { Mára, sing. subs. adj., m. f. n. / Mára dausi. Dual / Mára dau. Plural }
What, rel., Mára
Whát, correl., Maem
Dual and plural, Like
Interrogative for both
Whoever, } Gisko, subs. adj. m. f. n.
Whatever, }
Dual, Gisko dausi, } ditto
Plural, Gisko dau, }
As many, Gisko, } ut supra
How many? Gisko, }
So many, Metti
Dual, Metti dausi
Plural, Metti dau
Either, Yemka. Myemka
Dual, Yemka dausi. Myemka dausi
Plural, Yemka dau. Myemka dau
Both, Nimpho, subs. and adj. m. f. n.
Several. No word
My, Wá' ‡
Thy, I'
His, her, its, A'.

Dual.

Our, Wási, excl.‡ I'-si, incl.
Your, I'-si
Their, her, its, A'si

Plural.

Our, Wake, excl. Ike, incl.
Your, Ini
Their, A'ni
Mine, Wáke

---

* See note (*) on previous page.

† Gyem takes the á prefix and is used interrogatively in a relative sense: which of these persons or things will you take? A-gyemme ládi, wherein the disjunct form is employed, gyemme.

‡ The words father and mother in conjunction with their pronominal adjuncts are irregular,

a-pa	{ wasi-po / isi-po	wake-po	} Singular, Dual, and Plural.
i-po	isi-po	ike-po / ini-po	
a-po	asi-po	áni-po	

Other relations, as popo, uncle, though but iterations of po, are regular, *e.g*, wá-popo, i-popo, a-popo, &c.

Thine, I'ke
His, her, its, A'ke

Dual.

Ours, Wasike, excl. Isike, incl.
Yours, I'sike
Theirs, A'sike

Plural.

Ours, Wakke, excl. Ikke, incl.
Yours, I'nike
Theirs, A'nike
Own, Dauboke
1. My own, Wa dauboke
2. Thy own, I' dauboke
3. His, her, its own, A' dauboke

Dual.

1. { Wasi dauboke, excl. / I'si dauboke, incl.
2. I'si dauboke
3. A'si dauboke

Plural.

1. { Wake dauboke / I'ke dauboke
2. Ine dauboke
3. A'ne dauboke
1. Mine own, Wake dauboke
2. Thine own, I'ke dauboke
3. His, her, its own, A'ke dauboke, &c., like the disjunctive mine

BÁHING VERBS.

Cause, Páto, tr. Pápáto, its causal *
Cause not, Má páto
Can it, be able for it, { Cháppo, tr. / Chamso, intr. †
Do not can it, Má chápo. Má chámso.
Cause to can or enable { Chámpáto, tr. / Chámpáso, intr. / Chámpáyi, passive / Chámpápáto, causal, tr. / Champápáso, intr. causal / Chámpápáyi, pas. causal
Enable not, Má champáto, &c.
Be born, Gikko, n.
Give birth to or beget, { Kiko, trans. / Kingso, reflex / Kingyi, passive
Give birth to or beget, { Gingpáto, tr. causal / Gingpáso, intr. causal / Gingpáyi, passive causal
Cause to beget or produce, { Kingpáto, tr. / Kingpáso, reflex / Kingpáyi, passive
Be not born, Má gikko, Neg.
Beget or produce not, Má kikko, Neg.
Live, { Blęnno, n. / Blenpáto, tr. causal / Blenpáso, intr. causal / Blenpáyi, passive
Live not, Má blenno
Die, { Byákko, n. / Byangpáto, tr. causal / Byangpáso, intr. causal / Byangpáyi, passive
Kill, { Sáto, tr. / Sáso, reflex tr. / Sáyi, passive / Sapáto, tr. causal / Sápáso, reflex causal / Sápáyi, passive
Be (sum), Ká. Khe. Gno. Irreg. Defec.
Be ‡ (maneo), { Bwakko, n. (sit) / Bwangpáto, tr. causal / Bwangpáso, intr. causal / Bwangpáyi, passive
Become, Cause to become, { Dyúmmo, n. / Dyúmpáto, tr. causal / Dyúmpáso, intr. causal / Dyúmpáyi, passive / Thyumto. Dyumpato §
Have, possess, { Thiwo / Bwálá
Have not, or want, { Má thi'wo / Ma bwala
Make to have, Cause to possess, { Thiyáto, tr. / Bwálápáto, tr.
Do, make, perform, { Páwo, tr. / Páso, reflex / Páyi, passive ‖ / Pápáto, tr. c. / Pápáso, intr. c. / Pápáyi, passive, c.
Keep doing, { Páwomukho bwákho, n. / Pásogno bwákho, n.
Cease doing or to do, Pácho pléno, n.
Suffer, { Tyárro, tr. / Tyárso, reflex. tr. / Tyári, pas.

---

* Páto is the causative of all verbs, and is derived from the root pá, to do or make. It answers to the Háyu form, "do for another." In Báhing it is the causative, also bearing that sense. Do, or make, is pawo.

† These are = wonto and woncho of Háyu, the definite and indefinite of Hungarian; in English, can it, or be able for it, and be able simply. Chápo forms the potential of all verbs.

‡ Be in a certain place = sit. Sheer entity is expressed by ka, khe, gno, defectives.

§ Neuter dyum becomes normally transitive and causal thyum. Both take the ordinary causative, which with the latter makes a double causal thyumpato, cause to cause to become; or, at pleasure, even a treble one, thyumpapato. Sogikko become : kikko, whence kingpato and kingpapato.

‖ Observe, once for all, that the three forms of the transitive (primitive and causal alike) refer to him (any one), to self and to me (the speaker). Thus sá-to, kill him or it; sá-so, kill thyself; sá-yi, kill me; that in verbs like to do, the sense is modified of necessity, but without essential change; and that the passive has no imperative of the second or third person. Hence the entry under the first, and hence, as will be seen in the Grammar, the existence in the language of certain special forms of the verb subsidiary to the so-called passive.

Cause to suffer,
- Tyárpátó, tr.
- Tyarpáso, reflex
- Tyárpáyi, passive

Observe or Examine,
- Kwó-gno, tr. (see)
- Kwó-so, reflex
- Kwó-yi, passive
- Kwó-páto, tr. causal
- Kwó páso, intr. causal
- Kwó-páyi, passive, causal

Understand, Know, Think,
- Teuto. Jokko. Mimto, tr.
- Teuso. Jongso. Mimso, reflex
- Teuti. Jougyi. Mimti, passive

Cause to understand, Explain,
- Teupáto. Jongpáto. Mimpáto, tr. c.
- Teupáso. Jongpáso. Mimpáso, intr. c.
- Teupáyi. Jongpáyi. Mimpáyi, pas. c.

Feel, Be sensible of, bodily,
- Limléto, trans.
- Limléso, reflex
- Limléyi, passive

Remember,
- Mimto, trans.
- Mimso, reflex
- Mimti, passive
- Mimpáto, tr. causal
- Mimpáso, reflex causal
- Mimpáyi, passive, causal

Forget,
- Plendo, tr.
- Plenso, tr. reflex
- Plendi, passive
- Plen-pá-to-so-yi, causal

Desire, Lust for, love,
- Dwakko, intr.
- Dwakto, tr.
- Dwangso, reflex
- Dwakti, passive
- Dwangpá-to-so-yí, c.

Hate,
- Grámdo, tr.
- Grámso, reflex
- Grámdi, passive
- Grámpá-to-so-yi, c.

Recognise,
- Syanto, trs.
- Syanso, reflex
- Syanti, passive
- Syanpáto, &c., c.

Be modest, Gnúne bókko, n.

Make modest,
- Gnúne bong-pá-to-so-yi, tr., or
- Gnúne pok-ko-so-yi, tr.*

Laugh, Riso, n.
Make laugh, Risipá-to-so-yi, c.
Laugh at, irride, Rito. Riso. Riti, tr.
Weep, Gnwákko, n.
Make weep, Gnwángpá-to-so-yi, c.
Dance, Silimóvo,† tr.
Make dance, Silimópá-to-so-yi, c.
Sing, Swálong páwó, tr.
Make sing, Swálong pápáto-so-yi, c.
Hope. No such word
Fear, Gnito, n.

Frighten,
- Gnipáto, tr. c.
- Gnipáso, reflex c.
- Gnipáyi, passive

Cause to frighten,
- Gnipápáto, tr.
- Gnipápáso, reflex
- Gnipápáyi, *passive*

Tremble,
- Khiwo, n.
- Khipáto, causal
- Khipáso, c. reflex
- Khipáyi, c. p.

Be good, Nyúwo or *N*yúba bwákko, n.
Become good, Nyúba dyúmmo, n.

Make good,
- Nyúto, tr.
- Nyúso, reflex
- Nyúni, passive
- Nyúba dyumpáto, tr. c.
- Nyúba dyumpáso, refl. c.
- Nyúba dyumpáyi, p. c.‡

Be glad, I'thim nyúlá. Gyerso.

Gladden,
- A'thim nyúpáto, tr.
- I'thim nyúpáso, reflex
- Wáthim nyúpáyi,§ passive
- Gyérsi páto-páso-páyi

Be vexed, sad,
- I'thim má nyúla
- Deukha giso

Vex, sadden,
- Deúkha giwo
- A'thim mányúpáto

Be satisfied, Rúgno, n.
Satisfy, Rúpáto, c.

Utter, speak, Articulate,
- Bwakko, n.
- Bwangpáto, c. tr.
- Bwangpáso, c. reflex
- Bwangpáyi, c. passive

Relate, tell, speak to or of,
- Só-gno. Sódo, tr.
- Só-so. Sóso, refl.
- Sóyi. Sódi, pas.

Cause to relate, tell, &c. (For both the above)
- Sopáto, tr.
- Sópáso, refl.
- Sópáyi, p.

---

* As dyum becomes thyum, so bokko becomes pokko-bongpato; and from pokko, double causal pong-pato. (See Grammar.)

† Sili = a dance. The verb móvo has the separate sense of to fight, but is used with many nouns to verbalise them.

‡ Add as synonymes of dyumpato, &c.:—
Nyuba thyumto, tr. Nyuba thyumso, refl. Nyuba thyumyi, pas.
Nyú vel Neu. French eu, as before explained.

§ Means, may I be gladdened. Be gladdened, the sheer passive, cannot be expressed. I, thou, he, is gladdened = Wáthim nyúpáyi, I'thim nyúpáne, A'thim nyúpáda. The last = he gladdens and is gladdened. Gyérso and gyérsipáto are much closer expressions for be glad and gladden. The others are formed from thim or theum, the heart, and the conjunct pronouns. Opposite is the phase of the active and passive voices.

Active.	*Passive.*
A'thim nyúpádu	Wáthim nyúpáyi
A'thim nyúpádi	I'thim nyúpáne
A'thim nyú pada	A'thim nyúpáda

(For thim read theum, French *eu*.)

Talk, make discourse, { Ló páwo, tr.
Ló páso, reflex
Ló páyi, passive

Cause to talk, { Ló pápáto, tr.
Ló pápáso, reflex
Ló pápáyi, passive

Tell my, thy own, his, tale, { Wá ló sógno
I' ló sógno
A' ló sógno

Be silent, Liba bwakko, n.

Silence, { Liba bwangpáto, tr.
Liba bwangpáso, reflex
Liba bwangpáyi, p.

Cause to silence, { Liba bwang pápáto, tr.
Liba bwang pápáso, reflex
Liba bwang pápáyi, p.

Call, summon, { Bréto, tr.
Bréso, reflex
Bréti, passive

Cause to summon, { Brépáto, tr.
Brépáso, reflex
Brépáyi, passive

Shout, vociferate, { Syanda páwo, tr.
Syanda páso, refl.
Syanda páyi, p.

Learn = teach thyself, Cháyi*n*so, n.
Teach, Cháyi*n*do, tr.
Teach thyself, Cháyi*n*so, reflex tr.
Cause thyself to be taught, } Cháyi*n*sipáso, c. r.
Teach me, Cháyi*n*di, passive
Cause me to be taught, Cháyi*n*sipáyi, c.p.

Read, { No such word. Kwo-gno = see, is used

Write, { Ryakko, tr.
Ryangso, tr. reflex
Ryangyi, p.
Ryakti, p. = write for, or to me

Cause to write, { Ryángpáto, tr.
Ryángpáso, reflex
Ryángpáyi, p.

Ask, question, { Hilo páwo, tr.
Hilo páso, reflex
Hilo páyi, p.

Cause to ask, or question, { Hilo pápáto, tr.
Hilo pápáso, reflex
Hilo pápáyi, p.

Answer, Só-gno, tr. (see Tell)

Beg, solicit, { Punno, tr.
Punso, refl.
Punyi, p.

Cause to beg, { Pun páto, tr.
Pun páso, reflex
Pun páyi, p.

Get, obtain, find, { Tá-wo, tr.
Tá-so, reflex
Tá-yi, p.

Cause to get, &c. { Tá-páto, tr.
Tá-páso, reflex
Tá-payi, p.

Approve, like, { Dwakto, tr.*
Dwangso, reflex
Dwakti, p.

Cause to like, &c. { Dwang páto, tr.
Dwang páso, reflex
Dwáng páyi, p.

Dislike, Disapprove, { Mádwakto
Mádwangso, &c.
Mádwakti

See, { Kwó-gno, trans.
Kwó-so, reflex
Kwó-yi, passive

Show, { Kwó páto, tr. c.
Kwó páso, reflex c.
Kwó páyi, p.

Hide, lie hid, Khleúso, n. and reflex
Hide it, Khleúto, tr.
Hide me, Khleúti, p.†

Cause to be hid, or to be concealed, { Khleu páto, tr.
Khleu páso, reflex
Khleu páyi, p.

Cause to cause to be hid, { Khleu pápáto, tr.
Khleu pápáso, refl.
Khleu pápáyi, p.

Hear, { Ninno, tr.
Ninso, reflex
Ninyi, pas.

Cause to hear, { Nin páto, tr.
Nin páso, reflex
Nin páyi, passive

Taste, { Dapto, tr.
Damso, reflex
Dapti, passive

Cause to taste, { Dam páto, tr.
Dam páso, reflex
Dam páyi, passive

Blow, apply breath, { Múto, tr.
Múso, reflex
Múyi, passive

Cause to blow, { Mú páto, tr.
Mú páso, reflex
Mú páyi, passive

Smell, { Nammo, tr.
Namso, reflex
Námyi, passive

Cause to smell, { Nam páto, tr.
Nam páso, reflex
Nam páyi, passive

Touch, { Khúto, tr.
Khúso, reflex
Khúti, passive

Cause to touch, { Khú páto, tr.
Khú páso, reflex
Khú páyi, passive

Eat, { Jáwo. Báwo, tr.
Jáso. Báso, reflex
Jáyi. Báyi, passive

Cause to eat, = feed, { Já páto, tr. Bapato, tr.
Já páso, refl. Bapaso, refl.
Já páyi, pas. Bapayi, pas.

---

* The intransitive is dwakko ≒ approve, whence transitive dwakto, approve *it*, like the Hungarian determinate and indeterminate.

† In this, as in most verbs, the three forms refer respectively to me (*khleuti*), to him, or it, any being or thing (khleuto), and to self (thyself) (khleuso); and so precisely in the causal also, khleu páyi, khleu páto, and khleu páso.

Drink, { Túgno, tr. / Túso, reflex / Túyi, pas.
Cause to drink, { Tundo, tr. / Tunso, reflex / Tundi, pas.
Be intoxicated, Dúkko.* Neutro, pas.
Make intoxicated, or intoxicate, { Dung páto, tr. / Dung páso, reflex / Dung páyi
Vomit, { Méwo, tr. / Méso, reflex / Méyi, pas.
Cause to vomit, { Mé páto, tr. / Mé páso, reflex / Mé páyi, pas.
Sleep, Ippo, n.
Cause to sleep, { Im páto, tr. c. / Im páso, reflex c. / Im páyi, pas. c.
Cause to sleep, { Ipto, tr. / Ipso, refl. / Ipti, pas. } These are equal in sense to the last, and exhibit a second mode of making causals.
Wake, Syáyinso, n.
Awaken, { Syáyinsi páto, tr. / Syáyinsi páso, reflex / Syáyinsi payi, pas.
Dream, { Gnámung mówo, tr. / Gnámung móso, reflex
Cause to dream, { Gnámung mópáto, tr. / Gnámung mópáso, reflex / Gnámung mópáyi, pas.
Fart, Piso, n. Pisipáto, &c., causal
Fart at him, Pito. Piso. Piti, tr.
Shit (caca), Wáso, intr.
Cause to shit (caca), Wási páti, &c., c.
Caca supra ali quid vel aliquem, Wáto, tr.
Piss (minge), { Chárso, n. / Chársi páto, causal
Imminge, Chárto, &c., tr.
Kiss (give and take oscula), { Chuppáwo, tr. / Chuppáso, reflex / Chuppáyi, pas.
Cause to kiss, Chuppá páto, &c., c.
Kiss (coë), { Leuwo, tr. (French eu) / Leuso, reflex / Leuyi, pas.
Be kissed, Leupáso, reflex causal †
Sneeze, { Háchhún mówo, &c., tr. / Háchhún mópáto, &c., causal
Spit, { Téwo, tr. / Téso, reflex / Téyi, pas.
Cause to spit, { Té páto, tr. / Té páso, reflex / Té páyi, pas. / Té pápáto, &c., D.C.‡
Belch, { Byamne mówo, &c., tr. / Byamne mópáto, &c., causal

Cough, { Syókhé mówó, tr. / Syókhé mópáto, &c., c.
Hiccup, { Dikumi dokto, &c., tr. / Dikumi dongpáto, &c., c.
Swallow, { Dwakko, tr. / Dwangso, reflex / Dwangyi, pas.
Yawn, { Hapsa mówo, tr. / Hapsa mópáto, &c., c.
Lick, { Tukko, tr. / Tungso, reflex / Tungyi, pas
Cause to lick, { Tung páto / Tung páso / Tung páyi
Suck, { Bippo, tr. / Bimso, reflex / Bimyi, passive
Cause to suck, { Bim páto, tr. / Bim páso, reflex / Bim páyi, pas.
Bite, { Kráto, tr. / Kráso, reflex / Kráyi, pas.
Cause to bite, { Krá páto, tr. / Krá páso, reflex / Krá páyi, pas.
Kick, Tá-to, tr. Tá-so, reflex. Ta-yi, pas.
Cause to kick, { Tá páto, tr. / Tá páso, reflex / Tá páyi, pas.
Strike, { Teuppo, tr. (French eu) / Teumso, reflex / Teumyi, pas.
Cause to strike, { Teum páto, tr. / Teum páso, reflex / Teum páyi, pas.
Scrape or scratch (violently), { Khwáro, tr. / Khwárso, reflex / Khwáryi, pas. / Khwárpáto, &c., c.
Scratch (for ease, itching), { Bapto, tr. / Bamso, reflex / Bapti, pas. / Bampáto, &c., causal
Push, Shove, { Nyapto, tr. / Nyamso, reflex / Nyapti, pas. / Nyampáto, &c., causal
Pull, { Syallo, tr. / Syalso, reflex / Syalyi, pas. / Syal páto, &c., causal
Walk, Gwakko, n.
Cause to walk, { Gwang páto, tr. / Gwang páso, reflex / Gwang páyi, pas.
Walk about, Take the air, { Khirso, n. / Khirsi páto, &c., c.
Run, Wanno, n. Wanpáto, &c., c.

* This neuter is conjugated as a passive, dungi, dunge, duga.
† The causal reflex is always used to express an act voluntarily suffered by the party addressed.
‡ D. C. stands for double causal.

Run away, flee, { Júkokáto, n. / Júnguikápáto, &c., c.
Creep, Búsa khwongo gwakko, n. = Snake-like walk
Jump, hop, leap, { Prókko, n. / Prong páto, &c., c.
Fly, Byérro, n. Byer páto, &c., c.
Swim. No such word
Cross over, { Hamba glúgno, n. / Hamba glúpáto, &c., c.
Wade across, Gwaktako or Gwaksomami-bamba glúgno,* n.
Sink, Wamto, n.
Drown or cause to sink, Wampáto, &c., tr.
Bathe, Chiso, n. Chisipáto-páso-páyi, c.
Cause to bathe or bathe him, { Chikto, tr. / Chikso, reflex. / Chikti, pas.
Wash, { Syappo, tr. / Syamso, reflex. / Syamyi, pas. / Syampáto, &c., c.
Dress = dress thyself, { Phiso, reflex / Phisipáto-páso-páyi, c.
Cause to dress, = dress him, { Phikto, tr. / Phingso, reflex. / Phikti, pas.
Cause to cause to dress or have dressed, { Phing páto, tr. / Phing páso, reflex. / Phing páyi, pas.
Undress, { Kleuto, tr. / Kleuso, reflex. / Kleuyi, } / Kleuti, } pas.† / Kleupáto-páso-páyi, c.
Be naked, Iklaucho dyúmmo, n.
Make naked, A'klaucho páwo, tr.
Cause to make naked, { A'klaucho-pá-páto, tr. c.
Be hungry, { Sólyumi byakko, n. / = hunger by die.
Make hungry, { Solyumi byáng páto, &c., tr. c.
Be thirsty, { Pwáku dwakko, n. / Pwáku dwaktimi, byakko.
Make thirsty, { Pwáku dwáng páto, &c., tr. c.
Be sleepy, Myeldo, n. Ipthi dwánglá, n.
Make sleepy, { Myel páto,*tr. c. / Myel páso, reflex. c. / Myel páyi, pas. c. / Ipthi dwang páto-páso-páyi.
Be cold (to sentient being), { Júmi byakko, n. / = cold by die.
Make cold (ditto), { Júmi byang páto-páso-páyi, c.
Be warm or hot, Gluglum dyúmmo, n.
Make warm or heat, { Gluglum páwo-páso-páyi, tr. / Gluglum dyúm páto-páso-páyi, c. or / Gluglum thyúmto-thúmso-thumyi, c.
Be dirty, Kékém dyúmo, n.
Make dirty, { Kékém páwo, &c., tr. / Kékém dyúmpáto, &c., or / Kékém thyumto, &c.
Be clean, Búbúm dyúmmo, n.
Make clean, cleanse, Búbúmpáwo or bubum dyúm páto, tr., or Bubum thyumto.
Cause to cleanse, { Bubum pápáto, / Bubum pápáso, / Bubum pápáyi, / or Bubum thyum páto, } double causal.
Be angry, Sokso páso, tr. reflex.
Make angry, Sokso páwo, tr.
Cause to make angry, Soksopápáto, &c., c.
Abuse, revile, Abase, Humble, Humiliate, { Khryakko, tr. / Khryangso, reflex. / Khryangyi, pas. / Khryang páto-páso-páyi, causal.
Quarrel, { Khiwo, tr. / Khiso, reflex. / ——— pas.
Cause to quarrel, { Khi páto, tr. / Khi páso, reflex. / Khi páyi, pas.
Be reconciled, Deuwo, n.
Reconcile, { Deu páto, tr. / Deu páso, reflex. / Deu páyi, pas.
Fight, { Mó-wo, tr. / Mó-so, reflex. / ——— pas.
Cause to fight, { Mó páto, tr. / Mó páso, reflex. / Mó páyi, pas.
Be victorious or win, Glwaugno, n.
Make victorious or make win, { Glwau páto. tr. / Glwau páso, reflex. / Glwau páyi, pas.
Be conquered, yield, succumb, lose, { Sheóto, or / Syeúto, or / Shyóto, n.
Cause to succumb or lose, { Syeú páto, tr. / Syeú páso, reflex. / Syeú páyi, pas.
Work, { Rú páwo, tr. / Rú páso, reflex. / Rú páyi pas.‡
Cause to work, { Rú pápáto, tr. / Rú pápáso, reflex. / Rú pápáyi, pas.

* Literally, having walked issue on that side.

† My informants say kleuyi can only be said by the clothes, and that a man must say kleutigi, or kleuti, = give me undressed or undress me. So also kleuso is objected to. Thus to Hindí Or and Tain answer Utár, not Utar.

‡ Rupáyi, says the work, do me; rúpáti, says the man, do for me. Compare Háyu pósung and pásung. So work is rúpáwo, and work for him rúpáto. Rú is a substantive = work.

Play, Chamso, n. or reflex.

Cause to play, { Chamsi páto, tr. / Chamsi páso, reflex. / Chamsi páyi, pas.

Amuse, divert, = cause to play, { Chamto, tr. / Chamso, reflex. / Chamti, pas. / Cham páto-páso-páyi,* causal.

Be tired, Bállo, n.

Tire { Bal páto, tr. / Bal páso, reflex. / Bal páyi, pas.

Cause to tire, { Bal pápáto, / Bal pápáso, / Bal pápáyi, } double causal.

Take rest, Náso, n. or intr.

Give rest, { Nasi páto, tr. / Nasi páso, reflex. / Nasi páyi, pas. } causals.

Move, Dúkko, n.† Yóngso, reflex.

Cause to move, or move it, { Dung páto. Dukto, tr. / Dung páso. Dungso reflex. / Dung páyi. Dukti, pas.

Cause to cause to move or cause it to be moved, { Dung pápáto, tr. c. / Dung pápáso, refl. c. / Dung pápáyi, pas. c.

Remove, { Yokto, tr. / Yongso, reflex. / Yokti, pas.

Be still, Be firm or steady, { Jáso, ac. intr. / Má dukko.

Make still, stabilitate, or steady, { Má dukto, tr. neg. / Játo, tr. / Jáso, reflex. / Játi, pas.

Cause to make still, or firm, { Má dung páto, c. tr. / Já páto, c. tr.

Be quick, Grukko, n.

Quicken, { Grung páto. Grukto. / Grung páso. Grungso. / Grung páyi. Grukti.

Be slow, Wákha dyúmo, n.

Make slow, Wákha páwo, tr.

Stay, stop,‡ Jáso, n. act. intr.

Stop it or stay it, Játo, tr.

Stop me, Játi.

Cause to be stopped, or cause to cause to stop, { Jápáto, tr. / Jápáso, reflex. / Já páyi, pas.

Let him depart, { Lácho giwo, / Lá páto, } tr.

Let me depart, { Lácho giyi, / Lá páyi, } pas.

Let thyself depart, { Lácho giso, / Lá páso, } refl.

Be intoxicated, { Dukko, n. / Dukba dyumo or paso, n.

Make intoxicated, { Dukba páwo tr. / Dukba páso, reflex. / Dukba páyi, pas. / Dung páto-paso-páyi, c.

Tell the truth, A'je bwakko, n.

Cause to tell truth, { A'je bwáng páto, tr. / A'je bwáng páso, reflex. / A'je bwáng páyi, pas.

Tell falsehood, { Limo { -challo, n. / -bwakko, n.

Cause to tell, &c. { Limo bwang páto, or Limo chal páto.

Believe, Obey, { Bito, tr. / Biso, reflex. / Biti, passive. / Bipáto, &c., causal.

Disbelieve, Disobey, { Má bito, / Má biso, / Má biti, } Negative.

Present, Offer, { Jeullo,§ tr. (put down, place.) / Jeulso, reflex. / Jeulyi, pas. / Jeul páto-páso-páyi, causal

Accept (= take), { Bláwo, tr. / Blaso, reflex. / Bláyi, pas. / Blápáto, &c. causal.

Refuse or forbid, { Má bláwo, Neg. / Sheomi cyakko, tr.‖ / Sheomi tyangso, reflex. / Sheomi tyangi, pas. / Sheomi tyang páto, &c., causal.

Prevent, Restrain, hinder, { Tyakko, tr. / Tyangso, reflex. / Tyangyi, pas. / Tyangpáto, &c., c.

Cherish, { Theullo, tr. / Theulso, reflex. / Theulyi pas. / Theulpáto-paso-páyi, causal.

Abandon, desert, { Wárdo, tr. (= throw away), / Wárso, reflex. / Wárdi, pas. / Wárpáto, &c. causal.

Set at liberty, { Plenno, tr. / Plenso, reflex. / Plenyi, pas. / Plenpáto, &c. causal.

Confine, imprison, { Tyákko. See Prevent.

Have, { Bwálá, n. irreg. / Thiyelá, n. reg. / Thiwo, n. reg.

---

* See Be glad and gladden, and note thereon, p. 334. Initial í and á are the conjunct pronouns or pronominal or definitives of the second and third persons.

† Dukko, if leave not place. Yóngso, if you do.

‡ Stay, remain, don't go, is Bwáko = sit.

§ Jeullo vel jyullo, as afore explained; and so also teuppo vel tyuppo, strike.

‖ Literally, hinder by mouth.

Cause to have or possess, { Bwakba / Thiba } -páwo, tr. { Bwakba / Thiba } páso, refl. { Bwakba / Thiba } -páyi, pas. { Bwakba / Thiba } -pápáto, &c., c. Thipáto-páso-páyi

Want, { Má bwála / Má thiyela / Má thiwo

Give, { Giwo, tr. Giso, reflex. / Gii (Giyi), pas. / Gipáto-páso-páyi, causal

Give back = return, { Léti giwo-giso-giyi, ut supra

Give again (more), { Anaiyo giwo-giso-giyi, ut supra

Take, { Bláwo, tr. / Bláso, reflex. / Bláyi, pas. / Blápáto-páso-páyi, causal

Take back (see Return), { Léto, tr. / Léso, reflex. / Léti, pas. / Lépáto-páso-páyi, caus.

Take again (more), { Anaiyo bláwo-bláso-bláyi, ut supra.

Be saved, Blénno (see Live), n.

Save, { Blenpáto, tr. / Blenpáso, refléx. / Blenpáyi, pas. / Blenpápáto-pápáso-pápáyi, c.

Be well, Neuwo or Nyuwo, n.

Cure, make well, { Neupáto. Neuto, tr. / Neupáso. Neuso, reflex. / Neupávi. Neuti, pas. / Neupápáto-pápáso-pápáyi, causal of neuter / Neupáto-páso-páyi, c. of tr.

Spoil, destroy, mar, { Khlamto. tr. / Khlamso, reflex. / Khlamti, pas. / Khlam páto-páso-páyi, c. / Khlampápáto, double c.

Be handsome, { Rimmo, n. / Rimba dyúmmo, com. gender / Rimsókpa dyúmmo, mas. / Rimsóngma dyummo, fem.

Make handsome, adorn, { Rim páto, tr. / Rimba páwo, com. gender / Rimsókpa páwo. mas. / Rimsongma páwo, fem.

Be mature, adult, { Swálocha dyúmo, mas. / Swálomi dyúmo, fem. (no neuter)

Make mature, or adult, { Swálocha páwo, mas. / Swálomi páwo, fem.*

Be strong, { Sokticha dyúmmo, mas. / Soktimicha dyúmmo. fem. (no neuter)

Make strong, strengthen, { Sokticha páwo, mas. / Soktimicha páwo, fem.

Grow, Báro, n.

Grow it, or cause to grow, { Bár páto, tr. / Bár páso, reflex. / Bár páyi, pas. / Bár pápáto-pápáso-pápáyi, double c.

Decay, Syówo or Sheówo, n.

Decay it, make decay, { Syá páto, tr., or Sheó-páto, &c. / Syó páso, reflex. / Syó páyi, pas. / Syó pápáto, &c., causal

Steal, rob, { Kúwo, tr. / Kúso, reflex. / Kúyi, pas. / Kúpáto, &c., causal / Kúpápáto, double causal

Murder, Sáto (see Kill)

Deceive, cheat, { Hanto, tr. / Hanso, reflex. / Hanti, pas. / Hanpáto, causal

Accompany (Nung needs a noun or pronoun), { Nung láwo, n. / Kwángkho láwo, n.

Cause to accompany, { Kwángkho lápáto-páso-páyi, tr. causal.

Leave, quit, { Wáto, tr. / Wáso, reflex. / Wáyi, pas. / Wápáto, &c., causal

Remain with, Kwángkho bwakko, n.

Cause to remain with, { Kwángkho bwaugpáto, causal.

Sit, Niso, n., compare with the next

Seat or set down, { Nito, tr. / Nisipáto, causal

Seat, { Nito, tr. / Niso, reflex. / Niti, pas. / Nitpáto, causal. / Nipápáto, double causal

Stand, Rappo, n.

Make stand, Rámpáto, causal

Remain standing, { Rapsógno bwakko, n. / Ráppo mokho bwakko, n.

Keep him standing, { Rám páto mokho bwakko.† / Rápsógno bwápáto.

Be erect, { Bwókko or Bokko, n. (to recumbent) / Rápo (to sitter)

Stoop, Khúmmo

Make stoop, Khúm páto, &c., causal

Lie down, Glése, n.

---

* Compare Newári lyá-hma ju and lyáse ju, lyá-hma juye-ki or yá and lyáse juyeki or yá. Also Háyu bang-cho dum, bang-mi dum, bang-cho páko or thumto, and baugmi thumto or pakó. The Báhing verbs dyummo and páwo have the usual characteristics, given often before. Rimmo is a primitive neuter, whose causal is rimpáto.

† In conjugation, this compound verb preserves the transitive of rampáto and the neuter of bwakko blended in one conjugation. See Grammar.

Lay down, Glésipáto-páso-páyi, causal
Get up (to a sitter), Ráppo, n. (see Stand)
Get up (to a recumbent), Bwókko, n. (see Be erect)
Make get up, Bwong páto. Rám páto
Fall (being), Dokko, n.
Cause to fall, Dóng páto-páso-páyi, c.
Slip down, slide down, Bhlúwo, n.
Cause to slip or slide, { Bhlúpáto-páso-páyi, causal
Get on, mount, Wógno, n.
Cause to mount, Wópáto-páso-páyi, c.
Dismount, Yúwo, n.
Cause to dismount, Yúpáto-páso-páyi, c.

Put, place, put down, deposit, { Jyúllo, tr. Jyúlso, reflex. Jyúlyi, pas. Jyúlpáto, causal Jyúlpápáto, d. c.

Take up, lift, raise, { Bokto. Guppo, tr. Bongso. Gúmso, reflex. Bokti. Gumyi, pas.

Cause to take up, { Bong páto, &c., c. Gum páto, &c., c.

Throw, { Grepto, tr. Grepso, reflex, Grepti, pas. Grem páto, &c., causal

Catch as thrown, { Dáto, tr. Dáso, reflex. Dáti, pas. Dápáto, &c., causal

Keep, Jyullo, tr. (see Place).

Snatch away, { Réto, tr. Réso, reflex. Réti, pas. Ré páto, &c., causal

Throw away, squander, } Wárdo, tr. (see Abandon)
Be near, Nentha dyúmmo, n.
Approximate, Nentha dyúmpáto, tr.
Be distant, Brábá dyúmmo. Bráwo, n.

Distance, { Brápáto, &c., tr. Brábá dyumpáto, causal tr.

Bring (see Come, piwo; pito is trans. or causal = make come, { Pito, tr. Piso, reflex. Piyi, pas. Pipáto, &c., causal

Bring down (see Yúwo = come down), { Yúto, tr. Yúso, reflex. Yúti, pas. Yúpáto, &c., causal

Bring up (see Kúwo = come up), { Kúto, tr. Kúso, reflex. Kúti, pas. Kúpáto, &c., causal

Fetch, Blátha diwo, n. (to take go).
Cause to fetch, { Blátha dipáto-páso-páyi, tr. causal

Take away, { Láto, tr. Láso, reflex. Láyi, pas. Lápáto, causal

Send, { Phli-gno, tr. Phli-so, reflex. Phli-yi, pas. Phli-páto, &c., causal

Carry, bear, { Kúrro, tr. Kúrso, reflex. Kúryi, pas. Kúrpáto, &c., causal

Hold, take in hand, grasp, { Siwo, tr. Siso, reflex. Siyi, pas. Sipáto, &c., causal

Hold up, support, { Játo, tr. Jáso,* reflex. Játi, pas. Jápáto, &c., causal

Let it fall, U'cho giwo
Fall (thing), U'to, n. and a.
Make fall or fell, U'páto, c., and U'to, tr.
Enter, Wógno, n.
Cause to enter, { Wópáto, causal
Admit, insert, { Wondo, tr.
Issue, Glúgno, n.
Cause to issue, Glúpáto. Glúndo †
Ascend = climb tree, Wógno, n.
Ascend = come up, slope, Kúwo, n.
Ascend = go up, slope, Háteu láwo, n.
Descend = come down, Yúwo, n.‡
Descend = go down, Háyu láwo, n.
Descend = climb down tree, Glúgno, n.

Arrive, { Jwákdiwo, Jwákpiwo, } n., there, here; Jwákko, n. §

Cause to arrive, { Jwángdipáto Jwánghipáto Jwángpáto

Depart, Glúgno (issue)
Cause to depart, Glúpáto, &c.
Precede, Gnalla yóngso, intr.
Cause to precede, Gnalla yongpáto or yokto, reflex.
Follow, Nótha yóngso, intr.

---

* Jáso gives jáse, it is (self) supported; and Jáso or jápáso must be used for "be supported," though there be a passive formed from játi = support me. All this results from the imperfect development of the passive voice, which has no imperative of the second person.

† Transitive and causal glúndo from neuter glúgno, as wondo from wogno. From the former we have normally the double causals glúndáto and wonpáto. See on to pp. 345 f.

‡ See notes aforegone on the expedients for eking out the lack of true adverbs. One is the use of the gerunds as instanced in "wade across" at p 337. Endless samples occur. Another is the use of verbs minutely specific, and which include the adverbial sense, as we say enter, to come in; but enter means also go in, as ascend does equally come up and go up. But kúwo and yúwo can only be used in the senses of come up, and come down, not go up or down.

§ Jwakko = arrive simply. The adjuncts tell whether by going (diwo), or by coming (piwo).

Cause to follow, { Nótha yongpáto, ref. / Nóthá yokto, causal }
Attend on, Kwongkho bwakko, n.
Disappear, Khleuso, reflex. (see Hide)
Cause to disappear, { Khleuto, tr. / Khleuti, pas. }
Appear, Kwai*n*so páso, reflex.
Make appear, Kwai*n*so páwo, tr.
Make me appear, Kwai*n*so páyi, pas.
Be lost, lose, Shéoto, n. and a.
Cause to lose, lose it, Shéopáto-páso-páyi, c.
Search, { Lamo, tr. / Lamso, reflex. / Lamyi, pas. }
Cause to search, { Lam páto, tr. / Lam páso, reflex. / Lam páyi, pas. }
Find, { Táwo, tr. / Táso, reflex. / Táyi, pas. }
Cause to find, { Tá páto, tr. / Tá páso, reflex. / Tá páyi, pas. }
Begin, Prénso, n.
Cause to begin, { Prénsi páto, tr. / Prénsi páso, reflex. / Prénsi páyi, pas. }
End, Be ended, { Ryippo, n. / Ryim páto, &c., tr. }
End it, Cause to be ended, or finish, { Theummo, tr. / Theumso, reflex. / Theumyi, pas. / Theum páto, &c., causal }
Come, Piwo, n. Ráwo, n.
Cause to come, { Pipáto. Rápato, tr. / Pipáso. Rápáso, reflex. / Pipáyi. Rápáyi, pas. / Pipápáto. Rápápáto, d. c. }
Go, Diwo,* n. Lawo, n.
Cause to go, { Lápáto. Dipáto, tr. / Lápáso. Dipáso, reflex. / Lápáyi. Dipáyi, pas. }
Continue, Bwakko, n. (sit)
Cause to continue, { Bwángpáto, tr. / Bwángpáso, reflex. / Bwángpáyi, pas. }
Get out of the way, or clear the way, { Yongso, n. / Lam plénno, tr. }
Cause to clear the way, or make get out of the way { Yokto, tr. Lamplénpáto, tr. / Yongso, reflex. Lamplénpáso, reflex. / Yokti, pas. Lamplénpáyi, pas. }
Wait, Bwakko, n. (sit)
Cause to wait, Bwángpáto-páso-páyi

Wait for, Expect, { Rimdo, tr. / Rimso, reflex. / Rimdi, pas. / Rimpáto. &c., causal }
Arrive, { here, { Jwang diwo, n. / there, { Jwang piwo, n. }
Cause to arrive, { Jwang dipáto, &c. / Jwang pipáto, &c. }
Depart, { Glugno, n. (issue) / Láwo, n. (go) }
Cause to depart or dismiss, { Glúpáto, &c., causal / Lápáto, &c., causal }
Return, Léto, n. } See Take back
Cause to return, Lépáto, &c., } See Take back
Be high, grow, Barro, n.
Make high, or grow it, { Bár-páto-páso páyi, c.
Be large, big, Gnólo dyúmmo, n.
Make big or enlarge, Gnólo thyumto or dyúmpáto, &c., causal
Be fat, Syénéúwo,† n.
Fatten, Syéneúpáto, &c., causal
Be thin, Ryammo, n.
Make thin, Ryampáto, &c., causal
Increase, Barro, n.
Cause to increase, Bár páto, &c., causal
Decrease, Syó-wo, n.
Cause to decrease, Syó páto, &c., causal
Be good, Neuwo, n.
Make good, { Neuto, tr. / Neuso, reflex. / Neuti, pas. / Neú páto, &c., causal }
Be bad, Má neuwo, neg.
Make bad, Má neuto, &c., c. n.
Add to, or augment, { Gapto, tr. / Gapso, reflex. / Gapti, pas. / Gampáto, &c., causal }
Deduct from or lessen, Syó páto, tr. (decrease)
Cultivate (earth), { Chó-gno, tr. / Chó-so, reflex. / Chóyi, pas. / Chópáto, &c., causal }
Dig, { Kókk, tr. def. / Kóngso, reflex. indef. / Kóngyi,‡ pas. / Kóng páto, &c., causal }
Plough, { Jóto, § tr. / Jóso, reflex. / Jóti, pas. / Jópáto, &c., causal }
Sow, { Phúto, tr. / Phúso, reflex. / Phúyi,‖ pas. / Phú páto, &c., causal }

---

* See "Take away," láto = cause to go, but not used so.

† Syé = flesh; neuba = good; neuwo = be good, whence neugna, I am good (neu vel nyú).

‡ Kongyi, says field, dig me. Dig for me is koktigí, and dig for him koktigíwo.

§ Jóto is Hindi. So that we have here apparently an Arian word thoroughly incorporated and assimilated.

‖ The reflex and passive forms of the verbs to dig, to plough, to sow, and all such are eschewed, because incapable of application by or to a human being, and the constructio ad

Transplant, { Khleummo, tr. Khleumso, reflex. Khleumyi, pas. Khleum páto, &c., causal

Reap, { Rikko, tr. Riugso, reflex. Ringyi, pas. Ring páto, &c., causal

Gather, pluck flowers, greens, { Náto, tr. Préto, tr. Náso, reflex. Préso, reflex. Náyi, pas. Préyi, pas, Nápáto, &c., c. Prépáto, &c., c.

Eradicate, { Rukko, tr. Rungso, reflex. Rungyi, pas. Rungpáto, &c., causal

Fall, Be felled, } U'to, n. and tr.

Fell, { U'to, tr. U'yi, pas.

Cause to fell, { Upáto, tr. Upáso, reflex. Upáyi, pas.

Breed cattle, { Theúllo, tr. Theúlso, reflex. Theúlyi, pas. Theúlpáto, &c., causal

Slaughter cattle, { Chwárro, tr. (cut) Chwárso, reflex. Chwáryi, pas. Chwárpáto, &c., c.

Graze, { Chári páwo, tr. Chári páso, reflex. Chári páyi, pas. Chári pápáto, causal

Flay or decorticate or peel { Wókko, tr. Wóngso. reflex. Wóngyi, pas.* Wóngpáto, causal

Shear, { Krito, tr. Kriso, reflex. Kriti, pas. Kripáto, &c., causal

Shave, { Khwárro, tr. Khwárso, reflex. Khwáryi, pas. Khwárpáto, causal

Buy, { Jyappo, tr. Jyamso, reflex. Jyamyi, pas. Jyampáto, &c., causal

Sell, { Légno, tr. Léso, reflex. Léyi, pas. Lépáto, c.

Change or exchange, { Pháto, tr. Pháso, reflex. Pháyi. pas. Phápáto, c.

Lend, { Jyár giwo, tr. Jyár giso, reflex. Jyár giyi, pas. Jyár gipáto, &c., c.

Borrow, { Jyár bláwo, tr. Jyár bláso, reflex. Jyár bláyi, pas. Jyár blápáto, c.

Pay debt, { Chó-gno, tr. Chó-so, reflex. Chó-yi, pas. Chó-páto, c.

Count, { Hikko, tr. Hingso, reflex. Hingyi, pas. Hing páto, &c., c.

Measure or weight, { Thápo, tr. Thámso, reflex. Thámyi, pas. Thám páto, &c., c.

Plaster (wall), { Khlyakko, tr. Khlangso, reflex. Khlangyi, pas. Khlang páto, &c., c.

Make house, Khim páwo (see Make)

Make clothes, Wá páwo (see Make)

Spin, { Sále panno, tr. Sále panso, reflex. Sále panyi, pas. Sále panpáto, &c., c.

Weave, Wá páwo (supra)

Sew, { Phyérro, tr. Phyérso, reflex. Phyéryi, pas. Phyérpáto, &c., c.

Grind, { Khri-to, tr. Khriso, reflex. Khriyi, pas. Khripáto, &c., c.

Work mine, Kháni kokko (dig)

Work iron, Syal teuppo (beat)

Work wood, { Singchokko, tr. (plane) Singchongso, reflex. Singchongyi, pas. Singchongpáto, &c., c.

Work clay, { Khápi lwákto, tr. (knead) Khápi lwángso, reflex. Khápi lwákti, pas. Khápi lwángpáto, &c., c.

Cook, { Kiwo, tr. Kiso, reflex. Kiyi, pas. Kipáto, &c., c.

Be cooked, be prepared (rice), } Ming-gno, n.

Cause to be cooked, Ming páto, &c. causal

Be ripe (fruit), Jiwo, n.

Ripen, Jipáto, &c., c.

...nsum still overruling any feeling of grammatical uniformity with my unsophisticat... informants. The transitive and reflex forms of such verbs often tally with Hungari... definite and indefinite.

* Wongyi, says the skin, and wongso, says man to skin, wokti or woktigí, says one m... to another, strip off my skin. So also of "shear," &c.

Boil, Kiwo, (cook)

Roast, { Grémdo, tr.
Grémso, reflex.
Grémdi, pas.
Grémpáto, c. }

Grill, { Cheowo, tr.
Cheoso, reflex.
Cheoyi, pas.
Cheo páto, &c., c. }

Cut with knife by one blow, } Chwárro (slaughter)

Cut with scissors, Krito (shear)

Cut by frequent drawing, or saw { Séwo, tr.
Séso, reflex.
Séyi, pas.
Sepáto, &c., c. }

Perforate or pierce, { Hóto, tr.
Hóso, reflex.
Hóyi, pas.
Hópáto, &c., c. }

Be torn, Jito, n.

Tear, { Chito, tr.
Chiso, reflex.
Chiyi, pas.
Chipáto, &c., c. }

Be split, Yéso, reflex.

Split, { Yéto, tr.
Yéyi, pas.
Yépáto, &c., c. }

Be broken, Jingso, reflex.

Break, { Jikko, tr. and n.
Jingso, reflex.
Jingyi, pas.
Jingpáto, &c., c. }

Be burst, Bukko, n.

Burst it, { Pwákko or Pukko, tr.
Pwangso, reflex. Pungso, ref.
Pwangyi, pas. Pungyi, pas.
Pwangpáto, &c., c. }

Brew, { Kiwo, tr. (cook)
Kiso, reflex.
Kiyi, pas.
Kipáto, &c., causal }

Distil, { Hóto, tr.
Héso, reflex.
Héyi, pas.
Hépáto, &c., c. }

Filtrate, defecate, { Thyakto, tr.
Thyangso, reflex.
Thyangyi, pas.
Thyangpáto, &c., c. }

Be sharp, Syamso, reflex.

Sharpen, { Syappo, tr.
Syamso, reflex.
Syamyi, pas.
Syampáto, &c., c. }

Be blunt, Khlamso, reflex.

Make blunt (or spoil), { Khlamto, tr.
Khlamso, reflex.
Khlamti, pas.
Khlampáto, &c., c. }

Be shaken, Dungso, reflex. Dukko, n.

Shake, { Dukto, tr.
Dungso, reflex.
Dukti, pas.
Dungpáto, &c., c. }

Be still, be firm, } Jaso, reflex.

Make still, make firm, { Játo, tr.
Játi, pas.
Jápáto, &c., c. }

Be contained, Ringso, reflex.

Contain, hold, { Rikto, tr.
Ringso, reflex.
Rikti, pas.
Ringpáto, &c., c. }

Be sustained, Jáso (see Be firm)

Sustain, Játo (see Make firm)

Be retained, Tyangso, reflex.

Retain, keep in, { Tyakko, tr.
Tyangso, reflex.
Tyangyi, pas.
Tyangpáto, &c., c. }

Ooze out, Chappo, n.

Make ooze out, { Cham páto, tr.
Cham páso, reflex.
Cham páyi, pas.
Cham pápáto, c. }

Be full (belly), Rú-gno, n.

Fill (belly), { Rú páto, tr.
Rú páso, reflex.
Rú páyi, pas.
Rú pápáto, &c., c. }

Be full (vessel), Dyammo, n.

Fill (vessel), { Dyam páto, tr.
Dyam páso, reflex.
Dyam páyi, pas.
Dyam pápáto, c. }

Be empty, Asyéti dyúmmo, n.

Empty, { Asyéti páwo, tr.
Asyéti páso, reflex.
Asyéti páyi, pas.
Asyéti pápáto, &c., c. }

Shine, Chyárro, n.

Cause to shine, Chyarpáto-páso-páyi, c.

Be dark, Namrikko, n.

Darken, { Namring páto, tr.
Namring páso, reflex.
Namring páyi, pas.
Namring pápáto, &c., c. }

Be luminous, Hauhau dyúmmo, n.

Make luminous, Hauhau páwo, tr.

Blow as wind, Khito, n. Byéro, n. (fly)

Cause to blow, { Byér páto, &c., c.
Khi páto, &c., c. }

Flow as water, Gwákko (go)

Cause to flow, Gwang páto, &c., c.

Flower, Bóto, n.

Cause to flower, Bópáto, &c., c.

Fruit, Sito, n.

Cause to fruit, Si-páto, &c., c.

Be ripe (fruit only), Jiwo, n.

Ripen, Jipáto, &c., c.

Be ripe as grain, &c., Ming-gno, n.

Ripen, Ming páto, &c., c.

Be hot, Glé-wo, n.

Heat, Glépáto, &c., c.

Be cold (thing only), Chhikko, n.

Make cold, Chhing páto, &c., c.

Be rotten, Jippo, n.

Make rotten, Jimpáto, &c., c.

Be raw, Achekhli dyúmmo, n.

Make raw, Achekhli páwo, tr.
Be lighted (lamp), Hówo, n.

Light (lamp), { Hópáto, tr. / Hópáso, reflex. / Hópáyi, pas. / Hópápáto, c.

Be kindled (fire), Khryamso, reflex.

Kindle (fire), { Khryapto, tr. / Khryamso, reflex. / Khryamti, pas. / Khryam páto, c.

Be burnt (destroyed by fire), Deuppo, neuter

Burn it, { Deum páto, tr. / Deum páso, reflex. / Deum páyi, pas. / Deum pápáto, c.

Burn (corpse), { Chwé-wo, tr. / Chwé-so, reflex. / Chwé-yi, pas. / Chwé-páto, &c., c.

Be buried (= bury thyself), Thimso, reflex.

Bury it, { Thimmo, tr. / Thimso, reflex. / Thimyi, pas. / Thimpáto, &c., c.

Be melted (= melt thyself), Yóngso, reflex.

Melt it, { Yóng páto, tr. / Yóng páso, reflex. / Yóng páyi, pas. / Yóng pápáto, &c., c.

Be congealed, Jámidyúmmo, n.
Congeal it, Jámi páwo, tr.

Collect, bring, or put together, { Khuppo, tr. / Khumso, reflex. / Khumyi, pas. / Khum páto, &c., c.

Be collected, Khumso, supra

Spread, { Hammo, tr. / Hamso, reflex. / Hamyi, pás. / Hámpáto, &c., causal

Share out, apportion, { Yokko, tr. / Yongso, reflex. / Yongyi, pas. / Yong páto, &c., causal

Separate, set apart without division, { Phwakko, tr. / Phwangso, reflex. / Phwángyi, pas. / Phwang páto, &c., c.

Set together, Khuppo (see Collect)

Divide (by cutting), &c., what whole), { Chyakko, tr. / Chyangso, reflex. / Chyangyi, pas. / Chyangpáto, &c., causal

Unite, join, what divided or broken, { Khryapto, tr. / Khryamso, reflex. / Khryamyi, pas. / Khryam páto, c.

Knot it; join by knot, { Sapto, tr. / Samso, reflex. / Sapti, pas. / Sampáto, &c., causal

Unknot, loosen, unseam, unfold, { Prwákko, tr. / Prwángso, reflex. / Prwángyi, pas. / Prwáng páto, causal

Scatter, { Brá-wo, tr. / Bra-so, reflex. / Bráyi, pas. / Brápáto, &c., causal / Brápápáto, double causal

Mix, { Húl-do, tr. / Húl-so, reflex. / Húl-di, pas. / Húl-páto, &c., causal

Unmix, separate what mixed, } Phwakko (see Separate)

Acquire, gain by labour, or earn, { Grókso páwo, tr. / Grókso páso, reflex. / Grókso páyi, pas. / Grókso pápáto, c.

Save (what earned). See Collect. { Blenpáto. Khuppo, tr. / Blenpáso. Khumso, reflex. / Blenpáyi. Khumyi, pas. / Blenpápáto. Khumpáto, c.

Squander, { Wárdo, tr. / Wárso, reflex. / Wárdi, pas. / Wárpáto, causal / Wárpápáto, double causal

Fold, { Plepto, tr. / Plemso, reflex. / Plepti, pas. / Plempáto, &c., causal

Unfold, { Prwakko, tr. / Prwangso, reflex. / Prwangyi, pas. / Prwang páto, &c., causal

Open, { Hókko, tr. / Hongso, reflex. / Hóngyi, pas. / Hóng páto, &c., causal

Shut, { Tyákko, tr. / Tyángso, reflex. / Tyángyi, pas. / Tyáng páto, causal

Press, squeeze, depress, { Timto, tr. / Timso, reflex. / Timti, pas. / Timpáto, causal / Timpápáto, double causal

Compress or express, { Nippo, tr. / Nimso, reflex. / Nimyi, pas. / Nimpáto, &c., causal

Turn over carefully, { Lipto, tr. / Limso, reflex. / Lipti, pas. / Limpáto, &c., causal

Turn topsy-turvy, Hóldo tr. (mix)

Roll up, { Tyallo, tr. / Tyalso, reflex. / Tyalyi, pas. / Tyal páto, &c., causal

Unroll, { Prwakko, tr. (see Unfold) / Prwangso, reflex. / Prwangyi, pas. / Prwang páto, &c., causal

Be loose, slack, Thyelvimdyúmmo, n.

Loosen, slacken, Thyelvim páwo, tr. / Thyelvim páso, reflex. / Thyelvim páyi, pas. / Thyelvim pápáto, c.

Be tight, Muske dyúmmo, n.

Tighten, Muske páwo, tr.

Bind, Chúkko, tr. / Chúngso, reflex. / Chúngyi, pas. / Chúng páto, &c., causal

Unbind, Prokko, tr. / Prongso, reflex. / Prongyi, pas. / Prong páto, causal

Pack, Kúra páwo, tr. / Kúra páso, reflex. / Kúra páyi, pas. / Kúra pápáto, causal

Unpack, Prwákko (see Unrol)

Climb, or get up tree, &c., Wógno, n. / Wópáto.

Come down, Yúwo, n.

Put on (fire), Kwádo, tr. / Kwáso, reflex. / Kwádi, pas.

Take off (fire), Nito, tr. / Niso, reflex. / Niti, pas.

Put in (solid), Pikko, tr. Wondo / Pingso, r. Wonso / Pingyi, p. Wonyi / Pingpáto, &c. Wonpáto — See Wogno, get in

Pull out, take out, Glúndo, tr. / Glúnso, reflex. / Glúndi, pas. / Glúnpáto, &c., c. — See Issue, Glugno*

Pour in (liquid), Pikko (supra)

Catch as poured, Dáto, tr. / Dáso, reflex. / Dáti, pas. / Dápáto, &c., causal

Take down or bring down, Yuto, tr. / Yúso, reflex. / Yúyi, pas. / Yúpáto, &c., c. — See Yuwo, come down

Put up above, Lwakto, tr. / Lwangso, reflex. / Lwakti, pas. / Lwangpáto, &c., causal

Bring up, Kúto, tr. / Kúso, reflex. / Kúyi, pas. / Kúpáto, tr. c. — See Kuwo, come up

Stop, stay (to going man), Jáso (reflex. or intrans.)

Stop him, stay him, Játo, tr.

Stay or stop me, Játi, pas.

Cause him to stop, stay, Jápáto-páso-páyi, causal

Stay, stop, one who flees, or a road, Tyákko, tr. / Tyángso, reflex. / Tyángyi, pas. / Tyáng páto, &c., c.

Prevent, hinder, forbid, Tyákko, supra

Let go, Lácho giwo

Enable to go, Láne chapba páwo, tr. / Láne chapba páso, reflex. / Láne chapba páyi, pas. / Láne chapba pápáto, &c., d. c.

Rub, Yállo, tr. / Yálso, reflex. / Yályi, pas. / Yálpáto, causal

Polish, Phélephéle páwo, tr. / Phélephéle páso, reflex. / Phélephéle páyi, pas.

Be polished, Phélephéle dyúmmo, n.

Cause to be polished, Phélephéle dyúmpáto-páso-páyi, causal

Cover, Sheummo, tr. / Sheumso, reflex. / Sheumyi, pas. / Sheum páto, &c., causal

Uncover, Hokko, tr. / Hongso, reflex. / Hongyi, pas. / Hongpáto, &c., causal

Shoot, Appo, tr. / Amso, reflex. / Amyi, pas. / Ampáto, &c., causal

Wring, Twist neck, cloth, &c. Chyúrdo, tr. / Chyúrso, reflex. / Chyúrdi, pas. / Chyúrpáto, &c., causal

Twist or make rope, Chéwo, tr. / Chéso, reflex. / Chéyi, pas. / Chépáto, causal

Be like, resemble, Deu-wo, n.

Make like, Deu páto-páso-páyi, causal

Be white or clear, Bubum dyúmmo, n.

Make white or clean, whiten and cleanse, Bubum páwo, tr. / Bubum páso, reflex. / Bubum páyi, pas. / Bubum pápáto, d. c.

Be wet, Jiso, reflex.

Wet it, make wet, Jito, tr. / Jiso, reflex. / Jiti, pas. / Jipáto, &c., causal

Be dry, Syeu-wo, n.

Make dry, Syeu-páto-páso-páyi, causal

Dry in sun, Bláto, tr. / Bláso, reflex. / Bláti, pas.

Dry at fire, Gramdo, tr. / Gramso, reflex. / Gramdi, pas. / Grampáto, &c., causal

---

* Glú-gno, n., gives glú·ndo, tr. The ú sound is here the same in both. An u in superb is nearer than u in sure. Eu vel yú, *i.e.*, u in puling, which I write pyuling; but never eu vel ú. French eu in pour, heur, is often nearer.

Be flavoursome, Brógno, n.
Make flavoursome or flavour it, { Brópáto, tr. Brópáso, reflex. Brópáyi, pas.
Be sweet, Jijim dyúmmo, n.
Make sweet, { Jijim dyúmpáto, tr. c. Jijim páwo, tr.
Be sour, Phokko, n.
Make sour, Phong páto-páso-páyi, causal
Be bitter, Káwo, n.
Make bitter, Kápáto-páso-páyi, causal
Be knotted, Khingso, reflex.
Knot it, make knotted, { Khikto, tr. Khingso, reflex. Khikti, pas. Khingpáto, &c., c.
Be great, Gnólo dyúmmo, n.
Make great, Gnólo páwo, tr.
Be small, Yáke or Kachim dyúmmo, n.
Make small, Yáke or Kachim páwo, tr.
Be heavy, Hyallo, n. Hyalba dyúmmo, n.
Make heavy, Hyalpáto, tr.
Be light (levis), { Hammo, n. Hamba dyúmmo, n.
Make light, Hampáto, tr. Hampápáto, c.
Be hard, Tingko dyúmmo, n.
Harden, Tingko páwo, tr.
Be soft, Lobo dyúmmo, n.
Soften, Lobo páwo, tr.
Be straight, Dyámmo, n.
Straighten, Dyampáto-páso-páyi, c.
Be crooked, Gúkko, n.
Crook it, { Kúkko, tr. Kúngso, reflex. Kúngyi, pas. Kúng páto, &c., c.
Be rich = have, { Khiwo ór Khiba dyúmmo, Bwála, } n.
Enrich = make, have, { Thipáto, &c., c. Thiba dyumpáto-páso-páyi, c. Bwálapáto
Be poor, { Má thiwo Má thiba dyúmmo Má bwála
Impoverish, { Má thiba páwo Má thi páto Má bwála páto

ADVERBS AND PREPOSITIONS COMPARED.

Come, Piwo
Come in (into the house), { Khyimá gwáre piwo or wógno
Come out (of the house), { Khyimátola piwo or Glúgno.*
Come back, to rear, Nótha piwo
Come on, to front, Gnálla piwo
Come up, Yákhateu piwo or Kúwo
Come down, Yákhayeu piwo or Yúwo
Come back = return, { Létoko piwo, or Léto
Come again (repeating), { Anaiyo or Ana-piwo
Come once, Kwá bálá piwo
Come twice, Nip pálá piwo
Come thrice, Sap pálá piwo
Come four times, Lep pálá piwo
Come five times, Gnó pálá piwo
Come six times, Rú pálá piwo
Come seven times, Chá pálá piwo
Come eight times, Yá pálá piwo
Come nine times, Ghú pálá piwo
Come ten times, Kwaddyum pálá piwo
Come together (place), { Kwádo pine or ráne, (verbs in plural)
Come at once, (time), { Kwá bala pine, or ráne
Come near, Nentha piwo
Come close to him, Wáke púmdi piwo
Come apart, Hare piwo
Come far away, Brába piwo
Come with, Kwongkho piwo
Come with me, Gó nung piwo
Come alone, Giche piwo
Come without, me, thee, him, { Go manthi piwo Ga manthi piwo Harem manthi piwo
Come towards me, thee, him, { Wáke lá piwo Ike lá piwo Ake lá piwo
Come as far as this or here, that or there, } Eke sambh piwo Meke sambh piwo
Come quickly, instantly, Bácheu piwo
Come slowly, Wákha piwo
Come by and by, { Ghyárkwángmi piwo
Come silently, Liba piwo
Come noisily, { Bréso or Bresomami or Brésoko †—piwo
Come early, Bácheu piwo
Come late, Wákha piwo
Come at sun-rise, Namdhamna † piwo
Come at sun-set, Nam wamtana † piwo
Come loiteringly, { Wakhawákhagwak koko † piwo
Come over (by top), Khwátoko † piwo
Come under by beneath { Háyu lang glúgnoko † piwo.
Come through (by middle), { A'lam láng piwo
Come between, A'limbu láng piwo
Come across, { Glúgnoko piwo Glúso piwo

* Khyim á gwárè piwo, house its inside in come; Wogna, enter; Khyim á tolá piwo, house its outside to come; Glúgno, issue. In the former phrases Khyim may be omitted, but its forthcomingness would be implied by the pronominal definitive (á). The lack of proper adverbs and prepositions is made up in one of these two ways.

† These and all similars are imperatival gerunds. See Verbs. When the expression is imperative, the gerund sign is affixed to the imperative form of the verb; when it is indicative, to the indicative form. Come loiteringly is having loitered, come. This is one of the many affinities with the Dravidian tongues.

Come to, { this / that } side, { Yése hamba / Háre hamba } piwo
Come constantly, Pisogno bwakko
Come sometimes, Káyikáyi piwo
Come ever, Sadai, { ráwo / piwo }
Come never, Gyanaiyo má piwo
Never come again, Gyanaiyo ána má piwo
Come to, at, this side, Yékhola piwo
Come by this side, Yékholáng piwo
Come to, at, that side, Mékholá piwo
Come by that side, Mékholáng piwo
Come on the right, Jumrolá piwo
Come by the right, Jmmroláng piwo
Come on the left, Pérola piwo
Come by the left, Péroláng piwo
Come to the east, Namdhapdi khálá piwo
Come from the west, Nam wamdikhaláng piwo
Come towards the house, Khyimlá piwo
Come from towards the house, Khyim láng piwo
Go towards the plains, { Dhepdelá láwo / or diwo }
Go as far as Népál, Népál sambh láwo
Give a little, Akachi giwo
Give much, Eko giw o
Give secretly, Khleuso giwo
Give openly, Kwainso páso giwo
Give gladly, Gyarscho giwo
Give sulkily, Má gyarscho giwo
Give to-day, A'na giwo
Give to-morow, Dilla giwo
He gave yesterday, Sanamti gipta
Give mutually, Gi mose *
Hit mutually, Tyeum mose
Kiss mutually, Leú mose
Kill mutually, Sá mose
Give continually, Giso gno bwakko
Hit continually, Teupsogno bwakko
Sleep continually, Ipsogno-bwakko
Strike forcibly, Soktimi teuppo
Strike gently, Wákha teuppo
A house, Khyim
Of a house, Khyim kem Khyim dim
To a house, a house, Khyim (no signs)
In a house, Khyim di
From a house, Khyim ding
By (inst.) house, Khyim mi
Into (inside) house, Khyimá gwáre
Out of (outside) house, Khyimá tola
As far as house, Khyim sambh
Towards or at the house, Khyim lá
From vicinity of house, Khyim láng
Before the house, in front, Khyim á gnalla
Behind the house, in rear of, Khyim á notha
On the house (touching), Khyim a tauredi
Above the house (remote), Khyim ding hatyu
Under, Beneath, the house (close), Khyim háyu
Below the house (apart), Khyim ding háyu
From under house, Khyim ke háyu láng or hayu ding
In the under of house, Khyim ke háyu { la / di † }
In the above of house, Khyim á taure di or lá.
Near the house,‡ { Khyim ke nentha or / Khyim nentha.‡ }
Far from house, Khyim ding bràba
At the house, { Khyim á pumdi / Khyim nentha }
On account of house, Khyim dáso
In lieu of house, or in exchange for house, Khyim á phle
Through the house, Khyim á limbu láng
Beyond the house, { Khyim á gnalla = house its beyond }

PREPOSITIONS.

At this time, Yekhonadi
At that time, Myekhonadi
At this place, Yekedi
At that place, Myekedi
In this year, Yem tho'di
In that year, Myem tho'di
In a little while, Gyer Kwongmidi
During, pending this year, { Yem thomálá theum / Yem —— thobwáná }
Pending his coming, Haremma pi thiu
At home, Khyim di
In, within, the house, Khyim gwáre
In the wilderness, Sabala di
In my hand, Wá gu di
In, at Dorjiling, Dorjiling di
Go into the house, Khyim gwáre láwo
In me, in thee, in him, { Godi. Wáke di§ / Gadi. Ikedi / Haremdi, Akedi }
He gave to me, Go giwa

---

* Most dual of mowo, which apart = fight: in composition of several verbs = do, make.

† Lá expresses vicinity. Khyim lá, near, towards, at, the house; whence lá-m, of vicinity and lá-ng, from vicinity. So Di expresses inness, khyim di, in the house; whence di-m, of in and di-ng from in. M or me final is attributive. See adjectives and participles, *e.g.*, piba-me, I who come, I the comer, and kwágná me, the other one, and lala-m, red.

‡ Khyim nentha = the house is near and near the house, but the latter is better with genitive sign; so also of khyim pumdi. Khyim á pumdi, the house its side in, also prevents the equivoque and is the true form for near the house. Nentha having lost its sense as a noun cannot take the á. Nouns of place, however, take dim rather than á, as Khyim dim pumdi, literally, house in of side in. For possessive and genitive signs see p. 321 supra, and infra in Grammar.

§ More usual and correct perhaps are the inflective forms standing second. But wáke is also equal to my, wákedi, in me or mine, and wákeding, from me or from my.

He took it from me, thee, him, { Go ding-* / Ga ding- / Harem ding- } blapta
He struck thee, Ga teupta
Come into the house, Khyim gwáre piwo
Go into the house, Khyim gwáre láwo
Go into the water, Pwáku di wogno
Come out of the water, Pwáku ding glugno
The inside of the house, Khyim á golá
The outside of the house, Khyim á tolá
Come from the outside of the house, Khyim ke á tolang piwo
Come from the inside of the house, Khyim á golang glugno
Come out from the house, Khyim ding á tolá piwo, or Khyim ding glugno
Go with me, Go nung láwo
Sit by me, Wake pumdi bwakko
Come near me, Wake pumdi piwo
Sit beside me, Wake lá bwakko
Sit on my knee, Wa phyemtodi bwakko
Sleep in his bosom, Aphyemtodi ipo
Put on thy shoulder, I' balamdi jeullo
Throw in or into the fire, { Me di piko / Mi gware piko }
Put on the fire, Mi taure jeullo
Take off from the fire, Mi taureng bláwo
Put on, upon, the table, Mej táure jeullo
Take off from the table, Mej taureng bláwo
Get on, or mount, the horse, Ghora taure wogno
Get off, or dismount from, the horse, Ghora taureng glugno
Put on the horse (goods), Ghora taure jeullo
Take off from the horse (goods), Ghora taureng glundo or bláwo
On the head, Piya taure
Under the feet, { Kholi yeu† / Kholi gwayeu }
Put your cap on your head, Itáki i piya taure jeullo
Put grass under his feet, A' kholi gwayeu (nichasmen) jim jeullo
Above, higher than, his head, A' piya ding hateu
Beneath, lower than, my feet, Wa kholi ding hayeu
Above your house is the cantonment, Ikhyim ding hateu la tilanga bwagdikha
Below your house is the bazaar, I khyim ding háyeu la ledikha jyapdikha
Above the mouth is the nose, Sheö hateu la neu bwa
Below the mouth is the chin, Sheö ha yeu la yóli bwa
To, as far as, Nerá. Pumdi

As far as him, { Harem pumdi / Harem néra }
As far as Népál, Népál pumdi
Towards Népál, Népál pumla. Népál la
North of Népál, Népál ding hateu la
Near Népál, Népal nentha
Far from Népál, Népál ding brába
Towards night, Namringna (day setting)
Towards morning, Nam sona (day being born)
In the night, Teugnachidi
In the day, Namtidi
Cruel towards his children, Tamitawake la deukha giba
Be kind towards me and mine, { Wake la neuwo / Wa ta ke la neuwo }
Sit above me, Wake ding hateu la bwakko
Sit between us two, Wasike alimbu di bwakko
Sit below him, A'ke ding hayeu la bwakko
Put on me, Wake taure jyúllo
Put on him, A'ke taure jyúllo
The water comes from above and goes below, Pwáku hateu lang yú, hayeu la lá
On the top of the hill, Syerte á gware di
In the midst of the hill, Syerte á limbudi
At the bottom of the hill, Syerte á pumdi
From top of hill, Syerte á gware ding
From middle of hill, Syerte á limbu ding
From the bottom of the hill, Syerte á pum ding
He dwells below me, Wake ding hayeu la bwá
He dwells above me, Wake ding hateu la bwá
Sit on me, Wake taure bwakko
Press under me, Wake hayeu lam chimna
Underneath, under the chair, Khosingba gwayeu or a gwayeu
Above, upon, the hand, Gu taure, or Gu á taure
Put under, below, the table, Mej á gwayeu jyullo
Take out from under the table, Mej á gwá yeung bláwo
Go through the door, Lapcho lang láwo, or Lapcho á limbu lang láwo
Come through the house, Khyim gwárim piwo, or Khyim á gwa lang piwo
Go through the hole, A'lam lang glugno
Go through the river (wading), Pwáku di gwakso glugno
Go over the couch, Ipdikha khwakso láwo
Go over the river in boat, Dunga di woso glugno
Go under the couch, Ipdikha likso glugno
Come with me, Go nung piwo

---

* See note (§) on previous page.

† Gware = in, gwayeu = under. To the last answers ha-yeu, the one meaning what touches, the other, what touches not, but lies below; so taure and háyeu, as to what is above.

Go with him, { Am- or Harem, } nung láwo
Why should I go with thee? { Ga nung márcho lágna
Go without me, Go manthi láwo
Strike with force, Sokti mi teupo
Strike without force, Sokti manthi teupo
Sit before me, Wa gnalla di bwakko
Sit behind me, Wa notha di bwakko
Before, behind the door, { Lapcho á gnalla di / Lapcho á notha la
Opposite, Vis-a Vis-me, { Wa gnalla la / Wa gnalla di
Sit at my side, Wake pumdi bwakko
Towards his side, A'ke á pumla
In the middle, A'limbu di
To, at, the side, Apumdi
Before night, { Namrikso gnalla / Teugnachi dyumtheum / Nammá riktheum / Nammá wamtheum / Nam rikcho beladi
At nightfall, { Nam- { rigna / wamtana / Nam wancho beladi
After nightfall, { Nam-wamso / Namrikso } notha. / Nam wamtako / Nam riktako
Since dawn, Didila mekeng
Before dawn, Didila gnalla
After dawn, Didila notha
Since I came, Gopitina mekeng
Before my arrival, Gojokpicho gnalla
After my arrival, Gojokpicho notha
After to-morrow, Dilla mekeng
Before to-morrow, Dilla ma dyumtheu
By nightfall, { Nam ringna / Nam wamtana
Until night or Up to night, { Teugnachi sambh / Nam wamtana sambh
Towards the house, Khyim lá
Towards me, Wake lá
Towards night, Nam rikcho páwana
Towards dawn, { Teugnachi lána / Nam dhamna
At dawn, Nam dhamna
During the night, Teugnachi dyumna
By the time I arrive, Pignána
By the time thou arrivest, Piyena
By the time he arrives, Pina *
After my arrival, Go piso notha
After thy arrival, Ga piso notha
Round about the house, } Khyim harela yesela
About the house, Khyim apumdi
In the middle of the village, } Dyel á limbu di
On this side the river, Gulu yem pumdi
On that side the river, } Gulu myem pumdi

He pierced him through the body, { Ram hotáko sáta
He went through the door, { Lapcho lang glutako láta
Go by the door, Lapcho lang láwo
Go by the road, Lamlang láwo
Far from the house, Khyim ding brába
Near the fire, { Mi nentha / Mi pumdi / Mi á pumdi
Near me, Wake pumdi
After this, that, { Yem ding notha / Myem ding notha
Before this, that, { Yem ding gnalla / Myem ding gnalla
Instead of, in lieu of, that, } Myem ke áphle
For the sake of me, Wake dáso
For the love of thee I did it, { *Dwaktana* kopátong
For the love of me he did it, { Dwakti kopapto
As far as the house, Khyim á pumdi
Short of, not so far as, the house, } Khyim yesela
Beyond the house, Khyim hárela
With a house there may be a marriage { Khyim dyumna groche dyum
Without (wanting) a house there cannot be a marriage, { Khyim manthi groche má dyum
With a house he will marry if he have, &c., } Khyim thi kheda groche páwa
Without a house he will not marry, { Khyim manthi kheda (or manthi) groche má páwa
With me, Go nung
Without me, Go manthi
With thy father, I po nung
Without my father, A'pá manthi
I go not, Ma lágna
A child without father, an orphan, { A'pomanthiba tawo. Apomanthime tawo
For the purpose of building a house, { Khyim pácho dáso
In the middle of the house, } Khyim á limbudi
Even with, on level with, the house, { Khyim nung kwang khome
With a will (bongre), { Gyerstako / Gyerscho
Without against the will (malgre), { Mágyerstako / Mágyerscho
Willy, nilly, Gyerscho má gyerscho
In spite of her husband, { Wancha má visthim
For the love of her husband, { Wancha dwak tako
After the manner of the Néwárs, { Néwar dau khwog no †

---

* Sample of personated gerunds. See on to Grammar, p. 377.
† Khwogno = like; the word for manner or form is kho. For dau, plural sign, read daü.

In the form of fish, Gná khwogno
After the manner of the Tibetans, { Leucha dau khwogno
In the disguise of a Tibetan, } Leucha khwogno

CONJUNCTIONS.

And. No word for it
Also, likewise, Yo
Or. No term for it
Nor. No word
Nor this, { Yam ye má
Nor that, { Myam ye ma
Moreover. Besides, Myam taure
Than (comp.), Ding
As, Gyekho
So, Mekho
As, so, like, this, that, { Yé khwogno / Mé khwogno
How? what like, Gye khwogno
How? in what way, Gyé-khopáso
As well as, Yé khome neuba
As ill as, Yé khome-má neuba
But, Náká
Nevertheless. Notwithstanding, Náká
Though, yet, still, Náká
If, Khéda.—Khédda
If not, unless, Má kheda
Except, Wáso
Whether or not, Bwála má bwála
In the meanwhile, Yékhona. Mékhona
Thereon, Myem taure
To wit, that is to say, { Dáso dáta / Mára dayena
Why, { Márcho / Máragna
Because, since, as, { Yem paptako / Myem paptako

Yes, Aje (true)
No, Máá (it is not)

Verbal negative, Má
Verbal prohibitive, Má
Noun privitive, Má

ADVERBS.

Adverbs of time.

To-day, A'na
To-morrow, Dillá
Yesterday, Sanamti
Day after to-morrow, Niti
Day before yesterday, Nikhabol
This year, Yemthoche
Last year, Sántho
Year before last, Niware
Coming year, Máta
Year after that, Niwa

Now, Yékhona
Then, Mékhona
When? Gyóna
When, rel., Gyóna
Then, correl., Mékhona
Instantly, Bachéu
By and by, Gyer kwongmi
At once, at one time, Kwongkhó
Before, priorly, Gnalla
After, afterwards, Nóla
Since, Gyóna
Till, until. No word. It is expressed by theum added to the root and the negative, or by the negative gerund *
Till now, Hitherto, } A'na sambh (sambh is Khas)
Till then, Metti namti
Till when? how long? Giskonamti
Formerly, long ago, Nyéshè
At present, nowadays, A'nampilli
Whilst, Mim, added to a verb, or the gerund simply †
Henceforth, Hereafter, } A'namekeng
Thenceforth, Thereafter, } Memnamtimekeng
Ever. No word
Never, Genaiyo
Often, Yáko pala
How often, Gisko pala
Sometimes. No word
Once or twice, Kwá bále nippále
Once, Kwá bále
Twice, Nippále
Thrice, Sáj á
Four times, Seppále
Five times, Gnó pále
Six times, Rú pále
Seven times, Chá pále
Eight times, Yá pále
Nine times, Ghú pále
Ten times, Kwaddyum pále
Early, Bachem pasomami
Late, Wákha pasomami,
In the day, Nam bwoktáná
At night, In the night, } Teugnáchi dyumtana
All day, Nam dongmókho
Daily, Namtike namti
At sunrise, Namdhamna
At cock-crow, { Bá griná / Bá gricho pawáno
At dawn, Hauhaudyumchopawana
At sunset, { Nam wamtana / Nam wamcho pawana
At dusk. No word
At nightfall, { Nam rigna / Teugnachi dyumna
From night till morn, { Teugnachi mekeng didila sambh
At noon, Namhelschodi

---

* *e.g.*, stay till I come, gómá pignana, or gó má pi theum, bwákkó.
† *e.g.*, whilst he lives I will not go, Harem blenmim gó má lágna. Whilst he was walking he fell down, Harem gwaktana dokta.

At midnight, Teugnachi helschodi
To-morrow morning, Dilla didiladi
Yesterday at night, Sanamtiten gnachidi
In two or three days, Nikkha sakkhá
In three or four days, Sakkha sekkha
In four or five days, Sekkha gnokkha
How long? Gisko namti
As long, rel., Gikso namti
So long, correl., Metti namti
Again, repeatedly, Anáiyo
Again, returning, Létako

Adverbs of Place.

Here, Yóke
There, Myéke
Where? Gyéke
Where, rel., Gyéke
There, correl., Méke. Mekegnó
Here and there, Hárela yesela
Hither, Hereward, } Yékholá
Thither, Thereward, } Myékholá
Hence, Yékeng
Thence, Myékeng
Whence? Gyélang
Whence, rel., Gyélang
Thence, correl., Myekeng
By what way? Agyem lamlang
By this way, Yem lamlang
By that way, Myem lamlang
How near? Gisko nentha
How far? Gisko brába
How far? *i.e.*, to what limit? } Gyéla (where)
This far, Yeke (here)
That far, Myéke (there)
Near, Nentha
Far, Brába
How near? Gisko nentha
How far? Gisko brába
From after, Brába lang
From near, Nentha lang
In the near, Nentha di
In the far, Brába di
This near, Yeti nentha
That near, Myeti nentha
Nearer, { Anaiyo nentha / Yemdinganaiyo nentha
Nearest, very near } Haupped ing nentha / Thé nentha
Rather near, Dekho nentha
Rather far, Dekho brába
Very far, Thé brába
Up or upwards (an acclivity whence water comes), } Hateula / Yakayeula
From up, from above of slope, } Hateu lang
From down, from below of slope, } Hayeu lang
Up (perpendicular), Taúre
Down (ditto), { Gwáre / Gwáyeu * / Apumyeu
From above (perpendicular), Taureng
From below (ditto), { Apumyeung / Gwáreng / Gwáyeung
Upwards (ditto), Taurela
Downwards (ditto), Gwáyeula. Yeula
Upwards (on slope), Hateula
Downwards (on slope), Hayeula
On the top, Ajujudi †
In, at, the bottom, Apumdi
From the top, { Ajujuding / Ajuju lang
From the bottom, Apumding
Out (issuing), Gluko. Glutako
In (entering), Wóko. Wotako
Out, outside, A'tola (with noun)
In, within, Gwáre. A'gware
Towards this side, Yesehamba la
Towards that side, Hare hamba la
On this side, Yese hamba di
On that side, Hare hamba di
On both sides, { Hare hamba di / Yese hamba di
Round, Khirsoko
Before, Gnalla
After, Nótha
Opposite, vis-à-vis, Gnalla
Abreast, Kwongkho
Straight onwards. No word
Onwards, forwards, Gnálla lá
Backwards, Nothalá.

Adverbs of Manner, Cause, Quality, Quantity,

How? in what way, { Yékho / Yekhopasa
Thus, in that way, { Myekho / Myekhopasa
Why? for what reason, { Gyegná / Máragná / Marha
For this reason, Yé gna?
For that reason, Myé gna?
How? what like? Gyekhome
This like, Yekhome
That like, Myekhome
How much? how many? Gisko
As many, as much, Gisko. ? Caret
So many, so much, Metti
How often? Gisko pála
How great? Gisko gnólo
How small? Gisko yáke

---

* Taúre and gwáre (see p. 348) are chiefly prepositions, and gwá-rè means rather in below. Gwáyeu is better for the latter, or yeu; but none of them quite answers. The verbs express the meanings.

† A' juju di, its summit in. Juju is tree-top or house-top, Hill-top is gnári.

Well, rightly, { Neuba pawoko / Neuba paso / Neuba pasomami / Neuba pawako / Neuba paptako *

Ill, badly, wrongly, Máneuba páso, &c.

Wisely, { Josko and Joksomami, &c. / Teuso and Teusomami, &c.*

Foolishly, { Majoksomami / Mateusomami †

Hungrily, Solimi

Thirstily, Pwáku dwaktimi

Angrily, { Soksomi pawoko / Sokso paso, &c.

Gladly, joyfully, { Gyersimi. Gyersipaso / Gyersoko

Strongly, Soktimi. Soktipawoko, &c.

Weakly, Sokti manthimi

Gently, Wákha paso or pawoko, &c.

Noisily, { Syandami yandapaso or pasoko or pawoko

Silently, Liba dyumso

With blows, Teupsomami. Teuptako

Evenly, on level with, Deuso

Evenly, straightly, smoothly, Deuso

Much, a great deal, { Dhékwóng / Dhékong

A little, Dékho

Neither more nor less, Mádékho ma thé

Less, Dékho

More, Thé

Again (afresh), Gapti. Anaiyo

Back (the same), Ḷeti. Letako

Thoroughly, completely, { Theumsomami / Yáko. Hauppe

Partially, { Dékho bwaso / Dékho jyulsomami / Dékho jyultako

Heavily, { Helpasoko / Helpasomami / Helpattako * / Helpawako

Lightly, { Hampaso / Hampasomami / Hampattako. Hampawóko *

Tightly, { Khipso / Khipsomami / Khiptako

Slackly, { Thyelvim paso * / Thyelvim pasomami / Thelvim paptako / Thelvim pawako *

Greatly, Dhekong

Slightly, trivially, Dékho

In cowardly way, { Gnimami. Gnitako / Gniko

Bravely, { Gnima manthimi / Mágniko / Mágnitako

Modestly, { Gnunemi. / Gnune pawoko

Impudently, Gnune manthi

Secretly, Khleuscho mami

Openly, { Kwainsopascho / Kwainsopaschomami

Jestingly, Rischomami

Seriously, Ajedaso mami

Slowly, Wákha

Hastily, { Gruksomami / Grukso / Gruktako

Mortally, Byaktam sambh

Skin-deep, A'koktesambh,

Together, Kwongkho

Separately, Wang wang

Singly or one by one, { Kwong kwong paso

Solitarily, I'gicha

With a companion, Warcha nung

Afoot, Gwakoko. Gwakso

On horseback, Wognoko

Truly, { Aje dásomami / Aje dyumsomami

Falsely, Limochelso

---

* All these are gerundial, like the great majority of the adverbs; but if imperation is involved, the gerund sign is added to the imperative, not to the indicative.

† Or with main verb in indicative, ma jogako for present and ma joktako for preterit sense (see note at "Wisely"). This is merely the negative form of the same word, obtained by prefixing the particle of negation, or má.

B.—BÁHING GRAMMAR.

DECLENSION OF BÁHING PRONOUNS AND OF NOUNS.

1. Of Pronouns.

First Personal Pronoun.

1. Nom. I, Go
2. Gen. Of me — Conjunct. Wa = my / Disjunct. Wake = mine
3. Dat. / Ac. — To me / Me — Go. No sign
4. Loc. — In me / Within me — Wake gwáre (interior)
5. Loc. — Into me / In me — Wake di (entering, resting in)
6. Abl. From me, Wake ding (removal)
7. All. Towards me, Wake la (nearing)
8. —— From towards me, Wake lang (departing)
9. —— Towards me, Wake taure (behaving)
10. Soc. With me — Wakenung / Gonung — (society)
11. Priv. Without me — Wake manthi / Gomanthi — (privation)
12. Inst. By me, Go mi
13. Loc. At, by me, Wa pumdi * (proximity. H. pás)

Dual.

1. Gósi, incl. Gósúkú, excl.
2. Conjunct. Ïsi, incl. / Wási, excl. — Disjunct. Ïsike, incl. / Wásike, excl.
3. Gósi, incl. Gósúkú, excl.
4. Ïsikegwáre, incl. Wásikegwáre, excl.
5. Ïsike di, incl. Wásike di, excl.
6. Ïsike ding, incl. Wásike ding, excl.
7. Ïsike la, incl. Wásike la, excl.
8. Ïsike lang, incl. Wásike lang, excl.
9. Gosi taure, incl. Gosuku taure, excl.
10. Gosi nung, incl. Gosuku nung, excl.
11. Gosi manthi, incl. Gosuku manthi, excl.
12. Gosi mi, incl. Gosuku mi, excl.
13. Isi- / Wasi- — pumdi — incl. / excl.

Plural.

1. Gó-i, incl. Góku, excl.
2. Conjunct. Ike, incl. / Wake, excl. — Disjunct. Ikke, incl. / Wakke, excl.
3. Gó-i, incl. Góku, excl.
4. Ïkegwáre, incl. Wakegwáre, excl.
5. Ïke di, incl. Wake di, excl.
6. Ïke ding, incl. Wake ding, excl.
7. Ïke lá, incl. Wake lá, excl.
8. Ïke lang, incl. Wáke lang, excl.
9. Ïke taure, incl. Wake taure, excl.
10. Góï nung, incl. Goku nung, excl.
11. Góï manthi, incl. Goku manthi, excl.
12. Goï mi, incl. Goku mi, excl.
13. Ike- / Wake- — pumdi — incl. / excl.

Second Pronoun.

1. Ga
2. Conjunct. Ï — Disjunct. Ïke
3. Gá. No sign
4. Ïke gwáre
5. Ïke di
6. Ike ding
7. Ike la
8. Ike lang
9. Ïke taure
10. Ga nung
11. Ga manthi
12. Ga mi
13. Ï pumdi

---

* See remark in sequel. Tau, gwá, and púm, as substantives or quasi such, naturally take thu genitival pronoun; and perhaps also la and lang = taraf and tarafse of Urdu; but not so-mi, di, and nung, which soem to be sheer case signs. La, meaning proximity, approach, has possessive lam and ablative lang; di, meaning inness, contact, has similarly dim and ding; ke, meaning relation, belongingness, kem and keng. Ke is probably borrowed. Suffix m or me is its probable equivalont. Compound prepositions are formed by la and di, like those of Urdu and Hindi—*e.g.*, Khyim dim = ghar meṅ ka; khyim ding, ghar men se.

Dual.

1. Gasi
2. { Conjunct. { Disjunct; Ísi { Isike
3. Gasi. No sign
4. Ísi gwáre or Ísike gware
5. Ísike di
6. Ísike ding
7. Ísike la
8. Ísike lang
9. Ísi taure or Ísike taure
10. Gasi nung
11. Gasi manthi
12. Gasi mi
13. Ísi pumdi

Plural.

1. Gani
2. { Conjunct. { Disjunct; Íni { Ínike
3. Gani. No sign
4. Íni gwáre
5. Ínike di
6. Ínike ding
7. Ínike la
8. Ínike lang
9. Íni taure
10. Gani nung
11. Gani manthi
12. Gani mi
13. Íni pumdi

Third Personal.

1. Harem (all genders)
2. { Conjunct. { Disjunct; Á { Áke; Haremke, common
3. Harem. No sign
4. { Ágwáre or Ákegwáre; Haremke gwáre
5. Ákedi. Haremdi
6. { Ákeding; Harémke ding
7. { A'ke la; Haremke la
8. { A'ke lang; Haremke lang
9. { A'ke taure; Haremke taure
10. Harem nung
11. Harem manthi
12. Harem mi
13. A'pumdi. Haremke pumdi

Dual.

1. Hárem dausi
2. { Conjunct. { Disjunct; A'si. { A'sike; Harem dausike, common
3. Harem dausi. No sign
4. { A'si gwáre or A'sike gwáre; Harem dausike gwáre
5. A'sike di. Harem dausike di
6. A'sike ding. Harem dausike ding
7. A'sike la. Harem dausike la
8. A'sike lang. Harem dausike lang
9. A'si taure. Harem dausike taure
10. Harem dausi nung
11. Harem dausi manthi
12. Harem dausi mi
13. { A'si pumdi; Harem dausike pumdi

Plural.

1. Harem dau
2. { Conjunct. { Disjunct; Ani { Anike; Harem dauke, common
3. Harem dau. No sign
4. { Ani gware. Anike gware; Harem dauke gware
5. Anike di. Harem dauke di
6. A'nike ding. Harem dauke ding
7. Anike la. Harem dauke la
8. Anike lang. Harem dauke lang
9. A'nike taure. Harem dauke taure
10. Harem dau nung
11. Harem dau manthi
12. Harem dau mi
13. { Ani pumdi; Harem dauke pumdi

Near demonstrative. This.

1. Yam * (all genders)
2. { Conjunct. { Disjunct; Yamke. { Yamke meke
3. Yam. No sign
4. Yámke gware or Yam gware
5. Yam di
6. Yam ding
7. Yamke la. Yam la
8. Yamke lang. Yam lang
9. Yamke taure. Yam taure
10. Yam nung
11. Yam manthi
12. Yam mi
13. Yámke pumdi

Dual.

1. Yam dausi †
2. { Yam dausike; Conj. and disj.
3. Yam dausi. No sign
4. Yam dausike gware
5. Yam dausi di
6. Yam dausi ding
7. Yam dausike la
8. Yam dausike lang
9. Yam dausike taure
10. Yam dausi nung
11. Yam dausi manthi
12. Yam dausi mi
13. Yam dausike pumdi

* Yam or yem, and so Myam or myem. All vowel sounds are extremely vague. G-yem, the relative, is evidently a derivative of yem.

† For dausi and dau read daüsi and daü; *i e.*, da with the pausing tone.

Plural.

1. Yam dau *
2. { Yam dauke / Conj. and disj.
3. Yam dau. No sign
4. { Yam dau gware / Yam dauke gware
5. Yam dau di
6. Yam dau ding
7. Yam dau (ke) la
8. Yam dau (ke) lang
9. Yam dauke taure
10. Yam dau nung
11. Yam dau manthi
12. Yam dau mi
13. Yam dauke pumdi

Remote Demonstrative.

1. Myam † (all genders)
2. { Myamke, conj. / Myamk meke, disj.
3. Myam. No sign
4. Myamke gwáre
5. Myam di
6. Myam ding
7. Myamke la
8. Myamke lang
9. Myamke taure
10. Myam nung
11. Myam manthi
12. Myam mi
13. Myamke pumdi

Dual.

1. Myam dausi
2. { Myam dausike / Conj. and disj., &c., like singular

Plural.

1. Myam dau
2. { Myam dauke / Conj. and disj., &c., ut supra

Interrogative and Distributive.

Who? What person? Any one: m. and f. Substantival and adjectival.‡

1. Sú
2. { Suke / Conj. or disj., or / Sukemeke, disj.
3. Su. No sign
4. Su gware
5. Su di
6. Su ding
7. Sula. Sukela
8. Su lang. Suke lang
9. Su taure. Suke taure
10. Su nung
11. Su manthi
12. Su mi
13. { Su á pumdi / Suke pumdi

Dual.

1. Su dausi
2. Su dausike, &c.

Plural.

1. Su dau
2. Su dauke, &c.

Interrogative and Distributive Neuter.

What? What thing? Any thing: § Substantival and adjectival.

1. Mára
2. Márake, &c.

Dual.

1. Mára dausi
2. Mára dausike, &c.

Plural.

1. Mára dau
2. Mára dauke, &c.

Relative of all genders.

He, she, who; that, which: substantival and adjectival.‖

1. Gyem
2. Gyemke

Dual.

1. Gyem dausi
2. Gyem dausike, &c.

Plural.

1. Gyem dau
2. Gyem dauke

Reflective. Self.

1. Daubo or Dwábo
2. Dwábo ke
3. Dwábo. No sign
4. Dwábo gware
5. Dwábo di
6. Dwábo ding
7. Dwábo la
8. Dwábo lang
9. Dwábo taure
10. Dwábo nung
11. Dwábo manthi
12. Dwábo mi
13. Dwábo pumdi

Dual and plural as before.

So also are declined hwappe or hauppe = all and every; gisko = how many, and

* See note † on preceding page.
† Myam or myem.
‡ Equal kon and koí. Hindi and Urdu.
§ Equal kyá and kúcch.
‖ Equal jón and jó. The correlative is myam = tón and to. The relative pronoun is rarely used because of the relative character of the participles. Indeed its existence at all may be safely denied, and the correlative is nothing more than the remote demonstrative.

as many; metti = so many; dhé kono = many and much; dékho = a few, a little; gisko = whoever and whatever; kwángnáme = other, another; myem = the same (see *that*); nimpho = both; and, in a word, all primitive or personal pronouns. Possessive pronouns are formed from the genitives, except in the case of the three leading pronouns. I, thou, he or she or it, each of these has two distinct forms quite separate from the personals; thus go has wá = mei and meus, in English, of me and my; and wake = English mine. So also ga, the 2d pronoun, has í and íke; and harem, the 3d, has á and áke. The first of these two possessive or genitival forms are pronominal adjectives, or rather adjuncts of nouns and verbs (and adverbs also) by prefix and suffix respectively. The second are pronouns proper, like mine, thine, in English.* The former are indeclinable; the latter are declinable, like all other proper possessives, though with some confusion, originating in the imperfect development of the inflective element, its frequent coincidence with the genitive sign, and the variableness of that sign.

However, the case signs generally and their mode of annexation being uniform, out of this essentially one declension order is obtained, despite the disturbing causes adverted to. I give here, as a sample of the possessives:—

Dauboke = own

1. Dauboke
2. { Caret ? / Dwabokeke †
3. Dauboke
4. Dauboke gware
5. Dauboke di
6. Dauboke ding
7. Dauboke la
8. Dauboke lang
9. Dauboke taure
10. Dauboke nung
11. Dauboke manthi
12. Dauboke mi
13. Dauboke pumdi or Daubo á pumdi

Daubo = áp; dauboke = apna. *Apnaka* can only be separately expressed by the cacophonous iteration of the guttural. Nor is this defect remedied by the use of the conjunct pronouns, wá, í, á; for wádwábo, myself, gives wádwáboke, of myself and my own; and ídwábo, thyself, gives ídwáboke, of thyself or thy own. See more on the genitive in the sequel.

2. Declension of Nouns.

Substantives proper.

Wainsa, a man, m.

1. Wainsa
2. { Wainsake, disjunct, or / Wainsa á, conjunct
3. Wainsa. No sign
4. { Wainsa gware, or / Wainsa á gware
5. Wainsa di
6. Wainsa ding
7. Wainsa la
8. Wainsa lang
9. Wainsa á taure
10. Wainsa nung
11. Wainsa manthi
12. Wainsa mi
13. Wainsa á pumdi

Dual.

1. Wainsa dausi
2. { Wainsa dausike, disjunct / Wainsa ási, conjunct
3. Wainsa dausi
4. { Wainsa dausike gwáre / Wainsa dausi ási gware
5. Wainsa dausi di
6. Wainsa dausi ding
7. Wainsa dausi la
8. Wainsa dausi lang
9. { Wainsa dausike taure / Wainsa dausi ási taure
10. Wainsa dausi nung
11. Wainsa dausi manthi
12. Wainsa dausi mi
13. Wainsa dausi ási pumdi

Plural.

1. Wainsa dau
2. { Wainsa dauke, disjunct / Wainsa dau áni,‡ conjunct

* The formation of these from the my, thy series, by the addition of "ki" or "ke," is quite Turkic. Wa = my, wá-ke = mine. So Turki benim = my, benim-ki = mine. Only Báhing uses the conjunct form merely (quasi im, imki) of the pronoun, which in that tongue, moreover, is a prefix, in Turki an affix, of nouns. The existence of disjunct and conjunct forms of the pronouns, and the use of the latter as verbal formatives as well as to give the possessive sense to nouns, are traits of language very widely diffused, since they are found in the Egyptian and Semitic tongues. And it is queer that the vulgar or spoken Egyptian (Coptic) prefixes these verbal formatives, whereas the learned, or hieroglyphic, suffixes them.

† Compare uskaka in Hindi and Urdu.

‡ A', ási, and áni are the conjunct forms attaching to nominative which follows genitive, thus wainsa dau áni ming, or wainsa dauke áni ming = the wife of several men; literally, men (of) their wife or woman. The use of the same form in the next case proves gwá to be a substantive used as a preposition, like *bhitar* in Hindi, áni gware = their interior.

3. Wainsa dau. No sign
4. { Wainsa dauke gware / Wainsa dau áui gware }
5. Wainsa dau di
6. Wainsa dau ding
7. Wainsa dau la
8. Wainsa dau lang
9. { Wainsa dau ke taure, or / Wainsa dau áni taure }
10. Wainsa dau nung
11. Wainsa dau manthi
12. Wainsa dau mi
13. Wainsa dau áui pumdi

So also is declined mincha, a woman, and ming, a wife, and all feminine nouns.

Declension of a Neuter.

Substantive.

Grokso, a thing.

1. Grokso
2. { Groksoke, disjunct / Grokso-á, conjunct }
3. Grokso
4. Grokso á gware
5. Grokso di
6. Grokso ding
7. Grokso la
8. Grokso lang
9. Grokso á taure
10. Grokso nung
11. Grokso manthi
12. Grokso mi
13. Grokso á pumdi

Dual.

1. Grokso dausi
2. { Grokso dausike, disjunct / Grokso dausi ási, conjunct }
3. Grokso dausi, &c.

Plural.

1. Grokso dau
2. { Grokso dauke, or / Grokso dau áni, &c. }

It results from the above that there is but one declension; that gender has no grammatical expression; that number, like case, is expressed by separate postpositions, number going first; that all nouns and pronouns take the signs of number, neuters as well as others; that some of the signs of case are still significant (gware, the interior; taure, the top; púm, the side); that *ke* is the general genitive sign, but rarely used save when the noun stands alone, as in reply to a question, thus, whose?—the man's, is suke, wainsake; that when two substantives come together the former is the genitive, and has properly no sign (no qualitive ever has), though the "ke" be sometimes superadded to the special denotator, which is á, the third pronoun (his, her, its), or dim, whose sense is in, of. Dim expresses a relation of locality or inness (what is contained); á, almost all other sorts of relation. Dim is used conjunctively and disjunctively, as, of where the tooth? gyelame khleu: of the mouth, sheödim. Both precede the second substantive or nominative—thus wainsa á ning = the man's name; grokso á syanda = the thing's sound; rú dim khán = vegetables of the garden; bazar dim shéri = bazaar rice, or rice of the bazaar; pu dim pwáku, water of the cup; so that this latter may be called the general way of expressing the relation of two substantives which are both named—the former the general way of expressing relation when the qualitive noun only is named, for genitives are all qualitives, *e.g.*, singke = wooden, ramke = bodily. Lastly, that pronouns and nouns are declined throughout and in all respects in the same way, there being no difference whatever between them. As to the genitive relation, it should be further noted that the first of two substantives is by position alone a genitive; that very close connection and dependence is expressed by á, *e.g.*, the calf of the cow, bing á támi; that "ke" can be used with á, as wainsake á ning, the man's his name; that where ke is formative—as singke = wooden, from sing, wood—its conjunctive use is indispensable, like that of the ba and na, the participial formatives; thus, syelke bétho, the iron blade;* neubá muryu, the or a good man (properly, the man who is good), from syel = iron (subs.), and neu, to be good. Observe, further, that the topical sign di both asks and answers, as ru dim khan, garden vegetables; and, of where? the garden's, gyélam (or gyélame), rúdim.

In this latter instance we may observe that, gyéla being where, the final m or me of gyélam, gyélame, has, in respect of adverbs, a genitival force, and so in di-m, of in—m, possessive, ng, fromness, formatives; ke also takes the formative m (see note at p. 353) and la also; and in qualitives we constantly find a similar termination (bubum = white, lalam = red, kwágname = other, &c.), so that the m final is shown to be generally possessive; and more especially as its iteration (bubu-

* Observe that the iron of the blade is bétho á syel or betho ke syel. But the point or haft of the blade is necessarily bétho á juju and betho á rising. See note ‡ at p. 347, with the places therein referred to.

mme = the white one, lala-mme = the red one, kwágnamme = the other one) expresses the disjunct form of the same relation. Thus, which one will you have? the red one or the green? agyeme blávi, lalamme ki gigimme, a sample wherein the possessive á is welded to the relative pronoun gyem. By turning to the participles it will be seen that all those which have not a sign of their own (ba or na) are made participles by the annexation of the m or me particle—juju-m, chho-me.* This is, in fact, the general attributive affix, and its suffixture transforms all qualitives (including adverbs) into substantives or words used substantivally, like the hma gu affix of Newari, and like also the Dravirian van, val, which seem to me to be the unquestionable prototypes of the Prakritic wan, wal, war (gaon-wár, sheto-wala, gári wán, marne wala, &c.) I subjoin a few comparative samples, drawn from Báhing and Newári, which will also show that nearly any word in these tongues can be used substantivally, and that all qualitives, in particular, can by the appropriate affix be made substantival, *e. g.*, singke, wooden; singkeme or singkem, the wooden one.

---

* At all events, the participles in chome would seem to be formed from the infinitives in cho, the general infinitival sign; *e.g.*, jácho, to eat; jachome, edible; pácho, to do; pachome, double; dakcho, to desire; dakchome, desirable. But see the various examples of words in m or me in the vocabulary. Infinitives are regarded as nouns substantive (*e.g.*, dakcho, desire), and such nouns take m, me, to make them qualitive, *e.g.*, juju, a point; juju-m pointed; chho, the body; chhome, bodily. Thus m, me, is formative and possessive, and it can be added to case signs wherever possessiveness is implied, but it is no sign itself any more than ke, *e.g.*, juju-m = singkem, why not singem or singme? agyeme? à-gyè-mè, gyo, what? lalam? lala-m? lala, what?

English.	Báhing.	Newári.	Hindi.
1. The one	Kwong-me, m. n. Kwong nimame, f.	1. Chha-hma, m. f. Chha-gu, n.	1. Caret]
2. Mine or my one	Wake-me, m. n. Wake nimame, f.	2. Ji-hma, m. f. Ji-gu, n.	2. Mera wala, m. n. Meri wali, f.
3. The black	Kyakya-me, m. n. Kyakya nimame, f.	3. Hyáku-hma, m. f. Hyaku-gu, n.	3. Kala wala, m. f. Kali wali, f.
4. The striker. The striking one or one that strikes	Teupba-me, m. f. Teupba nimame, f. Teupcho-me, n.	4. Da-hma, m. f. Da-gu, n.	4. Kutne wala, m. n. Kutne wali, f.
5. The wooden one	Singke-me, m. n. Singke-nimame, f.	5. Sínya-hma, m. f. Sínya-gu, n.	5. Kath wala, m. n. Kath wali, f.
6. The anterior one	Gnalla-me, m. n. Gnalla-nimame, f.	6. Nhápaya-hma, m. f. Nhápaya-gu, n.	6. Áge wala, m. n. Áge wali, f.
7. The posterior one	Notha-me, m. n. Notha nimame, f.	7. Lipaya-hma, m. f. Lipaya-gu, n.	7. Píche wala, m. n. Píche wali, f.
8. The here one	Eke-me, m. n. Eke-nimame, f.	8. Thanaya-hma, m. f. Thanaya-gu, n.	8. Íhan wala, m. n. Íhan wáli, f.
9. The there one	Meke-me, m. n. Meke-nimame, f.	9. Ánaya-hma, m. f. Ánaya-gu, n.	9. Úhan wala, m. n. Úhan wali, f.
10. The to-day's one	Ána-me, m. n. Ána nimame, f.	10. Thá wúnya-hma, m. f. Thá wúnya-gu, n.	10. Áj wala, m. n. Áj wali, f.
11. The comer, the coming one	Píba-mé, m. n. Píba nimame, f.	11. Wó-hma, m. f. Wo-gu, n.	11. Áne wala, m. n. Áne wali, f.
12. The manlike one	Wainsákho-me, m. n. Wainsakho nimame, f.	12. Mijangsu-hma, m. f. Mijangsu-gu, n.	12. Mardsa wala, m. Mardsa wali, f.
13. The masculine one	Wainsake-me, m. n. Wainsake nimame, f.	13. Mijangya-hma, m. f. Mijangya-gu, n.	13. Mardana wala, m. Mardana wali, f.
14. The lowland (being) one	Dheptecha-me, m. n. Dheptecha nimame, f.	14. Kobiya-hma, m. f. Kobiya-gu, n.	14. Madhes wala, m. n. Madhes wali, f.
15. The highland (being) one	Syertecha-me, m. n. Syertecha nimame, f.	15. Choya-hma, m. f. Choya-gu, n.	15. Parbat wala, m. n. Parbat wali, f.

English.	*Báhing.*	*Newári.*	*Hindi.*
16. The handsome one	Rimba-me, m. n. Rimba nimame, f.; or Rimsokpa-me, m. Rimsongma-me, f.	16. Bangla-hma, m. f. Bangla-gu, n.	16. Sunder wala, m. Sunder wali, f.
17. The young one	Bebacha-me, m. Bebacha nimame, f.	17. Mochacha-hma Mochacha gu, m.	17. Chota wala, m. n. Choti wali, f.
18. The adult one	Swalocha-me, m. Swalomi-me, f.	18. Lyáyehma-hma, m. Lyásehma, f.	18. Siyán wala, m. Siyán wali, f.
19. The old one	Gnáwáme, m. Gnámi-me, f.	19. Jyatha-hma, m. Jyíthi-hma, f.	19. Budha wala, m. Budhi wali, f.
20. The Tibetan one (being)	Leucha-me, m. Leucha nimame, f.	20. Sanya-hma, m. f.	20. Bhot wala, m. n. Bhot wali, f.
21. *Tibetan one (thing)*	Leucha *dyaldim-me*, n.	21. Sanya-gu, n.	21. Bhotka wala
22. *The household one* The domestic one	Khyimcha-me, m. Khyimcha nimame, f.	22. Chheṇya-hma, m. f. Chheṇya-gu, n.	22. Gharwala, m. n. Ghar wali, f.
23. The wild one	Sabalacha-me, m. n. Sabalacha nimame, f.	23. Guṇya-hma, m. f. Guṇya-gu, n.	23. Jangal wala, m. Jangal wali, f.
24. The good one	Neuba-me, m. n. Neuba-nimame, f.	24. Bhing-hma, m. f. Bhing-gu, n.	24. Achha wala, m. n. Acchi wali, f.
25. The white one	Bubu jokpa-me, m. Bubu jongma-me, f.; or Bubum-me, m. n. Bubum nimame, f.	25. Toyu-hma, m. f. Toyu-gu, n.	25. Shéto wala, m. n. Shéti wali, f.
26. The bowman's	Líchake-me, m. Lícha nimakeme, f.	26. Lipajonghmaya-hma, m. f. Lipajonghmaya-gu, n.	26. Dhanuk walaka, m. Dhanuk walika, f.
27. The son-in-law's The daughter-in-law's	Dyel chake-me, m. Dyel mikeme, f.	27. Jichaya-hma, m. f. Jichaya-gu, n. Bohumochaya-hma, m. f. Bohumochaya-gu, n.	27. Dámád wala, m. Dámád wali, f. Patho wala, m. Patho wali, f.

Remark.—The above list affords, it will be seen, collateral information as to the formation of gender in qualitives used substantivally. It also shows that the formative suffix cha is apt to be equivalent for the suffix me, m; and as cha still leaves a substantival word (*e.g.*, khyim-cha = householder; lí-cha = bowman), the genitival sign ke is often introduced before final me, to express possessiveness, as, whose bow is that? the bowman's, suke lí, líchakeme. But lícha being bowman, líchame may be used for bowman's. Newári avoids all vagueness by its hma and gu signs, repeated toties quoties with the genitive sign ya, *e.g.*, Ji-hma, mine, m. and f.; Ji-gu, mine, n.; Ji hma ya hma, Ji hma ya gu, Ji hma ya hma ya, Ji hma ya gu ya, Ji gu ya hma ya, Ji gu ya gu ya, &c., express any number of variations in the possession of beings and things; and so also in all qualitives used substantively, thus: toyu hma ya hma, the white man's animal; toyu hma ya gu, the white man's thing; toyu hma ya gu ya, of the white man's thing, &c. Compare Báhing khyim-cha-me with Newári chhen-ya-hma, and it will be seen that cha = ya has a quasi-adjectival force, though khyimcha means householder. Such vagueness is normal.

CLASSIFICATION OF BÁHING VERBS.*

I. Transitives in "wo."—Infinitive Bla-cho, to take. Imperative Bla-wo, take it.

Indicative active, sing. number. *Present.*	*Preterite.*	*Indicative passive, sing. number.* *Present.*	*Preterite.*	*Causal imperative.*
1. Bla-gna	1. Blaptong	1. Blayi (i)	1. Blati	Bla-páto, tr.
2. Blayi (i)	2. Blapteu	2. Blaye (e)	2. Blate	Bla-paso, r.
3. Blawa	3. Blapta	3. Blawa	3. Blata	Bla-payi, p.†

Thus are conjugated mówo, to vomit; cheuwo, to grill; gíwo, to give; séwo, to saw; chwéwo, to burn corpse; bráwo, to scatter; táwo, to get or find; jáwo and báwo, to eat; khí-wo, to quarrel with; kú-wo, to steal; kíwo, to cook; pá-wo, to do; leu-wo, to kiss (coitus); sí-wo, to seize; té-wo, to spit on; mó-wo, to fight; wódipa-wo, to assay; and all compounds of like kind, *i.e.*, of a noun and the verb to do or make.

Intransitives in "wo."—Infinitive Pícho, to come. Imperative Pí-wo, come.

1. Pí-gná	Pí-tí	...	...	Pí-pato, tr.
2. Pi-yé (e)	Pí-té	...	...	Pí-paso, ref.
3. Pí	Pí-tá	...	...	Pí-payi, pas.

Thus are conjugated rá-wo, to come; glewo, to be hot; hó-wo, to be lighted; ká-wo, to be bitter; lá-wo and dí-wo, to go; kú-wo, to come up (slope); yú-wo, to come down (slope); khí-wo, to tremble; neu-wo, to be good; deu-wo, to be reconciled; shéo-wo, to decrease or decay; syé neuwo, to be fat; bhlú-wo, to slip or slide down; shú-wo, to itch; jí-wo, to be ripe, &c.

II. Transitives in "gno."—Infinitive Kwó-cho, to see. Imperative Kwógno, see it.

1. Kwó-gnú	Kwó-tóng	1. Kwó-yí (í)	Kwó-tí	Kwó-pa-to, tr.
2. Kwó-gní	Kwó-t-eu	2. Kwó-gné (é)	Kwó-té	Kwo-pa-so, refl. or middle.
3. Kwó	Kwó-tá	3. Kwó	Kwó-ta	Kwó-ka-yi, pas.

Thus are conjugated só-gno, to tell; lé-gno, to sell; tú-gno, to drink (water); chó-gno, to cultivate and to pay debt; phlí-gno, to send, &c.

---

* See observations at p. 285.

† The causal forms are the same throughout: pato, following the mutable transitives in "to;" paso, all intransitives whatever in "so;" and páyi (pá-í), all passives in í, yí for euphony.

This classification rests on the indicative singular. The infinitive and imperative and causal are given chiefly as clues to the root and to the euphonic changes. The form of the classification is throughout the same—1, 2, 3 refer to the three persons. See on to p. 285.

Intransitives in "gno."—Infinitive, Glwau-cho, to win. Imperative, Glwau-gno, to win.

Indicative active, sing. number.		*Indicative passive, sing number.*		*Causal*
Present.	*Preterite.*	*Present.*	*Preterite.*	*imperative.*
1. Glwau-gna	Glwau-ti	...	...	Glwau-pa-to, tr.
2. Glwau-gne	Glwau-te	...	...	Glwau-pa-so, refl.
3. Glwau	Glwau-tá	...	...	Glwau-pa-yi, pas.

Thus are conjugated rú-gno, to be filled (belly) or satisfied; lé-gno, to return; wo-gno, to enter; glú-gno, to issue; ming-gno, to be ripe; bro-gno, to be flavoursome.

III. Transitives in "ko."—Infinitive, Pok-cho, to make get up, or raise (not lift). Imperative, Pokko, raise him.

1. Pog-ú	Pók-tóng	1. Póng-yi ? (í)	Pók-tí	Pong-páto	ut supra
2. Pog-í	Pók-teu	2. Pong-ye (é) Pó-nyé	Pók-té	Pong-páso	
3. Pog-á	Pók-ta	3. Pó-gá	Pók-tá	Pong-páyi	

Thus are conjugated tuk-ko, to lick; chuk-ko, to bind; rik-ko, to reap; kik-ko, to beget; hik-ko, to count; kúk-ko, to crooken; yók-ko, to share out; prwak-ko, to unknot; nok-ko, to rub; tok-ko, to make fall; hok-ko, to open; jik-ko, to break; pwak-ko vel pukko, to burst; ryak-ko, to write or colour; jak-ko, to know; khryak-ko, to enrage and to revile; rik-ko, to reap; kok-ko, to dig; ruk-ko, to eradicate; tyak-ko, to hinder; wok-ko, to flay; khlyak-ko, to plaster; phwak-ko, to separate; chyak-ko, to divide; pik-ko, to pour or put in; dwak-ko, to swallow.

Intransitives in "ko."—Infinitive, Bok-cho, to get up. Imperative, Bok-ko, get up.

1. Bóng-gna	Bók-ti	...	...	Bong-pa-to	ut supra
2. Bóng-gne, nye	Bók-te	...	...	Bong-pa-so	
3. Bóng	Bók-ta	...	...	Bong-pa-yi	

Thus are conjugated gruk-ko, to be quick; jwak-ko, to arrive; jik-ko, to be broken (n. and a.); buk-ko, to be burst; bwak-ko, to remain and to speak; gúk-ko, to be crooked; phok-ko, to be sour; gwak-ko, to walk; duk-ko, to move or shake; prok-ko, to jump or leap; byak-ko, to die; gik-ko, to be born; gnwak-ko, to weep; dwak-ko, to desire; dok-ko, to fall from aloft (being only).

IV. Transitives in "ro."—Infinitive, Phyér-cho, to sew. Imperative, Phér-ro, sew it.

1. Phyér-ú	Phyér-tóng	1. Phyér-yí (i)	Phyér-tí	Phyér-páto	ut supra
2. Phyér-í	Phyér-t-eú	2. Phyér-é	Phyér-té	Phyér-páso	
3. Phyér	Phyér-tá	3. Phyér	Phyér-tá	Phyér-páyi	

Thus are conjugated chwarro, to cut; kurro, to carry; tyarro, to suffer, endure; khwarro, to shave or scrape or scratch (violently).

Intransitives in "ro."—Infinitive, Byar-cho, to fly. Imperative, Byarro, fly.

1. Byar-gná	Byar-t-í	...	...	Byar-páto	ut supra
2. Byar-é	Byar-t-é	...	...	Byar-páso	
3. Byar	Byar-t-á	...	...	Byar-páyi	

Thus are conjugated bárro, to increase; chyárro, to shine, as sun, &c.

V. Transitives in "lo."—Infinitive, Jyul-cho, to place. Imperative, Jyullo, place it.

1. Jyul-ú	Jyul-tóng	1. Jyul-yí (i)	Jyul-tí	Jyul-páto	ut supra
2. Jyul-í	Jyul-teú	2. Jyul-é	Jyul-té	Jyul-páso	
3. Jyul	Jyul-tá	3. Jyul	Jyul-tá	Jyul-páyi	

Thus are conjugated syallo, to snatch away; theullo, to cherish; yallo, to rub; limo challo, to tell lies.

Intransitives in "lo."—Infinitive, Bál-cho, to be tired. Imperative, Bállo, be tired.

Indicative active, sing. number. *Present.*	*Preterite.*	*Indicative passive, sing. number.* *Present.*	*Preterite.*	*Causal imperative.*	
1. Bál-gná	Bál-tí	...	...	Bál-páto	ut supra
2. Bál-ó	Bál-té	...	...	Bál-páso	
3. Bál	Bál-tá	...	...	Bál-páyi	

Thus are conjugated hyállo, to be heavy, &c.

VI. Transitives in "po."—Infinitive, Teup-cho, to beat. Imperative, Teuppo, beat him.

1. Teub-ú	Teup-tóng	1. Teum-yí (i)	Teup-tí	Teum-páto	ut supra
2. Teub-í	Teup-teú	2. Teum-é	Teup-té	Teum-páso	
3. Teub-á	Teup-tá	3. Teub-á	Teup-tá	Teum-páyi	

Thus are conjugated gup-po, to lift (a light thing); bippo, to suck; syappo, to wash and sharpen; khuppo, to collect; jyappo, to buy; thappo, to weigh; chappo, to can it, to be able for any work; nippo, to express; appo, to shoot.

Intransitives in "po."—Infinitive, Rap-cho, to stand. Imperative, Rappo, stand up.

1. Ram-gná	Rap-tí	...	...	Ram-páto	ut supra
2. Ram-é	Rap-té	...	...	Ram-páso	
3. Ram	Rap-tá	...	...	Ram-páyi	

Thus are conjugated ippo, to sleep; ryippo, to be ended or to end, n.; dhappo, to shine as sun; deuppo, to be combust; jippo, to be rotten, &c.

VII. Transitives in "mo."—Infinitive, Lam-cho, to search. Imperative, Lammo, search for it.

1. Lam-ú	Lam-tóng	1. Lam-yí (i)	Lam-tí	Lam-páto	ut supra
2. Lam-í	Lam-teú	2. Lam-é	Lam-té	Lam-páso	
3. Lam	Lam-tá	3. Lam	Lam-tá	Lam-páyi	

Thus are conjugated nam-mo, to smell; theum-mo, to finish or cause to become; khleummo, to transplant; phemmo, to take in one's arms; sheummo, to cover; thimmo, to bury; hammo, to spread. This conjugation agrees with IV. and V. (see remark at VIII.)

Intransitives in "mo."—Infinitive, Dyum-cho, to become. Imperative, Dyummo, become.

1. Dyum-gná	Dyum-tí	...	...	Dyum-páto	ut supra
2. Dyum-é	Dyum-té	...	...	Dyum-páso	
3. Dyum	Dyum-tá	...	...	Dyum-páyi	

Thus are conjugated rimmo, to be handsome; dyammo, to be full; hammo, to be light (levis); khummo, to stoop; ryammo, to be emaciated or thin.

VIII. Transitives in "no."—Infinitive, Pun-cho, to beg. Imperative, Pun-no, beg it.

1. Pun-ú	Pun-tóng	1. Pun-yí (i)	Pun-tí	Pun-páto	ut supra
2. Pun-í	Pun-teú	2. Pun-é	Pun-té	Pun-páso	
3. Pun	Pun-tá	3. Pun	Pun-tá	Pun-páyi	

Thus are conjugated ninno, to hear; plenno, to release or set at liberty; salepanno, to spin, &c.

N.B.—This agrees with the last. Hence IV., V., VII., VIII. are one, and it seems likely that the common imperative sign should be "o," however near that be to "wo" or the sign of the very different first conjugation. The four specified agree, moreover, in not being subject to any euphonic changes in conjugation. They might be unitised as transitives in a liquid or nasal.

Intransitives in "no."—Infinitive, Wan-cho, to run. Imperative, Wan-no, run.

Indicative active, sing. number.		*Indicative passive, sing. number.*		*Causal imperative.*	
Present.	*Preterite.*	*Present.*	*Preterite.*		
1. Wan-gná	Wan-ti	...	...	Wan-pato	ut supra
2. Wan-é	Wan-te	...	...	Wan-paso	
3. Wan	Wan-ta	...	...	Wan-payi	

Thus are conjugated Blenno, to live, &c.

IX. Transitives in "to."—Infinitive, brécho, to summon. Imperative, Bré-to, summon him.

1. Brét-ú	Bréttóng	1. Brét-í	Brétti	Bré-páto	ut supra
2. Brét-í	Brétteú	2. Brét-é	Bretté	Bré-páso	
3. Brét-á	Brettá	3. Brét-á	Brettá	Bré-páyi	

So are conjugated ríto, to laugh at; dáto, to catch; níto, to set down; khleuto, to conceal; neuto, to make good; mú-to, to blow (breath); khúto, to touch; grúk-to, to quicken; bí-to, to obey; rok-to, to lift; dwak-to, to approve; khryapto, to kindle; rik-to, to contain; gap-to, to add to; duk-to, to shake it or cause to shake; grepto, to throw; dapto, to taste; nyapto, to shove; mimto, to remember; bláto, to dry at fire; jíto, to wet; chamto, to amuse; teuto, to know; yokto, to remove; le-to, to take back; syanto, to recognise; hanto, to cheat; jąto, to stop, detain; khlamtó, to spoil; lwakto, to put upon; bapto, to scratch for ease; plepto, to fold; timto, to squeeze; lipto, to turn over. *N.B.*—Those which have a consonant before the sign, as rok-to, dap-to, dwak-to, cham-to, han-to, and khlam-to, &c., do not double the "t" in the preterite of either voice; and consequently in the passive there is no mark of the distinction of time, *e.g.*, dapti, is I am tasted and I was tasted;* and again, daptu is I taste, daptong, I tasted, but dapta is he tastes or he tasted—the last, however, is a general trait.

X. Transitives in "to" which change the "t" into "d."—Infinitive, Sá-cho, to kill. Imperative, Sá-to, kill him.

1. Sád-ú	Sátong	1. Sáyi	Sáti	Sá-páto	ut supra
2. Sád-í	Sáteu	2. Sáné	Sáté	Sá-páso	
3. Sád-á	Sáta	3. Sádá	Sátá	Sá-páyi	

Thus are conjugated wá-to, abandon or leave; tá-to, to kick; yóto, to split: úto, to fell; lá-to, to take away; páto, to do for another; krá-to, to bite; kléö-to, to undress; móto, to tell; chíto, to tear; píto, to bring; kú-to, to bring up; limléto, to feel; yú-to, to bring down; já-to, to make steady or firm; phú-to, to sow; náto and préto, to gather; phá-to, to exchange; khrí-to, to grind; hó-to, to pierce; hé-to, to distil.

Intransitives in "to."—Infinitive, Gní-cho, to be afraid. Imperative, Gní-to, be afraid.

1. Gní-gná	Gní-tí	...	...	Gní-páto	ut supra †
2. Gní-né	Gní-té	...	...	Gní-páso	
3. Gní	Gní-tá	...	...	Gní-páyi	

So are conjugated jí-to, to be torn; khá-to, to be in pain; ú-to, to fall (on ground); sheö-to, to lose; léto, to return; jyukokáto, to flee; héto, to be sharp; bré-to, to vociferate.

XI. Neuters in "to."—Infinitive, Bo-cho, to flower. Imperative, Bo-to, flower.

1. Bót-u	Bótti	...	...	Bó-pato	ut supra
2. Bót-i	Bótte	...	...	Bó-paso	
3. Bót-a	Botta	...	...	Bó-payi	

* In such cases the sense is determined by the use of the separate prefixed pronouns in the instrumental and objective respectively. Difference of time by an adverb.

† U'to and sheöto, like jikko elsewhere, are both neuter and transitive. See them under the respective heads. Khíwo, to tremble, is neuter; to quarrel is transitive. Bré-to, to cry out, is neuter; bré-to, to summon, is active.

Thus are conjugated khíto, to blow as wind; síto, to fruit; wamto, to sink or set as sun. But the last gives, owing to the consonant before the sign, wamtu, wamti, wamta; wamti, wamte, wamta; infinitive, wam-cho (see kwádo and sódo). Sí-to is often conjugated sidu, sidi, sida; siti, site, sita.

XII. Transitives in "do."—Infinitive, Gram-cho, to hate. Imperative, Gram-do, hate him.

Indicative active, sing. number.		*Indicative passive, sing. number.*		*Causal imperative.*	
Present.	*Preterite.*	*Present.*	*Preterite.*		
1. Gramdú	Gramtong	1. Gramdí	Gramtí	Gram-páto	ut supra
2. Gramdí	Gramteu	2. Gramdé	Gramté	Gram-páso	
3. Gramdá	Gramta	3. Gramdá	Gramtá	Gram-páyi	

Thus are conjugated chyurdo, to wring; rimdo, to expect; cháyindo, or chyéndo, to teach; kwádo, to put on the fire; wando, to put or pour in; wárdo, to throw away; plendo, to forget; chamdo, to divert, amuse; glundo, to extract or take out; jyuldo, to place for another; tundo, to cause to drink; sódo, to tell for another; gremdo, to roast; heldo, to mix. But kwádo and sodó, having no consonant before the sign, double the t, as in IX., thus—

1. Só-du	Sóttong	1. Só-di	Sótti	Só-pato	ut supra
2. Só-di	Sótteu	2. Só-de	Sótte	Só-paso	
3. Só-da	Sótta	3. Só-da	Sótta	Só-payi	

N.B.—This, like sógno of Conjugation II., makes infinitive só-cho and causal só-pato, &c.; and in fact the various modifications of the verbs by voice, and in the peculiar manner here in question (so-gno, tell; so-do, tell for another), are sadly deficient in correspondent forms of the infinitive and participles. See on.

Intransitives in "do."—Infinitive, Myel-cho, to be sleepy. Imperative, Myel-do, be sleepy.

1. Myeldu	Myelti	...	...	Myel-pato	ut supra
2. Myeldi	Myelte	...	...	Myel-paso	
3. Myelda	Myelta	...	...	Myel-payi	

N.B.—This nearly agrees with XI., only that the root having a final consonant, the preterite "t" is not doubled. So are conjugated (I have found no other verbs of this conjugation).

XIII. Intransitives in "so."—Infinitive, Nis-cho, to sit. Imperative, Niso, sit down.

1. Nísi-gna	Ní-s-ti	...	...	Nísi-pato	ut supra
2. Ní-se	Ní-s-te	...	...	Nísi-paso	
3. Ní-se	Ní-s-ta	...	...	Nísi-payi	

This conjugation interposes its reflex sign, or "s," between the root and the ordinary intransitive conjugational forms. Nearly all transitives can be conjugated in this form as a middle voice. But it has also many primitives, as will be seen by the instances given. So also are conjugated wáso, cacare; chárso, mingere; píso, crepitum facere; náso, to take rest; chyénso or chayinso, to learn; khleuso, to lie hid; syínso or shayínso, to wake; sáso, to kill one's self; teumso, to beat one's self; bamso, to scratch one's self; ríso, to laugh; gléso, to lie down; chiso, to bathe; phiso, to dress; chamso, to play; prénso, to begin.

CONJUGATION OF BÁHING VERBS.

I.—Paradigm of Verbs Transitive in "wo."

Root, Já, to eat. Imperative, já-wo.

ACTIVE VOICE.

Imperative Mood.

1. *Singular of Agent.*	*Dual of Agent.*	*Plural of Agent.**
Já-wo, eat it	Já-se, ye two eat it	Já-ne, ye all eat it

* See note * next page.

2. *Dual of Object.*	*Dual of Object.*	*Dual of Object.**
Já-wosi, eat them two	Já-sesi, ye two eat them two	Já-nési, ye all eat them tw
3. *Plural of Object.*	*Plural of Object.*	*Plural of Object.*
Já-womi, eat them all	Jásemi, ye two eat them all	Jánémi, ye all eat them all

Negative Form.

By má prefixed, má já wo, &c., and so in all the subsequent moods.

INDICATIVE MOOD.

Present and Future Tenses.

Singular of Agent.	*Dual of Agent.*	*Plural of Agent.*
	First Person.	
1. Já-gna, I eat or will eat it	Já-sa, incl. Ja-suku, excl. We two eat it	Já-ya, incl. Já-ka, excl. We all eat it
Dual of Object.	*Dual of Object.*	*Dual of Object.*
2. Ja-gna-si, I eat them two	Ja-sa-si, incl. Ja-sukusi, excl. We two eat them two	Já-ya-si, incl. Já-ka-si, excl. We all eat them two
Plural of Object.	*Plural of Object.*	*Plural of Object.*
3. Ja-gna-mi, I eat them all	Ja-sa-mi, incl. Ja-suku-mi, excl. We two eat them all	Ja-yami, incl. Ja-ka-mi, excl. We all eat them all †
	Second Person.	
1. Já-(y) í	Já-si	Ja-ni
2. Já-(y)-i-si	Já-si-si	Já-ni-si
3. Já (y)-i-mi	Já-si-mi	Já-ni-mi
	Third Person.	
1. Ja-wa	Já-se	Já-me
2. Já-wa-si	Já-se-si	Já-me-si
3. Já-wa-mi	Já-se-mi	Ja-me-mi

Preterite Tense.

	First Person.	
1. Já-tong	Já-tá-sá, incl. Já-tá-súku, excl.‡	Ján-tá-yo, incl. Ják-tá-ko, excl.
2. Já-t-óng-si	Já-tá-sá-si, incl. Já-tá-súkú-si, excl.	Ján-tá-yo-si, incl. Ják-tá-kó-si, excl.
3. Já-t-óng-mi	Já-tá-sá-mi, incl. Já-tá-sú-kú-mi, excl.	Ján-tá-yó-mi, incl. Ják-tá-kó-mi, excl.

N.B.—The intercalated n and k are devious. See on.

	Second Person.	
1. Jáp-t-eu	Já-tá-si	Ján-tá-ni
2. Jáp-t-eu-si	Já-tá-si-si	Ján-tá-ni-si
3. Jáp-t-eu-mi	Já-ta-si-mi	Ján-tá-ni-mi

N.B.—The intercalated p and n are devious.

---

* See note ‖ at p. 283. The peculiarities in question hold as to both tongues, and are even more developed in Báhing than in Váyu.

† The form of the conjugation in the remaining persons of the indicative mood being the same as in the first person (and also in the imperative), it is needless to load the paper with repetitions of the names of the numbers, agentive and objective, or with the English equivalents.

‡ Observe that the separation of the syllables is merely to facilitate the student's comprehension, and that I shall do so no further, for the genius of the language is averse to any such treatment of its finely-blended elements.

Third Person.

1. Jáp-t-a	Já-ta-se	Jám-ta-me
2. Jáp-t-asi	Já-tá-se-si	Jám-ta-me-si
3. Jáp-t-a-mi	Já-ta-se-mi	Jám-ta-me-mi

N.B.—The intercalated p and m are devious.

INFINITIVE MOOD.

Já-cho, to eat or to have eaten, aoristic.*

PARTICIPLES.

(Take notice that all the participles are essentially relative, and that they correspond as to sense with nouns, substantival or adjectival, ad libitum.)

1.—PARTICIPLE OF THE AGENT.

Impersonal form.

Já-ba, the eater, who eats, or ate, or will eat; aoristic.

N.B.—This participle has no personated equivalent.

2.—PARTICIPLE OF THE OBJECT AND OF THE INSTRUMENT, ALSO EXPRESSIVE OF HABIT AND OF FITNESS.

Present and future time.

Impersonal form.

Jácho-me, eatable, what is usually eaten or is fit to eat (to be eaten), what or whom any one eats or will eat (food), and what he eats or will eat with (teeth).

3.—PARTICIPLE OF THE OBJECT AND OF THE INSTRUMENT.

Past time.

Impersonal form.

Já-na, eaten, what or wherewith any one ate (also what has been eaten).

4.—PERSONATED EQUIVALENT OF SECOND PARTICIPLE, SUPRA.

First Person.

Singular of Agent.	*Dual of Agent.*	*Plural of Agent.*
1. Ja-gnáme, the one that I eat	Jasame, incl. Jasukume, excl. the one that we two eat	Jayame, incl. Jakame, excl. the one that we all eat
Dual of Object.	*Dual of Object.*	*Dual of Object.*
2. Jagnasime, the two that I eat	Jasasime, incl. Jasukusime, excl. the two that we two eat	Jayasime, incl. Jakasime, excl. the two that we all eat
Plural of Object.	*Plural of Object.*	*Plural of Object.*
3. Jagnamime, the all that I eat	Jasamime, incl. Jasukumime, excl. the all that we two eat	Jayamime, incl. Jakamime, excl. the all that we all eat

Second Person.

1. Jayime	Jasime	Janime
2. Jayisime	Jasisime	Janisime
3. Jayimime	Jasimime	Janimime

---

* Where purpose is involved the sign tha takes the place of the sign cho; *e.g.*, he went to summon, for the purpose of summoning, bretha láta.

Third Person.

1. Jawame	Jaseme	Jameme
2. Jawasime	Jasesime	Jamesime
3. Jawamime	Jasemime	Jamemime

These (second and third person) of course mean respectively what or wherewith thou and he (or she) eats or will eat, &c. See note to first person of indicative mood.

5.—Impersonated equivalent of Third Participle, supra.

First Person.

1. Já tongme, the one that I ate	Játasame, incl. / Játasukume, excl.	Jántayome, incl. / Jáktakome, excl.
2. Játongsime	Játasasime, incl. / Játasukusime, excl.	Jántayosime, incl. / Jáktakosime, excl.
3. Játongmime	Játasamime, incl. / Játasukumime, excl.	Jántayomime, incl. / Jáktakomime, excl.

Second Person.

1. Jápteume	Játasime	Jántanime
2. Jápteusime	Játasisime	Jántanisime
3. Jápteumime	Játasimime	Jántanimime

Third Person.

1. Jáptame	Játaseme	Jámtameme
2. Jáptasime	Játasesime	Jámtamesime
3. Jáptamime	Játasemime	Jántanimime *

GERUNDS.

Gerund of the present and future time impersonal. There is none.

Gerund of present and future time personated.

1.—With main Verb in Present or Future Time.

First Person.

Singular of Agent.	*Dual of Agent.*	*Plural of Agent.*
1. Jagnana, I eating it, shall do so and so.	Jasana, incl. / Jasukuna, excl.	Jayana, incl. / Jakana, excl.
Dual of Object.	*Dual of Object.*	*Dual of Object.*
2. Jagnasina	Jasasina, incl. / Jasakusina, excl.	Jayasina, incl. / Jakasina, excl.
Plural of Object.	*Plural of Object.*	*Plural of Object.*
3. Jagnamina	Jasamina, incl. / Jasukumina, excl.	Jayamina, incl. / Jakamina, excl.

Second Person.

1. Jayina	Jasina	Janina
2. Jayisina	Jasisina	Janisina
3. Jayimina	Jasimina	Janimina

Third Person.

1. Jawana	Jasena	Jamena
2. Jawasina	Jasesina	Jamesina
3. Jawamina	Jasemina	Jamemina

---

* The above forms of the participle and gerund add merely the respective formative particles to the several tense forms; being "me" for the participle and "na" for the gerund.

2. Same gerund personated with main verb in the preterite.

First Person.

1. Jatongna, I eating it, did so and so	Jatasana, incl. Jatasukuna, excl.	Jantayóna, incl. Jaktakóna, excl.
2. Jatongsina	Jatasasina, incl. Jatasukusina, excl.	Jantayósina, incl. Jaktakósina, excl.
3. Jatongmina	Jatasamina, incl. Jatasukumina, excl.	Jantayómina, incl. Jaktakómina, excl.

Second Person.

1. Japteuna	Jatasina	Jantanina
2. Japteusina	Jatasisina	Jantanisina
3. Japteumina	Jatasimina	Jantauimina

Third Person.

1. Japtana	Jatasena	Jamtamena
2. Japtasina	Jatasesina	Jamtamesina
3. Japtamina	Jatasemina	Jamtamemina *

Gerund of past time, impersonal, Jáso and Jásomami.†

1. Same gerund personated with main verb in present or future.

First Person.

Singular of Agent.	*Dual of Agent.*	*Plural of Agent.*
1. Jagnako, I having ate it, will do so and so	Jasako, incl. Jasukuko, excl.	Jayako, incl. Jakako, excl.
Dual of Object.	*Dual of Object.*	*Dual of Object.*
2. Jagnasiko	Jasasiko, incl. Jasukusiko, excl.	Jayasiko, incl. Jakasiko, excl.
Plural of Object.	*Plural of Object.*	*Plural of Object.*
3. Jagnamiko	Jasamiko, incl. Jasukumiko, excl.	Jayamiko, incl. Jakamiko, excl.

Second Person.

1. Jayiko	Jasiko	Janiko
2. Jayisiko	Jasisiko	Janisiko
3. Jayimiko	Jasimiko	Janimiko

Third Person.

1. Jawako	Jaseko	Jameko
2. Jawasiko	Jasesiko	Jamesiko
3. Jawamiko	Jasemiko	Jamemiko

2. Same gerund with main verb in the preterite.

First Person.

1. Jatangko, I having ate it, did so and so	Jatasako, incl. Jatasukuko, excl.	Jantayoko, incl. Jaktakoko, excl.
2. Jatongsiko	Jatasasiko, incl. Jatasukusiko, excl.	Jantayosiko, incl. Jaktakosiko, excl.
3. Jatongmiko	Jatasamiko, incl. Jatasukumiko, excl.	Jantayomiko, incl. Jaktakomiko, excl.

---

* The above forms of the participle and gerund add merely the respective formative particles to the several tense forms, being "me" for the participle, and "na" for the gerund.

† See remark in the sequel on Jásógno with the auxiliary.

Second Person.

1. Japteuko	Jatasiko	Jantaniko
2. Japteusiko	Jatasisiko	Jantanisiko
3. Japteumiko	Jatasimiko	Jantanimiko

Third Person.

1. Japtako	Jataseko	Jamtámeko
2. Japtasiko	Jatasesiko	Jamtamesiko
3. Japtamiko	Jatasemiko	Jamtamemiko *

REFLEX TRANSITIVE, OR MIDDLE VOICE † OF THE TRANSITIVE VERB TO EAT.

Imperative Mood.

Singular.	*Dual.*	*Plural.*
Jáso, eat thyself	Jás-che, ye two eat yourselves	Jásine,‡ ye all eat yourselves

Indicative Mood.

Present and Future Tense.

	Singular.	*Dual.*	*Plural.*
1st Per.	Jásigna	Jás-cha, incl. Jás-chuku, excl.	Jásiya, incl. Jásika, excl.
2d Per.	Jáse	Jás-chi	Jásini
3d Per.	Jase	Jás-che	Jásime

Preterite Tense.

1st Per.	Jasti	Jastasa, incl. Jastasuku, excl.	Jastayo, incl. Jastako, excl.
2d Per.	Jaste	Jastasi	Jastani
3d Per.	Jasta	Jastasa	Jastame

Infinitive Mood.

Jascho, to eat, or to have eaten one's self, aoristic.

Participles.

1. Participle of the agent, impersonal.

Jásiba, the self-eater, one who eats, or will eat or ate himself, aoristic.

2. Participle of the object and instrument, present and future time, impersonal form.

Jaschome, his own that any one eats or will eat, self-eatable, what is self-eaten or wherewith to eat self.

---

* Here, as before, the gerundial impersonated forms are constructed by merely adding the past gerund sign or "ko" to the several forms of the tenses; and as in the indicative mood there are thirty-three personal forms proper to either time (present or future and preterite), so there are sixty-six forms of the gerund of past time, and in like manner are there sixty-six of the gerund of the present time, besides two impersonal forms—in all, 134. Of the participles there are sixty-six personated and three impersonate forms of the latter, making in all sixty-nine! This is a more than Manchuric luxuriance of participial and gerundial growth. I have now gone through the most essential and characteristic forms of the verb, and shall reserve the less essential, or the several other so-called moods, &c., for the sequel, proceeding first to the reflex or middle voice, and then to the passive, upon the present model. The gerunds are purely verbal, with no touch of the noun, and they are essentially continuative, serving in lieu of the conjunction "and."

† There are a great many primitives or neuters in "so," besides the derivatives or reflex forms of the transitives, which I call their middle voice. All transitives make their middle voice by changing their appropriate sign into "so." This form is perfectly uniform for all primitives and derivatives. The French amuser and s'amuser, = cham-cho and cham-s-cho, give a good idea of it.

‡ There are of course no objective forms of an intransitive verb, and all verbs in "so," whether primitively neuter or derived, as here, from transitives, are so regarded. See and compare the transitive forms in the active voice aforegone.

3. Same participle of time past, impersonal.

Jasina, his own (flesh) that any one ate, or what has been self-eaten by any one; and wherewith it has been self-eaten,* or his own (teeth) wherewith any one ate.

4. Impersonated equivalent of participle second in "chome."

	Singular.	*Dual.*	*Plural.*
1st Per.	Jasigname, my own that I eat or eat with	Jaschame, incl. Jaschukume, excl.	Jasiyame, incl. Jasikame, excl.
2d Per.	Jaseme	Jaschime	Jasinime
3d Per.	Jaseme	Jascheme	Jasimeme

5. Impersonated equivalent of participle third in "na."

1st Per.	Jastime, my own that I ate	Jastasame, incl. Jastasukume, excl.	Jastayome, incl. Jastakome, excl.
2d Per.	Jasteme	Jastasime	Jastanime
3d Per.	Jastame	Jastaseme	Jastameme

GERUNDS.

Gerund of present and future time, impersonal. There is none.

1. Gerund of present and future time, personated with main verb in same time.

	Singular.	*Dual.*	*Plural.*
1st Per.	Jasignana, I eating my own flesh, shall do so and so	Jaschana, incl. Jaschukuna, excl.	Jasiyana, incl. Jasikana, excl.
2d Per.	Jasena	Jaschina	Jasinina
3d Per.	Jasena	Jaschena	Jasimena

2. Same gerund personated with main verb in past tense.

1st Per.	Jastina, I eating my own flesh, did so and so	Jastasana, incl. Jastasukuna, excl.	Jastayona, incl. Jastakona, excl.
2d Per.	Jastena	Jastasina	Jastanina
3d Per.	Jastana	Jastasena	Jastamena

Gerund of past time, impersonal. There is none.

1. Same gerund personated with main verb in present or future.

1st Per.	Jasignako, I having eaten my own flesh, shall do so and so	Jaschako, incl. Jaschukuko, excl.	Jasiyako, incl. Jasikako, excl.
2d Per.	Jaseko	Jaschiko	Jasiniko
3d Per.	Jaseko	Jascheko	Jasimeko

2. Same gerund with main verb in the preterite.

1st Per.	Jastiko, I having eaten my own, did so and so	Jastasako, incl. Jastasukuko, excl.	Jastayoko, incl. Jastakoko, excl.
2d Per.	Jasteko	Jastasiko	Jastaniko
3d Per.	Jastako	Jastaseko	Jastameko

PASSIVE VOICE OF THE SAME VERB.

(Basis, Jayi = eat me.)

IMPERATIVE MOOD.

	Singular of Object.	*Dual of Object.*	*Plural of Object.*
1.	Jáyi, eat me thou	Jásiki, eat us two thou	Jáki, eat us all thou

* The participles in cho-me and in na are scarcely usable in derivative verbs in "so" like jaso, but more freely in primitives of the same formation, such as wáso = caco, *e.g.*, was-chome khli, voidable ordure; and wásina khli = voided ordure, that is, the ordure which will be and has been voided. This shows the passive bent of these participles, and the affinity of neuter verbs to passives. See Classification of Verbs.

Dual of Agent.	*Dual of Agent.*	*Dual of Agent.*
2. Jáyisi, eat me ye two	Jasikisi, eat us two ye two	Jákisi, eat us all ye two
Plural of Agent.	*Plural of Agent.*	*Plural of Agent.*
3. Jáyini, eat me ye all	Jásikini, eat us two ye all	Júkini, eat us all ye all *

INDICATIVE MOOD.

Present and Future Tense.

First Person.

Singular of Object.	*Dual of Object.*	*Plural of Object.*
1. Jáyí, eats me he = I am eaten by him	Jáso, incl. Jásiki, excl. We two are eaten by him	Jáso, incl. Jáki, excl. We are all eaten by him
Dual of Agent.	*Dual of Agent.*	*Dual of Agent.*
2. Jayisi, I am eaten by them two	Jasosi, incl. Jasikisi, excl. We two are eaten by them two	Jasosi, incl. Jakisi, excl. We all are eaten by them two
Plural of Agent.	*Plural of Agent.*	*Plural of Agent.*
3. Jayimi, I am eaten by them all	Jasomi, incl. Jasikimi, excl. We two are eaten by them all	Jasomi, incl. Jakimi, excl. We all are eaten by them all

N.B.—The agent is always of the third person, he, she, or it; if it be second person the conjugation is another.

Second Person.

1. Jaye	Jasi	Jani
2. Jayesi	Jasisi	Janisi
3. Jayemi	Jasimi	Janimi

Third Person.

1. Jawa	Jawasi	Jawami
2. Jase	Jasesi	Jasemi
3. Jame	Jamesí	Jamemi

Preterite Tense.

First Person.

1. Jati	Jataso, incl. Jatasiki, excl.	Jataso, incl. Jáktaki, excl.
2. Jatisi	Jatasosi, incl. Jatasikisi, excl.	Jatasosi Jáktakisi
3. Jatimi	Jatasomi, incl. Jatasikimi, excl.	Jatasomi Jaktakimi

Second Person.

1. Jate	Jatasi	Jantani
2. Jatesi	Jatasisi	Jantanisi
3. Jatemi	Jatasimi	Jantanimi

* Observe that of the active voice of the transitive the object is him or her or it; of the middle voice the object is self, and of the passive the object is me; but that the order of arrangement of agent and object is reversed in the passive as compared with the active voice, and so also in the indicative mood. This is done in conformity to the genius of this language, which requires the attention to be primarily fixed on the agent in one voice, on the object in the other. It will be seen in the sequel that there are further special forms of the verb to denote the action which passes from me to thee, and from thee to me. These are necessary complements of the passive voice in a language, which makes the mention of agents and patients inseparable from that of the action. Compare note ‖, p. 283.

Third Person.

1. Japta	Japtasi	Japtami
2. Jatase	Jatasesi	Jatasemi
3. Jamtame	Jamtamesi	Jamtamemi

INFINITIVE MOOD.

There is none properly so called.

The sense is conveyed by placing the separate pronoun in the objective case before the verb in the active voice; gó jácho = to eat me = to be eaten.

PARTICIPLES.

1. Participle of the agent in "ba" is of course wanting.

2. Participle of the object in "chome" is rather passive than active, though used in both voices; as we say in English, what (or whom) any one eats or is wont to eat, or what is wont to be eaten by any one.

3. Participle in "na" is yet more purely passive; ja-na, what has been eaten. But it is used with more than English license, as though it belonged to the active voice, what any one hath eaten.

4. Personated equivalent of the second of the above. It is formed by adding the formative suffix "me" to the several tense forms of the indicative present and future of this voice, *e.g.*

Singular of Agent.	*Dual of Agent.*	*Plural of Agent.*
1. Jayime	Jasome, incl.	Jasome, incl.
	Jasikime, excl.	Jakime, excl.

and so on through the whole of the thirty-three forms above given in the indicative.

5. Personated equivalent of the third of the above participles, or that in "na." It is formed, as above, by adding the formative "me" to the several forms of the preterite indicative of this voice, *e.g.*

1. Jatime	Jatasome, incl.	Jatasome, incl.
	Jatasikime, excl.	Jatakime, excl.

and so on through all the thirty-three forms of the three persons of the preterite passive. Jayime means I who am the eaten of him, and jatime, I who was the eaten of him; and so on of all the rest.

N.B.—The impersonal forms in this, and of the active and middle voices, are declinable like nouns. The personated in "me," which take so much of the verb character, are indeclinable. Both are thoroughly and intrinsically relative in sense.

GERUNDS.

Gerund of future and present time impersonal. There is none.

1. The same gerund personated with the main verb in same time.

It is formed by the addition of the appropriate formative, or "na," to the several forms of the present and future indicative of this voice, *e.g.*,

Singular.	*Dual.*	*Plural.*
1. Jayina	Jasona, incl.	Jasona, incl.
	Jasikina, excl.	Jakina, excl.

and so on through all the thirty-three forms of the three persons of the indicative.

2. The same gerund personated with the main verb in the preterite.

It is formed by suffixing the "na" to the preterite indicative forms, *e.g.*

1. Jatina	Jatasona, incl.	Jatasona, incl.
	Jatasikina, excl.	Jatakina, excl,

Samples of the sense—Being eaten I shall cry out, jayina bregna; being eaten I cried out, jatina breti.*

Gerund of past time, impersonal. There is none.

---

* Observe that the root bre, to cry out, is here conjugated as an intransitive. Elsewhere I have given the same root conjugated as a transitive in the sense of to summon. The infinitive and imperative (bre-cho, bre-to) are identical. This double indicative conjugation from the same root of words having nearly identical senses is very common, as uto, to fall and to fell, jikko, to be broken and to break, &c. Breto, the intransitive, is conjugated like gnito, to be afraid, the type of regular intransitives in "to."

1. Same gerund personated with main verb in present or future.

It is formed by adding the formative "ko" to the several forms (thirty-three) of the indicative present and future, *e.g.*,

	Singular.	*Dual.*	*Plural.*
1.	Jayiko	Jasoka, incl.	Jasoko, incl.
		Jasikiko, excl.	Jakiko, excl.

2. Same gerund with the main verb in the preterite.

It is formed, as above, by adding "ko" to the several forms of the indicative preterite, *e.g.*,

1.	Jatiko	Jatasoko, incl.	Jatasoko, incl.
		Jatasikiko, excl.	Jatakiko, excl.

and so on through all the thirty-three forms of the indicative preterite of this voice. The senses respectively of jayiko and jatiko are, having been eaten I shall be, and, having been eaten, I was or have been (forgotten); and so of the rest.

PARADIGM.

Of certain special forms of conjugation supplementary of the passive, and denoting, first, the action that passes between me as the agent and thee as the patient; second, that in which thou art the agent and I the patient. The first of these forms is very distinct, but is confined to the indicative (and subjunctive) mood. It has no imperative or infinitive. The second runs much into the ordinary passive, and has an imperative. See on.

First Form, I—Thee.

(Verb Ja, to eat, as before.)

Indicative Mood.

Present and Future Tense.

*Singular of Agent.**	*Dual of Agent.*	*Plural of Agent.*
1. Jana, I eat thee, or thou art eaten by me	Jayesi, we two eat thee	Jayemi, we all eat thee
Dual of Object.	*Dual of Object.*	*Dual of Object.*
2. Janasi, I eat you two	Jasisi, we two eat you two	Jasimi, we all eat you two
Plural of Object.	*Plural of Object.*	*Plural of Object.*
3. Janani, I eat you all	Janisi, we two eat you all	Janimi, we all eat you all

Preterite Tense.

1. Jantana, I ate thee, or thou wast eaten by me	Jatesi, we two ate thee	Jatemi, we all ate thee
2. Jantanisi, I ate you two	Jatasisi, we two ate you two	Jatasimi, we all ate you two
3. Jantanani, I ate you all	Jantanisi, we two ate you all	Jantanimi, we all ate you all

Participles.

There are none of the impersonal form.

Participle of the future personated. It is formed, as in the ordinary conjugation, by adding the appropriate particle of "me" to the forms of the indicative, *e.g.*

Singular.	*Dual.*	*Plural.*
Janame	Jayesime	Jayemime †

and so on through all the nine forms above given in the indicative present.

Participle of the past personated. It is formed from the preterite by adding the "me," *e.g.*,

---

* This form is rather allied to the passive than active, and may be called the supplement of the former, which is very incomplete, and alien to the genius of the tongue, being cramped at the threshold by taking the first person objective for its starting-point; thus, jayi = eat me. There is no Be thou eaten. And here jana and its participial janame look to the object chiefly, thou art eaten by me and thou who art the eaten of me.

† The "y" is merely to keep the vowels apart.

Singular.	*Dual.*	*Plural.*
Jantaname	Jatesime	Jatemime

and so on through the above nine forms of the preterite.

The sense of janame is, thou who art the eaten of me; of jantaname, thou who wert the eaten of me; and so of all the rest.

Gerunds.

There are none whatever not personated.

The personated forms are, as in the ordinary conjugation, four, two of the present and two of the past, and they are constructed, as before, by adding respectively "na" and "ko" to the tense forms above; *e.g.*,

Gerund of the future and present with the main verb in same time.

Singular.	*Dual.*	*Plural.*
Janana	Jayesina	Jayemina

and so on through all the nine forms of the tense.

Same gerund with the main verb in the preterite.

Jantanana	Jatesina	Jatemina

and so on through all the nine forms above.

Gerund of the preterite with main verb in the past time.

Jantanako *	Jatesiko	Jatemiko

and so on through the nine tense forms.

Second Special Form, Thou—Me.

Imperative Mood.

Singular of Agent.	*Dual of Agent.*	*Plural of Agent.*
1. Jayi,† eat me thou, or let me be eaten by thee.	Jayisi	Jayina
Dual of Object.	*Dual of Object.*	*Dual of Object.*
2. Jasiki	Jasikisi	Jasikini.
Plural of Object.	*Plural of Object.*	*Plural of Object.*
3. Jaki	Jakisi	Jakini

N. B.—This tallies with the ordinary passive, as will be seen by reading the vertical columns of the one with the horizontal of the other.

Indicative Mood.

Present and Future Tense.

1. Jayi, thou eatest me, or I am eaten by thee	Jayisi	Jayini
2. Jasiki	Jasikisi	Jasikini
3. Jaki	Jakisi	Jakini

Preterite.

1. Jati	Jatasi	Jatini
2. Jatasiki	Jatasikisi	Jatasikini
3. Jaktaki	Jaktakisi	Jaktakini

N.B.—These agree respectively with the present and preterite of the passive, save, first, that there are here no inclusive forms; and, second, that the personal sign ni stands here in the place of the passive mi.

---

* Samples of the above gerunds. Eating thee I shall fill my belly, janana rugna; eating thee I filled my belly, jantana ruti; having eaten thee I will go, janako lagna; having eaten thee I slept, jantanako ipti; we all having eaten thee, were pleased, jatemiko gyerstako; we two, having eaten thee, will flee, jayesiko juksukasuku; we all eating thee, fled, jatemina jukkatako.

† This is the formula of the passive, because the passive only requires that the first person be the patient, allowing the second or third to be the agent, and hence the indicative of this form so nearly tallies with that of the passive, jayi, eat me he or thou, &c.

Infinitive Mood.

Wanting: the ordinary infinitive is used with the separate pronouns in the instrumental and objective cases, gami go jacho.

Participles.

There are none of the non-personated kind.

The personated are formed, as usual, by the "me" suffix added to the tense forms, *e.g.*

Singular.	*Dual.*	*Plural.*
Jayime	Jayisime	Jayinime

and so on through the nine tense forms.

Jatime	Jatisime	Jatinime

and so on through the nine tense forms above.

The senses of jayime and jatime are, I who am the eaten of thee, and I who was the eaten of thee. The sense would be equally expressed by thou who art my eater; but eater, jaba, is purely active, and cannot be admitted into an agento-objective verb.

Gerunds.

Unpersonated, there are none.

The personated of the present are formed, as before, by "na" suffixed to the several tense forms, and those of the past by "ko" similarly affixed; *e.g.*, jayina, jatina, and jayiko, jatiko, equivalent to thou eating me wilt do so and so, and did so and so; and thou having ate me wilt do, and did, so and so.

Paradigm of Transitives in "to," not changing the "t" into "d."*

Root Bre, to summon.

ACTIVE VOICE.

Imperative Mood.

Singular.	*Dual.*	*Plural.*
1. Breto	Bretise	Bretine
Dual of Object.	*Dual of Object.*	*Dual of Object.*
2. Bretosi	Bretisesi	Bretinesi
Plural of Object.	*Plural of Object.*	*Plural of Object.*
3. Bretomi	Bretisemi	Bretinemi

Indicative Mood.

Present and Future Tense.

First Person.

1. Bretu	Bretisa, incl.	Bretiya, incl.
	Bretisuku, excl.	Bretika, excl.
2. Bretusi	Bretisasi, incl.	Bretiyasi, incl.
	Bretisukusi, excl.	Bretikasi, excl.
3. Bretumi	Bretisami, incl.	Bretiyami, incl.
	Bretisukumi, excl.	Bretikami, excl.

Second Person.

1. Breti	Bretisi	Bretini
2. Bretisi	Bretisisi	Bretinisi
3. Bretimi	Bretisimi	Bretinimi

Third Person.

1. Breta	Bretise	Bretime
2. Bretasi	Bretisesi	Bretimesi
3. Bretami	Bretisemi	Bretimemi

* Those that change the ti of the imperative into d in the indicative do not take the incrementive ti of the dual and plural present, nor the double t of the preterite, and they have i, not ti, in the passive. These peculiarities are in fact confined to the transitives in unchanging "to," but are partially shared by the changing transitives and by the neuters.—See Classification of Verbs, pp. 361–365. For paradigm of transitives in "to" which change t into d, see on to p. 390 ff.

Preterite.

First Person.

1. Brettong	Brettasa, incl.	Brettayo, incl.
	Brettasuku, excl.	*Brettako, excl.*
2. Brettongsi	Brettasasi, incl.	*Brettayosi, incl.*
	Brettasukusi, excl.	Brettakosi, excl.
3. Bréttongmi	Brettasami, incl.	*Brettayomi, incl.*
	Brettasukumi, excl.	Brettakomi, excl.

Second Person.

1. Bretteu	Brettasi	Brettani
2. Bretteusi	Brettasisi	Brettanisi
3. Bretteumi	Brettasimi	Brettanimi

Third Person.

1. Bretta	Brettase	Brettame
2. Brettasi	Brettasesi	Brettamesi
3. Brettami	Brettasemi	Brettamemi

INFINITIVE MOOD.

Bre-cho, to call or to have called, &c.

PARTICIPLES.

1st, in ba, Bre-ba, who calls or called

2d, in chome, Brechome, { whom any one calls or will call / who will be called

3d, in na, Bre-na, { whom any one has called / who has been called

4th, in me, Bretume, &c., { whom I call or shall call / who will be called by me

5th, in me, Brettongme, &c., { whom I called / who has been called by me

Gerund of the past, impersonal, Breso or Bresomami. None of the present.

GERUNDS PERSONATED.

1st, in na, Bretuna, &c., I calling (will do so and so)
2d, in na, Brettongna, &c., I calling (did so and so)
3d, in ko, Bretuko, &c., I having called (will do so and so)
4th, in ko, Brettongko, &c., I having called (did so and so)

MIDDLE VOICE.

Bréso, call thyself. Precisely like Jaso.

PASSIVE VOICE.

IMPERATIVE MOOD.

1. Bréti	Bretisiki	Bretiki
2. Brétisi	Bretisikisi	Bretikisi
3. Brétini	Bretisikini	Bretikini

INDICATIVE PRESENT.

First Person.

1. Breti	Bretiso, incl.	Bretiso, incl.
	Bretisiki, excl.	*Bretiki, excl.*
2. Bretisi	Bretisosi, incl.	*Bretisosi, incl.*
	Bretisikisi, excl.	*Bretikisi, excl.*
3. Bretimi	Bretisomi, incl.	*Bretisomi, incl.*
	Bretisikimi, excl.	*Bretikimi*, excl.

Second Person.

1. Brete	Bretisi	Bretini
2. Bretesi	Bretisisi	Bretinisi
3. Bretemi	Bretisimi	Bretinimi

Third Person.

1. Breta	Bretasi	Bretami
2. Bretise	Bretisesi	Bretisemi
3. Bretime	Bretimesi	Bretimemi

Preterite.

First Person.

1. Bretti	Brettaso, incl. Brettasiki, excl.	Brettaso, incl. Brettaki, excl.
2. Brettisi	Brettasosi, incl. Brettasikisi, excl.	Brettasosi, incl. Brettakisi, excl.
3. Brettimi	Brettasomi, incl. Brettasikimi, excl.	Brettasomi, incl. Brettakimi, excl.

Second Person.

1. Brette	Brettasi	Brettani
2. Brettesi	Brettasisi	Brettanisi
3. Brettemi	Brettasimi	Brettanimi

Third Person.

1. Bretta	Brettasi	Brettami
2. Brettase	Brettasesi	Brettasemi
3. Brettame	Brettamesi	Brettamemi

INFINITIVE MOOD.

Brecho, precisely as in the last verb *

PARTICIPLES.

1st, in ba, Wanting, as in the last
2d, in chome, Brechome, precisely as in the last
3d, in na, Brena, ditto, ditto
4th, in me, Bretime, &c., as before
5th, in me, Brettime, &c., as before

GERUNDS.

1st, in na, Bretina,
2d, in na, Brettina,
3d, in ko, Bretiko,
4th, in ko, Brettiko,
} &c., as before

SPECIAL FORM I.

Indicative Present.

1. Bretina	Bretesi	Bretemi
2. Bretinasi	Bretisisi	Bretisimi
3. Bretinani	Bretinisi	Bretinimi

Preterite.

1. Brettana	Brettesi	Brettemi
2. Brettanasi	Brettasisi	Brettasimi
3. Brettanani	Brettanisi	Brettanimi

INFINITIVE MOOD.

None. Gomi ga brecho expresses the sense.

PARTICIPLES.

Impersonal, none.

1st personated, Bretiname, &c. 2d personated, Brettaname, &c.

---

* See remark at p. 375. There is no infinitive passive in Báhing any more than in Váyu, nor any unpersonated gerund; but of the three unpersonated participles, two, or those in chome and na, are essentially passive.

GERUNDS.

Impersonal, none.

1st personated,	Bretinana, &c.	3d Personated,	Bretinako, &c.
2d ,,	Brettanana, &c.	4th ,,	Brettanako, &c.

SPECIAL FORM II.

Imperative.

1. Breti	Bretisi	Bretini
2. Bretisiki	Bretisikisi	Bretisikini
3. Bretiki	Bretikisi	Bretikini

Indicative Present.

1. Breti	Bretisi	Bretini
2. Bretisiki	Bretisikisi	Bretisikini
3. Bretiki	Bretikisi	Bretikini

Preterite.

1. Bretti	Brettisi	Brettini
2. Brettasiki	Brettasikisi	Brettasikini
3. Brettaki	Brettakisi	Brettakini

INFINITIVE MOOD.

There is none. Gami go brecho expresses the sense.

PARTICIPLES.

Impersonal, none.

1st personated, Bretime, &c., }
2d ,, Brettime, &c., } as before, by "me" added to the tense forms.

GERUNDS.

Impersonal of the past (none of present), Bréso or Brésomami.

Ditto personated.

1st personated, Bretina, &c., }
2d ,, Bréttina, &c., }
3d ,, Brétiko, &c., }
4th ,, Bréttiko, &c., } as before, by "ná" added to the several forms of the tenses.

PARADIGM OF VERBS INTRANSITIVE OR NEUTER.

Not having the sibilant sign.

A neuter in "wo," Pi-wo, come thou.

IMPERATIVE MOOD.

Singular.	*Dual.*	*Plural.*
Piwo	Pise	Pine

INDICATIVE MOOD.

Present and Future Tenses.

1st *Per.*	Pigna	Pisa, incl. / Pisuku, excl.	Piya, incl. / Pika, excl.
2d *Per.*	Piye	Pisi	Pini
3d *Per.*	Pi	Pise	Pime

Preterite Tense.

1st *Per.*	Piti	Pitasa, incl. / Pitasuku, excl.	Pintayo, incl. / Piktako, excl.
2d *Per.*	Pite	Pitasi	Pintani
3d *Per.*	Pita	Pitase	Pimtame

INFINITIVE MOOD.

Picho, to come or to have come, aoristic.

PARTICIPLES.

First of the Agent, impersonal, aoristic.

Piba, who or what comes, or will come or came.

Second of the object and instrument.

Present or future, impersonal.

Pichome, fit to come by (road), and fit for coming with (feet), and what any one will come by (road).

Third the same, past time, impersonal.

Pina, what any one came by (road), and what he came with (feet).

Impersonated form of second and third.

It is formed by "me" added to the several forms of the tenses, pignáme, pitime, &c.*

GERUNDS.

That of present tíme (future).

Pígnana,† &c., with main verb in same time.

Pítina, &c., with main verb in preterite.

That of past time.

Pígnako, &c., with main verb in future.

Pítiko, &c., with main verb in past.

All intransitives not having "so" in the imperative are conjugated as above, except certain ones in "to," which I shall distinguish as neuters, and which are conjugated as follows:—

PARADIGM OF NEUTERS IN "TO."

Root Bó, to flower. Imperative, Bó-to.

IMPERATIVE MOOD.

Singular.	*Dual.*	*Plural.*
Bóto	Bótise	Bótine

INDICATIVE MOOD.

Present and Future.

	Singular	Dual	Plural
1st Per.	Bótú	Bótisa, incl. / Bótisuku, excl.	Bótiya, incl. / Bótika, excl.
2d Per.	Bóti	Bótisi	Bótini
3d Per.	Bóta	Bótise	Bótime

Preterite.

	Singular	Dual	Plural
1st Per.	Bótti	Bottasa, incl. / Bóttasuku, excl.	Bóttayo, incl. / Bóttako, excl.
2d Per.	Bótte	Bóttasi	Bóttani
3d Per.	Bótta	Bóttase	Bóttáme

INFINITIVE MOOD.

Bó-cho.

PARTICIPLE of the agent in "ba."

Bóba, what flowers, or will flower, or has flowered.

N.B.—The second and third participles in "chome" and "na" are wanting,‡ and so also their derivatives in "me."

---

* *e.g.*, Pignáme kholi, the feet which I come with; pignáme lam, the road which I come by; pitime kholi, the feet which I came with; pitime lam, the road which I came by.

† *e.g.*, Pignana pagna = I will come and do it; literally, I coming will do it.

‡ These participles can rarely be used with intransitive or neuter verbs, never with such of the latter as relate to the action of things. They imply an agent who produces that effect on a thing which these participles express relatively to future and past time respectively. Out of the vast number of intransitives enumerated elsewhere hardly a dozen make use of these participles. Some of these exceptions are bwakko, to speak, which gives bwangna ló = spoken words; bokko, to get up, whence bongna blocho, = the bed whence any one has risen; niso, to sit, whence nisina-khosingba, the chair on which any one has sat, &c.

GERUNDS.

1. Bótuna.	Bótina	Bótana, &c.
2. Bóttina	Bottena	Bóttana, &c.
3. Bótuko	Bótiko	Bótako, &c.
4. Bóttiko	Bótteko	Bóttako, &c.

What, as opposed to the above, called neuters (see conjugation XI.) for distinction's sake, I have elsewhere called intransitives in "to," as jíto, kháto, &c. (conjugation X.), are all regular and conjugated like the verb to come above given. In fact, all the so-called intransitives, whatever their sign, have one uniform conjugation, those in "so," merely interpolating the reflex sibilant, as may be seen by comparing the aforegone samples of both. But the neuters in "to," here ensampled by bóto, are quite unique, leaning to the model of unchanging transitives with the same sign, for which see breto aforegone.

By comparing the above samples of complete conjugation with the summary view of the same subject which precedes it,* it will be seen that there is at bottom but one conjugation, because all transitives and intransitives follow the one general model, with the material exception, however, of the singular indicative. Of that the various forms are therefore brought together in the classification of so-called conjugations; and it is only necessary to add, that beyond the singular indicative of transitive verbs there are no deviations from the one model of conjugating in the three voices. The whole force of conjugation is, it will be seen, thrown upon the actors who do and suffer. Of the action itself there is little comparative heed, only two moods and two times being developed, and the active and passive voices being perplexed. There are not in fact any inflexional or inherent verbal forms to express the various modifications of the action. Nevertheless these modifications, of course, have periphrastic means of expression; I shall call them moods, and now proceed to enumerate them.

SUBJUNCTIVE OR CONDITIONAL MOOD.

If, or should, I come.

Indicative Present.

Singular.	*Dual.*	*Plural.*
1st *Per.* Pígna khedda	Písa khedda, incl. Písuku khedda, excl.	Píya khedda, incl. Píka khedda, excl.
2d *Per.* Píye khedda	Písi khedda	Píni khedda
3d *Per.* Pí khedda	Píse khedda	Píme khedda

Preterite.

1st *Per.* Pígnáwa khedda	Písawa khedda, incl. Pisukuwa khedda, excl.	Píyawa khedda, incl. Píkawa khedda, excl.
2d *Per.* Piyéwa khedda	Písiwa khedda	Píniwa khedda
3d *Per.* Píwa khedda	Písewa khedda	Pímewa khedda

The negative is formed, as usual, by má prefixed.

Another negative, allied if not equivalent, is impersonal, and substitutes the particle theum for khedda, adding the separate pronouns personal in lieu of the pronominal suffixes of verbs.

Should I not come, &c.

Present Tense.

1st *Per.* Gó má pítheum	Gósi má pítheum, incl. Gósuku má pítheum, excl,	Góyi má pítheum Góku má pítheum
2d *Per.* Ga má pítheum	Gasi má pítheum	Gani má pítheum
3d *Per.* Harem ma pítheum	Harem dausi má pítheum	Harem dau má pítheum

The preterite of this is formed by adding the "wa" above gone to the correlative part of the sentence; as, had I not come, he would not have come, gó má pítheum, harem má píwa.

In the present or future it is gó ma pítheum, harem má pí=should I come not, he will not come. In both forms of the conditional, wá, added to the indicative, takes the place of the regular preterite piti, pite, pita.

---

* To wit, Classification of Verbs, pp. 361–365.

CONTINGENT MOOD.

I may (perhaps) go.

It is expressed by the future in the alternative way, *e.g.*, lágna má lágna, má teutu = I shall go, shall not go, I don't know = I may go, or perhaps I shall go, perhaps not (root, la, to go).

POTENTIAL MOOD.

It is formed by adding ne to the root of any main verb (*e.g.*, la, to go), and then subjoining the several conjugational forms of the subsidiary verb to can, which is a regular transitive in "po." This not having been given above, shall be fully set down here, though it differ not much, save euphonically, from the foregone samples of transitives, especially bréto.*

Root, Chap, to can. Infinitive, Chap-cho.

Imperative.

Singular.	*Dual.*	*Plural.*
1. Láne chappo	Láne chapse	Láne chamne
2. Láne chapposi	Láne chapsesi	Láne chamnesi
3. Láne chappomi	Láne chapsemi	Láne chamnemi

Indicative Present (Future).†

First Person.

Singular	Dual	Plural
1. Láne chabu	Láne chapsa, incl.	Láne chamya, incl.
	Láne chapsuku, excl.	Láne chapka, excl.
2. Láne chabusi	Láne chapasi, incl.	Láne chamyasi, incl.
	Láne chapsukusi, excl.	Láne chapkasi, excl.
3. Láne chabumi	Láne chapsami, incl.	Láne chamyami, incl.
	Láne chapsukumi, excl.	Láne chapkami, excl.

Second Person.

Singular	Dual	Plural
1. Láne chabi	Láne chapsi	Láne chamni
2. Láne chabisi	Láne chapsisi	Láne chamnisi
3. Láne chabimi	Láne chapsimi	Láne chamnimi

Third Person.

Singular	Dual	Plural
1. Láne chaba	Láne chapse	Láne chamme
2. Láne chabasi	Láne chapsesi	Láne chammesi
3. Láne chabami	Láne chapsemi	Láne chammemi

Preterite.

First Person.

Singular	Dual	Plural
1. Láne chaptong	Láne chaptasa, incl.	Láne chaptayo, incl.
	Láne chaptasuku, excl.	Láne chaptako, excl.
2. Láne chaptongsi	Láne chaptasasi, incl.	Láne chaptayosi, *incl.*
	Láne chaptasukusi, excl.	Láne chaptakosi, *excl.*
3. Láne chaptongmi	Láne chaptasami, incl.	Láne chaptayomi, *incl.*
	Láne chaptasukumi, excl.	Láne chaptakomi, excl.

Second Person.

Singular	Dual	Plural
1. Láne chapteu	Láne chaptasi	Láne chaptani
2. Láne chapteusi	Láne chaptasisi	Láne chaptanisi
3. Láne chapteumi	Láne chaptasemi	Láne chaptanimi

Third Person.

Singular	Dual	Plural
1. Láne chapta	Láne chaptase	Láne chaptame
2. Láne chaptasi	Láne chaptasesi	Láne chaptamesi
3. Láne chaptami	Láne chaptasemi	Láne chaptamemi

---

* Compare chap-cho, chap-po, chab-u, chab-i, chab-a, chap-tong, cham-i, with bré-cho, bré-to, brét-u, brét-i, brét-a, brét-tong, bre-ti; and observe in regard to the former that its radical p becomes b before a vowel and m before a nasal (n. m.), but remains p before a sibilant or hard dental. It is so in all transitives in po, of all which chappo is a perfect sample.

† There is no present tense. The present is regarded as an inappreciable time. An act is not such till it is performed; hence the past is the main tense. But an act can be contemplated as during in intention and preparation; a blow falling till it has actually descended—future tense.

INFINITIVE MOOD.

Láne chapcho.

PARTICIPLES.

1st, in ba, Láne chapba, 2d, in chome, Láne chapchome, 3d, in na, Láne chamna,	Impersonal, as before.
4th, in me, Láne chabume, &c., 5th, in me, Láne chaptongme, &c.,	Personated, and formed by adding "me" to the tense forms.

GERUNDS.

1st, in na, Láne chabuna, &c., 2d, in na, Láne chaptongna, &c., 3d, in ko, Láne chabuko, &c., 4th, in ko, Láne chaptongko, &c.,	Personated all, and constructed as before by adding na or ko to the several tense forms. The impersonate past gerund is Láne chápso or chapsomami.

MIDDLE VOICE.

Lána chamso, and so on, precisely as in the verbs to eat and to summon.

PASSIVE VOICE.

IMPERATIVE MOOD.

1. Láne chamyi	Láne chapsiki	Láne chapki
2. Láne chamyisi	Láne chapsikisi	Láne chapkisi
3. Láne chamyini	Láne chapsikini	Láne chapkini

Indicative Present.

First Person.

1. Láne chamyi	Láne chapso, incl. Láne chapsiki, excl.	Láne chapso, incl. Láne chapki, excl.
2. Láne chamyisi	Láne chapsosi, incl. Láne chapsikisi, excl.	Láne chapsosi, incl. Láne chapkisi, excl.
3. Láne chamyimi	Láne chapsomi, incl. Láne chapsikimi, excl.	Láne chapsomi, incl. Láne chapkimi, excl.

Second Person.

1. Láne chamye	Láne chapsi	Láne chamni
2. Láne chamyesi	Láne chapsisi	Láne chamnisi
3. Láne chamyemi	Láne chapsimi	Láne chamnimi

Third Person.

1. Láne chaba	Láne chabasi	Láne chabami
2. Láne chapse	Láne chapsesi	Láne chapsemi
3. Láne chamme	Láne chammesi	Láne chammemi

Preterite.

First Person.

1. Láne chapti	Láne chaptaso, incl. Láne chaptasiki, excl.	Láne chaptaso, incl. Láne chaptaki, excl.
2. Láne chaptisi	Láne chaptasosi Láne chaptasikisi	Láne chaptasosi Láne chaptakisi
3. Láne chaptimi	Láne chaptasomi Láne chaptasikimi	Láne chaptasomi Láne chaptakimi

Second Person.

1. Láne chapte	Láne chaptasi	Láne chaptani
2. Láne chaptesi	Láne chaptasisi	Láne chaptanisi
3. Láne chaptemi	Láne chaptasimi	Láne chaptanimi

Third Person.

1. Láne chapta	Láne chaptasi	Láne chaptami
2. Láne chaptase	Láne chaptasesi	Láne chaptasemi
3. Láne chaptame	Láne chaptamesi	Láne chaptamemi

INFINITIVE.—It is wanting, as in all the passives.

PARTICIPLES.

1st, in ba, wanting	4th, in me, Láne chamyime, &c.
2d, in chome, Láne chapchome	5th, in me, Láne chaptime, &c.
3d, in na, Láne chamna	

GERUNDS.

1st, in na, Láne chamyina, &c.	3d, in ko, Láne chamyiko, &c.
2d, in na, Láne chaptina, &c.	4th, in ko, Láne chaptiko, &c.

Remark.—The precedent is given in full, first, because it affords a sample of transitives in "po;" second, because it demonstrates that these so-called moods are merely compound verbs, which (like the case signs) can be multiplied ad infinitum, but have little to do with grammar.

Duty, necessity; I must, or ought.

It is expressed by the impersonal use of the verb dyúm, to become, put after the main verb in the regular infinitive, with the separate objective pronoun preceding both.

IMPERATIVE—wanting.

INDICATIVE MOOD.

	Singular.	*Dual.*	*Plural.*
1st *Per.*	Gó lácho dyum *	Gósi lácho dyum, incl. Gósuku lácho dyum, excl.	Góyi lácho dyum Góku lácho dyum
2d *Per.*	Ga lácho dyum	Gasi lácho dyum	Gani lácho dyum
3d *Per.*	Harem lácho dyum	Haremdausi lácho dyum	Haremdau lácho dyum
		Preterite.	
1st *Per.*	Gó lácho dyumta	Gósi lácho dyumta Gósuku lácho dyumta	Góyi lácho dyumta Góku lácho dyumta
2d *Per.*	Ga lácho dyumta	Gasi lácho dyumta	Gani lácho dyumta
3d *Per.*	Harem lácho dyumta	Haremdausi lácho dyumta	Haremdau lácho dyumta

OPTATIVE MOOD.

Wish, desire.

Indicative Present.

	First Person.	
1. Wa lála dwáng	Isi lála dwáng, incl. Wasi lála dwáng, excl.	Íke lála dwáng Wake lála dwáng
	Second Person.	
2. Í lála dwáng	Ísi lála dwàng.	Íni lála dwáng
	Third Person.	
3. Á lála dwáng	Ási lála dwáng	A'ni lála dwáng
	Preterite.	
1. Wá lála dwakta	Ísi lála dwakta, incl. Wasi lála dwakta, excl.	Íke lála dwakta, incl. Wake lála dwakta excl.
2. Í lála dwakta	Ísi lála dwakta	Íni lála dwakta
3. Á lála dwakta	Ási láa dwakta	Áni lála dwakta

Formed of the conjunct possessives of lála, a verbal noun from lá, to go, and of dwáng, dwakta, the third person of the intransitive dwákko, to be desirous. Present and preterite used impersonally.

PRECATIVE MOOD.

Oh! that I might go.

Let me go.

Imperative.

1. Lácho giyi	Lácho gisiki	Lácho giki
2. Lácho giyisi	Lácho gisikisi	Lácho gikisi
3. Lácho giyini	Lácho gikisi	Lácho gikini

* Quasi mihi ire fit, *i.e.*, decet vel necesse est, in Khas, manlai janu parcha.

Indicative present.

First person.

1. Lácho gíyi	Lácho gíso Lácho gísiki	Lácho gíso Lácho gíki
2. Lácho gíyisi	Lácho gísoki Lácho gísikisi	Lácho gísosi Lácho gíkisi
3. Lácho gíyimi	Lácho gísomi Lácho gísikimi	Lácho gísomi Lácho gíkimi

And so on, conjugating the transitive gíwo, to give, in the passive voice, like the passive of jáwo, to eat, aforegone. Lácho gíyi = let me go, give me to go. But observe, that in order to say let *him* go, you must use the active voice, as below.

Singular.

Let me go, lácho gíyi
Let him go, lácho gíwo

Dual.

Let us two go, lácho gísiki
Let them two go, lácho gíwosi

Plural.

Let us all go, lácho gíki
Let them all go, lácho gíwomi

Remark.—If to these forms we add those of the middle voice, S. Lácho gíso, D. Lácho gísche, P. Lácho gísine, we have a good clue to the character of the three voices in this language, which are based upon the idea of me, the speaker, being the exponent of the passive; of self, the spoken to, being that of the middle; and of him, or her, or it, the spoken of, being that of the active voice. Gí-wo = give him: gí-so = give thyself: gí-yi = give me, are respectively the starting-points of the active, middle, and passive voices.

Interrogative Mood.

It resembles the indicative, lágná, I shall go, or shall I go?

Prohibitive and Negative Mood.

There is no separate form of the negative verb as in Dravidian tongues, nor even any prohibitive particle distinct from the negative.

Má prefixed expresses verbal negation and prohibition, and also nominal privation; *e.g.*, má jáwo, eat not; má jágna, I do not eat; má neuba, not good = bad.

Inceptive Mood.

It is formed by subjoining to the ordinary infinitive form (cho) of the main verb the subsidiary intransitive verb prénso, to begin, or the transitive páwo, to do, to make: *e.g.*, túcho páwo, begin to drink; túcho papta, he began to drink; jácho prénso, begin to eat; jácho prensigna, I begin to eat.

Finitive Mood.

It is formed as above, but substituting for páwo or prénso the transitive theummo (conficio), *e.g.*, jácho theummo, finish eating; jácho theumtong, I have done eating. Sometimes "ne" * replaces the infinitival "cho" of the main verb.

N.B.—The neuters ryipo (desino) and dyummo (fio), to be ended or to end, cannot be used in this way, and prénso, to be begun or to begin (self), is much rarer in such use than páwo. Ryipcho páwa is, it nears its end, literally it makes to an end, or to be ended.

Continuative Mood.

It is formed by adding sógno (sense doubtful) to the root of the main verb, and therewith conjugating the intransitive verb bwakko, to remain (see conj. III.), *e.g.*, continue eating, jásogno bwakko. *N.B.*—The definite present and past are also thus expressed.

Imperative.

Singular.	*Dual.*	*Plural.*
Jáso-gno bwakko, eat continuously or keep eating	Jáso-gno bwakse, incl.	Jáso-gno bwangne

* The infinitival sign varies, not always intelligibly. Where purpose is meant "tha" is the sign, as játha láti, I went to drink, *i.e.*, for the purpose of drinking. Where commencement and end are expressed, "ne" is more frequent than "cho," jáne prénsigna, jáne theumu, I shall begin to eat, and I shall have done eating. So also where wish is expressed, jáne dwaktong, I wished to eat. But cho is the common form, and always used alone, as jácho má jácho ágyom neu, which is better to eat or not to eat.

Indicative present.

	Singular.	*Dual.*	*Plural.*
1st *Per.*	Jáso-gno bwang-gna	Jásogno bwaksa, incl. Jásogno bwaksuku, excl.	Jásogno bwangya Jásogno bwakka
2d *Per.*	Jasogno bwangye	Jasogno bwaksi	Jasogno bwangni
3d *Per.*	Jasogno bwang	Jasogno bwakse	Jasogno bwamme *

Preterite.

1st *Per.*	Jasogno bwakti, I ate continuously, or I was eating	Jasogno bwaktasa, incl. Jasogno bwaktasuku, excl.	Jasogno bwaktayo Jasogno bwaktako
2d *Per.*	Jasogno bwakte	Jasogno bwaktasi	Jasogno bwaktani
3d *Per.*	Jasogno bwakta	Jasogno bwaktase	Jasogno bwaktame

Infinitive.

Jasogno bwakcho.

Participles.

1st, in ba, Jasogno bwakpa (ba). (Surd requires surd.)
2d, in chome, Jasogno bwakchome.
3d, in na, Jasogno bwangna.
4th, in me, Jasogno bwanggname, &c., eleven forms, ut supra.
5th, in me, Jasogno bwaktime, &c., ditto, ditto.

Gerunds.

1st, in na, Jasogno bwanggnana, &c., eleven forms.
2d, in na, Jasogno bwaktina, &c., ditto.
3d, in ko, Jasogno bwanggnako, &c., ditto.
4th, in ko, Jasogno bwaktiko, &c., ditto.

Remark.—The above is given in full as an exemplar of intransitives in "ko." The transitives of the same conjugation (III.) have the like *euphonic* changes, and for the rest their conjugation may be determined by analogy with the help of the premises already supplied. The indicative present singular alone varies, and that is set down in the classification of verbs. The radical "k" becomes "g" in the active voice, and "ng" in the passive and causal, *e.g.* pók-ko, póg-u, póng-yi, póng-páto.

ITERATIVE MOOD.

Raise repeatedly, pókko, mókho, bwákko.

It is formed by adding to the imperative of the main verb, whether transitive or intransitive, the word mókho (sense unknown), and to it subjoining the verb bwakcho, to remain, as in the last mood to which this is very nearly allied in sense. There, however, we have compound conjugation according to the sense of the primary and secondary verbs, which are both conjugated with mókho, immutable, between them, *e.g.*

Ípo mókho bwákho, sleep repeatedly	Pókko mókho bwákko, raise repeatedly
Ímgna mókho bwanggna, I sleep repeatedly	Pógu mókho bwanggna, I raise repeatedly
Ípti mókho bwakti, I slept repeatedly	Póktong mókho bwakti, I raised repeatedly

And so on through the whole of the intransitive conjugation in "po" (VI.) and of the transitive in "ko" (III.) The definite sense of the present and preterite, I am sleeping, I was sleeping, I am raising, I was raising, is likewise thus expressed.

Conjugation with auxiliar and substantive Verb and Participle.

Of the four substantive verbs, ká, khé, gnó, and bwá, the three first express essence and entity, the last presence, being in a certain place, corresponding respectively to the Khas ho and cha, and to the Newári kha and du, or chóna. Of the Báhing four, the last, or bwá, is alone used as an auxiliar, and it is compounded with the (apparent) participle or gerund aforegone, or jasogno, in order to make a definite present (or future) and past tenses of any and every verb in the manner

* Observe the change of the radical k into ng and m, bwak-ko, bwang-gna, bwam-me It is constant in all verbs neuter in "ko."

there seen, *e.g.*, písogno bwanggna, I am coming; písogno bwakti, I was coming; teupsogno bwanggna, I am beating; teupsogno bwakti, I was beating.

Remark.—Jásógno, which gives the continuative and the definite form of the tenses above, seems to spring from the impersonal past gerund in "so," jaso vel jasomami. But that is not clear, though it *be* so that, whatever else jasogno is, it is a form of every verb usable with the auxiliar in conjugation.

Jásogno bwanggna = I am eating.	Písogno bwakti = I was coming.
Jásogno bwakti = I was eating.	Brésogno bwanggna = I am summoning.
Písogno bwanggna = I am coming.	Brésogno bwakti = I was summoning.

Compound Verbs with each element conjugated.

Jwagdíwo, to arrive.*

IMPERATIVE MOOD.

	Singular.	*Dual.*	*Plural.*
	Jwagdíwo †	Jwagdíse	Jwagdíne
		Indicative present.	
1st Per.	Jwanggnadígna	Jwaksadísa, incl. / Jwaksudísuku, excl.	Jwangyadíya, incl. / Jwakkadíka, excl.
2d Per.	Jwanggnedíye	Jwaksidísi	Jwangnidíni
3d Per.	Jwangnidí	Jwaksedíse	Jwangmedíme
		Preterite.	
1st Per.	Jwaktidíti	Jwaktasadítasa / Jwaktasudítasuku	Jwaktayodíntayo / Jwaktakodíntako
2d Per.	Jwaktedíte	Jwaktasidítasi	Jwaktanidíntani
3d Per.	Jwaktadíta	Jwaktasedítase	Jwaktamedímtame

INFINITIVE MOOD.

Jwakchodícho.

Participles.

1st, in ba, Jwakpadíba.
2d, in chome, Jwakchodíchome, &c.
3d, in na, Jwangnadína, &c.
4th, in me, Jwanggnamedígname, &c.
5th, in me, Jwaktimedítime, &c.

Gerunds.

Impersonal of the present none.
Impersonal of the past, Jwaksomamidísomani or Jwaksodíso.

Personated Gerunds.

1st, Jwanggnadígnana, } present.
2d, Jwaktidítina, } present.
3d, Jwanggnadígnako, } past.
4th, Jwaktadítako, } past.

Causal Verbs.‡

All verbs whatever can be made causal by adding to their root the transitive verb páto, from pá,§ to do or make. But pá makes its regular transitive in "wo," páwo.

* Jwákko is an intransitive in "ko," meaning to arrive, and it can be conjugated separately; but, with that love of specialisation which is so characteristic of Kiránti verbs, it is always used in conjunction with the verb to come (píwo) or to go (díwo). Jwagdíwo as a single word can be also so conjugated. The remarkable thing is that each verb of the compound can be conjugated.

† You can also say Jwakkodíwo, using the full form of each verb in the imperative as in the indicative.

‡ Besides its ordinary use, the causal form of the verb is frequently used, especially in its middle voice, as a passive. Thus, jápáso is be thou eaten, or suffer thyself to be eaten, implying voluntariness on the part of the patient; and so hémpáso is let thyself be kissed. All three voices, however, can be used thus, and frequently are so, whenever the complex pronominalisation of the primary verb causes embarrassment. The passive use of the causal is very common in Himálaya, and is often, as in Newári, the only substitute for a passive. This is not wonderful in so crude a tongue as Newári: it is so, however, in the Kiránti language, which possesses the great secret of the most refined conjugation in its neat personal suffixes and its power of euphonic compounding. Owing, however, to too much attention to the agents and too little to the action, the Kiránti verb, with all its constructive richness on one side, shows equal poverty on another, and hence the passive use of the causal form.

§ The root pá, pí, in Váyu, an allied Himálayan tongue, is the same as the Dravidian causative.

Páwo is do; páto, do for him, on his behalf; and this leads me to observe that every transitive verb, save those in "to," has the following six forms:—

1. Teuppo, strike him, active transitive in "po."
2. Teum-so, strike thyself, reflex transitive, or middle, in "so."
3. Teum-yi, strike me, passive in "i."
4. Teup-to, strike it for him, active transitive in "to."
5. Teum-so, strike it for thyself, middle in "so."
6. Teupti, strike it for me, passive in "ti."

So also pá, to do, has pá-wo, páso, páyi; páto, páso, and páti: and kwó, to see, has kwógno, kwóso, kwóyi; kwoto, kwoso, and kwoti: and pok, to raise, has pokko, pokso, pongyi; pokto, pokso, pokti; and in like manner every other transitive, except those in "to" as the primary form. It is the secondary form of the transitive of the verb to make, or páto, which is used for constructing causals, but yet it takes the passives in "i," not "ti," when thus employed, though, when used separately, it assumes its regular form in "ti"—an anomaly, like that of the use of the reflex or middle voice in one form and two senses (2, 5).

But besides the regular causal formed by páto added to the root of the main verb (*e.g.*, kwopáto, cause to see), there are other means of constructing causals, which shall be first mentioned before proceeding to exhibit the conjugation of the former.

These means are, first, the hardening of the initial consonant of an intransitive, as—

Dokko, fall.	Tokko, cause to fall
Dyúmmo, become	Thyúmmo,* cause to become
Gúkko, be crooked	Kúkko, crooken or make crooked
Gíkko, be born	Kíkko, beget or give birth to
Jíto, be torn	Chíto, tear
Bokko, get up	Pokko, raise, or make get up
Bukko, be burst	Pukko, burst

Second, by dropping the intransitive sign, whatever it be, and substituting the transitive sign in "to," or "ndo" (do).

Píwo, come	Píto, bring
Ráwo, come	Ráto, bring
Díwo, go	Díto, take away
Láwo, go	Láto, take away
Kúwo, come up	Kúto, bring up
Yúwo, come down	Yúto, bring down
Dwakko, be desirous or long	Dwaktō, desire it, or long for it
Túgno, drink	Túndo, cause to drink
Wogno, issue	Wondo, extract
Glúgno, enter	Glúndo, insert
Cháyinso, learn	Cháyindo, teach, *i.e.*, cause to learn
Níso, sit	Níto, set down, or seat him, or cause to sit
Khleuso, lie hid	Khleundo, hide it

I need not point out what an important analogy with the Dravidian tongues the first (nay, both) of these two processes presents, but I may add that this analogy is in perfect keeping with the further habit of this Himálayan language of hardening or doubling the indicative present sign by way of making a preterite, as

Myelda, he is sleepy	Myelta, he was sleepy
Sáda, he kills	Sáta, he killed
Kwáda, he puts on the fire	Kwáta, he put on the fire
Gramda, he hates	Gramta, he hated
Teuba, he strikes	Teupta, he struck
Bréta, he summons	Brétta, he summoned
Khleuta, he conceals	Khleutta, he concealed
Soda, he tells it	Sotta, he told it

Add the absence of conjunctive (relative) pronouns, and of conjunctions proper (and), with the manner in which these are replaced, and all sentences held together,

* Perhaps tyummo; hardening or aspirating, rarely both. But there are a few instances of it in Báhing and also in Váyu—as dum, become; thumto, cause to become.

by participles carrying an inherent relative-pronoun sense, and by gerunds which are essentially copulative. It is, however, but fair to add that these are traits by no means exclusively Dravidio-Himálayan. Still they are a sound part of the answer which may be given to those who, like Caldwell, assert that there is nothing Dravidian in the languages of Himálaya.*

Add to these analogies the common habit of Báhing and Támil of annexing the conjugational sign to the imperative, and that that sign is differently applied to intransitives and transitives (leaving the style of the indicative to difference them); and further that the conjunct pronomenalisation of their verbs and nouns is by prefixing in regard to the nouns and suffixing in regard to the verbs, not to mention several other analogies cited in the sequel, and Messrs. Müller and Caldwell will find it difficult to maintain their assertion that there is nothing Dravidian in the structure of the Himálayan tongues!

Many verbs identical in form in the imperative, yet differ in sense, as khiwo, n., tremble, and khíwo, a., quarrel; úto, n., fall, úto, a., fell. Many, again, materially change their sense in passing into the causal or transitive form from the intransitive or neuter; and, lastly, the causal form of neuters and of transitives, though very generally of the normal construction in páto added to the root (ippo, sleep; impáto, cause to sleep), yet in the case of many verbs of both sorts in "po" and in "gno" is not so, the alteration being effected by changing their sign into the transitive "to" vel "do" sign, as ippo, sleep; ipto, cause to sleep (a synonyme of impáto); túgno, drink; túndo (= tupáto), cause to drink. When the sense is much altered in such transition, the derivative causal of a neuter is constantly regarded as an independent word and primitive verb, and the neuter takes the normal causal form, thus láwo, n. = go, has láto for its causal; but láto being used to signify take away, lápáto is made to express the precise sense of cause to go.

All this shows, when taken in connection with the general transformability of all transitives not primitively in "to" into that form, the pre-eminent transitive and preterite character of that widely-diffused sign.

It also shows how apt causal is to be equivalent to transitive, another widely-prevailing Turanian trait, and one harmonising with the almost identity of neuter and intransitive. And here we may remark another special characteristic common to the Himálayan and Dravidian tongues, viz., double causation. Thus, in Báhing (and it is the same in many others of our tongues), ippo, sleep; impáto, cause to sleep; impápáto, cause to cause to sleep. Gikko, be born; kikko or gingpáto, cause to be born; kingpáto or gingpapáto, cause to cause to be born; to which we may add kingpápáto, expressing causation in the *third* degree from the primitive gikko; and the like holds good with regard to every neuter undergoing a similar change with gikko.

I proceed now to exhibit an exemplar of the normal causative form of verbs, taking the instance of the verb to eat. Root, já; causal transitive, jápáto; causal reflex, jápáso; causal passive, jápáyi. The prefixed root does not affect the grammatical form of the auxiliars save as above stated. Páto, therefore, in this combination, will afford a sample of all transitives in "to" which change the t into d. Of the unchanging transitives in "to" I have given a model in bréto. I shall here give páto in full in its combination with já, as a sample of the changing conjugation in "t" (see conjugation X.), merely premising that páso, as an intransitive in "so" (see conjugation XIII.), and páyi, as a passive in "i" (yi to keep the vowels apart merely†), have already been given in full, as also the passive in "ti" (vide bréto).

---

* See note at p. 356.

Teub-u, I strike	Wa popo, my uncle	*Remark.*—Wa, i, a, the pronominal adjuncts, are perfectly distinct from the separate pronouns; and wa being = u, the adjuncts of verb and noun tally to identity. Here, then, is the alleged diagnosis of Dravidianism more fully developed than in any Dravidian tongue.
Teub-i, thou strikest	I popo, thy uncle	
Teub-a, he strikes	A popo, his uncle	
Pog-u, I raise	Wagu, my hand	
Pog-i, thou raisest	I gu, thy hand	
Pog-a, he raises	A gu, his hand	
Bret-u, I summon	Wa daubo, myself	
Bret-i, thou summon'st	I' daubo, thyself	
Bret-a, he summons	A daubo, himself	

† M also requires the y; for example, teum-yi, strikes me, he, or thou = I am struck; see remarks aforegone. It is because the *agent* may be he *or* thou (any one) in the passive, that the passive runs so near parallel with the second *special* form of the verb.

Paradigm of a Causal Verb.

ACTIVE VOICE.

Imperative Mood.

	Singular of Agent.	*Dual of Agent.*	*Plural of Agent.*
1.	Jápáto	Jápáse	Jápáne
	Dual of Object.	*Dual of Object.*	*Dual of Object.*
2.	Jápátosi	Jápásesi	Jápánesi
	Plural of Object.	*Plural of Object.*	*Plural of Object.*
3.	Jápátomi	Jápásemi	Jápánemi

Indicative Mood.

Present and Future Tense.

First Person.

	Singular.	*Dual.*	*Plural.*
1.	Japadu	Jápása, incl. Jápasúkú, excl.	Jápáya, incl. Jápáka, excl.
2.	Jápádusi	Jápásasi, incl. Jápásúkúsi, excl.	Jápáyosi, incl. Jápákosi, excl.
3.	Jápádumi	Jápásami, incl. Jápásúkúmi, excl.	Jápáyomi, incl. Jápákomi, excl.

Second Person.

1.	Jápádi	Jápási	Jápáni
2.	Jápádisi	Jápásisi	Jápánisi
3.	Jápádimi	Jápásimi	Jápánimi

Third Person.

1.	Jápáda	Jápáse	Jápáme
2.	Jápádasi	Jápásesi	Jápámesi
3.	Jápádami	Jápásemi	Jápámemi

Preterite.

First Person.

1.	Jápátong	Jápátasa, incl. Jápátasuku, excl.	Jápátayo, incl. Jápátako, excl.
2.	Jápátongsi	Jápátasasi, incl. Jápátasukusi, excl.	Jápátayosi, incl. Jápátakosi, excl.
3.	Jápátongmi	Jápátasami, incl. Jápátasukumi, excl.	Jápátayomi, incl. Jápátakomi, excl.

Second Person.

1.	Jápáteu	Jápátasi	Jápátani
2.	Jápáteusi	Jápátasisi	Jápátanisi
3.	Jápáteumi	Jápátasimi	Jápátanimi

Third Person.

1.	Jápáta	Jápátase	Jápátame
2.	Jápátasi	Jápátasesi	Jápátamesi
3.	Jápátami	Jápátasemi	Jápátamemi *

* Observe for a moment the singular neatness, euphony, and precision of these forms. The single words jápátamesi and jápátamemi must be rendered into English by they all fed them two and they all fed them all; into Newári, by amisang, aminihma yata nakala, and amisang amita nakala. And but for the happy term to feed in English the distinction would be greater still. In Khas the equivalents are, uni heru le ú uwi lai khuwaiyo and uni heru le ú heru lai khuwaiyo, or seven words for one!

INFINITIVE MOOD.

Jápácho, aoristic as usual.

Participles.

1st, in ba, Jápába, who feeds or will or did feed.

2d, in chome, Jápáchome, feedable, whom or with what any one feeds or will feed.

3d, in na, Jápána, fed, whom or with what any one has fed.

4th, in me, Jápádume, &c., thirty-three forms. Feedable by me; whom or with what I feed or will feed, &c.

5th, in me, Jápátongme, &c., thirty-three forms. The fed of me; whom or with what I fed, &c.

N.B.—1–3 are impersonal, as before; 4–5 are personated.

Gerunds.

Non-personated of the present and future, none.
Non-personated of the past, Jápáso, or Jápásomami.

Personated Present.

1st, in na, Jápáduna, &c., thirty-three forms.
2d, in na, Jápátongna, &c., thirty-three forms.

Personated Past.

1st, in ko, Jápádúko, &c., thirty-three forms.
2d, in ko, Jápátóngko, &c., thirty-three forms.

SPECIMEN OF THE KÍRÁNTI LANGUAGE (BÁHING DIALECT).

Kwóng múryeu hópo ke di brétha * látá. Gyékhopáso brétha dáyána. Wa khyim di kwóng múryeu, rásogno bwaktako, wa ming nung dwángmóse. Gó harem gyánaiyo má tágna, syú, syú. Íke nyau ásra jajulso, myem sícho, láma, dáso, binti † pápta.

Mokoding hópomi harem kwóng rí nyúba gyáwa dyampattame sísi giptako chyanta, yem sísi í ming giptako, syúyo má giwo, dáso, lópáso, gíwo. Hárem múryeumi myem khógno pápṭa. Hópomi yo chíwacha dau brétamiko chyantámi. Syuke di rínyuba gyáwa rínám, myem rácho.

Mékeding ryamnípo béla † kwósomami ming ke di díta. Myem mingmi wádi rínyúba gyáwa khlyakti giptáko mócho prénsta, mára dáyana, wa wancha mi syú (or sú) má gíwo mótime bwá. Naka ga wa ram khome bwagne, i kamdi mára khéda syu ke kam di ra data

---

* See note on the infinitive at p. 367.

† *N.B.*—Nyau, ásra, binti, and béla are Hindi terms having no precise equivalent in the Kiránti tongue. Though it would be easy to turn the phrases so as to replace them by pure Kiránti terms, I leave them as samples of a process everywhere going on in the Central Himálaya, whose still primitive languages will probably in time become first mixed and then obsolete.

(or móta). Mékeding ryamnípo khyim ding glutana chìwachadaúmi á rí tamtameko, myem simtámeko, hópo ke di chótha dimtame.

Mékeding hópomi á wancha brétako, móta, yem í ryamnipo, dwákti khedda chyáro, dwakti khedda plyénti gíwo (or plyenotako) dáso dáta.

TRANSLATION.

A certain person went to his prince to complain of a man who was in the habit of coming constantly to his house to make love to his wife, but whom he could never contrive to identify. To his sovereign he said, "Relying on your justice, I appeal to you to have this man arrested." The Rájah thereon gave the petitioner a phial filled with scented oil, and said to him, "Give this phial to your wife, and caution her at the same time not to give it to any one." The man did as he was bade, and the Rájah, when he was gone, instructed his spies to look after the matter, and to seize and bring to his presence any person they might detect coming from the plaintiff's house whose clothes had the scent of atter.

By and by, the lover, finding an opportunity, went as before to his mistress, who rubbed the atter on his clothes, and said to him, "My husband desired me to give this atter to no one, but you are my life, my soul, how should I refuse it to you? If you like it, take it. I can have no other use for it."

As the lover, thus anointed with atter, thereafter left the house of his mistress, the spies of the Rájah, who were on the look-out for him, seized him and carried him to the Rájah.

The Rájah thereon sent for the woman's husband, and said to him, "This is your wife's lover. If you please, kill him; if you please, let him go."

END OF BÁHING GRAMMAR.

V.

ON THE VÁYU OR HÁYU TRIBE OF THE CENTRAL HIMÁLAYA.

THE Váyus, vulgarly called Háyús, inhabit the central Himálaya, and the central region of that part of the chain.* They are subjects of Népál, tenanting the basin of the river Kósi between the confines of the great valley of Népál proper and that point where the Kósi turns southwards to issue into the plains. The Váyus belong to that interesting portion of the Himálayan population which, in the essay adverted to, I have denominated the broken tribes—tribes whose status and condition, relatively to those of the unbroken tribes, sufficiently demonstrate that they are of much older standing in Himálaya than the latter. The Váyus are in an exceedingly depressed condition, gradually passing to extinction probably. Their numbers do not now exceed a few thousands—how many, I have no means of ascertaining.

Their high antiquity and the complex character of their language, give them, especially in connection with other tribes of Himálaya similarly characterised, very great interest as an element of Himálayan population. They consider themselves as a single people distinct from all their neighbours. Their language, which has no marked dialects, and is quite unintelligible to any but themselves, supports this view. So also does their perfect community of habits and customs, though they recognise certain distinctions among themselves, of no practical importance, but marked by specific designations, of which the chief are Yákúm, Dóphóm, Konsino, Bálung, Phoncho, Kámaléchho, &c.

Bálung, I know, means exorcist in the Váyu tongue; and the other terms probably point to some perhaps now forgotten avocations. At all events, the people cannot now explain the force of the terms.

They have a tradition of a very remote time when they were a numerous and powerful people; but never having had the use of writing, their remote past is too vague for ascertain-

* See new edition of Essay on Physical Geography of Himálaya, printed under the auspices of Government.

ment: no foreign and cultivated people having ever noticed and recorded * their existence. The religious ideas of the Váyus are extremely vague, nor does their language afford any term for *the* Deity, or even for *any* deity; though they have, as usual, an exorcist, who is their only priest and physician, and to whom they look for relief from all those evils which malignant influence, whatever it be, afflicts them with. They are a very inoffensive industrious race, employed in the cultivation of the earth. Their use of the plough is noticeable from its rarity in these regions.

As it has been the chief object of this paper to illustrate the highly interesting language † of the Váyus, I shall not at present say more of their status, manners, and customs than by a reference to their own account of these conveyed in the statement subjoined to the language, as a sample thereof, and of which translation was there furnished. ‡

But the physical traits of the Váyu are of an importance second only to that of his language, and the following description will help to illustrate them:—

Dimensions of a man named Páte, a Váyu of the Yákúm caste, aged twenty-eight years, in the service of Captain Gajráj Thápa of Népál. §

	ft.	in.
Height, ...	5	0
Crown of head to hip, ...	1	11½
Hip to heel, ...	3	0½
Length of arm and hand, . . .	2	2½
Girth of head, ...	1	9
Girth of arm, ...	0	9
Girth of forearm, ...	0	9½
Girth of thigh, ...	1	6
Girth of calf, ...	1	1
Girth of chest, ...	2	11

* Are not our Háyús, or Haiyus, the Haivas of Lakshmídhara's Shadbháshâchandriká, wherein he truly calls them Mountain barbaroi? See Muir's Sanscrit Texts, *ii.* 59. See also *i.* 181, *voce* Haihayas, Haihayas = Haivas = Haiyus = Háyus = Váyus.

† *I meant to have prefaced the linguistic details by a few general remarks under the usual heads of Article, Noun, Pronoun, &c.; but time runs short, and the philological reader will readily apprehend these from the details themselves, whilst other classes of readers are little likely to pay any attention to the matter.*

‡ See pp. 317–19.

§ See xxvii. Report for several of the other tribes.

Páte is rather below than above the standard height of his fellows, which may be taken at about five feet three inches. His colour is a pure isabelline brown, without the least trace of ruddiness in the skin or hair. The eye is dark hazel, and the hair long, straight, black, ample on the head, scant everywhere else.

Vertical view of the head oblate ovoid, rather wider behind than before, but not much, and flattish behind.

Bachycephalic. Facial angle very good, the mouth being only moderately salient, and the forehead of good height, forwardness, and breadth, but the chin defective. Eyebrows even, scantish. No beard or whisker, and a very small moustache. Eyes small, flush with the cheek, oblique, very wide apart, drooping upper lid bent down at the inner angle. Nose rather short, straight, depressed between the eyes, moderately salient elsewhere, broad at end, and having large round nostrils. Mouth moderately salient, the peculiar thickening of the upper gum, which chiefly causes the saliency, being not great, and the lips not tumid, only moderately full. Teeth vertically set, strong, white. Chin retiring and small. Zygomata and cheek-bones very salient to the sides, and profile flat. Front view of the face squarish, owing to the large angular jaws, which are as salient laterally as the zygomata.

Remark.—This young man's physiognomy is distinguished by the full Turanian breadth of head and face. Two others of his race whom I examined—a man of fifty-eight years and another of thirty years—had not the same breadth nor the same perfectly Kalmac eye. These men measured nearly five feet five inches, and were several shades darker in colour than Páte; and upon the whole I incline to regard them as more normal samples of the race than Páte. In a word, I think that I have sufficient grounds for concluding that the Váyus are in general somewhat darker and of a less decidedly Mongolic cast of countenance than the Lepchas (for example), from whose perfectly Turanian type they lean towards the Túrkic and Dravidian sub-types, which again approach the Arian, and are seen in the Kiránti tribe of the Himálaya more clearly and more frequently than in the Váyu tribe.

The elder of the two individuals above adverted to I was

enabled to examine rapidly whilst Mr. Scott photographed him. He was five feet four inches and a half in height, moderately fleshy, and dark brown. Vertical view of the head oblate. Wider and flat behind, greatest breadth between the ears, rising pyramidally from the zygomata to the crown of the head. Facial angle not bad, the forehead retiring, and narrowing only slightly, the mouth not being porrect, nor the chin retiring but pointed. Eyes remote, not small, but the upper lids flaccid and somewhat down-curved at the inner canthus. Nose pyramidal, not levelled between the eyes nor the extremity much thickened, but the nares large and round. Mouth large but well formed, with neatly-shaped lips and vertical fine teeth.

The younger man above alluded to was five feet five inches, and as dark as an ordinary native of the plains, whom he further resembled in his unflattened face, though his eye wanted the fulness and shapeliness of that of the lowlanders beside whom I placed him.

When these Háyús were placed beside some Dhángars of the Uráon tribe, the impression made upon me by a comparison of the whole was, that the physical type is one and the same in the highlanders and lowlanders; that the type is flexible to a large extent; and that the general effect of the northman's residence for ages in the malarious and jungly swamps of the plains is to cause the Turanian type to incline toward the Negro type, but with a wide interval from the latter. The Uráon, compared with the Váyu, has less breadth of head and face, more protuberance of mouth, and a better-shaped, larger eye, not down-curved next the nose; and it is thus, I conceive, that the Negro type differs from the Turanian.

VI.

ON THE KIRÁNTI TRIBE OF THE CENTRAL HIMÀLAYA.

It has been the main purpose of one of the preceding papers to examine the grammatical structure of the Kiránti language, as a second sample of that class of Himálayan tongues (the

Váyu tongue, already examined, being the first) which I have elsewhere denominated the pronomenalised or complex.*

The opinion of such scholars as Müller and Caldwell, that the Himálayan tongues have nothing Dravidian about them, can thus be tested, and, I think, shown to be a mistake; and it will be further demonstrated, I trust, by these and other investigations which I hope soon to complete, that the Himálayans are closely connected as well with the southern as with the northern members of the family of Túr—members by no means so disjoined and dissimilar as it is the fashion to represent them.

As a supplement to the grammatical details, I will now give such a sketch of the Kiránti people, as at present existing in Népál, as will, I hope, add to the interest and value of the philological portion of my essay.

The Kirántis, on account of their distinctly traceable antiquity as a nation and the peculiar structure of their language, are perhaps the most interesting of all the Himálayan races, not even excepting the Néwárs of Népál proper.

By means of the notices contained in the classics of the East and West, we are assured that the Kiránti people was forthcoming in their present abode from 2000 to 2500 years back, and that their power was great and their dominion extensive, reaching possibly at one time to the delta of the Ganges. Moreover, the general tenor of these classical notices is confirmed by the Vansávalis, or chronicles of Népál proper, which show a long line of Kiránti sovereigns ruling there from the mythic age of the Shepherd kings (Gópál) down to the fourteenth century of our era. And, lastly, these distinct historical data harmonise with a well-known tradition, which assigns a very unusual (in these regions) amount of power and population to the "many-tongued" Kiránti. We know not when the Kirántis were expelled from the plains of India; if indeed they ever held permanent possession there. But it was the Mall dynasty of Népál proper which, about the middle of the fourteenth century, expelled them from the great valley; and the Sáhs of the eastern or Vijayapur branch of the Makwánis, by whom their independence in the mountains, probably about the same period, was

* See Essay on Physical Geography of Himálaya, and other papers, issued under the auspices of Government.

greatly trenched on; whilst the Sáhs of the house of Gorkha, now sovereigns of the modern kingdom of Népál, completed the subjection of the Kirántis about a century ago.

Adverting to the high recorded antiquity of the terms Kirát or Kiránt and Kiráti or Kiránti (vague nasal), as applied respectively to the country and people even to this hour, it is remarkable that the Kirántis themselves do not readily admit the genuineness or propriety of those terms, but prefer the names Khwombo vel Khombo and Kiráwa as their general personal designations, and seem to have none at all for their country. But the Kirántis, always ignorant of letters, have been now for a long time depressed and subdued; and, huddled as they now are into comparatively narrow limits, they are yet divided among themselves into numerous tribes and septs, speaking dialects so diverse as not to be mutually intelligible; and hence they are wont to think only of their sectional names, and to forget their general or national one.

It is difficult, owing to the varying limits at diverse eras, to ascertain the precise force of the territorial term Kiránt in the view of the people themselves. But the following statement of boundaries, divisions, and included septs may, I believe, be considered sufficiently accurate for all present purposes:—

Kiránt.

1. Wallo Kiránt or Hither Kiránt.	2. Mánjh Kiránt or Middle Kiránt.	3. Pallo Kiránt or Further Kiránt.*
	Respective tribes.	
Yákha.	Bontáwa.	Chourasya.
Límbu.	Ródong.	
Lóhorong.	Dungmáli.	
Chhingtáng.	Kháling.	
	Dúmi.	
	Sángpáng.	
	Báláli.	
	Lambichhong.	
	Báhing.	
	Thúlung.	
	Kúlung.	
	Waling.	
	Nachhereng.	

* Khas terms, and bearing topical reference to the Khas metropolis in the valley of Népál proper.

This is Kiránt in the larger sense, and including Khwombuán or Kiránt proper, and Limbuán or the country of the Limbus. The popular inclusion of the latter people is important and, I believe, well founded, as also that of the Yákhas, though both are often alleged to be not Kirántis. They are at all events closely-allied races, having essential community of customs and manners with the Kirántis, and they all intermarry; nor, probably, do the dialects of the Limbus and Yákhas differ much more from the Khwombu * tongue, than that tongue now does from itself, as seen in the several dialects of the septs set down above under "Middle Kiránt." The comparative vocabulary already submitted to the Society will go far to decide these questions, when taken in connection with that grammatical analysis of the Limbu tongue which I am now engaged on. The boundaries of Kiránt, in its three subdivisions, are:—

1. Súnkósi to Likhu, } Khwombuán.
2. Likhu to Árun, }
3. Árun to Mêchi and Singilela ridge, } Limbuán.

Such are the territorial limits of the extant Kiránti race, in the larger sense. Their numbers probably do not now exceed a quarter of a million; but the tradition, which I referred to above, assigns two and a quarter millions as the amount of their population at some remote and not well ascertained period, when their country was customarily spoken of as the "no lákh Kiránt," and the phrase was interpreted to mean that a house-tax, at two annas per family, yielded nine hundred thousand annas, whence, if we allow five souls to a family, we shall obtain two and a quarter millions of people for the Kirántis, inclusive of the Limbus and Yákhas, † and possibly the Váyús

* Potius Khambo. The intercalated "w" is a dialectic peculiarity of Báhing. Khombo = Khampa, whence we may infer that the Kirántis came from Eastern Tibet or Kham.

† See Tennant's "Ceylon," voce Aborigines, and there called Yakkhos. The identity of name is at all events curious, more especially as there is much resemblance of form, manners, and customs between the aborigines of the Himálaya and of Ceylon; *e.g.*, the "devil dance" of the Yakkhos of Ceylon tallies wonderfully with a similar ceremony described by me in the essay on the "Kócch, Bódo, and Dhimál," vol. i. 133 f. The Mahavansa refers to a certain Yakho who dwelt in Himálaya and became a teacher of Buddhism. This, too, is significant, and imports that one of the Yakha tribes of Himálaya was converted and instructed by some Bauddha sage or Vihar establishment, and sent into the hills to make proselytes among the hill-men.

also. The Kirántis occupy the central or healthful region of the mountains, and never descend, to dwell there, into the lowest and malarious valleys of that region. Consequently, they are not reckoned among the Áwalias, or tribes inured to malaria. Nor can they be placed among the broken tribes, great as is their antiquity and devoid as they long have been of political independence, and, moreover, allied as they are by the character of their language to the above two sections of the population of Himálaya or the Áwalias and the broken tribes (see Essay referred to above). The chiefs, or kings, of the Kirántis were called Hang or Hwang. There are, of course, none such now, nor have been for five centuries. Their village headman they still denominate Pasung, equivalent to Rai in the Khas tongue of their present masters the Gorkhalis. The Pasung has still, under the Gorkhali dynasty, a good deal of authority over his people. He collects their taxes and adjusts their disputes with but rare reference or appeal to the Rajah's courts.

Unlike most of the subjects of Népál, the Kirántis retain possession of the freeholds of their ancestors, which they call walikha, and the owner, thangpung hangpa. Each holding is extensive, though not generally available, owing to the high slope of the surface, for the superior sort of culture. The boundaries of an estate are defined by the run of the water. The tax paid to the Government by each landholder, or thangpung hangpa (literally, lord of the soil), is five rupees per annum, four being land-tax, and one in commutation of the corvée.

The general style of cultivation is that appropriate to the uplands, not the more skilful and profitable sort practised in the level tracts; and though the villages of the Kirántis be fixed, yet their cultivation is not so, each proprietor within his own ample limits shifting his cultivation perpetually, according as any one spot gets exhausted.

Arva in annos mutant et superest ager. The plough is sometimes used, but very rarely, and the use of it at all is recent and borrowed, nor has the language any term for a plough. The produce is maize, buckwheat, millets, pease, dry rice, and cotton. The general, almost exclusive, status of this people is that of agriculturists. They did not till lately take military or menial service.* They have no craftsmen of their own tribe, but buy iron implements, copper utensils, and ornaments for their women from other tribes, and supply most of their simple wants themselves. The useful arts they practise are all domestic; fine arts they have none, nor ever had; no towns, and only small villages of huts raised obliquely on the outer side on wooden posts some three to six feet, so as to get a level on the slope of the hill, size small, because the children separate on marriage, walls of thick reed, plastered, and the pent roof of grass. Each family builds for itself. The women spin and weave the cotton of native growth, which constitutes their sole wear, and the men and women dye the clothes with madder and with other wild plants—whereof one, a climber, yields a fine black colour. They make fermented and distilled liquors for themselves, and use the former in great quantities—the latter moderately.

The Kirántis have not, nor ever had, letters or literature.† Their religious notions are very vague. They have no name for the God of gods, nor even for any special deity whatever, though the term "mang" may be construed deity, and that of "khyimmo" or "khyimmang," household deity or penate. Nor is there any hereditary priesthood, or any class set apart and educated for that office. Whom the mang inspires, he is a priest, and his duty is to propitiate the Khyimmang or Penate of each family by an annual worship celebrated after the harvest, and also to perform certain trivial ceremonies at marriages and deaths, but not at births. The priest is named Nakchhong, and he has, moreover, once a year, to make offerings to the manes (samkha) of the ancestors of each householder, or rather to all the deceased members of each family.

The Kirántis believe heartily in the black art, and call its professor Krákrá, Kúnyamayáwo, &c. The professional anta-

* Jang Bahadur has lately raised some Kiránti regiments. He is wise, and has seen in time and provided against the risk of a too homogeneous army. The Kirántis have of late freely taken menial service with us in Sikim.

† The Limbus, like the Lepchas, have an alphabet seemingly original, but neither people has made much use of it. I submitted these alphabets to the native and English scholars of Madras, Ava, and Arrakan, and was told they could not be traced to any Indo-Chinese or Dravidian source. I had priorly received a like disclaimer from the Lamas of Tibet.

gonist of this formidable person, who undoes the mischief, bodily or mental, which the other had done, who is at once exorcist and physician, is named in the various dialects, Janicha, Mangpa, &c.

There are only two religious festivals per annum: one to the Khyimmo or Penate, and the other to the samkha or souls of the deceased.

As already said, birth is not attended by any religious observances.

The Kirántis buy their wives, paying usually twenty-five to thirty rupees, frequently in the shape of copper household utensils. If they have no means, they go and earn their wife by labour in her father's family. They marry usually at maturity —nay, almost universally so. Divorce can always be had at the pleasure of either party; but if the wife seek it, she or her family must give back the price paid for her, and all the children will remain with the husband in every event of divorce. The marriage ceremony is as follows:—The priest takes a cock in his left hand and strikes it on the back with the blunt side of a sickle till blood flows from its mouth. According as the blood marks the ground, the priest prophesies that the offspring will be boys or girls; and if no blood flow, that the marriage will be childless. This is the essence of what passes, and it seals the contract.

The Kirántis bury their dead on a hill-top, making a tomb of stones loosely constructed. The burial takes place on the day of decease. The priest must attend the funeral, and as he moves along with the corpse to the grave he from time to time strikes a copper vessel with a stick, and, invoking the soul of the deceased, desires it to go in peace and join the souls that went before it. The law of inheritance gives equal shares to all the sons, and nothing to the daughters, unmarried or married. Concubines are unknown. Polygamy is allowed and not uncommon. Polyandry unheard of and abhorred.

Tattooing is unknown. Boring of ears and nose common with the women; rare with the men. The hair is usually worn long and so as to hide the Hindu-like top-knot that is, however, always forthcoming. The general character of the Kirántis is rather bad among the other tribes, who consider them to be somewhat fierce and prompt at quarrelling and blows, especially in their cups,—a state very frequent with them. But at Darjiling they have now for fifteen years borne an excellent character as servants, being faithful, truthful, and orderly, so that their alleged fierceness should, I think, be called manly independence, or be referred to their long-past days of political independence and martial habits.

I proceed now to the physical character of the tribe. Premising that I have long been habituated to these physical observations, by no means confined to the hills, I would repeat once * more that the Himálayan type, though upon the whole Mongolian, is not to be judged (any more than the African one by the Negro) by the Kalmak exaggeration of that type; and, moreover, that the type exhibits here, as to the north and to the south of us, a large range of variation, indicating, like the lingual type, that the Himálaya has been peopled by successive immigrations of northmen belonging to many, probably to all, of the various sub-families into which the restless progeny of Túr has been (I think prematurely) divided by European philologists and ethnologists. I think, moreover, that I can discern this sort of accord between the physical and lingual types, to wit, that the tribes with simple languages have more, and the tribes with complex languages have less, of the Mongolian physical attributes, after careful elimination of the presumed effects of mixture of breed (and such facts are always notorious on the spot) where such mixture has taken place. Thus a Lepcha, or Gurung, or Magar, or Murmi, to a simple language unites a palpable Mongolian physiognomy and frame; whilst a Kúswár, a Dhimál, or a Kiránti, with a language much allied to the higher Túrkic, Ugrofinnic, and Dravidian types † possesses a face and form tending the same way.

* See my Essay on Kócch, Bódo, and Dhimál, p. 113 ff.

† The complex pronomenalisation of the Kiránti verb points to a special connection with Müller's subdivision, embracing, as far as we yet know, the Hó, the Sontal, and the Munda proper. The numerous traits of resemblance of the pronomenalised Himálayan tongues to the cultivated Dravidian have been pointed out, here and there, in the course of the foregoing analyses of two samples of the former. But observe that Hó and Sontal, like Túrki and Kúswár, suffix personal signs to noun and verb. Váyu and Kiránti, like Dhimáli, follow the Dravidian rule of prefixing to noun, suffixing to verb. This difference seems great, but is not perhaps really so, for the vulgar and sacred dialects of Egyptian, which were, says Poole, one tongue, nevertheless had this difference.

I will now describe my samples, adding, lest I should be supposed to have selected them unfairly, that they are men long in my own service.

Dimensions in English feet and inches.

	(1) *Bontáwa.*		(2) *Báhing.*		(3) *Thúlung.*	
Total height, ...	5	4	5	0	5	2
Crown to hip, ...	2	5	2	2	2	3
Hip to heel, ...	3	2	2	11	3	0
Fore-and-aft length of head, .	0	9⅛	0	8¾	0	8¼
Side-to-side width of ditto, .	0	6	0	6¼	0	6
Girth of ditto, ...	1	9¼	1	9½	1	8
Breadth of face, . . .	0	5⅛	0	5⅜	0	5¼
Length of arm and hand, .	2	5	2	3½	2	4
Girth of arm, ...	0	10	0	9¾	0	9¼
Ditto of fore arm, . . .	0	9¼	0	9¾	0	10
Girth of thigh, ...	1	6	1	6	1	6½
Ditto of calf, ...	1	0½	1	0½	1	0¾
Girth of chest, ...	2	9½	2	10	2	10½

No. 1. A Bontáwa, age 55. Head long, narrow, vertical view elliptic, equally wide fore and aft, widest between the ears. Front view of the head and face oval, with the cheek-bones little protruded and the forehead not narrowing upwards. Profile or side view good, nearly vertical, the mouth not being at all inclined to prognathism, and the forehead very little retiring, but chin somewhat defective. Forehead of good height and breadth, nearly as wide as the cheek-bones. Eyes of good size, remote; upper lid flaccid, but hardly perceptibly bent down next the nose. Nose long, straight, pyramidal, well elevated though thick, and with the nostrils elongated, not round. Mouth well formed, not protuberant, of good size, and having shapely lips and vertical teeth not at all exposed, chin not retiring, but not advanced, and rather defective. Jaws neither heavy nor square. Colour a clear light brown, deeper and less olive than usual. No trace of ruddiness. Hair jet black, ample, straight, glossy, strong but not coarse. Moustache full and jet black. No whisker. Eyebrows scanty and horizontal. No hair on chest. Figure good, but trunk and arms long, and legs short. Very

moderate development of bone or muscle for a highlander, and scarcely more than in a plainsman.

No. 2. A Báhing,* 30 years old. Head broader and shorter, vertical view oblate ovoid, wider behind than before, but not flattened behind. Front view of the face shows (like the head) more breadth than in No. 1, and is somewhat square, owing to the projection of the cheek-bones and of the angles of the jaws. Profile vertical, as in the last, with very little saliency of the mouth, a vertical but somewhat narrow forehead, and a chin flush with the front of the jaw. Forehead less fine than in the last, vertical to the front, but somewhat narrow, or rather seeming so, owing to the lateral projection of the jaws and cheek-bones. Eyes of good size remote, showing faintly but distinctly the usual flaccidity and deflection towards the nose, of the upper lid. Nose, as in the last, long, straight, pyramidal, broad, but not depressed. Nostrils large and round. Mouth of good size and shape, with moderately full lips, of which the upper has a tendency to advance more than the lower, owing to the normal thickening of the gum. Teeth fine and vertical, and not at all exposed. Chin devoid of the prominent roundness of the part, flush with the jaw in front. Jaws heavy and angular. Colour, as in the last, pale ruddy brown, deeper and less dull than the usual isabelline colour. Hair jet black, straight, strong. No whisker. A scanty moustache. Eyebrows full. Chest, legs, and arms hairless. No more development of bone or muscle than in the last, and figure, as before, good, but noticeable for length of trunk and arms.

No. 3. A Thúlung, 22 years old, has the breadth of head and face of the last, vertical view of the head showing great and remarkably uniform width in proportion to length. Profile line vertical, as before, and all the details of the features wonderfully similar, as in a strong family likeness, and figure also and colour.

* Is our Báhing the Bábik of Muir's Sanscrit Texts, ii. 482? His Aratta may be the Aratt of Sikim, and his Khas is no doubt the now dominant tribe of Népál. Muir's authority indeed says that the Báhik were a Sanscrit-speaking race, but that may be accounted for by the ignorance displayed by Brahmanical writers on this subject, and by their determination to find degraded Kshatriyas in all the great nations and peoples bordering on Aryavartta; *e.g.*, the Burmese are with them degraded Kshatriyas!!

General Remark.—All these three men have a depth of colour and defect of bone and muscle assimilating them to the lowland Turanians, generally and differencing them from the highlanders generally, but especially from the Palusen or Cis-himalayan Bhotia, the Gúrung, the Súnwár, the Múrmi, the Magar, and the Lepcha; and the Bontáwa has a head and face carrying on the resemblance with the lowland Turanians, and which I believe to be so frequent among the Kirántis as to deserve to be called the rule, not the exception. In conclusion, I may perhaps be permitted to say, as the result of long years of practised observation, that the effect upon the Turanian northmen of passing from the cold high-and-dry plateau of "Asie Centrale," down the various steps of the Himálayan ladder into the hot and moist plains of India, is to diminish the volume of bony and muscular development, to diminish also the extreme breadth of head and face, with the consequent wide separation of all the double organs of sense, and to modify the defects of the eye, giving it a freer and straighter aperture and less flaccid upper lid; moreover, that such tribes as, in the throng of successive immigrations, have been broken, barbarised, and driven to seek refuge in malarious tracts, seem to manifest a tendency to pass from the low Turanian to the low African or Negro type;* and lastly, that after these effects have been produced in the course of numberless ages, it must always be unsafe to dogmatise upon physiological or philological grounds only respecting the *special* relations and characteristics of any given tribe without abiding advertence to the general relations and characteristics of such tribe, and to the proof of both that may be had by carefully seeking out and weighing all the available evidence, whether physiological or philological, moral or traditional.

The evidence of any reflux towards the north of the great tide of Turanian population flowing wave after wave over India, through the numberless passes of the Himálaya, and also, perhaps, round the Western and Eastern extremities of the

* Narrowness of head and face and projection of mouth are the great marks of the Negro type. Now, I have an Uráon in my service in whom these marks united to a very dark skin are conspicuous, and his lips are very thick and his eye good, and his hair crisply curled, but not at all woolly.

chain, is faint, seeming to be confined to the Néwár tribe of Népál proper, who have a tradition of their return to Népál after having reached so far south as Malabar. Nor are there wanting coincidences of arbitrary customs, of the shape and use of agricultural and other implements, and of words, and even of grammatical forms, to countenance and uphold that tradition, as I have already adverted to in my paper on the Nilgirians.

END OF VOLUME I.